From the Grassroots to the Supreme Court

Constitutional Conflicts

A SERIES WITH THE

INSTITUTE OF BILL OF RIGHTS LAW AT

THE COLLEGE OF WILLIAM & MARY

*Series editors:* Neal Devins and

Mark Graber

PETER F. LAU, EDITOR

# From the Grassroots to the Supreme Court

*Brown v. Board of Education* and American Democracy

*Duke University Press  Durham and London  2004*

R0408995279

*For Sophie, Emmie, and Thompson*

# Contents

# Acknowledgments

On 14 June 2002 the contributors to this book gathered at the University of South Carolina to discuss drafts of essays and sharpen the thematic approach of the proposed collection, thanks to the generous support of the university's Institute for Southern Studies and African American Studies Program, as well as the Virginia Foundation for the Humanities. In attendance were various members of the University of South Carolina community, along with Joseph A. DeLaine Jr. and his brother, Brumit B. (B.B.) DeLaine. Both men are sons of the late Reverend Joseph Armstrong DeLaine, the man celebrated in Richard Kluger's magisterial *Simple Justice* (1976) for encouraging the African American residents of rural Clarendon County, South Carolina, to demand equality in their public schools and to become a driving force behind the U.S. Supreme Court's landmark decision in *Brown v. Board of Education* (1954). Historians in their own right, the DeLaine brothers have been actively leading efforts to educate the public about the history and legacy of *Brown* and the Clarendon County contribution to it, *Briggs v. Elliott*. During the daylong discussion of essays, the DeLaines offered their insight into the past, and they led all of us on a memorable bus excursion to Clarendon County the following day.

Down highways and back roads, we traversed the Black Belt county. We viewed the plantation lands that drove the region's economy in days past and the black churches, most notably Liberty Hill A.M.E. and St. Marks A.M.E., that hosted mass meetings to rally support for litigation aimed at equalizing and then integrating the county's public schools. We saw the modern schools that have replaced the small, often ramshackle, one- and two-room schoolhouses that were the most visible signs of Jim Crow injustice and some of the most important symbols of black resolve in the years before *Brown*. We visited the land of the Pearson family, one of the black families that anchored support for the county's civil rights struggles, and we stood under a tree in front of Hammett Pearson's home to absorb the surroundings and meet members of the local community. Our day was capped by a splendid barbeque dinner with community members, including descendents of the litigants who risked their lives to tear down the legal edifice of racial segregation. Amid the clamor of the festive event, we talked about our scholarly work and community members shared their stories of struggle and perseverance. Although Clarendon County remains one of the poorest counties in the nation fifty years after *Brown*, the spirit of its people suggests that hope for a better tomorrow is undiminished and that the struggle for equality continues. Ensuring that the stories of people like those we met in Clarendon are heard and understood is one of the primary reasons for this collection. A special thanks is owed to the DeLaine brothers and to all of those engaged in struggle who have been willing to share their stories for all the world to hear and learn.

There are many people to thank for helping to produce this book. Foremost are the writers who agreed to contribute original essays and who have worked diligently to revise numerous drafts, incorporating the thoughts of each other and the anonymous readers at Duke University Press, as well as my own. The collection received crucial institutional and financial support from the Institute for Southern Studies (ISS) under the direction of Walter Edgar, the African American Studies Program under the direction of Cleveland Sellers, and the Virginia Foundation for the Humanities. Bob Ellis of the ISS provided the administrative work that made the writers' meeting in Columbia possible and created the index. Bobby Donaldson, Valinda Littlefield, and Dan Littlefield, all members of the History Department and African American Studies Program at USC, graciously contributed their time and expertise in African American history to the project. Tom Brown, the associate director of the ISS, first approached me about creating a collection of essays in commemoration of *Brown* nearly two years ago. Not only did he coordinate the writers' gathering in Columbia in June 2002, he also read drafts of each essay, passed along his thoughts about the organization of the book, and supported my efforts to move the collection along. Steven Lawson and David Levering Lewis, good friends and mentors, provided timely comments on the manuscript. Steven's urging years ago to understand the history of the African American struggle for civil rights in an "interactive" manner, incorporating perspectives that are "bottom-up" and "top-down," informs this entire collection.

Duke University Press has proved an excellent choice to publish the book. The anonymous readers for the press offered insight that made individual essays stronger and helped make the collection work. Dave Douglas guided me to the press and Neal Devins helped usher the manuscript into the review process. Throughout, Valerie Millholland has demonstrated patience, skill, and grace as an editor. Fred Kameny spearheaded the copyediting of the manuscript. His insightfulness and laserlike editing have improved each essay and the book as a whole.

Lastly, I would like to thank Sophie Glenn Lau and our daughter, Emmie, for their support and encouragement during the production of this book. Each in her own way provided me with the space, time, and motivation needed to see the project through to completion. There are few words that can fully express my gratitude to them both.

PETER F. LAU

# Introduction

℘ Few legal decisions have been as hotly contested in courtrooms, legislatures, and the streets as the U.S. Supreme Court's decision in *Brown v. Board of Education* (1954). In a short and unemotional ruling crafted by Chief Justice Earl Warren, a unanimous court struck down the legal doctrine of "separate but equal" in public education. The decision decisively undercut the constitutional justification of Jim Crow segregation established by the Supreme Court fifty-eight years earlier in *Plessy v. Ferguson*. But *Brown* was much more than a legal decision. It was also a social, political, and cultural event that presented—as it still does today—a powerful symbol of the possibilities and limitations of American democracy and a reference point for ongoing battles over questions of segregation, schools, and equality.

This collection of original essays brings together innovative scholarship about *Brown* that combines the tools of legal analysis with those of social, political, and cultural history. It aims to shed new light on the history and legacy of *Brown* by placing studies of the law and national institutions in dialogue with studies of the everyday lives of grassroots activists and ordinary members of communities marginalized over the course of more than a century. As a collection, it adopts a perspective that is at once "top-down" and "bottom-up," allowing for sustained inquiry into the relationship between law and society and between institutional and social change. More than any existing studies of *Brown*, this collection also seeks to extend the discussion of segregation and public schools beyond the parameters of black-white race relations.

Some writers in the collection emphasize views from above. They analyze the development of national organizations such as the National Association for the Advancement of Colored People (NAACP) and the Supreme Court. They look at *Brown* in relationship to broad shifts in American liberal thought and judicial decision making during the early cold war years and explore how constitutional conflicts embedded in the decision subsequently informed legal and political debates over issues from school desegregation to affirmative action. Other writers emphasize views from below. Through oral histories, memoirs, personal papers of movement activists, and archives combed for evidence of grassroots social struggles, these scholars consider the lives of African Americans, Mexican Americans, Puerto Ricans, Asian Americans, and Native Americans in relationship to issues of segregation, schools, and equality. Perspectives from the bottom up show both how grassroots movements led directly to *Brown* and how local struggles around segregation and schools existed independently from the formal challenge to the doctrine of separate but equal. They also illuminate how the legal decision informed the future course of collective social activism and provide insight into the ways in which the decision shaped the lives of ordinary individuals and their communities. Still other writers in the collection adopt perspectives that are explicitly top-down *and* bottom-up. These scholars show how the NAACP's legal strategy to destroy the doctrinal underpinnings of Jim Crow segregation and its efforts to implement the desegregation mandate of *Brown* were inextricably intertwined with a broader social insurgency from below.

It is important to note that few of the essays contained in this collection adopt perspectives that are top-down or bottom-up exclusively. The differences in perspective are marked more by emphasis than by one-sided choices, by professional discipline and methodology rather than blindness to the richly complex history and impact of *Brown*. But differences in perspective do exist. These differences reflect traditional disciplinary divisions between the legal and historical professions and between political and social historians. Because this collection brings these perspectives together in one volume, it offers an opportunity not only to enrich our understandings of pathways to and from *Brown* but also to debate how various academic approaches inform broader understandings of the decision and its legacy.

In an important sense, the dialogue between top-down and bottom-up explorations of *Brown* represents an extension of a debate that first achieved critical attention from scholars in the mid-1980s. By that time, a number of books concerned with the history of the African American civil rights movement of the 1950s and 1960s had been published and many more were on their way to publication. In an effort to grapple with the movement's enormous importance in American life, many of these books focused on the key leaders, institutions, events, and legislative achievements of a movement that achieved iconic status as the Civil Rights Movement. Though scholars seldom intended for this to happen, the Civil Rights Movement soon found itself confined historically and in the popular imagination to a discrete period between *Brown v. Board of Education* and the passage of the Civil Rights Act (1964) and Voting Rights Acts (1965), or between the rise of Martin Luther King Jr. during the Montgomery bus boycott (1955–56) and his assassination in Memphis (1968). This emphasis on legal and legislative victories or on the life of one major leader threatened to detach the movement from the rich history of African American activism and community life. More significantly, the top-down emphasis on the movement threatened to submerge, once again, the voices, aspirations, and actions of the ordinary men, women, and children who gave the movement life and continued to struggle over a range of social and economic concerns that did not disappear in the wake of legal and legislative triumphs, or with the decline of mass demonstrations, or with the death of King, or with the waning interest of the national media.[1]

By the middle of the 1980s, a full-fledged effort to write the history of the civil rights movement from the bottom up was well under way. Casting the civil rights movement more broadly as part of an ongoing struggle by everyday African Americans and their allies to secure full citizenship rights and redefine the meaning of freedom, scholars writing from the bottom up stretched the parameters of historical inquiry back in time and revealed a complex history of black protest and activism that did not fit neatly within the dominant narrative of the Civil Rights Movement. Scholars emphasized the agency of local people and the importance of local institutions from schools to churches to NAACP branches in bringing about social change. Rather than write about one single Civil Rights Movement, scholars pointed toward the existence of many movements. And rather than define these movements as struggles for civil rights, scholars began defining them as freedom struggles, adopting the language most often utilized by movement participants themselves. Community studies of black activism in Greensboro, North Carolina, Tuskegee, Alabama, and St. Augustine, Florida, emerged first, along with an important sociological study of the black church and so-called movement halfway houses that served as incubators of local activism. These studies were followed by important monographs that detailed black activism in cities such as Norfolk, Virginia, and Memphis and in states such as Mississippi and Louisiana. At the same time, a growing body of scholarship concerned with black migration and black women's activism issued a sharp challenge to understandings of the Civil Rights Movement as an event confined to a discrete period or dominated by male ministers and leaders of national civil rights organizations.[2]

Writing the history of the African American struggle for civil rights and freedom from the bottom up has proved a valuable endeavor. It has brought to the surface the voices, actions, and aspirations of African Americans who seldom attracted the attention of the national media in the past or of scholars in the present. It has shown how ordinary people struggled for survival, sustained families and communities amid the horror of Jim Crow, battled for economic justice, and agitated for an end to racial oppression across time and space. In focusing attention on the quality of activism at the grassroots level, it has also helped to enlarge understandings of what constitutes political activity. While traditionally politics has been defined by political parties, vote tallies, and the actions of lawmakers, the history of African American activism written from the bottom up has expanded our understanding of politics by making religion and the church, grassroots organizing and protest, fraternal associations and women's club work, as well as migration and networks of family and kin, a central part of the discussion. Most importantly, this history has shown that the African American struggle for civil rights has been about a lot more than securing legal and legislative victories. As important as these victories were, viewed from the grassroots they were only pieces in a larger human quest for dignity, self-determination, and economic security.

Bottom-up histories have, however, almost always privileged the local over the national, the social over the institutional, and the particular over the representative in their examination of struggles for civil rights and freedom. Despite warnings about the perils of local history and despite calls for "interactive" histories of the movement that combine top-down and bottom-up approaches, it has been more than a decade since the publication of an overarching treatment of the Civil Rights Movement. And it has been more than a decade since the publication of an edited collection of essays that offered a framework for a dialogue across scholarly divides within the field of civil rights studies. With the rapid expansion of work in the field of African American civil rights history and the simultaneous, though largely parallel, expansion of scholarship concerned with the struggles of Latinos and Asian Americans for civil rights and freedom, the need for dialogue and broad reflection is urgent.[3]

*From the Grassroots to the Supreme Court* takes the occasion of the fiftieth anniversary of *Brown v. Board of Education* to work across the divides of discipline and geography and to assess both the meaning of the legal decision and its connection to the larger struggle over access to and application of civil rights in American history. In contrast to a number of recently published and important books on *Brown*, its aim is not only to dissect the intricacies of the legal decision *or* to provide a synthetic treatment of its troubled legacy *or* to detail its broken promises. It includes legal analysis and evaluates long-term legacies. But it also introduces new evidence and perspectives that situate the decision in the context of community activism and social life across the twentieth century.[4]

*From the Grassroots to the Supreme Court* is divided into four parts that cut across the late nineteenth and twentieth centuries and alternate between views from the bottom up and views from the top down. Part I situates

*Brown* in the history of grassroots social struggles dating to the second half of the nineteenth century. It shows how battles over segregation and schools traversed lines of race, ethnicity, and region and were connected to battles for voting rights, economic justice, and human dignity. Blair L. M. Kelley's essay opens the collection by exploring the ways in which the doctrine of "separate but equal" established in *Plessy v. Ferguson* emerged from the complicated racial and political matrix of New Orleans in the late nineteenth century and how differences among African Americans obstructed efforts to thwart Jim Crow segregation. It was in New Orleans that African Americans, differentiated by class, color, and culture, joined for a time in a battle to resist the rise of legalized segregation, but increasingly came into conflict over the value and efficacy of racial integration. As Kelley shows, the city's Creoles, a population of French-speaking, Catholic, mixed-race descendents of free people of color, viewed integration as the sine qua non of equality, while darker-hued descendents of enslaved African Americans placed a premium on preserving autonomous black institutions in their fight for liberation.

While Kelley reminds readers that African Americans have not been of one mind about how to battle segregation or achieve equality, Vicki Ruiz brings to life the vibrant tapestries of resistance to school segregation in the western United States woven by Mexican Americans, Asian Americans, and American Indians in the century preceding *Brown*. Battles to resist segregation and secure access to quality schools, she reveals, were neither waged by African Americans alone nor confined to the South. To the contrary, the efforts of Mexican Americans, Asian Americans, and American Indians in the West ran parallel to and intersected with the struggles of African Americans in sometimes surprising ways. In one telling moment, Latino parents in Orange County, California, sued to desegregate four local school districts. The case, *Méndez v. Westminster* (1946), struck a blow to the practice of school segregation in Orange County and was upheld by the U.S. Court of Appeals for the Ninth Circuit in 1947. Although the decision is seldom mentioned in discussions of *Brown*, as Ruiz makes clear, its connection to the decision is both tangible and significant.

The final three essays of Part I turn the discussion to the southeastern United States in the years before *Brown*. Raymond Gavins, Kara Miles Turner, and Peter Lau place the voices of everyday African Americans at the center of their historical narratives and show how the issue of educational equality was tied to the broad concerns and aspirations of black southerners in the era of Jim Crow. Each scholar relies extensively on oral testimony, much of it collected as part of Duke University's oral history project "Behind the Veil: Documenting African American Life in the Jim Crow South."

In his study of North Carolina, Gavins demonstrates how African Americans waged a ceaseless campaign, individually and collectively, through organizations such as the NAACP and the North Carolina Teachers Association (NCTA), for "the ballot, the book, and the buck" across the twentieth century. In an explicit challenge to depictions of the Civil Rights Movement as a movement of "seamless demonstrations and speeches," Gavins deftly shows how generations of teaching, aspiration, debate, and civil rights organizing informed challenges to Jim Crow in the 1950s and beyond.

Similarly, Turner explains how black high school students in Prince Edward County, Virginia, managed to withstand the crushing power of Jim Crow and waged a concerted campaign to destroy the inequities that it supported. Led by a sixteen-year-old high school junior, Barbara Johns, students at the Robert R. Moton high school struck for better school conditions in the spring of 1951 and ultimately became litigants in one of five cases included in *Brown*. As Turner shows, Jim Crow neither cowed nor broke the students psychologically. Instead, students drew strength from black institutions and generations of African Americans who lived lives informed by what one graduate of R. R. Moton called "liberating lifescripts."

Like Turner's essay, Lau's examination of Clarendon County, South Carolina, revisits the history of an African American community that produced a case included in *Brown*. And like Turner, Lau demonstrates that the effort of African Americans to destroy Jim Crow through the court system was tied to a larger, longer, and still lingering fight for self-determination and equality. In contrast to previous scholars of *Brown*, Lau situates events in the rural, Black Belt county of Clarendon in the context of a broader social movement under way in South Carolina and the South from the beginning of the 1940s. Despite the rural context and oppressive conditions, African Americans in Clarendon were active participants in early efforts to revive the NAACP in South Carolina, secure voting rights, and smash the all-white Democratic primary in the years before the county became the focus of litigation aimed at overturning *Plessy*. Read along with the essays by Gavins and Turner, Lau's sheds new light on the important role of the NAACP in supporting a broadly based grassroots social movement concerned with a multitude of issues in the years before *Brown*. Indeed, African Americans utilized the NAACP at the grassroots level as a vehicle for achieving far more than school desegregation.

Part II of the collection provides a bridge between studies of grassroots activism and studies of the advocates and judges who were instrumental in litigating and adjudicating *Brown*. Although the essays in this part focus on the thinking and actions of élites, they powerfully suggest the inseparability of top-down and bottom-up approaches to understanding the case. Read in conjunction with Turner's essay in Part I, Lara Smith's essay on black NAACP attorneys in Virginia is a case in point. Smith's essay shows how a vanguard group of black attorneys helped till the ground for civil rights activism in the years preceding the student-led strike for better school conditions in Prince Edward County. In Virginia, she explains, black NAACP attorneys were far more than lawyers who litigated civil rights cases. During the 1930s and 1940s black attorneys such as Oliver Hill and Spottswood Robinson, III "helped to organize NAACP branches . . . organized voter registration campaigns and ran for political office in hopes of inspiring African Americans to vote." NAACP attorneys in Virginia were both lawyers and grassroots organizers, and their actions "shaped the scope of civil rights activism in Virginia and ultimately influenced the trajectory of the NAACP's national strategy in challenging inequalities in education."

Essays by Patricia Sullivan, Christopher Schmidt, and Michael Klarman turn the collection's historical lens at a more decisively top-down angle. In Sullivan's examination of the NAACP's legal strategy, Schmidt's of a federal court judge's career, and Klarman's of the U.S. Supreme Court, each scholar connects the history of Brown to broader changes in American political, intellectual, and judicial thought and practice. Sullivan and Schmidt, in particular, are interested in the ways in which Brown embodied both the promises and the limitations of postwar racial liberalism. Sullivan discerns a significant shift during the NAACP's formative years (1909–34) in the way the organization framed the issue of race and segregation, with important consequences for racial reform in postwar America. The NAACP, Sullivan explains, viewed race and racial discrimination in national terms in its early years. Despite its limited resources, the organization worked to publicize and address "the routine violation of constitutional rights in the South" and "patterns of racial discrimination and equality in the North." But the NAACP began shifting course in 1934, Sullivan argues, as it launched a legal campaign to destroy Jim Crow through an attack on segregated education in the South. In making the shift, the NAACP achieved new levels of support among African Americans and white liberals and finally secured its greatest victory in Brown. At the same time, however, the organization contributed to a narrowing of its objective of combating racial discrimination in all its forms on a national scale, helping to reframe "the problems of race and racial discrimination [in the United States] as a distinctly southern problem."

In his essay on J. Waties Waring, a federal judge who wrote a dissenting opinion in Briggs v. Elliott, the Clarendon County case included in Brown, Schmidt expands on Sullivan's critique of the trajectory of postwar racial liberalism. Waring was a native South Carolinian, schooled in the white South's Jim Crow traditions, whose personal and judicial transformation in the 1940s, Schmidt argues, reflected the promises and perils of liberal ideas about race and reform. As a member of the U.S. District Court for the Eastern District of South Carolina, Waring presided over the key court cases filed by black South Carolinians in their expanding struggle for civil rights discussed throughout this book. In opinions mandating the equalization of white and black teachers' salaries, demanding the end of the all-white Democratic primary, and finally declaring that, "Segregation is *per se* inequality," Waring became an ardent critic of Jim Crow and an uncompromising advocate of racial integration. On the bench he became an increasingly self-conscious member of "a dynamic, expanding community of racial liberals from around the country." Schmidt argues that Waring's liberal views on race, like those of his contemporaries, would prove "a crucial weapon of reform," but simultaneously contained "blind spots" and "potentially conservative tendencies." They placed, Schmidt writes, "too much faith in rationally-derived, top-down reform," gave "too much attention" to "changing attitudes without addressing structural or institutional concerns," and relied too extensively "on psychological models of racism."

Klarman's essay extends Schmidt's analysis to the U.S. Supreme Court and shows how the justices arrived at their unanimous and highly controversial decision in *Brown*. The essay reconsiders the court's behind-the-scenes deliberations to explain how a less than secure majority of justices in favor of overturning *Plessy* in December 1952 resulted in a 9–0 ruling striking down the doctrine of "separate but equal" in May 1954. Klarman shows how public opinion, liberal thought, the cold war, and the social status of the justices all played significant roles in shaping the decision's outcome. In Klarman's analysis, Supreme Court justices were neither isolated from American society at large nor certain in their conviction that the traditional tools of judicial decision making—legal precedent, historical intent, and custom—could invalidate the constitutionality of the doctrine of "separate but equal." To the contrary, Klarman explains, even key justices such as Felix Frankfurter and Robert Jackson, who "loathed" segregation, believed that it was constitutional. Indeed, Klarman argues, a 5–4 majority in favor of invalidating *Plessy* was in doubt through the appointment of Earl Warren to the court to fill the vacancy created by the death of Chief Justice Fred Vinson in September 1953. Provocative in his insistence that "*Brown* was not inevitable in 1954," Klarman's work also makes it clear that the justices were deeply influenced by the "dramatic political, economic, social, and ideological forces affecting race relations" and the climate of public opinion by the opening years of the 1950s. "Thus," he concludes, "*Brown* is not an example of the Court resisting majoritarian sentiment, but rather of its converting an emerging national consensus into a constitutional command."

Parts III and IV begin a rethinking and reassessment of *Brown*—its impact on local communities and the modern civil rights movement, black thought and American culture, as well as the law and public school education. Part III opens with an essay by Tomiko Brown-Nagin that explicitly ties local history to American legal history and returns to the issue of *intra*racial conflict raised in the opening essay of the collection by Blair Kelley. With a focus on efforts to implement *Brown* in Atlanta, Brown-Nagin, like other contributors to this book, looks at the roles played by NAACP branches in the African American struggle for civil rights. As Brown-Nagin explains, the internal social dynamics of Atlanta's black community "exerted an enormous influence on the NAACP Legal Defense Fund's (LDF's) effort to desegregate the city's schools." Although the relationship between NAACP national officials and local NAACP branches had never existed without tension, on the road to *Brown* the close working relationship between NAACP attorneys and local communities proved crucial for successful litigation efforts. But in the years after *Brown*, Brown-Nagin shows, an investigation by the Internal Revenue Service into the connections between the tax-exempt LDF and the non-tax-exempt NAACP led to the formal severing of ties between the two organizations, with serious consequences for the NAACP and its efforts to implement *Brown*. According to Brown-Nagin, the split helped to erode the relationship between LDF attorneys and members of the NAACP's grassroots constituency in Atlanta, creating "significant barriers for the school desegregation campaign" there and perhaps elsewhere in the South. Not only did the split help to confine school desegregation efforts to the courtroom, but the "absence of a close lawyer-client relationship," Brown-Nagin writes, also "enabled Atlanta's biracial elite, rather than civil rights lawyers and their clients, to control the terms, and eventually, the outcome of the fight against segregated schools." In much the same way that differences among African Americans constrained effective resistance to the rise of Jim Crow in the 1890s, so too did differences limit the shape and speed of Jim Crow's undoing in the years after *Brown*.

Essays by Christina Greene, Laurie Green, and Madeleine Lopez continue to explore the influence of *Brown* at the grassroots level. What they show, along with earlier essays by Turner and Lau, is that the Supreme Court decision informed grassroots social struggles in ways that varied widely across time and space. In Prince Edward and Clarendon counties the decision proved devastating rather than liberating. Massive white resistance to public school integration in those counties and elsewhere in the South exacted a heavy price on individual litigants and local black communities. Challenges to Jim Crow were met by economic sanctions, school closings, physical intimidation, overt violence, and legislation aimed at destroying the NAACP. Massive resistance did not end black resistance to racial subjugation, however, nor the African American struggle for civil rights, which continued to grow during the early years of the cold war. Greene's essay challenges conventional views of civil rights activism and political leadership by focusing attention on the often behind-the-scenes work performed by black women and youth in the cause of black freedom in Durham, North Carolina. Black female beauticians and tobacco workers, as well as members of various women's clubs and the NAACP, Greene shows, provided the networks that allowed African American civil rights struggles to expand in the wake of *Brown* and created the "critical grassroots foundation for the sit-ins, boycotts, and demonstrations that emerged in the 1960s."

In her essay on African American activism in Memphis and the surrounding rural Mississippi Delta, Laurie Green explains that *Brown* is best understood in the broad context of a "triangular relationship" between rural and urban activism and national civil rights politics. In Green's formulation, the Supreme Court's decision occurred at the precise moment when the divide between the rural and urban South was vanishing, with profound consequences for traditional black leadership, civil rights politics, and ideas about equality and democracy. For African American activists who journeyed back and forth between the rural Delta and urban Memphis, *Brown* was viewed as a "crucial federal sanctioning of racial justice." But, Green explains, neither the decision's "mandate for desegregation nor its definition of equality" fully defined African Americans' understandings of democracy. School desegregation became part of a multifaceted struggle against police brutality, and for voting rights, economic justice, dignity, and cultural respect in which rural and migrant African Americans played leading roles. *Brown*, in other words, did not define or determine the nature of the African American struggle for freedom in Memphis or the Delta, but it did inform it in significant ways.

In keeping with the theme of migration and movement developed by Green, Madeleine Lopez pushes understandings of *Brown* in new directions by analyzing the ways in which Puerto Rican migrants and residents of New York City interpreted the decision and fought to make it relevant to their lives and futures. At the same moment that southern African Americans migrated to the urban North in growing numbers in the 1940s and beyond, a growing number of Puerto Ricans migrated from the island of Puerto Rico to New York City. The Puerto Rican "Great Migration," Lopez explains, was a defining event for Puerto Ricans and New York City, and *Brown* would prove to be one as well. Although the black-white focus of public policy debates over integration and school reform in New York City marginalized Puerto Ricans during the 1950s and 1960s, rapidly changing demographic realities and increasingly assertive Puerto Rican educators and community activists began shifting the terms of debates about *Brown* by the middle of the 1960s. In battling to have their voices heard, Lopez demonstrates, Puerto Ricans not only placed their concerns about bilingual and bicultural education on the school reform agenda. In the process of working to "personalize the debate and reform efforts that flowed from *Brown*" they also created a voice of their own in New York City politics.

Essays in the final section of the volume take the most sweeping views of *Brown* and its legacy. Waldo E. Martin Jr. explores the influence of *Brown* on the thought and consciousness of African Americans who came of age amid the growing civil rights insurgency of the 1950s and 1960s. Through an analysis of black autobiography and memoir, Martin shows how a generation of African Americans experienced and understood *Brown* in relation to two concurrent historical events—the brutal and highly publicized lynching of a black teenager named Emmett Till in Money, Mississippi, and the Montgomery bus boycott of 1955–56. Hope and hardship, victory and violence, celebration and dread, Martin demonstrates, presided over the same historical moment in mid-1950s America. He argues that Till's lynching and the Montgomery bus boycott—horrific white violence and assertive black action—shaped the fears and aspirations of a generation at least as much as *Brown*. In the same way that the violence and slow pace of change in the wake of *Brown*—and the realization among young African Americans of the "possibilities and perils of concerted mass black social protest," as exemplified by Montgomery—inspired more aggressive black activism in the early 1960s, the slow pace of change after the Civil Rights Act of 1964 and the Voting Rights Act of 1965 fueled the Black Power movement of the late 1960s and 1970s. Although the Civil Rights and Black Power movements continue to be viewed by many as starkly opposed, Martin concludes by emphasizing what they had in common: a deeply held belief among many African Americans in the transformative and liberating power of education, and the memory of the historical moment signified by *Brown*, informed by the experience and spirit of Till and Montgomery.

In Martin's formulation, *Brown* continues to reside in the present through the memory and writings of African Americans who came of age during the *Brown* moment and through the institutionalization of African American, ethnic, and third world programs and departments in universities across the United States.

As Mark Tushnet demonstrates in his essay, the warring constitutional ideas embedded in *Brown* and the Supreme Court's "Ruling on Relief" (1955), commonly referred to as *Brown II*, also continue to inform American legal and political discourse in our own time. *Brown* and *Brown II*, he argues, contained at least two legitimate if seemingly counterpoised views of equality and interpretations of the Equal Protection Clause of the Fourteenth Amendment. According to one view, which embodies what legal scholars call the anti-discrimination principle, the Fourteenth Amendment mandates colorblind decision making by government officials. In this view *Brown* has been understood as a mandate for equal opportunity and as a prohibition on the use of race by official decision makers in educational and other policy matters. According to the second view, which embodies what legal scholars call the anti-subordination principle, the Fourteenth Amendment bars governments from taking actions that sustain patterns or systems of racial subordination. As a general rule, adherents of the anti-subordination principle have supported judicial and political measures aimed at achieving measurable equality outcomes by making race a positive factor in remedying past and ongoing racial discrimination. Although muted in current debates, Tushnet concludes, the latter principle has not entirely faded from the nation's legal-political landscape. To the contrary, from affirmative action and voting rights to the Americans with Disabilities Act of 1990 and the Religious Freedom Restoration Act of 1993, the "anti-subordination principle" has informed legal and policy decisions in the United States in substantive ways. "*Brown*," Tushnet concludes, "identified the possibility that the Equal Protection Clause embodied *either* the anti-discrimination principle *or* the anti-subordination principle" and refused to "choose between them." Partly as a consequence, both approaches to issues of equality remain available to policymakers and the public in the early years of the twenty-first century.

The collection concludes with an essay by Davison M. Douglas that considers the impact of *Brown* on the educational and life opportunities of minority children in the United States. In it he traces the ways that the Supreme Court and the elective branches of the federal government have interpreted and sought to fulfill the promise of *Brown*. As Douglas makes plain, African Americans and the nation as a whole have made tremendous strides in the field of education in the years since the decision. For a time, at least, *Brown* helped make schools in the United States more diverse places of learning and socialization, especially in the formerly segregationist South. *Brown*, the threat of court-mandated integration, and the nation's growing financial commitment to education in the 1950s and beyond also helped to direct new resources toward the once extremely underfunded education of African Americans. In the decades since *Brown*, black graduation rates from high school and college have increased dramatically and African American students have made significant strides in educational achievement as well. But such advances tell only a portion of the larger story. African Americans and other people of color continue to make up a disproportionate share of those living in poverty or on meager wages with little hope for advancement. Many of the nation's cities and rural areas continue to hurt, and hurt badly; long-term economic trends, troubled schools, and budget shortfalls combine to ensnare far too many people in poverty and despair. Indeed, whether measured by access to equal educational opportunities or racial integration, too many young people of color, Douglas writes, remain "largely unaffected by the educational reforms provoked by the Court's decision in *Brown*." Perhaps, as Douglas explains, present-day inequities ought to raise serious questions about "whether education can in fact be the instrument of liberation that African Americans and other racial minorities have long hoped for."

Persistent inequities between those who have and those who have not raise serious questions about the distribution of opportunity and social power in the United States and pose major challenges to the nation's democratic practices. *Brown*, however, has always been about far more than educational reform or the achievement of racial integration in the larger society. As a historic event—as the product of a specific moment in the historical past—*Brown* brought together and came to embody a number of human struggles, ideas, and trends. By the opening years of the 1950s, an expanding black struggle for civil rights and equality, a worsening cold war, shifting currents of liberal and judicial thought, the rapid erosion of the rural countryside, dramatic migrations and population shifts, industrial and urban decline, and the rise of an increasingly knowledge-based service economy marked life in the United States and the larger world. As this book demonstrates, *Brown* was shaped by and in turn informed each of these developments in significant ways. In doing so, *Brown* left its imprint on the historical landscape in ways large and small—in ways that scholars have only just begun to fully appreciate.

Despite and perhaps because of the persistence of racial and ethnic segregation in American life, continued disparities in educational opportunities, and seemingly intractable gaps in economic opportunities and outcomes, a fresh view of *Brown* has much to contribute to current debates about the state of education, access to economic opportunity, and the theory and practice of democracy in the United States. By including perspectives on the legal decision that are top-down, bottom-up, and interactive, and that are informed by the disciplines of legal, social, political, and cultural history, this collection of essays reinforces long-held views of the decision's seminal importance and revolutionary nature. But it does more than merely declare *Brown* a revolution. Instead, it carefully historicizes the ways in which the decision emerged from decades of social ferment and legal action, was informed by major historical changes in the United States and the world, and subsequently shaped the civil rights and freedom struggles, American politics, the law, and the lives of individuals across the divides of race, class, gender, ethnicity, and geography. It shows that change—indeed, revolutionary change—is possible and that it is the product of conflict between individuals and groups, people and institutions, society and the law. Seldom does significant change occur from any single source or emanate from any single direction; that is a key lesson of this book.

For more than a century, segregation and struggles to confront its destructive force have been central to the history of the United States. Collectively, segregation and the confrontation with it have transformed the lives of lawyers, judges, and ordinary people of all racial and ethnic backgrounds. *Brown* was the key legal event in a century-long struggle with segregation and it continues to touch the lives of individuals and American society as a whole. *Brown* stands as a living testament to the centrality of segregation and discrimination in American life *and* to the power of human beings to confront and achieve victories over both. At the same time, *Brown* is a testament to the price paid for change and to the realization that the struggle against segregation and discrimination and for greater equality and democracy is a struggle without end.

## Notes

1 Key works which focused on well-known leaders, national institutions, events, and legislative achievements include Taylor Branch, *Parting the Waters: America in the King Years, 1964–1968* (New York: Simon and Schuster, 1988); Clayborn Carson, *In Struggle: SNCC and the Black Awakening of the 1960s* (Cambridge: Harvard University Press, 1981); David J. Garrow, *Bearing the Cross: Martin Luther King, Jr. and the Southern Christian Leadership Conference* (New York: William Morrow, 1986); Richard Kluger, *Simple Justice* (New York: Alfred A. Knopf, 1976); Steven F. Lawson, *Black Ballots: Voting Rights in the South, 1944–1969* (New York: Columbia University Press, 1976); August Meier and Elliott Rudwick, *CORE: A Study in the Civil Rights Movement, 1942–1968* (New York: Oxford University Press, 1973). The PBS documentary series "Eyes on the Prize: America's Civil Rights Years, 1954–1965" (1987), a production of Henry Hampton and Blackside, Inc., helped establish popular understandings of the civil rights movement as an event defined by the "King years."

2 Clayborne Carson's essay "Civil Rights Reform and the Black Freedom Struggle," in Charles Eagles, ed., *The Civil Rights Movement in America* (Jackson: University Press of Mississippi, 1986), issued the most coherent call for writing

the history of the "black freedom struggle" from the "bottom up." Key early community studies include William Chafe, *Civilities and Civil Rights: Greensboro, North Carolina and the Black Freedom Struggle* (New York: Oxford University Press, 1980); David Colburn, *Racial Change and Community Crisis, St. Augustine, Florida, 1877–1980* (New York: Columbia University Press, 1985); Robert J. Norrell, *Reaping the Whirlwind: The Civil Rights Movement in Tuskegee* (New York: Alfred A. Knopf, 1986). On the black church and movement "halfway houses," see Aldon Morris, *The Origins of the Civil Rights Movement: Black Communities Organizing for Change* (New York: Free Press, 1984). Important local and state studies published in subsequent years include Earl Lewis, *In Their Own Interests: Race, Class, and Power in Twentieth Century Norfolk, Virginia* (Berkeley: University of California Press, 1991); Michael Honey, *Southern Labor and Black Civil Rights: Organizing Memphis Workers* (Urbana: University of Illinois Press, 1993); John Dittmer, *Local People: The Struggle for Civil Rights in Mississippi* (Urbana: University of Illinois Press, 1994); Charles M. Payne, *I've Got the Light of Freedom: The Organizing Tradition in the Mississippi Freedom Struggle* (Berkeley: University of California Press, 1995); Adam Fairclough, *Race and Democracy: The Civil Rights Struggle in Louisiana, 1915–1972* (Athens: University of Georgia Press, 1995). For an overview of the work in black migration see Joe William Trotter Jr., ed., *The Black Migration in Historical Perspective* (Bloomington: Indiana University Press, 1991). Some of the most important works concerned with African American women's activism are: Vicki L. Crawford, Jacqueline Anne Rouse, and Barbara Woods, eds., *Women in the Civil Rights Movement: Trailblazers and Torchbearers, 1941–1965* (Bloomington: University of Indiana Press, 1993); Melinda M. Chateauvert, *Marching Together: Women of the Brotherhood of Sleeping Car Porters* (Urbana: University of Illinois Press, 1997); Evelyn Brooks Higginbotham, *Righteous Discontent: The Women's Movement and the Black Baptist Church, 1880–1920* (Cambridge: Harvard University Press, 1993); Tera Hunter, *To 'Joy My Freedom: Southern Black Women's Lives and Labors after the Civil War* (Cambridge: Harvard University Press, 1997); Deborah Gray White, *Too Heavy a Load: Black Women in Defense of Themselves* (New York: W. W. Norton, 1999).

3 The most notable call for "interactive" histories of the African American struggle for civil rights is Steven F. Lawson's "Freedom Then, Freedom Now: The Historiography of the Civil Rights Movement," *American Historical Review* 96 (1991): 456–71. It is important to note that previously cited works by Branch, Garrow, and Kluger, although top-down in focus, pointed toward a more interactive approach to understanding the African American struggle for civil rights. Synthetic portraits of the Civil Rights movement include Robert Weisbrot, *Freedom Bound: A History of America's Civil Rights Movement* (New York: W. W. Norton, 1990); Steven F. Lawson, *Running for Freedom: Civil Rights and Black Politics in America since 1941* (Philadelphia: Temple University Press, 1991); Manning Marable, *Race, Reform, and Rebellion: The Second Reconstruction in Black America, 1945–1990*, 2d ed. (Jackson: University Press of Mississippi, 1991); Harvard Sitkoff, *The Struggle for Black Equality, 1954–1992*, rev. ed. (New York: Hill and Wang,

1993). The last essay collection explicitly concerned with surveying the state of the field of civil rights studies was Armstead L. Robinson and Patricia Sullivan, eds., *New Directions in Civil Rights Studies* (Charlottesville: University Press of Virginia, 1991). For a comprehensive overview of the state of Mexican American and Chicano and Chicana history see Vicki L. Ruiz, "*Morena/o, Blanca/o y Café con Leche*: Racial Constructions in Chicana/o Historiography," *Estudios Mexicanos/ Mexican Studies* (forthcoming). Some key works in the field include David Gutiérrez, *Walls and Mirrors: Mexican Americans, Mexican Immigrants, and the Politics of Ethnicity in the Southwest, 1910–1986* (Berkeley: University of California Press, 1995); Vicki L. Ruiz, *From Out of the Shadows: Mexican Women in Twentieth-Century America* (New York: Oxford University Press, 1998); George J. Sánchez, *Becoming Mexican American: Ethnicity, Culture, and Identity in Chicano Los Angeles, 1900–1945* (New York: Oxford University Press, 1993); Guadalupe San Miguel, *Brown, Not White: School Integration and the Chicano Movement in Houston* (College Station: Texas A&M University Press, 2001). Key works in Asian American history include Valerie J. Matsumoto, *Farming the Home Place: A Japanese American Community in California, 1919–1982* (Ithaca: Cornell University Press, 1993); Ronald Takaki, *Strangers from a Different Shore: A History of Asian Americans* (Boston: Little, Brown, 1989); Frank H. Wu, *Yellow: Race in America beyond Black and White* (New York: Basic Books, 2001); Judy Yung, *Unbound Feet: A Social History of Chinese Women in San Francisco* (Berkeley: University of California Press, 1995).

4 The recently published treatments of *Brown* are: Austin Sarat, ed., *Race, Law, and Culture: Reflections on Brown v. Board of Education* (New York: Oxford University Press, 1997); Jack M. Balkin, ed., *What "Brown v. Board of Education" Should Have Said: The Nation's Top Legal Experts Rewrite America's Landmark Civil Rights Decision* (New York: New York University Press, 2001); James T. Patterson, *Brown v. Board of Education: A Civil Rights Milestone and Its Troubled Legacy* (New York: Oxford University Press, 2001); Peter Irons, *Jim Crow's Children: The Broken Promise of the Brown Decision* (New York: Viking, 2002).

# PART I

# Historical Contexts: Views from the Grassroots

BLAIR L. M. KELLEY

# *Plessy* and Early Challenges to the Doctrine

# of "Separate, but Equal"

*Plessy v. Ferguson* (1896) represents the legal and historical benchmark for Jim Crow legislation. The ill-fated case established the precedent of "equal, but separate" which shaped African American legal battles against segregation throughout the first half of the twentieth century. Numerous legal scholars have probed the arguments of Plessy's attorney, Albion Tourgee, before the U.S. Supreme Court, highlighting the difficulties of establishing rights in the obscurities of the Fourteenth Amendment to the Constitution. Similarly, historians have aptly outlined the Court's reluctance to defend black rights in a time of legal and social repression, and examined the terrible consequences of segregation law in the South.[1]

However, the broader social circumstances from which *Plessy* emerged have been less well probed. *Plessy v. Ferguson* was the result of the collective organizing efforts of important men of color in New Orleans. After the joint efforts of black freedmen and Afro-Creole leaders had failed to block the passage of a Louisiana law separating black and white train passengers, a small group of leading Creoles of color[2] established the Citizens' Committee for the Annulment of Act No. 111 Commonly Known as the Separate Car Law. The Committee engaged Homer Plessy, a working-class Afro-Creole resident of New Orleans, to be arrested and press a test case against the East Louisiana Railroad in the summer of 1892.

The committee's efforts to contest the onslaught of segregation included exceptional efforts to promote integrationist ideals and advance a vision of American citizenship transcendent of racial boundaries. Drawing on their own racial ambiguities as the fair-skinned descendants of European and slave forebears, the Afro-Creole leaders of New Orleans questioned the logic of segregation in a mixed-race society, cogently challenging the meaning of categories that classified some white-skinned people as "Negro." Central to their effort to dispute racial categories, Afro-Creole leaders also sought to defend the citizenship rights of all Americans no matter their color and to establish coalitions with sympathetic whites. At a moment when it might have been more politic to argue for their own exceptional social status, members of the Citizens' Committee argued on behalf of all African Americans. But increasingly, their argument against Jim Crow and in favor of an integrated society brought them into conflict with the community of freed blacks. Afro-Creole efforts to defend integration eventually led them to deplore all-black institutions as symbols of a growing system of legal segregation, rather than of African American autonomy. As Creoles of color were increasingly excluded from integrated spaces, they resented being shunted into black institutions. But Americanized blacks outside the Creole community had worked hard to create and defend black schools and churches, and although they vigorously contested segregated public accommodations, they gained strength within their own institutions.

This chapter examines the divides of color and culture that complicated the efforts of African Americans in New Orleans to contest the Louisiana state law segregating railroads by race in the 1890s. Although most African-Americans at the turn of the century were concerned with achieving equality and social justice, sought to maintain citizenship rights through the ballot, and desired safe and just recognition in the broader public sphere, they disagreed on how to achieve these ends. Creoles of color believed that the fight for equality and the fight for integration were inextricable. For the members of their unique community, integration was not merely a tactical means of gaining equality but a connection to their past as free people of color in a slave society. Fair inclusion was their legacy, and they sought to defend the limited liberties they had enjoyed as free people during the age of slavery.

Much like the NAACP attorneys who argued before the Supreme Court in *Brown* more than sixty years later, Creoles of color contested segregation as a stigmatizing system that marked people of color as inferior. They believed that an ideal society would be an integrated one, one where color did not matter. From public accommodations to primary schools, colleges, churches, and neighborhoods, Creoles of color believed that distinctions based on color had no place.

The story of *Plessy v. Ferguson* marks an odd but telling moment in African American history. As we reflect on the legacy of *Brown v. Board of Education* and what it has meant for African Americans and the larger nation, and as we debate the meaning of equality and the merits and possibilities of creating a "colorblind society," we would do well to recall the historical moment when the doctrine of "equal, but separate" came into being. Though the rise of Jim Crow had many sources, the constitutional doctrine was itself the product, in part, of a particular social struggle among African American communities in the city of New Orleans over the best way to advance in an era of constrained choices. The history of organizing that predated *Plessy* provides a historical lens through which to examine the messy complexity of the contemporary debate over equality and inclusion.

## A Divided People: The Histories of Two African American Communities in New Orleans

Histories of the antebellum Creoles of color emphasize their distinctive in-between status. Afro-Creoles had a unique legacy marked by differences of culture, color, and language. The cosmopolitan and racially diverse city of New Orleans had once been home to alternatives to strict racial segregation. The French-speaking descendants of free people of color, *gens de couleur libres*, or Creoles of color, were a unique community. Their legacy could be traced to the French and Spanish colonial era, when racially mixed slaves and free black émigrés from Haiti moved to New Orleans, where they gained a degree of social and political freedom in the late eighteenth century. The colonial era in Louisiana was distinctive: French and Spanish colonists were permitted to free and educate the children whom they had fathered with black slave women. As a result, Louisiana was home to thousands of free descendants of mixed unions.

During the antebellum period, free people of color gained a stronger economic and social foothold. Some became skilled tradesmen, purchasing both land and slaves, while seeking education at home and in Europe. Others became part of the city's vibrant working class, finding employment as longshoremen, draymen, and factory workers. White Creoles, mixed French and Spanish descendants of white colonists, never identified with their colored counterparts. However, members of their community began to gradually blend into Creole society, integrating Creole neighborhoods and Catholic churches and schools. Free people of color created a distinct niche in New Orleans society, one that allowed for greater autonomy and freedom than black slaves enjoyed.[3]

Although Creoles of color enjoyed the privileges of liberty, segregation laws and customs increasingly circumscribed their freedom after Louisiana became part of the United States in 1803. Theaters were the first public accommodations to be legally segregated in 1816, followed by jails in the 1830s. While a privileged few Creoles of color had been educated in the private schools of New Orleans, they were officially barred from the public school system when it was initiated in the 1840s. Philanthropists from the community such as Thomy Lafon and Aristide Marie founded and financed a number of private institutions, providing increased opportunities for education to both poor and privileged students of color. But Creoles of color always resisted racial separations, and whenever they could they sought to slip past the city's color lines through artful persuasion or silently passing for white.[4]

Afro-Creoles existed in the murky middle between free white society and enslaved blacks, and they suffered a severe erosion of their citizenship rights as fears of slave insurrections led by free people of color peaked in the mid-nineteenth century. But despite these challenges, Creoles of color enjoyed a more liberated existence than other free black people and black slaves in the American South. With this second-class citizenship, Afro-Creoles were able to build a society rich in culture and relatively sheltered from most of the barbs of race prejudice and violence that slaves and rural free blacks faced. After emancipation, Creoles of color became the reluctant leaders of the less fortunate former slaves. But identity in New Orleans remained distinctively marked, divided by color, language, and heritage.[5]

Afro-Creole legislators led the fight to dissolve the color line, successfully passing laws desegregating public schools and accommodations during the Constitutional Convention of 1867–68. In the postwar period, Creoles of color took full advantage of their newly affirmed rights as citizens, integrating public schools and participating in the city's public life. Not only did people of color in New Orleans gain a sure foothold on citizenship, they also became more fully ingrained in a network of racial integration— attending Catholic mass with white congregants, living in racially integrated neighborhoods in the French Quarter, attending Carnival festivities, public plays, and sporting events, and riding freely on public conveyances. This is not to suggest that the lives of Creoles of color were free from discrimination and oppression; race remained a tremendous barrier to even the most successful. And the systematic violence of white repression that threatened African American voters in rural Louisiana reverberated in the cities as well.

Unless they chose to separate from their family, friends, and communities and pass for white, Afro-Creoles in New Orleans could not escape the larger social reality of race.[6] Some light-skinned Creoles of color desired the privileges usually connected with white skin, and deeply resented their invisible connection to blackness. In 1877 an angry Creole of color wrote anonymously about his social discomfort. He believed that there was no racial middle ground, even for those who appeared to be white. He angrily complained that "a person having a few drops of african blood in his veins, no matter how white he may be is considered a nigger." Pressing the viewpoint of the Afro-Creoles who had decided to pass permanently as white citizens, he continued, "I think that man has a right to choose for himself, weather [sic] he will be a white man or a nigger. So it is, the moral suffering of a man having a little Negro blood in his veins is something terrible—for he is always in hot water."[7] Some descendants of free people of color felt enslaved by their black heritage and sought ways to distance themselves, not only from other African Americans but also from black identity.

But the majority of Afro-Creoles were not as bitter about their racial status. Not all Creoles of color were pale-skinned enough to pass for white, but more importantly, most did not want to break with their family, friends, culture, and community simply to become white. Rather than choose the social isolation and personal risk that came with passing for white, they chose to emphasize their unique place in society and the history of New Orleans and fought to maintain their tenuous hold on middle-ground status.

Although much of the historical record focuses on the élite Creole leaders, as a group Creoles of color were also separated into classes, along lines of wealth, employment, and privilege. Most Creoles of color were not wealthy and propertied: they lived their lives in circumstances similar to those of Homer Plessy. Like Plessy, most Afro-Creole people in New Orleans were literate, skilled laborers employed in cigar factories, or artisans such as metal workers and stonemasons. When litigation began, Plessy's occupation was listed as shoemaker; by 1902 the city directory listed him as a laborer. Plessy held a variety of jobs during his working life; his biographer reports that he was employed as a clerk, a warehouse laborer, and an insurance collector in his lifetime. The labor of working-class Creoles was distinct; their jobs separated them from the élite Afro-Creole professional class as well as from the masses of unskilled black workers. And although working-class Creoles of color lived in integrated neighborhoods on the French side of Canal Street, they seldom resided in the city's more exclusive sections. Like many, Plessy lived in the city's Tremé section along with his wife in a rented house near the famed Congregation Hall.[8] Plessy's Creole status and light skin may have allowed him some intracommunity privilege, but he was far from élite.

Homer Plessy was part of a community of color with a unique legacy and an unusual approach to questions of race. The majority of Creoles of color had battled hard to break down the color line and valued colorblind inclusion in the city of their birth. They approached the fight against turn-of-the-century Jim Crow laws with a distinct outlook and a belief in the value of an integrated society. But opportunities for African Americans of both Creole and American descent began shrinking in the 1890s with the advent of more formal laws barring blacks from public accommodations. Afro-Creoles united with newly freed blacks to contest the growth of segregation.

But these two communities had different origins and their views on the problem of segregation were distinct.

The descendants of the freed slaves who resided in New Orleans or migrated to it faced more difficult circumstances than the Creoles of color. After emancipation, freed slaves were attracted to the city, seeking work and the security of an urban setting. This migration continued in the decades after Reconstruction. Between 1880 and 1900, more than twenty thousand new black migrants moved to the expanding city from the rural counties of Louisiana and Mississippi. But dire circumstances faced the migrants. Nearly half the black population of New Orleans was illiterate in 1890. Lynching and racial violence increasingly threatened the black populace, as did dismal urban living conditions. By the turn of the century the hot and often-flooded city had no sewage system, so sickness and disease plagued the poorest residents.[9] But the poor and working class gained a sure hold on citizenship during Reconstruction and the decades that followed, fighting hard to maintain their right to vote and fair representation in every aspect of public life.[10]

Black residents of New Orleans had only continued to progress because of autonomous efforts to improve their communities. By 1890 black illiteracy had dropped dramatically, aided in part by black educators who supplemented the poor system of public education through black churches and mutual aid societies. Black communities established church schools and Sunday schools to meet the tremendous need for education. Care for the physical health of poor black residents also improved. Community efforts to organize black hospitals and black mutual aid and benevolent societies helped brighten a bleak black public health record. Numerous societies of middle-class and poor African Americans made valiant attempts to address the needs of their community.[11]

Blacks in New Orleans also built some coalitions with white residents. Many noted politicians who emerged as leaders in the Republican Party were not part of the Creole élite. During Reconstruction, blacks successfully worked alongside white politicians for more than fifteen years. The black electorate's support of the Republican Party held back the tide of white supremacy and violence during Reconstruction. Coalition building also buttressed the city's working class. Interracial unionism among the city's dockworkers dramatically improved conditions for black and white longshoremen. During the general strike of 1892, twenty thousand black and white longshoremen and dockworkers united to improve pay and working conditions.

But most of the progress that black people experienced grew out of autonomous improvement efforts. A black middle class slowly emerged from the population of former slaves and their children in the closing decades of the nineteenth century. A class of educators, preachers, merchants, and businesspeople nurtured by black churches and schools grew prominent and more successful, serving as community leaders for blacks who lived outside the Vieux Carré or "French City." Thus over time New Orleans developed a divided black leadership class, one Creole and one non-Creole. These two communities not only maintained separate societies but distinctly different approaches to the questions of race, equality, and integration.[12]

### The Battle against Segregated Railroads in New Orleans

In Louisiana, African Americans fought the segregation of the state's railways throughout the decades following the Civil War. Some African Americans were forced to ride in smoking cars near the soot-spewing engine at the front of the train, barred from sleeping cars, and many black women were excluded from ladies' cars. Despite Reconstruction laws that prohibited discrimination, conductors arbitrarily barred black riders who had purchased first-class tickets from seats in first-class cars.[13] As a result, African Americans developed creative solutions to counter railroad segregation. Instead of merely fighting segregation case by case, black lawmakers of the early 1870s pushed to include prohibitions against racial discrimination in railroad charters. So attempts to segregate blacks in Louisiana were met not only with damage suits but also with reviews of the offending railroad's charter. The African American legislator P. B. S. Pinchback, for example, sued the Jackson railroad when his wife was denied admission to a Pullman berth, and he threatened to have the railroad's charter revoked. After the threat of a damage suit, the Jackson railroad, along with the other railroad companies in Louisiana, usually honored first-class tickets purchased by black patrons, a practice that continued into the 1870s.[14]

The "redemption" of Louisiana politics in 1877 by white Democrats and the repeal of state constitutional provisions protecting black rights to public accommodations in 1879 did, however, present new challenges to black travelers in the 1880s. Uneven policies governed the rails of Louisiana. Some railroads regularly operated integrated cars, to the chagrin of segregationist newspaper editors who highlighted "the indiscriminate commingling of the races in travel." But some segregated cars were put into operation with various levels of enforcement. During this turbulent period, the experience of black passengers varied from carrier to carrier and sometimes from day to day.[15]

Nevertheless, New Orleanians of color pushed for equal accommodations by sheer will, indignation, and legal protest, forcing railroads to adopt more flexible standards for seating African American passengers throughout the 1880s. After all, it was cheaper for the railroad to seat the few first-class, respectable passengers of color among white riders than to establish and run entirely separate first-class cars. New Orleans had many élite Afro-Creole passengers who were as respectable and by appearance as white as the most respected white citizens.

The white writer and sympathetic racial advocate George Washington Cable put forth the idea of class segregation, arguing that "neither race . . . wants to see the civil rewards of decency in dress and behavior usurped by the common herd of clowns and ragamuffins." Instead he asserted that élite African Americans had earned the "rights of gentility by the simple act of being genteel."[16] Although the city's famous resident was heralded for his historical fiction about the people of New Orleans, he may have hinted at the silent truth held by some élite whites in New Orleans. Whites of the city may have grown accustomed to a few élite people of color in their midst. Cable saw no harm in allowing these privileged few to flourish. He believed that the city's educated and propertied African Americans, particularly Creoles of color, should be respected because they had, over time, earned class-based civil privileges.

Cable wanted a class-based hierarchy in southern society and rejected racial segregation as an illogical divider. He asserted that "these distinctions on the line of color are really made not from any necessity, but simply for their own sake—to preserve the old arbitrary supremacy of the master class over the menial without regard to the decency or indecency of appearance or manners in either the white individual or the colored." Segregation, Cable argued, made "the average Southern railway coach more uncomfortable than the average railway coaches elsewhere," forcing the "average Southern white passenger to find less offense in the presence of a profane, boisterous, or unclean white person than in that of a quiet, well-behaved colored man or woman."[17] But he was one of just a handful of whites who were willing to argue on behalf of respectable black citizens. When segregation law and popular white opinion turned against the rights of respectable black railcar patrons, there were few white southerners who supported flexible racial policies. The statute requiring separate railcars, once introduced in the state legislature, threatened the tenuous compromise that had been established in New Orleans. The quiet concessions of the earlier decade were increasingly threatened by growing white sentiment that connected integration with "race mixing" and the threat of social equality.

### Defending "Right and Justice": Organizing against Segregation

African American leaders quickly responded to the threats to equal citizenship. Initially Afro-Creole and Americanized blacks united their disparate voices in the fight against segregation. But each community adopted its own unique approach to the question of segregation. In 1889 Louis Martinet, a Creole attorney of color, founded the weekly publication *Crusader* to counter the rising tide of hostility in New Orleans. The editors described the newspaper as an "organ of justice and equal rights, the enemy of wrong and injustice, the friend and defender of right and justice." Martinet, along with the Afro-Creole writer Rodolphe Desdunes, used a fiery progressivism to push for maintaining civic equality for citizens of color.

Desdunes did not accept the notion that the *Crusader* was a "Negro paper." Challenging traditional assumptions about race, Desdunes asserted that the newspaper's editor, Martinet, was "as white as the editor of the [New Orleans] Times-Democrat, as any who will see both together can judge." Questioning the racial "purity" of his critics, Desdunes went on to provocatively assert that the *paper's* Creole of color "proprietors are men of as pure Caucasian blood as any, and perhaps purer than some on the T[imes]-D[emocrat] staff." Although Desdunes made proprietary claims of whiteness, his arguments targeted what he believed were false dichotomies between black and white in the age of segregation. Desdunes and others in the Afro-Creole community wanted to avoid being stigmatized by blackness linked to a slave legacy, but they also did not want to erase their unique legacy in order to become white. Rather they sought to embody the literal meaning of Creole—a complicated blend of historic cultures and communities that emerged from a unique, and free, legacy.

Martinet's fiery weekly was the voice of politically engaged Creoles of color, not only presenting a unique vision of race but also emphasizing egalitarian principles and a deep belief in the racial integration of institutions such as Catholic schools and churches.[18] As evidenced in the pages of the *Crusader*, Afro-Creoles were a conservative people who clung to their antebellum status, seeking to maintain their place in an integrated civic world. The Creole of color community opposed segregation of every sort, even the establishment of all-black colleges and churches that most non-Creole African Americans favored. Creoles of color had become invested in a lifestyle that allowed them to participate in many of the institutions of public life in New Orleans.

Segregated facilities, even when encouraged by black American leaders or founded to further black education and independence, were an anathema to the Afro-Creoles. At a time when most African American communities were rallying to defend black elementary and high schools against attacks from white state legislatures questioning the need to educate black children, the Afro-Creoles of New Orleans battled to keep their children in majority-white public and private schools. Creoles of color had been the greatest beneficiaries of remarkable efforts to desegregate public schools during Reconstruction. Despite efforts to oust children of color from public schools in the 1880s and 1890s, many Creole children of color light enough to pass remained in the white public school population.[19] The greatest strength of most southern black communities was their independent churches, but Creoles of color in the Parish of New Orleans fought the efforts of the Catholic Church to establish a separate sanctuary for African American congregants. Although Afro-Creoles sought to provide instrumental leadership for the African American community after emancipation, they also rejected any efforts that threatened their unique social status. They hoped that through an egalitarian and integrated New Orleans they might be able to maintain their distinct identity.

Black Americans in New Orleans also monitored closely the erosion of equal access to public conveyances and responded to local white efforts by taking advantage of federal law. A principal medium for their views was the long-running black newspaper the *Southwestern Christian Advocate*. Although the *Advocate*, a black Methodist Episcopal publication, was a denominational organ that contained church news and Christian instruction, it also tracked shifting political currents for the city's black residents. The paper faithfully reported shifts in the law and the encroachment of segregation on the city, as well as general political news of the city, state, and nation. The black American middle class in New Orleans battled the changes facing their burgeoning community. The *Advocate* spoke out against both local and national challenges to black voting rights and regularly published accounts of lynchings in Louisiana, boldly reporting that prominent and successful blacks were most often the targets of white violence. The editor of the weekly, the Reverend A. E. P. Albert, tried to address the systematic threats to the health of black citizenship, demonstrating the ways that the inequities faced by blacks in New Orleans would systematically render African Americans voiceless.[20]

The *Advocate* tracked state legislators' attempts to segregate southern rails. Reporting on the U.S. Supreme Court decision in *Louisville, New Orleans, and Texas Railway v. Mississippi* (1890), Albert bemoaned that "one by one all the results of the [Civil] [W]ar secured at such tremendous cost in life and property, are being frittered away by the Supreme Court." The Court held in the decision that interstate segregation was constitutional, reversing an earlier decision that in effect had limited the southern states' ability to pass segregation laws applicable to railroads that spanned more than one state. Albert reported that local white segregationists resolved to make hay of the new opportunity.

But central to the efforts of Americanized blacks to fight segregation was the fight to improve conditions within their own communities. The *Advocate* vigilantly reminded black readers of the need to improve black schools with increased funding and competent black educators, and it promoted black independence and self-help as the best ways to further African American progress. Rejecting the idea that mere inclusion was the path to African American success, the *Advocate* embraced community-based efforts to improve from within, publicizing mutual-aid and church societies.

Despite their differences, Afro-Creole and black American community leaders united in the effort to highlight injustices and began to organize collectively on behalf of their communities. In response to a proposal put forward at the National Colored Convention, held in Washington in February 1890, Pinchback, who had been the most prominent representative sent to the convention by the Louisiana State Convention of Colored Men, formed a state branch of the American Citizens' Equal Rights Association. Although Pinchback was very light-skinned and the descendent of a free black mother and a white father, he was not a native of the state and hence not a Creole of color. However, four hundred men of both Creole and non-Creole descent attended the convention as representatives of state and local districts. Pinchback assumed a leadership position in the convention and in an organization of Louisiana blacks.[21] Following the model of the National Colored Convention, Pinchback "organized a central association for the state of Louisiana." The state organization elected leading Afro-Creoles and black Americans to head the group, including Albert as its president. Leadership was shared by the two groups: J. Lewis and William J. Rudolphe were the organization's vice presidents, while Pinchback and Louis A. Martinet, editor of the *Crusader*, were ex-officio members.[22]

The cautious, newly founded state association attempted to bridge the gap between the Afro-Creole and black American communities by drawing its leadership from both groups. Although Creoles of color may have sought to maintain a distinct identity throughout the post-emancipation period and into the 1890s, some Creoles initially respected the experience of political elders like Pinchback and new voices like Albert, who had similar approaches to working for the benefit of people of color. Albert was even welcomed as the sole black American in the Crusader Publishing Company, the group that published the Afro-Creole newspaper in the 1890s. Adversity in a city where white segregationists cared little about the different origins of the people of color drew embattled communities together. Even if Afro-Creoles and members of the black middle class did not share birth languages, they were both familiar with the language of disfranchisement and racial segregation.[23]

Both communities agreed that education, thrift, and moral behavior were the best remedies for white arguments about the inferiority of the African race. Believing that hard work was the path to substantial change, Albert cautioned his readers to "let us have less show and feathers, and more comfortable homes, nice churches, and substantial schools," things similar to what Afro-Creoles had already established for themselves.[24] In an argument similar to that of Creoles of color, Pinchback asserted that African American political success depended on behavior: "to vitalize our efforts to secure civil equality and political influence we must improve our condition in wealth by frugal industry, our intelligence by study, [and] our moral force by fidelity to truth and to principle." In the battle against legal segregation, the Creole and non-Creole communities did adopt some shared terms and shared approaches to protest. But Pinchback also hinted at the autonomous black American spirit when he stated, "we must do not only well for ourselves, but rely on ourselves."[25]

Although the American Citizens' Equal Rights Association (ACERA) had a conservative approach to the race problem, it sought to make a statement to white segregationists that African Americans would not simply accept the legal and extra-legal deterioration of black citizenship. Pinchback asserted that African Americans "demand protection, because we are American citizens."[26] When the Louisiana General Assembly considered "a statute inspired by the court's ruling and modeled after the one in Mississippi"[27] that required separate accommodations for black passengers on railroads, ACERA immediately organized to confront the offensive bill. It formed a committee of Creole and non-Creole leaders "to draw up protests against the proposed class legislation now pending before the Legislature." The committee composed a written protest that would be presented by a black legislator to the Assembly. ACERA also sent a delegation "to visit Baton Rouge and exert all influence" to defeat the proposed segregation law. The editor of the *Advocate* was "selected to address the Legislature in behalf of the Association."[28]

The association submitted its protest to the Louisiana Assembly through T. T. Allain, a state legislator and Creole of color. The document called the separate-car law "unconstitutional, un-American, unjust, dangerous and against sound public policy." Citing the Declaration of Independence and the Golden Rule, the association connected an integrated public sphere to the "American principles" that were the fundamental basis of citizenship.

Segregation was not the natural organization of society but rather the expression of "unreasonable prejudice." People of color were "respectable, useful, and law-abiding," representative of "a considerable percentage of the capital and almost all the labor of the state," and deserved better. The document argued that black Louisianans, working-class and élite alike, had made profound contributions to the state and should not be denied first-class citizenship: "We do not think that citizens of a darker hue should be treated by law on different lines than those of a lighter complexion. Citizenship is national and has no color."[29]

Despite the best effort of the delegation, the association met defeat in July 1890 when the separate-car act passed.[30] The association did continue organizing throughout the fall, but only around issues that divided the leadership. ACERA called on delegates from local churches and community organizations to meet concerning the improvement of black schools in New Orleans, and the group successfully pushed for New Orleans to hire black teachers to teach in segregated African American schools.[31] The former slaves viewed opportunities to gain education and build religious institutions in all-black surroundings as opportunities to strengthen the status of freedmen. Creoles of color did not support such efforts to improve segregated schools. Instead they advocated integrated schools and the mixing of white students with students of color. The Creole of color community sought to maintain access to New Orleans society on an equal basis, not to improve conditions in segregated facilities. Creoles of color opposed segregation in all forms and detested being lumped with the freedmen and pushed outside the white public realm.

Philosophical differences had always plagued ACERA's leadership. At the Colored Convention in Washington in February 1890, Martinet had worked, unsuccessfully, to "keep the word 'colored' out of the [ACERA] preamble." To Martinet, segregation in any form, including the exclusion of sympathetic whites from a mostly black political organization, was fundamentally wrong.[32] Some Creole of color members even withdrew from leadership positions in ACERA. And after the failure of ACERA to block the passage of the separate-car law, the coalition tentatively forged by the association finally failed. The venerable Senator Pinchback would continue to agitate against segregation, but as a resident of New York State.[33]

Martinet, a founding member of the Louisiana American Citizens' Equal Rights Association, commented negatively on the demise of the organization in 1891: "the American Citizens' Equal Rights Association has about gone down, the proper men were not at the head. Its last . . . national convention was turned into a purely political resolution machine." Martinet had joined the organization with the aim of starting a national daily newspaper that would inform Northerners about "the conditions and affairs in the South," and he was disturbed by what he perceived as the desire of most delegates to organize without building coalitions with sympathetic whites. A disappointed Martinet blamed "politicians [and] . . . that other clan not much better—those preachers who see in their profession the means of earning a livelihood or making money only" and asserted that ACERA's leadership was concerned with nothing beyond "the honor and prestige of the moment." Despite Pinchback's and Albert's long-term commitment to struggle, Martinet believed that many African American leaders of the period were attracted to politics for selfish gain and that the fight against segregation would be best served by selfless, egalitarian leaders willing to build a long-term, national, cross-racial coalition. His beliefs became the hallmark of his effort in the Citizens' Committee.[34]

Others, such as Rodolphe Desdunes, were proud of this first protest effort and viewed it as just a beginning. In 1892 Desdunes sent Albion Tourgee a letter with an attached copy of the ACERA protest document. "Now that we have begun action in the separate car case, it appears to me proper to send you a copy of our protest to the General Assembly of Louisiana against the passage of class legislation," he wrote. "The paper has the merit of showing the first step taken and by whom, against the passage of that infamous act." For Desdunes, the next move was into the court system. Blaming Republican Party insiders for the failure of the first efforts, he saw the courts as a way to consolidate their efforts and make an effective end run around party politics.

With the advent of segregation law in the 1890s, Afro-Creoles began to withdraw from cross-community organizations, seeking instead to lead a more independent fight against segregation law. Afro-Creoles sought to organize alone, cutting themselves off from a broader constituency and from outside opinions. An élite group of Creoles of color came together to form an organization that would raise funds for pressing a test case and continuing the fight against Jim Crow cars. The small group of like-minded men decided to take a top-down approach to fighting legal segregation.[35]


The Plessy Case and the Work of the Citizens' Committee


A new organization, the Citizens' Committee, became the leader of the ensuing legal challenge to segregated rails beginning in 1891. Martinet, committed to developing an interracial coalition against segregation, cited racial exclusiveness as the major cause of the failure of the American Citizens' Equal Rights Association. Martinet believed that "the North needs to be educated as to conditions in the South and its disloyalty and rebellious tendencies. And we need to do the work soon." For the members of the Citizens' Committee, the key to challenging Jim Crow policy was to petition the federal courts and establish a new national consensus against segregation law. They believed that if Northern whites were aware of the plight of African Americans in the South, they would put pressure on southern legislators to protect black citizenship. Segregationists were better tuned to the national pulse, which was increasingly turning a blind eye to discriminatory southern politics.[36]

The Citizens' Committee was composed exclusively of leading men from the Afro-Creole community of New Orleans,[37] and formed with the encouragement of Aristide Marie, an Afro-Creole legislator from the Reconstruction era. Marie was a philanthropist and elder statesman by the 1890s, whose conflicts with the non-Creole leader P. B. S. Pinchback over the founding of Southern University as a separate state-funded university for African Americans had led to an ongoing rivalry between the two leaders.[38] This tactical disagreement mirrored the conflicts that prompted leading Creoles of color to organize outside the American Citizens' Equal Rights Association.

The Citizens' Committee formed specifically to respond to the separate-car law. Eighteen leaders of the Creole of color community banded together to take "some definite action towards offering legal resistance" to segregation on Louisiana's rails by preparing a test case to challenge Jim Crow railcars. Unlike ACERA, the committee had a singular purpose and a closed membership; its founders had "invited" "a few citizens representing various interests" within the Afro-Creole community to participate. Three key members of ACERA joined the Citizens' Committee, a group that included the main voices of the *Crusader*, Rodolphe Desdunes and Louis Martinet, and the Reconstruction-era politician Laurant August. The well-established weekly the *Crusader* was the voice of the newly formed organization. And it was in the newspaper's office that the members of the Committee held their first meeting to plan "offering legal resistance to [the Jim Crow Car's] operation."[39]

The group published "an appeal, to the public" soon after its initial meeting. The document informed the larger community that the committee would wage "an earnest effort to vindicate the cause of equal rights and American manhood. If honored with the confidence of the people, we pledge our best exertions to pursue the object of the mission to its legitimate end." The committee insisted that the character of American citizenship was threatened if African Americans did not force the issue of segregation into the courts. They saw Jim Crow as part of a slippery slope toward "every manner of outrage, up to murder, without redress." Even though committee membership was exclusive, the group still sought the support of all people concerned with the future of American citizenship, publishing the appeal in English rather than the more exclusive Creole language of French. But despite such efforts to speak broadly, the élite bent of the committee's message was unmistakable.[40]

The committee's hopes that local and national leaders might support its efforts were not borne out. Desdunes wrote that the committee's efforts were mocked not only by local white "Democratic journals" but also by "Negro leaders—National Leaders" who "refused aid or encouragement." Desdunes reported that Frederick Douglass, "the greatest of all Negroes," refused to support the work of the Citizens' Committee because "he was opposed to making decisions and establishing precedents against his race." Desdunes did not recognize Douglass's foresight and dismissed him as "unpardonably ignorant . . . of the constitutional rights of his race." As the struggle against segregation continued, the divide between Creoles of color and other African Americans would further widen.[41]

Early organizing centered on raising the funds necessary to support a test case. Members of the committee called for financial support from citizens of all races and from all walks of life; they hoped that the contributions would demonstrate popular support for their cause: "Our countrymen without regard to age, color or condition, may, through their offering, as a medium of communication, express their indignation as well as their desire to test in the courts the constitutionality of this law." By the end of October the committee had raised more than $1,400 to fund the test case and had committed to hiring Tourgee as its lead counsel. Martinet believed that the committee's financial success was due to Tourgee's relationship to the organization. He wrote to Tourgee in early October 1891: "the revival of interest in the Jim Crow car matter is owing to you more than to anyone else. I only hope that the people of other places will do as well as our friends here."[42]

Tourgee was a leader in the Republican Party, a popular writer, and a national voice on behalf of black civil rights. His affiliation with the fledgling Citizens' Committee attracted both local and national attention. Tourgee provided the connection with concerned northern whites that the organization desperately sought, and he was able to highlight the work of the *Crusader* and the Citizens' Committee in his column in the Republican newspaper the *Inter-Ocean*. Martinet was appreciative of Tourgee's efforts, which boosted the circulation of the *Crusader* and helped to develop the cross-cultural, nationwide attention that Martinet believed was crucial. Martinet felt that the committee's fight could only succeed if the problems of segregation were revealed to white Northerners, just as the civil rights movement of the 1950s built a critical consensus against the injustice of segregation by engaging the entire nation in the fight.[43]

The separate-car law called for train officials to set up two first-class cars, a requirement which increased the cost of running trains in Louisiana. Railroad employees were also burdened with the awkward task of deciding if boarding passengers were white or black, a difficult proposition in a city with a large population of phenotypically white people of color. Martinet believed that whites could not necessarily assign passengers quickly and accurately to segregated cars, explaining, "if you were not informed you would be sure to pick out the white for colored and the colored for white."[44] Although conductors had maintained informal discriminatory practices before 1890, their decisions now had the force of law. Conductors would fear accidentally seating light-skinned African Americans in cars designated for white passengers, just as they would fear insulting dark-featured whites by seating them in colored cars. Such awkward situations made the company vulnerable to suits from both sides. To the railroad companies, segregation was a liability: they could be fined for seating blacks with whites, censured for insulting white passengers, and sued because of unequal facilities in the separate colored car.[45]

The committee decided that the case could only work with the agreement of railroad officials. The effort to work with Louisiana rail companies revealed the uneven application of the law. One rail company contacted by committee members informed them that it "did not enforce the law." The railroad displayed "the sign required by law" and "the conductors were instructed to show the car" to African American passengers. "If they refused," conductors were instructed "not to be violent in any way." Martinet characterized the messy situation on this railroad as "a victory already." Yet the ambiguous situation was still unfair at best and dangerous at worst. African American riders intimidated by the law would be forced to sit in the colored car, while more indignant ones could perhaps be tolerated in the car for white riders. This informal policy did not guarantee that blacks could ride in the first-class car, nor did it guarantee the safety of blacks who sat in the "white" car and risked becoming the victims of angry white passengers personally seeking to enforce the unjust law. Another rail company agreed that the law was "bad . . . [and they] would like to get rid of it," but the company did attempt to follow the law.[46] Black passengers in Louisiana did not know what to expect when they boarded trains, a condition which must have created confusion and anxiety about railroad travel.

The committee was eventually successful in coming to an agreement with the railroads. The railroad decided to allow the protest to proceed as planned on their train.[47] With everything in place, the committee had to choose a representative to be arrested on the train in violation of the segregation law, ultimately settling on Homer Plessy. Although nothing is known about how Plessy came to volunteer to press the case, he was selected by the committee in part because he was phenotypically white. Tourgee insisted that a light-skinned subject would highlight the difficulty of defining race in a society where not all people of color were easily identifiable. In fact, a key part of Tourgee's argument was that Plessy was denied his rights as a "mostly" white man simply because he had a trace of black blood. Tourgee was fascinated by the blurred color line in New Orleans, and he sought to exploit the light skin of Afro-Creoles to his advantage in the courtroom.

A challenge to the committee's legitimacy quickly came when a minister in New Orleans accused the organization of élitism and exclusivity. The all-Creole committee was attacked by blacks who felt that its light-skinned leaders did not represent their race and were merely trying to remove the barriers that kept an élite few from white privilege. The minister "charged that the people who support our movement were nearly white, or wanted to pass for white and that in 'succumbing' to our fund they did not sign their names." Martinet replied that most people did donate to the cause by name, that only a few were "earnest . . . but modest." Hurt by the accusation that his supporters were ashamed of their heritage, Martinet said that he had begun to think that the greatest hindrance "the race has to contend with [came from] . . . within our ranks."[48] Afro-Creoles shared more than their pale skin tones: they also valued racial integration as a way of insuring African American citizenship, an approach that differed from the beliefs of many non-Creole black Americans. But perhaps the committee could have shown greater depths of leadership; in its efforts to promote integration and interracial coalitions it failed to generate mass support and build coalitions within the larger African American community. The committee never invited local black leaders to take part and failed to give sufficient credit to non-Creole leaders and their willingness to speak out against the discriminatory law. In the effort to defend integrationism, they muddled the fight against segregation. The effort of the committee might have been stronger had its members included a broader range of viewpoints on how best to challenge Jim Crow. Division weakened the fight against segregation in New Orleans, causing African Americans in New Orleans to direct some of their political energy against one another.

At least in part the committee's failure to organize mass support for its efforts stemmed from its members' great faith in the "strong power of the courts" to halt the rising tide of legalized segregation. Thus they pushed ahead with a test case in June 1892, believing that the law would work in their favor. On 7 June Homer Plessy purchased a first-class ticket to a destination within the state and boarded the train. He found a seat in the white car, told the conductor that he was colored, refused to move to the colored car, and was arrested by a private detective before the train left the station for its short journey. Plessy was soon found guilty of violating the separate-car law in both city and state courts. The path to the U.S. Supreme Court was, however, a longer and more trying one during which the committee struggled to stay afloat. As the committee waited for the legal process to run its course, the political climate in New Orleans worsened and racial hostility increased. African Americans across the color and culture divide had to battle attempts at legal disfranchisement and faced a rapid escalation of extralegal violence.

Plessy's case finally reached the U.S. Supreme Court in 1895. As the lead attorney, Tourgee argued that any limitations on Plessy's ability to purchase a first-class ticket and ride in the first-class car were an abridgment of his rights. Tourgee's case rested on two points. First, segregation was a violation of Plessy's rights under the Thirteenth and Fourteenth Amendments to the Constitution, which made slavery illegal and guaranteed citizenship to all persons born or naturalized in the United States. Here Tourgee attacked the provision in the law that allowed black servants attending to white children or the infirm to ride in first-class cars. The goal of the law was not complete separation but removing individuals who were not servile, he argued. To Tourgee, this exception affirmed that the segregation law sought to maintain a hierarchical racial status. Segregation was not about mere separation. Rather, it was about reaffirming racial divisions born in slavery.

The second and more controversial argument hinged on the second part of Section 1 of the Fourteenth Amendment, which asserted that "no State shall make or enforce any law which shall abridge the privileges or immunities of citizens . . . nor . . . deprive any person of life, liberty, or property." Interestingly, Tourgee argued that the separate-car law denied Homer Plessy "the reputation of being white" and that whiteness was not simply a status but also a form of property. Much like the anonymous Creole of color who wanted the right to choose his race, Tourgee believed that the separate-car law gave Plessy's right to self-chosen identity to train conductors who arbitrarily assigned passengers to one car or another based on their own judgment. Although it was clever of Tourgee to exploit the unique, racially ambiguous population of New Orleans, his approach fell short of offering a more universal solution to the problem of Jim Crow. Tourgee's argument undercut the notion that African Americans, regardless of skin color, deserved protection under the banner of equitable citizenship, and that systematic exclusion degraded the nature of black citizenship no matter how white an individual's heritage might be.[49]

While waiting for the decision the Citizens' Committee encountered internal difficulties, and its greatest spokesperson, Louis Martinet, became increasingly discouraged by these battles and by the problem of race in America. He questioned his place in the nation, feeling trapped between a hostile white South and a black population from which he felt distant and estranged by culture, belief, custom, and approach to politics. Within a decade W. E. B. Du Bois would describe this feeling as one of "two-ness." Martinet wrote:

> I feel at times as if I could tear the flag—the stars and stripes—into shreds. Yet I am not a bad citizen—as long as I live within its jurisdictions I shall be loyal to the country. . . . And yet why this feeling? I have no special love for the Negro—never perhaps had—only sympathy. As an individual I have been treated better than a great many . . . I have always been respected by those with whom I have come in contact. . . . I do not hanker for companionship or social relations with those who do not want to associate with me, nor do I desire unduly the personal advantages that accrue from unreserved association with one's fellow beings. I'm foolish enough to think that I am above those who view a man's worth through the glass of color prejudice. All I want is my civil rights, privileges as a citizen, and simple justice for all who are denied it. I want to *enjoy* rights and don't want to be *tolerated* merrily.

His anger and frustration left Martinet alienated, angry at the failed promises of American citizenship, and bitter at having organized on behalf of a people to whom he often felt superior and from whom he felt separate.[50]

The fight of the Citizens' Committee came to its disappointing climax in May 1896 when the majority of the Supreme Court found separate but equal accommodations to be within the bounds of the Constitution. Substantive correspondence between members of the Citizens' Committee and Tourgee ended before the decision, but their disappointment must have been tremendous. The case that the committee had hoped would reaffirm African American citizenship instead became a federal endorsement of racist southern laws and practices. Although the Citizens' Committee went on to protest against lynching and racial violence in Louisiana, its viability as an organization soon came to an end. Martinet's mouthpiece, the *Crusader*, ceased publication in 1897, one year after the decision.

After the failure of *Plessy*, Creoles of color withdrew from the forefront of the fight against segregation. When black citizens began to protest against the segregation of city streetcars in 1902, Afro-Creoles remained silent. They also continued their efforts to maintain their unique place in an integrated society, contesting the Catholic Church's attempts to segregate parishioners and parochial school students, and at the same time utilizing the advantages of color to keep their pale-skinned children enrolled in public schools. Hundreds of Creole of color children remained in majority-white schools into the twentieth century. When the New Orleans school board attempted to " 'weed out' the 'white colored' children from the public schools for whites" in 1900, it had a difficult time separating students by color. Not only could fair-skinned people of color pass undetected, but also "dark white people" might be falsely targeted for ejection. As the *Advocate* stated, "the question of determining 'which is which' is a great one here at all times."[51]

But passing was not integration, and the practice further exacerbated tensions between Creoles of color and other black people. Fair-hued Creoles of color as well as light-skinned blacks could avoid segregation by passing for white. But their passing proved a tacit acceptance of the color line and of the regime of Jim Crow. In the end, there could be no real middle ground for advocates of integration in the age of segregation. Choice was not an option in the Jim Crow era.

The difficulties and debates that plagued organizing efforts in turn-of-the-century New Orleans resonate in contemporary debates. In particular, the debate over the value and purpose of integrated schools, set against arguments for "neighborhood schools," race-based charter school programs, and vouchers, continues to inspire coalition building and division among both African Americans and Americans more generally. Although the legal strictures of Jim Crow segregation have been dismantled and the *Brown* decision sought to remedy racial inequity inherent in segregated systems, the debates that divided the unique African American communities of New Orleans continue to challenge Americans today.

## Notes

1 Some examples include: C. Vann Woodward, "The National Decision against Equality," *American Counterpoint: Slavery and Racism in the North-South Dialogue* (Boston: Little, Brown, 1971); Charles A. Lofgren, *The Plessy Case: A Legal-Historical Interpretation* (New York: Oxford University Press, 1987); Otto H. Olsen, "Reflections on the Plessy v. Ferguson Decision of 1896," *Louisiana's Legal Heritage*, ed. Edward F. Haas (Pensacola: Perdido Bay, 1983).

2 I have employed the terms Afro-Creole and Creole of color to denote the

French-speaking, Catholic, mixed-race descendents of free people of color in New Orleans to distinguish them from non-Creole African Americans; the terms black American and black to mean non-Creole populations in New Orleans; and African American as an overarching term for both communities. The terms available to describe the complexities of community are limited; however, I have adopted this language as a way of better outlining the distinctions of identity in post-emancipation New Orleans.

3 Caryn Cosse Bell, *Revolution, Romanticism and the Afro-Creole Protest Tradition in Louisiana, 1718–1868* (Baton Rouge: Louisiana State University Press, 1997); Charles Barthelemy Rousseve, *The Negro in Louisiana: Aspects of His History and His Literature* (New Orleans: Xavier University Press, 1937).

4 Roger A. Fischer, "Racial Segregation in Ante Bellum New Orleans," *American Historical Review* 74, no. 3 (1969): 926–37; Rodolphe L. Desdunes, *Our People and Our History*, ed. and trans. Dorthea Olga McCants (Baton Rouge: Louisiana State University Press, 1973).

5 John W. Blassingame, *Black New Orleans, 1860–1880* (Chicago: University of Chicago Press, 1973).

6 For a closer look at passing in New Orleans see Arthe Anthony, " 'Lost Boundaries': Racial Passing and Poverty in Segregated New Orleans," *Louisiana Purchase Bicentennial Series in Louisiana History* 15, "Visions and Revisions: Perspectives on Louisiana Society and Culture," ed. Vaughan Burdin Baker (Lafayette: Center for Louisiana Studies, University of Louisiana, 2000), 125–41.

7 "Justice to Cable," 24 February 1887, in Dale A. Somers, "Black and White in New Orleans: A Study in Urban Race Relations," *Journal of Southern History* 40 (1974): 29.

8 Arthe A. Anthony, "The Negro Creole Community in New Orleans, 1880–1920: An Oral History" (diss., University of California Irvine, 1978); Keith Weldon Medley, "The Sad Story of How 'Separate but Equal' Was Born," *Smithsonian*, February 1994, 106–7; *Soard's City Directory* (New Orleans, 1900), Williams Research Center, New Orleans; Keith Weldon Medley, "The Life and Times of Homer Plessy and John Ferguson," *Times-Picayune*, 18 May 1996.

9 Zane L. Miller, "Urban Blacks in the South, 1865–1920: The Richmond, Savannah, New Orleans, Louisville, and Birmingham Experience," *The New Urban History: Quantitative Explorations by American Historians*, ed. Leo Schnore (Princeton: Princeton University Press, 1975), 189, 192; William Ivy Hair, *Carnival of Fury: Robert Charles and the New Orleans Race Riot of 1900* (Baton Rouge: Louisiana State University Press, 1976), 69–71.

10 Olsen, "Reflections on the Plessy v. Ferguson Decision of 1896," 167.

11 Claude F. Jacobs, "Benevolent Societies of New Orleans Blacks during the Late Nineteenth and Early Twentieth Centuries," *Louisiana History* 29, no. 1 (1988): 21–24; Somers, "Black and White in New Orleans," 32; Eric Arnsen, *Waterfront Workers in New Orleans: Race, Class, and Politics* (New York: Oxford University Press, 1991).

12 Somers, "Black and White in New Orleans," 32; Arnsen, *Waterfront Work-*

ers in New Orleans; August Meier, "Negro Class Structure and Ideology in the Age of Booker T. Washington," *Phylon* 31 (1970): 261.

13  Blassingame, *Black New Orleans*, 190–91.

14  *Id.* at 191–92.

15  Henry C. Dethloff and Robert R. Jones, "Race Relations in Louisiana, 1877–98," *Louisiana History* 9, no. 1 (1968): 314.

16  George Washington Cable, "The Silent South, 1885," *The Negro Question* (New York, 1888), 98.

17  George Washington Cable, "The Freedmen's Case in Equity, 1884," *The Negro Question*, 71–72.

18  *Daily Crusader*, 22 June 1895, 1; *Crusader*, 16 July 1891; *Crusader* clippings, Rodolphe Desdunes Papers, Special Collections, Xavier University, New Orleans.

19  For more on conditions in New Orleans schools see Louis Harlan, "Desegregation in New Orleans Public Schools during Reconstruction," *African Americans and the Emergence of Segregation, 1865–1900*, ed. Donald G. Nieman (New York: Garland, 1994), 155–67; "Race Identity in New Orleans," *Southwestern Christian Advocate*, 19 July 1900, 8.

20  A. E. P. Albert, Editorial Notes, *Southwestern Christian Advocate*, 13 March 1890, 1; A. E. P. Albert, "Colored Schools of New Orleans," *Southwestern Christian Advocate*, 20 March 1890, 4; A. E. P. Albert, Editorial Notes, *Southwestern Christian Advocate*, 27 February 1890, 1.

21  J. W. Smith, "Our Washington Letter: Topical Talk about Persons and Things: The Convention—Bishop Jones," *Star of Zion*, 13 February 1890, 2; James Haskins, *Pinkney Benton Stewart Pinchback* (New York: Macmillan, 1973), 253–56.

22  A. E. P. Albert, "The State Convention of Colored Men," *Southwestern Christian Advocate*, 23 January 1890, 5; A. E. P. Albert, "American Citizens' Equal Rights Association," *Southwestern Christian Advocate*, 13 March 1890, 4.

23  Masthead, *Daily Crusader*, 22 June 1895, 2.

24  A. E. P. Albert, Editorial Notes, *Southwestern Christian Advocate*, 3 April 1890, 1.

25  P. B. S. Pinchback, "Speech of Senator Pinchback: On Taking the Chair of the National Equal Rights Convention," clippings file, P. B. S. Pinchback Papers, Manuscript Division, Moorland-Spingarn Library, Howard University.

26  Pinchback, "On Taking the Chair."

27  Olsen, "Reflections on the Plessy v. Ferguson Decision of 1896."

28  A. E. P. Albert, "American Citizens' Equal Rights Association," *Southwestern Christian Advocate*, 29 May 1890, 5; "American Citizens' Equal Rights Association Letter to Members, February 12, 1890," P. B. S. Pinchback Papers, Manuscript Division, Moorland-Spingarn Library, Howard University.

29  "Protest of the American Citizens' Equal Rights Association of Louisiana, against Class Legislation," *Southwestern Christian Advocate*, 5 June 1890, 4.

30  Pinchback, "On Taking the Chair"; "Political Review," *Southwestern Christian Advocate*, 17 July 1890, 4.

31  "A Convention," *Southwestern Christian Advocate*, 17 July 1890, 4.

32  L. A. Martinet to A. Tourgee, 5 October 1891, item 5760, Albion W. Tourgee Papers, 1801–1924, Micro-Photo Division, Bell & Howell Company, Cleveland, 1967.

33  Afro-American Council, "An Appeal to Officers of Southern States," P. B. S. Pinchback Papers, Manuscript Division, Moorland-Spingarn Library, Howard University.

34  L. A. Martinet to A. Tourgee, 5 October 1891, item 5760, Albion W. Tourgee Papers, 1801–1924, Micro-Photo Division, Bell & Howell Company, Cleveland, 1967.

35  R. L. Desdunes to A. Tourgee, 28 February 1892, item 6064, Albion W. Tourgee Papers, 1801–1924, Micro-Photo Division, Bell & Howell Company, Cleveland, 1967.

36  L. A. Martinet to A. Tourgee, 5 October 1891, item 5760; L. A. Martinet to A. Tourgee, 25 October 1891, item 5768, Albion W. Tourgee Papers, 1801–1924, Micro-Photo Division, Bell & Howell Company, Cleveland, 1967.

37  *Soard's City Directory* (New Orleans, 1900), Williams Research Center, New Orleans.

38  Foreword, *Our People and Our History*, xvii; Pinchback, "On the Need for Equality in Education," n.d., P. B. S. Pinchback Papers, Manuscript Division, Moorland-Spingarn Library, Howard University.

39  "Report of Proceedings of the Citizens' Committee for the Annulment of Act No. 111 Commonly Known as the Separate Car Law," Plessy v. Ferguson Records, Amistad Research Center, Tulane University, New Orleans.

40  *Id.*

41  Rodolphe Desdunes, "Jim Crow Is Dead," *Crusader*, 28 May 1892, *Crusader* Clippings, Desdunes Papers, Special Collections, Xavier University, New Orleans.

42  "Report of Proceedings of the Citizens' Committee for the Annulment of Act No. 111," Plessy v. Ferguson Records; L. A. Martinet to A. Tourgee, 11 October 1891, item 5763; L. A. Martinet to A. Tourgee, 5 October 1891, item 5760, Albion W. Tourgee Papers, 1801–1924, Micro-Photo Division, Bell & Howell Company, Cleveland, 1967.

43  L. A. Martinet to A. Tourgee, 5 October 1891, item 5760, Tourgee Papers.

44  *Id.*

45  May v. Shreveport Traction Co., 127 La. 420, 53 So. 671, 1910 La. LEXIS 838 (1910).

46  L. A. Martinet to A. Tourgee, 7 December 1891, item 5837, Albion W. Tourgee Papers, 1801–1924, Micro-Photo Division, Bell & Howell Company, Cleveland, 1967.

47  Letter from L. A. Martinet to A. Tourgee, 28 December 1891, Plessy v. Ferguson Records.

48  L. A. Martinet to A. Tourgee, 7 December 1891, item 5837, Albion W. Tourgee Papers, 1801–1924, Micro-Photo Division, Bell & Howell Company, Cleveland, 1967.

49 For an edited account of the legal battle over *Plessy v. Ferguson*, see *Plessy v. Ferguson: A Brief History with Documents*, ed. Brook Thomas (Boston: Bedford, 1997). For a close analysis of the case law, the best account available is found in Lofgren, *The Plessy Case*.

50 L. A. Martinet to A. Tourgee, 20 May 1893, item 6998, Tourgee Papers.

51 "Race Identity in New Orleans," *Southwestern Christian Advocate*, 19 July 1900, 8.

VICKI L. RUIZ

# Tapestries of Resistance

## Episodes of School Segregation and Desegregation

## in the Western United States

"We always tell our children they are Americans ..."

—Felícitas Méndez

In 1945, nine years before *Brown*, Latino parents in Orange County, California, led by Gonzalo and Felícitas Méndez, sued four local school districts for segregating their children. This case, *Méndez v. Westminster* (1946), would foreshadow the landmark Supreme Court case in several ways, including its judicious use of social science research, the application of the Fourteenth Amendment, and the involvement of Thurgood Marshall, a co-author of the amicus curiae brief filed by the NAACP. Landing a blow for segregation in California, the Méndez case would also serve as a precedent for judicial decisions in Texas and Arizona. Though relatively unknown on a national level, *Méndez v. Westminster* places the struggles for civil rights across regional, racial, and ethnic temporalities. Moving beyond a black-white binary, this chapter explores how diverse groups in the western United States developed parallel strategies for addressing injustice, though often in isolation from one another, which came together most visibly in *Méndez*.

As a land of encounters and conquests, the western United States encompasses multiple and overlapping histories. This chapter focuses on selected episodes involving educational segregation and desegregation in the western United States through the stories of people of color, especially Asian Americans, Mexican Americans, and American Indians. Behind the court cases, legislation, and public policy are real people who struggled against discrimination for the sake of their children and their communities. When possible, I privilege the voices and memories of the children themselves, such as American Indians, who as boarding school students far from home experienced not only segregation but also literal incarceration.

## Patterns of Segregation

The codification of school segregation in the western United States came early. In 1852, two years after California became a state, the legislature passed a bill barring African American children from schools. The First State Convention of Colored Citizens of the State of California met in 1854 and in a public pronouncement chafed against this discriminatory measure. "You have been wont to multiply our vices and never to see our virtues . . . [Y]ou receive our money to educate your children and refuse to admit our children into the common schools." By 1870 California had devised a formula of ten. When African American, Asian American, or American Indian students numbered ten, a school district was empowered to create separate schools for white and nonwhite children. In Visalia, California, for example, when Daniel Scott, an African American teacher from the East, opened a school for black children, local school officials offered him "a small fee" to enroll the Mexican American pupils also barred from the local public school.[1]

Private institutions run by the black community, sometimes with the support of northern charities, often provided the only avenues for education. Although Texas mandated segregation in 1875, Euro-American Texans proved loath to support "colored" schools. By the 1880s most black Texans were taught in "churches, barns, and other rented buildings." Protesting the segregation of African American children in Kansas, William Eagleson of the *Topeka Colored Citizen* wrote, "We hear of no Irish schools, no German schools, no Swedish schools. No, not one."[2]

Fought at the local level, African Americans launched numerous campaigns to provide equal access to education for their children. In the 1860s and 1870s, the sons of Frederick Douglass, Lewis and Frederick Jr., mobilized Denver's black community for the cause of school integration. In 1872 parents in Virginia City, Nevada, proved successful in enrolling their children in the common schools. Parents understandably desired equitable treatment for their children, as evidenced by a letter to a local newspaper from an African American woman in Park City, Utah: "My children's skin may be a shade darker than his, but in all other respects, they are equal." Quintard Taylor underscores the importance of education to black westerners, considering it "the premier weapon in the campaign for both economic advancement and racial equality."[3]

School segregation was a fact of life throughout much of the western United States by the end of the nineteenth century, but legal challenges continued as both African Americans and Chinese immigrants pushed for educational opportunities for their children. In 1872 Harriet Ward attempted to enroll her daughter Mary Frances in an all-white school in San Francisco. When the principal refused to admit her, Ward filed suit. *Ward v. Flood* (1873) was California's first case challenging educational segregation. In its ruling the state supreme court foreshadowed the logic of the U.S. Supreme Court in *Plessy v. Ferguson* (1896) by establishing "the principle of 'separate but equal.' "[4] *Ward v. Flood* nevertheless heartened African American leaders, in that the court affirmed the right of African Americans to any public education at all.

In 1875 the San Francisco school board integrated African Americans into the local public schools and in 1880 Political Code 1662 was significantly amended, dropping race as a qualifier for public education. This measure represented a milestone, for as Charles Wollenberg contends, "blacks never again were specified in the school law and thus never again subjected to *de jure* segregation." De facto segregation, however, remained.[5]

The Chinese community took notice of the revision of the school code in 1880. Since 1859 Chinese children had generally been taught in private missionary schools, such as the one operated by the Presbyterian Board of Home Missions. Intentions were modest and the education superficial and segregated, consisting of a rented room with a single teacher; even this so-called school closed its doors in 1871. Emphasizing their position as taxpayers who supported public education, Chinese merchants and their compatriots petitioned the state assembly to establish schools for their children, but to no avail. In 1885 the case of *Tape v. Hurley* would force local and state officials to address public education for Chinese youth. In 1884 Joseph and Mary Tape, both immigrants from China, attempted to enroll in the neighborhood public school their daughter Mamie, who had been born in the United States. The principal, Jennie Hurley, refused admittance and the Tapes filed suit.[6]

The Tapes were an unusual middle-class Chinese couple. Joseph Tape was an "expressman, drayman, and interpreter for the Chinese consulate." Arriving in 1869, he quickly adopted western fashion and customs, as well as Christianity. His wife Mary grew up in an orphanage in Shanghai and arrived in San Francisco under the auspices of Protestant missionaries. Fluent in English and Chinese, Mary Tape was well educated for her time and displayed talents as a "photographer, painter, and telegraph operator." The Tapes sought to give every advantage to their four children, all born in the United States, including a public education with their Euro-American neighbors. Given that Mamie came from a thoroughly acculturated Victorian family, was native-born, and spoke English with greater ease than Chinese, and that the school code had been amended, the Tapes pursued their case vigorously. The state superior court confirmed the right of Mamie Tape to attend the neighborhood school: "The Fourteenth Amendment . . . secures equal protection, rights and privileges of every nature to all persons born within the United States."[7]

Unbowed by this early application of the Fourteenth Amendment, the school board appealed, but two months later the California Supreme Court upheld the ruling. Within the city of San Francisco, school board members and the school superintendent, Andrew Jackson Moulder, reflected the xenophobia toward the Chinese that three years earlier had culminated in the Chinese Exclusion Act. According to the legal scholar Charles McClain, Moulder held particularly virulent views toward Chinese women, considering them "all prostitutes . . . [who] only wanted to attend school so that they could learn English and thereby increase their market value."[8] While awaiting the decision by the California Supreme Court, Moulder lobbied the legislature for an amendment to the school code. The legislators responded resoundingly by adding to Political Code 1662, after a phrase noting "infectious diseases," a statement of their purpose "to establish separate schools for children of Mongolian or Chinese descent." As a result, the Chinese Primary School opened in San Francisco, thus ending all recourse for Mamie Tape to attend her local school. For Chinese residents of the city, "separate but equal" remained the order of the day. An outraged Mary Tape wrote an impassioned letter to the San Francisco school board, a letter that also appeared in a local newspaper. "Dear sirs, Will you please tell me! Is it a disgrace to be Born Chinese? Didn't God make us all!!!" She continued, "May you Mr. Moulder never be persecuted like the way you have persecuted little Mamie Tape. Mamie Tape will never attend any of the Chinese schools of your making! Never!!"[9] Belying notions of both the fragile, submissive Victorian lady and the secluded Chinese middle-class wife, Mary Tape, as noted by Judy Yung, "shines as an early example of an emancipated Chinese American woman." Tape did revisit her position, as Mamie and her brother Frank became two of the first children to enroll in the Chinese Primary School. Indeed, the segregation of Chinese children in northern California continued into the twentieth century.[10]

For Mexican Americans, education during the late nineteenth century, when available, often boiled down to a debate over private versus public instruction. Parochial institutions were traditionally the primary means of formal education. In the early 1870s Jacinto Armijo, a territorial legislator in New Mexico, introduced a bill providing for public education. His measure provoked a storm of controversy. Catholic priests in New Mexico voiced intense opposition and Archbishop Lamy of Santa Fe "threatened to withhold the sacraments from children who attended these coeducational secular schools." Father Gasparri, editor of *La Revista Católica* and an ardent foe of women's suffrage, articulated his concern that coeducational classrooms would " 'remove any brakes to contain the passions of the human heart.' "[11] Although they couched their opposition in moral terms, local clerics realized that free public education provided an alternative to parochial school tuition.

In 1871 Don Estevan Ochoa met similar clerical concerns when the Safford-Ochoa Act, which provided for public schools, was approved by the Arizona territorial legislature. Perhaps to quell criticism, state-supported schools in Tucson were initially single-sex facilities. However, Mary Bernard Aguirre, a former St. Louis belle and widow of a Mexican rancher who was one of Arizona's first schoolmarms, described her charges at the Tucson Public School for Girls as "the most unruly set the Lord had ever let live," and she attributed their behavior to the "violent opposition to the Public Schools from Catholic priests." Far from being shy and retiring, Aguirre engaged in a contest of wills with her Catholic pupils. With a steely persistence, she continued to teach and in time commanded the community's respect. "I was pretty well known thro' Arizona and Sonora, *then*," she noted. "So . . . by degrees some of the better Mexican families sent their girls to me and finally the priest's nieces came to me and that settled the matter."[12] Mary Bernard Aguirre acted as a bridge, someone who traveled in both Euro-American and Mexican circles. Yet her role seemed circumscribed by class, as she frequently used the phrase "the better Mexican families" in the text of her narrative. Despite a flurry of protests, public education had come to stay in the Southwest, and in the following decades Mexican Americans and Mexican immigrants alike sought equitable educational opportunities for their children.

For rural Tejanos, *rancho* schools were the rule. With classes conducted in crude *jacales* (shacks), students were hampered by limited materials and poorly trained teachers. Like their African American neighbors, Tejanos began to experience segregation, but segregation based on neighborhood and language as well as stereotypes. School segregation of Mexican Americans was implemented by local district rules rather than by legislative fiat. At times policies of exclusion were couched in terms of language differences, but comments about smelly, lice-infested Tejano children also found their way into the rationale of board members. Despite restricted opportunities, Tejanos valued education and a small group negotiated the system to become teachers themselves, laboring in segregated schools for decades to come. Reflecting on schooling for Mexican Americans in Texas at the turn of the twentieth century, the education scholar Guadalupe San Miguel commented that "schools were usually segregated, overcrowded, and lacked adequately trained teachers." He continued, "Despite their deficiencies, Tejanos flocked to them for knowledge."[13]

One of the first boarding schools for Native Americans was not created by the federal government but by the Cherokee National Council of Oklahoma. Founded in 1851, the Cherokee Female Seminary was intended to provide schooling for the daughters of élite mixed-bloods, and after 1871 the children of less affluent full-bloods, with a curriculum similar to that of Mount Holyoke College. Students took courses in Latin, French, trigonometry, political economy, and literary criticism (to name a few). From Homer to Shakespeare, these young women received a very traditional upper-crust course of study, a curriculum that precluded any discussion of Cherokee culture or language. Pupils staged dramatic productions, held music recitals, and published their own newsletter evocatively entitled *A Wreath of Cherokee Rosebuds*. Devon Mihesuah has demonstrated how this institution helped shape an acculturated Cherokee identity that allowed young graduates to become "educators, businesswomen, physicians, stock raisers, and prominent social workers." In a response to tribal criticisms that the seminary students were ill prepared to take their places as farmers' wives, the curriculum shifted somewhat by 1905 to include classes in "domestic science," with the two Cs—cooking and cleaning—prominently featured. Across five decades over three thousand young women attended the Cherokee Female Seminary, and their lives there "helped to strengthen their identities as Cherokees although there was differences in opinion as to what a Cherokee really was."[14]

The legacy of boarding schools off the reservation can be traced to the ideas and efforts of one man: Captain Richard Henry Pratt. A cavalry officer who had commanded African American troops against American Indians in western campaigns, Pratt developed his notion of assimilation through total immersion while in charge of incarcerated Indians at Fort Marion, Florida. Unlike many of his contemporaries, Pratt did not believe in the innate genetic inferiority of American Indians. Using a specious analogy, Pratt contended that just as slavery had assimilated African Americans, boarding schools away from reservations could accomplish the same result for indigenous peoples. In 1879 Pratt got a chance to test his experiment: an old army barracks in Pennsylvania was transformed into the Carlisle Indian School.[15]

With Pratt as both founder and superintendent, Carlisle became the model for boarding schools that proliferated across the Midwest and Southwest during the late nineteenth century. By 1902 there were twenty-five federally supported, nonreservation boarding schools for American Indians across fifteen states and territories with a total enrollment of six thousand. Replicated at other sites, the Carlisle curriculum emphasized vocational training for boys and domestic science for girls. In addition to reading, writing, and arithmetic, Carlisle students learned how to make harnesses, shoe horses, sew clothes, do laundry, and craft furniture and wagons. Given that the federal government funded the boarders' education at $167 per student per year, it is not surprising that American Indian children, some as young as six years of age, should have put in long hours providing items for school use and for the market. Carlisle also pioneered the system of "outing," the summer placement of young people in the homes of neighboring farmers or townspeople, providing cheap labor for local residents.[16]

How were children recruited or lured into boarding school life? What were the fears and motivations of their parents? Major Haworth, the person in charge of the Chilocco Indian Industrial School in Oklahoma, traveled far and wide in search of pupils among the Cheyenne, Comanche, Arapaho, Kiowa, and closer to the school the Pawnee. Later selected Chilocco students, in the company of teachers, would themselves venture to distant reservations to expound upon the benefits of their school. For some students, temptation came not in flowery testimony but in the form of good, old-fashioned candy. As Luther Standing Bear (Lakota), one of Carlisle's first students, recalled: "When they saw us peeping in at the window, they motioned for us to come inside. But we hesitated. Then they took out some sticks of candy . . . and that was a big temptation."[17]

Although federal legislation mandated compulsory schooling for American Indians, children could not be taken off reservations without "the full consent" of their parents. How consent was obtained at times amounted to pure coercion, even violence. In 1892 the Indian agent S. J. Fischer at Fort Hall, Idaho, did not disguise his use of force in procuring children, even physically assaulting " 'a so-called chief into subjection.' " At some reservations, quotas were set for the number of children to be enrolled in boarding schools, with Indian policemen given the detail of deciding which children would be sent from which family. As Adams reveals, these law enforcement officials "might put the agonizing question to a mother—which child to give up, which to hold back?"[18]

Some parents resisted sending their children by running away from the reservation or hiding their sons and daughters. Given the mortality rates in boarding schools, they feared for their children's health and certainly realized that if their children traveled to a distant state, years would pass before they and the children would be reunited. Conversely, if the school were near, as was the Phoenix Indian school in relation to the Pima and Maricopa, for example, the decision could be less wrenching. Other parents coped with separation by holding fast to the belief that they were giving their daughters or sons an opportunity to succeed in the white world. Parental aspirations, whether well founded or ultimately misplaced, can be discerned in the following passage taken from a father's letter to his daughter: " 'Why do you ask for moccasins? I sent you there to be like a white girl and wear shoes?' "[19]

As they arrived by wagon, train, and later automobile, new boarding school students found themselves adapting to changes at every turn. As in contemporary boot camp, young people were initiated into military discipline. Cropped hair and school uniforms became the first order of business, with daily drill practice and scheduled routines. Especially in the early years, children received English names based either on loose translations of their traditional names, Anglo-American historical figures, or lists randomly written on a blackboard. Life was regimented from sunup to after sundown, with strict discipline and swift punishment.[20] The emphasis on vocational education remained a constant in boarding school education along with the afternoon chores of producing items for school use and for sale. In 1924, for instance, the young women at the Chilocco Indian School in Oklahoma produced "505 aprons . . . 85 brassieres, 608 pillowcases, 755 nightgowns, 623 shirts, blouses, and nightshirts, 3,071 sheets, 436 undershirts, 1,430 dresses, and 75 skirts." Loneliness was of course endemic to a life far away from home.[21]

Certainly homesickness was not the only illness stalking boarding school students. Tuberculosis, trachoma, measles, smallpox, whooping cough, influenza, and pneumonia roamed the halls of poorly funded schools. Harshly critical of school conditions, the Meriam Report in 1928 noted that meager food budgets (11 cents per child per day), overcrowded facilities, inadequate health care, and overwork of children contributed to the spread of diseases. American Indians had a death rate six and a half times that of other racial and ethnic groups.[22]

## Threads of Change

The Meriam Report sparked the beginning of reform. Curricular innovations included the creation of bilingual teaching materials, the preservation of native cultures (including religion), and the end of military trappings. Vocational education, however, was seriously outdated. By the 1930s training students to be blacksmiths and harness makers seemed oddly antiquated, if not downright irresponsible. Enrollment in the boarding schools dropped precipitously, in large measure because of the entry of native students into the public school system. Nationally, before the onset of the Depression over 8,000 students remained in federal non-reservation boarding schools, compared to over 34,000 American Indians in local public schools.[23]

Memories of boarding school life vary, from visions of Shangri-La to recollections of hunger, from the experience of a star athlete to that of a desperate runaway. Alumni frequently recall with merriment social events, teachers, and close friends, as well as the times they got away with some mischief. Young people often met their future spouses on campus. According to Steve Crum, the Stewart Indian School in Nevada fostered intermarriage between Shoshone and Paiute students. Circumscribed in their daily routines, students looked forward to amusements outside the school. Going into town to shop or see movies was a special treat, although in Phoenix, American Indian students had to sit in the segregated aisles reserved for people of color. Sports teams promoted school pride and the Haskell Institute produced the legendary athlete Jim Thorpe. Even young women "were encouraged to become involved in the 'genteel' sports of basketball and tennis." Beloved educators, such as Ella Deloria (Lakota) and Ruth Bronson (Cherokee), made life more bearable.[24]

Though laden with contradictions, with hardships and hopes, boarding schools "created community." Esther Horne, a graduate of Haskell Institute and an educator for over thirty years in Indian schools, articulated how Haskell shaped her life: "Most of us who are alumni of Indian boarding schools feel a great pride and sense of belonging to a unique and special group . . . Even though boarding schools took children away from their homes . . . we created our own community at the school."[25] Fostering a sense of connection and building alliances across tribal affiliations, the boarding school environment cultivated (if unintentionally) a pan-Indian unity. Wade Davies and Peter Iverson offer the following observation: "Rather than a prelude to assimilation and disappearance, the boarding school could underscore the need for different peoples to work together in the future."[26]

During the early decades of the twentieth century, school segregation policies affected Asian Americans differentially depending on their heritage and locale, and on the prevailing social climate. In 1900 the federal census counted 89,863 people of Chinese birth or descent living in the United States, most on the West Coast. Residents of Chinatown in San Francisco felt the sting of Political Code 1662, which mandated school segregation for the Chinese. From 1900 to 1935, however, they pushed against exclusionary educational policies and practices. Living with his family outside Chinatown, Dr. Wong Him enrolled his daughter Katie in a neighborhood school, but soon she was instructed to attend the Chinese Primary School. The doctor filed suit, noting that the San Francisco school board permitted blacks, American Indians, and Japanese to attend local schools while targeting only Chinese for discriminatory treatment. In *Wong Him v. Callahan* the U.S. District Court disagreed, upholding the idea of "separate but equal." The San Francisco earthquake of 1906 destroyed the Chinese Primary School, and in considering a new building the board promulgated a new policy, first changing the name of the Chinatown school to the Oriental Public School and then remanding to it "all Chinese, Japanese, or Korean children." Although there were sporadic legal challenges to segregation, change occurred in small, almost imperceptible ways. As Victor Low has related, "The board of education's unwritten policy was to allow Chinese children who lived outside of the Chinese quarter to go to neighborhood schools as long as white parents did not object."[27] By the late 1920s, owing to community mobilizing in Chinatown, the school board began to implement new policies, including deliberately ignoring Political Code 1662. The first step came in 1924, when the Oriental Public School was rechristened Commodore Stockton School, thus erasing the stigma of the term "Oriental." Soon thereafter, by the time of the Depression, students who lived in Chinatown attended several local elementary and secondary schools.[28]

By 1910 over 72,000 persons of Japanese birth or descent lived in the continental United States and Hawaii. After the earthquake of 1906, when the San Francisco school board specifically required Japanese children to attend the "Oriental" school, this new policy sparked an international incident. Japanese residents challenged the mandate, drawing support from the Japanese ambassador and consul in helping to secure the rights of their American-born (Nisei) children. President Theodore Roosevelt personally intervened, calling the segregation of Japanese students "a wicked absurdity." Cognizant of Japan's rise as a military power after its defeat of Russia, Roosevelt sought to avoid strained diplomatic relations.[29]

In Hawaii the question of segregation was expressed somewhat differently from the way it was on the mainland. By 1900 the Japanese represented the largest racial or ethnic population in the Hawaiian Islands, and not surprisingly a sizable segment of the public school population. Instead of segregating students of color under the mantle of "separate but equal," the territorial legislature created "select" or English Standard schools for the Euro-American minority. With superior facilities and funding, these schools educated less than 10 percent of Hawaii's youth. While only 3 percent of whites attended regular public schools, they represented 50 percent of pupils who sat at desks in English Standard classrooms. For Japanese children, the figures were almost reversed, as they represented only 3 to 8 percent of "select" school students during the period 1925 to 1927. Roger Daniels contends that the English Standard schools "eerily prefigure some of the less violent devices used by southern school systems in their attempts to resist integration after 1954."[30]

Like the German immigrants in the American heartland, the Japanese created after-school language schools both in Hawaii and on the mainland. The education scholar Eileen Tamura has traced the tenacity of Hawaii's Japanese community in maintaining and defending these classes despite nativist attempts to curb them. During the First World War and after, with rising anti-immigrant sentiment, twenty-two states abolished "foreign language schools." A similar attempt was made in Hawaii with legislation that sought to circumscribe these community-based institutions through permits, regulations, and additional taxes. Resisting these restrictions, the schools filed suit. In *Farmington v. Tokushige* (1926), the U.S. Court of Appeals for the Ninth Circuit ruled in favor of the language classes. Speaking for the court, Judge Frank Rudin remarked, " 'The children . . . do attend the public schools . . . and when they have done this we take it for granted that they have an undoubted right to acquire a knowledge of foreign language, music, painting . . . and such other accomplishments.' " The court based its decision in part on *Meyer v. Nebraska* (1923), a case that also upheld the right of language schools to exist.[31]

At the same time that Japanese communities in Hawaii were defending their language schools, Nisei children in California and Arizona were subject to de jure segregation (though not always enforced). In 1921 the California school law, Political Code 1662, was amended once again, to include the Japanese. However, only four towns (Walnut Grove, Courtland, Florin, and Isleton) duly segregated Japanese and other Asian American youth into "oriental" schools; all four were small farming outposts in the San Joaquin River Delta of northern California. Interestingly, in all four communities the Nisei represented the majority of students. In Walnut Grove, for example, over two hundred pupils filled the Asian school while the elementary school reserved for whites contained only sixty-two and the "migratory school" (read: Mexican) just under thirty.[32]

In some areas, Japanese and Mexican children attended the same segregated facility. El Monte was a small enclave in the shadows of Los Angeles, a town with a population of under ten thousand (75 percent Euro-American; 20 percent Mexican; and 5 percent Japanese). Despite its small size, El Monte had clearly marked racial divisions in housing, schools, and public facilities. Mexicans and Japanese were segregated from Euro-American El Monte. The children of Japanese farmers and Mexican farm workers attended the same segregated school, Lexington Elementary, and in the town's premier movie palace they were relegated to the same side of the aisle, away from Euro-American patrons. This sharing of social space in the classroom or the cinema led to an environment in which relations between growers and campesinos were familiar, but not friendly. According to Señora Jesusita Torres, "[The Japanese farmers] would work in the field, but you knew they were the *boss*."[33]

Similarly in Arizona, school officials routinely exercised the prerogative of establishing separate classes for children of color, at times creating separate schools. In 1925 the Arizona legislature debated the merits of House Bill 31, intended to segregate white and "colored" youth in the state's high schools. The bill that passed, however, placed the "matter of segregation to the vote of the people living in the district concerned." A year later the *Arizona Teacher and Home Journal* reported that the Cartwright School in Phoenix had hired Edna Hanson to teach "Mexican and Japanese" children in their own classroom. Susie Sato, a native of Arizona, revealed that segregation extended beyond the schoolyard. Asian Americans, Mexican Americans, African Americans, and American Indians were not permitted to swim in the Tempe public pool, and throughout the Phoenix area movie theaters practiced a strict policy of segregation.[34]

Despite these examples of exclusion, Charles Wollenberg contends that in California the overwhelming majority of Nisei youth attended integrated classes in integrated schools. Growing up in the San Joaquin Valley community of Cortez, California, the Nisei residents, interviewed by Valerie Matsumoto, spoke fondly of their school experiences but also noted the discrimination they faced. The Nisei developed friendships across racial lines with peers of the same gender; conversely, interracial dating "was unthinkable for most." The taboo against interracial relationships had roots in both the Issei (first-generation) and Euro-American worlds. Indeed fourteen states, including California, banned marriages between whites and Asian Americans.[35]

The unwritten social rules for high school, however, proved to be the least of the problems facing Nisei youth in 1942. With a pen's stroke, President Franklin Delano Roosevelt signed Executive Order 9066, "authorizing the removal of 110,000 Japanese and their American-born children from the western half of the Pacific Coast states and the southern third of Arizona." For Japanese Americans in Phoenix, the side of the street on which they lived determined whether they stayed or left. The ten internment camps were conglomerations of hastily assembled barracks situated in isolated, desolate locales. Subjected to the sweltering summers typical of Arizona, the Poston Camp was subdivided into three areas, known by the unflattering (though appropriate) sobriquets of "Toaston, Roaston, and Duston."[36]

Schools were set up within the camps, staffed by over 550 Euro-American and 25 Nisei educators. The Amache Camp in Colorado provides a glimpse of the economies of scale involved in the task of organizing a small school district with fifty-one teachers, forty-one Nisei aides, and almost two thousand students. For many children, it was their first taste of segregation. Nisei writers and poets have crystallized the surreal high school milieu, complete with cheerleaders, sports teams, and yearbooks. In "The Watch Tower," the poet Mitsuye Yamada recalls the inherent contradictions: "We loved and we lived. / just like people." The War Relocation Authority did permit Nisei college students to transfer to Midwestern and eastern institutions. Along with being recruited into the U.S. military, Nisei graduates of internment high schools applied to colleges and sought sponsorship for jobs further inland, eager for opportunities to prove themselves. By 1945, for instance, over 60 percent of Nisei women sixteen years and older had left the barbed wire behind.[37]

During the dawning decades of the twentieth century, as the Japanese built communities on western soil, immigrants from Mexico also arrived, often with their dreams and little else. Between 1910 and 1930 over one million Mexicanos (one-eighth to one-tenth of Mexico's population) migrated northward. Pushed by the economic and political chaos generated by the Mexican Revolution and lured by agribusiness and industrial jobs in the United States, they settled into existing barrios and created new ones in the Southwest and Midwest. In 1900 from 375,000 to perhaps as many as 500,000 Mexicans lived in the Southwest. Within a short space of twenty years, Mexican Americans were outnumbered at least two to one and their colonias became immigrant enclaves. In some areas, this transformation appeared even more dramatic. Los Angeles, for example, had a Mexican population ranging from three thousand to five thousand in 1900. By 1930 approximately 150,000 persons of Mexican birth or heritage resided in the city's expanding barrios. As David Gutiérrez has so persuasively argued, immigration from Mexico in the twentieth century has had profound consequences for Mexican Americans in terms of "daily decisions about who they are—politically, socially, and culturally—in comparison to more recent immigrants from Mexico." Indeed, a unique layering of generations has occurred in which ethnic and racial identities take many forms, from the identities of the Hispanos of New Mexico and Colorado, whose roots go back to the eighteenth century, to those of the recently arrived who live as best they can in the canyons of northern San Diego County.[38] Such a heterogeneous Mexican community is not new. Throughout the twentieth century, a layering of generations can be detected in schools, churches, community organizations, work sites, and neighborhoods.

During the teens and twenties, religious and state-organized Americanization projects aimed at the Mexican population proliferated throughout the Southwest and Midwest. While these efforts varied in scale from settlement houses to night classes, curriculum generally revolved around cooking, hygiene, English, and civics. Frequently segregated schools were touted as tools in the cause of Americanization. In 1899 the Arizona territorial legislature enacted Title XIX, a bill stipulating English as the language of instruction in the public schools. Title XIX would later be used as the legislative foundation for local school districts to segregate Spanish-speaking pupils, who not coincidentally represented over 50 percent of the territory's school-age population.[39]

While some school districts did not segregate Mexican youth, residential and educational segregation often went hand in hand. Albert Camarillo has demonstrated that in Los Angeles restrictive real estate covenants and segregated schools increased dramatically between 1920 and 1950. In the tiny hamlet of Fort Stockton, Texas, the street separating the Euro-American community from the Mexican barrio and the white school from the "Mexican" school was aptly named Division Street. On the eve of the Depression, Phoenix represented a western apogee of segregation, with George Washington Carver High School, the Phoenix Indian School, and several "Mexican" elementary schools sprinkled across the Valley. The Tempe Eighth Street School was "restricted to 'Spanish American' or 'Mexican American'" youth and staffed primarily by student teachers from the neighboring normal school (now Arizona State University).[40]

In the memories of pupils past, "Mexican" segregated schools were not necessarily conducive to either self-esteem or collective identity. Throughout the Southwest, Spanish-speaking children had to sink or swim in an English-only environment. Even on the playground, students were punished for conversing in Spanish.[41] As Mary Luna stated: "It was rough because I didn't [speak] English. The teacher wouldn't let us talk Spanish. How can you talk to anybody? If you can't talk Spanish and you can't talk English? . . . It wasn't until maybe the fourth or fifth grade that I started catching up. And all that time I just felt I was stupid."[42] Yet Luna credited her love of reading to a Euro-American educator who had converted a small barrio house into a makeshift community center and library. Her words underscore the dual thrust of Americanization—education and consumerism. "To this day I just love going into libraries . . . there are two places that I can go in and get a real warm, happy feeling; that is, the library and Bullock's in the perfume and make-up department."[43]

But what type of training was associated with Americanization? As in other segregated facilities across the nation, the curriculum in "Mexican" schools was vocational. Many teachers and administrators believed that their students possessed few aspirations and fewer abilities beyond farm and domestic work. One article on Americanization, focusing on a home economics class for Mexican Americans, typifies this view: "These girls are very enthusiastic and are learning in this class, things which will make it possible for them to be efficient domestic help, when they go into American homes to work." In the abstract, education held out hope, but in practice it trained students for low-status, low-paying jobs. Perhaps some Americanization proponents had their own doubts about their enterprise, as noted by the provocative title to the article, "Does it Pay to Educate a Mexican?"[44]

Schools in some instances did raise expectations. Imbued with the American dream, young people believed that hard work would bring material rewards and social acceptance. One California grower disdained education for Mexicans because it would give them " 'tastes for thing they can't acquire.' " Some teenage women aspired to college while others planned careers as secretaries. "I want to study science or be a stenographer," one Colorado adolescent related. "I thinned beets this spring, but I believe it is the last time. The girls who don't go to school will continue to top beets the rest of their lives." The impact of Americanization was most keenly felt at the level of personal aspiration. "We felt that if we worked hard, proved ourselves, we would become professional people," Rose Escheverria Mulligan asserted.[45]

Braced with such idealism, Mexican Americans faced prejudice, segregation, and economic segmentation. Though they perceived themselves as Americans, others perceived them as less than desirable foreigners. The *Saturday Evening Post*, for example, ran a series of articles urging the restriction of Mexican immigration. The titles tell the story: "The Mexican Invasion," "Wet and Other Mexicans," and "The Alien on Relief." With the onset of the Depression, rhetoric gave way to action. Between 1931 and 1934 an estimated one-third of the Mexican population in the United States (over 500,000 people) were either deported or repatriated to Mexico even though the majority (an estimated 60 percent) were native U.S. citizens. Mexicans were the only immigrants targeted for removal. Proximity to the Mexican border, the physical distinctiveness of *mestizos*, and easily identifiable barrios induced immigration and social welfare officials to focus their efforts solely on the Mexican people. From Los Angeles to Gary, Indiana, Mexicans were either summarily deported by immigration agencies or persuaded to depart voluntarily by duplicitous social workers who greatly exaggerated the opportunities awaiting them south of the border.[46] Policies of segregation in public facilities compounded the climate surrounding deportations and repatriations. Citing a survey conducted in 1931, Francisco Balderrama mentions "that more than 80 percent of the school districts in southern California enrolled Mexicans and Mexican Americans in segregated schools."[47]

Even under these circumstances Mexican parents sought educational equity for their children. Before 1931 Mexican American and Euro-American youngsters in Lemon Grove, California, a sleepy agricultural community east of San Diego, attended the same school. In January 1931 the local school board built a separate facility for Mexican pupils across the tracks in the barrio. The "new" two-room facility resembled a barn hastily furnished with secondhand equipment, supplies, and books. Forming El Comité de Vecinos de Lemon Grove, local parents voted to boycott the school and seek legal redress. Except for one household, every family kept its children home. With the assistance of the Mexican Consul, the Comité hired attorneys on behalf of the eighty-five children affected and filed suit. Using the Americanization banner, board members justified their actions on the grounds that a separate facility was necessary to meet the needs of non-English-speaking children. To counter this argument, students "took the stand to prove their knowledge of English."[48] In *Alvarez v. Lemon Grove School District* (1931), Judge Claude Chambers ordered the "immediate reinstatement" of Mexican children in their old school. During a reign of deportations and repatriations, Mexican immigrants had mustered the courage to protest segregation in education and had won. Comadres and compadres had banded together for grassroots political action. These immigrant parents, moreover, had sought the assistance of the Mexican consul in their effort to provide equal opportunities for their children born in the United States. Equally important, *Alvarez* may represent "the first successful court action in favor of school desegregation in the United States." Certainly it was an early victory.[49]

Efforts at school desegregation cut across class and generational divisions within Mexican American communities. A year before the Lemon Grove case, a Texas state court in *Independent School District v. Salvatierra* upheld the right of the Del Rio school district to separate Tejano children from Euro-American Texans. Represented by the League of United Latin American Citizens (LULAC), Tejano parents had argued against "the complete segregation of . . . children of Mexican descent . . . from children of other white races." The superintendent, conversely, unctuously invoked the "decided peculiarities" of Tejano students to justify segregation. Accepting the district's rationale of separation in furtherance of Americanization (and making no distinction between children born in Mexico and the United States or between Spanish and English speakers), the court ruled that Mexican children were not segregated on the basis of race. Not surprisingly, LULAC members shifted their focus to inequities in school funding.[50]

While el Comité de Vecinos de Lemon Grove represented the hopes of working-class Mexicano neighbors, LULAC emerged as a regional middle-class Mexican American civil rights organization. Founded by Tejanos in 1929, LULAC struck a chord among Mexican Americans, and by 1939 chapters could be found throughout the Southwest. Envisioning themselves as patriotic "white" Americans pursuing their rights, members of LULAC restricted their organization to English-speaking U.S. citizens. As David Gutiérrez notes, LULAC took a page from the early NAACP in stressing the leadership of an "educated elite" who would lift their less fortunate neighbors by their bootstraps. He continued, "From 1929 through World War II LULAC organized successful voter registration and poll tax-drives . . . and aggressively attacked discriminatory laws and practices . . . More important . . . , LULAC also achieved a number of notable legal victories in the area of public education."[51]

Gonzalo Méndez, a naturalized U.S. citizen, and his Puerto Rican–born wife Felicitas attempted to send their three children, Sylvia, Gonzalo Jr., and Geronimo, to the 17th Street School, the elementary school Gonzalo had himself attended as a child. But times had changed; the Westminster school district, like its counterparts throughout Orange County, California, had drawn boundaries around Mexican neighborhoods, ensuring de facto segregation. The placement of children, furthermore, was also based on Spanish surnames and phenotypes. As noted by Carey McWilliams, the preeminent commentator on California life, "Occasionally the school authorities inspect the children so that the offspring of a Mexican mother whose name may be O'Shaughnessy will not slip into the wrong school." After their children were turned away, Gonzalo and Felicitas Méndez organized other parents and "persuaded the school board to propose a bond issue for construction of a new, integrated school." When the measure failed, the school board refused to take further action. Méndez then enlisted the help of LULAC and hired an attorney, David Marcus. On behalf of their children and five thousand others, Gonzalo and Felicitas Méndez and four other families in 1945 filed suit against the Westminster, Garden Grove, Santa Ana, and El Modena school districts in Orange County.[52]

The superintendents reiterated both the tired stereotypes of the nineteenth century and the rhetoric of twentieth-century Americanization. The Garden Grove superintendent baldly asserted: " 'Mexicans are inferior in personal hygiene, ability and in their economic outlook.' " Youngsters, he asserted, needed separate schools given their lack of English proficiency: they "were handicapped in 'interpreting English words because their cultural background' prevented them from learning Mother Goose rhymes."[53] The court transcript is replete with images of "dirty" Mexican children. For example, Kent recited a list of hygienic deficiencies said to have been peculiar to Mexican children, including "lice, impetigo, tuberculosis, generally dirty hands, face, neck, and ears." Marcus queried, "Are all children dirty?" Kent answered, "No sir." Marcus pushed the issue: "Do you keep a record of dirty hands and face?" "No" was the response.[54]

Marcus devised a twofold strategy: he questioned the constitutionality of educational segregation and called in expert witnesses—social scientists who challenged these assumptions about Mexican American children and the supposed need for separate schools. Sylvia Méndez, an eight-year-old, took the stand, later recalling, " 'I had to testify because [school authorities] said we didn't speak English.' " With simple poignancy, Felícitas's testimony summed up her family's struggles: "We always tell our children they are Americans." After taking almost a year to formulate his decision, Judge Paul McCormick "ruled that segregation of Mexican youngsters found no justification in the laws of California and furthermore was a clear denial of the 'equal protection' clause of the Fourteenth Amendment."[55]

The school district appealed the decision, alleging that the federal court had lacked jurisdiction. The importance of Judge McCormick's ruling was not lost on civil rights activists. Amicus curiae briefs were filed by the American Jewish Congress, the ACLU, the National Lawyers Guild, the Japanese American Citizens League, and the NAACP (whose brief was partly the work of Thurgood Marshall, later the lead attorney for the plaintiffs in Brown). The state attorney general, Robert W. Kenney, even filed his own supporting brief. Nationally, hopes were high that the case would be a test case before the U.S. Supreme Court. In McWilliams's words, "the decision may sound the death knell of Jim Crow in education." When the U.S. Court of Appeals for the Ninth Circuit in 1947 upheld McCormick's ruling, the Orange County school districts decided to desegregate and drop the case, dashing these expectations.[56]

Méndez v. Westminster has national significance for four interrelated reasons. First, according to the historian Rubén Flores, there are "clear and unmistakable" links between Méndez and the NAACP's decision to deploy "social science arguments." Second, the social science arguments were not just advanced by the plaintiffs but accepted by the court: Judge McCormick in his decision relied on social science and education research in addition to legal precedent. As Charles Wollenberg noted, "much of the social and educational theory expressed by Judge McCormick anticipated Earl Warren's historic opinion in the Brown case." Third, Méndez marked "the first time that a federal court had concluded that the segregation of Mexican Americans in public schools was a violation of state law" and unconstitutional under the Fourteenth Amendment because of the denial of due process and equal protection. Finally, as the direct result of the *Méndez* case, the Anderson bill (1947), signed into law by Governor Earl Warren (later the Chief Justice when the U.S. Supreme Court handed down *Brown*), repealed all California school codes mandating segregation.[57] *Méndez v. Westminster* was certainly a crucial case in the multiple struggles for school desegregation, one that forecast the rationale of the Warren Court in *Brown v. Board of Education*.

We learn from each other's stories as we seek a fuller recounting of the American past, with all of its contradictions, complexities, pain, and promise. While many problems remain and debates continue over school financing, residential segregation, and equitable access to quality education (to name a few), the multiple and overlapping narratives of school desegregation remind us that individuals in concert with others do make a difference. Though their stories have remained largely unheralded in the annals of civil rights history, American Indians, Asian Americans, and Mexican Americans for well over a century have woven tapestries of resistance against school segregation and discrimination.

## Notes

1 Eleanor M. Ramsey and Janice S. Lewis, "A History of Black Americans in California," *Five Views: An Ethnic Site Survey for California* (Sacramento: California Department of Parks and Recreation, 1988), 61–62, 84; Quintard Taylor, *In Search of the Racial Frontier: African Americans in the American West, 1528–1990* (New York: W.W. Norton, 1998), 91–92; Charles Wollenberg, *All Deliberate Speed: Segregation and Exclusion in California Schools, 1855–1875* (Berkeley: University of California Press, 1976), 14.

2 Taylor, *In Search of the Racial Frontier*, 209, 215–16, 219.

3 *Id.* at 202, 215, 217.

4 *Id.* at 215; Ramsey and Lewis, "A History of Black Americans in California," 63; Wollenberg, *All Deliberate Speed*, 22–23.

5 Wollenberg, *All Deliberate Speed*, 23–25; Victor Low, *The Unimpressible Race: A Century of Educational Struggle by the Chinese in San Francisco* (San Francisco: East/West, 1982), 50.

6 Low, *The Unimpressible Race*, 13; Charles J. McClain, *In Search of Equality: The Chinese Struggle against Discrimination in Nineteenth-Century America* (Berkeley: University of California Press, 1994), 134–36; Patricia Hogan, "*Tape v. Hurley*," *Encyclopedia of the American West*, ed. Charles Phillips and Alan Axelrod (New York: Macmillan, 1996), 1536–37; Judy Yung, *Unbound Voices: A Documentary History of Chinese Women in San Francisco* (Berkeley: University of California Press, 1997), 171, 173.

7  Yung, *Unbound Voices*, 171; Low, *The Unimpressible Race*, 62–63; McClain, *In Search of Equality*, 141.

8  Low, *The Unimpressible Race*, 60–64; McClain, *In Search of Equality*, 141.

9  Low, *The Unimpressible Race*, 67; Yung, *Unbound Voices*, 174–75.

10  Yung, *Unbound Voices*, 175; McClain, *In Search of Equality*, 143.

11  Richard Griswold del Castillo, *La Familia: Chicano Families in the Urban Southwest, 1848 to the Present* (Notre Dame: University of Notre Dame Press, 1984), 81, 83–84.

12  Alleen Pace Nilsen with Margaret Ferry and L. J. Evans, eds., *Dust in Our Desks: Territory Days to the Present in Arizona Schools* (Tempe: ASU Centennial Commission and College of Education, 1985), 6; Mary Bernard Aguirre, "Public Schools of Tucson in the 1870s," Aguirre Family Papers, Arizona Historical Society Library, Tucson.

13  Guadalupe San Miguel Jr., *"Let Them All Take Heed": Mexican Americans and the Campaign for Educational Equality in Texas, 1910–1981* (Austin: University of Texas Press, 1987), 11–12, 54–55; Mario T. García, *Desert Immigrants: The Mexicans of El Paso, 1880–1920* (New Haven: Yale University Press, 1981), 110–11; Arnoldo de León, *The Tejano Community, 1836–1900* (Albuquerque: University of New Mexico Press, 1982), 188–94.

14  Devon A. Mihesuah, "Too Dark to Be Angels: The Class System among the Cherokees at the Female Seminary," *Unequal Sisters: A Multicultural Reader in U.S. Women's History*, 3d ed., ed. Vicki L. Ruiz and Ellen Carol DuBois (New York: Routledge, 1999), 183–204; Devon A. Mihesuah, *Cultivating the Rosebuds: The Education of Women at the Cherokee Female Seminary, 1851–1909* (Urbana: University of Illinois Press, 1993), 55, 74–75, 83, 101–2, 116.

15  Robert A. Trennert Jr., *The Phoenix Indian School: Forced Assimilation in Arizona, 1891–1935* (Norman: University of Oklahoma Press, 1988), 5; K. Tsianina Lomawaima, *They Called It Prairie Light: The Story of Chilocco Indian School* (Lincoln: University of Nebraska Press, 1994), 4; David Wallace Adams, *Education for Extinction: American Indians and the Boarding School Experience, 1875–1928* (Lawrence: University Press of Kansas, 1995), 38–43, 51–53.

16  Trennert, *The Phoenix Indian School*, 7–9; Lomawaima, *They Called It Prairie Light*, 4–5; Adams, *Education for Extinction*, 57–59, 149–50, 155–63.

17  Adams, *Education for Extinction*, 97, 142–48; Lomawaima, *They Called It Prairie Light*, 9–10.

18  Adams, *Education for Extinction*, 63–65, 211, 216.

19  *Id.* at 210–17, 241, 248–51; Trennert, *The Phoenix Indian School*, 48–49; Brenda J. Child, *Boarding School Seasons: American Indian Families, 1900–1940* (Lincoln: University of Nebraska Press, 1998), 16–17, 20.

20  Adams, *Education for Extinction*, 100–124; Lomawaima, *They Called It Prairie Light*, 13, 41–46, 101–12; Child, *Boarding School Seasons*, 39–41.

21  Lomawaima, *They Called It Prairie Light*, 81–93; Child, *Boarding School Seasons*, 75–85; Esther Burnett Horne and Sally McBeth, *Essie's Story: The Life and Legacy of a Shoshone School Teacher* (Lincoln: University of Nebraska Press, 1998),

35, 48–49. The Meriam Report of 1928 stated bluntly, "The question may very properly be raised whether much of the work of Indian children in boarding schools would not be prohibited in many states by child labor laws." Margaret Connell Szaz, *Education and the American Indian: The Road to Self-Determination since 1928* (Albuquerque: University of New Mexico Press, 1974), 20.

22  Child, *Boarding School Seasons*, 55–68; Szaz, *Education and the American Indian*, 18–20; Lomawaima, *They Called It Prairie Light*, 31.

23  Szaz, *Education and the American Indian*, 67–73; Lomawaima, *They Called It Prairie Light*, 31, 104; Trennert, *The Phoenix Indian School*, 208; Adams, *Education for Extinction*, 320, 331–32.

24  Child, *Boarding School Seasons*, 2–4, 17; Adams, *Education for Extinction*, 115; Lomawaima, *They Called It Prairie Light*, 41, 94–99, 121, 158–67; Steven J. Crum, *The Road on Which We Came: A History of the Western Shoshone* (Salt Lake City: University of Utah Press, 1994), 65; Trennert, *The Phoenix Indian School*, 128–29, 132–33; Horne and McBeth, *Essie's Story*, 32–33, 42, 45–47, 52–53, 58.

25  Horne and McBeth, *Essie's Story*, 52–53.

26  Adams, *Education for Extinction*, 336; Trennert, *The Phoenix Indian School*, 210; Wade Davies and Peter Iverson, "American Indian Identities in the Twentieth Century," *American Stories: Collected Scholarship on Minority History from the OAH Magazine of History* (Bloomington: Organization of American Historians, 1998), 111.

27  Judy Yung, *Unbound Feet: A Social History of Chinese Women in San Francisco* (Berkeley: University of California Press, 1995), 293; Low, *The Unimpressible Race*, 84–87, 92–93, 96–98, 100, 106, 110, 116–22, 120–31; Wollenberg, *All Deliberate Speed*, 54.

28  Low, *The Unimpressible Race*, 114–20, 122–23, 131–32; Yung, *Unbound Feet*, 127.

29  Yung, *Unbound Feet*, 127; Low, *The Unimpressible Race*, 88–89, 93–94; Wollenberg, *All Deliberate Speed*, 48–49, 54–61, 66–67.

30  Eileen H. Tamura, *Americanization, Acculturation, and Ethnic Identity: The Nisei Generation in Hawaii* (Urbana: University of Illinois Press, 1994), xi, 5, 110–15.

31  *Id.* at 147–50, 275.

32  Isani Arifuku Waugh et al., "A History of Japanese Americans in California," *Five Views*, 196; Wollenberg, *All Deliberate Speed*, 72–73.

33  Charles S. Spaulding, "The Mexican Strike at El Monte, California," *Sociology and Social Research* 18 (1933–34): 571; Ronald W. López, "The El Monte Strike of 1933," *Aztlán*, spring 1970, 103; Rodolfo F. Acuña, *Occupied America: A History of Chicanos*, 2d ed. (New York: Harper and Row, 1981), 220; *Los Angeles Times*, 27 September 1992; Interview with Jesusita Torres by Vicki L. Ruiz, 8 January 1993.

34  *Arizona Teacher and Home Journal* 13, no. 6 (February 1925): 16–18; *Arizona Teacher and Home Journal* 15, no. 1 (September 1926): 28; Valerie Jean Matsumoto, "*Shikata ga nai*: Japanese American Women in Central Arizona, 1910–1978" (honors thesis, Arizona State University, May 1978), 20–21.

35  Wollenberg, *All Deliberate Speed,* 73; Valerie J. Matsumoto, *Farming the Home Place* (Ithaca: Cornell University Press, 1993), 75–76; Valerie J. Matsumoto, "Japanese American Women and the Creation of Urban Nisei Culture in the 1930s," *Over the Edge: Remapping the American West,* ed. Valerie J. Matsumoto and Blake Allmendinger (Berkeley: University of California Press, 1999), 298.

36  Valerie J. Matsumoto, "Japanese American Women during World War II," *Unequal Sisters,* 480–81; Matsumoto, *"Shikata ga nai,"* 23–24.

37  Wollenberg, *All Deliberate Speed,* 76–78, 80; Matsumoto, *Farming the Home Place,* 24–125, 132–35, 140–43; Mitsuye Yamada, *Camp Notes and Other Poems* (Lathan, N.Y.: Kitchen Table: Women of Color Press, 1992), 22.

38  Oscar J. Martínez, "On the Size of the Chicano Population: New Estimates, 1850–1900," *Aztlán,* spring 1975, 56; Albert Camarillo, *Chicanos in a Changing Society* (Cambridge: Harvard University Press, 1979), 200–201; George J. Sánchez, *Becoming Mexican American* (New York: Oxford University Press, 1993), 18; David Gutiérrez, *Walls and Mirrors: Mexican Americans, Mexican Immigrants, and the Politics of Ethnicity in the Southwest, 1910–1986* (Berkeley: University of California Press, 1995), 6.

39  Nilsen, Ferry, and Evans, *Dust in Our Desks,* 4, 26; Laura Muñoz, " 'Does It Pay to Educate a Mexican?': Americanization in Arizona, 1914–1925" (graduate seminar paper, Arizona State University, 1998).

40  Albert Camarillo, "Mexican American Urban History in Comparative Perspective," Distinguished Speakers Series, University of California, Davis (26 January 1987); María Eva Flores, "The Good Life, the Hard Way: The Mexican American Community of Fort Stockton, Texas" (diss., Arizona State University, 2000); *Arizona Teacher and Home Journal* 15, no. 2 (October 1926): 62; Muñoz, " 'Does It Pay to Educate a Mexican?' "

41  Vicki L. Ruiz, "Oral History and La Mujer: The Rosa Guerrero Story," *Women on the U.S.-Mexico Border: Responses to Change* (Boston: Allen and Unwin, 1987), 226–27; Interview with Belen Martínez Mason, *Rosie the Riveter Revisited,* ed. Sherna Berger Gluck (Long Beach: CSULB Foundation, 1983), 23:24–25; Interview with Erminia Ruiz by Vicki L. Ruiz, 18 February 1993; an excellent overview is Gilbert González, *Chicano Education in the Era of Segregation* (Philadelphia: Balch Institute, 1990).

42  Interview with Mary Luna, *Rosie the Riveter Revisited,* 20:10.

43  *Id.* at 20:9.

44  San Miguel, *"Let Them All Take Heed,"* 46–47; Gilbert González, "Racism, Education, and the Mexican Community in Los Angeles, 1920–30," *Societas* 4 (autumn 1974): 287–300; Muñoz, " 'Does It Pay to Educate a Mexican?' "

45  Interview with Rose Escheverria Mulligan, *Rosie the Riveter Revisited,* 27:16–17; Ruiz, "Oral History and La Mujer," 227–28; Paul S. Taylor, *Mexican Labor in the United States* (Berkeley: University of California Press, 1929, 1932), 1, 79, 205–6; Paul S. Taylor, "Women in Industry," field notes for his book *Mexican Labor in the United States,* Bancroft Library, University of California.

46  Roy L. Garis, "The Mexican Invasion," *Saturday Evening Post,* 19 April 1930, 43–44; Kenneth L. Roberts, "Wet and Other Mexicans," *Saturday Evening*

*Post*, 4 February 1928, 10–11, 137–38, 141–42, 146; Raymond G. Carroll, "The Alien on Relief," *Saturday Evening Post*, 11 January 1936, 16–17, 100–103; Kenneth L. Roberts, "The Docile Mexican," *Saturday Evening Post*, 10 March 1928, 39, 41, 165–66; Albert Camarillo, *Chicanos in California* (San Francisco: Boyd and Fraser, 1984), 48–49; Francisco Balderrama and Raymond Rodríguez, *Decade of Betrayal: Mexican Repatriation in the 1930s* (Albuquerque: University of New Mexico Press, 1995), 16–20.

47  Francisco Balderrama, *In Defense of La Raza: The Los Angeles Mexican Consulate and the Mexican Community, 1929–1936* (Tucson: University of Arizona Press, 1982), 56.

48  "The Lemon Grove Incident" (1985), documentary produced by Paul Espinosa; Balderrama, *In Defense of La Raza*, 58–61; Robert Alvarez Jr., *Familia: Migration and Adaptation in Baja and Alta California, 1800–1975* (Berkeley: University of California Press, 1987), 152–55; Robert Alvarez Jr., "The Lemon Grove Incident: The Nation's First Successful Desegregation Court Case," *Journal of San Diego History* 32, no. 2 (spring 1986): 118, 124–25, 129–30.

49  "The Lemon Grove Incident" (1985); Balderrama, *In Defense of La Raza*, 60–61; Alvarez, *Familia*, 152–55; Alvarez, "The Lemon Grove Incident," 131–34.

50  San Miguel, *"Let Them All Take Heed,"* 78–81. For an example of LULAC's efforts with regard to equity in school funding, especially those of Elueterio Escobar in San Antonio, see Mario T. García, *Mexican Americans: Leadership, Ideology, and Identity, 1930–1960* (New Haven: Yale University Press, 1989), 65–83.

51  Benjamin Márquez, *LULAC: The Evolution of a Mexican American Political Organization* (Austin: University of Texas Press, 1993), 17–38; García, *Mexican Americans*, 35; Gutiérrez, *Walls and Mirrors*, 74–87.

52  Frank Barajas, "On Behalf of . . ." (seminar paper, Claremont Graduate School, 1994), 1, 12, 26; Carey McWilliams, "Is Your Name Gonzales?," *Nation*, 15 March 1947, 302; José Pitti et al., "A History of Mexican Americans in California," *Five Views*, 238; *Los Angeles Times*, 10 September 1996.

53  *Los Angeles Times*, 10 September 1996; McWilliams," Is Your Name Gonzales?," 303.

54  Reporter's transcript of proceedings, *Gonzalo Méndez v. Westminster School District of Orange County*, file folders 4292-M, box #740, Civil Cases 4285–4292, RG 221, Records of the District Court of the United States for the Southern District of California, Central Division, National Archives and Records Administration (Pacific Region), Laguna Niguel, Calif., 5, 85–87, 116–19, 120, 122–23. The exchange between Marcus and Kent is at 116–18.

55  McWilliams, "Is Your Name Gonzales?," 302; Wollenberg, *All Deliberate Speed*, 127–28, 131–32; *Los Angeles Times*, 10 September 1996; Reporter's transcript of proceedings, *Méndez v. Westminster*, 460, 468; Barajas, "On Behalf of . . . ," 33–34.

56  McWilliams, "Is Your Name Gonzales?," 302; *Los Angeles Times*, 10 September 1996; "A Family Changes History: *Méndez v. Westminster*" (1998), fiftieth

anniversary commemorative program book, University of California, Irvine, Division of Student Services, Office of the Vice-Chancellor, 8.

57 Rubén Flores, "Social Science in the Southwestern Courtroom: A New Understanding of the Development of the NAACP's Legal Strategies in the School Desegregation Cases" (B.A. thesis, Princeton University, 1994), 105–16; Wollenberg, *All Deliberate Speed*, 128, 131–32; Barajas, "On Behalf of . . .," 33; San Miguel, *"Let Them All Take Heed,"* 119; Pitti et al., "A History of Mexican Americans," 239.

RAYMOND GAVINS

# Within the Shadow of Jim Crow

## Black Struggles for Education and

## Liberation in North Carolina

℞ African Americans in North Carolina, the Tar Heel State, battled for education and equality against the forces of segregation. The State Constitution of 1868 mandated that "the children of the white race and the children of the colored race shall be taught in separate public schools." Segregation, known by the shorthand of Jim Crow, lasted until the *Brown* decision and the civil rights revolution. Black North Carolinians, who accounted for a third of all North Carolinians and were the South's sixth-largest black population in 1880 and the second-largest by 1960, resolved to "secure the blessings of liberty to ourselves and our posterity." Education was the sine qua non of this vision.[1] Oral and written sources reveal not only that black North Carolinians fought for the right to learn, but also how learning was integral to their liberation movement.

Building institutions and solidarity, they aspired to be educated and equal. Philanthropic allies helped considerably, while black communities sustained the crusade to build schools. Founded in 1881, the North Carolina Teachers Association (NCTA) promoted "the mental, moral, and physical education of the Negro youth of North Carolina." Indispensable from the nadir of racial inequality (1876–1901) through the first half of the twentieth century, NCTA merged with the white North Carolina Education Association in 1965. Today, it is virtually omitted from Tar Heel history books.

NCTA was critical in forging black literacy, however. Between Reconstruction and the First World War, it garnered black parents' backing and persevered despite unfair levels of state funding. Self-help and philanthropy therefore were crucial to maintain schools. From 1920, together with National Association for the Advancement of Colored People (NAACP) branches and the eventual State Conference of NAACP Branches, NCTA led the drive for school equity. By the 1940s the NAACP Legal Defense and Educational Fund, Inc. (LDF) was suing the state for equalization. Complaints about North Carolina schools were similar to those from South

Carolina or Virginia. My purpose is to explore the long struggle, interplaying the voices of local people and educators. Underappreciated historical actors, differing in status but linked by experience and a shared goal, they did much to guide black North Carolina on the road to *Brown*.

Let me begin with oral testimony to depict their culture of aspiration and its ideals. I will refer to three narrators who typify the 378 North Carolinians in the collection at Duke University "Behind the Veil: Documenting African American Life in the Jim Crow South." Narrators averaged seventy-two years of age when interviewed in the summers of 1993–95. They were diverse in gender (57 percent female), occupation (sharecroppers to teachers), educational level, region, and civic affiliation.[2] Their testimonies vividly detail black schooling and striving, and provide the contexts of educators' evolving agenda.

York D. Garrett Jr. (1894–1998) was born in Princeville, North Carolina, a son of former slaves. Longtime pharmacist and "race man," he expressed a sublime belief in education. Using his interview for "Behind the Veil," *U.S. News and World Report* featured him as "The Man Who Outlived Bigots." The Durham television station WTVD profiled him in 1996 as one of the city's most productive and revered senior citizens.[3] Trained at Elizabeth City State Normal School and Howard University, where he earned a degree from the School of Pharmacy in 1920, Garrett was a veteran of the First World War. "I went in as a company clerk, which was the biggest job in the Army then unless you were an officer," he recounted. "It was segregated. I was in charge of the whole company, 250 blacks." Returning, he pursued democracy at home. He referred early in the interview to his enslaved grandfather York. A harness maker who refused to be whipped, he escaped and was never seen again. Dr. Garrett's father, York Garrett II, was born in 1863. He attended a Freedmen's Bureau School, worked at a white grocery store in Tarboro, and later purchased it. A staunch Republican, he was elected to a town office in 1896, when the ex-slave George H. White (1852–1918), riding the wave of Republican-Populist fusion, won in the "Black Second" Congressional District. He was the fourth black congressman from North Carolina and the last until 1992.[4]

York Sr. resided in Princeville, founded as Freedom Hill, the oldest incorporated black town in America. He was a good provider for his wife, ten children, and ex-slave mother. Every child graduated from a college in North Carolina. The eldest was Beatrice Garrett Burnett (b. 1893), a physical education teacher. Her biographer notes: "[She] stands in the shoes of her father, 'a politican from the sole of his feet to the top of his head.' She, more than any other person, is responsible for the establishment and growth of the NAACP in eastern North Carolina. She urged blacks in Edgecombe

County to register and vote, giving strong encouragement to women after passage of the 19th Amendment. During fifty years of teaching in Tarboro public schools, she introduced children to . . . organized recreation and team sports in vacant fields."[5] Mrs. Burnett modeled dignity. "My father often said, 'You're as good as anybody else' and I have never taken low either," she testified.[6]

York Jr. was a trailblazer too. He passed the state pharmacy examination in 1921 and, backed by his father, opened a drugstore in Tarboro. In 1932 he moved to Durham and there until 1977 operated Garrett's Drugstore at the black-owned Biltmore Hotel. Displaced by urban renewal, he reopened in College Plaza near North Carolina College (NCC). He was a pillar of White Rock Baptist Church and civically active. Prominent in professional circles, he served as president of the National Pharmaceutical Association.

Garrett absorbed African American traditions of discipline and self-help. Praising the Yankee principal of Princeville Graded School, he recalled: "[John Jones] took a particular interest in me and he tutored me for four years. I was the first boy from his tutoring that graduated." Dr. Garrett knew his ex-slave grandmother, who told him about bondage and emancipation. York Sr., who died in 1928, personified independence: "So I've never known my father to work for anybody because he was in business for himself when I was born and continued to be in business for himself until he died."

The color line was pervasive. "There was no black [drug]store in Tarboro . . . and the law was that no black person be served at any white place because it would be illegal," he commented. Jim Crow laws had multiplied since the Supreme Court decreed the "equal, but separate" doctrine in *Plessy v. Ferguson* (1896). White supremacists then fueled the Wilmington racial pogrom and coup of 1898. Constitutional disfranchisement hit in 1900. Now voteless, blacks were barred from school committees, juries, and skilled jobs. Reporting a population that was 51 percent black in his county, one registrar submitted: "Negroes do not serve on juries in our county, nor are they allowed to vote or take any part in county or municipal affairs." The death toll in 1898 (reportedly there were "Wagon loads of Negro bodies"), property destruction, and recent claims for reparations remain controversial. A similar troubled memory surrounds the riots in Fayetteville and Winston-Salem of 1918, hitherto ignored by North Carolina historians. Both were ignited by economic conflict and police brutality in the black ghetto.[7]

Dr. Garrett conveyed the pride behind "the Veil that hung between us and Opportunity" (quoting W. E. B. Du Bois). He cast down his bucket in North Carolina. "Most of my friends went north after college. The big difference between the regions was that in the North if you looked white, nobody asked you, 'Are you white or colored?' My wife's family is very light, and the only one who didn't 'go white' is my wife, Julia," he remembered. "She could have gone either way. Her parents opposed her marrying me because I was darker skinned. But we made it." The Garretts saved and schooled four children. Their contemporaries flocked to graded and normal schools, and increasingly to colleges. Dr. Garrett's brothers and sisters studied at Elizabeth City Normal, Shaw University, and St. Augustine's College. Educators emphasized ideas of racial manhood and womanhood. Graduates augmented the élite of black professionals and entrepreneurs catering to farmers and urban wage workers. "For thirty years before my father died he was the treasurer of the statewide . . . secret societies like Masons."[8] Dr. Garrett credited fraternal orders, churches, and women's clubs for promoting education.

His generation faced coerced ignorance and poverty. Black families not only strove for self-sufficiency. They also answered the call of the Raleigh teacher Edward A. Johnson (1859–1944) to capitalize the "N" in Negro, and despite use of the words "nigger" and "negress" to use the prefixes Mr. and Mrs. Some joined the first North Carolina branches of the NAACP in 1917. Parents in the meantime subjected themselves to "double taxation" to obtain better schools, supplementing their direct taxes with donations of cash, land, labor, or produce to match grants from the school building program of the Rosenwald Fund; these voluntary contributions accounted for 17 percent of the cost of the program throughout the South.[9] The parents struggled for both citizenship and their children's future. Literacy would imbue the children with a sense of self-esteem, refuting notions of black inferiority.

Lillie P. Fenner (b. 1907), who grew up poor in Halifax County, broadens our view of rural black education. Fieldwork overwhelmed her childhood. "I was spending about two good months in school. Along then it won't no strict laws for children to go to school no way," she confirms. "So I never could go. But I didn't worry about that. I just stayed home and I tried to learn, read books at home."[10] Halifax was in the eastern Black Belt, where cotton and tobacco planters ruled. Thousands of black residents left when the Democrats regained state power in 1876 and the Landlord and Tenant Act was enacted in 1879; perhaps three thousand were Exodusters to Kansas and Indiana. In 1889, sparked by an election law that all but disfranchised them, nearly fifty thousand blacks dispersed to Arkansas, Texas, and Oklahoma. Tens of thousands more boarded trains in the 1914–18 Great Migration to the North.[11]

The great majority stayed. In 1950 thirteen counties in eastern North

Carolina domiciled 40 percent of all blacks in the state's one hundred counties. They averaged 59 percent of the population in eight counties, including Halifax, where croppers endured fraud and the whip. Those who disputed landlords when settling up or broke contracts rarely received protection. Tenants accounted for most of the state's 101 lynching victims (1882–1968). Most schools had one room and a lone teacher. Counties did not furnish buses and children frequently walked several miles to school. Books were scarce, so teachers had to be creative. One collected "all of the materials" she could "to let the children know of the accomplishments of the people of their race."[12]

The Fenners yearned to breathe free. "I never knowed my grandparents on my father's side. Never did know them. They had passed before I was large enough to know who they were," she explains. Yet she recalled how the family scrimped to get by. "We never had no land of our own. We'd sharecrop with the white people." They searched for security. "We moved around different places in Halifax County . . . Well, I don't know," she confessed. "Seemed like my daddy and the man he worked with couldn't agree on different things. So he would get up and move somewhere else. We'd stay there awhile until it looked like we couldn't agree and then he'd get up and move somewhere else." Braving the odds, her parents schooled nineteen children. "All of them got to go but me and my oldest brother . . . Some of them graduated and some went in [army] service," she remembered. Her parents thus never gave up. A nucleus of blacks in the county became landowners and sent their children to the private Bricks School in Enfield.[13]

Work was the common denominator. Folks labored "on the farm . . . in the log woods. That's the way they made their living," she recalled. They cooperated to subsist. "My daddy was a member of the lodge called the Knights of Gideon and they would go to the lodge at night, he and my mama. It was some kind of meeting. They would meet and discuss different things. When somebody would pass in the family they would always give them a certain portion of money to help them. Then they would fix food and carry to the house . . . Won't no insurance or nothing. So different ones would pitch in and help them." After marrying at seventeen in 1927, Fenner and her husband sharecropped on one farm thirty-four years. Parents of six schoolchildren, they were surrounded by good neighbors. People developed a co-op and assisted each other in getting Resettlement Administration relief. During illness "the people in the community would come and see about you."[14]

Fenner echoes the survivors of *Growing Up in the Black Belt* (1941), the classic ethnography by Charles S. Johnson of Fisk University. She did not relocate in the Second Great Migration from the 1930s to the 1960s. North Carolina cities, the destination of many migrants, were 31 percent black in 1940. From 1940 to 1950 about 128,000 blacks migrated to the North and West. Fenner and her neighbors stayed on the land, acquiring few material goods. Still, they forged a moral economy of sharing and sacrificed to educate their children.[15]

William T. Childs (b. 1919) mirrors black perseverance in Wilmington after its riot. Black schools somehow survived. "The old Williston school property on Seventh Street, worth approximately $3,000.00, is the only investment the public school system has made in the way of buildings for the education of the colored people," the superintendent admitted in 1917, "and this is so insignificant that we ought to be ashamed to mention it." Blacks were restoring their neighborhoods and seeking opportunity, although a "fear of mob violence and uncontrolled outlawry" lingered. Childs describes a milieu of mistrust. "They did not really want to talk too much about the riot of 1898. They did not like to talk too much about that," he says of his grandparents (ex-slaves) and parents. "There was . . . a lot of information about it. But they did not like to talk about it." He heard little about the atrocities until he "started going to [Peabody] school. And I later learned there was a real traumatic kind of thing and many blacks who lived through that era were quieted. They were not expected to talk too much about it . . . blacks were driven out of the town." But there was "an old minstrel man" who witnessed the mobs and "used to talk about what happened."[16]

An intergenerational household instilled precepts of character, education, and service. The adults were "positive people that looked forward rather than back." Childs's father was a train car cook and "not that formally educated . . . But he had this thing about reading and learning." Childs and five siblings followed the golden rules of St. Stephen African Methodist Episcopal (AME) Church and the schools. Teachers stressed the value of "Negro heritage" and achievement. The boxing champion Joe Louis, the Wilmington-born opera singer Caterina Jarboro, and Congressman Oscar DePriest of Illinois "were some of our models then," Childs states. "They had achieved in a world that wasn't easy to achieve [in]. They had something special, extra, in order to do it."

Childs was among three children to finish college. He completed Williston High School in 1937 (when only 26 percent of Tar Heel blacks between the ages of fourteen and seventeen could expect to do so) and North Carolina A&T College in 1941. His brothers finished A&T and Shaw. Taught "to cope" and maintain some semblance of dignity, they sought white-collar employment to no avail. "There were a whole lot of problems that really needed to be squared away" in Wilmington.[17] Childs shows the interplay of home, church, and school in molding black consciousness. Such sanctuaries nurtured his identity, his opposition to caste, and his duty as one of the college-trained.[18] A shipyard messenger, he experienced blatant bigotry before his induction in 1942 into the army. He returned in 1947 to teach Social Studies at Harnett County Training School. Pressured by the NAACP and by returning black soldiers in 1948, Wilmington hired him and three black policemen. Childs was the "juvenile court probation officer and the attendance counselor officer for the board of education. I had two jobs in one."[19]

As a state employee Childs could ill afford to oppose white racism publicly. Rather, he resisted its indignities through the "offstage culture." He networked with many teachers who were, as the Durham Manifesto of 1942 proclaimed, "fundamentally opposed to the principle and practice of segregation in our American society."[20] School was foremost for him. "Every time that they arrested a black child they called me and it was my decision usually as to whether he would go back home or whether he would be locked up," Childs recalled. "And usually those kids went back home . . . I had a reputation for picking them up and taking them to school." They would be encouraged to reach their highest potential.[21]

While Garrett, Fenner, and Childs emphasized the importance of education at the grassroots, the NCTA and NAACP made formal efforts to promote it. The leadership of these organizations, members of the "talented tenth," were also witnesses of black school conditions and framed the key issues for white society. Communities crusaded "for universal schooling" during the nadir of racial inequality. Race, ethnic, and class inequalities persisted. Among those addressing the crisis was John C. Dancy Jr. (1857–1920), co-founder of the NCTA and twice collector of customs for the Port of Wilmington. There is no record of his graduation speech in 1899 at the Gregory Normal Institute, a missionary-supported school in Wilmington. At the Colored Industrial Fair in Raleigh in 1901, however, he told blacks to climb. They were vital to the economy. Whether farm or urban dwellers, they must be industrious and thrifty. "In reference to education, I urge eternal vigilance along that line. We need to keep every school house open to us, filled with our children." For longer school terms, for scholastic and vocational instruction, "we need to make sacrifices." Dancy concluded: "If we succeed along these lines, we will have taken another step in the solution of our great problem."[22] Garrett, Fenner, and Childs embraced those core values.

Progress was uphill, step by step. Illiteracy rates were 76 percent among blacks and 45 percent among whites in 1880; 32 percent for blacks and 10 percent for whites in 1920. NCTA proved to be a chief mover, hiring a black assistant in what would become the state Division of Negro Education. The group approached major donors, notably the Peabody Educational Fund, which George F. Peabody of Boston had launched in 1867 to assist the war-ravaged South. The Slater Fund, created by John F. Slater of Connecticut in 1882, financed Christian and industrial education among black southerners. Its direct beneficiaries were the Slater Normal and Industrial School of Winston-Salem and county training schools. Established at Asheville, North Carolina, in 1901, the Southern Education Board united northern industrialists and southern reformers to foster "public education for all groups."

Other foundations delivered as well. Created in 1902 and based in New York, the General Education Board benefited four-year high schools, among other aims. Anna T. Jeanes, a Quaker from Pennsylvania, established the Jeanes Fund in 1905 to benefit "rural, community, [and] country schools for southern Negroes." The Phelps Stokes Fund, founded by a bequest of Caroline Phelps Stokes of New York, started donating to country districts in 1910. The same year the Chicago philanthropist Julius Rosenwald launched the Rosenwald Fund, best known for its schoolhouses. The Durham tobacconist Washington Duke and his sons assisted black colleges in North and South Carolina before and after the formation in 1924 of the Duke Endowment.[23]

While steering proposals to the General Education Board, the NCTA grappled with the curriculum. Should it be classical, industrial, or both? What is its function in cultivating black manhood and womanhood? In enfranchising the race? How should teachers neutralize or oppose inequality? Or meet objectives defined by philanthropies and the state? Self-help surely was not enough to sustain and upgrade schools in this "emergency period" of extreme privation. Government tax dollars were denied or unequal. Philanthropies extended a helping hand, accepting Jim Crow, but their gifts contributed to black empowerment. Operating into the 1960s, the Jeanes Fund furnished thirty-nine supervisors to forty-one of the poorest counties by 1928–29. They supervised 1,368 schools and 2,278 teachers. Without such assistance, most blacks in Fenner's native Halifax County could have been illiterate. Probably "the most influential philanthropic force that came to [the] aid of Negroes at that time" was the Rosenwald Fund. By 1933 it had supplemented the construction of over eight hundred schools, eight shops, and eighteen teacherages in North Carolina.[24]

Missionary philanthropy was no less significant. Of the seventy-two private schools in North Carolina counted by the federal survey of Negro education in 1917, sixty-three were church related. Ten white religious bodies funded forty-one, with the American Baptist Home Mission Society, the

American Church Institute for Negroes (Episcopal), and the American Missionary Association (Congregational) leading the way.[25] Other religious bodies such as the AME, AME Zion, and General Baptist State Convention sponsored twenty-two schools, whose total income was only half that of the top thirteen white schools. In addition, black churches rallied supporters like the Prince Hall Masons, the Order of Eastern Star, and the United Order of Tents.[26]

The First World War and its aftermath saw more and more protests. By the "Red Summer" of 1919, eleven communities had chartered NAACPS. Chartered in 1921, the Halifax County branch was the state's second-largest by 1945 (756 members). Branches enlisted farmers, laborers, and teachers. They addressed urgent concerns: anti-lynching, the right to vote, and fair hiring. And they allied with the NCTA to demand public high schools, increasing the number from one in 1918 to 119 by 1930. The allies (who divided on tactics in the 1930s) put all public schools on notice. Like the Wilmington branch, they pledged: "To educate that better and fuller facilities may be provided for the children; to educate that men and women will be better and law-abiding citizens; to educate that men and women may know how to qualify and then exercise all the rights and privileges of citizenship. To unite that we may eradicate the illiteracy, ignorance and disregard of the laws which now exist, and that all efforts for the good and the uplift of humanity, of which we are unquestionably a part, may have the strong and sturdy support necessary to accomplish the same."[27]

Local blacks, embracing the "New Negro Movement," mobilized for fairness. In 1920 the Rocky Mount NAACP partnered in getting approval for secondary courses at Lincoln School, but the superintendent balked. Accordingly, he summoned the principal, Oliver R. Pope (1876–1973), who recalled their conversation, beginning with the superintendent's remarks:

"I don't believe in niggers studying Latin and Algebra in public schools— and some white children don't need these for that matter. I want the niggers to have a high school suited to their peculiar needs . . . drop Latin and Algebra. . . . All right, Pope, what have you to say?" "Mr. Banner, I believe you and I could sit down together and work out a course of study flexible enough to meet the needs of both races . . . but we can't. I wish we could. We have only the state course of study, which makes no distinction between the races. And, just as you told me last spring, it's the law." "Pope, is that the way you feel about this thing?" And I answered truthfully, "It certainly is." "Well, Pope, if that's the way you feel about it," he answered as he looked at me after more than a minute, although it seemed twice that long, "go on with your high school. That's not saying I'm endorsing it. So don't get your hopes too high."[28]

Pope was diplomatic but forthright. He was determined to combat the status quo, as were his comrades in the NCTA. Members numbered about 1,000 at the war's end and 2,400 in seventy-five chapters by 1924. Three-quarters of the state's 5,700 certified black teachers belonged in 1929, constituting "one of the largest organizations of its kind in the United States."[29] The NCTA inspired "hope of reaching higher opportunities," declared Annie W. Holland (1871–1934), state supervisor of Negro Elementary Schools. She traveled widely for demonstration classes and fundraisers. In 1928 she organized the North Carolina Congress of Colored Parents and Teachers. Rural folk particularly valued the congress, which raised funds for books, buses, food, health clinics, janitors, and repairs.[30] Importantly, it was in primary grades that Garrett and Childs acquired a foundation for high school and college. White schools, nonetheless, had far superior instructional support.

The NCTA demanded equitable treatment. It targeted poor facilities, short sessions, and unjust teacher salaries—$466.14 black and $833.61 white in 1929. Nor was it derailed by a sunny report from southern superintendents ranking North Carolina third (after Texas and Virginia) in the valuation of black school property. Even so, "more money was spent in 1929–30 for school buses for white children than was spent for new schools for black children."[31] The NCTA formed an action committee. Equality was an idea whose time had come. "It is our plain duty to make no discrimination in the matter of public education," insisted Simon G. Atkins (1863–1934), president of the NCTA and Winston-Salem Teachers College (formerly Slater Normal). "I cannot too strongly urge upon you the importance of this consideration." Nondiscrimination was "both a race and State need."[32] But what did equality mean? Could it happen in the framework of *Plessy*? Would attacking inequities spark a bloody backlash? Yield more than a gesture of reform? The NCTA agonized, argued, and compromised on these questions, on how to leverage its political capital. How the organization responded reveals dilemmas in black ideology and strategy during the two decades preceding *Brown*.

Raleigh demurred on the NCTA demands. State officials seemed smug, hailing the news in 1930 that North Carolina now surpassed Texas and Virginia in allocations for black education. The governor did not confer with the NCTA's subcommittee and its white director of Negro education until *Hocutt v. Wilson* (1933) forced his hand. Through the Durham NAACP, Thomas R. Hocutt, a graduate of NCC, sued for admission to the University of North Carolina (UNC) School of Pharmacy. Rumor of a "salary challenge" soon spread. Hocutt's petition, arguably the "genesis" of *Brown*, incensed the doves in the NCTA, led by the president of NCC, James E.

Shepard (1875–1947). His refusal to release a transcript aborted the suit. "It is the duty of citizen-teachers to continue to work within the bounds of the state by every legitimate means and specially through the . . . appeal at the bar of public conscience," Shepard contended. The NAACP counsel and some of the NCTA officers split, but the rank and file held on to the NAACP.[33] *Hocutt* signaled "the beginning of an eighteen-year campaign in North Carolina to open the state's graduate and professional institutions to its black citizens." Moreover, it "portended a concerted campaign to end segregated education all over the South."[34]

Authorities finally acted in 1934. The governor invited fourteen panelists, five from the NCTA, to name a biracial fact-finding commission. It would ascertain "the facts and not propaganda," the "best judgment of the leaders of both races." Issued in 1935, the report confirmed black grievances. "Many colored children, practically half of the rural ones, are poorly—some miserably—housed. Two-thirds of the urban children are reasonably well housed," the document explained. It detailed everything from inferior equipment to the absence of advanced degrees. Besides standard high schools and an eight-month session, it recommended improved college appropriations, graduate preparation, and a subsidy "to be used toward meeting the tuition charges for those whose scholastic attainments enable them to pursue the work which is provided for whites, but which the State does not make available to Negroes." Salary gaps should "be reduced approximately 50 percent in 1935" and "eliminated within a period of three to five years."[35]

Gaps between programs were large. Curricula at UNC, the Women's College (Greensboro), and North Carolina State College lacked black equivalents. Black "professional work" was scanty. Shaw's law, medicine, and pharmacy departments had been closed since 1918. Eight private black colleges offered training for the ministry and in nursing, pre-dentistry, engineering, medicine, law, social work, and teaching. Only four were bona fide offerings, and just three reported enrollments. Saint Augustine counted forty-one students in nursing and social work, Shaw four, and Johnson C. Smith nineteen in ministry. Five black state colleges had agronomy, commerce, engineering, trades, pre-dentistry, medicine, and teacher training. Teaching and trades predominated. Of 1,464 state-college students, 1,127 were preparing to teach.[36]

The legislature stalled on reforms, but two events prodded it. In 1938 Pauli Murray (1910–1985), alumna of Hillside High School (Durham) and Hunter College, applied to the UNC Graduate School, fueling another "bitter controversy." Then, in *Gaines v. Canada* (1938), the Supreme Court required Missouri to equalize the plaintiff's school or admit him to the

University of Missouri School of Law. Posthaste, legislators approved master's degrees in liberal arts and a law school at NCC. They authorized the Department of Public Instruction to begin equalizing teachers' salaries. Equal pay would be announced in 1944, yet "where it was formally achieved, devices such as city supplements had the effect of creating the disparity once more." A bill allowing out-of-state tuition "loans to negro medical students" passed in 1945.[37]

Educators echoed the debates underlying blacks' growing consensus to attack Jim Crow. Rose Butler Browne of NCC preached: "Find a point of entry where you can fight segregation. Never give up principle, but don't be too proud to act with compassion toward those who treat you unjustly." Wary of the militants, Shepard believed it "unwise to go outside the state for legal aid . . . to do what we should do for ourselves." He clung to negotiation, hoping to mold NCC into a college "for the colored people which would stand for the same high ideals as Trinity College stands among the whites." Pope wanted to pressure the authorities. "How are we to get out of this dilemma? . . . By sporadic and unsupported appeals? By wishing and waiting for that deceptive something we call the psychological moment? . . . I tell you, No. Never! We have got to intelligently organize." He added that "we have resources without. We have many friends at our disposal." Meanwhile, the NCTA was gaining backers in biracial labor unions and women's associations as well as the outspoken North Carolina Committee on Negro Affairs. It aimed to "present a solid front for the solution of our common problems." Affiliates emerged in Durham and Wilmington, where Garrett and Childs were registered voters. Childs also championed students. Formed in 1940, the LDF proved to be the NCTA's strongest friend. And "many individual teachers made anonymous contributions" to it.[38]

Battles after 1940 expanded the groundwork laid by the NCTA and NAACP and included court challenges that foreshadowed *Brown*. Consider the Durham Manifesto (1942), the southern black declaration of war on segregation, formulated at NCC by fifty-nine conferees. Thirty-four were educators such as Charlotte Hawkins Brown (1882–1961), founder of Palmer Memorial Institute in Sedalia, currently the only North Carolina historic site named for an African American. The manifesto's education section condemned injustices that the NCTA had exposed in 1929. Its agriculture and employment sections described the "color line" marking black life chances. Formed in 1943, the State Conference of NAACP Branches played a paramount role. Among its priorities were adjustments in teachers' salaries (1944) and "school boycotts" in Kinston and Lumberton (1946). Its president Kelly M. Alexander (1915–85), a native of Charlotte, pushed organization building and school lawsuits. The Asheville schoolteacher Leila B. Michael (1875–1965) became the group's state organizer, and the Durham attorney Conrad O. Pearson (1902–1984), co-counsel in *Hocutt*, headed the legal committee.[39]

Michael demonstrated a strong bond between education and civil rights. "This is what amazed me so. Now they at that time were working hard, and they were schoolteachers," a protégée reflected. Michael was the leader of an activist cadre of women teachers and cafeteria workers in the Asheville NAACP. She taught at Hill Street Elementary School, where her husband was principal, while rearing four children. During her branch presidency (1938–45), membership rose from 108 to 409. Writing to the NAACP National Office, she sighed: "You know . . . this is strictly a southern city and I was advised many times by my most intimate friends that I should resign as president, as it was thought my activities along this line would jeopardize my teaching position." She was not fired, but black state employees had to hide their NAACP memberships. As an organizer, she increased the number of branches from twenty-two with 5,700 members in 1945 to eighty-three with 9,300 members by 1955.[40]

Pearson, Howard School of Law '32 and a respected member of LDF's national team, kept abreast of anti–Jim Crow litigation in North Carolina and neighboring states. He enjoyed the favor of Louis E. Austin (1898–1971), militant editor in Durham of the *Carolina Times* and an LDF liaison. Together they countered the white press, recruited litigants, and arranged a protest by NCC law students at the State Capitol in 1949. Students carried placards reading "WE'RE CITIZENS" and "DO SOMETHING NOW!" Filing "equal protection" petitions like those in Clarendon County, South Carolina, and Prince Edward County, Virginia, Pearson litigated important cases. *Blue v. Durham Board of Education* (1951) enjoined the board to end black-white school "disparities" forthwith. *McKissick v. Carmichael* (1951), won in the U.S. Court of Appeals for the Fourth Circuit, ordered the UNC School of Law to admit Floyd B. McKissick (1922–91), an alumnus of NCC and veteran of the Second World War who ended white-only admissions at Chapel Hill. In Wilmington *Eaton v. New Hanover County Board of Education* (1952) brought an order from the Federal District Court comparable to that issued in Durham in *Blue*. The Wilmington Committee on Negro Affairs defrayed the bulk of expenses and the NCTA donated $500. Board attorneys "alluded to the race riots of 1898 . . . as an effort to intimidate—to warn that it could happen again," reports the plaintiff Hubert A. Eaton (1916–91). Yet, he concludes, the "Negro community had found a new degree of unity."[41] On the verge of overcoming statutory Jim Crow, blacks would never turn back.

Hope abounded in 1954. That fall the NAACP state convention explored "The Meaning of Segregation in American Society." Alexander assured the delegates that "we can get rid of segregation in all areas . . . without violence; we can do it without breaking laws." Before adjourning the attendees agreed to flood the governor's office with letters protesting his segregationist education proposals. New battle lines were drawn.

Equality was the lodestar. Almost forgotten are the parents and children who braved racist reprisals to desegregate schools. Nor do we remember the courageous steps by the NCTA and NAACP to implement school desegregation before the sit-ins and the case of *Swann* (1965) in Charlotte took center stage.[42] The NCTA initiated forty-six suits against black teacher dismissals in 1964–65 alone. Promoting racial tolerance and cooperation, it also agreed to a plan of merger with its white counterpart.

Black North Carolina's past was prologue. Aspirations for "the ballot, the book, and the buck" deeply informed black school crusades from Reconstruction to *Brown*. The advances and setbacks of earlier generations enlarge our understanding of the interplay of African American ideologies, institutions, and movements. Parents, teachers, and the coalition of NCTA and NAACP were essential movers. But they are oddly understudied. Recovery of their roles should recast the official Tar Heel civil rights narrative.

"The Civil Rights Movement in North Carolina 1945–1975," an exhibit commemorating the fiftieth anniversary of *Brown* in 2004, is a welcome start. Its sponsor, the North Carolina Museum of History, set out to provide a multimedia presentation of the community "stories . . . that lay at the heart of the cause." For example, photographs of black and white schools helped to explain locally based antecedents of the court decisions of the 1950s.[43] "White Only" signs and oral histories situated non-élite families and neighborhoods in the sea change of the civil rights movement, often depicted simply as a series of mass demonstrations and speeches. Blacks' education and liberties were indivisible. School campaigns, in the shadow of the plantation and the veil, significantly shaped their dialogue on organizing and stride toward freedom.

In my exploration, black North Carolinians exemplify schools' centrality to their aspirations and democratic struggles. They illustrate the responses and self-activity of the oppressed, enabling us to link the agency of the masses and the intelligentsia. They represent an aspiring "world that white people hardly knew and cared about even less." It was "Behind the Veil" that schools trained those who would strive for black freedoms. Here men and women (sharecroppers, factory workers, educators, organizers) debated priorities and strategies. As the NCTA and NAACP show, they ultimately consolidated their energies to confront the state. Overmatched within "a dominant system and a wardship . . . without authority," they remained resilient and resourceful in the encounter. Historians of modern North Carolina are just beginning to reexamine Jim Crow's "statutory discriminations,"[44] its milieu of anti-black violence, and its effects on contemporary race policy. Looking "within the shadow," they will discover the likes of Garrett, Fenner, and Childs. They will find the NCTA and NAACP, empowering the disfranchised, speaking truth to power, reaching out to create working-class alliances, struggling for integrated education and justice.

## Notes

1 Jeffrey J. Crow, Paul D. Escott, and Flora J. Hatley, *A History of African Americans in North Carolina* (Raleigh: Division of Archives and History, North Carolina Department of Cultural Resources, 1992), 120; Raymond Gavins, "Fear, Hope, and Struggle: Recasting Black North Carolina in the Age of Jim Crow," *Democracy Betrayed: The Wilmington Race Riot and Its Legacy*, ed. David S. Cecelski and Timothy B. Tyson (Chapel Hill: University of North Carolina Press, 1998), 187, 194; Frenise A. Logan, *The Negro in North Carolina 1876–1894* (Chapel Hill: University of North Carolina Press, 1964), 139–63; Pauli Murray, ed. and comp., *States' Laws on Race and Color* (1951; reprint, Athens: University of Georgia Press, 1997), 329.

2 Ken Chujo, "The Black Struggle for Education in North Carolina" (diss., Duke University, 1988), 177–80; Percy Murray, *History of the North Carolina Teachers Association* (Washington: National Education Association, 1984), 115, 138; "Behind the Veil: Documenting African American Life in the Jim Crow South," *Duke University Libraries* 9 (spring 1996): 2–6.

3 For the "race man, an individual who was proud of his race and always tried to uphold it," see Horace R. Cayton, *Long Old Road* (New York: Trident, 1965), 250; "The Man Who Outlived Bigots," *U.S. News and World Report*, 28 August–4 September 1995, 90, 93; Interview with York Garrett, Durham, N.C., 3 June 1993, "Behind the Veil: Documenting African American Life in the Jim Crow South," Rare Book, Manuscript, and Special Collections Library, Duke University, Durham; Funeral Program, White Rock Baptist Church, Durham, 3 January 1999.

4 Interview with Garrett; Raymond Gavins, "Recasting the Black Freedom Struggle in Wilmington, 1898–1930," *Carolina Comments* 48 (November 2000): 145.

5 Emily Herring Wilson and Susan Mullany, *Hope and Dignity: Older Black Women of the South* (Philadelphia: Temple University Press, 1983), 87.

6 *Id.*

7 Cecelski and Tyson, eds., *Democracy Betrayed*, ix–xvi; Interview with Garrett; Gavins, "Fear, Hope, and Struggle," 190; Gavins, "Recasting the Black Freedom

Struggle in Wilmington," 143, 148; Glenda Elizabeth Gilmore, *Gender and Jim Crow: Women and the Politics of White Supremacy in North Carolina, 1896–1920* (Chapel Hill: University of North Carolina Press, 1996), 91–118; H. Leon Prather Sr., *We Have Taken a City: Wilmington Racial Massacre and Coup of 1898* (1984; reprint, Wilmington: NU World, 1998), 9–12.

8  W. E. B. Du Bois, *The Souls of Black Folk* (1903; reprint, New York: New American Library, 1969), 102; Interview with Garrett.

9  James D. Anderson, *The Education of Blacks in the South, 1860–1935* (Chapel Hill: University of North Carolina Press, 1988), 152, 153, 156, 183–85; Gavins, "Recasting the Black Freedom Struggle in Wilmington," 144.

10  William H. Chafe, Raymond Gavins, and Robert Korstad, eds., *Remembering Jim Crow: African Americans Tell about Life in the Segregated South* (New York: New Press, 2001), 208–11, 328; Interview with Lillie Fenner, Halifax, N.C., 26 June 1993, "Behind the Veil: Documenting African American Life in the Jim Crow South," Rare Book, Manuscript, and Special Collections Library, Duke University, Durham.

11  Raymond Gavins, "The Meaning of Freedom: Black North Carolina in the Nadir, 1880–1900," *Race, Class, and Politics in Southern History: Essays in Honor of Robert F. Durden*, ed. Jeffrey J. Crow, Paul D. Escott, and Charles L. Flynn Jr. (Baton Rouge: Louisiana State University Press, 1989), 178–80; Daniel M. Johnson and Rex R. Campbell, *Black Migration in America: A Social Demographic History* (Durham: Duke University Press, 1981), 59, 63.

12  Chafe, Gavins, and Korstad, *Remembering Jim Crow*, 119, 154, 255, 256, 293; John R. Larkins, *The Negro Population of North Carolina, 1945–1955* (Raleigh: North Carolina State Board of Public Welfare, 1957), 1–5; Robert L. Zangrando, *The NAACP Crusade against Lynching, 1909–1950* (Philadelphia: Temple University Press, 1980), 5–8.

13  Chafe, Gavins, and Korstad, *Remembering Jim Crow*, 170; Interview with Fenner; Crow, Escott, and Hatley, *African Americans in North Carolina*, 157.

14  Interview with Fenner.

15  Chafe, Gavins, and Korstad, *Remembering Jim Crow*, 89; Larkins, *The Negro Population of North Carolina*, 1–5; Charles S. Johnson, *Growing Up in the Black Belt: Negro Youth in the Rural South* (1941; reprint, New York: Schocken, 1967), 274, 319.

16  Interview with William T. Childs, Wilmington, N.C., 12 July 1993, "Behind the Veil: Documenting African American Life in the Jim Crow South," Rare Book, Manuscript, and Special Collections Library, Duke University, Durham; Gavins, "Fear, Hope, and Struggle," 190, 196.

17  Interview with Childs; Gavins, "Recasting the Black Freedom Struggle in Wilmington," 147–48; William M. Reaves, *Strength through Struggle : The Chronological and Historical Record of the African-American Community in Wilmington, North Carolina, 1865–1950*, ed. Beverly Tetterton (Wilmington: New Hanover County Public Library), 52.

18  Interview with Childs; Adam Fairclough, " 'Being in the Field of Education

and Also Being a Negro . . . Seems . . . Tragic': Black Teachers in the Jim Crow South," *Journal of American History* 87 (June 2000): 83–84.

19 Interview with Childs; Reaves, *Strength through Struggle*, 360.

20 Raymond Gavins, "The NAACP in North Carolina during the Age of Segregation," *New Directions in Civil Rights Studies*, ed. Armstead L. Robinson and Patricia Sullivan (Charlottesville: University Press of Virginia, 1991), 109; James C. Scott, *Domination and the Arts of Resistance: Hidden Transcripts* (New Haven: Yale University Press, 1990), 6.

21 Interview with Childs; James L. Leloudis, *Schooling the New South: Pedagogy, Self, and Society in North Carolina, 1880–1920* (Chapel Hill: University of North Carolina Press, 1996), 227–28; Vanessa Siddle Walker, *Their Highest Potential: An African American School Community in the Segregated South* (Chapel Hill: University of North Carolina Press, 1996), 3.

22 Gavins, "Recasting the Black Freedom Struggle in Wilmington," 144; Helen G. Edmonds, *The Negro and Fusion Politics in North Carolina, 1894–1901* (Chapel Hill: University of North Carolina Press, 1951), 212–13; Reaves, *Strength through Struggle*, 166–67.

23 Anderson, *The Education of Blacks in the South*, 239, 240, 245, 247; Hugh Victor Brown, *A History of the Education of Negroes in North Carolina* (Raleigh: Irving Swain, 1961), 29; Robert Korstad, "Duke, James (1856–1925)," *The Oxford Companion to United States History*, ed. Paul S. Boyer (New York: Oxford University Press, 2001); J. Morgan Kousser, "Progressivism—For Middle-Class Whites Only: North Carolina Education, 1880–1910," *Journal of Southern History* 46 (May 1980): 82–83, 186; *Laws and Resolutions of the State of North Carolina . . . 1900* (Raleigh: Edwards & Broughton and E. M. Uzzell, 1900), 58; Murray, *History of the North Carolina Teachers Association*, 27; U.S. Bureau of the Census, *Fourteenth Census, 1920: North Carolina* (Washington: Government Printing Office, 1923), 52; Richard Barry Westin, "The State and Segregated Schools: Negro Public Education in North Carolina, 1863–1923" (diss., Duke University, 1966), 342–56.

24 For the debate see *Proceedings of the Twentieth Annual Session of the North Carolina Teachers Association*, Kittrell, N.C., 12–17 June 1901 (Elizabeth City: E. F. Snakenberg, 1901), 6, 16–17, 25–26. Cf. Brown, *A History of the Education of Negroes in North Carolina*, 52, 58; Thomas W. Hanchett, "The Rosenwald Schools and Black Education in North Carolina," *North Carolina Historical Review* 65 (October 1988): 387, 426; Neil R. McMillen, *Dark Journey: Black Mississippians in the Age of Jim Crow* (Urbana: University of Illinois Press, 1989), 98; Murray, *History of the North Carolina Teachers Association*, 31.

25 The other seven bodies: Board of Freedmen's Missions of the United Presbyterian Church; Board of Missions for Freedmen of the Presbyterian Church; Christian Local Conventions; Freedmen's Aid Society of the Methodist Episcopal Church; Lutheran Board of Missions; Society of the Methodist Episcopal Church; Society of Friends.

26 Gavins, "Recasting the Black Freedom Struggle in Wilmington," 145–46;

Murray, *History of the North Carolina Teachers Association*, 32; U.S. Bureau of Education, *Negro Education: A Study of the Private and Higher Schools for Colored People in the United States*, Bulletin 1916, no. 30 (Washington: Government Printing Office, 1917), 1:384, 2:389.

27 Gavins, "The NAACP in North Carolina during the Age of Segregation," 106–7, 110; David Levering Lewis, *When Harlem Was in Vogue* (New York: Penguin, 1979), 17–20; Reaves, *Strength through Struggle*, 201.

28 Oliver R. Pope, *Chalk Dust* (New York: Pageant, 1967), 103–4 (O. R. Pope Elementary School, Rocky Mount, is named for him); Obituary, Rocky Mount *Evening Telegram*, 16 December 1973, 2; Funeral Program, Camphor Memorial United Methodist Church, Philadelphia, 18 December 1973.

29 Murray, *History of the North Carolina Teachers Association*, 33, 151; *Minutes of the Forty-Fourth Annual Session . . .*, Wilmington, N.C., 26–28 November 1924 (Raleigh: North Carolina Educational Association, n.d.), 24, 32; *Report of the Governor's Commission for the Study of the Problems in the Education of the Negroes in North Carolina* (Raleigh: North Carolina Department of Public Instruction, 1935), 7–8, 88, 93.

30 Crow, Escott, and Hatley, *African Americans in North Carolina*, 156; N. C. Newbold, *Five North Carolina Negro Educators* (Chapel Hill: University of North Carolina Press, 1939), 17, 70–76; Walker, *Their Highest Potential*, 141–69.

31 John Hope Franklin and Alfred A. Moss Jr., *From Slavery to Freedom: A History of African Americans*, 8th ed. (New York: McGraw-Hill, 2000), 446; Murray, *History of the North Carolina Teachers Association*, 44; Samuel L. Smith, *Builders of Goodwill: The Story of the State Agents of Negro Education in the South, 1910–1950* (Nashville: Tennessee Book, 1950), 52–53.

32 Report of Committee on Teachers' Salaries, *North Carolina Teachers Record* (March 1930), 1:8; N. C. Newbold, *President's Address, S. G. Atkins . . .*, Goldsboro, N.C., 23 November 1927, 9; Newbold, *Five North Carolina Negro Educators*, 5–6, 15. Cf. Adam Fairclough, *Teaching Equality: Black Schools in the Age of Jim Crow* (Athens: University of Georgia Press, 2001), 14–15.

33 Wade Hamilton Boggs, "State Supported Higher Education for Blacks in North Carolina, 1877–1945" (diss., Duke University, 1972), 248–53; Murray, *History of the North Carolina Teachers Association*, 44–45, 48; Mark V. Tushnet, *The NAACP's Legal Strategy against Segregated Education, 1925–1950* (Chapel Hill: University of North Carolina Press, 1987), 52–53, 58; Gilbert Ware, "Hocutt: Genesis of Brown," *Journal of Negro Education* 52 (summer 1983): 227–33; Gilbert Ware, *William Hastie: Grace under Pressure* (New York: Oxford University Press, 1984), 46–54, 55–57.

34 Augustus M. Burns III, "Graduate Education for Blacks in North Carolina, 1930–1951," *Journal of Southern History* 46 (May 1980): 195.

35 Murray, *History of the North Carolina Teachers Association*, 46; Newbold, Abstract, *Report of the Governor's Commission for the Study of the Problems in the Education of the Negroes in North Carolina*, 7–9, 23–24, 49–50, 53, 56, 80–83, 96; Smith, *Builders of Goodwill*, 52–53.

36  Murray, ed. and comp., *States' Laws on Race and Color*, 342; *Report of the Governor's Commission for the Study of the Problems in the Education of the Negroes in North Carolina*, 7–8, 43, 72, 76–77, 79–86, 88, 93.

37  Augustus Merrimon Burns III, "North Carolina and the Negro Dilemma, 1930–1950" (diss., University of North Carolina at Chapel Hill, 1968), 128–30; Pauli Murray, *The Autobiography of a Black Activist, Feminist, Lawyer, Priest, and Poet* (Knoxville: University of Tennessee Press, 1987), 64, 114–20; Murray, ed. and comp., *States' Laws on Race and Color*, 338; Murray, *History of the North Carolina Teachers Association*, 49–50.

38  Rose Butler Browne and James English, *Love My Children: An Autobiography* (New York: Meredith, 1969), 115–17; Ralph J. Bunche, *The Political Status of the Negro in the Age of FDR*, ed. Dewey W. Grantham (Chicago: University of Chicago Press, 1973), 315–16; Hubert A. Eaton, *Every Man Should Try* (Wilmington, N.C.: Bonaparte, 1984), 46; Murray, *History of the North Carolina Teachers Association*, 48–49; "Shall We Retreat, Compromise, or Attack? Annual Address of President O. R. Pope," *North Carolina Teachers Record* 4 (May 1933): 48, 55.

39  Du Bois, *The Souls of Black Folk*, xi; Raymond Gavins, "North Carolina," *Civil Rights in the United States*, ed. Waldo E. Martin Jr. and Patricia Sullivan (New York: Macmillan, 2000), 2:566–69; August Meier and Elliott Rudwick, *Along the Color Line: Explorations in the Black Experience* (Urbana: University of Illinois Press, 1976), 360; Charles W. Wadelington and Richard F. Knapp, *Charlotte Hawkins Brown and Palmer Memorial Institute: What One Young African American Woman Could Do* (Chapel Hill: University of North Carolina Press, 1999), 212–16; Ware, *William Hastie*, 54.

40  Gavins, "The NAACP in North Carolina during the Age of Segregation," 110, 117; Raymond Gavins, "Black Female Reformers in the Age of Segregation: The Emergence of Civil Rights in the Old North State," 21–24 (unpublished paper for the Women and the Civil Rights Movement Conference, 31 May–2 June 1989, University of Virginia, Charlottesville).

41  Eaton, *Every Man Should Try*, 45, 51; Gavins, "The NAACP in North Carolina during the Age of Segregation," 105, 110–11; Crow, Escott, and Hartley, *African Americans in North Carolina*, 165; Frank Emory et al., eds., *Paths toward Freedom: A Biographical History of Blacks and Indians in North Carolina by Blacks and Indians* (Raleigh: Center for Urban Affairs, North Carolina State University, 1976), 130, 132, 173, 178; Waldo E. Martin Jr., ed., *Brown v. Board of Education: A Brief History with Documents* (Boston: Bedford, 1998), 168–74; Obituary of Pearson, Durham *Morning Herald*, 27 June 1984, § A, pp. 1–2.

42  Davison M. Douglas, *Reading, Writing, and Race: The Desegregation of the Charlotte Schools* (Chapel Hill: University of North Carolina Press, 1995), 107–15; Program, Eleventh Annual Convention, North Carolina State Conference of NAACP Branches, Lumberton, 15–17 October 1954, and Press Release, 15 October 1954, box 23, folder 1953–65, Kelly M. Alexander Papers, Special Collections, J. Murrey Atkins Library, University of North Carolina, Charlotte; "Can North Carolina Lead the Way?," *New South* 11 (March 1955): 9.

43  Research Areas, Civil Rights Exhibit, North Carolina Museum of History; Doris McLean Bates, "Coming Soon: The Civil Rights Exhibition," *Cornerstone and Program Calendar*, October–December 2001, 6–7; Molly Hennessy-Fiske, "Signs of the Struggle," Raleigh *News and Observer*, 22 May 2002, § B, pp. 1, 6.

44  Project brochure (1993), "Behind the Veil: Documenting African American Life in the Jim Crow South," Rare Book, Manuscript, and Special Collections Library, Duke University, Durham; Charles S. Johnson, *Patterns of Negro Segregation* (New York: Harper and Brothers, 1943), 12–25; "Shall We Retreat, Compromise, or Attack?," 57.

KARA MILES TURNER

# "Liberating Lifescripts"

## Prince Edward County, Virginia, and the Roots

## of *Brown v. Board of Education*

Around 11:00 A.M. on Monday, 23 April 1951, the students at R. R. Moton, the segregated black high school in Prince Edward County, Virginia, filed into the auditorium for what most assumed to be a routine assembly. When the stage curtain opened, however, students saw a small group of their peers on stage, rather than the principal, who normally convened school meetings. The main speaker, a sixteen-year-old junior named Barbara Rose Johns, informed her classmates that the assembly's purpose was to initiate a protest against the severely overcrowded and unequal conditions at their school. Inspired by her forceful speech, the entire student body marched out of the school and into history. The student protest resulted in a lawsuit by the NAACP to end school segregation in the county (*Davis v. County School Board*), which became one of the cases subsumed under the now-famous heading *Brown v. Board of Education of Topeka, Kansas*. By shining a national spotlight on the county through its role in *Brown*, the strike also led indirectly to the tragic and unprecedented closing of all public schools in the county to prevent desegregation between 1959 and 1964.

The school strike was indisputably justified. Moton High was most assuredly separate from the all-white Farmville High, but the schools were not even remotely equal. Moton did not have a cafeteria. Instead, "you walked up these stairs, you got a brown bag and you walked down these stairs with your little brown bag and you went outside or sat somewhere and ate your lunch."[1] As the school did not have locker rooms, athletes "changed in a classroom some place."[2] Basketball games had to be held outside because there was no gymnasium. Other amenities enjoyed at Farmville High but absent at Moton included a nurse's office and fixed seats in the auditorium. In a county with a roughly equal number of black and white residents, white students received their education in a multistory, block-long building, while the 450-odd students at Moton were crammed into a small, one-story building built to hold 180 students. The school was so overcrowded that some recall classes being held in school buses.[3] Two to three classes at a time were held in the auditorium. In 1948 the school board addressed the black community's constant complaints about the overcrowding at Moton by building temporary buildings that blacks derided as "tarpaper shacks." The roofs leaked, the heat was provided by dangerous and uncomfortable pot-bellied stoves, and the buildings were often mistaken for chicken coops by passers-by. One strike organizer, Barbara Johns, characterized the shacks as "depressing, demeaning places."[4]

Despite the obvious justification for the student protest, it was still an incredible act for its time and place. This chapter will explore how teenagers in 1951, in the segregated, white supremacist Black Belt region of Virginia were able to conceptualize, plan, and successfully carry out this momentous action. Johns, the niece of the militant civil rights leader Vernon Johns, played a crucial role in mobilizing and inspiring her fellow students and adults. The Reverend L. Francis Griffin was a critical adult leader. He used his esteemed position in the community to shore up support among those who were initially unsure of or against the strike's continuance. It was Griffin who directed the student protesters to the Richmond NAACP lawyers Oliver Hill, Spottswood Robinson, and Martin A. Martin. He also organized strike-related meetings and opened his church (First Baptist in Farmville) for them.[5] Yet to place all credit for the success of any mass action on the shoulders of leaders is misguided. The people who stand behind the leaders are every bit as important. At every stage of the Moton protest, a link in the chain could easily have been broken. Unwilling to face possible suspension, expulsion, or parental punishment, the student leaders whom Barbara Johns approached with her idea could have refused to participate, or the students could have remained in their seats when asked to follow the strike committee out of the school. Fearful of reprisals, parents could have forced their children to return to school, or refused to sign the NAACP's legal petition for school desegregation. Community members could have denounced the strike as the actions of brash troublemakers. This chapter argues that the success of the school strike was largely due to the activism and cultural groundwork laid by forefathers and foremothers.

In a paper written in 1990, Grace Ward of the class of 1948 talked of the "lifescript" that her slave-born paternal grandparents, Robert Henry Scott and Alice Gilliam Carrington Scott, had laid out for their progeny. There were seven main legacies: to "keep a spiritual center"; to value and seek education ("Formal education was denied both my grandparents, but highly prized by them. It is expected that family members will attend school and receive an education."); to keep close ties with one's extended family; to work hard and spend wisely; to have "a sense of progressivism" like Ward's grandparents ("They were joiners and supported civic and political groups for the betterment of their family, their race, and their community."); to look for pleasure and meaning in life through work and caring for others, rather than through chemical or material means; to "live actively until you die." Ward considers this lifescript, passed down through the generations of her family, "the most liberating lifescript" that she could imagine.[6]

Exemplifying the type of "liberating lifescript" that Ward described, blacks in Prince Edward County had for generations been laying the foundation for the actions of the students in 1951. The very existence of a black high school for the students to walk out of was largely due to the activism of previous black generations. In the late 1920s and early 1930s, blacks had paid the teachers' salaries for high school grades, until the county finally took over the responsibility. Parents paid for private transportation to the school and lobbied the school board for nearly a decade to provide adequate public transportation. The black PTA was instrumental in getting funds from the Public Works Administration to build Moton High, the county's first free-standing high school for blacks, in 1939. When the students staged their walkout in 1951, the PTA was in the middle of a frustrating years-long battle with the school board to relieve severe overcrowding by building a new school.[7]

The lifescripts that members of the black community handed down to their children enabled the strike generation to take educational activism to another level. Behind the veil of segregation, black people had for generations constructed and passed on empowering messages to posterity. They imparted to their children the consciousness that they were worthy of, and had a right to, equality. Children learned that justice would come only through black insistence. County blacks also instilled self-confidence in their youth, a necessity for planning and executing the school strike. Finally, institutions and individuals gave the students the courage to execute their daring plan, by assuring them that if they did their community would be holding a net.

In Black Belt Virginia of the early 1950s, it could not be taken for granted that black children would believe themselves entitled to equality with whites. They were surrounded by negative signals about black abilities, intelligence, and attractiveness. While the county newspaper, the *Farmville Herald*, was packed with accounts of white accomplishments, black achievements were generally consigned to a brief Colored News Column. Pictures of white brides, athletes, and civic and political leaders regularly graced the paper's pages, whereas pictures of blacks, for any reason, were rare. One of the few photographs of blacks printed in the *Herald* was of an old black man, recognized for having been a "house boy" for a prominent Virginia family.[8] The few advertisements using black images were stereotypical. One for a Farmville restaurant featured a black mammy figure holding a sign reading "Home Cooking."[9] The paper also regularly featured offensive jokes like one about a "Master" who taught a "little pickaninny" to recite the line, "It is I. Be not afraid." The little boy went to the platform "ashy with stage fright," and nervously choked out, "Tain't nobody but me. Doan' git skeared."[10] Even in their all-black schools, children encountered negative depictions of their race. Willie Shepperson remembered that at Moton High all the movies shown featured all-white casts. The one film with an almost exclusively black cast was a film on personal hygiene. "And all the people who got gonorrhea and syphilis were black. The only white person in the film was the doctor. And all the white kids, in my head, when they would look at that film and then they would look at me, they would see the worst that society has to offer."[11]

Real-life experiences also bombarded black youth with messages of their inferiority. As James Samuel Williams recalled, "Didn't see anybody in my day, black folk, on the cash register and in other positions that were nonmenial, you didn't see that."[12] There were also the ubiquitous moments in every black child's life, usually by the age of seven or eight, when they first became aware of segregation. Downtown with his mother, John Stokes approached a water fountain, but "mama said 'no, you can't go there.' And I said why and she said 'because it's for white only' and then she took me to the other fountain. And I knew then that we were living in a world that had differences in individuals due to color."[13] Some children experienced even more jarring encounters with the reality of their inferior status. As a young boy, Willie Shepperson accidentally bumped into a white lady's leg while playing around in a store in Chester, Pennsylvania. Shepperson recalls that "her boyfriend, husband, whatever—a white man—he grabbed me and threw me down on the floor . . . and kicked me in the face and dislocated this jaw."[14]

Growing up in a society that tried mightily to convince them of their inferiority, black children could have been irreparably crippled psychologically. That the students of R. R. Moton High School were conscious of their innate equality and therefore desirous of actual material equality was due to the ways in which their families, schools, and churches counteracted the myriad pernicious influences of the larger society.[15] In vital, diverse ways, parents positively shaped their children's racial development. *Ebony* magazine, which Sammy Williams's parents began subscribing to shortly after it went into circulation in 1945, was "one of the things that began to give me strength in my people": "*Ebony* was the first publication that depicted black people positively. Everything else was Steppin Fetchit, Bojangles, stepping, smiling, big nose, big lips, that kind of stuff, ugly and all that. *Ebony*, it was like look at those black people, look at that Cadillac, 15 dresses, that started revolutionizing your thinking."[16]

Another strike leader, John Watson, remembered his mother standing up to whites. A washwoman, she once cursed the editor of the *Farmville Herald*, J. Barrye Wall, "up one side and down the other . . . Next week there he was back with his laundry, and he was totally respectful of her."[17] Barbara Johns admired how her famously militant uncle, Vernon Johns, "didn't care who you were if he thought that something was right" and "the way he would handle white men who would have an argument with him."[18] The attitudes of several other strong, race-conscious family members also contributed to Barbara's impatience with the inequalities at Moton. Her mother Violet engaged in a "verbal fight almost every day" with white customers to the Johns store who called her by her first name.[19] Barbara characterized her paternal grandmother, Sally Johns, as being "not the slightest bit subservient to whites."[20]

Willie Shepperson's mother turned her son's queries about the inequities at his school into challenges to him to excel. When he asked his mother why the answers had already been written in his school books, she said, "don't worry about . . . the writing in the book . . . see if they're right."[21] Irene Taylor inquired why only the white children had buses; her father soft-pedaled the reason, saying simply, "you are going to school . . . get an education and do better. Make it better . . . one day it's going to be different."[22] John Watson's family also minimized the importance of racism: "We didn't spend a lot of time talking about that." As a result, "I didn't grow up feeling like a second class citizen. To me it was like, alright, I'm in a segregated society and I'm going to be treated negatively by certain people, but that's their problem, that's not my problem."[23] Not dwelling on the inequities, or the rationale behind those inequities—white beliefs of black inferiority—could be just as effective in building black children's self-esteem as directly addressing racial injustice and teaching by example to fight it.

Another powerful way that children gained knowledge of their racial self-worth was through black history lessons. Joan Johns remembered her uncle Vernon Johns quizzing the children daily. "He would become upset if you really didn't know . . . he would say, 'you should know this, you know. This is part of your history.' "[24] Schools celebrated Negro History Week with assemblies on topics like "Interesting Negroes of Farmville and Prince Edward County," Negro history quizzes, scrapbook contests, and public lectures, including one by Vernon Johns in 1945.[25] Black history lessons were not limited to one week in February, however. Barbara Stiles, Moton class of 1958, recalls, "In every subject matter you studied, you were told about your people in that particular category."[26] It had been the same when her mother, Elizabeth Stiles, had attended school in the county. "We talked about ourselves all the time and it was impressed upon you at home and you got the same thing at school."[27] John Stokes proudly asserted, "we had black history year, because we couldn't walk in the school on one day unless a teacher within our curriculum would speak about from whence we'd come."[28]

The black history that he learned at Mary E. Branch Elementary School in Farmville profoundly affected Sammy Williams. His sixth-grade teacher, Arthur Jordan, "couldn't teach any subject in and of itself. . . . If you're teaching arithmetic he's going to hook up Benjamin Banneker . . . everyday his class was blackness." The students did not always believe Jordan's stories of blacks with exotic names like P. B. S. Pinchback, Sojourner Truth, Benjamin Banneker, and Henry O. Flipper. Williams explained that "we were used to Mary Jones or Betty Johnson, something like that, but names like that we thought he was lying . . . he would name these people and we used to fall out laughing at him in class." Nonetheless, Jordan's lessons "began to transform my whole thinking."[29] Before the school year was over, "he had won us over quite a bit . . . I began to feel elated, really elated, really exalted and really proud of myself for having been black."[30]

The next year, the school principal, L. L. Hall, built on the foundation laid by Jordan. Hall would cover Sammy's seventh-grade class once a week while the teacher performed registrar duties. During this time he would teach black history "to let them know that Negroes have made some contributions to this world, that it isn't all white."[31] Williams remembers Hall's visits vividly: "He would come and turn a desk backward and sit right up on the desk and open a book and teach Negro history and that is the first time that any of us had ever seen anything positive in print about black people . . . And I looked for that, every whatever day of the week that it was I looked for it more than I did anything in school . . . this was groundbreaking stuff to me."[32] Because of these lessons, "You didn't grow up [believing] that black people were all dumb and all ignorant and all totally inferior," Williams explained.[33] Barbara Stiles concurred about the effect of these lessons: "I can do it too. I have the ability to do it."[34]

Teachers were crucial purveyors of self-confidence. Elizabeth Stiles, a 1936 graduate, remembered learning "how to improve yourself, to prove to whites that you were just as good as anyone else . . . you were taught at home and at school that if you had good character, proper manners and whatnot, you were just as good as anybody else. That was emphasized much, very much."[35] John Watson credited his achievements to the Moton teachers: "[they] were on us all the time." He recalls doing poorly on a test once. The teacher said, " 'This is not acceptable. You can do better than that.' She made me take the test over. That's the kind of teachers we had."[36] Caring, demanding, and inspiring teachers instilled confidence in students like Bessie Daugherty, class of 1955: "you can do whatever you want to do . . . you can't let segregation or anything hold you back . . . their attitude was showing you how you can get over . . . that feeling of nothingness" caused by Jim Crow.[37]

Children also gained self-confidence through school activities. Performances in class plays, operettas, and debates allowed students to display their intellectual and artistic talents, hone their public speaking skills, and, given the assuredly warm reception accorded by proud relatives and neighbors, bolster their self-esteem.[38] Extracurricular clubs and athletic teams also provided outlets for students' talents and built self-esteem. Additionally, these organizations offered opportunities to hold leadership positions, interact with people in other communities, and discover conditions in other places. The year of the strike, one of its principal leaders, John Stokes, was vice-president of the student council, business manager of the school paper, president of the Virginia New Farmers of America, and an award-winning competitor in track and field and oratory.[39] In addition to the maturity and confidence gained from these activities, travels made in connection with them exposed John to black schools that were far superior to Moton. On these trips he was "teased constantly by other schools . . . even by other faculty members of other schools" about his "tar paper shacks" and "chicken coops."[40] Barbara Johns traveled quite a bit as a result of her positions in the drama guild, New Homemakers of America, the chorus, and the student council. Seeing handsome black schools like Huntington High in Newport News, Solomon Russell High in Lawrenceville, and Ralph Bunche High in King George made the conditions at Moton seem much worse than they would have seemed otherwise.[41]

Along with consciousness of their right to equality, and the confidence to believe that they could transcend the barriers placed before them, children learned another vital concept—the ability and responsibility of blacks to work at destroying racial inequity. This concept was instilled more fervently than ever during and after the Second World War, as black adults became even more determined to become full citizens. In churches throughout the county, by 1948 voting rights and NAACP membership were being emphasized.[42] Sammy Williams, a senior at the time of the strike, learned from his pastor, L. Francis Griffin of First Baptist Church, that "there was something wrong morally and ethically" about segregation, and that blacks must "organize and fight to get this wrong changed."[43] Dr. Kennell Jackson concurred about Griffin's impact, remembering that he, "from the pulpit, told us early on about the fights against colonial injustice in places like India, and Gandhi."[44] Some students would have heard the inestimable Reverend Dr. Vernon Johns speak, as he visited churches in his home county from time to time.[45] Barbara Johns's certainty that her strike plan was "divinely inspired" played a large role in her determined execution of it. "It had been given to me. All I had to do was do it."[46] From religious spaces, then, it was possible not just to gain a positive sense of self and hope for a better day, but to understand the importance of facilitating the arrival of that new day.

Moton High participated in a civic education program begun by the Virginia Teachers Association (VTA) in 1942 to produce "a body of vote conscious young people who may face the future determined to participate in the affairs of government." The principal, Joseph Pervall, reported to the VTA in 1942 that teachers "discussed the methods of qualifying [to vote] in Civics class pointing out the advantages of voting in a Democracy." A student paper written for the class was printed in the school newspaper.[47] In 1948 a voter registration project that a teacher of government, Pelton Abbott, undertook with his students resulted in the registration of more than a hundred citizens.[48] Moton made student elections "as realistic as possible," further inculcating in its students the importance of democratic participation.[49] Candidates were divided into Democrats and Republicans and elections were held on the same day as national elections. In 1948 John Stokes was elected vice-president on a Democratic ticket. He and two students elected council representatives that year, Hodges Brown and Carrie Stokes, would become members of the strike planning committee.[50]

The activism of parents shaped children's consciousness too. Grace Ward knew that her "father was a NAACP man." Often in her home, "people at the dining room table would be sitting there learning how to write their names so they could vote." She was also aware that her father, Otis Scott, and pastor, the Reverend Carter, "were always doing something for uplifting the black people . . . they were always down at the board of education and county board of supervisors, lobbying for bus service." Once she accompanied her father to the school board to request a new school.[51] Though Ward finished school several years before the school strike, her knowledge of her father's activism exemplifies the lessons that some of the striking students learned from their parents.

While few parents were leaders like Grace Ward's father, many children still developed a consciousness of the importance of black action through their parents' involvement in community organizations and support for community projects. Edwilda Allen Isaac, a strike participant, "was aware of how blacks could get things done," because she had "been to enough [fund-raising] chicken dinners and fish fries to know that when they want to get something that they get out there and get it done."[52] Even students whose parents were in no way involved in community action could be exposed to the idea at organizational meetings. PTA and NAACP meetings often included performances by student groups. Just two years before the strike, for instance, the Moton High School chorus furnished the music for a Negro History Week program, the speaker for which was Oliver Hill, later one of the lawyers in the quest for desegregated schools.[53] Attending such functions exposed children to the determined efforts of blacks to oppose racial inequities, helping them to understand that the status quo was not the way things should be, and that change came through advocacy.

Students also learned the need for black action through their own participation in school improvement efforts. School No. 14 received electricity through money raised by plays written and performed by Barbara Johns and her cousins (Vernon Johns's daughters).[54] Nellie Coles prepared sandwiches and pies to raise money for supplies like crayons and paper for her school.[55] School clubs regularly sponsored fund-raisers to pay for school equipment. A popularity contest at Branch Elementary in 1946 raised $306.71 toward playground equipment, for example.[56]

Students learned from some teachers to critique racism. Sammy Williams, a third grader at the time, recalled that the refusal of one sixth-grade teacher, Arthur Jordan, to kowtow to whites left a mark on his conscience. As students were filing out of an assembly one day:

Mr. Jordan said, "open those doors over there" . . . so students could come out you know. So one teacher on the other side said, "Mr. McIlwaine [the superintendent] said for one of those doors to be closed." [Jordan] said "I don't care if Mr. *Hacilwaine* said, I said open both of those doors." . . . Now here the white superintendent . . . coming down with a directive and all of us have always so-called obeyed him—when he and others come from downtown oh we're singing God Bless, Star Spangled, all that stuff. But here comes a man, a black preacher, a black teacher, see, overruling, overriding, what the superintendent had said . . . it was the first time I had seen or heard of a black person going against a white man and especially in authority . . . And then nobody came back—see if someone had came back and told him "you gonna lose your job"—his word was the last word and the doors were opened. I never will forget that.[57]

Teachers also exposed children to the inequalities of their schools vis-à-vis the white schools. Teachers talked to the students about the insufficient, unequal, and often hand-me-down equipment and materials they had to use, "in such a way that we knew they didn't like it."[58] Inez Davenport Jones, a music teacher, not only discussed the inequities with her students but encouraged them to do something about it, a suggestion that Barbara Johns took to heart. She recalled telling Jones that "there was no reason we should be treated so shabbily." Jones responded, "Sometimes in life, you have to do something about your conditions."[59] Johns mulled the advice for some time before coming up with the idea of a strike: "I spent many days in my favorite hangout in the woods on my favorite stump, contemplating it all . . . I would dream that some mighty man of great wealth through his kind generosity built us a new school building or that our parents got together and surprised us with this grand new building and we had a big celebration. And I even imagined that a great storm came through and blew down the main building and splattered the shacks to splinters . . . then there were times I just prayed, 'God, please grant us a new school.' "[60]

In her class, Johns recounts, "we always ended up talking about the school . . . we did a lot of that." One day she told her students of an article in a music educator's journal about a student strike in Massachusetts for higher teachers' salaries. "If they can do that, so could you," she told her class. Barbara Johns approached her teacher after class and asked if she really thought the students could have a strike. Jones replied, "Why not? You think about it." According to Jones, the next day Barbara asked if she would help her organize a protest. Jones recalled, "My positive response made her smile and I knew then that a strike would indeed be a reality because she was a focused, determined young lady." Communicating by notes left in a textbook on the teacher's desk, so as not to arouse suspicion, Jones advised Barbara on how to organize the protest.[61]

Jones had gotten her own activist spirit from the milieu of her childhood years. "See I came from a family—my father was the person who fought for free bus transportation and he'd go to the PTA meetings and complain . . . So that was sort of instilled in me that you don't just sit there and take things, so I think that's how it all started," she explained.[62] Her husband, M. Boyd Jones, the school's principal, was also instrumental in setting the stage for the strike. Though he did not know about the students' plan, he had been "training them for four years" to stand up for their rights and "to become dissatisfied with mediocrity, with hand-me-downs."[63] He elaborated on his philosophy of developing the students' critical thinking: "you're looking at what the blacks had from the public coffers and then compare that to what the whites got and these students could develop their own judgments when they looked at that. Their parents paid taxes as was required of them and the whites paid taxes. But the blacks were left with the short end of the stick and we helped our students develop that thought and it was fundamental . . . when it comes to the student strike."[64]

In these ways, and surely many others, the black community in Prince Edward County raised children capable of initiating and implementing a major act of civil disobedience years before doing so became an accepted mode of mass struggle. They showed their children by example the necessity of working for civil rights and educational goals, and taught them through many means that they were every bit as valuable, intelligent, and capable of success as white children were. As Carl Allen remembers of his childhood in the county, "teachers, parents . . . the community in general, [and leaders] in church" constantly told them "that no one is better than you . . . And that's what kept us going."[65]

The ways in which black institutions molded children's consciousness and self-concept contributed to a third factor that made the student walkout possible: courage. Though Virginia was a place of relatively little racial violence, it still took amazing courage to protest racial inequality in such a dramatic way.[66] Barbara Johns's sister, Joan, was "frightened" by the strike plan, "because I knew that what [Barbara] was doing would have severe consequences. And I sort of thought all of us would be hurt, harmed, physically, or something."[67] Edwilda Allen Isaac too "was very nervous. Even as young students we knew this was a serious thing."[68]

The bravery required of the leaders to plan and put such an act into motion, and of the listeners to agree to carry it through, was bolstered by the implicit and in some cases explicit approval of respected adults. Lorita Branch Graham felt, "we had so much support for whatever was going on— a play, concert, whatever, parents were there, community people were there . . . we just knew they supported education and wanted to improve . . . In the back of our minds, I would say, we had the assurance that the parents, the community people were always with us."[69]

One reason why Irene Taylor gave her full cooperation to the plan was that she knew she had her father's backing. "I knew he would take care of me."[70] Edwilda Allen consulted her father about the planned protest. He "in essence said you've got to do what you've got to do."[71] John Stokes also discussed the plan with his mother, who told him, "I'm praying for you and you all be careful . . . I'm sure everything will work itself out."[72]

Several teachers besides Mrs. Jones also knew about the strike in advance, including the algebra teacher Ernest Parker, the vocational teacher Thomas Mayfield, and the principal of Branch Elementary, L. L. Hall.[73] By not divulging the students' plan, the teachers implied their consent. The strike planners' courage to take on the white power structure was also bolstered by the knowledge that they were not alone in wanting better facilities. Astute, mature student leaders such as Barbara Johns and John Stokes were likely aware that blacks across the state were struggling for equitable conditions. The year before the student strike, the struggle for an equal school in neighboring Cumberland County had made the front page of the *Herald* twice.[74] The attorney Martin A. Martin and a group of blacks had recently tried to swim at the white-only beach in the town of Colonial Beach.[75] Awareness of the actions of blacks in other places, and the support they had received from the NAACP, certainly made it easier for blacks in Prince Edward County to act themselves.

If the actions and values of older generations were important to the initiation of the strike, they were even more critical to its ultimate success. Jones was known to be a no-nonsense principal who "ran the school just like an army," according to one former teacher, Connie Rawlins.[76] If Jones had entered the auditorium and commanded students to return to class immediately, he likely could have "snuff[ed] out the uprising in its larval stage."[77] Instead, he comprehended what was going on and acquiesced. Rawlins recalls, "I was so happy down in here, I could cry."[78] Though Jones pragmatically tried to convince the students that a strike was not the way to get their goals met, when Barbara Johns asked him to go back to his office, he complied.[79] He also let the leaders know secretly that he supported them, visiting John Stokes's home to say, "You all have to do what you have to do. I'll find a job . . . this is bigger than any of us."[80] Teachers showed their support by not hindering the students' action. As Willie Shepperson points out, "They could have walked into this classroom and shouted out, 'alright everyone of you go back to your classes' . . . If a teacher commanded you to do something, your immediate reaction was to go do it. So why didn't they walk in here and command all of us to get up and walk out [back to class]? And Barbara and those kids would have been probably standing over there by themselves . . . But they never did it . . . Because they approved of what [the students] were doing."[81]

Though Jones and the faculty were soon forced by the superintendent to send a letter to parents requesting that they send the children back to school, they subtly demonstrated their solidarity with the students' cause. When the buses rolled onto campus on Wednesday, 25 April, and the students proceeded to walk down to First Baptist, teachers did not induce them to come to school. The students' protest posters and signs remained up inside and outside the building also.[82]

Parents' support was likely the most critical component to the strike's continuation. Students' need for their parents' approval is clear from the discussion that P. H. Shepperson's children had with their father the night of the strike. The eldest son, Lester, said, "Daddy, we've done something today and I don't know whether you're going to approve or not." After listening to the explanation of what they had done, Shepperson responded,

"I think it's the right thing" and assured his son that he would not force the students to go back.[83] Sammy Williams's mother, a teacher in neighboring Cumberland, questioned the wisdom of the strike. Cumberland and Prince Edward shared a school superintendent, T. J. McIlwaine, and she surely feared for her job. Nonetheless, Williams recalls, "Mama never did say don't be a part of it, I'll lose my job . . . It wasn't a thing we debated or argued."[84] In this time of much stronger parental discipline, where children "were scared of our parents . . . We didn't talk back—you'd be getting off the floor," if parents had demanded that children return to school the next day, the strike undoubtedly would have crumbled.[85]

Instead, parents generally "were proud as punch" at their children's brave action, though concerned about possible retaliation.[86] Bessie Daugherty's mother, who had always said "because this is the way it is" when her children questioned segregation, reacted to her daughter's excited account of the strike with an exclamatory "good!" Though Daugherty considers her mother's contribution "nothing outstanding," the support of the masses of people like her mother, who attended meetings, contributed when collections were taken up to help the cause, and allowed their children to attend strike meetings was crucial to the effort.[87] Irene Taylor is aware that her father's willingness to ensure that she "got into town everyday and back home" from strike rallies represented "a lot of support."[88] John Stokes recently saluted the parents "who stood tall and signed the petitions and risked everything . . . Our petitions would not have gone before the Supreme Court if those parents had not had the fortitude . . . to support us."[89]

The children who initiated the school strike were able to do so because their churches, schools, community organizations, and families all contributed to a "positive lifescript which seeks to develop the individual talent for the greatest public good . . . fosters self-love and acceptance . . . allows me to think, encourages me to dream, comforts me in failure, and assumes my success."[90] In 1951 one young woman inspired her fellow classmates to apply the lessons imparted by their elders, touching off one of the most significant battles in civil rights history. The success of the student protest led to a desegregation lawsuit, *Davis v. County School Board*, that became one of the *Brown* cases and indirectly caused the infamous school closings of 1959–64. This dramatic development was rooted in generations of local black educational activism and "liberating lifescripts" created by the strike generation's forebears.

# Notes

1 Edwilda Isaac, interview by author, Prince Edward County, Va., 15 October 1997, tape recording in author's possession.

2 John Watson, interviewed in *Farmville: An American Story*, Richard Wormser and Bill Jersey, producers (Berkeley: Quest Productions and Videoline, forthcoming).

3 M. Boyd Jones, interview by author, Virginia Beach, Va., 3 June 1998, tape recording in author's possession; Hodges Brown, interviewed in *Farmville: An American Story*.

4 *Richmond Times-Dispatch*, 7 July 1988.

5 R. C. Smith, *They Closed Their Schools: Prince Edward County, Virginia, 1951–1964* (Chapel Hill: University of North Carolina Press, 1965), 51.

6 Grace Scott Ward, "The Scott/Carrington Family: Themes and Legacies," unpublished paper, January 1990, copy in author's possession.

7 For a detailed discussion of earlier educational black self-help efforts in the county, see Kara Miles Turner, " 'It Is Not at Present a Very Successful School': Prince Edward County and the Black Educational Struggle, 1865–1995" (diss., Duke University, 2001).

8 *Farmville Herald*, 3 November 1944.

9 *Farmville Herald*, 22 March 1946.

10 *Farmville Herald*, 3 November 1944.

11 Willie Shepperson, interviewed in *Farmville: An American Story*.

12 James Samuel Williams, interview by author, Prince Edward County, Va., 7 January 1998, tape recording in author's possession.

13 John Stokes, interviewed in *Farmville: An American Story*.

14 Willie Shepperson, interview by author, Prince Edward County, Va., 27 October 1999, tape recording in author's possession.

15 Because the central importance of the black church has been much studied, I will not dwell on its role in promoting black self-esteem here.

16 James Samuel Williams, interview by author, 7 January 1998.

17 John Watson, interviewed in *Farmville: An American Story*.

18 Smith, *They Closed Their Schools*, 28. Barbara emphatically denied, however, that Vernon Johns played any role in conceiving the strike. She wrote in a twenty-two-page memoir shortly before she died in 1991: "I didn't consult my Uncle Vernon because he wasn't around." *Farmville Herald*, 1 September 2000.

19 Smith, *They Closed Their Schools*, 29.

20 Smith, *They Closed Their Schools*, 28; Richard Kluger, *Simple Justice* (New York: Vintage, 1977), 454.

21 Willie Shepperson, interview by author, 27 October 1999.

22 Irene Taylor McVay, interviewed in *Farmville: An American Story*.

23 John Watson, interviewed in *Farmville: An American Story*.

24 Joan Johns Cobbs, interviewed in *Farmville: An American Story*.

25  *Farmville Herald*, 25 February 1944, 16 February 1945.

26  Barbara Stiles Dixon, interview by author, Prince Edward County, Va., 7 August 1997, tape recording in author's possession.

27  Elizabeth Stiles, interview by author, Prince Edward County, Va., 5 September 1997, tape recording in author's possession.

28  John Stokes, interviewed in *Farmville: An American Story*.

29  James Samuel Williams, interview by author, 7 January 1998.

30  James Samuel Williams, interviewed in *Farmville: An American Story*.

31  Hall had minored in history and taken four classes under two eminent historians of black history, Luther Porter Jackson and James Hugo Johnston Jr., while a student at Virginia State College for Negroes. L. L. Hall, interview by author, Prince Edward County, Va., 9 June 1998, tape recording in author's possession.

32  James Samuel Williams, interview by author, 7 January 1998.

33  *Id.*

34  Barbara Stiles Dixon, interview by author, 7 August 1997.

35  Elizabeth Stiles, interview by author, 5 September 1997.

36  John Watson, interviewed in *Farmville: An American Story*.

37  Bessie Daugherty, interview by author, Prince Edward County, Va., 5 November 1997, tape recording in author's possession.

38  A teacher at Caswell County Training School in North Carolina explained that these activities were "an institutional way of caring and implementing the school philosophy . . . to prepare the student to go back into the community and be an effective citizen . . . It develop[ed] self-esteem, who I am, why I'm here and where am I going." Vanessa Siddle Walker, *Their Highest Potential: An African American School Community in the Segregated South* (Chapel Hill: University of North Carolina Press, 1996), 108.

39  *Farmville Herald*, 15 September 1950.

40  John Stokes, interviewed in *Farmville: An American Story*.

41  Smith, *They Closed Their Schools*, 30–31.

42  M. Boyd Jones to Luther Porter Jackson, 21 June 1948, VTA Civic Education Prince Edward, box 30, folder 801; Letter to L. P. Jackson, 30 June 1948, IBPOEW Prince Edward, box 43, folder 1238; Emma Hicks to L. P. Jackson, 29 March 1949, Virginia Voters League (VVL), box 18, folder 523, Luther Porter Jackson Papers, Johnston Memorial Library, Virginia State University, Petersburg.

43  James Samuel Williams, interview by author, 7 January 1998.

44  Kennell Jackson, interviewed in *Farmville: An American Story*.

45  Smith, *They Closed Their Schools*, 10–11.

46  *Farmville Herald*, 1 September 2000.

47  Joseph B. Pervall to L. P. Jackson, 16 May 1942, VTA Civic Education Prince Edward, box 30, folder 801, Luther Porter Jackson Papers. The Virginia Teachers Association was an all-black teachers association.

48  Jones to Jackson, 21 June 1948, Luther Porter Jackson Papers.

49  Jones to Jackson, 23 November 1948, Luther Porter Jackson Papers.

50 *Farmville Herald*, 19 November 1948.

51 Grace Scott Ward, interview by author, Prince Edward County, Va., 5 December 1997, tape recording in author's possession.

52 Edwilda Allen Isaac, interview by author, 15 October 1997.

53 *Farmville Herald*, 4 February 1949.

54 Smith, *They Closed Their Schools*, 29–30.

55 Nellie Coles, interview by author, Prince Edward County, Va., 3 October 1997, tape recording in author's possession.

56 *Farmville Herald*, 29 March 1946.

57 James Samuel Williams, interview by author, 7 January 1998.

58 Nellie Coles, interview by author, 3 October 1997; Clara Ligon, interview by author, Prince Edward County, Va., 26 September 1997, tape recording in author's possession; Barbara Stiles Dixon, interview by author, 13 August 1997; Joan Johns Cobbs, interview by author, Richmond, Va., 2 October 1999, tape recording in author's possession.

59 *Richmond Times-Dispatch*, 7 July 1988.

60 *Farmville Herald*, 1 September 2000.

61 Jones did not publicly reveal her role in the strike until 1999. A few people close to Barbara Johns, who died in 1991, doubt that Jones's role was as large as she makes it out to have been: Barbara credited her only with challenging Barbara to "do something about" the inequalities about which Barbara was complaining. *Farmville Herald*, 1 September 2000. Others, including the strike planners John Watson and John Stokes, had always felt that someone was advising Barbara, but assumed it was her Uncle Vernon. *Farmville Herald*, 2 June 1999. I interviewed Jones the year before her public announcement and found her account credible. It is entirely plausible that Barbara never mentioned Jones's role to protect Jones from retaliation. According to Jones, she had sworn Barbara to secrecy, and it may well be that Barbara was just keeping her promise. Inez Davenport Jones, interview by author, Virginia Beach, Va., 3 June 1998, tape recording in author's possession; *Richmond Times-Dispatch*, 30 May 1999.

62 Inez Davenport Jones, interview by author, 3 June 1998.

63 *Washington Post*, 30 May 1999.

64 M. Boyd Jones, interview by author, 3 June 1998.

65 Carl Allen, transcript, *Farmville: An American Story*.

66 W. Fitzhugh Brundage, *Lynching in the New South: Georgia and Virginia, 1880–1930* (Urbana: University of Illinois Press, 1993), 140–43, for instance, points out that more lynchings occurred in Georgia in 1919 alone than in Virginia throughout the twentieth century.

67 Joan Johns Cobbs, interview by author, 2 October 1999.

68 *Richmond Times-Dispatch*, 24 August 1998.

69 Lorita Branch Graham, interview by author, 12 April 2000.

70 Irene Taylor McVay, interviewed in *Farmville: An American Story*.

71 Edwilda Allen Isaac, interview by author, 15 October 1997.

72 John Stokes, interviewed in *Farmville: An American Story*.

73  L. L. Hall, interview by author, 9 June 1998; John Stokes, interviewed in *Farmville: An American Story*; Ernest Parker, interview by author, Richmond, 21 November 1997, tape recording in author's possession; Thomas Mayfield, interview by author, Prince Edward County, Va., 8 August 1997, tape recording in author's possession.

74  *Farmville Herald*, 25 April 1950, 16 May 1950.

75  *Richmond Times-Dispatch*, 31 May 1951. Direct action against segregation in public accommodations was occurring across the North and in several southern locales throughout the 1940s and early 1950s. Additionally, as August Meier and Elliott Rudwick point out in *Along the Color Line: Explorations in the Black Experience* (Urbana: University of Illinois Press, 1976), numerous school strikes had occurred in the preceding thirty years, including one in the South (Lumberton, North Carolina in 1946). Though none of my interviewees recall knowing of any of these actions, it is possible that some may have been aware of them contemporarily.

76  Connie Rawlins, interview by author, Prince Edward County, Va., 26 April 1997, tape recording in author's possession.

77  Kluger, *Simple Justice*, 469.

78  M. Boyd Jones, interview by author, 3 June 1998.

79  Smith, *They Closed Their Schools*, 38.

80  John Stokes, interviewed in *Farmville: An American Story*. Jones also secretly told Barbara that he was "going to have to make certain statements to the school administration," but that no matter what he said publicly, "you remember this—I am on your side. I am your principal, and I protect you as best I can." *Richmond Times-Dispatch*, 30 May 1999.

81  Willie Shepperson, interviewed in *Farmville: An American Story*.

82  Kluger, *Simple Justice*, 475.

83  Smith, *They Closed Their Schools*, 53.

84  James Samuel Williams, interview by author, 7 January 1998.

85  Bessie Daugherty, interview by author, 5 November 1997.

86  Mary Redd, interview by author, Prince Edward County, Va., 5 December 1997, tape recording in author's possession.

87  Bessie Daugherty, interview by author, 5 November 1997.

88  Irene Taylor McVay, interviewed in *Farmville: An American Story*.

89  *Farmville Herald*, 9 September 1988.

90  Ward, "The Scott/Carrington Family."

PETER F. LAU

# From the Periphery to the Center

## Clarendon County, South Carolina, *Brown*, and

## the Struggle for Democracy and Equality in America

In its most elemental sense, the landmark Supreme Court victory of the NAACP in *Brown v. Board of Education* sounded the death knell for the doctrinal underpinnings of Jim Crow segregation in the public schools. It culminated the NAACP's decades-long campaign to destroy the Jim Crow system through a strategic legal assault on public school segregation. As a legal victory, *Brown* was a tremendous triumph and as a symbolic blow to a virulent form of white supremacy its value was magnified exponentially. But the NAACP's legal campaign was about far more than securing legal victories or landing symbolic blows to white supremacy, no matter how important each was. For those who signed their names to the lawsuits and organized to secure their rights through the court system, the NAACP's campaign that culminated in *Brown* was just one piece of a larger quest for empowerment and equality. Although *Brown* is often understood as an event that sparked the mass civil rights movement of the 1950s and 1960s, it is better understood in light of a broader social movement that had achieved heightened form by the early years of the Second World War. Considered as the opening salvo in the movement of the 1950s and 1960s, *Brown* is too easily reduced to a decision aimed at tearing down legal forms of racial segregation. But situated as a key event in a decades-old and multi-faceted struggle waged by African Americans for empowerment and equality, *Brown* takes on even greater significance as an event aimed at destroying Jim Crow and revolutionizing the meaning and practice of democracy in America.

In the standard narrative account of the road to *Brown*, the rural, Black Belt county of Clarendon, South Carolina, plays the leading role, and justly so. It was there that a heroic A.M.E. minister, the Reverend Joseph Armstrong (J. A.) DeLaine, rallied the county's African American community to challenge Jim Crow segregation and to become, ultimately, the sole representatives from the Deep South in the NAACP's Supreme Court triumph. In this account, the Clarendon County story begins in 1947 when the Reverend DeLaine attended a rally in the state capital, Columbia, and decided to take up the challenge issued by the president of the state NAACP to secure plaintiffs for a legal attack on inequities in black and white public school education. The problem with this version of the story is that it presents Clarendon County as somehow frozen in time, seemingly cut off from the main currents of history, until the NAACP's legal campaign to destroy Jim Crow in public school education increasingly came to dominate the civil rights movement in South Carolina and the nation. But the people of Clarendon County had neither been frozen nor cut off. For decades, African Americans in Clarendon County had battled to survive a declining cotton economy, resist the brutalities of legalized white supremacy, and secure a better life for themselves and their children. And their efforts had begun to find new avenues for expression and collective action through a resurgent black freedom movement in South Carolina and the nation by the first years of the 1940s.[1]

Buoyed by a climate of reform fostered by the New Deal and the war for democracy in Europe and Asia, by the early 1940s black South Carolinians had begun a renewed struggle to secure their constitutional rights and participate fully in the life of their communities and the nation. They joined the NAACP in growing numbers, created numerous citizenship clubs, and formed their own political party, the Progressive Democratic Party (PDP). In doing so, black South Carolinians articulated and fought for an expansive conception of equality and demanded the remaking of American democracy. The right to vote, protection from arbitrary and state-sanctioned violence, and access to public facilities, jobs, and quality education were frontline issues in a far larger fight for self-determination and meaningful participation in the decisions that governed their lives. Black residents of Clarendon County were central actors in this multifaceted battle and provided shape and substance to the movement in South Carolina and the nation from 1942 onward. To understand this is to begin to see Clarendon County as the embodiment of both the promises and the limitations of the changing landscape of postwar America. It is to begin to see *Brown* as one moment, although a revolutionary one, in a far more expansive and unfinished drama at the center, not the periphery, of America's struggle with the idea and practice of democracy.

Conditions in Clarendon County were brutally oppressive in 1947, the year when J. A. DeLaine joined forces with the leadership of the South Carolina NAACP State Conference to find a suitable case through which to challenge persistent inequities in the state's funding of public education for black children. African Americans accounted for better than 70 percent of Clarendon County's population in 1950, the highest percentage in South

Carolina. White people owned 85 percent of the land in the county, where two-thirds of the black households earned less than $1,000 a year and a mere 280 earned as much as $2,000. Born in Summerton in 1922, Minnie Ida Wright recalled the difficulties growing up in Clarendon. "It was rough then," she explained, "because they bring us up the rough way, hard way." Wright's father was a sharecropper who plowed "from sunrise to sundown," and her mother worked as a domestic servant for a white family. But while disfranchised and living life under the regime of white supremacy in the midst of the South Carolina Black Belt, the Wrights battled in myriad ways to earn a living, build and sustain networks of family and friends, and secure a better life for themselves before the NAACP made inroads into the county. Working in a chronically depressed cotton economy, the Wrights held education in high regard and struggled to send each of their eight children to Scott's Branch School in Summerton. They sold corn to purchase clothes and books for school and the children split time in the classroom and the cotton fields, returning home at the end of each school day to labor in the fields to support the family.[2]

Formal and state-funded schooling was however hard to come by for the vast majority of Clarendon County's black residents. During the 1949–50 school year the state spent $179 for each white child to attend one of twelve schools, while it spent only $43 for each black child to attend one of sixty-one single-teacher and two-teacher schools scattered across the county. Most of the schools were little more than makeshift structures, usually constructed in the shadow of a black church. "That's how most of the schools got their name, because it started in the church first," Joseph Richburg Sr. remembered. "Then the parents got together and built a little shack." Schools operated to the rhythms of cotton production. While the county paid for a portion of the school year, black parents pooled resources to extend it, a practice known as "running pay school." The Richburg family, along with the Pearsons and Levys, were among a handful of black families in Clarendon who owned substantial tracts of land. Although land ownership elevated the Richburgs' economic and social status relative to families such as the Wrights, the hardships of agricultural life and the desire for education cut across economic lines. Richburg attended school, but the demands of cotton production and the patriarchal prerogatives of his father drew him back to the fields. "I finished the eighth grade," he noted, "and Daddy tell me I'll have to come home and feed the rest of the children . . . I had to plow."[3] Voting too remained out of the question for the county's black residents. African Americans remained thoroughly disfranchised in Clarendon County at the end of the 1940s, the decade that witnessed the legal end of the white primary.[4]

Like most of the county's black residents, J. A. DeLaine grew up working the land and was schooled in the value of education. Unlike most, his life path took him from the land to the ministry, and on to a career of civil rights activism. Born in July 1898 to Henry Charles and Tisbia Gamble Delaine, J. A. was reared on a large tract of family-owned land outside the town of Manning, Clarendon's county seat, northeast of Summerton. A landholder, minister, and funeral director, Henry Charles DeLaine was a model of thrift and racial uplift and pushed his children hard in all endeavors. In 1912, after refusing to accept punishment for fighting two white boys who had been harassing his younger sister, J. A. left his father's home for four years and labored in sweatshop conditions in Atlanta and Baltimore. Upon his return, he enrolled in high school in Columbia at Allen University, which was affiliated with the A.M.E. church. There he graduated from high school, earned a B.A., entered the ministry, and commenced work toward the eventual completion of a divinity degree by 1931. That year he married Mattie Belton of Columbia and the two began teaching careers in Orangeburg County. Like his father, J. A. soon turned to a career in the ministry. Between 1934 and 1939 he served as the pastor of the Spring Hill A.M.E. Church near Summerton. At the same time, he was the principal and one of three teachers at the Bob Johnson School in the nearby village of Davis Station. In 1940 he was assigned to the A.M.E. Church's Pine Grove Circuit, with responsibilities for ministering to the Pine Grove and Society Hill A.M.E. Churches in the lower end of Clarendon County. He also moved his family into a newly constructed home in Summerton, where he continued to work as a teacher at the Liberty Hill School, and where his spouse began work as an elementary school teacher at the Scott's Branch School. As Richard Kluger has noted, along with Joseph Richburg's uncle, the Reverend E. E. Richburg of Liberty Hill A.M.E., DeLaine fast became "one of the two best-known and most respected black ministers in the county."[5]

As DeLaine established his ministerial reputation in the late 1930s and early 1940s, the NAACP had just begun to reemerge from the wreckage of the Depression years as a force for democratic change in South Carolina and the nation. Formally organized in 1910 as a predominantly white and board-dominated organization dedicated to winning full citizenship rights for African Americans through legal and legislative action, the association saw its reins seized by African Americans by the end of the First World War. Black South Carolinians helped lead this shift in power when residents of Charleston and Columbia chartered branches in early 1917. In short order, the somewhat stodgy legal-rights organization inspired the imaginations of black South Carolinians statewide, from the relatively élite venues of Charleston and Columbia, to the piedmont town of Anderson, to the low country town of Beaufort and the nearby coastal sea islands, to the rural Black Belt county of Calhoun. Through the NAACP, African Americans organized collectively, demanded access to better schools, battled for the right to vote, and envisioned mounting a statewide challenge to their continued exclusion from the state's political decision-making process. But the brutal 1920s, years characterized by a rising level of violent white resistance to black advancement, economic turmoil, large-scale out-migration, and natural disasters, turned back the mounting tide of NAACP activism. By the onset of the Depression the organization was in effect moribund, and it would remain so until the fall of 1939.[6]

It was in that year that black South Carolinians began piecing together a statewide NAACP that would provide the key institutional basis for reorganizing old NAACP branches and creating new branches across the state in the 1940s. In 1941 the South Carolina State Conference of NAACP Branches circulated a pamphlet, entitled "Exhortation for Solid Voluntary Action," in which it set forth their raison d'être. "The day of rugged individualism is said to have passed," it declared. "The only action that has a chance in the world today is mass action." The purpose of the organization, its leaders explained, was to inspire "social solidarity—A Great American Negro Need" and to encourage black men and women to emancipate themselves from "the present evil of social, economic, and political slavery." In its most revolutionary and remarkable passage, the pamphlet declared: "What the Negro needs is INTEGRATION, instead of SEGREGATION . . . They are to each other as plus is to minus. The one affirms, the other denies. All the blessings of life, liberty and the pursuit of happiness are possible in integration, while in segregation lurk all forces destructive of these values." Demonstrating the need for the organization and support for it, NAACP membership topped the ten thousand mark in 1945 and the number of branches in the state increased from fifteen to forty-nine between 1943 and 1946.[7]

The growth of participation in the NAACP was due in large measure to the organization's efforts on the educational and voting rights fronts during the early 1940s. In 1941 and 1942 Osceola E. McKaine, a native of Sumter, South Carolina, and veteran of the First World War, led the early fight for equal salaries for black teachers in South Carolina's public school system. In the spring of 1943 the State Conference assumed responsibility for the fight, which proved largely successful in a series of court decisions between 1944 and 1946. At the same time, the association made substantial headway in the battle for the right to vote. At its annual state gathering in 1942, State Conference members pledged to focus their efforts on breaking into the white primary and formed the Negro Citizens' Committee of South Carolina (NCC) to raise money and rally support for the campaign. Created in part to avoid the charge that the NAACP was encouraging lawsuits, the NCC served as the organization's voting rights arm, a front for the NAACP's political activities. As the organization made plain from its inception, black South Carolinians wanted the right to vote and access to the white primary for reasons greater than mere inclusion in the existing American social and political system. As a promotional pamphlet of the NCC put it, "THE NEGRO CITIZENS' COMMITTEE OF SOUTH CAROLINA believes that DEMOCRACY— equal rights and privileges for all—and not the so-called 'American Way of Life' which so often compromises, discriminates, or even denies where Negroes are concerned, should come into full play for all Americans." What they wanted, in other words, was the transformation of the "American way of life," and their full inclusion was to be but a first step in that process.[8]

By early 1942 DeLaine had become interested in the NAACP through McKaine's grassroots organizing campaign for equalizing teachers' salaries, and he paid membership dues to the Sumter branch of the organization that summer. Inspired by the efforts of the Negro Citizens' Committee to secure the right to vote, he soon commenced the arduous and dangerous task of piecing together a full-fledged branch in Clarendon County, the heart of the state's Black Belt. Taking a cue from the Negro Citizens' Committee, DeLaine dubbed the organization-in-the-making the Citizens' Committee. "We use the name Citizens Committee," he explained, "but it is really the NAACP."

In a letter to the national office in January 1943 DeLaine provided insight into the difficulties he confronted. "I want you to mail all mail to me in plain envelopes," he wrote. "You see I am a preacher in this county and a public school teacher too. My living largely depend[s] upon the ones that fear and hate the N.A.A.C.P. My activities have already been under question." Indeed, it would take DeLaine five additional years to secure a formal NAACP charter, which according to NAACP bylaws required fifty members. The repressive rural context in which DeLaine organized, as elsewhere in the state, militated against turning the NAACP into a mass organization in Clarendon County. So too did DeLaine's health. By early 1944 DeLaine had begun suffering from pleurisy, the painful inflammation of the membrane surrounding his lungs, and his organizational work ground to a near standstill. "My work with the Church, School, and [the] effort to work the folks up to want full citizenship," he noted, "was more that I could take under the war strain and privation."[9]

Such difficulties did not mean that the NAACP ceased to exist or portend future mass action in Clarendon. During the mid-1940s the NAACP continued to operate as a loosely jointed, underground organization, supported and maintained by a small band of dedicated individuals working through the association and its various organizational fronts. For the Richburgs, joining the NAACP was a family affair. Joseph joined on his own in the 1930s and recalls that his father and two uncles, L.B. Rivers and the Reverend Richburg, were all members of the organization. A. Maceo Anderson, the principal of the Scott's Branch School, helped lead efforts on the voting rights front through the Citizens' Committee, while a future vice president of the Clarendon County NAACP, Sarah Daniels, a home demonstration agent for the National Youth Administration (NYA) and president of the Clarendon County Teachers' Association, organized two women's auxiliaries of the Progressive Democratic Party and led local voter registration efforts. "I am hoping to help every teacher of Clarendon County," she wrote in late 1946, "see the work of this organization and at least register."[10]

Organized in the spring and summer months of 1944, the Progressive Democratic Party (PDP), like the NCC, was a vehicle through which NAACP activists could advance their broader political agenda without compromising the NAACP's nonpartisan status or opening the organization to the charge that it was soliciting lawsuits. "The fact is," its brash, thirty-two-year-old founder John H. McCray later put it, "those in [the] NAACP, the Citizens Committee, and in the Progressive Democrats were one and the same people." In the wake of *Smith v. Allwright* (1944), the Supreme Court decision that marked the legal end of the all-white Democratic Party primary, McCray organized the PDP with the expressed purpose of smashing the white primary in practice and securing the right of self-representation for black South Carolinians. In August 1944 the PDP challenged the seating of the all-white South Carolina delegation at the Democratic National Convention in Chicago. Although PDP delegates were unable to convince the DNC that they represented South Carolina's only lawfully constituted delegation, their convention challenge represented a remarkable demonstration of the desire of black southerners to achieve the right to vote. It also signaled that black South Carolinians had emerged at the forefront of the African American fight for self-representation and empowerment by the closing years of the Second World War. And black residents of Clarendon County, following the lead of men and women such as DeLaine and Sarah Daniels, were very much a part of that fight.[11]

The lives of black residents of Clarendon County were intimately connected to the institutions and social forces giving shape to the resurgent black struggle for full citizenship rights and empowerment of the 1940s. As early as 1943, DeLaine had begun discussions with Levi and Hammett Pearson about the condition of black schools in the county, especially the need for adequate transportation, the subject of a campaign that would converge with the NAACP's broader legal campaign in 1947. Levi Pearson owned some 175 acres of land near the town of Jordon. At the time, a number of his children attended the Mount Zion school, a cement-block structure with four classrooms approximately eight miles from their home. Pearson and other family members regularly drove local children to school in the back of an old pickup truck, a routine made all the more galling because the county paid for bus transportation for white children. First in 1945 and then again in 1946, the Pearson brothers and DeLaine organized local parents to purchase an old school bus from the county and transport children to the Scott's Branch School, where three of Levi Pearson's children attended by that time. Ferdinand Pearson, one of Levi's eldest sons, remembers returning home in full uniform from overseas service in the U.S. Army in 1946 to see DeLaine and his father discussing the issue of bus transportation.[12]

The war also gave shape to the emerging movement in Clarendon County, as it had elsewhere. At twenty-three, Ferdinand Pearson gained from his experience in the military a sharpened sense that life had to change in the county. "It made me feel like something was wrong with our society," he explained. "Came back here and found that America was still segregated . . . was just the same as it was before I went away." "I am over there putting my life on the line to help save a country," he continued, "that is goin' to segregate me back home . . . I didn't want my sons and daughters to see those kind of conditions." Upon his return to South Carolina he became part of a cohort of black veterans, including his cousin Jessie, dedicated to improving life in Clarendon County. With the aid of DeLaine, the veterans drew up a petition to secure state funding for agricultural training classes as part of the GI Bill and began adult education classes at the Scott's Branch School. As Pearson recalled it, the GI Bill classes doubled as a vehicle for recruiting new members to the NAACP.[13]

By the spring of 1947, the day-to-day and largely behind-the-scenes activism in Clarendon County converged with the search by the state and national offices for a suitable case through which to challenge inequities in public education and perhaps address the constitutionality of segregation itself. While attending the Benedict-Allen Summer School, where he was enrolled in George Singleton's course on "Race and Culture," DeLaine listened to the president of the NAACP State Conference, the Reverend James M. Hinton, address a Thursday evening gathering of summer school enrollees. Hinton decried the state of black schools in South Carolina, argued that black South Carolinians would never advance without quality education, and, as DeLaine remembered it, challenged his audience to take the lead in the fight against discrimination in the state's public schools. Virginians had already launched such a campaign, he declared. But "No teacher or preacher in South Carolina has the courage," he exclaimed, "to get a plaintiff to test the School Bus Transportation practices of discrimination against Negro children."[14] Prodded by Professor Singleton, DeLaine returned to Clarendon and that Sunday held a meeting with his son, Joseph A. DeLaine Jr., and Levi and Hammett Pearson to discuss a legal challenge to the problem of bus transportation. Eight days later, DeLaine and Levi Pearson traveled to Columbia and met with the State Conference's attorney, Harold Boulware, the Reverend Hinton, and A. J. Butler of the Sumter NAACP. Together they resolved to put the resources and energies of the state NAACP behind a campaign to end discrimination in public school bus transportation in Clarendon County. Afterward, DeLaine and Pearson returned home to file a petition in Pearson's name with the County Superintendent of Education, the County School Board, and the State Board of Education, requesting that the county provide school bus transportation for DeLaine's children and the other black children residing in School District 26. In a note that he later jotted at the bottom of a letter to Boulware, DeLaine declared, "This is the *legal* beginning of the movement set in motion by me for the benefit of Negro children."[15]

Although the South Carolina NAACP and the national office were rapidly moving toward disclaiming support for legal cases aimed at equalization rather than outright repeal of "separate but equal," for the time being at least they remained willing to move against Jim Crow incrementally. The South Carolina State Conference was already on record as opposed to legal segregation. But Pearson's petition proved insufficient to push either effort forward. State officials simply ignored Pearson's petition for months. In Clarendon County, where the work of the NAACP remained clandestine, support for the bus transportation suit waned among African Americans. "Many questions are being asked me about when the Bus Transportation case will start," DeLaine wrote to Reverend Hinton. "I had a pretty good sentiment worked up for financial help but everything is growing cold and wandering now." Still feeling the effects of illness and mindful that broad public knowledge of his NAACP activities would likely end his teaching career, DeLaine remained largely in the background. In an act that indicated his growing disillusionment, DeLaine sent the balance of the branch's treasury, $83.20, to the State NAACP in early February 1948. "It looks like our officers," he wrote, "are not going to do anything further. In fact I think it will be well to get all of the money out of the hands of the officers." DeLaine felt certain that the bus transportation case could revive local activism, but he also believed that those with the means, those who did not depend on white people for their livelihood, had to take the lead in the fight. "When the Bus Transportation case breaks to the public," he explained, "it will give courage to many who are waiting on leadership." But, he added, "Nothing short of a new organization is needed here." "Who will take the leadership is a problem to me. There are a number of the folks about in the county who want to do something but don't have the ability to take the leadership."[16]

As a large landowner, Pearson had agreed to lead the way; Harold Boulware and Thurgood Marshall filed suit on his behalf in the U.S. District Court in Florence that March. In the meantime, the Reverend Hinton took matters into his own hands. He appointed Pearson "temporary president" of the Clarendon NAACP branch and asked him to notify Sarah Daniels that she was to serve as vice president, with DeLaine as secretary and the Reverend J. W. Seals of St. Mark A.M.E. as treasurer. But even before the case, *Pearson v. County Board of Education*, reached the courtroom for its scheduled opening session on 9 June, it was dismissed. Clarendon County officials had discovered that Pearson paid property taxes in School District 5, not District 26. Pearson's property straddled the two districts, but the new evidence left him without legal standing to sue in the district where the NAACP charged that his children were denied state-funded bus transportation. Although the case went nowhere, its immediate effect was to expose the undercover activities of the faltering NAACP branch in Clarendon and open local activists to reprisal. "Somebody had to suffer for the eyes of the people being opened," DeLaine later wrote, "so the School Board discharged Mr. A. M. Anderson the principal of Scott's Branch School during the last 18 years." Sarah Daniels, similarly, lost her post as a home demonstration agent. That spring, Pearson's credit was revoked at white-owned stores and banks. In the fall, white cotton gin owners refused to gin his cotton and white farmers refused to lend him equipment to harvest his crops; Pearson was forced to watch his wheat, oats, and beans rot in the field. Even some of the local black "folks were afraid to be seen talking with him on the street or in public places," his son recalled.[17]

At the beginning of the 1948–49 school year, further work on the civil rights front in Clarendon was seriously in doubt. Officials in Summerton took new steps to enforce school district boundaries, demanding that parents submit applications so that their children would attend school in the right district. In late September, DeLaine wrote to Hinton and Boulware, informing them that something must be done quickly to jump-start the legal campaign. "We are getting knocks on every side," he explained. "I am trying to hold every thing together as best I can." With activism on the school issue in Clarendon seemingly at a standstill, Thurgood Marshall and his legal staff were prepared to cease their work and move on to other cases by March 1949. In the words of Eugene Montgomery, the State Conference's first full-time and paid staff member, "Clarendon County almost never happened." "They were dragging their feet in New York," he recalled, until Hinton instructed him to get in touch with the people in the national office and set them straight. The state NAACP wanted to know what the national office was going to do. "[I]f you're not going to go for it," they declared, "let us know. We'll drop the whole thing." Soon enough, however, Marshall and his staff held a meeting in Columbia with state NAACP officials and representatives from Clarendon County. At that meeting, Marshall clearly established the terms and conditions of his legal staff's continued involvement. He informed the Clarendon contingent that the NAACP would no longer support a fight to win equal bus transportation alone and that if the case in Clarendon were to proceed it would need to do so as an effort to win "Equal Educational Opportunities and Facilities for Negro Children." As DeLaine remembered it, Marshall "threatened to pull up from Clarendon County" unless he could secure a sufficient number of plaintiffs willing to lend their names to the lawsuit. The terms set, DeLaine and his compatriots took up the gauntlet. They returned to Clarendon and organized a series of community meetings in black churches to rally support for the equalization suit and to encourage parents to sign their names to a petition requesting that state officials equalize school facilities.[18]

Despite rousing meetings in area churches, securing signatures proved slow going during the months of March and April. However, the determination of students in the senior class at the Scott's Branch School provided black parents with a tangible example of the issues at stake in the suit and helped propel the equalization campaign forward during the early weeks of June. The 1948–49 school year was the first when the Scott's Branch School offered a twelfth grade to its students. For members of the school's first senior class, like Robert Georgia Jr. and Abraham Smith, the additional year of school came as a welcome surprise. Georgia and Smith were accustomed to hard work and sacrifice just to attend school regularly. Milking cows, collecting wood, and working in the cotton fields before and after school were a normal part of their daily routine. But their senior-year experience stretched the limits of their expectations for hard work and fairness. Although students regularly contributed out-of-pocket funds for school supplies and books, the school board's replacement principal for the beloved A. Maceo Anderson, I. S. Benson, raised fees and, students complained, failed to supply them with the promised equipment. Students and parents held rallies to raise funds for the school, but the money vanished. Benson rarely showed himself in the classroom. As the end of the school year approached, he levied a $2.50 charge for state certificates for each student and threatened to withhold the transcripts of seniors who complained about the prohibitive fee. Benson, DeLaine explained, had "misjudged the feelings, intelligence and courage of students and parents." With DeLaine's assistance, students organized and drew up a petition detailing their charges against Benson that they submitted to the superintendents and trustees of School District 22 and Clarendon County. When officials ignored the petition, DeLaine noted, "a flame of anger" ignited the passions of students, teachers, and parents and led to a dramatic mass meeting on 8 June.[19]

DeLaine later wrote that the meeting, held in the St. Mark A.M.E. Church, proved to be "the Psychological Meeting which conditioned the minds of the mass of parents in District 22." The 1948–49 school year and the student grievances vividly encapsulated the issues underlying their lawsuit in the making. Not only did Benson's tenure as principal highlight the blatant and persistent inequities in funding and facilities between white and black schools, but it also laid bare the lack of black representation and power in school affairs. The school itself had been created as an extension of the St. Mark A.M.E. Church. But because of the state's inadequate funding of the school, the community's investment in Scott's Branch had been substantial over the years and the school came to serve as a focal point of civic life among the county's black residents. Parents wanted an acknowledged role in governing the school, including the selection of a principal. They also wanted permission to hold civic meetings on school grounds. They sought, in short, the power to help craft a better future for their children. By meeting's end, those in attendance agreed that support for the NAACP's legal campaign, even if it meant a battle all the way to the U.S. Supreme Court, would be crucial for the success of their ongoing battles at the local level.[20]

In the short term, the efforts of the Committee on Action to address the concerns of African Americans in Clarendon County sparked a second round of white reprisals aimed at preserving white supremacy. On 9 June DeLaine presented the parents' grievances to Clarendon school officials and two days later he was relieved of his teaching and administrative duties in the county. In July parents petitioned the superintendent and trustees of District 22 in an effort to stem the tide of school firings in the wake of their June actions. Although school officials refused to terminate Benson's employment, parents managed to force Benson's resignation by the following October. In the meantime, efforts to secure sufficient signatures for the NAACP's school equalization petition proceeded apace. In a last-ditch effort to halt mounting black activism, the superintendent of schools, H. B. Betchman, offered DeLaine the principal's post at the Scott's Branch School. As DeLaine remembered it, Betchman did not hide his intentions. "You must stop this fight," he told DeLaine. "These colored people are doing what you tell them to do and you must give them a better leadership than this." After

DeLaine refused the offer, his wife, Mattie, "was drafted" by the county to serve as the school's principal, a post which over the course of the following school year passed through the hands of four more temporary appointees as school officials desperately sought a way to stop the rebellion emanating from the school.[21] In December DeLaine was informed that the Ku Klux Klan was "going to take him to ride if he didn't shut his mouth." By then DeLaine was posting an armed guard outside his home and warning "innocent persons" not to approach his residence at night for fear that he might inadvertently shoot them. Next DeLaine became the target of a $20,000 slander suit stemming from the ouster of I. S. Benson from his post as principal of Scott's Branch and ultimately was ordered to pay him $2,700 in damages. That spring, the A.M.E. synod transferred DeLaine to the St. James A.M.E. Church in Lake City in Florence County, just as the movement in Clarendon verged on total collapse. In October his Summerton home went up in flames as the local fire department stood by and watched.[22]

DeLaine was not the only person targeted for reprisal. On 11 November 1949, after six earlier petitions citing specific issues related to Benson's tenure at the Scott's Branch School brought no relief, black parents submitted a petition to school officials asking for "equal opportunities for Negro children." The petition fulfilled DeLaine's promise to Marshall and launched, once again, the legal campaign to secure equal educational opportunities for black children. It also launched another round of mass reprisals. Harry Briggs, the son of sharecroppers and a veteran of the Second World War, signed the petition and was fired from his job as an attendant at a local filling station. His wife, Eliza Briggs, lost her job as a maid at the Summerton Motel. So too did Annie Gibson. Massie Solomon lost her job as a maid and her family was thrown off its land. Others who lost their jobs included William "Bo" Stukes, from a local automobile repair shop; James Brown, after ten years working for the local Esso; and William "Mich" Ragin and the Reverend Seals, from jobs teaching GI classes at the Scott's Branch School. At the end of the school term, those teachers who signed their names to the petition were not offered contract renewals. When Harry Briggs sought to make ends meet by working twenty acres of rented farmland, he was denied access to credit and could not find a gin owner willing to gin his cotton. Virtually across the board, those who dared to sign the petition faced crushing economic sanctions. Many lost access to credit and to farm and business supplies. Some lost their jobs, while others had bank loans called in or were thrown off their land. Harry Briggs attempted to remain in Summerton, but by 1953 he was forced to migrate to Florida in search of work to support his family. Indeed, to openly challenge white supremacy in Clarendon County quickly became associated with leaving town. "A lot of our colored people had to leave Summerton," Minnie Ida Wright recalled, "and go off from here to get jobs to make a living. Couldn't stay here." "A lot of people had to move off the white man's place," Milison Green remembered, "a good many." "If you was an NAACP man," Joseph Richburg explained, "if you was on that man's place sharecropping, or if you were renting, you had to move ... It wasn't funny."[23]

The winter of repression only marked the beginning of a struggle that would successfully challenge both the social and the symbolic power of white supremacy in South Carolina and the United States. By May 1950 the equalization movement in Clarendon had come to a halt and the NAACP branch hardly existed at all. "We really dont have a real branch," DeLaine wrote to the national office in May, and now "[m]ost of the Negroes are afraid to be connected in any way whatsoever." But as local efforts ended and recourse to local institutions was exhausted, NAACP lawyers again carried the battle into the federal court system. On behalf of twenty adult petitioners, including Harry Briggs, and the forty-six children who managed to withstand (at least for the time being) the unrelenting intimidation and economic sanctions of the winter months, NAACP attorneys filed *Briggs v. Elliott* in U.S. District Court. In a matter of months, the case, which began as a local challenge to the inequitable practice of Jim Crow, would be transformed into a direct assault on the legal foundation of racial segregation. It ultimately became one of five cases included in the U.S. Supreme Court's *Brown* decision in May 1954, striking down the fifty-eight-year-old doctrine of "separate but equal."[24]

For black South Carolinians, however, the legal end of Jim Crow schools did not usher in a period of enlightened racial reform. Rather, the effective impact of *Brown* and the Supreme Court's "Ruling on Relief" of May 1955, which famously instructed lower courts to implement its decision with "all deliberate speed," was to inaugurate a vicious and sustained campaign to resist school integration, crush the NAACP, and curtail the black freedom movement in South Carolina. White businessmen and other leading public officials began forming White Citizens' Councils across the state in the summer of 1955 to exert economic and political pressure against black insurgency. Some fifty-five Citizens' Councils were in operation by July 1956. At the same time, the South Carolina legislature took steps to vigorously oppose the full implementation of *Brown* and vanquish proponents of integration. At the behest of the Gressette Committee, an advisory committee named for its chairman, State Senator L. Marion Gressette, the legislature repealed the state's compulsory school attendance law. It empowered local school officials to sell or lease school property and prohibited automatic renewal of teachers' contracts. In 1956 the legislature passed an "interposition resolution" declaring that the state of South Carolina maintained the right to "interpose" its authority "between its people and the federal government."

The legislature then took aim at the NAACP, borrowing heavily from the tactics used to persecute alleged Communist Party members and sympathizers earlier in the decade. It charged the organization with advocating an agenda "contrary to the principles upon which the economic and social life of our state rests." Lawmakers unanimously adopted a resolution requesting that the U.S. attorney general list the NAACP "as a subversive organization so that it may be kept under the proper surveillance and that all citizens of the United States may have ample warning of the danger to our way of life which lurks in such an organization." Next, they barred NAACP members from employment in local, county, and state government. As a condition of employment, teachers were required to divulge their personal and family ties to the association and declare their personal views on school integration.[25]

For black residents of Clarendon County the post-*Brown* racist counterinsurgency struck with particularly horrifying force. The NAACP's campaign for equality in public education and an end to Jim Crow reached a peak just as an increasing number of small-scale farmers, sharecroppers, and laborers found it virtually impossible to make a living in South Carolina and across the region. In the twenty years after the *Brown* decision, the number of black farmers in the county plummeted, while the share of the total population that was black declined by 10 percentage points. As the need for black labor fell, little was left to hold back a merciless terror campaign. On 5 October 1955 DeLaine's Lake City church was torched. Three days later DeLaine received a death threat warning him to leave town voluntarily or by force of dynamite. Then, on the night of 10 October, DeLaine and his wife were awakened by gunshots fired into their home. After whisking his wife out the back door with the help of a neighbor, Webb Eaddy, DeLaine grabbed his rifle and stood guard outside under cover of darkness. Once again, a passing car fired shots toward his home. This time, DeLaine returned fire. "Then," he recalled, "I made up my mind to run for my life." DeLaine jumped in his car and headed for Florence, eluding would-be-assailants along the way. The next day he was reunited with his wife, and friends spirited the couple across the state border to Charlotte, North Carolina. Ultimately, DeLaine would make his way to New York, where he learned that officials in Florence had charged him with assault and battery with a deadly weapon. Now a fugitive from South Carolina justice, DeLaine remained in New York for the remainder of his life, never to return to the state he had fought so hard to change.[26]

While DeLaine was forced to make his final exit, the White Citizens' Council in Clarendon stepped up efforts to resist school integration and crush the local black insurgency. The force of white economic sanctions, the threat of massive violence, and the decline of necessary agricultural labor proved devastating to African Americans and wreaked havoc on the county's long-term social and economic well-being. "It dried Summerton up," Joseph Richburg explained, "it dried them up . . . See, it wasn't much money out in the field, but it was so many of them, you know. A lot of people leave and went up North just like I did." Like so many others, Richburg and his family left Clarendon in search of a better life elsewhere. For the Briggs family, life in Clarendon turned increasingly bleak. Harry and Eliza Briggs had hoped that their efforts would improve their children's educational and life opportunities. "My children didn't get [the education]," though, Eliza Briggs later explained. Even worse, she thought, was that her husband's efforts and the crushing economic sanctions imposed on him in Clarendon meant that their children "didn't have a chance to raise up with their daddy" because "he had to leave." Indeed, by the time Clarendon County finally submitted to a token desegregation plan in 1965, after yet another lawsuit brought by black parents, the Briggs children were grown. They had packed their bags and headed North to New York City. Harry and Eliza Briggs would eventually join them. Harry found work as a parking attendant and, as she had in Clarendon, Eliza took a job as a chambermaid. Back in Clarendon, white resistance to school integration persisted. Under a court order issued in 1970 to achieve a more equitable racial balance in the county school system, white parents entirely withdrew their support from the public schools. With a single exception, white children enrolled in Clarendon Hall, a Baptist parochial school, and other private academies, or left the county altogether. By 1980 the county had the lowest per capita income and lowest median family income of any county in the state, helping to earn it an official designation as a "distressed area."[27]

In the short term, the efforts of white South Carolinians to cripple the NAACP and the black fight for full citizenship and empowerment were highly effective. With the Clarendon County case as a rallying call, the NAACP had expanded its organizational base in South Carolina from sixty-nine to eighty-four branches between 1948 and the first years of the 1950s. The association extended its reach into the state's backwoods, cotton fields, and rural county churches. In the wake of *Brown*, however, those numbers spiraled downward. Between 1955 and 1957 the number of NAACP branches in South Carolina fell from eighty-four to thirty-one, the lowest total since the organization began its rapid expansion in 1943. Accordingly, statewide membership in the organization plunged from more than 8,266 to 2,202, threatening to return the organization to the brutal days and ineffectual ways of the 1920s and early 1930s.[28] The NAACP's travails in South Carolina were by no means isolated. In the NAACP's southeast region alone, an area encompassing Florida, Georgia, Mississippi, Alabama, Tennessee, North Carolina, and South Carolina, massive resistance helped cut the organization's membership nearly in half between 1955 and 1957, from 52,375 to 26,955. In Alabama the organization was banned, while in Louisiana and Texas state-imposed injunctions decimated NAACP activity and slashed membership rolls. Nationally, under pressure from southern members of Congress, the Internal Revenue Service launched an investigation into the relationship between Marshall's tax-exempt Legal Defense Fund (LDF) and the tax-paying NAACP, forcing their complete separation. At precisely the moment when the NAACP ought to have been working to turn its monumental legal victory over Jim Crow into a sustained effort to mobilize a broader mass insurgency, the organization was thrown on the defensive. Rather than expand its membership, publicize its decades-long work on behalf of African Americans, and turn its revolutionary legal victory into meaningful reforms, the NAACP was forced to fight a rearguard battle against massive resistance.[29]

The NAACP and the African American fight for full citizenship and empowerment had of course suffered similar setbacks before. The organization and the movement had each been in a long and constant process of reinvention in an effort to secure the basic legal rights afforded by the Constitution and the meaningful application of those rights. From the First World War to the 1920s and the Depression to the Second World War and beyond, African Americans confronted the exclusions and limitations of both the theory and practice of democracy in America and searched for a way forward. Winning the right to vote and gaining full access to the nation's public schools were important issues in their own right. At the same time, these single-issue battles were part of a far larger struggle for self-determination and equality. Long before they joined the NAACP's legal campaign to destroy Jim Crow, African Americans in Clarendon County were active participants in this larger struggle. The people of Clarendon County have always been part of the fabric of American life, and their struggles have registered both the promises and limitations of American democracy, even if their voices have not always been heard. Today there are signs of improved educational opportunities for the county's African American children, and yet the segregated realities of everyday life and bleak economic prospects continue to limit the life chances of another generation. To continue to ignore these hardships and to relegate the voices of the county's residents to the periphery of national discourse is to leave the promise of American democracy and the concept of equality unfulfilled fifty years after *Brown*.[30]

## Notes

1 The standard narrative account of Clarendon County's role in *Brown* remains Richard Kluger, *Simple Justice* (New York: Vintage, 1977). Subsequent scholarship has relied extensively on Kluger's account of events in Clarendon. The most recent examples include James T. Patterson, *Brown v. Board of Education: A Civil Rights Milestone and Its Troubled Legacy* (New York: Oxford University Press, 2001), 23–27; Peter Irons, *Jim Crow's Children: The Broken Promise of the Brown Decision* (New York: Viking, 2002), 46–50.

2 Interview with Minnie Ida Wright by Gregory Hunter, Summerton, S.C., n.d., Behind the Veil: Documenting African American Life in the Jim Crow South Oral History Project, Center for Documentary Studies (Rare Book, Manuscript, and Special Collections Library, Duke University, Durham), hereafter cited as Behind the Veil Oral History Collection.

3 Interview with Joseph Richburg Sr. by Mary Hebert, 26 June 1995, *id*. Also see interview with Moses Levy Sr. by Kisha Turner and Blair Murphy, 29 June 1995, *id*. A special thanks and debt of gratitude are owed to Blair Murphy (Kelley) for her field work and conversations and for a paper she wrote on oral history and Clarendon County, "To Tell a Bigger Story," for a panel we did together at the annual meeting of the Organization of American Historians in 2000.

4 Kluger, *Simple Justice*, 6–8. On access to voting rights in Clarendon County, see J. A. DeLaine to Harold Boulware, 6 March 1948, folder 2, Joseph Armstrong DeLaine Papers (South Caroliniana Library, University of South Carolina, Columbia), hereafter cited as DeLaine Papers; J. A. DeLaine to Harold Boulware, 9 April 1948, DeLaine Papers.

5 DeLaine's personal history is detailed in Kluger, *Simple Justice*, 3–14. For a more recent account informed by new documents and conversations with family members, see Julie Magruder Lochbaum, "The Word Made Flesh: The Desegregation Leadership of the Rev. J. A. DeLaine"(diss., College of Education, University of South Carolina, 1993), especially 75–85. The account here also has benefited from Joseph A. DeLaine Jr.'s "Recollections of His Father, Reverend Joseph Armstrong DeLaine Sr. and the Civil Rights Struggle of Clarendon County, SC," copy in author's possession, and the author's conversations with Joseph DeLaine Jr.

6 For a view of the NAACP's transformation at the national level, see August Meier and Elliott Rudwick, "The Rise of the Black Secretariat in the NAACP," *Along the Color Line: Explorations in the Black Experience*, ed. Meier and Rudwick (Urbana: University of Illinois Press, 1976), 94–127. For a view from South Carolina and the curtailment of NAACP activity in the 1920s, see Peter F. Lau, "Freedom Road Territory: The Politics of Civil Rights Struggle in South Carolina

during the Jim Crow Era" (diss., Rutgers, The State University of New Jersey, 2002), 1–72, 73–113.

7 On the creation of the South Carolina NAACP State Conference of Branches, see Lau, "Freedom Road Territory," 172–234. Quotes are from "Exhortation for Solid Voluntary Action by All People of Cheraw, S.C. in the Matter of Support for the Only and Greatest Organizational Champion of Negro Rights in America—National Association for the Advancement of Colored People," South Carolina State Conference File, II-C-181, Papers of the National Association for the Advancement of Colored People (Manuscript Division, Library of Congress, Washington), hereafter cited as NAACP Papers. Membership numbers are from Report and Recommendations on Membership and Staff, 1957, III-A-37, NAACP Papers.

8 On McKaine and the fight for equal teachers' salaries, see Miles Spangler Richards, "Osceola E. McKaine and the Struggle for Black Civil Rights, 1917–1946," (diss., University of South Carolina, 1994), 103–50. Also see Tushnet, *The NAACP Legal Strategy against Segregated Education, 1925–1950* (Chapel Hill: University of North Carolina Press, 1987), 992–93; Tinsley E. Yarbrough, *A Passion for Justice: J. Waties Waring and Civil Rights* (New York: Oxford University Press, 1987), 42–46. On the NCC see Lau, "Freedom Road Territory," 207–9. Quotes are from the NCC pamphlet "Which Do You Want—Democracy or the 'American Way of Life,'" ca. 1942–43, S.C. State Conference File, II-C-181, NAACP Papers.

9 J. A. DeLaine, "August 1962: Some Reminiscence of My Life: Vacation Reflections," Persons: J. A. DeLaine, reel 9, John H. McCray Papers (South Caroliniana Library, University of South Carolina, Columbia), collection hereafter cited as McCray Papers and document hereafter cited as "Reminiscence"; Richards, "Osceola E. McKaine and the Struggle for Black Civil Rights," 117; National Association for the Advancement of Colored People, Sumter Branch Minute Book, 28 June 1942, 147 (South Caroliniana Library, University of South Carolina, Columbia). Quotes are from: J. A. DeLaine to Flutie Boyd, 7 April 1948, folder 2, DeLaine Papers; J. A. DeLaine to NAACP, 17 January 1943, Clarendon County Branch File, II-C-177, NAACP Papers; J. A. DeLaine, "Reminiscence." The DeLaine family dates the creation of an NAACP branch in Clarendon to 1941. See Joseph A. DeLaine Jr.'s "Recollections of His Father."

10 Interview with Joseph Richburg Sr. by Mary Hebert; Officers of South Carolina Branches, 20 January 1944, State Conference Files, II-C-176, NAACP Papers; Report of Election of Officers, Clarendon County, 2 September 1948, Clarendon County Branch File, II-C-177, NAACP Papers; Bessie House to John H. McCray, 19 February 1945, Places: Clarendon County, reel 10, McCray Papers; Sarah E. Daniels to John H. McCray, 1 December 1946, Places: Clarendon County, reel 10, McCray Papers.

11 Histories of the PDP include Kari Frederickson, *The Dixiecrat Revolt and the End of the Solid South, 1932–1968* (Chapel Hill: University of North Carolina Press, 2001), 42–46; Lau, "Freedom Road Territory," 211–22; Richards, "Osceola E. McKaine and the Struggle for Black Civil Rights," 155–206; Patricia Sullivan, *Days of Hope: Race and Democracy in the New Deal Era* (Chapel Hill: University of

North Carolina Press, 1996), 133–92. McCray quoted in Lau, "Freedom Road Territory," 212–13.

12 Interview with Ferdinand Pearson by Blair Murphy and Kisha Turner, Manning, S.C., 14 June 1995, Behind the Veil Oral History Collection; J. A. DeLaine Jr., "*Briggs v. Elliott*: Clarendon County's Quest for Equality," (Pine Brook, N.J.: O. Gona Press, 2002), 6–7, copy in author's possession.

13 Interview with Ferdinand Pearson by Blair Murphy and Kisha Turner; Jessie Pearson et al. to W. A. Schiffley, 6 July 1946, folder 1, DeLaine Papers; Lochbaum, "The World Made Flesh," 84–85.

14 Kluger, *Simple Justice*, 13–14. Quote from J. A. DeLaine and others, "The Clarendon County School Segregation Case," in Joseph A. DeLaine file no. 9-28873, Federal Bureau of Investigation, Freedom of Information/Privacy Acts Section, Washington.

15 J. A. DeLaine to John H. McCray, 14 December 1961, McCray Papers, University of South Carolina, Columbia; Kluger, *Simple Justice*, 13–14; Harold Boulware to J. A. DeLaine, 29 July 1947, folder 1, DeLaine Papers (DeLaine's hand notes), emphasis mine.

16 J. A. DeLaine to James Hinton, 5 February 1948, folder 1, DeLaine Papers; Harold Boulware to J. A. DeLaine, 16 February 1948, folder 2, DeLaine Papers (DeLaine's hand notes); J. A. DeLaine to Harold Boulware, 9 April 1948, folder 2, DeLaine Papers.

17 James M. Hinton to Levi Pearson, 12 March 1948, folder 2, DeLaine Papers; Harold Boulware to J. A. DeLaine, 16 February 1948, folder 2, DeLaine Papers (hand notes); J. A. DeLaine to Harold Boulware, 6 March 1948, folder 2, DeLaine Papers; J. A. DeLaine to Harold Boulware, 9 April 1948, folder 2, DeLaine papers; Kluger, *Simple Justice*, 17; interview with Ferdinand Pearson by Blair Murphy and Kisha Turner.

18 J. A. DeLaine to James Hinton and Harold Boulware, 30 September 1948, folder 3, DeLaine Papers; interview with Eugene Alonzo Randolph Montgomery by Charles Houston Jr., Orangeburg, S.C., 2 August 1994, Behind the Veil Oral History Collection; DeLaine and others, "The Clarendon County School Segregation Case"; Harold Boulware to J. A. DeLaine, 8 March 1949, folder 3, DeLaine Papers (hand notes); Thurgood Marshall to Harold Boulware, 28 February 1949, Legal File B, 1948–49, II-B-3, NAACP Papers, Manuscripts Division, Library of Congress, Washington; Joseph A. DeLaine Jr., "Recollections of His Father"; also see Tushnet, *Making Civil Rights Law: Thurgood Marshall and the Supreme Court, 1936–1961* (New York: Oxford University Press, 1994), 154.

19 Interview with Robert James Georgia Jr. and Abraham Smith by Mary Hebert and Blair Murphy, Summerton, S.C., 14 June 1995, Behind the Veil Oral History Collection; interview with Hauleen Green Smith by Kisha Turner, Summerton, S.C., 14 June 1995, Behind the Veil Oral History Collection; Petition Submitted to Superintendents and Trustees of Clarendon County and District Number 22, 1949, Clarendon County Board of Education Complaints against Principles, 1949–50, South Carolina Department of Archives and History, Columbia, hereafter cited as Complaint Files.

20  DeLaine and others, "The Clarendon County School Segregation Case"; Minutes of 8 June 1949 meeting taken by the Reverend E. E. Richburg, folder 3, DeLaine Papers, herafter cited as Richburg Minutes; Harold Boulware to J. A. DeLaine, 8 March 1949, folder 3, DeLaine Papers (hand notes). For more on the concerns of black parents in Clarendon County schools see Complaint Files.

21  Robert Georgia et al. to County Board of Education, 9 July 1949, Complaint Files; R. M. Elliott et al., summary of 24 June 1949 meeting, Complaint Files; Parents of Scott's Branch School Petition to Superintendent and Trustees, 25 July 1949, Complaint Files; Parents of School District 22 to Trustees of School District 22, Trustees of County Board, & State Board of Education, 18 September 1950, Complaint Files; Parent Committee on Action to Superintendent and Trustees, 13 April 1950, Complaint Files. DeLaine quoted from "The Clarendon County School Segregation Case."

22  "Please Announce This in Your Church," ca. December 1949, folder 3, DeLaine Papers (hand notes); DeLaine and others, "The Clarendon County School Segregation Case"; Kluger, *Simple Justice*, 25; Lochbaum, "The World Made Flesh," 121–22, 129–30.

23  DeLaine and others, "The Clarendon County School Segregation Case"; J. A. DeLaine, "An Open Letter: A Summary of Incidents in the Summerton School Affair," January 1950, folder 4, DeLaine Papers; interview with Eliza Gemble Briggs by Mary Hebert, 16 June 1995, Summerton, S.C., Behind the Veil Oral History Collection; interview with Robert Georgia Jr. and Abraham Smith by Mary Hebert and Blair Murphy, Summerton, S.C., 14 June 1995, Behind the Veil Oral History Collection; Kluger, *Simple Justice*, 23–24; interview with Minnie Ida Wright by Gregory Hunter, Summerton, S.C., n.d., Behind the Veil Oral History Collection; interview with Melison Beatrice Green by Mary Hebert, Summerton, S.C., 4 July 1995, Behind the Veil Oral History Collection; interview with Joseph Richburg Sr. by Mary Hebert, Summerton, S.C., 26 June 1995, Behind the Veil Oral History Collection.

24  J. A. DeLaine to NAACP, 3 May 1950, Clarendon County Branch File, II-C-177, NAACP Papers.

25  The most cogent argument on the devastating short-term effects of *Brown* in the South is Michael J. Klarman, "How *Brown* Changed Race Relations: The Backlash Thesis," *Journal of American History* 81 (June 1994): 81–118. On the formation of White Citizens' Councils in South Carolina see Howard H. Quint, *Profile in Black and White: A Frank Portrait of South Carolina* (Westport: Greenwood, 1958), 45–54. On the formation of White Citizens' Councils across the South see Numan V. Bartley, *The Rise of Massive Resistance: Race and Politics in the South during the 1950s* (1967; reprint, Baton Rouge: Louisiana State University Press, 1999); Neil R. McMillen, *The Citizens' Council: Organized Resistance to the Second Reconstruction, 1954–1964* (1971; reprint, Urbana: University of Illinois Press, 1994). On the Gressette Committee and the state's legislative efforts to smash the NAACP see Quint, *Profile in Black and White*, 95–97, 103, 105–10.

26  Statistical data are from Raymond Wolters, *The Burden of Brown: Thirty*

*Years of School Desegregation* (Knoxville: University of Tennessee Press, 1984), 130–31. On economic changes across the South see Gavin Wright, *Old South, New South: Revolutions in the Southern Economy since the Civil War* (New York: Basic Books, 1986), 239–74. Economic changes in South Carolina are detailed in Peter A. Coclanis and Lacy K. Ford, "The South Carolina Economy Reconstructed and Reconsidered: Structure, Output, and Performance, 1670–1985," *Developing Dixie: Modernization in a Traditional Society*, ed. Winfred B. Moore Jr., Joseph F. Tripp, and Lyon G. Tyler Jr. (New York: Greenwood, 1988), 93–110. On DeLaine's final exit see Joseph A. DeLaine Jr.'s "Details regarding Rev. De Laine's Escape via Florence, SC," 1996, copy in author's possession; Lochbaum, "The Word Made Flesh," 130–37; Kluger, *Simple Justice*, 3, 525; Quint, *Profile in Black and White*, 36; DeLaine and others, "The Clarendon County School Segregation Case"; J. A. DeLaine to J. Edgar Hoover, 13 October 1955, in Joseph A. DeLaine, FBI File. A copy of the death threat can be found in folder 8, DeLaine Papers.

27 Interview with Joseph Richburg Sr. by Mary Hebert, Summerton, S.C., 26 June 1995, Behind the Veil Oral History Collection; interview with Eliza Briggs by Mary Hebert, Summerton, S.C., 16 June 1995, Behind the Veil Oral History Collection. On desegregation efforts in Clarendon County see Wolters, *The Burden of Brown*, 150–51, 166, designation as "distressed area" found on p. 131.

28 Membership numbers are from Report and Recommendations on Membership and Staff, 1957, NAACP Papers. On the growth of NAACP branches in South Carolina between 1948 and 1955 see Lau, "Freedom Road Territory," 287–89.

29 Report and Recommendations on Membership and Staff, 1957, NAACP Papers. On the repression of the NAACP in the South see Aldon Morris, *The Origins of the Civil Rights Movement: Black Communities Organizing for Change* (New York: Free Press, 1984), 30–35; Tushnet, *Making Civil Rights Law*, 247–300. On repression of the NAACP in Louisiana and Mississippi after *Brown* see, respectively, Adam Fairclough, *Race and Democracy: The Civil Rights Struggle in Louisiana, 1915–1972* (Athens: University of Georgia Press, 1995), 187–233; John Dittmer, *Local People: The Struggle for Civil Rights in Mississippi* (Urbana: University of Illinois Press, 1994), 41–89. On the split of the LDF and NAACP see Tushnet, *Making Civil Rights Law*, 310–13, and Tomiko Brown-Nagin's chapter in this book.

30 For two views on the current conditions of life in Clarendon County, see Irons, *Jim Crow's Children*, 331–37; Patterson, *Brown v. Board of Education*, 206–7.

# PART II

# Advocates, Judges, and the Making of *Brown*

LARISSA M. SMITH

# A Civil Rights Vanguard

## Black Attorneys and the NAACP in Virginia

℞ "The eradication of racial segregation and discrimination in public education has long been a major objective of the NAACP," wrote the Virginia attorney Spottswood W. Robinson III in 1951. "Steady progress, unique successes, and an endless improvement of procedural techniques have characterized this magnitudinous undertaking." "Virginia," Robinson asserted, "has been the chief proving ground for the techniques utilized" to challenge educational inequalities in elementary and secondary schools.[1] Indeed, beginning in the 1930s Virginia emerged as one of the chief arenas in which the NAACP waged its battle against segregation in schools. Central to this fight was a critical mass of highly trained and motivated lawyers, twelve in all, who were committed to the NAACP and its goal of securing black people's citizenship rights. These attorneys, most notably Robinson and Oliver W. Hill , used the NAACP litigation campaign as an organizing vehicle through which African Americans struggled for their first-class citizenship rights. They assisted local communities in initiating legal challenges, helped to organize NAACP branches, filed countless petitions and court documents, and coordinated litigation with lawyers from the NAACP national office. Hill and Robinson pioneered many of the litigation techniques the NAACP would use in its education cases. Moreover, these attorneys actively participated in the broader civil rights struggles during the New Deal and the Second World War. In the 1940s, Hill and his fellow attorneys attacked the system of segregation from multiple directions. They challenged not only discrimination in education but also discrimination in transportation and employment; they organized voter registration campaigns and ran for political office in hopes of inspiring African Americans to vote. These lawyers understood the education campaign to be the centerpiece of a much broader assault on segregation in all arenas of southern life. Their work not only shaped the direction of civil rights activism within the state of Virginia but also proved essential to laying the groundwork for *Brown*.

Charles H. Houston played a central role in creating a cadre of lawyers who would lead civil rights struggles in Virginia and in shaping the litigation strategy that those lawyers would pursue in the 1940s. When appointed dean of Howard University Law School in 1930, Houston sought to train a generation of black lawyers who would wage civil rights struggles in the South. He transformed the law school from an unaccredited night program into a full-time, accredited day program. Houston charged his students with the mission to be "social engineers" and "group interpreters." "Due to the Negro's social and political condition," he observed, "the Negro lawyer must be prepared to anticipate, guide, and interpret his group advancement."[2] Houston instructed his students to take the lead in organizing their communities and in engineering struggles to gain full equality before the law for African Americans. Houston also advised his students to return to their southern communities after completing their law education. In an article published in 1935 entitled "The Need for Negro Lawyers," Houston asserted that in the entire South there were no more than a hundred black lawyers devoting full time to practice. In Alabama, according to 1930 census lists, there were four lawyers to attend to the legal needs of 944,834 blacks in the state. In Virginia, fifty-seven lawyers served a black population of 650,155, and Houston estimated that the actual number of lawyers practicing full-time was closer to fifteen. White southern lawyers had too many conflicting interests to "wage an uncompromising fight for equal rights for Negroes," Houston believed, and therefore black lawyers needed to go south.[3]

A handful of students crossed the Potomac River into Virginia to practice what Houston preached. Robinson, Hill, J. Byron Hopkins, Robert Cooley, Raymond Valentine, and Martin A. Martin all graduated from Howard during the 1930s and practiced law in Virginia. These men—along with Leon Ransom, Eddie Lovett, William H. Hastie, and Thurgood Marshall—maintained ties with Howard University Law School and assisted Houston as he initiated the NAACP's legal campaign to fight educational inequalities. These men served at various times as Houston's scouts, ambassadors, lieutenants, and eventual successors in the NAACP's legal campaign.

In July 1935 Charles Houston left his job as dean of Howard University Law School and joined the NAACP national office as special counsel in charge of implementing a legal campaign against educational inequalities in the South. The campaign began in 1930, when the American Fund for Public Service (AFPS) granted the NAACP $100,000 to launch a variety of taxpayer suits: to challenge dual school systems in the South, protect blacks' civil liberties, seek the end of segregation and jury exclusion, and fight American imperialism in Haiti and Nicaragua.[4] The campaign was soon narrowed to focus on discrimination in education and transportation.

With the onset of the Depression, however, the AFPS substantially reduced the size of the grant to $10,000, and the NAACP asked Houston to prepare a memorandum suggesting the best way for the money to be spent.

Houston proposed spending all the money on a campaign to fight discrimination in education. He argued that while discrimination in transportation was significant, inequalities in public education had been exacerbated by the Depression. Feeling the economic pinch, southern governments were sacrificing black education to save white education, and "the ideals and efficiency of an entire generation" of African Americans were "at stake."[5] For Houston, discrimination in education was "merely part of the general pattern of race prejudice in American life" and an attack on educational inequality, he believed, had to be waged in conjunction with the association's anti-lynching campaign and economic programs.[6]

Houston envisioned the NAACP's multifaceted program as enabling southern blacks to mobilize in defense of their own rights. The support of local communities was essential to the legal campaign he planned. Houston knew that initiating a campaign to fight segregated schools would cost much more than the initial AFPS grant. Not only did the NAACP need the financial support that local groups could provide, but it also needed members of local communities to volunteer to be plaintiffs. Being a plaintiff in a court case entailed great economic and social risk, and if the plaintiff did not have support from the black community, the results could be disastrous. Therefore Houston insisted, "The general policy of the NAACP should be to lend a hand in contests already undertaken or proposed by the local communities themselves, rather than to precipitate a struggle on a community which does not want it." "The inspirational value of a struggle," Houston reminded, "is always greater when it springs from the soil than when it is a foreign growth."[7]

Working with local communities interested in challenging educational inequalities meant that Houston had to be flexible about where and when court cases would be litigated. Yet he did have a basic strategy for attacking segregated education. It was clear that white and black public schools were grossly unequal in facilities, transportation, equipment, teachers' salaries, and per capita spending on students. Houston's tactic was to force southern government officials to equalize spending between black and white schools. Ultimately, Houston believed that officials would be financially unable to afford two separate school systems and would combine them. "For purely technical reasons" though, Houston wanted to start with cases challenging the lack of graduate education for blacks.[8] Before demonstrating that "separate but equal" facilities were far from equal in secondary education, Houston wanted to begin where there was no question of inequality: separate graduate programs did not even exist for blacks in southern states. While gathering information and evidence about the myriad ways in which secondary schools were unequal, Houston also moved to challenge inequalities in teachers' salaries, for discrepancies in salaries were clear-cut and relatively simple to litigate.[9]

In looking for potential plaintiffs for court cases challenging the lack of graduate programs for blacks and inequalities in teachers' salaries, Houston turned to Virginia. If the South was to be Houston's battleground, then Virginia was to be his beachhead. With his permanent home in Washington, it was easier for Houston to litigate cases in Virginia or Maryland than elsewhere. Moreover, as the legal historian Mark Tushnet points out, Houston litigated his first cases in the upper South because he "may have shared a common intuition . . . that it would be easier to litigate and win lawsuits" there.[10] There may have existed a greater chance in the upper South of finding white officials who agreed at least in principle that discrimination and inequalities in black and white education were wrong. After all, white Virginians prided themselves on their "amicable race relations."[11] Élite white Virginians, including state politicians, perceived themselves as being firmly in control of the pace of reform. They did not mind granting African Americans a modicum of rights as long as they did not threaten social stability or white political power. Moreover, in the late 1920s and early 1930s African Americans in Virginia had won court cases challenging residential segregation and their exclusion from the white primary.[12]

Furthermore, by 1935 Houston had already established a reputation for himself and developed important connections with African American activists in Virginia. He had done some of his earliest work for the NAACP as lead counsel in the murder trial of George Crawford in Loudon County in 1933. After the trial, Houston received acclaim from both the white and black presses in Virginia for his professional manner and legal knowledge. Houston hoped that these qualities would serve him well as he launched the legal campaign against segregated education. As he told the editor of the *Richmond Planet*, "The state of Virginia gave me applause in the Crawford case for refusing to pervert justice and sticking to the truth, the whole truth, and nothing but the truth. It is going to be interesting to see what they are going to do now that I am determined to tell the truth about Southern education."[13]

Apart from Houston's personal experience, Virginia proved fertile ground for the legal campaign because of the emerging presence of the NAACP in the state. In 1929 P. B. Young, editor of the *Norfolk Journal and Guide*, the largest African American newspaper in the state, declared that the "scant support" black Virginians gave the NAACP was a "cause for shame."[14] All that began to change in the 1930s. The Depression exacerbated African Americans' already precarious social and economic position, and the NAACP provided a means through which African Americans could wage their local struggles, while linking up with national efforts to gain their citizenship rights. With encouragement from members of the NAACP national office, African Americans turned local community citizens' leagues, voters' leagues, and other existing community organizations into NAACP chapters. African Americans rejuvenated branches in Richmond, Hampton, Norfolk, and Newport News in 1930 and 1931. By 1934 black Virginians had organized branches in Alexandria, Hampton, Norfolk, Petersburg, Portsmouth, Richmond, and Roanoke, and a college chapter at Virginia Union University. Moreover, the association's emerging litigation campaign dovetailed with the concerns of African American Virginians about the lack of educational opportunities for their children and the inequalities in salaries between black and white teachers. In 1931, for instance, Thomas L. Dabney, an outspoken black principal of an African American school in Buckingham County, circulated a petition among teachers in twenty-five counties and five cities calling for the state to correct racial salary differentials.[15]

From 1933 to 1935 Charles Houston laid the groundwork for the NAACP litigation campaign by investigating school facilities and raising community awareness about the legal campaign. He relied on local NAACP activists and educators, like Thomas L. Dabney and Luther P. Jackson, a history professor at Virginia State College for Negroes, to survey school conditions quietly in their area and seek out potential plaintiffs for graduate education and teachers' salary cases.[16] Houston also contacted young lawyers in Virginia trained at Howard, such as J. Byron Hopkins in Richmond and Raymond Valentine in Petersburg. Hopkins, who was legal counsel for the Richmond NAACP branch, made investigative trips with Houston; they traveled across the state of Virginia, taking photographs to record school conditions.[17] In November and December 1935 Houston made an eleven-day speaking tour of the state. His itinerary testifies to his commitment to education and to impressing on the public the importance of the legal campaign. He spoke at NAACP branch meetings in Petersburg, Richmond, and Roanoke; at a citizens' meeting in Louisa; at Virginia Union University; and at the initial organization meeting of a NAACP branch in Lynchburg.[18] Through these speaking engagements, Houston sought to stimulate the formation of an organizational network that would support the association's fight against segregated schools.

The litigation campaign became the vehicle through which the NAACP in Virginia grew and strengthened in the late 1930s. In 1935 black activists organized the Virginia State Conference of Branches. The purpose of the conference was to support local branches and coordinate statewide voter registration campaigns and challenges to discrimination. In January 1935 the board of directors of the Virginia State Conference of Branches held its first meeting in Richmond. The board planned to bring a case in state court to test the unequal salaries paid to black and white teachers, as well as to test the legality of blacks' exclusion from institutions of higher learning. In a letter to Walter White, the state conference asked for assistance from the national office to direct the legal attack they wanted to make.[19] Although local NAACP leaders in Virginia were responsible for organizing the state conference, they launched a legal campaign that clearly reflected Houston's influence. This dynamic between Houston and Virginia NAACP leaders makes sense, if viewed through Houston's understanding that the NAACP national office could not force a fight against discrimination upon any community. In June 1935 Houston met jointly with the Virginia State Teachers Association and the Virginia state conference of the NAACP to muster support for the legal campaign.

That December the state conference held its first annual meeting; it convened the day after the annual meeting of the State Teachers Association. During the State Teachers Association meeting, Leon "Andy" Ransom, an attorney whom Charles Houston had dispatched to the meeting as his substitute, led a session of the division of rural teachers on "Points of Approach to the Problems Facing Negro Teachers of Virginia." Later that evening, Ransom met with NAACP branch presidents and state leaders such as Professor Luther P. Jackson. Ransom discussed with them the situation confronting the NAACP in Virginia, as well as the potential problems they might encounter in the coming year as they developed the legal campaign. The next day, before the meeting of the state conference officially opened, Ransom caucused with a group of NAACP leaders to develop a slate of officers for the state conference "which would most effectively carry out the program desired" by Houston and his colleagues. Later that afternoon, during the meeting of the state conference, Ransom succeeded in getting officers elected who would support the legal campaign. As Ransom wrote to Houston, "I am proud to say that [the slate of officers] represents my selection, although I may be accused of being somewhat czar-like in the matter of suggestion for the slate."[20]

The public education campaign that Houston and other NAACP activists had conducted began to pay off, as black teachers in communities throughout Virginia wrote to the NAACP asking for advice and declaring their readiness to fight for higher wages. In September 1937 a teacher in Mecklenburg County reported that the school situation had not improved much since she had talked with Houston two years earlier. The teachers had petitioned the school board to raise their salaries, and they were granted a small increase, but salaries were still not on par with what white teachers were paid.[21] The president of the NAACP branch in Middlesex County related that the teachers in his county were meeting to plan a fight for higher salaries. He was meeting with the teachers, and since only five teachers belonged to the NAACP chapter, he saw this as a good opportunity to have the teachers become members of the branch.[22]

Indeed, NAACP activists in Virginia used the teachers' salary equalization fight as the basis for organizing and invigorating branches around the state. Thomas L. Dabney revitalized the Lynchburg branch as a way to get local citizens to support the fight against educational inequalities. "A group here," he told Walter White, "would like to reestablish the Lynchburg branch of the Association to strengthen the State Conference of the NAACP for our fight to equalize the salaries of Negro and white teachers."[23] After his visit to the annual meeting of the Virginia State Conference of Branches in 1937, E. Frederic Morrow, the branch coordinator from the NAACP national office, noted that the "teachers salary fight has given the needed impetus to ailing branches." Moreover, he was "overwhelmed by the militancy of the delegates" and vowed that the national office "intend[ed] to assist the officers in every possible way to make the Virginia Conference a Gibraltar in the South."[24]

By 1937 Charles Houston had turned over the bulk of the legal work in Virginia to Thurgood Marshall, his former student from Howard, who had joined the association as assistant special counsel in 1936. Houston needed help with the burgeoning caseload of the Association. He desired to build a team of lawyers to wage the legal campaign, so he could "keep free to hit and fight wherever circumstances call for action."[25] Having grown up in Baltimore, Marshall served as Houston's field marshal in Maryland, handling the details of litigation in the Donald Murray case, which succeeded in gaining Murray's entrance to the University of Maryland Law School in 1935. In 1936 Marshall also litigated a successful teacher salary equalization suit in Montgomery County and was setting in motion additional equalization suits in other counties in Maryland.[26] By the summer of 1937 Marshall was looking to extend the association's work in Maryland down into Virginia. "Our southern states further down are desirous of filing such cases," Marshall explained to J. M. Tinsley, president of the Virginia State Conference of Branches, "but we would prefer to go from Maryland into Virginia, then into Carolina and Kentucky on down." Marshall knew that people in Virginia were interested in equalizing teachers' salaries, and he asked whether the NAACP state conference and the State Teachers Association were ready.[27]

In November 1937, in Hampton, Virginia, Marshall appeared at the annual meetings of the State Teachers Association and the state conference of the NAACP to garner support for the teachers' salary fight.[28] At that meeting Marshall helped to organize a Joint Committee on the Equalization of Teachers' Salaries to coordinate and supervise the litigation campaign. The committee was composed of five members each from the Teachers Association and the State Conference of Branches. J. M. Tinsley would be recognized publicly as the chairman of the committee, but the names of all other members would be kept secret to avoid any retaliation from white officials. The committee would administer a defense fund, which the State Teachers Association had established. The fund was intended to pay legal expenses and to compensate a plaintiff in the likely event that the teacher lost his or her job because of involvement in a lawsuit. The State Teachers Association, representing four thousand members, had pledged $1,000 toward the fund, and each member would be asked to contribute one additional dollar to bring the total to $5,000. In response to the teachers' action, Thurgood Marshall commented to Walter White, "Here we have an example of four thousand Negroes in the south in a group fighting for their rights—willing not only to support the cases but also to put up money for a defense fund to protect the plaintiffs."[29]

Although the teachers were willing to pledge money to a defense fund, few were willing to volunteer to be plaintiffs in a salary equalization case. Concerned about maintaining their jobs in difficult economic times, many teachers were conservative and discouraged other teachers from volunteering. It took until October 1938 before Marshall had found a plaintiff, a high school teacher from Norfolk named Aline Black. At the end of October, Marshall and J. Thomas Hewin Jr., a member of the state conference's legal committee in Richmond, took the first step in the equalization case by filing a petition with the Norfolk Board of Education, asking to raise the salaries of black teachers to the level of white teachers.[30] The school board denied Black's petition in early December, and Marshall and Hewin initiated court proceedings in February 1939. In response, the city of Norfolk, although admitting to paying white and black teachers different salaries solely on the basis of race, argued that Black had waived her rights to contest the salary once she signed her teaching contract. In June the circuit court judge agreed with the city of Norfolk and dismissed the case. Marshall quickly filed an appeal, but before the case could make its way to court the Norfolk Board of Education, in a not wholly unexpected move, declined to renew Aline Black's contract for the coming school year.[31] With Black's dismissal, the NAACP lawyers believed that Black no longer had standing to bring suit against the school board, so they turned to another plaintiff, Melvin O.

Alston. Like Black, Alston taught at Booker T. Washington High School; he also headed the Norfolk Teachers Association and was vice-president of the Norfolk branch of the NAACP.

The switch to Alston as a plaintiff resulted in a change in the litigation team as well. Throughout the Black case, Marshall had relied on J. Thomas Hewin Jr. as the lawyer on the ground in Virginia. Hewin, along with J. Byron Hopkins, constituted the legal staff of the Virginia state conference of the NAACP. They had succeeded in winning some defense cases, and Hopkins especially had been helpful in organizing NAACP branches around the state. By the late 1930s, however, Hewin and Hopkins appeared unreliable and inconsistent and a clear rift had emerged between the NAACP state conference and Hopkins.[32] As a result, Marshall asked his old law school classmate and friend Oliver W. Hill to join the litigation team.

Born in 1907, Hill spent most of his childhood in Roanoke, living with family friends while his mother and stepfather worked out of town. In 1923 he joined his parents in Washington, where he attended Dunbar High School. Finishing high school in three years, he entered Howard University, where he took classes from young professors such as Ralph Bunche and Abram Harris. During his sophomore year in college his step-uncle, who had been a lawyer, died, and Hill inherited his set of the U.S. Code Annotated and some other law books. In reading the books, Hill learned that it had been the Supreme Court that had taken away African Americans' rights in the late nineteenth century. He decided to go to law school to learn how to win back those rights. At Howard at the time, a student could finish his last year of undergraduate coursework while beginning his first year of professional training. Hill entered Howard Law School in September 1930, where he came under the tutelage of Charles Houston and met his classmate Thurgood Marshall.[33]

On graduating from law school in 1933, Hill returned to Roanoke and attempted to establish his own practice. Starting a law practice during the Depression proved a difficult task. Working with another lawyer in Roanoke, he handled a few divorce cases, collected unpaid debts, and served several times as a court-appointed defense lawyer. While in Roanoke, Hill joined the local NAACP branch and also served on the nominating committee at the organizational meeting of the Virginia State Conference of Branches in 1935. The NAACP national office referred black citizens in southwest Virginia to Hill, and he also participated in the research phase of the NAACP's litigation campaign, investigating school conditions and taking pictures of the one-room schools in the counties around Roanoke. By 1936, though, Hill gave up on his practice in Roanoke and returned to Washington, where his wife taught in the public schools. He worked as a waiter, attempted to organize a union of waiters and cooks, and generally tried to save money to resume his law practice.[34]

The impetus for Hill's return to Virginia and the law came in 1939, when his former professor Andy Ransom called him to consult on a murder case with two lawyers from Richmond. Those two lawyers happened to be J. Thomas Hewin Jr. and J. Byron Hopkins. Hopkins invited Hill to form a legal firm with him and Hewin. Hill agreed, but upon arriving in Richmond he learned that Hewin had not approved the idea. Hill then set up a small law office in the building next door. Apparently Hill was sympathetic about Marshall's problems with Hopkins and especially Hewin. In his autobiography, Hill recalls how on several occasions Hewin would disappear for days, and then reappear right before a case went to court.[35] As a student of Charles Houston, Hill understood the significance of the salary equalization cases, and he became the legal counsel for the Joint Committee on Teachers' Salary Equalization. Marshall lobbied to tie Hill closer to the association. In a memorandum to Roy Wilkins, he insisted that the association pay Hill fifty dollars for his services in the case. "We have had a tremendous amount of difficulty with local lawyers in Virginia," Marshall explained, "and at last we have one whom we can work with. We should do all we can to continue his good will."[36]

Marshall and Hill, working with Andy Ransom and William Hastie, argued Alston's case before Judge Luther Way of U.S. District Court in early February 1940. Way acknowledged that the school board had discriminated against Alston but decided that since Alston had signed a contract with the school board, the court had no jurisdiction in the case and dismissed it.[37] The lawyers filed an appeal with the Circuit Court of Appeals. In June 1940 the Circuit Court overturned Way's dismissal and remanded the case for hearing in the District Court. The Circuit Court held that the teachers had not waived their constitutional rights when they signed their contracts, and that they had the right to take the school board to court. Moreover, in his opinion Judge John Parker declared that the Norfolk salary scale was clearly discriminatory and unconstitutional: "This is as clear a discrimination on the ground of race as could well be imagined and falls squarely within the inhibition of both the due process and the equal protection clause of the 14th Amendment."[38]

The settlement reached in Alston reveals the challenges that NAACP attorneys faced in litigating these education cases and in negotiating with local black and white communities. Black attorneys could use the law as a tool to advance African Americans' citizenship rights, but they confronted the reality that white people controlled the rules of the game. Court officials made it difficult for the NAACP lawyers to file court documents. Alfred

Anderson, the Norfolk city attorney, created as many opportunities as possible to delay hearings and negotiations in the case. Norfolk city officials also pressured local black leaders to settle for less than the full and immediate equalization of salaries. They proposed that for the year 1941, teachers would be paid a sum of $30,000, and that their salaries would be equalized by 1943. City leaders argued that if they delayed equalizing teachers' salaries, then the African American community could get a new elementary school and funding for the black hospital.[39] More conservative black leaders, like P. B. Young, editor of the *Norfolk Journal and Guide*, were used to negotiating with white officials in this manner. Young had fashioned himself as an "ambassador" between the white and black communities in Norfolk, and he saw the immediate promise of a new elementary school and hospital funding as more important than the goal of equalizing teachers' salaries.[40] Young used his social power in the black community to induce the teachers to vote against their own immediate interests and accept the city's offer "for the benefit of maintaining good racial relations."[41] Joining Young were African Americans who were particularly vulnerable to pressure from city officials, like Winston Douglas, the principal of Booker T. Washington High School. He also urged teachers to accept the equalization plan proposed by the city.[42]

Pressured by their local leaders and against the advice of the lawyers, the teachers accepted the city's plan of gradual equalization. Marshall was livid: "It is the joint opinion of Hastie, Ransom, Hill and myself that this is the most disgraceful termination of any cases involving Negroes in recent years," he told Walter White and Roy Wilkins. Yet the NAACP lawyers did not abandon the teachers in Norfolk. As Marshall explained to L. F. Palmer of the Virginia Teachers Association, he and his colleagues wanted to keep the teachers' salary equalization a "moving fight." If they did not then the fight would die out, and in Marshall's view the lawyers would not feel as if they had completed their job until all the cities and counties in Virginia were equalized.[43] Although the teachers bargained away their financial compensation, they did vote to retain the consent decree drafted by the NAACP lawyers, which stated that the city agreed not to discriminate and to pay black and white teachers equal salaries in the future.[44]

Despite the challenges in Norfolk, the *Alston* decision set an important precedent, establishing that different salary scales for white and black teachers violated the Fourteenth Amendment. In addition, *Alston* cemented Hill's position as the lead lawyer in Virginia upon whom the NAACP would rely. Marshall praised Hill's work and explained his important role in the litigation campaign to members of the NAACP National Office and to other black leaders in Virginia. In a letter to L. F. Palmer, executive secretary of the

Virginia State Teachers Association, Marshall commented that Hill "has worked hard throughout the case and he has given us better cooperation than any other local attorney we have ever had in any of our teachers' salary cases throughout the country." Marshall noted that this comment was not for public consumption, "because it might hamper our other cases, but I want you to know how we feel about Hill." He believed that Hill would "bolster the courage of the teachers to realize that they have an attorney in Virginia on hand at all times for whatever problems might come up."[45]

By the end of 1940 Thurgood Marshall had turned over all the teachers' salary equalization cases to Oliver Hill.[46] In pursuing the education cases, the NAACP lawyers responded to the needs and demands of local African American communities. Parents in those communities desired much more than equal salaries for their black teachers; they desired better educational opportunities for their children. In the wake of the *Alston* decision, Hill worked to educate African Americans about how to achieve their demands. It was "up to the Negroes of Virginia," he insisted, "to see to it that this decision is made effective in every city and county in Virginia." He distributed a memorandum about the procedure local communities should use to equalize teachers' salaries. Hill laid out in plain language the steps involved: organizing a local committee of citizens to lead and coordinate the challenge; making a preliminary investigation of the salary schedule for the teachers; educating the local community about the existing inequalities and the planned challenge; and petitioning the school board to equalize salaries. These steps were to be taken in consultation with Hill. If the school board refused to allow black citizens to see the board's records, then Hill would intervene. Hill also planned to attend school board meetings at which the citizens' petition would be considered. In the memo, Hill emphasized the broader significance of the teachers' salary equalization effort. He encouraged local leaders to explain to their community that the "fight to equalize salaries" was a "fight not only for the teachers but for equal expenditures for schools." "Let this fight," Hill declared, "be the opening gun in a sustained fight to fully equalize school facilities in the community."[47]

The *Alston* case, along with Hill's presence, emboldened black teachers throughout Virginia to initiate campaigns for salary equalization. Following on the heels of the *Alston* decision, African Americans in the cities of Roanoke, Richmond, Newport News, Danville, Lynchburg, and Portsmouth and in Princess Anne County initiated campaigns to equalize teachers' salaries.[48] Teachers in Chesterfield County, Accomac County, Loudoun County, Sussex County, and Norfolk County and in the cities of Clifton Forge and Suffolk also pressed for salary equalization.[49] In several of these communities, the school board responded to the teachers' demands and issued plans to equalize salaries. Where school boards resisted, Hill, along with other NAACP lawyers, sued on the teachers' behalf. They won in court, and then typically negotiated plans under which the school board would equalize salaries over a period of three years.

By stressing the importance of educating the local community about the legal challenge, Hill continued Houston's work of using the legal cases as an organizing vehicle for the NAACP. As he explained, "I was identified with NAACP people, Doc Tinsley and all the rest of them and even the Teachers' Association people. So I just took over the joint committee and . . . I spent practically every weekend riding around in communities developing community support for telling people what we were and what we were planning to do." As Oliver Hill recalled, he and Tinsley "used to ride around to counties on Sunday to organize the NAACP."[50] Hill's work with the NAACP state conference contributed to its growth and strength. During 1941, NAACP leaders helped to organize an additional nine branches, which grew out of the teachers' salary equalization fight.[51] Thurgood Marshall was so impressed with the work of the state conference, he told Roy Wilkins in the national office, that he saw it and the state conference in Oklahoma as "the only two state conferences worth a dime."[52] By 1941 Virginia, with thirty-nine NAACP chapters, had the largest number of branches in the nation.[53]

What emerges in Virginia is a picture of a litigation campaign that moved in many directions at once, as Hill developed strategies for challenging inequalities in education. As early as March 1940, while *Alston* was still pending, Hill began to expand the litigation campaign beyond teacher salary equalization. He traveled to Emporia to discuss with members of the Greensville County league a case to gain bus transportation for black children.[54] In 1941, in Norfolk County, black residents complained about inequalities in teachers' salaries, inequalities in the high school curriculum, and the lack of bus transportation for their children; they had formed an NAACP branch in December 1940 to lead the fight in the community. Before initiating court proceedings, Hill took a group of black students to the white high school in an attempt to enroll them in courses not offered at the black high school. As expected, the white principal refused to register them. In a similar move, Hill, accompanied by a group of black students and local NAACP leaders, stopped a white school bus in the Bowers Hill section of the county and demanded that the bus driver allow the black students onto the bus. The bus driver agreed, until he spotted a photographer from the *Norfolk Journal and Guide*. Afraid of losing his job, the bus driver demanded that the black students get off the bus.[55] Hill soon initiated legal action against the school board in Greensville County.

As Hill worked with local communities, he also cultivated relationships with other African American attorneys in Virginia. Martin A. Martin, a graduate of Howard Law School, class of 1938, worked out of Danville.[56] In 1939, as president of the Danville NAACP branch, Martin had coordinated the efforts to get a high school for African Americans built in the southern part of Pittsylvania County. The county maintained sixteen standardized high schools for white children and one for black children.[57] Martin also began to mount a challenge to the discriminatory teacher salary scale in Danville, and to investigate school facilities and the lack of adequate transportation in surrounding Pittsylvania County.[58] In late 1940 Thurgood Marshall encouraged Martin to work with Hill and the Joint Committee for the Equalization of Teachers' Salaries on the Pittsylvania County cases, so that all the cases in Virginia could be coordinated and financed by the Joint Committee.[59] By 1941 the legal staff of the Virginia state conference of the NAACP included Hill, Martin, and the Petersburg attorneys Robert H. Cooley Jr. and Raymond J. Valentine, both Howard Law School graduates. During 1941 these lawyers were involved in twenty-seven court cases; by November, seven were still pending and they had lost only three.[60] Most significantly, during this time Hill also forged ties with Spottswood W. Robinson III. Born in Richmond in 1916, Robinson attended Virginia Union University and earned his law degree from Howard in 1939. After graduation, he taught at Howard Law School while practicing law in Richmond.[61] According to Hill, he persuaded Robinson to form a firm with him before Hill was inducted into the service in 1943.[62] Soon after, Martin A. Martin joined the firm. Working closely with the Virginia state conference of the NAACP and the NAACP national office, these attorneys would lead civil rights challenges throughout the state for the next two decades.

America's entry into the Second World War had contradictory effects on civil rights activism in Virginia. On the one hand, the war slowed the momentum of activism, as Oliver Hill and others were drafted and as African Americans concentrated on the war effort. Wartime rationing of gas and rubber restricted organizing activities, like driving to meetings in rural counties. Yet at the same time, the democratic rhetoric of the war galvanized African Americans to demand their first-class citizenship rights and challenge segregation directly. On an individual basis, African Americans increasingly refused to comply with segregated seating on public transportation. Working through NAACP branches and voters' leagues, African Americans lobbied at the state and national levels to enact legislation that would eliminate the poll tax. Black activists also increasingly emphasized political participation and voting.

NAACP attorneys not only defended the legal rights of African Americans who challenged segregation but also participated in the emerging assault on segregation in all areas of southern life. During the war, while Oliver Hill was in the army, Spottswood Robinson assumed responsibility for many of the NAACP cases in the state. Robinson, along with Andy Ransom and William Hastie, litigated school cases such as the one in Newport News, where three black principals had been dismissed for their involvement in the movement to equalize teachers' salaries. Robinson also litigated *Morgan v. Virginia* in the lower courts: the case reached the Supreme Court in 1946 and led to the legal abolition of segregated interstate transportation. In another transportation case, Robert Cooley and Raymond Valentine represented Pauli Murray, who had been arrested and jailed in Petersburg for refusing to follow the directions of a bus driver. Cooley and Valentine, working with Luther P. Jackson, a professor at Virginia State College, also organized the Virginia Voters League to coordinate and stimulate black voter participation around the state. They often threatened court action against officials who refused to register black voters. The activities of the Virginia Voters League, as it worked closely with the Virginia state conference of the NAACP, helped to increase the number of African Americans registered to vote. Between 1943 and 1946 close to sixteen thousand black citizens were added to those qualified to vote in Virginia; by 1946 approximately 13 percent of African Americans of voting age were qualified to vote.[63] Moreover, in the years following the Second World War black lawyers such as Oliver Hill, Victor Ashe, and Raymond Valentine ran for political office in hopes of stimulating black voter participation. In 1948 Hill won election to the Richmond City Council, becoming its first black member in the twentieth century.[64]

Yet the NAACP's campaign against inequalities in education emerged as the centerpiece of the postwar assault on segregation. In a memorandum to state conferences of branches in June 1945, Thurgood Marshall asserted, "Education is one of the most important factors being considered in all post-war programs." Noting that states were "making elaborate plans for education" after the war, he urged the state conferences to make the equalization of educational opportunities "the first order of business." "The policy of discrimination against Negroes will continue," Marshall warned, "unless we move and move fast."[65] In December 1945 the president of the Virginia state conference, J. M. Tinsley, called upon the executive board to meet with the conference's legal staff and Thurgood Marshall in January 1946 to discuss the "possibility of waging a fight against the educational system of Virginia."[66]

After that meeting, Robinson and Hill initiated cases that would challenge inequalities in elementary and secondary education. They hammered out the strategy and procedure for litigating these cases at a conference called by Thurgood Marshall. Held in Atlanta in April 1946, the conference included members of the national legal staff and lawyers working in the South, such as Arthur D. Shores of Birmingham and A. P. Tureaud of Louisiana. The attorneys discussed the progress in cases challenging the lack of graduate and professional education for African Americans. The focus then shifted to the question of how to litigate the equalization of elementary and high school facilities, school terms and curriculum, and equipment and bus transportation. In these discussions Hill and Robinson played a leading role. Hill proposed that lawyers seek an "injunction to restrain school boards from denying to Negroes because of race and color equal educational opportunities that are afforded to white[s]." Marshall and the other lawyers agreed that this method would be used both in Louisiana and in Virginia to challenge the lack of high school facilities for African Americans or to bring black schools up to par with the white schools. Marshall asserted that the "question of how to determine equality" was one the lawyers might have to confront down the road but not yet.[67]

As Charles Houston had envisioned the legal campaign back in the early 1930s, the goal of the equalization suits was not to actually equalize the school facilities, because doing so would make the association complicit in perpetuating segregation. Rather, through equalization suits the NAACP hoped to make maintaining two equal but separate school systems so expensive that southern school boards would decide to abandon segregation altogether. In pursuing these equalization cases, what the NAACP attempted to do was first, demonstrate that inequalities existed, and second, ask the court for an injunction barring the school board from discriminating against African Americans any further. The lawyers employed a litigation strategy that left the choice of remedy to the defendants. In other words, the NAACP asked the court to prevent a school board from treating African American students unequally, but then it became the school board's responsibility to figure out how to achieve equal school facilities.[68]

By November 1946 Robinson and Hill had school facilities cases at various stages of preparation in six counties and had filed suit in King George County. They planned to take legal action in an additional seven counties. In Chesterfield County, directly south of Richmond, they planned to challenge inequalities in teachers' salaries; this was the first case against the "discriminatory rating system" employed by counties to pay black teachers less money than white teachers.[69] The work that Robinson and Hill had already commenced moved Thurgood Marshall to choose Virginia as the site of an intensive campaign to attack inequalities in school facilities at the elementary and secondary school levels in November 1947. As Mark Tushnet has argued, Marshall understood that a direct attack on segregated education would depend on the readiness of NAACP members to support the litigation, as well as on the outcome of a series of graduate school cases that were then making their way to the Supreme Court. Therefore, Marshall decided to test the logistics of what an equalization campaign would cost in terms of money and manpower.

In late 1947, with support from the national office, the state conference launched an all-out attack on segregated education. Virginia was selected because of the "efficiency and fund-raising record of its state NAACP conference, and because of the glaring inequalities in its school system."[70] Indeed, the Virginia State Conference of Branches was positioned to support a sustained legal campaign. By 1946 the state conference had grown to ninety-one branches with 24,843 members, leading the organization to hire W. Lester Banks, a former school principal and veteran of the Second World War, to serve as its first full-time executive secretary. In the late 1940s Banks logged over thirty thousand miles a year, canvassing the state. He often drove through rural areas with the letters "NAACP" boldly displayed on the rear window of his car, raising support for the organization and its litigation campaign.[71] The state conference also expanded its legal staff from six to eleven lawyers. By 1947 the state conference had a member of the legal staff within easy reach of any part of the state. Moreover, in preparation for the litigation campaign, the Virginia state conference had gained approval from the NAACP board of directors to establish a defense fund. Of each dollar raised, fifty cents would go to the state conference, thirty cents would go to the branches, and twenty cents would go to the national office. Normally, the NAACP divided funds evenly between the branches and the national office, with no money going to the state conference.[72]

Spottswood W. Robinson III, who took leave from teaching at Howard Law School, and Lester Banks, executive secretary of the Virginia NAACP, shared responsibility for much of the work of the equalization campaign. Banks took primary responsibility for mobilizing the community, asking local residents to conduct preliminary investigations of school facilities and securing prospective plaintiffs for a case. Robinson participated in many of these meetings, but his main charge was the legal aspect of the equalization campaign, and thus he spent much of his time investigating school inequalities, petitioning school boards, and initiating court action.[73] Like Charles Houston during the 1930s, Banks and Robinson went to some lengths to educate local communities about the NAACP's program. As Banks explained in his annual report in 1949, during the initial mass meeting held to discuss a possible challenge to educational inequalities in a county, "the Association's program is explained and the people are asked what they want—piecemeal improvements or their children's constitutional rights."

"I can assure you this is no easy task," Banks added. "While most of our parents want someone else to get for them and their children their constitutional rights, it becomes a different problem when they are told that the national office, nor the State Conference, nor the local branch can do the job for them." Banks had nothing but praise for the "lay citizens" around the state who were willing to "roll up their sleeves" and do what was required to initiate legal action.[74] Through Robinson's and Banks's efforts, the NAACP initiated actions in seventy-five school districts.[75]

By the end of January 1948, the Virginia NAACP had entered four cases that addressed inequalities in elementary and secondary schools. Three of the cases involved school facilities in counties in the Tidewater (Gloucester, King George, and Surry), the fourth inequalities in teachers' salaries in Chesterfield County, which bordered the city of Richmond.[76] At the end of March 1948, Judge Sterling Hutcheson made a sweeping decision in the Surry County case in Federal District Court. He ordered the school board and the superintendent to "immediately make plans to equalize the educational facilities and opportunities for Negro children in Surry County." Hutcheson permanently enjoined the school board from discriminating against black children in "providing and maintaining school facilities, including buildings, equipment, bus transportation, libraries, and qualified instructional and janitorial personnel." He also ordered the school board to equalize salaries between white and black teachers in the county by the school year 1949–50.[77] The Surry County decision, in the opinion of one scholar, was as significant as the *Alston* decision, because it established a precedent that NAACP lawyers could use in other cases, and it motivated other parents and NAACP branches to challenge inequalities in their own schools.[78] Less than two weeks later, Judge Hutcheson issued similar decisions in the cases in Chesterfield, Gloucester, and King George counties. The *Richmond Times-Dispatch*, in evaluating the Surry County decision, noted that Hutcheson's decision "serves to stress the unconstitutionality and illegality of discriminatory educational facilities for white and colored children in the public schools of Virginia." "Either schools for the two races will be made substantially equal, or the State may be ordered by the Federal courts to operate a single system, and to admit all children, irrespective of race," warned the *Times-Dispatch*. "The handwriting on the wall seems plain, in light of Judge Hutcheson's decision. We must act accordingly." In the wake of these decisions, Thurgood Marshall in early 1949 announced that the litigation fight would increase to bring cases in 124 school jurisdictions in Virginia.[79]

By 1950 the NAACP attorneys had won favorable injunctions or declarations in most of the equalization suits they had brought, but they spent countless hours making "equality" real, by forcing school boards to comply with the court orders. It was clear that the equalization strategy had outlived its usefulness. "This equalization method of fighting them one case at a time failed to produce enough results," Oliver Hill observed in an interview in the 1970s. Yet the *Washington Post* reported that the NAACP's equalization campaign had increased teachers' salaries by $50 million and improved transportation and school facilities for African Americans.[80] In 1951 Spottswood Robinson gave a compelling explanation of the weaknesses in the equalization campaign. The equalization approach stressed the physical inequalities of segregated education but overlooked "its adverse psychological and other intangible consequences." "We won legal victories without measurably increasing the Negro student's share in the educational wealth," he insisted. "We refined the judicial concept of the equal protection of the laws but in practice it was not applied. We wrote the meaning of equality under the Constitution into the case reports but failed to get it into the public schools. There was the even greater danger that, in those instances in which our suits were followed by construction of Negro school facilities, we were nailing the lid on our own coffin by the production of newer and costlier monuments to segregation as by-products of our efforts." Therefore, a change in strategy, Robinson concluded, was "inevitable."[81]

In 1950, soon after the Supreme Court's decisions in the *Sweatt* and *McLaurin* cases, the NAACP announced that it would abandon the equalization suits and only sue on the grounds that segregated education was itself unconstitutional.[82] It was on this basis that Hill and Robinson agreed to sue the school board in Prince Edward County in April 1951. A high school junior named Barbara Johns had called Hill and Robinson after she led her fellow students at Robert R. Moton High School in a strike, protesting against the terribly unequal school conditions they had to endure. Hill and Robinson had not intended to litigate a case in rural, southside Virginia, but after meeting with the students and parents they agreed to take the case on the condition that they would sue to desegregate the schools rather than to equalize facilities. The Prince Edward County case became one of the five cases subsumed under *Brown v. Board of Education*, in which the Supreme Court in 1954 declared segregated education unconstitutional.

The energy and commitment of black attorneys shaped the scope of civil rights activism in Virginia and ultimately influenced the trajectory of the NAACP's national strategy in challenging inequalities in education. Hill and Robinson developed litigation strategies in teachers' salary and school equalization cases that were adopted and used in other states. They also played a signal role in the NAACP's litigation campaign. Robert L. Carter, who was assistant special counsel for the NAACP from 1944 to 1956, has observed that the firm of Hill, Robinson, and Martin was the only group of local lawyers that the national office worked with regularly.[83] Hill and Robinson collaborated with other attorneys to litigate school cases in Atlanta and Durham, North Carolina. By the late 1940s Spottswood Robinson was virtually a member of the association's national legal staff; in late 1950 he was named its southeastern regional counsel. Thurgood Marshall acknowledged how important the Virginia lawyers were to the association's legal campaign. In late 1948 he suggested that a young lawyer named Marshall Tate, who would be running the legal campaign in Texas, go to Virginia to watch Robinson and the other Virginia lawyers prepare for trial in two education cases. "The Virginia lawyers did the best job of any group I know of in preparing these education cases," Marshall observed, "and the experience will be invaluable to Tate."[84] Marshall was not the only one who knew how valuable the Virginia lawyers were: Virginia politicians believed that targeting the attorneys was the most effective way to undercut the power of the NAACP in the state. In 1955 and 1956, as part of its program of massive resistance, the Virginia General Assembly passed a series of anti-NAACP laws that greatly restricted the actions of NAACP lawyers.[85] Consequently, the association's national legal staff devoted a great deal of energy during the post-*Brown* era to challenging, and eventually overturning, these anti-NAACP laws in court.

When seen from the perspective of Virginia, a more complete picture of the NAACP litigation campaign that culminated in *Brown* emerges. This campaign was not planned and directed solely by legal staff in the NAACP national office. It did not move forward at a lockstep pace; it was driven neither from the top down nor from the bottom up. Rather, it was a collaborative enterprise, shaped fundamentally by the experiences of lawyers in Virginia who worked with local communities and litigated cases. During the era of segregation, these attorneys served as a civil rights vanguard, tapping into the aspirations of black communities across Virginia and helping create a sustainable, organized struggle for first-class citizenship rights.

## Notes

1 "Policy in the Program against Jim Crow Education," *Historical Souvenir Program of the 16th Annual Convention of the State Conference of Branches*, Richmond, 12–14 October 1951, 41, group II, box C-212, Papers of the National Association for the Advancement of Colored People, Manuscripts Division, Library of Congress, Washington (hereafter cited as NAACP Papers).

2 Charles H. Houston, "Personal Observations on the Summary of Studies in Legal Education as Applied to the Howard University School of Law," unpublished manuscript, 28 May 1929, quoted in Genna Rae McNeil, *Groundwork: Charles Hamilton Houston and the Struggle for Civil Rights* (Philadelphia: University of Pennsylvania Press, 1983), 71.

3 Charles H. Houston, "The Need for Negro Lawyers," *Journal of Negro Education* 4 (January 1935): 52.

4 McNeil, *Groundwork*, 114–17.

5 Charles H. Houston, "Memorandum for the Joint Committee of the NAACP and the American Fund for Public Service, Inc.," 26 October 1934, group I, box C-199, NAACP Papers.

6 Charles H. Houston, "Educational Inequalities Must Go," *Crisis* 42 (October 1935): 300.

7 Houston, "Memorandum for the Joint Committee."

8 Houston, "Educational Inequalities Must Go," 301.

9 Mark V. Tushnet, *The NAACP's Legal Strategy against Segregated Education, 1925–1950* (Chapel Hill: University of North Carolina Press, 1987), 42–43.

10 *Id.* at 43.

11 "The Problem Remains," *Richmond Times-Dispatch*, 14 February 1929.

12 For discussion of the legal struggles of African Americans in the 1920s, see Larissa M. Smith, "Where the South Begins: Black Politics and Civil Rights Activism in Virginia, 1930–1951" (diss., Emory University, 2001), 49–65. For discussion of white élites' attitudes toward race relations, see J. Douglas Smith, "Managing White Supremacy: Politics and Culture in Virginia, 1919–1939" (diss., University of Virginia, 1998).

13 Charles H. Houston to M. A. Norrell, 11 September 1935, group I, box C-203, NAACP Papers.

14 "Cause for Shame," *Norfolk Journal and Guide*, 10 August 1929.

15 J. Douglas Smith, "Managing White Supremacy," 314–15. P. B. Young, "Clearing the Atmosphere," text of a speech he delivered at a citizens' protest meeting in the wake of Aline Black's dismissal from the Norfolk city schools, reprinted in the *Norfolk Journal and Guide*, 1 July 1939.

16 Charles H. Houston to Hazel W. Reid (Portsmouth branch), 26 September 1935, 4 October 1935, 11 October 1935, all in group I, box G-210, NAACP Papers; W. P. Milner (Norfolk branch) to Charles H. Houston, 10 October 1935, group I, box G-208, NAACP Papers; Charles H. Houston to W. P. Milner, 11 October 1935, group I, box G-208, NAACP Papers; Charles H. Houston to Thomas L. Dabney, 21 November 1935, group I, box G-207, NAACP Papers.

17 Charles H. Houston to Raymond Valentine, 17 October 1935, 31 October 1935, 20 November 1935, group I, box C-203, NAACP Papers; Charles H. Houston to J. Byron Hopkins, 1 November 1935, all in group I, box C-203, NAACP Papers. For an article based on the research conducted on that trip, see Charles H. Houston, "Senator Glass Aided School Inequalities," *Crisis* 43 (January 1936): 15.

18 Virginia Itinerary, 20 November 1935, box 163-39, folder 6, Charles H.

Houston Papers, Moorland-Spingarn Research Center, Howard University, Washington.

19  W. P. Milner to Walter White, 2 February 1935, group I, box G-206, NAACP Papers.

20  Leon Ransom to Charles Houston, 3 December 1935, group I, box G-206, NAACP Papers.

21  Alfreda A. Madison to Charles H. Houston, 2 September 1937, group I, box D-91, NAACP Papers.

22  James A. Jones to Thurgood Marshall, 5 December 1937, group I, box D-91, NAACP Papers.

23  Thomas L. Dabney to Walter White, 17 June 1935, group I, box G-207, NAACP Papers.

24  Memorandum from E. Frederic Morrow to Mr. White, Mr. Pickens, Mr. Wilkins, and Miss Jackson, 30 November 1937, group I, box G-206, NAACP Papers.

25  Charles H. Houston to William Houston, 14 April 1938, group I, box C-82, NAACP Papers, quoted in Tushnet, *The NAACP's Legal Strategy against Segregated Education*, 35.

26  Mark V. Tushnet, *Making Civil Rights Law: Thurgood Marshall and the Supreme Court, 1939–1961* (New York: Oxford University Press, 1994), 11–23.

27  Thurgood Marshall to J. M. Tinsley, 30 August 1937, group I, box D-91, NAACP Papers.

28  J. Rupert Picott, *History of the Virginia Teachers Association* (Washington: National Education Association, 1975), 107–8.

29  Draft of minutes, meeting of committee from Virginia State Teachers Association and Virginia State Conference of the NAACP, 26 November 1937, group I, box D-91, NAACP Papers; memorandum from Thurgood Marshall to Walter White concerning meeting with Virginia State Teachers Association, 2 December 1937, group I, box D-91, NAACP Papers.

30  Thurgood Marshall to P. B. Young, 31 October 1938, group I, box D-91, NAACP Papers; "First Step Taken in Norfolk to Equalize Salaries of White and Negro," *Richmond Times-Dispatch*, 1 November 1938.

31  "Virginia Teacher Loses in Lower Court; Appeals," *Crisis* 46 (1939): 213–14; Earl Lewis, *In Their Own Interests*, 159; "No Contract For Teacher Who Filed Pay Suit," *Norfolk Journal and Guide*, 24 June 1939.

32  J. M. Tinsley to J. Byron Hopkins, 7 March 1938, group I, box D-91, NAACP Papers; J. M. Tinsley to Thurgood Marshall, notation at bottom of letter from Marshall to Tinsley, 10 June 1938, group I, box D-91, NAACP Papers.

33  Oliver W. Hill Sr., *The Big Bang: Brown v. Board of Education and Beyond*, ed. Jonathan K. Stubbs (Winter Park, Fla: Four-G, 2000), 4, 36, 56. For why Hill decided to go to law school see 71–72; for meeting Thurgood Marshall see 73–74; for experiences during law school see 76–85.

34  *Id.* at 93, 98–100; "Conversations with Civil Rights Crusaders," *Virginia Lawyer* 37 (February 1989): 13.

35  Hill, *The Big Bang*, 101–2.

36 Thurgood Marshall to Roy Wilkins, 24 April 1940, group II, box B-181, NAACP Papers.

37 Thurgood Marshall to Carl Murphy, 13 February 1940, group II, box B-181, NAACP Papers.

38 "Along the NAACP Battlefront," *Crisis* 47 (September 1940): 290–91.

39 Thurgood Marshall to P. B. Young, 29 March 1940, group II, box B-182, NAACP Papers; Oliver Hill to Marshall, Hastie, and Ransom, 27 June 1940, group II, box B-181, NAACP Papers.

40 Henry Louis Suggs, *P. B. Young, Newspaperman: Race, Politics, and Journalism in the New South, 1910–1962* (Charlottesville: University Press of Virginia, 1988), 95.

41 Memorandum from Thurgood Marshall to White and Wilkins, 8 November 1940, group II, box B-182, NAACP Papers.

42 For additional discussion of the *Alston* case see Smith, "Where the South Begins," 153–67.

43 Thurgood Marshall to L. F. Palmer, 18 November 1940, group II, box B-182, NAACP Papers.

44 Thurgood Marshall to Melvin Alston, 4 December 1940, Marshall to members of Joint Committee on Teachers' Salaries, 8 January 1941, Alfred Anderson to Oliver Hill, 6 January 1941, all in group II, box B-182, NAACP Papers.

45 Thurgood Marshall to L. F. Palmer, 5 October 1940, group II, box B-182, NAACP Papers.

46 Thurgood Marshall to Walter Williamson, 21 January 1941, group II, box B-182, NAACP Papers.

47 "Memorandum of Program for Equalization of Teachers' Salaries in Virginia," included in Oliver Hill to Joseph Waddy, 3 December 1940, box 163–30, folder 12, Charles H. Houston Papers, Moorland-Spingarn Research Center, Howard University, Washington.

48 "Pay Suits Loom over South," *Norfolk Journal and Guide*, 14 December 1940; "Move Gains in States," *Norfolk Journal and Guide*, 28 December 1940.

49 "Chesterfield Citizens Back Pay Parity Move," "Accomac Teachers Ask for Pay Parity," "Clifton Forge May Adopt Year Plan for Equalization," "Norfolk County Teachers Petition for Pay Raises," all in *Norfolk Journal and Guide*, 21 December 1940; "Loudoun County Votes Equalization," "Norfolk County Board Petitioned," "Suffolk Teachers Submit Petition," "Sussex County Asks Equalization," all in *Norfolk Journal and Guide*, 28 December 1940.

50 "Conversations with Civil Rights Crusaders," 14; Oliver W. Hill interview with author, Richmond, 21 February 2001.

51 "Proceedings of the Sixth Annual Virginia State Conference of the NAACP," 8–9 November 1941, group II, box C-210, NAACP Papers.

52 Thurgood Marshall to Roy Wilkins, 14 February 1940, group II, box C-210, NAACP Papers.

53 Membership branch statistics, 1940–46, group II, box C-380, NAACP Papers.

54 Oliver Hill to Leon A. Ransom, 11 March 1940, group II, box B-181, NAACP

Papers; "Father Sues to Get Bus for School Child," NAACP press release, 14 March 1941, group II, box B-147, NAACP Papers; "Virginia County May Provide School Buses," NAACP press release, 21 March 1941, group II, box B-147, NAACP Papers.

55 "Norfolk County Teachers Petition for Pay Raises," *Norfolk Journal and Guide*, 21 December 1940; "Norfolk County Faces Suit over School Buses," *Norfolk Journal and Guide*, 22 November 1941.

56 Eric W. Rise, *The Martinsville Seven: Race, Rape, and Capital Punishment* (Charlottesville: University Press of Virginia, 1995), 72; Oliver W. Hill, *The Big Bang*, 104–5; Peter Wallenstein, " 'I Went to Law School to Fight Segregation': Oliver W. Hill and the Siege in Virginia against Jim Crow" (paper presented at annual meeting of the Southern Historical Association, 6 November 1992). I want to thank Professor Wallenstein for providing me with a copy of his paper.

57 Martin A. Martin to Thurgood Marshall, 10 August 1940, 9 September 1940, both in group II, box B-147, NAACP Papers; "Along the NAACP Battlefront," *Crisis* 47 (September 1940): 295.

58 Thurgood Marshall to Martin A. Martin, 10 December 1940, group II, box B-182, NAACP Papers. Also see telegrams from Martin to Marshall, 9 December 1940, Martin to Marshall, 11 December 1940, Marshall to Martin, 12 December 1940, group II, box B-182, NAACP Papers; Martin A. Martin to Thurgood Marshall, 16 September 1941, group II, box B-147, NAACP Papers.

59 Thurgood Marshall to Martin A. Martin, 10 December 1940, group II, box B-182, NAACP Papers.

60 Program of the Sixth Annual Conference of the Virginia State Conference of the NAACP, 8–9 November 1941, group II, box C-210, NAACP Papers; "Proceedings of the Sixth Annual Virginia State Conference," group II, box C-210, NAACP Papers.

61 W. Augustus Low, ed., *Encyclopedia of Black America* (New York: McGraw-Hill, 1981), 735.

62 Hill, *The Big Bang*, 191.

63 Luther P. Jackson, *Seventh Annual Report, Voting Status of Negroes in Virginia, 1946* (Richmond: Quality Printing, May 1947).

64 For discussion of the attorneys' participation in the civil rights struggles of the 1940s see Smith, "Where the South Begins," 171–92, 198–217, 277–81.

65 Thurgood Marshall to State Conference of Branches, 29 June 1947, group II, box B-67, NAACP Papers.

66 J. M. Tinsley to Executive Board, 28 December 1945, box 1, Esther I. Cooper Papers, Moorland-Spingarn Research Center, Howard University, Washington.

67 Robert L. Carter, "Digest of Proceedings in Atlanta Conference," 27 April 1946, group II, box B-137, NAACP Papers.

68 Tushnet, *The NAACP's Legal Strategy against Segregated Education*, 110–11. Also see Tushnet, *Making Civil Rights Law*, 127.

69 Report of the Legal Committee, 11th Annual Virginia State Conference of

Branches, 9–10 November 1946, Richmond, box 2, Esther I. Cooper Papers, Moorland-Spingarn Research Center, Howard University, Washington.

70 "Statewide School Suits Planned," *Norfolk Journal and Guide*, 8 November 1947. Also see Special Release, 31 October 1947, group II, box C-211, NAACP Papers.

71 Membership Branch Statistics, 1945–46, group II, box C-380, NAACP Papers; Robert A. Pratt, "New Directions in Civil Rights History," *Virginia Magazine of History and Biography* 104 (winter 1996): 152.

72 "VA NAACP Meets Next in Staunton," *Norfolk Journal and Guide*, 8 November 1947; "The Call to Action," 1947 [likely November or December], group II, box C-211, NAACP Papers; W. Lester Banks to Gloster Current, 24 August 1950, group II, box C-211, NAACP Papers.

73 "Virginia Testing Ground for Move against Jim Crow Schools," *Norfolk Journal and Guide*, 24 January 1948; "The Call to Action." Also see Tushnet, *The NAACP's Legal Strategy against Segregated Education*, 110.

74 W. Lester Banks, Secretary's Annual Report, 21 October 1949, group II, box C-211, NAACP Papers.

75 Richard Kluger, *Simple Justice* (New York: Vintage, 1977), 473–74.

76 "Virginia Testing Ground for Move against Jim Crow Schools," *Norfolk Journal and Guide*, 24 January 1948.

77 "Schools Ordered Equalized," *Norfolk Journal and Guide*, 3 April 1948.

78 Peter Wallenstein, "Seizing the 'Equal' in 'Separate but Equal': The NAACP and the Public Schools—Virginia in the 1940s" (paper presented at the annual meeting of the American Society for Legal History, Richmond, 18 October 1996; paper in author's possession), 14.

79 Kluger, *Simple Justice*, 473–74.

80 *Id.* at 474.

81 "Policy in the Program against Jim Crow Education," *Historical Souvenir Program*, 41, group II, box C-212, NAACP Papers.

82 Kluger, *Simple Justice*, 267–69, 280–84.

83 Robert L. Carter, interview with the author, Washington, July 2002.

84 Thurgood Marshall to Donald Jones, 13 October 1948, group II, box B-99, NAACP Papers.

85 On the Virginia General Assembly's attack on NAACP attorneys see Tushnet, *Making Civil Rights Law*, 274–82.

PATRICIA SULLIVAN

# Prelude to *Brown*

## Education and the Struggle for Racial Justice during

## the NAACP's Formative Decades, 1909–1934

*Brown v. Board of Education* is recognized as one of the most momentous Supreme Court decisions in American history, and a turning point in the modern struggle for civil rights. In recent years, however, a growing number of scholars have emphasized the limitations of the *Brown* decision—namely its failure to secure the transformation envisioned by Chief Justice Earl Warren in May 1954 when he issued the opinion striking down racial segregation in public schools. The phrases "broken promise" and "troubled legacy" frequently recur in public assessments of *Brown*. Rather than being viewed as a critical opening toward a decade of escalating civil rights protest that culminated in the fall of legalized segregation in the South, *Brown* has come to symbolize the failure of the civil rights movement to fundamentally alter structures of racial inequality and discrimination that continue to inhibit the educational opportunities of many black children. *Brown* indeed carries a heavy burden.[1]

Yet to fully assess the significance of *Brown* and its achievements, a deeper understanding of how *Brown* fit into the broader strategy designed by the NAACP is essential. This chapter will explore some of the factors that set the NAACP on "the road to *Brown*" in 1934, when Charles Houston launched the legal campaign that led to the *Brown* ruling two decades later. It is particularly notable that at this juncture the NAACP chose to mount a legal campaign focusing on school segregation in the South, with little attention to growing educational inequities in the North. This decision had several causes, not the least of which were constraints and scarcity of resources as well as an understanding of where the openings might be for mounting a sustained and effective challenge to the ideology and practice of white supremacy, a reality that by 1934 knew no regional boundaries. A fuller understanding of the assumptions, goals, and choices that shaped the legal campaign against racial discrimination in public schools is essential if one is to take a full measure of the historic significance of *Brown* and weigh what it achieved, what it failed to achieve, and why.

Segregation and public education were the subject of the first editorial published in the *Crisis*, the official magazine of the National Association for the Advancement of Colored People. Writing in the fall of 1910, its editor, W. E. B. Du Bois, noted a quiet trend toward establishing separate schools for black children in several northern cities, including Chicago; Philadelphia; Atlantic City, New Jersey; and Columbus, Ohio. This trend was part of a broader movement toward segregation in response to the steady migration of southern blacks to the urban North. Du Bois viewed this disturbing development as an effort to remove the burden of educating poorly prepared black students from the community at large, and appealed to blacks and whites to resist it. Racial segregation in the schools, Du Bois warned, would undermine a primary purpose of public education, which was to advance "human contact, human acquaintanceship, and human sympathy," and would also obstruct black advancement. It was "an argument against democracy and an attempt to shift public responsibility from the shoulders of the public" to the rising class of black people and their children.[2]

The issue of education and schools was considered within the broad framework of the NAACP's evolving program. During its formative years, the association directed its efforts toward containing the spread of racial discrimination and segregation in the North while building a foundation for mounting a national movement to advance racial justice. The organizational structure and strategies that would later be used to great effect in the legal campaign culminating in *Brown* were developed during this time. Another significant development was the evolution of Du Bois's ideas about segregation in schools as racial segregation became more deeply entrenched throughout the United States. A fuller explanation of both areas offers an important context for evaluating the considerations shaping the campaign for school desegregation that dominated the NAACP's program from 1934 to 1954.

The NAACP was established in 1909 at the initiative of a small group of white progressive reformers. The association was a self-consciously interracial enterprise, and its earliest members represented a broad spectrum of views. They were joined by a sense of urgency and a commitment to halt the downward spiral of black life and race relations that had proceeded unabated since the 1890s. From the beginning, the NAACP attempted to nationalize the race question both by emphasizing that the routine violation of constitutional rights in the South was a national issue and by exposing patterns of racial discrimination and inequality in the North.

The early program was dictated by efforts to grasp the totality of the challenge that the organization faced as it responded to some of the most egregious violations of civil rights while working to secure the support essential for survival. Early efforts focused on individual cases of lynching, peonage, and police brutality, discussions about how to enforce existing civil rights laws in the North, and thoughts about strategy for challenging segregation and disfranchisement laws in the South. Education was also an area of concern. Plans for a scientific study of black schools in the South were discussed early on, and a committee was established to investigate the issue of national aid to education. Early in 1911 the NAACP endorsed the revival of the Blair Bill, legislation sponsored by Senator Henry Blair of New Hampshire in the 1880s that provided large grants to the states apportioned in ratio to the rate of illiteracy.[3]

The ambitions of the early leaders of the NAACP vastly exceeded the resources they were able to marshal. Oswald Garrison Villard, chairman of the NAACP's board of directors, had assumed that $1 million would be sufficient to launch the program; after a year he had raised barely $1,000. With scant funding, the NAACP's early program lacked a strong focus, one that would have distinguished it as an organization capable of not only defining the problem but also of effectively challenging the growing assault on the lives and opportunities of black people in America. Most of the black press remained cool to this white-dominated enterprise, and few saw it as a vehicle for pushing against the tightening web of racial proscription and discrimination. This changed dramatically, however, when the NAACP rose to meet the spread of Jim Crow in the federal government after the inauguration of Woodrow Wilson and the ascendancy of "Southern Democracy" in the nation's capital.

The NAACP's response to Woodrow Wilson's segregationist policies was a major turning point for the fledgling organization. From 1913 to 1916 the organizational structure that would define the NAACP for the next fifty years took shape. During this period, the association established a lobbying presence in Washington, launched a program of fieldwork and branch building "to federate and organize the local battle against race prejudice," and began a systematic legal campaign to roll back discriminatory laws.[4]

The Wilson administration's expansion of segregation in the federal government galvanized the NAACP. Largely through the efforts of its secretary, May Childs Nerney, the association combined investigative reporting, publicity, and a nationwide mobilization campaign to frame the issue in the public mind and generate mass protests. Through its newly organized Washington branch, the NAACP moved decisively into the arena of national politics. The timing was critical. During Wilson's first term, southern Democrats in particular flooded Congress with discriminatory legislation, including bills that would ban interracial marriages, establish residential segregation and segregate the streetcars in Washington, make blacks ineligible for service in the Army or Navy, require segregation in the federal government, and bar people of African descent from immigrating to the United States. The Washington branch acted as the association's congressional office and led the local fight against hostile legislation, while Nerney, upon receiving word of discriminatory measures, alerted branches and members to telegram their representatives in protest against particular bills.[5]

The campaign against segregation in the federal government and anti-black legislation in Congress raised the national profile of the NAACP and generated growing interest and support for the organization. The *Washington Bee*, formerly a critic, hailed the NAACP as "the modern abolition movement." An infusion of financial support from blacks in Washington and other parts of the country lifted the association out of debt and left it with a balance of $1,000 in the treasury as of January 1914. In the fall of 1913 the association was able to hire a full-time attorney, thanks to special contributions raised by Nerney from ten branches that covered his salary for a year. By the end of 1913 membership had more than doubled, to upwards of three thousand, organized into twenty-four branches; 80 percent of the members were black. The association continued to encourage the enlistment of white members, but the requirement that branches include both black and white members was less rigorously enforced. The annual report for 1913 noted what had become obvious: if the NAACP was to succeed, "it must be increasingly supported by its colored members."[6]

The NAACP's fight against segregation in the federal government merged into a concerted effort to contain the spread of racial segregation and discrimination outside the South, providing the association with one of its most effective organizing tools. Even before the Great Migration during the years surrounding the First World War, a steady migration of blacks to cities in the North and the West, along with the growth of a small but prosperous group of black professionals, activated what Du Bois described as "the American leaven of race prejudice." Increasingly, blacks were barred from restaurants, theaters, hotels, and other places of public accommodation, often in violation of state civil rights laws. Cities, particularly in border states, sought to enact a variety of laws that would strictly limit where blacks could live, while mobs policed the boundaries of predominantly white neighborhoods. The trend toward segregating black children into separate schools steadily increased. Paralleling the flood of discriminatory legislation in the nation's capital, anti-intermarriage bills were debated in the state legislatures of New York, Pennsylvania, Ohio, California, Illinois, Michigan, Wisconsin, Washington, Colorado, Kansas, and Nebraska during 1913 and 1914.[7] The fight against this insidious trend, Du Bois editorialized in the spring of 1913, had to be waged collectively and continuously. "The blows of racial and color prejudices fall on all alike, rich and poor, educated and ignorant, and all must stand together and fight," he explained. Through its system of vigilance committees and branches, the NAACP offered a national structure for exchanging experiences, coordinating activities, and systematizing scattered local efforts against race prejudice into "steady, persistent, unwavering pressure." While branches provided the foundation and support for the national office, Du Bois explained, their main purpose was to organize the local fight against race prejudice.[8]

Under May Nerney's direction, a program of fieldwork was aimed at expanding the reach of the NAACP by increasing black membership and connecting the national office with the diverse realities of black life and evolving patterns of racial discrimination. The NAACP relied on leading figures from the national office, particularly Du Bois and Joel Spingarn, who succeeded Villard as chairman, to bring the program of the association to black communities across the country through speaking tours and mass meetings. With the hiring of a full-time lawyer late in 1913 to direct its legal campaign, the NAACP created another avenue for building on the publicity generated by the fight against segregation in the federal government and working with local communities to organize a legal challenge against the rising tide of racial discrimination.

While Du Bois and Spingarn preached the gospel of the "New Abolitionism," the NAACP's newly hired attorney, Charles Brinsmade, initiated a systematic legal campaign that bolstered efforts to engage local communities in the national fight against race discrimination. Brinsmade, a recent graduate of Harvard Law School, was hired on a one-year contract with funds raised from a special appeal to the branches. Working closely with Nerney and the NAACP's legal committee, Brinsmade implemented an expanded legal campaign which combined litigation aimed at building up a body of civil rights law with an active program of fieldwork. The overarching goal of the legal bureau was to secure a series of judicial decisions which would define the law on the matter of civil and political rights, molding it so far as possible to admit no distinction based on race or color. This ambitious program depended on cooperation with communities around the country, where the patterns of racial discrimination were given form and meaning.[9]

Working through branches and membership, the legal bureau aimed to establish the NAACP as a clearinghouse for cases of racial discrimination. Allowing that each locality had its peculiar problems—whether they concerned education, residential segregation, police brutality, job discrimination, public accommodations—Brinsmade explained that all should be regarded as manifestations of "the one evil we are fighting, namely, race discrimination." Race discrimination, he emphasized, was a national problem, the common denominator of seemingly local problems, and the primary focus of the NAACP's legal campaign. In a preliminary effort to coordinate a national program, Brinsmade collected information from each branch regarding its legal program and its arrangements with local attorneys, while also appealing to them and to the large readership of the *Crisis* to contact the national office with information about cases of race discrimination. While the national office was not in a position to provide financial assistance, it would offer legal advice. Not surprisingly, the office was quickly flooded with requests, through the mail and in person, for advice and assistance on a scale that it was impossible for one lawyer to meet.[10]

While the scope of the NAACP's legal interests far exceeded its ability to offer assistance, these early efforts helped to establish a framework for future growth. The focus of the new legal bureau was in line with the chief concern that had led to the founding of the NAACP and had heightened with the extension of segregation in the federal government under President Wilson—namely to counter the spread of segregationist ideas and practices in the North. The most immediate and pervasive expression of this trend was in the area of housing. The migration of blacks into border and northern cities fueled efforts by whites to contain black residents in racially defined areas, which were increasingly overcrowded and chronically underserved. At the same time, the scarcity of housing along with the growth of a small black professional class caused increasing numbers of African Americans to seek housing in exclusively or predominantly white neighborhoods. Mob terror and the destruction of black homeowners' property was the most common response when African Americans settled in areas considered "for whites only." Following the lead of Baltimore, a number of cities and towns experimented with residential segregation ordinances that sought to maintain existing racial boundaries under the force of law.

By the time Brinsmade joined the NAACP staff late in 1913, the trend toward residential segregation had accelerated. Legal ordinances as well as privately drawn plans were enacted or pending in cities around the country, from Birmingham, Alabama, to New York City, but primarily in the border states and the upper South. Brinsmade began looking for the best case for testing the constitutionality of residential segregation laws. Several factors were critical in making this determination, including the wording of the law and the presence of a unified black community willing to cooperate, through local counsel, with the NAACP's legal bureau in bringing a legal challenge. In the spring of 1914 the NAACP agreed to work with the National Urban League to help organize blacks in opposition to residential segregation laws in Richmond and Louisville. Nerney visited Richmond and Brinsmade visited Louisville to meet with local blacks active in the anti-segregation fight. Ultimately it was agreed that Louisville offered the most promising opportunity to mount a constitutional challenge.[11]

The legal campaign against residential segregation ordinances antici-pated the approach that Charles Houston would use in mounting the cam-paign against segregated schools. Fieldwork and branch building at the local level were essential counterparts to litigation. The NAACP's national office and its legal representative worked closely with blacks in Louisville who organized a branch in response to the residential segregation ordi-nance, and raised the money needed to support a legal challenge. While the Louisville case moved forward, representatives of the NAACP's national office visited several cities to support local efforts against residential segre-gation ordinances that had been enacted or were pending, and to link these efforts to a national campaign represented by the Louisville case. These local efforts were closely tied to membership campaigns and branch build-ing in cities like Baltimore, St. Louis, Richmond, and Dallas. In 1917 the U.S. Supreme Court ruled in *Buchanan v. Worley* that the Louisville residen-tial ordinance violated the Fourteenth Amendment, providing the NAACP with its first major legal victory.[12]

By the eve of the First World War, the NAACP had brought the fight against the rising tide of anti-black sentiment and practices into the na-tional arena. Its membership base had grown dramatically in response to the anti-segregation campaign, its role in orchestrating a nationwide pro-test against D. W. Griffith's film *The Birth of a Nation*, and its expanded program of fieldwork focused on African Americans. From 1912 to 1916 the organization grew from fewer than five hunded members to nearly ten thousand organized in sixty-three branches that stretched from coast to coast, while subscriptions to the *Crisis* climbed to more than thirty thou-sand. Most of the growth in membership took place outside the South, but tentative inroads had been made there as well. The gains made were all the more remarkable given the association's financial constraints. In spite of all the difficulties, May Nerney told the organization's annual meeting in 1916 that the pioneering work was done and the foundation had been laid. "We have achieved something that has never been done before. We have built up an organization of white and colored people who stand for equal oppor-tunity regardless of the color line."[13]

While the early growth of the NAACP was impressive, it paled next to the magnitude of the challenges. Nerney cautioned: "nowhere are we meet-ing the situation." "Nowhere," she said, was the NAACP "beginning to cope with the increase in prejudice and discrimination." In those instances where the NAACP did succeed in organizing a branch, people had come to understand the rudiments of organized effort and were beginning "to read and think about the race question in terms of democracy." But for the vast majority of people, civil rights, democracy, and the "new abolitionism" were only phrases. The association offered lofty principles for which it asked support "in the hope that some day an association will be built up to enforce these principles." A major challenge was getting people to sign on to a movement that did not offer any short-term, tangible gains. Yet by the very nature of the problem, Nerney conceded, "we cannot hope for very material results" for a long time to come "and certainly not for anything spectacular unless some great crisis arises."[14]

Nerney's prescription involved reinforcing work that had already begun as well as broadening the reach of the NAACP's program. She provided a blueprint that would help guide the NAACP's growth over the next three decades. Most importantly, she advised, branches needed "the stimulation of personal contact" from the national office. A competent and seasoned organizer, whose full time would be spent in the field supervising and studying branch activity, was essential to this effort. Equally critical to the work of branch building and to advancing the work of the association was a full-time, salaried lawyer who would spend most of his time in the field, keeping "in closest touch" with the legal work of the branches. Brinsmade's contract was not renewed for lack of funds, which left the legal work dependent upon the volunteer services of Arthur Spingarn and Charles Studin. Nerney advised that it should also become the declared policy of the NAACP to engage black lawyers to handle local cases of discrimination whenever possible.

While Nerney agreed that the legal campaign was necessarily a central focus of the NAACP's program, a six-week tour of branches in the Midwest convinced her that it was not sufficient, particularly in terms of building support at the local level. In many places, especially where there was a large southern-born black population, the feeling toward the NAACP was "one of indifference . . . or open hostility." Nerney found that the majority of blacks were most concerned with securing economic opportunities and advancement, and less interested in fighting legal disabilities. In a proposal that hewed closely to the work of the National Urban League, she advised that each branch include a small committee that would make a persistent effort to secure professional and industrial opportunities for African Americans, developing contacts with leading manufacturers, businessmen, and labor unions. In essence, if the work of the NAACP was going to take hold at the local level, the branches needed "a definite program suited to their local and individual needs."[15]

The NAACP was uniquely positioned to respond to the major transformations in black life generated by the First World War and the Great Migration. The war coincided with the association's recruitment of James Weldon Johnson as its first full-time field secretary. Under Johnson's initiative, the NAACP launched a major organizing campaign in the South, which resulted in a rapid growth of membership throughout the region. Overall membership grew nearly tenfold during the war and the immediate postwar period. By the end of 1919, the NAACP claimed a total membership of 91,203 organized in 310 branches. Membership was nearly equally divided between the South and the rest of the country.[16]

During the 1920s the program of the NAACP developed in response to the varied circumstances of black life and race relations around the nation. Major areas of activities reflected a regional divide. They included a campaign for anti-lynching legislation, efforts to expose peonage in the South, a major investigation into the disfranchisement of voters, the first legal challenge to the all-white Democratic primary, and a successful effort to overturn the conviction of farmers convicted of murder in the riot in Elaine, Arkansas. Outside the South, the struggle against housing segregation continued as white neighborhood associations developed other means for limiting black movement, such as restrictive covenant agreements, while mobs continued to police the color line. One of the NAACP's major Supreme Court cases in the mid-1920s involved the successful defense of Ossian Sweet, charged with the murder of a white man while defending his home in Detroit from a mob. There were also sporadic efforts to protest the establishment of separate schools for blacks.

The issue of schools and education in the South and North was an area of growing concern. The NAACP monitored pending bills providing for federal aid to education and lobbied the Harding administration to investigate the distribution of federal funds under the Smith Lever Act, a federal appropriation for agricultural extension work administered through agricultural colleges in the South. The organization urged the president to take action if, as suspected, these funds were not "reasonably expended" to provide for blacks as well as whites. In 1923 the NAACP set up a Committee on Education in Southern Schools, chaired by Du Bois and Florence Kelley, to implement a scientific study of black schools in the South, as proposed ten years earlier. Early in 1925 the NAACP and the *Crisis* secured a $5,000 grant from the Garland Foundation (also known as the American Fund for Public Service) to do a comparative study of public funds spent on the education of white and black children in the South.[17]

At the same time, the trend toward establishing separate schools for blacks in the North accelerated in response to the dramatic growth of the black population in urban areas in the Northeast and Midwest during the war and the postwar period. Local branches of the NAACP led the protest against the spread of school segregation in cities like Philadelphia; Springfield, Illinois; Cleveland; and Terre Haute, Indianapolis, and Gary, Indiana. Often, however, the black community was divided on this issue. For black teachers, barred in most places from teaching in integrated schools, black schools offered the only opportunity for employment. For many black parents, the presence of black teachers in segregated schools appeared to offer a better way to meet their children's educational needs than did the prospect of sending them off to confront racial tensions and discrimination in predominantly white schools. Du Bois, who continued to urge blacks and whites to fight the spread of segregation in public schools, described the paradox that black communities faced: "While we must oppose segregation in schools," he wrote in 1923, "we must honor and appreciate the color of the teacher in the colored school. . . . Small wonder that Negro communities have been torn asunder by this pitiable dilemma."[18]

In a series of articles published in the *Crisis* in 1923, Du Bois sounded the call for clear thinking and honest discussion about what the attitude of blacks and sympathetic whites should be toward school segregation. He reiterated the long-time policy of the NAACP to strongly oppose "compulsory segregation of any sort," noting that of all the forms of segregation and discrimination that existed, segregation in public schools was "the most dangerous, most insidious, the most far reaching." It sowed the seeds of race prejudice among the young and, Du Bois insisted, must be opposed by all who believed in democracy and broad human development.

Yet the reality was that segregation already existed, and that there was a large and growing number of public and private common schools, high schools, and colleges attended exclusively by black students and staffed wholly or largely by black teachers. While the educational plight of blacks was still precarious, the situation would be positively disastrous if not for "the self-sacrificing, efficient colored teacher of colored youth." Within their ranks, Du Bois wrote, there were some "of the finest trained men and women in the world and the black race can never repay them for the work they have done."[19] Another factor to be weighed was the experience of black students in mixed schools staffed exclusively by white teachers. Du Bois noted a disturbing trend: mixed high schools in Philadelphia and New York graduated only fifty black students a year, while all-black high schools in Washington and Baltimore graduated four hundred students a year, even though all four cities had black populations of similar size. Black students in mixed schools, Du Bois reported, often did not receive proper consideration or attention. In many mixed schools, particularly in border states, black students were deliberately mistreated and discriminated against, systematically discouraged, and "kept in something worse than ignorance." In more benign environments, they frequently received little inspiration or encouragement.[20]

Du Bois did not advocate segregation as a solution to these problems. Such an evil, he wrote in 1923, could not be outweighed by the few benefits that resulted from separate schools. But he did insist that the situation be faced squarely and aggressively, and that attention be directed at overcoming some of the problems confronting black students in mixed schools. Du Bois noted that New York was pointing the way toward what should be done. The city had nearly three hundred black teachers scattered through the school system from kindergarten through high school, teaching white children probably more often than black children. A pilot program was also under way in New York to monitor the course of black children in mixed schools, to work with them at home and in school, encouraging them to enroll in high school, and to identify and oppose teachers who discriminated against black students.[21]

Starting in 1925, supported by the grant from the Garland Fund, the *Crisis* focused considerable attention on conditions of black schools in the South. Based on investigations made on site by a team of researchers in five southern states, the *Crisis* documented the gross inequities in public spending on the education of black children. Findings were reported in a series of articles published between the fall of 1926 and the summer of 1928 and offered compelling evidence to support the charge that "funds devoted to education by the states and the nation" were systematically spent "so as to discriminate against colored children and keep them in ignorance." Particularly striking was the evidence in Deep South states from South Carolina to Mississippi, which Du Bois described as "shameless and impudent in their defiance of law and justice in Negro education." It was time, Du Bois proclaimed in 1929, "to start the crusade" for equal education, as a fundamental right of citizenship. Surely, he wrote, "there must be a way to bring . . . cases before the state and federal courts."[22]

The NAACP's secretary, Walter White, sought support from the Garland Fund to initiate a series of taxpayer suits aimed at forcing southern states to equalize expenditures for black and white schools, thus "making a dual system so prohibitive as to speed the abolition of segregated schools." The Garland Fund awarded the association $100,000 in 1930 for a broad-based legal campaign against racially discriminatory measures, including the unequal apportionment of school funds. Financial losses in the wake of the Depression caused the fund to reduce its award to $10,000. After considerable delay, Charles Houston, vice-dean of Howard University Law School, was hired in 1934 by the NAACP to mount a legal challenge to unequal school funding in the South and segregated railroad transportation.[23]

The same year that Charles Houston began mapping out plans for a legal attack on school segregation and educational inequality in the South, Du Bois initiated a debate in the pages of the *Crisis* on segregation as an opening toward a "new . . . philosophy concerning race segregation in the United States." Du Bois reiterated his oft-stated belief that the greatest human development took place by maintaining the widest human contact possible. But it was necessary, he cautioned, to deal with facts and not theory. And in 1934 racial prejudice in the United States, and "the . . . almost criminal propaganda" that supported it, made his goal increasingly difficult if not impossible to achieve. "Segregation with a vengeance," Du Bois wrote, marked black life in both South and North. The difference, he contended, was largely one of degree, however wide.

Among the most notable and disturbing developments since the founding of the NAACP some twenty-five years earlier, Du Bois observed, was that segregation in the North had become "more insistent, more prevalent, more unassailable." The limits of the law in reversing this trend had been demonstrated in the area of residential segregation. Legal action had steadied the foundation "so that in the future segregation [in the North] must be by wish and will and not law." Blacks in the North were confined by unyielding white opinion to a colored world. The efforts of the previous two decades had not made the slightest impression on the overwhelming mass of white Americans, who remained determined not to treat Negroes as men. "The dilemma is complete," Du Bois wrote, "and there is no escape."

What did this mean for schools? Again, Du Bois emphasized in an article for the *Journal of Negro Education* that integrated education was the ideal, and provided the intellectual basis for real democracy. It was something to be strived for. But it was not among the choices facing blacks in 1935. Du Bois estimated that four-fifths of black students attended separate schools, with the rest attending mixed schools that according to Du Bois placed them at a decided disadvantage. Racial prejudice made it almost impossible for black students to receive a proper education in mixed schools. A sympathetic understanding between teachers and students was essential to a nurturing learning environment, and even well-meaning white teachers lacked an informed appreciation of the surroundings and background of black students to develop such an understanding. Futhermore, Du Bois insisted, students needed to know the history "of the Negro race in America," which they seldom if ever received in white institutions. For the most part they were mistreated by classmates and teachers and served as little more than battering rams in the effort to secure a measure of racial mixing. "To endure bad schools and wrong education because the schools are mixed," DuBois claimed, "was a costly if not fatal mistake."[24]

There was little room for argument as to "whether the Negro needs separate schools or not," Du Bois contended. The plain choice was "either he will have separate schools or he will not be educated." How blacks approached this fact was of critical importance. Separate schools, he advised, should not be viewed as something "forced on us by grim necessity" but rather as an opportunity for racial uplift and a broad "new . . . effort at human education." Black communities should insist on shaping and controlling these schools, overseeing the hiring of the teaching force, the selection of textbooks, discipline, the expenditure of funds, and other administrative matters. Du Bois believed that Negro schools and colleges had a unique role to play in expanding the boundaries of knowledge and understanding, especially in the areas of history and the social sciences. Black scholars, he cautioned, should not try to parallel the history of white folk by making similar boasts about brown and black folk, but instead should pursue an honest evaluation of human effort and accomplishment.[25]

Du Bois criticized the NAACP, charging that it concentrated all its efforts on preventing the establishment of separate schools, "but scarcely a single cent to see that the division of funds between white and Negro schools, North and South, is carried out with some faint approximation of justice." While Du Bois failed to note that the NAACP was embarking on a campaign to force the equalization of spending on black and white schools in the South as a tactic to overturn segregation, his assessment was particularly relevant to the situation in the North. There the NAACP would attend only sporadically to the problem of schools, and only where the creation of separate schools violated state civil rights laws. In the meantime, de facto segregation patterns in the North became deeply entrenched, and separate and inferior schools for black children grew unchecked and largely unchallenged as the NAACP mounted its major, long-term campaign to overturn Jim Crow in the South.

As the NAACP prepared to launch its campaign against segregation in the South, Walter White and the board of directors made clear their unwillingness to equivocate on an anti-segregation program. Du Bois, however, would not be silenced. He resigned in 1934, just as Charles Houston joined the staff as head of the legal bureau. Under Houston's direction, the NAACP became even more deeply invested in the South. That, Houston told White, was where "the work of the next decade" must be focused.[26] The NAACP concentrated its attention and resources on chipping away at the legal structure of Jim Crow and on disfranchisement. The primary emphasis was on ending discrimination in schools, and this effort was linked to others

in the areas of transportation and voting. While Houston initially implemented a strategy aimed at equalizing schools, he made it clear from the
beginning that the program did "not intend to endorse the principle of
segregation." Rather, the plan was to fight segregation by making the dual
system so expensive to support that southern states would abandon it.[27]

The campaign launched by Houston was, as he explained, more than "a
bit of legal handiwork." Building upon the infrastructure created by the
NAACP, it aimed "to arouse and strengthen the will of the local community
to demand and fight for their rights." Houston emphasized the importance
of fieldwork and personal contact to ensure that cases were "vigorously and
carefully handled" and that local people remained actively involved and
committed. "The social and public factors," Houston wrote, "must be developed along with and, if possible, before the actual litigation commences."
During 1934 Houston traveled nearly five thousand miles around the South
"with a view of stirring up interest in their local educational situation . . . to
the point where the fight will be self-generated." He advised that it would
take at least five years before "full momentum" was reached. By the time
Houston passed the torch to his successor Thurgood Marshall in 1938, the
campaign was well under way, in the area of graduate and professional
schools and teachers' salaries. It was accompanied by a revival of NAACP
branch activity throughout the South, and rapid membership growth during the Second World War. But it would take twenty years of litigation and
organizing before the NAACP struck its decisive blow with *Brown v. Board*.

The NAACP's shift toward the South in 1934 coincided with the emergence of a coalition of liberal, labor, and black voters in the Democratic
Party, joined by their support for the expansive social and economic policies
of the New Deal. They found common opponents in the conservative southern Democrats who resisted labor and New Deal reforms, as well as any
initiatives in civil rights. And northern congressmen, responsive to the
growing power of black voters in key urban areas, were increasingly inclined to support a civil rights program that addressed problems of racial
discrimination and segregation in the South. All these factors conspired to
frame race as a distinctly southern problem, even as black migration to the
North continued to alter the demographic profile of race in America, and as
structures of racial segregation and inequity became more deeply fixed in
northern cities.

Until the mid-1950s, the national office of the NAACP gave scant attention to the problem of school segregation and educational inequities
in the North. There separate schools existed largely because district lines
were fitted to racially defined housing patterns. As Davison Douglas has
shown, after the Second World War, as the NAACP's attack on segregated

schools crested in the South, Thurgood Marshall took note of areas in the North where school boards supported dual systems of education in violation of local and state laws prohibiting school segregation. In the 1940s and early 1950s Marshall and his associates worked with uneven success to rouse local branches to take the lead in eliminating vestiges of government-sponsored segregation in the North. Marshall's comments to Roy Wilkins on the situation in Illinois suggest the limited nature of the contact between the national office and urban areas in the North concerning the issue of schools and school segregation. Marshall wrote to Wilkins: "I am beginning to doubt that our branch officers are fully indoctrinated in the policy of the NAACP in being opposed to segregation . . . We need to educate our branch officers and in turn the membership, and finally, the people in the need for complete support in this all-out attack on segregation."[28]

The governor of New Jersey and the state legislature in Illinois responded to these demands by threatening to withhold funds from school districts that failed to end blatant forms of segregation. Yet such political leadership came with little cost. As Douglas notes, attacks on northern segregation most often involved rural and small-town school districts, leaving school segregation in large urban areas unaffected. There the hardening of residential segregation patterns and school district lines relegated many African Americans to segregated, underfunded, and poorly equipped schools.[29]

The legal campaign that culminated in the *Brown* decision was at the center of a growing effort to dismantle state-sponsored segregation and disfranchisement in the South. Some scholars have questioned how important or even necessary *Brown* was to the mass protests that finally ended Jim Crow in the South.[30] As part of the broader challenge to racial discrimination as it was practiced in the South, *Brown* was the pivot on which the movement of the 1950s and 1960s turned. The litigation campaign, as orchestrated by Houston and Marshall, was also an organizing campaign, one that supported the growth of a regionwide infrastructure of NAACP branches and stoked rising expectations. When *Brown* struck the death knell to *Plessy*, few who were engaged in the movement—or determined to maintain segregation—missed its significance. Pauli Murray wrote on 18 May 1954, the day after the *Brown* ruling was announced: "How do you draw the line as to the damage done by feelings of inferiority," she asked. "If you must educate the child in a non-segregated school . . . do you then commit him to a segregated hospital when he is sick, send him to segregated areas of the bus on the way to school, have him go up to the gallery when he goes to the movies, and have him drink out of a fountain marked colored when he goes to the county courthouse? Do you make this great effort of integration of your school system only to tear it all down again once he leaves the school house?"[31]

Yet as a tool for advancing equal educational opportunity for black children, *Brown* offered a promise not easily realized. The questions that Du Bois had raised some two decades earlier would reemerge as civil rights lawyers and activists attempted to interpret and apply *Brown* to situations where black students were isolated in separate and unequal schools that had grown up in urban areas around the country. Reflecting back on *Brown*, Robert L. Carter, a leading NAACP lawyer who played a critical role in the school desegregation fight, acknowledged that in terms of education, most black children had benefited little from *Brown* "despite its being an almost total fulfillment of the strategy we devised." Carter acknowledged that the problem was in part related to a strategy that focused exclusively on uprooting legally mandated school segregation. "We were locked into a present that was already past," Carter concluded. The Supreme Court's decision "was designed to restructure an era that was dead as soon as the *Brown* decision became law although it was to linger on for at least two decades before finally giving up the ghost."[32]

In the immediate aftermath of *Brown*, Carter began working to expand the interpretation and application of the Court's mandate, namely "to establish through constitutional doctrine equal educational opportunity for black children in real life." In 1955 he and Kenneth Clark met with the New York City superintendent of schools to complain that schools with predominantly black students were not equal in resources or facilities to schools with predominantly white students. An investigation by the Public Education Association confirmed that there was a gap in achievement between black and white students, starting in the third grade and widening with each successive grade, a pattern that fit most school systems throughout the North. Carter, who became head of the NAACP legal office after the Legal Defense Fund officially separated from the NAACP, led the legal campaign against this northern form of school segregation. Carter and his associates sought unsuccessfully to expand the application of *Brown*, arguing that whenever school assignment policies or organization produced inferior education of blacks, whether intentional or not, that was a violation of the law. The courts did not follow.[33]

However, to admit the limits of *Brown* is not to suggest that the legal strategy devised and implemented by NAACP lawyers was fundamentally flawed. As Carter himself has written, it is difficult to see how there could have been significant movement against the broad and complex structures of racial discrimination, North and South, until *Plessy* "was dethroned as a national standard." The mistake, he acknowledges, may have been to "put all of our efforts on southern issues." In considering the current state of education and schools, Carter echoed Du Bois: "We cannot allow ourselves to be prisoners of dogma. While integration must remain our ultimate objective, alternative approaches must be explored." The immediate need is to improve the quality of education.

As we revisit *Brown* fifty years later, the measure of its achievement should be considered in light of the early history that shaped the legal struggle leading to *Brown*. Designed and implemented at a time when the great majority of black Americans lived under the regime of Jim Crow, the NAACP's legal campaign was part of a broad, improvisational strategy aimed at dismantling the crippling system of segregation and disfranchisement that was supported by state law with the sanction of the U.S. Supreme Court. While schooling and education was a major arena of struggle, the primary target was Jim Crow in all its manifestations. The *Brown* decision was critical to the ultimate demise of that system, and to the process of desegregation that for a time found schools more integrated in the South than in the North.

But the debate that Du Bois initiated in 1934 is instructive in considering the limits of the campaign that led to *Brown* and the broader movement it helped to define. From the New Deal era to the mid-1960s, the NAACP and its liberal allies increasingly framed the problems of race and racial discrimination as a distinctly southern problem, and looked toward integration as the solution. As scholars, policymakers, and others remember the promise of *Brown* and consider its limitations, attention should be given to the ways in which the NAACP's shift to a southern focus in 1934 narrowed the possibilities for addressing the ways in which race structured the educational opportunities of a growing number of black students outside the Jim Crow South.

## Notes

1 See for example Raymond Walters, *The Burden of Brown: Thirty Years of School Desegregation* (Knoxville: University of Tennessee Press, 1992); James Patterson, *Brown v. Board: A Civil Rights Milestone and Its Troubled Legacy* (New York: Oxford University Press, 2000); Peter Irons, *Jim Crow's Children: The Broken Promise of the Brown Decision* (New York: Viking, 2002).

2 "Segregation," *Crisis*, November 1910, 10.

3 James McPherson, *The Abolitionist Legacy: From Reconstruction to the* NAACP (Princeton: Princeton University Press, 1975), 128–30.

4 W.E.B. Du Bois, "The Vigilance Committees: A Call to Arms," *Crisis*, May 1913, 26–27.

5 NAACP, Fourth Annual Report (1913); *Crisis*, February 1915, 190, March 1916, 298.

6 NAACP, Fourth Annual Report (1913); NAACP, Fifth Annual Report (1914);

Oswald Garrison Villard to Francis Villard, 23 January 1914, box 1463, Oswald Garrison Villard Papers, Houghton Library, Harvard University.

7 "The Northward Migration," *Crisis*, June 1911, 56; NAACP, Fourth Annual Report (1913), 8–10; *Crisis*, June 1913, 91.

8 Du Bois, "The Vigilance Committees," 26–27; *Crisis*, April 1914, 285.

9 *Crisis*, December 1913, 90–91, January 1914, 139–40, April 1914, 291–92, May 1914, 36.

10 NAACP, Fourth Annual Report (1913), 29; *Crisis*, January 1914, 139.

11 "Legal Work," NAACP Fifth Annual Report (1914), reprinted in *Crisis*, April 1915, 289–90; Minutes, NAACP Board of Directors, 7 July 1914, part I, reel 1, NAACP Papers, Manuscript Division, Library of Congress, Washington.

12 Patrick Shaheen McElhone, "The Civil Rights Activism of the Louisville Branch of the NAACP, 1914–1960" (MA thesis, University of Louisville, 1976), 17–70; *Crisis*, August 1915, 198–99, September 1915, 243–44.

13 Minutes, NAACP Annual Meeting, 3 January 1916, series I, box A-8, NAACP Papers, Manuscript Division, Library of Congress, Washington.

14 Report of the secretary, presented to the NAACP board of directors, 13 December 1915, part I, reel 1, NAACP Papers, microfilm.

15 *Id.*

16 Charles Flint Kellog, *NAACP: A History of the National Association for the Advancement of Colored People* (Baltimore: Johns Hopkins University Press, 1967), 137

17 *Id.*

18 W. E. B. Du Bois, "The Tragedy of Jim Crow," *Crisis*, August 1923, 170.

19 *Id.*

20 *Id.*

21 *Id.*; W. E. B. Du Bois, "The Negro and Northern Public Schools," *Crisis*, March 1923, 205–8, "The Negro in Public Schools, II," *Crisis*, April 1923, 262–65.

22 "The Negro Common School in Georgia," *Crisis*, September 1926; "Education," *Crisis*, April 1929, 32, February 1930, 65. In addition to Georgia, other states investigated included North Carolina, South Carolina, Oklahoma, and Mississippi.

23 Mark Tushnet, *The NAACP's Legal Strategy against Segregated Education, 1925–1950* (Chapel Hill: University of North Carolina Press, 1987), 13–18.

24 W. E. B. Du Bois, "Does the Negro Need Separate Schools," *Journal of Negro Education*, March 1935, 328–35.

25 *Id.*

26 Charles Houston to Walter White, 1 November 1934, reel 16, NAACP Papers.

27 Charles Houston, "Educational Inequalities Must Go!" *Crisis*, October 1935, 300.

28 Davison M. Douglas, "The Limits of Law in Accomplishing Racial Change: School Segregation in the Pre-*Brown* North," 44 *UCLA Law Review* 677 (1997) (Marshall's quote at 738).

29  *Id.*

30  Michael Klarman, "How *Brown* Changed Race Relations: The Backlash Thesis," *Journal of American History*, June 1994, 81–118.

31  Pauli Murray to Caroline Ware, Pauli Murray Papers, Schlesinger Library, MC 412, 1818.

32  Robert L. Carter, "A Reassessment of *Brown v. Board*," in Derrick Bell, *Shades of Brown: New Perspectives on School Desegregation* (New York: Teachers College Press, 1980), 21.

33  Robert L. Carter, "Law and the Struggle for Racial Justice: The Memoir of Robert L. Carter," unpublished manuscript.

CHRISTOPHER W. SCHMIDT

# J. Waties Waring and the Making of Liberal

# Jurisprudence in Postwar America

And the truth is that the Warings are a million miles away from all this. They live in Charleston physically, but that is all. Psychologically they have left it, to live in the great world, the world represented by the out-of-town newspapers they eagerly read and clip each day, by the vast correspondence they carry on all over the country.—Samuel Grafton, "The Lonesomest Man in Town," *Colliers*, 29 April 1950.

On 26 January 1942, J. Waties Waring of Charleston, South Carolina, sixty-one, was sworn in as a federal judge for his state's Eastern District. In his acceptance speech, Waring gave the expected acknowledgments to holding "the scales of justice evenly" and providing "equal justice," without regard for "rank or position," words that in the Deep South of the day were generally understood to include the qualifier, unspoken in this case, "for whites only."[1] Probably no one in the audience that day envisioned that this high-sounding rhetoric would necessarily apply equally across all parts of society, certainly not with regard to the state's large African American population. No one, including Waring himself, who owed his judicial appointment to support from South Carolina's racist demagogue of a senator, "Cotton Ed" Smith, would have imagined that this new judge, in attempting to do just this, would become one of the most controversial figures in his city's history.

There was hardly a hint in Waring's background to indicate that he was destined to become a central figure in the struggle for African American equality and a pioneer of the modern civil rights movement. He was born and bred in the tradition-bound world of white, upper-class Charleston society, a member of a family that traced its Charleston ancestors back to the seventeenth century. Waring received his entire education in Charleston, attending a local private school before going on to the College of

Charleston. After passing the state bar examination, he established a law practice in town. In 1913 he married Annie Gammell, who came from another respected Charleston family, and together they set up home in a fashionable section of the city. He eventually served in a variety of public service positions in Charleston, where he made the necessary connections that opened the way for his appointment to the federal bench. In short, there was little particularly exceptional in his life and career before the mid-1940s. He was a prominent, respected member of the southern establishment who rarely, if ever, questioned the Jim Crow laws and customs of the South. Yet upon his retirement from the bench in 1952, he was reviled by practically all of Charleston's white population and was a hero to blacks and liberal whites around the nation.

The transition in Judge Waring's life began not long after he assumed his judgeship. Although there were several dramatic moments within the story of his racial awakening, it was basically a gradual, educative process that can be charted over the period between 1945 and 1951. The first evidence of Waring's transformation was a decision he wrote in 1945 ordering that black teachers be paid on a scale equal to that for white teachers, a ruling that might have raised the eyebrows of some of his Charleston friends but was hardly earth-shaking.[2] Yet Waring would see this decision, at least in retrospect, as a turning point in his understanding of the race question. After this ruling he made a number of changes in how his court was run: he ordered that jury lists no longer make reference to the race of potential jury members; he encouraged racially mixed seating in the courtroom and jury box; he ended the lawyers' practice of addressing black witnesses by their first names; and he appointed an African American as court bailiff.[3]

These actions were only the initial steps of the judge's journey toward civil rights activism. In 1947 Waring issued *Elmore v. Rice*, a dramatic voting-rights decision in which he ordered that the South Carolina Democratic primary, previously an all-white affair, be opened to black voters.[4] The decision drew national attention: here was a judge who dared to preach an aggressive brand of civil rights in the land of Dixie. That attention only grew in the following year with his ruling in *Brown v. Baskin*, in which he issued an injunction to ensure that his previous voting-rights decision would be implemented.[5] Waring's newfound prominence as an advocate of racial justice gained him numerous awards and invitations for interviews and speeches, all of which offered occasions to further his attack on discrimination and publicize his growing belief in the need for immediate desegregation.

Waring's most lasting contribution to American history was his role in *Brown v. Board of Education*. In 1951 Waring wrote a scathing dissent in *Briggs v. Elliott*, a case tried before a three-judge district court in which the majority upheld the legality of segregated schools in Clarendon Country, South Carolina.[6] With Waring's private encouragement, the NAACP team of attorneys that had argued the *Briggs* case, led by Thurgood Marshall, appealed the case to the Supreme Court, where along with cases from three other states and the District of Columbia it would be combined in the *Brown* opinion. Despite the failure of the Supreme Court's unanimous opinion to even mention Judge Waring's dissent, in many respects *Brown* followed the legal and moral reasoning that Waring had outlined three years earlier.

Waring paid a steep price for his commitment to racial justice. He had a cross burned on his lawn and bullets fired into his house—both incidents, Waring assumed, the work of the local Ku Klux Klan. Hate mail and harassing phone calls became a constant presence in his life. He was ostracized from the same white Charleston society that he had belonged to for over six decades of his life. "The man they love to hate" was also "the lonesomest man in town" and "an island in a sea of hate," to borrow from the titles of three magazine articles on the controversial judge.[7] He was, in a phrase that Waring frequently used, a "stranger in a foreign land." White Charleston's traditional ways and political conservatism stood out even in a region known for both. It was not surprising, then, that upon retiring in 1952 Waring decided to leave Charleston and make his home in New York City, where he remained until his death in 1968.

Most attempts to explain Waring's unexpected change in attitude on the race question focus on his personal life. Most Charleston whites attributed his new ideas to his abrupt divorce in 1945 from his wife of thirty-two years, followed by his marriage eight days later to Elizabeth Avery, a native of Detroit who had moved to Charleston with her second husband several years earlier. Elizabeth Waring's sudden entrance into Charleston high society received a decidedly cold reception. Elizabeth was an outspoken, opinionated woman unafraid to voice her liberal convictions in the parlors of the city's élite. This tendency, combined with a general disapproval of divorce (South Carolina did not even have a divorce law at the time—the Warings received their divorce in Florida), led to the beginnings of the Warings' isolation. The impact of the divorce and remarriage on Judge Waring's subsequent racial decisions was a subject of debate. Waring's critics contended that he began pushing for civil rights to punish Charleston society for refusing to embrace his wife. More charitable observers noted that Elizabeth's liberal views seemed to have a powerful influence on the judge. While these explanations tend to be reductive, the combined effect of Elizabeth's liberalism and the ostracism of the couple from white Charleston society certainly contributed at least in part to Waring's changed views.[8]

Another version, and the explanation Waring preferred, was that his new role as a judge led him to see old issues in a new light. A growing number of cases dealing with issues of racial discrimination came before his court, and as Waring often recounted, his conscience, coupled with an increased knowledge of the situation, led him to recognize the wrongness of Jim Crow. In short, his experience on the bench led to his racial awakening, an experience that he often described in religious terms.[9] In a revealing personal memorandum titled "The Result of the Break with South Carolina and Charleston in Terms of Losses and Gains," Waring wrote: "Of course the first great gain is the complete knowledge that one's actions have been right, not only right because, in the matter of court decisions, there have been affirmances and complete approval nationally, but right because the conscience of the world approves of these actions, and right because one's own conscience says so, and that is the greatest gain there is."[10] This emphasis on the importance of his personal convictions and sense of justice in shaping his new outlook on the race issue was a standard part of Waring's explanation.

While both these explanations help to elucidate Waring's racial conversion, they run the risk of letting his dramatic personal story overwhelm the significance of the historical context in which his transformation took place.[11] This conversion was of a piece with significant developments in the personal life of the man. Yet, his racial awakening was also a product of—and eventually a contribution to—the larger context of mid-century racial liberalism. The early years after the Second World War saw the formation of a distinctive worldview among liberals, a worldview premised on the recognition that racism threatened America's most cherished ideals and that a commitment to government-led reform was needed to address the threat. In this chapter I will argue that in understanding Waring one should not be too quick to underestimate the importance of the legal "affirmances," the "complete national approval," and the support of the "conscience of the world" that Waring placed second to his individual conscience and that his critics placed second to his personal adventures. A critical factor leading to Waring's crusade as a civil rights activist was the context of America in the 1940s, specifically the emergence of racial liberalism as a powerful, politically viable national phenomenon. The story of Judge Waring is not only the story of a courageous individual: it is also the story of a pivotal moment in the history of American race relations.

Waring's transformation was the product of his ability to re-envision his community. Rather than remain a part of the Charleston society to which he was born, he entered a dynamic, expanding community of racial liberals from around the country. He was a widely admired character in liberal circles, particularly in the North, and the support he received from these sources was central to his political development and to the confidence with which he established his positions on issues of civil rights. Without the support and encouragement he received from outside Charleston and outside the Deep South, his transformation would have been inconceivable. While Waring's dramatic personal circumstances made his vision of social reform a unique one, overall it was very much indebted to mainstream liberal thought. By and large, the strengths of Waring's vision were widely evident in the best characteristics of racial liberalism, even as its limitations were also an integral part of the worldview of liberal America. For all that there is to admire in Waring's fight against racial discrimination, there is also much in his understanding of race and reform that is less admirable. Paradoxically, the very parts of his thought that were the least attractive—notably, his tendency toward élitism and uncompromising self-righteousness—contributed most to his greatest accomplishments. The same can be said about mid-century racial liberalism in general. By studying how a paragon of the white southern establishment could become a crusader in the struggle for racial equality, one can better appreciate the reach, impact, and limitations of liberal racial thought in the postwar era. Waring's story also helps to explain how the Supreme Court, consisting of nine members of the white power establishment—including, in 1954, three southerners—would follow in this Charleston judge's footsteps with its momentous decision in *Brown*.

At practically every point of Waring's development into a civil rights crusader, he drew strength from the recognition that he was not alone in his views. Waring's day-to-day existence in Charleston after the mid-1940s, when most members of his earlier circle of acquaintances did their best to isolate and shun him, made this recognition all the more important. To counter the ostracism, he formed new connections and relationships. The most important of these was undoubtedly his bond with his new wife—by all accounts, this marriage was a mutually dependent and deeply sustaining relationship. The Warings also reached out to the local African American community. The dinner parties at which they entertained blacks were probably as controversial among Charleston high society as anything the judge declared from the bench. In addition to these local connections, Waring formed a powerful relationship with a national community of liberal thinkers, activists, and policymakers. These contacts were deeply heartening to a man who, when walking down the familiar streets of Charleston, found himself harassed or at best snubbed by people with whom he had lived all his life.

Waring's connections with liberal thought were forged in a number of ways. One of the most important was his reading of works by racial liberals. Waring's reading habits changed sharply around the mid-1940s, when he became interested, with his new wife's encouragement, in studies of the South and the American race problem. The two books whose influence he would most often cite were W. J. Cash's *The Mind of the South* (1941) and Gunnar Myrdal's *An American Dilemma* (1944).[12] Myrdal's exhaustive study of race in America was a central text of postwar liberalism and an important influence on Waring. In particular, Myrdal's work reinforced in Waring a faith in the importance of America's ideals of liberty and equality as a counterforce to the nation's social practice of racial discrimination. Cash's *The Mind of the South*, if not as nationally recognized or as long-lived as *An American Dilemma*, was also an essential text in its time, particularly among southern liberals. Waring felt a special connection to this work since it was written by a fellow southerner willing to take on the myths of the southern tradition. Cash described the South as psychologically scarred by its own violent, racist, myth-ridden heritage, an analysis that Waring would whole-heartedly embrace.

Although none of his other readings appeared to make as much of an impression on Waring as the books of Myrdal and Cash, he was well versed in the general arguments and positions of many prominent liberals of the day. He read and praised the work of the southern activist Lillian Smith, who like Waring and Cash found sickness and disease to be useful meta-phors for describing southern racism, and he lauded the movie version of William Faulkner's novel *Intruder in the Dust*.[13] His study of history was also guided by a new generation of scholarship on the Civil War and its aftermath. Waring left extensive annotations on a copy of Arthur Schle-singer Jr.'s essay "The Causes of the Civil War: A Note on Historical Senti-mentalism" (1949), in which Schlesinger argued against the dominant historical interpretation of the war as an unnecessary conflict that resulted from a failure of leadership. Schlesinger described abolitionism as a funda-mentally moral issue, going so far as to compare the anti-slavery movement to the struggle against Hitler. For Schlesinger, Waring, and most racial liberals of the day, a renewed appreciation for the efforts of the abolitionists was an important step in justifying their own efforts to reform society.[14]

In addition to scholarship, literature, and film that provided perspectives far different from those offered by his immediate surroundings, Waring kept close watch on the national press. Elizabeth Waring carefully recorded the reception outside the South to her husband's statements and actions. The couple received various northern papers from which Elizabeth clipped all articles mentioning her husband, eventually compiling seventy-two scrapbooks filled with news accounts of him, herself, and developments in the struggle for racial equality.[15] The Warings had little difficulty finding positive accounts in the out-of-town press, since practically all journalists outside the Deep South who took an interest in writing about Waring did so in a laudatory manner. The reporting of the national press was one of the best indications the Warings received as to the general attitude toward racial progress outside the South.

Waring also lifted himself out of his Charleston surroundings through friendships with outsiders, most of which were developed and deepened through correspondence. His most frequent correspondents in the late 1940s included: Walter White, the executive secretary of the NAACP; Thurgood Marshall, the head of the NAACP's Legal Defense Fund; Aubrey Williams, a New Dealer who returned to his native Alabama to publish *Southern Farmer*, a monthly newsletter that advocated an interracial style of populism; and James Dombrowski, director of the Southern Conference Education Fund, a liberal activist organization. In addition to this core group of friends, Waring occasionally corresponded with other prominent national figures, including Eleanor Roosevelt and Harry S. Truman. Waring clearly thrived on the sense of connection and belonging—and of being needed—that he received from these friendships. After his decisions in the South Carolina primary cases in 1947 and 1948, Waring's circle of friends and contacts dramatically expanded, giving him new learning opportunities and new forums in which to present his views.

The strength that Waring drew from his newfound friendships can be clearly seen in his personal musings and in interviews. For example, in his memorandum on the gains and losses of his break with South Carolina, he listed "outside contacts" as one of the benefits of his choice: "I feel that this ostracism here has allowed me to take part in what might be termed a true crusading movement in which many hundreds and thousands of good people in this country are enlisted and performing various parts."[16] In an interview in 1950, Waring returned to the topic. "It is an unpleasant situation to be in, to stand alone in a community," he noted. "But after experiencing it, and after my contacts with other communities, I feel that it is the happiest position I could be in."[17] Waring compensated for his hostile local environment by creating his own network of liberal ideas and personalities. As a result of these connections, he gained confidence in pursuing the goal of ending racial discrimination. It was during the period between 1948 and 1950 that Waring developed his uncompromising attack on efforts to promote incremental racial reform.[18]

Another way in which Waring interacted with the larger community of racial liberalism was through his frequent travels. With little to hold him in Charleston when his court was not in session, Waring took advantage of opportunities to serve as a judge on courts in New York and California, as well as to visit friends outside the South and attend award ceremonies in his honor. A brief snapshot of his schedule is revealing: After issuing his injunction opening the South Carolina Democratic primary to blacks in the summer of 1948, Waring spent a good part of the following months away from Charleston. From August through mid-October the Warings traveled and visited friends in California and New York. While in New York, Waring attended a luncheon given in his honor by the city's chapter of the National Lawyers Guild, an event he used as a forum to make an impassioned call for direct federal civil rights intervention in the South. After returning to Charleston, Waring was back north in early December, when he met with President Truman (an event that earned him a praising editorial in the *New York Times*) and Chief Justice Fred Vinson. Then in February Waring was back in New York to accept the National Lawyers Guild's Roosevelt Award for 1948, which, in addition to giving Waring an opportunity to enjoy the praise of his admirers, gave him another chance to voice his views on the situation in the South.[19] The opportunities that the Warings had to periodically escape the South had a cathartic effect on their psyches, as shown by their decision to permanently relocate to New York City upon Judge Waring's retirement in 1952.

Finally, Waring's place in the federal judiciary system gave him an institutional connection to the world outside Charleston. Of all the links between Waring and the national liberal community, the most influential, at least in terms of his legal decisions, were those resulting from his role as a judge within a system that was gradually adopting the liberal line on the race issue. It is important to recognize that for all the controversy surrounding this crusading judge, his most important legal decisions on racial issues were upheld by the higher courts.[20] Even if he could not walk from his home to the courthouse without wondering whether that day would be the day when someone decided to follow through on one of the many threats he received, he had the knowledge that even his most controversial decisions generally had the support of the federal judiciary. This was true of the white-primary decisions, which were upheld by the Fourth Circuit Court of Appeals and which the Supreme Court, by declining to review the case, allowed to stand.[21] In his meeting with Chief Justice Vinson several years after this case, Vinson told him that one of the Supreme Court justices thought they should have accepted Waring's primary case so as to strengthen it by affirming it, a piece of insider knowledge that could only have strengthened Waring's confidence in the high court.[22] And of course Waring's school segregation decision would receive the Supreme Court's approval in *Brown*, although Waring would be retired in New York City by then. Indeed, Waring was confident when he wrote his dissent in *Briggs* that the Supreme Court would support his stance.[23]

Although Waring tended to oversell the importance of putting on the judicial robes in his transformation into a liberal activist, his position as a federal judge offered his strongest connection to a system in which racially liberal opinions were increasingly being accepted. The simple fact that Waring became a judge says little about his future activism, but being a judge gave him a link to a community of people who would largely accept Waring's rulings. In particular, the precedents coming down from the Supreme Court in the 1940s and early 1950s were a constant source of inspiration for Waring. As a jurist, no less than as a citizen, Waring was being assured that he was a part of a movement that was not only right but also supported.

Although mid-century racial liberalism was the predominant influence on the development of Waring's racial thought, he was by no means a passive receptacle. An examination and analysis of Waring's most important legal decision demonstrate an adherence to widely held doctrines of racial liberalism, but also a distinct interpretation and application of these ideas. Waring's dissent in *Briggs v. Elliott*, the Clarendon County school segregation case, was an intensely personalized statement of belief—much of it was written in first person, and it revealed an obvious tone of moral outrage at the situation in the South.[24] Waring bluntly stated that segregated education failed to produce equal schools and was an "evil that must be eradicated." "[I]f the courts of this land are to render justice under the laws without fear or favor, justice for all men and all kinds of men," Waring wrote, "the time to do it is now and the place is in the elementary schools where our future citizens learn their first lesson to respect the dignity of the individual in a democracy." His rhetorical climax was contained in a single italicized sentence that stood as its own paragraph toward the end of the decision: "*Segregation is per se inequality.*"[25] This argument would be echoed in the more famous (and more limited) climactic line from Warren's *Brown* decision: "Separate educational facilities are inherently unequal."[26]

In addition to offering insight into its author's mind, Waring's dissent is an important representation of mid-century racial liberalism. Indeed, this dissent is a much better indication than the Supreme Court's unanimous opinion in *Brown* of the contours and shape of mainstream liberal thought as it pertained to racial concerns. As great a proclamation of liberal racial principle as *Brown* was, it was also severely constrained by the intensely political nature of its creation and intention. The Chief Justice's need to keep the eight other justices on board, his desire to write an opinion that would not offend the South, his fear of announcing a legal doctrine that would be ignored—all these factors were in play when Warren wrote his famous opinion. Waring, writing alone in dissent, faced no such restrictions. The *Brown* opinion certainly contains the marks of postwar liberal thought and culture, but these manifestations are clouded by the immediate circumstances of its creation. Waring's opinion offers a clearer lens into the world of liberal thought and culture.

By the time he heard *Briggs*, Waring had gone through a process of racial and legal education, one that while certainly unique for where it took place was far from unique among the larger community of racial liberals. In fact, the stages and experiences of Waring's development were mirrored in the recent history of the Supreme Court. To begin with, both Waring and the justices of the Supreme Court received an early exposure to the horrific consequences of racial injustice in criminal cases dealing with brutality against African Americans. The Supreme Court dealt with a number of such cases in the 1930s and 1940s, and these were critical events in the developing civil rights jurisprudence within the Court. The shocking examples of violence against African Americans in the South were particularly effective in mobilizing liberal opinion toward supporting at least some federal intervention to remedy the worst abuses of the southern criminal justice system.[27] While the Court confronted the issue when it expanded federal oversight of state-level criminal justice proceedings in major decisions such as *Chambers v. Florida* (1940) and *Screws v. United States* (1945), President Truman's policy was also affected by his exposure to violence against blacks in the South. His shock at reports of attacks on African Americans in the South, particularly returning war veterans, was a major factor in his decision to create a presidential commission to study the issue of civil rights.[28] Similarly, one of Waring's early exposures to racial brutality involved the case of Isaac Woodard Jr., an African American veteran returning home from military service in 1946 when he was viciously beaten and blinded by a constable for his alleged disorderly conduct on a bus in Batesburg, South Carolina. Waring presided over the jury trial of the constable. With the outcome of the trial in the hands of an all-white jury, the most Waring could do, knowing that the jury would quickly acquit, was to take a long walk once the jury began deliberating so as to make it appear that the jury took at least some time in considering the case. The entire experience was intensely frustrating to Waring.[29]

Another area in which the development of Waring's jurisprudence and that of the Supreme Court coincided was voting rights. Waring's much-noted voting rights decisions found a powerful precedent in the landmark Supreme Court ruling in *Smith v. Allwright* (1944), an 8–1 decision that declared unconstitutional the whites-only primary system in Texas. As Waring noted in 1947 in his own decision involving a white primary, the view of the Supreme Court on the question of whether the federal government had the right to supervise primary elections "has suffered a drastic and complete change." Working from *Smith*, and its key precedent, *United States v. Classic* (1941), Waring wrote, "it is clear . . . that the law of our land has been materially changed."[30] Based on the precedents of the Supreme Court, Waring could convincingly argue that he was only fulfilling his role as a federal judge in adhering to the supreme law of the land. In his mind, the primary cases were, as he recalled in a speech in 1949, "pretty simple."[31] He would later elaborate on his approach to the case: "Either you were going to be entirely governed by the white supremacy doctrine and just shut your eyes and bowl this thing through, or you were going to be a Federal judge and decide the law. That was the issue."[32] The choice to decide the case as he did, at least for a judge from South Carolina, involved much more than simply deciding law. Yet that he could portray the issue in such a way, both to himself and to his critics, was due largely to the previous actions of the Supreme Court. Even the most controversial lines of Waring's decision—"It is time for South Carolina to rejoin the Union. It is time to fall in step with the other states and to adopt the American way of conducting elections"—depended on an already established principle of what it meant to be a part of the Union and to conduct an election in the American way.

Additionally, like the Supreme Court, Waring initially accepted the separate-but-equal doctrine announced by the Court in *Plessy v. Ferguson* (1896) and attempted to use this doctrine to improve conditions for African Americans, before abandoning this approach as untenable. In Waring's first major race case, in 1945, he ordered the equalization of salaries for black and white teachers.[33] Two years later he used the same separate-but-equal principle in *Wrighten v. Board of Trustees of South Carolina*, in which he approved a plan to create a separate law school for blacks in South Carolina as an alternative to integrating the white school.[34] In this decision Waring noted that "the right to segregate has been assumed or tacitly acknowledged by many of our courts, including the Supreme Court of the United States," citing *Plessy* as a precedent. He also cited the Supreme Court decision of *Gaines v. Canada* (1938), which ruled that an African American resident of Missouri who sought to go to law school must be provided adequate educational facilities within his home state, if those facilities existed for white residents.[35] Following the Supreme Court's lead as set forth in *Gaines*, Waring's ruling in *Wrighten* was based on the notion inspired by *Plessy* that segregated facilities could still meet the requirements of the equal protection clause of the Fourteenth Amendment.

It was not long, however, before Waring became convinced that equality was impossible under a system of legalized segregation. The years between 1947, when he issued his first white-primary ruling and the *Wrighten* decision, and 1951, when he wrote his dissent in *Briggs*, saw him grow increasingly exasperated with what he saw as the fallacy of separate but equal. This frustration was reinforced by various pronouncements from the nation's capital. In his *Elmore* decision, Waring had quoted from a speech that Truman gave before a NAACP conference calling for federal involvement to end racial discrimination.[36] In October 1947, the president's Committee on Civil Rights released its report, titled *To Secure These Rights*, in which the committee, while not necessarily calling for desegregation of public schools, pointed out that separate but equal schooling had failed in practice.[37] Waring's esteem for the president only increased after his address to Congress calling for civil rights legislation and his executive order desegregating the military. Waring's support for Truman grew still more after his personal meeting with the president in December 1948. Although he would eventually become frustrated with Truman's inaction on the civil rights agenda in the early 1950s, the president's rhetoric and action in the late 1940s earned him Waring's respect and support.[38]

The most influential messages emanating from the nation's capital as Waring sat down to write his opinion in *Briggs*, however, were from the U.S. Supreme Court. He dedicated the bulk of the dissent to an exposition of how, during the course of the twentieth century, "the courts have generally and progressively recognized the true meaning of the Fourteenth Amendment," summarizing the promising trend in the Court's racial decisions in various fields, including jury selection, peonage, transportation, criminal justice, housing, labor, suffrage, and education.[39] For Waring, the culminating moment in this progression of decisions came on a single day in 1950 when the Court announced rulings in three separate segregation cases. In *Henderson v. United States*, the Court ruled that segregation in dining cars on interstate railroads violated the Interstate Commerce Act.[40] The other two cases, and the ones that most attracted Waring's attention, dealt with segregation in graduate education. *Sweatt v. Painter*, a law school case out of Texas, and *McLaurin v. Oklahoma*, a case involving segregation policies within the University of Oklahoma's graduate school of education, were critical victories for the NAACP's carefully orchestrated litigation campaign.[41] While neither decision went so far as to directly challenge *Plessy* or the doctrine of separate but equal, they both set the bar of equality so high as to threaten the entire outdated doctrine, at least as far as graduate education was concerned. For Waring these rulings were a watershed, not necessarily for how they affected his belief in the moral wrongness of segregation (which was already set in his mind by this point), but for how these land-mark decisions could be used to legitimize a judicial assault on segregated education on all levels. In *Briggs*, Waring argued that *Sweatt* and *McLaurin* "definitely and conclusively establish the doctrine that separation and seg-regation according to race is a violation of the Fourteenth Amendment."[42] (This was, to put it generously, a rather loose reading of two decisions that the Supreme Court carefully limited to avoid exactly this kind of over-reaching interpretation.) Waring's extension of the reasoning of *Sweatt* and *McLaurin* to the public schools formed the legal basis for his decision, as it would for the Supreme Court three years later.

All this analysis of precedent and constitutional interpretation, however, cannot be separated from the general discourse on the nature of American society and the problem of racial discrimination that made for the most memorable sections of the *Briggs* decision. A mark of Waring's jurispru-dence was the integration of legal analysis with social and moral commen-tary. It is primarily because of Waring's externalist approach to the law that the dissent is such a valuable window into Waring's thought and his place among racial liberals of the period. To begin with, the themes from Myr-dal's *An American Dilemma* were a constant, if somewhat muted, presence in the opinion. The central argument of Myrdal's work, probably the central tenet of mid-century racial liberalism, was that there was a coherent set of American ideals, an "American Creed," premised on the principle of hu-man equality. Although there was no room in *Briggs* for the thorough explication of Myrdalian thought that Waring offered in some of his non-legal statements and that informed his social vision, his belief that the American ideal of equality was a controlling principle in the case is clearly present.

Waring most explicitly fell back on Myrdal's thesis in his interpretation of the Fourteenth Amendment. In *Briggs* he asked whether segregated educa-tion could exist "under our American system as particularly enunciated in the Fourteenth Amendment to the Constitution of the United States."[43] This idea of an "American system," a term equivalent to Myrdal's "Ameri-can Creed," deriving from but not limited to the Fourteenth Amendment, formed the basis of Waring's constitutional interpretation. Rather than limit his reading of the amendment to the specific wording of the text, or even to the intentions of the amendment's framers, Waring took a broader approach, reading the amendment as a representation of an American ideal rather than the controlling articulation of that ideal. In other words, Waring implied that the ideal itself, the "American system," had an existence be-yond the language of the Constitution and was to be taken into account in all cases of constitutional interpretation. But Waring did not develop further this line of reasoning, preferring to fall back on a call for common sense (which, it could be argued, is itself a resort to a common understanding that could be attributed to the existence of an American Creed): "It seems to me that it is unnecessary to pore through voluminous arguments and opinions to ascertain" the meaning of the Fourteenth Amendment. "One of ordinary ability and understanding of the English language will have no trouble in knowing that when this Amendment was adopted, it was intended to do away with discrimination between our citizens." This "self evident" interpretation concluded: "it is undeniably true that the three great [Reconstruction] Amendments were adopted to eliminate not only slavery, itself, but all idea of discrimination and difference between American citizens."[44] Thus Waring's understanding of the Reconstruction amendments, using the interpretive filter of his understanding of the "American System," brought him to the colorblind ideal articulated most famously by Justice John Marshall Harlan in his dissent in *Plessy* over fifty years earlier, an ideal that found a new life during the mid-twentieth century.[45]

In embracing the "American System," Waring was very much a part of mainstream culture of the early postwar period, a culture derived from the patriotism of the Second World War and the victory over fascism, strengthened by postwar economic prosperity, and given new urgency with the onset of the cold war. This general feeling of comfort in the righteousness of American ideals and institutions, if not all its social realities, dominated the era. The more radical critiques of American institutions had receded since the 1930s, with the cold war and domestic anticommunist crusades making leftist positions even less likely to be heard. America's confrontation with fascism and communism led many Americans to look at their own democratic system with a more positive, oftentimes celebratory, outlook.[46] Waring considered himself a patriot, and while never an outspoken anticommunist, he always sought to insulate his crusade from any implications of communist influence.[47] While the conservative tendencies of this celebration of American ideals should be readily evident, Waring's particular use of this perspective for the purposes of social reform indicates that equating celebratory Americanism with conservatism is an oversimplification.

Waring's anticommunism led him to emphasize the importance of progress on civil rights as a defense against Soviet propaganda, which frequently publicized incidents of American racial oppression as evidence of the hypocrisy of America's claim to leadership of the "free world." The use of what the historian Mary Dudziak has termed the "Cold War imperative" as a weapon against segregation and discrimination was prevalent among liberals in the decades following the Second World War.[48] Not surprisingly, this line of reasoning appeared prominently in the conclusion to Waring's dissent in *Briggs*. The need to act against discrimination was particularly urgent, Waring explained, "at this time when our national leaders are called upon to show to the world that our democracy means what it says and that it is a true democracy."[49] The same point recurred constantly in Waring's writing.[50] The importance of world opinion became an additional source of support for Waring as he broke from local tradition. In rejecting South Carolina's system of legalized oppression, he looked to both national liberal opinion and what he saw as a worldwide consensus against racism. Considering Waring's need for support of his views in as many places as he could find it, his embrace of the cold war imperative is readily understandable.

The power of Myrdalian ideas over Waring's thought is further illustrated in one of the most fascinating paragraphs of the dissent. The paragraph, toward the end of the opinion, begins with a discussion of the expert witnesses the NAACP used to demonstrate the "deleterious and warping effect" that segregation had on African American children (a topic that the Supreme Court would famously pick up on in *Brown*). Midway through this discussion, Waring wrote, "This [damage of segregation] applies to white as well as Negro children"—a sentence that was not in the first draft of the decision.[51] Waring then noted that expert studies, including some conducted in Clarendon County, found segregation most harmful early in life. He continued: "And from their testimony as well as from common experience and knowledge and from our own reasoning we must unavoidably come to the conclusion that racial prejudice is something that is acquired and that that acquiring is in early childhood."[52] The subject of this key paragraph has shifted from the black child to the white child. In the first draft this shift was a subtle one; the addition of a sentence explicitly bringing in the white child made the shift more clear, but the reasoning of the paragraph is still puzzling. Waring implied that the psychologists presented studies of the damages that segregation caused in white children (the studies conducted in Clarendon County examined only black children), although he qualified this assertion by falling back on "common experience" and "our own reasoning." Nevertheless, Waring blended the two arguments about psychological damage before concluding the paragraph with a discussion of the transmission of prejudice. In other words, his line of reasoning, after wavering for most of the paragraph, settled on desegregation as necessary to save white children from the harm of being prejudiced. The idea that racism was essentially a white problem, an idea that lay at the heart of Myrdal's work and would become an orthodox assumption of racial liberalism, was a position toward which Waring's thought tended.[53]

The idea that segregation damaged whites is related to another prominent element of Waring's racial thought that appeared in his dissent in *Briggs*: that of prejudice as a disease or sickness. Of all the metaphors Waring used to describe the problem of racism, by far the most common were medical in nature: racism was a disease, a cancer, a contagion—at one point he even compared the white supremacist to an alcoholic.[54] This sort of argument was most famously articulated in Cash's *The Mind of the South*, one of Waring's favorite books. The disease metaphor contained an important corollary: if racial prejudice was a medical ailment, it could be cured. As Waring employed the metaphor in *Briggs*, while ending segregation in higher education only dealt with the "symptoms of disease," striking at segregation in the public schools would strike at the "cause of infection."[55] In his nonjudicial writings and speeches, Waring used this type of language over and over. He once compared the immediate action that he advocated to a surgical procedure: "It is painful. Of course it hurts to have an operation. It hurts to lance a boil or carbuncle, but that is the best way to get the festering infection out of your system."[56] Waring's various descriptions of the South, of prejudice, and of segregation in terms of pathology and disease became more frequent as he became more aggressive in his call for civil rights. His growing impatience with the gradualist approach favored by most southern liberals led him to frame the issue in more immediate terms, for which the analogy of an urgent medical issue fit well.[57] Waring admired what he considered scientific approaches to the race problem and embraced the psychological testimony offered by the NAACP in *Briggs*. Indeed, he seemed to envision the jurist as a kind of expert who is able to look beyond the immediate desires of the people to locate the larger imperatives of the nation and the world. The medical analogy had the far from insignificant ability to make the problem of segregation appear not only urgent but something that could be remedied with a committed and concerted effort.

A related idea was that prejudice was the product of irrationality or ignorance. This line of reasoning worked particularly well in the education cases like *Briggs*. Once integrated, a major American institution, its school system, would become a symbol of equality, while at the same time strengthening this principle through the educational process. Since, as Waring explained in *Briggs*, "[t]here is absolutely no reasonable explanation for racial prejudice," and "[i]t is all caused by unreasoning emotional reactions," then educational efforts, both in the schools and outside, were essential weapons against white supremacy.[58] If prejudice was a psychological ailment, then it could be treated by properly trained experts. This mentality fit well into a postwar culture in which psychology was seen as a tool for achieving social happiness. The therapeutic ethos was clearly evident among the social visions of postwar racial liberals, Waring included.[59] Perhaps the primary drawing power of psychological analysis for racial reformers was that like biological terminology, it described a problem that had a readily evident and viable solution.

Yet as subsequent history would make painfully clear, both the racism-as-cancer and the racism-as-irrational-behavior approaches were not just powerful tools for reform. They were dangerously simplistic. The assumption of Waring, and most other racial liberals of his generation, was that prejudice was predominantly an attitude, and discrimination a product of this attitude. Change the attitude, along with the laws that contribute to it, and both discrimination and prejudice should decline. While this process would be far from easy, as even the most optimistic of racial reformers would probably have recognized, it had the immeasurable benefit of appearing manageable. It is worth noting that both Waring and Warren saw their school desegregation cases as "easy" cases to decide.[60] Yet their approach, which emphasized curing a "disease" and shining the light of reason on prejudice, had a serious flaw: it failed to appreciate those elements of racial discrimination that were embedded in the very structures and institutions of American society. The liberal reform movement, premised on bringing American practices more in line with American ideals, was unprepared for a new wave of social critique contending that many of the ideals and institutions characteristic of the "American way of life" were themselves partly responsible for continued racial inequities.

One American ideal that Waring was willing to take on, if it may be described as an ideal, was states rights, which he saw as inextricable from white supremacy in the South. For Waring, the constitutional tool necessary to take on the states rights doctrine was the Fourteenth Amendment. As he wrote in *Briggs*, this amendment had been effectively used in recent years to strike down "the attempts made by state governments (almost entirely those of the former Confederate states) to restrict the Amendment and to keep Negroes in a different classification so far as their rights and privileges as citizens are concerned."[61] Rather than elaborate on or even defend his views on federalism, however, Waring simply ignored the issue. This was a blatant omission, considering that it was at the center of the segregationist defense and played a central role in the majority opinion in *Briggs*. By emphasizing the precedence of the "American system" over all other considerations, Waring bypassed the entire question of state power and assumed that federal interests were controlling.[62] In putting his faith for reform squarely in the hands of the federal government—of which he was, of course, a representative—Waring rejected the dominant approach of southern liberals, who sought to pursue improved protection of black rights while upholding the southern tradition of states rights. Waring would have nothing to do with such arguments. Having cut his ties with his local and state community—aside from a few activist blacks in Charleston—he put his full faith for progress in the intervention of the federal government.

Waring's belief that the federal government, particularly the federal judiciary, had made the most progress in recent years on the race issue—and therefore, assumedly, would continue to do so in the future—was a central component of his vision for social change, which was basically a top-down model. Although he occasionally applauded grassroots efforts, he generally saw lower-class whites as too deeply mired in their own prejudices to effectively take part in a movement, and most blacks as too weighed down by the damaging effects of these prejudices—economic insecurity, lack of education, fear of retribution—to contribute in any meaningful way. Waring never fully let go of the paternalist feelings that dominated his approach to the black community earlier in his life.[63] In the first draft of *Briggs*, for instance, he noted that racial discrimination resulted in "the poor underprivileged and often complacent attitude of the Negroes in the southern states." (He would later modify this line to read: "the poor under-privileged and frightened attitude of so many of the Negroes in the southern states.")[64] Elizabeth Waring wrote a scathing attack on African American intransigence to social change in a diary entry soon after *Briggs* was announced. "[E]nemies both White and Negro are rising up again, crawling out of their holes and spewing their venom around wherever they can reach," she recorded. "The Negro variety is usually politicians, Doctors and Dentists, preachers and worst and most vociferous of all SCHOOL TEACHERS. They believe they thrive, but at any rate they benefit from Segregation fearing to compete with better trained White Professionals." Her husband, she explained, similarly denounced "Negro traitors," telling her, "When one breaks one pane of glass in their prison window they cry out with terror that it will hurt them."[65] Although on occasion Waring would see hope in increasing black activism, he generally saw the most promising sort as coming from established national organizations, such as the NAACP. His paternalistic understanding of the African American condition blinded him to the possibility of a grassroots movement based in the black community. He and most liberals of the period saw the best hopes for reform in effective leadership, not mass movements.[66]

Waring's élitist bent is best illustrated in his faith in the law and legal process as a tool of reform. This attitude is not surprising considering the position he held. Yet his commitment to the rule of law as the key to racial progress was more than simply what one might expect from a judge. Waring argued, for example, that focusing the racial reform movement simply on modifying the sentiment of white racists was wrongheaded. Rather, discriminatory laws should be attacked first. For laws, Waring believed, had the ability to shape popular belief and action. "I think the fight in the South is primarily a fight of law," he would recall. "You can't wait for sentiment of people to change if it's unlawful for them to change."[67] If used properly, Waring and many racial liberals believed, reforming the law could lead the way to reforming society.[68]

Finally, a theme that Waring emphasized in *Briggs*, and one that can bring coherence to Waring's racial vision, is the theme of progress. Although Waring often portrayed racial redemption in the Deep South as a distant prospect, he saw the twentieth century as a period of steady progress toward racial equality.[69] His recognition of the complexity of the issue in the South was not always consistent with his call for reform, which tended to portray the problem as relatively easy to solve. In this sense, one can see a tension in Waring's thought, between a confidence in social engineering, which dominated much of postwar liberal thought, and an understanding of the intransigence of southern racial traditions. Even as Waring embraced much of what racial liberalism offered, his background and experience in the Deep South tempered his views, causing his work to blend a particular brand of southern realism with racial liberalism. Yet even though he implicitly accepted at least an element of a distinctly southern perspective on racial reform, in the end Waring was more a part of the mainstream, northern-based version of racial liberalism than any southern version—the southern adherence to states rights and gradualism made any reconciliation with this group impossible. Waring's optimism would, more often than not, triumph over his pessimism.

Waring's dissent in *Briggs* reveals much about both the context of mid-century liberalism and Waring's particular interpretation of this body of thought. Those aspects of racial liberalism that would make it particularly attractive to this southern judge are readily evident. Racial liberals often repeated the mantra that the race problem was really a white problem, a belief that contained an element of self-criticism but also implied that a solution to the problem could be effected without necessarily stretching the reach of the liberal imagination into the realm of black society and culture. This was basically an assimilationist approach to reform. It was also an establishment-focused, leadership-oriented approach to reform, which was particularly attractive to Waring, who sought to use his role as a judge to advance activism. One can readily perceive those aspects of racial liberalism that would make it particularly effective in moving a heretofore apathetic white establishment to at least begin to address racial inequality through the force of the federal government. The worldview of liberal racial thought that Waring began to embrace in 1945 was also the worldview that would dominate the justices of the Supreme Court as they deliberated on the cases of *Brown* in the winter and spring of 1954. For all its blind spots, for all its potentially conservative tendencies, racial liberalism proved, at least in the late 1940s and early 1950s, a crucial weapon of reform. Waring's dissent in *Briggs* exemplifies this point.

Strictly in terms of its legal argument, Waring's dissent, like *Brown*, was a rather uninspired document. The words that the legal scholar Alexander Bickel used to describe the Warren Court's jurisprudence fit Waring's as well: "They relied on events for vindication more than on the method of reason for contemporary vindication. . . . [T]hey bet on the future."[70] But as both Waring and the justices of the Warren Court knew, by the middle of the century taking a stance against racial discrimination was a pretty safe bet. Although the court-led effort at implementing school desegregation failed for the most part, at least until the other branches of the federal government committed themselves to the problem in the mid-1960s, the basic principle of the decision, and the basic principle of Waring's contribution—that racial equality was an American ideal worthy of protecting with the power of the state—would indeed be vindicated by subsequent history. Even if this particular vision of racial equality, based on ending overt discrimination, began to show its limitations almost as soon as it was proclaimed (many of the adherents to this vision of racial equality would be caught off guard by the rapid developments of the black freedom struggle of the 1960s), this vision, as embodied in Waring's life and work, as embodied in *Brown*, was an essential part of the modern struggle for racial equality.

America in the 1940s is not normally seen as a time of dramatic racial change, particularly compared to the revolutionary transformations that would occur in the 1960s. While these changes are not necessarily comparable in scope, there is a strong argument that the rise of racial liberalism in the 1940s and 1950s led to a significant conceptual shift among an ever-growing group of liberal Americans—both black and white, mostly in the North, but also to a limited extent in the South—that laid the groundwork without which the civil rights movement could never have achieved all it did in its relatively short life span. While Waring's life and work, along with *Brown*, are often seen as important precursors to the era of the civil rights movement, they should also be appreciated as culminating moments of an earlier era of social reform. The era of racial liberalism often appears to modern eyes as frustratingly moderate or even conservative. The limitations of the vision of racial liberals were significant, to be sure. There was too much faith in rationally derived, top-down reform, too much attention to changing attitudes without addressing structural or institutional concerns, too much reliance on psychological models of racism. But in the end these limitations were outweighed by the real changes that came of this shared vision of possibility. The era of racial liberalism was in fact a critical step away from the complacency toward civil rights and race relations that had marked most of the white establishment in the previous era.

After the ruling in *Briggs*, Aubrey Williams wrote Waring a letter of congratulations. Williams, himself a prominent activist on behalf of racial equality, expressed a measure of envy for the judge's opportunity to act on behalf of his convictions. "Truly," he wrote, "you are a man favored by the course of his times."[71] This is a striking description for someone who was ostracized, harassed, and attacked in the very city where he had made his home for over six decades. But it is also quite insightful. Waring was, by all counts that matter, extremely well favored by his times. His racial views, which appeared so revolutionary in South Carolina in the late 1940s, were becoming increasingly accepted by Americans around the nation. Waring's position in the midst of the white power structure of the Deep South made him a symbol of redemption and hope for a nation entering a promising new stage in its long and troubled history of race relations. Waring's ability to embrace the most significant conceptual shift of the era, the movement to end legalized racial inequality, made him not only a man of his times, but a man who was truly favored by these times.

## Notes

1 A copy of Waring's acceptance speech is found in the J. Waties Waring Papers, box 110-1, folder 8, Manuscript Division, Moorland-Spingarn Research Center, Howard University.

2 By the mid-1940s various southern courts had issued similar rulings. Davison M. Douglas, *Reading, Writing, and Race* (Chapel Hill: University of North Carolina Press, 1995), 20, 260 n. 101.

3 Reminiscences of J. Waties Waring, Columbia University Oral History Research Office, 1972 (microfiche), 235–46.

4 *Elmore v. Rice*, 72 F. Supp. 516 (E.D.S.C. 1947).

5 *Brown v. Baskin*, 78 F. Supp. 933 (E.D.S.C. 1948).

6 *Briggs v. Elliott*, 98 F. Supp. 529 (E.D.S.C. 1951).

7 "The Man They Love to Hate," *Time*, 23 August 1948, 17; Samuel Grafton, "The Lonesomest Man in Town," *Colliers*, 29 April 1950, 20–21, 49–50; Lillian Scott, "Judge Waring: An Island in a Sea of Hate," *Chicago Defender Magazine*, 20 November 1948.

8 For a summary of the "revenge" explanation see "The Man They Love to Hate."

9 Waring compared the donning of the judicial robes to "being born again."

Reminiscences of J. Waties Waring, 139a–140a, quotation from 139a. See also Grafton, "The Lonesomest Man in Town," 49.

10 Waring, "The Result of the Break with South Carolina and Charleston in Terms of Losses and Gains," undated memorandum, Waring Papers, box 110-2, folder 9.

11 Most studies of Waring have focused on the singular nature of his courageous rejection of the southern racist tradition. Robert Lewis Terry, "J. Waties Waring, Spokesman for Racial Justice in the New South" (diss., University of Utah, 1970); William B. Scott, "Judge J. Waties Waring: Advocate of 'Another' South," *South Atlantic Quarterly* 77 (1978): 320–34; David W. Southern, "Beyond Jim Crow Liberalism: Judge Waring's Fight against Segregation in South Carolina, 1942–52," *Journal of Negro History* 66 (autumn 1981): 209–27; Tinsley E. Yarbrough, *A Passion for Justice: J. Waties Waring and Civil Rights* (New York: Oxford University Press, 1987).

12 Gunnar Myrdal, with the assistance of Richard Sterner and Arnold Rose, *An American Dilemma: The Negro Problem and American Democracy* (New York: Harper and Row, 1944); W. J. Cash, *The Mind of the South* (New York: Alfred A. Knopf, 1941). For Waring's praise of these works see Waring, "The Struggle for Negro Rights," *Lawyers Guild Review* 9, no. 1 (winter 1949): 10; Reminiscences of J. Waties Waring, 405; Grafton, "The Lonesomest Man in Town," 49.

13 Waring to Aubrey Williams, 21 July 1949, Waring Papers, box 110-20, folder 614; Waring to Aubrey Williams, 21 March 1950, Waring Papers, box 110-20, folder 615.

14 Arthur M. Schlesinger Jr., "The Causes of the Civil War: A Note on Historical Sentimentalism," *Partisan Review* (October 1949): 969–81. Waring's annotated copy of this essay is found in Waring Papers, box 110-35, folder 1134. On the connection of historical interpretations of abolitionists and contemporary attitudes toward racial concerns, Peter Novick points out that declining levels of racism could be charted by noting the rising stock of abolitionists among academics. *That Noble Dream: The "Objectivity Question" and the American Historical Profession* (New York: Cambridge University Press, 1988), 351 n. 47.

15 These scrapbooks are found in the Waring Papers.

16 Waring, "The Result of the Break with South Carolina and Charleston."

17 Grafton, "The Lonesomest Man in Town," 50.

18 Untitled memorandum [ca. 1951], Waring Papers, box 110-31, folder 945.

19 On his meeting with Truman see editorial, "Advances toward Democracy," *New York Times*, 3 December 1948, 24; "Waring Calls on Truman," *New York Times*, 3 December 1948, 30; Waring to Truman, 6 December 1948 and 9 June 1952, and Truman to Waring, 10 December 1948, all in Waring Papers, box 110-19, folder 567. On his award from the National Lawyers Guild see *Lawyers Guild Review* 9, no. 1 (Winter 1949): 5–12.

20 Waring's record on appeal was forty-six cases affirmed, one modified and affirmed, two affirmed in part and reversed in part, two dismissed as premature, and ten reversed. A summary of Waring's record on appeal, 1943 to 1951, is found in Waring Papers, box 110-31, folder 965.

21  *Elmore v. Rice*, 72 F. Supp. 516 (E.D.S.C 1947), affirmed, 165 F.2d 387 (4th Cir. 1947), cert. denied, 333 U.S. 875 (1947).

22  Reminiscences of J. Waties Waring, 272.

23  For Waring's confidence in how *Brown* would be decided, see Reminiscences of J. Waties Waring, 33, 364–68; Waring to Thurgood Marshall, 27 November 1953, Waring Papers, box 110-15, folder 388; Waring to Aubrey Williams, 2 July 1951, Waring Papers, box 110-20, folder 616. Waring maintained that even if Warren had not replaced Vinson the decision would have been the same, with the Chief Justice in the majority. Reminiscences of J. Waties Waring, 364.

24  Several of the more personal references were cut in the editing process as well. Draft of *Briggs*, Waring Papers, box 110-24, folder 740.

25  98 F. Supp. 529, 548.

26  *Brown v. Board of Education*, 347 U.S. 483, 495 (1954).

27  See Michael J. Klarman, "The Racial Origins of Modern Criminal Procedure," 99 *Michigan Law Review* 48 (2000).

28  *Chambers v. Florida*, 309 U.S. 227 (1940), and *Screws v. United States*, 325 U.S. 91 (1945). On Truman's reaction to racial violence in the South, see Walter White, *A Man Called White: The Autobiography of Walter White* (New York: Viking, 1948), 322–33, and Kari Frederickson, *The Dixiecrat Revolt and the End of the Solid South, 1932–1968* (Chapel Hill: University of North Carolina Press, 2001), 56–58.

29  On Waring's recollections of the case see Reminiscences of J. Waties Waring, 215–24.

30  72 F. Supp. 516, 519, 523.

31  Waring, "The Struggle for Negro Rights," 11.

32  Reminiscences of J. Waties Waring, 256.

33  *Thompson v. Gibbes*, 60 F. Supp. 872 (E.D.S.C. 1945).

34  *Wrighten v. Board of Trustees of South Carolina*, 72 F. Supp. 948 (E.D.S.C. 1947).

35  *Gaines v. Canada*, 305 U.S. 337 (1938).

36  Harry S. Truman, "Address before the National Association for the Advancement of Colored People," 29 June 1947, *Public Papers of the Presidents of the United States: Harry S. Truman, 1947* (Washington: Government Printing Office, 1963), 311–13.

37  President's Committee on Civil Rights, *To Secure These Rights* (Washington: Government Printing Office, 1947), 63–65, 168.

38  For Waring's praise of the desegregation order, see untitled, undated memorandum, Waring Papers, box 110-31, folder 945.

39  98 F. Supp. 529, 542–44, quotation from 542.

40  *Henderson v. United States*, 339 U.S. 816 (1950).

41  *Sweatt v. Painter*, 339 U.S. 629 (1950); *McLaurin v. Oklahoma*, 339 U.S. 637 (1950).

42  Waring's quotation is at 98 F. Supp. 529, 544.

43  98 F. Supp. 529, 541.

44  98 F. Supp. 529, 541–42.

45  The NAACP, in its litigation campaign against segregated education, fre-

quently asserted a colorblind interpretation of the Constitution. See generally Andrew Kull, *The Color-Blind Constitution* (Cambridge: Harvard University Press, 1992).

46 The best study of this trend is found in Edward Purcell, *The Crisis of Democratic Theory* (Lexington: University Press of Kentucky, 1973), esp. 235–72.

47 Waring's anticommunism, implied in his idealization of American ideals, is made explicit in Waring to Walter White, 22 April 1949, Waring Papers, box 110-20, folder 601.

48 Mary L. Dudziak, *Cold War Civil Rights: Race and the Image of American Democracy* (Princeton: Princeton University Press, 2000).

49 98 F. Supp. 529, 548.

50 See for example Reminiscences of J. Waties Waring, 396–97; Waring to Harry S. Truman, 9 June 1952, Waring Papers, box 110-19, folder 567; undated, untitled memorandum, Waring Papers, box 110-2, folder 9.

51 This sentence is added in pencil to the first typed draft, which is found in the Waring Papers, box 110-24, folder 740. In the published opinion, this sentence is found at 98 F. Supp. 529, 547.

52 98 F. Supp. 529, 547.

53 Perhaps the somewhat awkward fit of this "white damage" argument into the line of reasoning of Waring's decision, as evidenced in the penciled addition to the first draft, explains why Warren excluded the argument from his opinion in *Brown*.

54 Undated, untitled memorandum, Waring Papers, box 110–31, folder 947.

55 98 F. Supp. 529, 548.

56 Waring, "The Struggle for Negro Rights," 12. See also "Race Bars Hit by S.C. Judge," *Daily News* (New York), 27 February 1950.

57 Quoted in "Jurist from South Assails Prejudice," *New York Times*, 12 October 1948, 31.

58 98 F. Supp. 529, 547.

59 See Ellen Herman, *The Romance of American Psychology: Political Culture in the Age of Experts* (Berkeley: University of California Press, 1995).

60 On Warren see Richard Kluger, *Simple Justice* (New York: Alfred A. Knopf, 1976), 678.

61 98 F. Supp. 529, 543.

62 In his dissent Waring did not even make reference to the majority decision until the concluding paragraph. 98 F. Supp. 529, 548. In other contexts, Waring was more explicit in his reliance on the federal government. In a letter to Truman, he argued that it "is necessary for the federal government to firmly and constantly keep pressure" on the South. Waring to Harry S. Truman, 6 December 1948, Waring Papers, box 110-19, folder 567. See also Waring's draft of a civil rights plank for the 1952 Democratic platform, Waring Papers, box 110-2, folder 9.

63 For Waring's description of his early attitude on race see Reminiscences of J. Waties Waring, 9–11.

64  Draft of *Briggs*, Waring Papers, box 110-24, folder 740; 98 F. Supp. 529, 542.

65  Elizabeth Waring Diary, entry from 12 June 1951, Waring Papers, box 110-3, folder 14.

66  The attitude of most postwar liberals toward mass movements ranged from dismissal to outright fear. The dismissal is well illustrated in the title of a chapter in *An American Dilemma*, "The American Pattern of Individual Leadership and Mass Passivity." The fear is perhaps best illustrated in the work of scholars who located the origins of McCarthyism in irrational and ignorant mass politics. See for example Daniel Bell, ed., *The New American Right* (New York: Criterion, 1955), and Will Herberg, "Government by Rabble-Rousing," *New Leader*, 18 January 1954, 13–16.

67  Reminiscences of J. Waties Waring, 398.

68  This thesis was extremely common in the work of racial liberals. Two prominent works that address this issue are Carey McWilliams, "Race Discrimination and the Law," *Science and Society* 9, no. 1 (winter 1945): 1–22, and Will Maslow, "Prejudice, Discrimination, and the Law," *Annals of the American Academy of Political and Social Science* 275 (May 1951): 9–17. Even a psychologist such as Gordon W. Allport found an important role for the law in changing prejudiced attitudes. See *The Nature of Prejudice* (Reading, Mass.: Perseus, 1954), 461–78. It is worth noting, however, that Myrdal tended to put less faith in the power of the law in American society, preferring to emphasize what he saw as a culture of disrespect for the rule of law, particularly in the South. Myrdal saw the greatest hope for reform in an "educational offensive against racial intolerance." *An American Dilemma*, 13–19, 523–72, quotation from 49. As much as Waring admired Myrdal's work, he could never feel as optimistic as Myrdal about the potential for re-educating the southern racist.

69  Both sides of Waring's thought are shown in a single memo, in which Waring wrote: (a) "The abolition [of segregation laws] in the deep South is, I am afraid, in the very far distant future"; and (b) "I believe that the prospect for the Negro in the next fifty years is brightening. . . . The old White Supremacists . . . will be driven to cover and die off." Untitled memo, Waring Papers, box 110-31, folder 945. For Waring's generally optimistic appraisal of racial progress, see Reminiscences of J. Waties Waring, 385–97.

70  Alexander M. Bickel, *The Supreme Court and the Idea of Progress* (New York: Harper and Row, 1970), 12–13.

71  Aubrey Williams to Waring, 29 June 1951, Waring Papers, box 110-20, folder 616.

MICHAEL J. KLARMAN

## Brown v. Board of Education

### Law or Politics?

When cases challenging the constitutionality of racial segregation in public schools reached the Supreme Court in 1951–52, the social and political context had changed dramatically since 1927, the last time the justices had (obliquely) considered the question. Several million blacks had migrated from southern farms to northern cities in search of greater economic opportunity and relative racial tolerance. One largely unintended consequence of this Great Migration was black political empowerment, as African Americans relocated from a region of pervasive disfranchisement to one of relatively unrestricted ballot access. Moreover, blacks in large northern cities frequently held the balance of power between the two major political parties.[1]

Demographic shifts, industrialization, and the dislocative impact of the Second World War produced an urban black middle class with the education, disposable income, and lofty expectations conducive to involvement in social protest. Economic gains enabled blacks to challenge the racial status quo by freeing them from white control and creating a powerful lever, the economic boycott, for extracting racial reforms. Economic progress also inclined blacks to contest traditional racial practices, by dramatizing the disparity between their economic and social status. Southern urbanization empowered blacks politically, because cities had looser restrictions on black suffrage. Urban blacks found it easier to coordinate social protest, because of less oppressive racial mores and the relative ease of overcoming collective-action problems, given better transportation and communication.

Ideological forces also helped transform American racial attitudes and practices. The war against fascism impelled many Americans to reconsider racial preconceptions, to clarify the differences between Nazi Germany and the Jim Crow South. The ensuing cold war pressured Americans to show noncaucasian Third World nations why they should not equate democratic capitalism with white supremacy. Finally, developments in transportation and communication—television, interstate highways, expanded air travel—bound the nation into a more cohesive unit. The homogenization of America hindered the white South from maintaining deviant social practices such as Jim Crow.

Potent as these background forces for racial change were, by the early 1950s they had yet to produce dramatic changes in southern racial practices. Southern black voter registration had increased dramatically since 1940, but even so 80 percent of southern blacks remained voteless in 1952, and a large number of Deep South counties with black majorities still disfranchised African Americans entirely. Many southern cities had instituted less offensive bus-seating practices, but none had desegregated. Others had desegregated police forces and minor league baseball teams, and disparities in public funding of black and white schools were rapidly decreasing. In large border-state cities—Baltimore, Kansas City, St. Louis, Louisville, Wilmington—segregation in public accommodations was eroding, and Catholic parochial schools were starting to integrate. Yet racial segregation in public grade schools remained completely intact in southern and border states and the District of Columbia. Public school segregation lay near the top of white supremacists' priorities. For the Court to invalidate it was certain to generate far greater controversy and resistance than striking down the white primary or segregation in interstate transportation.

Five cases challenging the constitutionality of public school segregation reached the Court in 1951–52 and were subsumed under the caption *Brown v. Board of Education*. Justices were unenthusiastic about confronting so quickly the question they had deliberately evaded in the university segregation cases in 1950, and the National Association for the Advancement of Colored People (NAACP) had not planned to force the issue this soon. Moreover, the five cases were hardly representative. Three were from jurisdictions where whites were not deeply committed to segregation—Kansas, Delaware, and the District of Columbia—and judicial invalidation would probably not cause great disruption. The other two, however, came from Clarendon County, South Carolina, where blacks were 70 percent of the population, and Prince Edward County, Virginia, where they were 45 percent of the population. Broad forces for racial change had barely touched these counties, where judicial invalidation of segregation could jeopardize public education. The NAACP's secretary, Roy Wilkins, later confided that Clarendon County "would be the last place" he would choose to integrate. Yet ironically, the NAACP's decision in 1950 no longer to accept equalization cases had pushed blacks in these counties to convert grievances against inferior schools and lack of bus transportation into broad desegregation challenges. The association would not abandon courageous blacks willing to challenge Jim Crow under oppressive conditions, but it did pressure them to attack segregation directly, which they otherwise probably would not have done. Some civil rights leaders questioned the wisdom of pushing a desegregation suit on the Court at this time, worrying that the strategy might backfire and produce a disastrous defeat. Why run the risk, they wondered, if narrower challenges to racial inequality were virtually certain to succeed? Even Thurgood Marshall had doubts whether the justices were yet prepared to invalidate school segregation. As we shall see, such concerns were well founded.[2]

On 17 May 1954, *Brown v. Board of Education* unanimously invalidated racial segregation in public schools. The Court emphasized the importance of public education in modern life, refusing to be bound by the views of the Fourteenth Amendment's drafters or late-nineteenth-century justices, most of whom held more benign views of segregation. Segregated public schools were "inherently unequal" and thus violated the equal protection clause of the Fourteenth Amendment. Because a practice just invalidated in the states could not possibly be permitted in the capital of the free world, the justices ruled in the companion case of *Bolling v. Sharpe* that the due process clause of the Fifth Amendment imposed identical restrictions on the District of Columbia.[3]

The Court's unanimity can be misleading. Some scholars have concluded that the decision was easy and that a contrary ruling in *Brown* was "scarcely imaginable" by 1954. This view is mistaken; the justices were deeply conflicted. When first argued in the fall of 1952, the school segregation cases had an uncertain outcome. Before analyzing why many justices found *Brown* difficult, let us reconstruct the deliberations as the Court first considered the constitutionality of school segregation.[4]

Fred Vinson began the discussion, as the Chief Justice traditionally does. Vinson was from Kentucky, a border state with southern leanings and a long tradition of segregated education. There is a "[b]ody of law back of us on separate but equal," Vinson announced, and "Congress has not declared there should be no segregation." It was "[h]ard to get away from [the] long continued interpretation of Congress ever since the Amendments." District of Columbia schools "have long been segregated." Vinson was making two points. First, a long line of precedent upheld segregation as constitutional. Second, the same Congress that wrote the Fourteenth Amendment and was responsible for its enforcement had allowed segregated schools in the District of Columbia for nearly a hundred years, implying that segregation was constitutional. He continued: "Harlan in his dissent in *Plessy* does not refer to schools." That the one justice who had condemned railroad segregation in 1896 had implied that school segregation was acceptable was "significant." Vinson found it hard to "get away from that construction by those who wrote the amendments and those who followed." Vinson also worried that the "complete abolition of public schools in some areas" was a "serious" possibility if the Court invalidated segregation. Though others "said we should not consider this," Vinson thought "we can't close our eyes to [the] problem." He also thought it "would be better" if Congress acted. To maintain confidentiality and preserve fluidity, justices decided not to take even a tentative vote at conference. Yet several kept informal tallies, and all but one recorded Vinson as probably voting to reaffirm *Plessy*.[5]

As the senior associate justice, Hugo Black spoke next. He was the only justice from the Deep South—Alabama—and had briefly belonged to the Ku Klux Klan in the mid-1920s. Black predicted "violence if [the] court holds segregation unlawful" and warned that "states would probably take evasive measures while purporting to obey." He warned that South Carolina "might abolish [its] public school system." Black worried that if the Court invalidated school segregation, district courts "would then be in the firing line for enforcement through injunctions and contempt." He did not believe in "law by injunction" (perhaps because injunctions had undermined labor union organizing earlier in the century, and Black was a strong union supporter). Yet Black believed that the intention of segregation laws was "to discriminate because of color," whereas the "basic purpose" of the Fourteenth Amendment was "protection of the negro against discrimination." He was inclined to conclude that "segregation per se is bad *unless* the long line of decisions bars that construction of the amendment." Black "would vote[] to end segregation," but he expressed doubt about his colleagues: "If equal and separate prevails," he would "give weight to findings in each state."

Stanley Reed, like Vinson, was from Kentucky. Of all the justices, he was the most supportive of segregation, as a matter of policy and constitutionality. Reed took a "different view" from Black, declaring that "state legislatures have informed views on this matter," "Negroes have not thoroughly assimilated," and states "are authorized to make up their minds." "[A] reasonable body of opinion in the various states [was] for segregation," which was "for [the] benefit of both [races]." After noting "constant progress in this field and in the advancement of the interests of the negroes," Reed opined that "states should be left to work out the problem for themselves." Because the Constitution's meaning was "not fixed," Reed asked when the changes would be made? He answered: when the "body of people think [segregation is] unconstitutional." He could not "say [that] time [has] come," when seventeen states still segregated their schools. and four more afforded localities the option of doing so. Reed predicted that "[s]egregation in the border states will disappear in 15 or 20 years." But in the Deep South, "separate but equal schools must be allowed." He thought that "10 years would make [the schools] really equal" in Virginia and urged his colleagues "to allow time for equalizing." Until then, he "would uphold separate and equal." Reed's statement was unambiguous: *Plessy* was good law and should be reaffirmed.

Felix Frankfurter was an Austrian Jew who immigrated to the United States as a child. He taught law at Harvard for a quarter-century before Franklin Roosevelt appointed him to the Court in 1939. Frankfurter and Black had feuded before over the meaning of the Fourteenth Amendment—specifically, whether it "incorporated" the Bill of Rights, making its guarantees applicable to the states (rather than simply to Congress, as intended at the founding). In a manner reminiscent of that dispute, Frankfurter now wondered how Black could "know the purpose of the 14th amendment." Frankfurter had "read all of its history and he can't say it meant to abolish segregation." He also wanted "to know why what has gone before is wrong." He was reluctant to admit that "this court has long misread the Constitution." Moreover, he could not say "it's unconstitutional to treat a negro differently than a white." Yet Frankfurter also discussed the remedy the Court might issue if it invalidated segregation: "These are equity suits. They involve imagination in shaping decrees." He "would ask counsel on re-argument to address themselves to problems of enforcement." Frankfurter appeared not to have made up his mind, conceding that he "can't finish on [the] merits and would reargue all [the cases]."

Frankfurter had no similar doubts regarding the District of Columbia case, which "raise[d] very different questions." To permit school segregation in the nation's capital was "intolerable," and Frankfurter was prepared "to vote today that [it] violates [the] due process clause." Paradoxically, Frankfurter was quicker to bar segregation where the legal argument against it was weaker. The Fourteenth Amendment binds states, not Congress, and the many slaveowners who endorsed the Fifth Amendment, which does constrain Congress, presumably would not have condemned segregation in public schools, had such schools existed when the amendment was ratified in 1791. Frankfurter found compelling the moral, not the legal, argument against segregation in the nation's capital. In the end, he favored "put[ting] all the cases down for re-argument," which he insisted was not "delaying tactics," but a "further maturing process." Even the District of Columbia case should be reargued, he believed, to allow the Eisenhower administration time to fulfill its promise to end racial segregation through administrative action, which Frankfurter thought would produce "enormous . . . social gains" and was preferable to judicial intervention.

William O. Douglas grew up in Washington state, where few black people lived, then traveled east for law school at Columbia University, after which he became a law professor, first at Columbia and then at Yale. In 1936 Roosevelt appointed him to the Securities and Exchange Commission, a position affording few opportunities to ponder race issues. As a justice, Douglas often had little trouble resolving legal problems that vexed his colleagues, and segregation was no exception. "Segregation is an easy problem," Douglas stated, and the answer was "very simple." He explained: "No classifications on the basis of race can be made. [The] 14th amendment prohibits racial classifications. So does [the] due process clause of the 5th [amendment]. A negro can't be put by the state in one room because he's black and another put in the other room because he's white. The answer is simple though the application of it may present great difficulties." Nobody could have doubted where Douglas stood on *Brown*.

Robert Jackson was raised in upstate New York, another area with few blacks and no school segregation. Jackson admitted that his upbringing afforded him "little personal experience or firsthand knowledge by which to test many of the arguments advanced in these cases." He was "not conscious of the [race] problem" until he moved to Washington in the 1930s to join the Roosevelt administration. Jackson's conference statement began bluntly: "Nothing in the text that says this is unconstitutional. [There is] nothing in the opinions of the courts that says it's unconstitutional. Nothing in the history of the 14th amendment [says it's unconstitutional]." "On [the] basis of precedent," Jackson concluded, "segregation is ok."

Jackson ridiculed the NAACP's brief as "sociology," not law. He noted that New York mandated school segregation in the 1860s (when the Fourteenth Amendment was passed) and still in the 1890s (when *Plessy* was decided). Jackson thought that it would "be bad for the negros to be put into white schools" and he doubted whether one could "cure this [race] situation by putting children [of different races] together." He would not "say it is unconstitutional to practice segregation tomorrow." Yet he predicted that "segregation is nearing an end. We should perhaps give them time to get rid of it." He "would go along on that basis. There are equitable remedies that can be shaped to the needs." What these final words meant is unclear, but apparently Jackson could imagine joining a decision invalidating segregation or threatening to do so under certain conditions. Jackson also wanted to invite the House and Senate Judiciary Committees to participate in the reargument, because "if stirred up . . . they might abolish [segregation]." Still, the thrust of his remarks suggests doubt as to the legal basis for invalidating segregation.[6]

Harold Burton was the sole Republican justice in 1952, though he had been appointed by a Democrat, Harry Truman. Burton had been a senator from Ohio, and before that mayor of Cleveland, in Ohio's Western Reserve, known for its long-standing racial egalitarianism. Burton spoke briefly and to the point: "*Sipuel* [and *Sweatt*] crossed the threshold of these cases. Education is more than buildings and faculties. It's a habit of mind."[7] Burton continued: "With [the] 14th amendment, states do not have the choice. Segregation violates equal protection. [The] total effect is that separate education is not sufficient for today's problems. [It is] not reasonable to educate separately for a joint life." Though Burton "would give plenty of time in this decree," he plainly favored barring segregation in public education.

Tom Clark was from Texas, in the peripheral South. Few blacks lived in West Texas, where whites' commitment to segregation was thin. East Texas, though, resembled the Deep South; many counties had majority or near-majority black populations, and most whites were deeply invested in Jim Crow. Clark declared that the "result must be the same in all the cases," probably evincing the typical sensitivity of southern whites to perceived anti-southern prejudice. He meant that if the Court invalidated segregation in South Carolina and Virginia, it must do so in Delaware and Kansas. Clark observed that "the problem [in Texas] is as acute as anywhere. Texas also has the Mexican problem. [A] Mexican boy of 15 is in a class with a negro girl of 12. Some negro girls get in trouble" (read pregnant). After this brief digression into Texas social history, Clark got to the point: "If we can delay action it will help. [The] opinion should give lower courts the right to withhold relief in light of troubles." He "would go along with that." Otherwise, Clark would say "we had led the states on to think segregation is OK and we should let them work it out."

Clark's statement is ambiguous. His willingness to "go along" with an opinion affording local courts discretion to withhold relief indicates a possible vote against segregation. Yet his concern that the Court "had led the states on" and thus perhaps should "let them work it out" suggests an opposite vote. Clark, like Frankfurter and Jackson, was probably undecided.

Sherman Minton was from Indiana, a northern state with southern racial views. He and Truman had been Senate cronies—apparently an important criterion for Truman's Court appointments. Like Burton, Minton was brief and to the point: "[A] body of law has laid down [the] separate but equal doctrine. That however has been whittled away in [*Sweatt* and *McLaurin*]. Classification on the basis of race does not add up. It's invidious and can't be maintained."[8] With regard to the District of Columbia case, Minton also observed: "Congress has authorized segregation but it's not legal. Our decree will cause trouble but the race carries trouble with it. The negro is oppressed and has been in bondage for years after slavery was abolished. Segregation is per se illegal." Minton left no doubt that he was voting to end school segregation.

This is approximately what the justices said, as they first collectively considered the school segregation cases. Figuring out how these statements would have translated into votes requires speculation, as the justices decided, contrary to their usual practice, not to vote after speaking. Absent a formal tally, commentators have disagreed as to how the justices would have voted in December 1952. My view is that four—Black, Douglas, Burton, and Minton—thought school segregation plainly unconstitutional. But Court majorities require five, and no other justice was equally certain. Two—Vinson and Reed—probably leaned toward reaffirming *Plessy*. The other three—Frankfurter, Jackson, and Clark—were apparently unsure.

Before trying to explain how a 4–3–2 split became a 9–0 ruling against segregation, I want to look more closely at each justice and speculate why he held the views that he did. Black's ready condemnation of segregation was perhaps the most extraordinary. In 1952 he was the only justice from the Deep South, and he had been a Klan member. Black appreciated better than his colleagues how intensely resistant white southerners would be to a judicial ban on segregation. The costs of that resistance also would be more personal for Black, whose immediate family in Alabama would feel the repercussions of his vote.

One cannot know why Black concluded that school segregation was unconstitutional. He often claimed to be a textual literalist, but a constitutional injunction not to deny "equal protection of the laws" does not plainly forbid separate but equal. Nor does the legislative history of the Fourteenth Amendment. Thus legal sources to which Black usually claimed allegiance seem to have better supported an opposite result. Accordingly, if he is to be taken at his word, Black's personal views, not his legal interpretation, must explain his vote. But why did Black personally condemn segregation when few white Alabamians of his age did so? Speculating why people hold certain views is risky. Maybe Black was just idiosyncratic; he certainly had a contrarian personality. Another possibility is that Black was so chastened upon his appointment in 1937 by public criticism of his former Klan membership that he dedicated his judicial career to rebutting it. Soon after joining the Court, Black hired a Catholic secretary and a Jewish law clerk, apparently to dispel suspicions of religious prejudice flowing from his Klan affiliation. Not long thereafter, he wrote the landmark opinion in *Chambers v. Florida* (1940), reversing a black man's conviction because his confession was coerced and celebrating the Court's role as the savior of oppressed minorities. Perhaps Black was like John Marshall Harlan, the former Kentucky slaveowner who seems to have partially dedicated his judicial career to gainsaying Radical Republican criticism of his appointment by resisting the Court's post-Reconstruction retreat from racial equality.[9]

Douglas's vote may be the easiest to explain. He was less committed than other justices to maintaining a distinction between law and judges' values, which is why he frequently found easy the issues that troubled his colleagues. For Douglas, segregation's immorality was the beginning and end of the legal inquiry. If it was wrong, then it was unconstitutional. Douglas had evinced no special racial sensitivity in his pre-Court years, but he was a quintessential northern liberal. Before the Second World War, such people generally were more interested in economic issues than racial ones. Afterward, racial egalitarianism became a defining characteristic of northern liberals. By 1952 the immorality of segregation was no longer debatable for someone of Douglas's political stripe.[10]

Burton's and Minton's anti-segregation votes are harder to explain. Neither was as liberal as Douglas. Their personal histories regarding race are thin. The little surviving evidence suggests that they shared neither Reed's support for segregation nor Frankfurter's passion for racial equality. On civil liberties issues generally they were the most conservative justices, nearly always siding with the government and celebrating judicial restraint.[11] Why would Burton and Minton, generally averse to civil *liberties* claims, have been so receptive to the civil *rights* claim in *Brown*? Perhaps the answer lies in a consideration emphasized in briefs, oral argument, and newspaper reaction but never mentioned at conference: the cold war imperative for racial change. Both Burton and Minton were fierce judicial cold warriors. Their enthusiasm for judicial restraint was most evident in cases challenging government loyalty and security programs, where they almost never found a constitutional violation. In *Brown* the cold war imperative put them in the unusual position of siding with individual claimants (and the federal government) against state legislatures. The Justice Department's brief invoked the cold war imperative as justification for invalidating school segregation: "Racial discrimination furnishes grist for the Communist propaganda mills." Reed's law clerk recalled the justice observing that he was hearing much on the subject of the cold war and that this was causing him to think (though he believed that such considerations should be irrelevant). After *Brown*, supporters boasted that America's leadership of the free world "now rests on a firmer basis" and that American democracy had been "vindicat[ed] . . . in the eyes of the world." Perhaps Burton and Minton, ever heedful of national security, concluded that barring segregation was service to that cause.[12]

Frankfurter and Jackson may have been the most conflicted over *Brown*, which posed for them a clash between law and politics. Both justices abhorred segregation, but were committed to maintaining the distinction between law and judges' personal values. Traditional legal sources to which they looked for guidance—text, original intent, precedent, and custom—pointed more toward reaffirming than overruling *Plessy*. Thus, as Jackson conceded, invalidating segregation could be defended only in "political" terms. *Brown* required these justices to choose between their aversions to segregation and to political decision making by judges. We shall further explore that conflict below.

Two justices, Vinson and Reed, were leaning toward reaffirming *Plessy*. Both came from Kentucky, which legally mandated school segregation. Reed endorsed segregation as a social policy. He refused to attend a Court party in 1947 because black messengers were invited, and he was appalled that "a nigra" might sit down beside his wife at a restaurant after the Court in 1952 desegregated public accommodations in the District of Columbia under an old civil rights statute. Less is known about Vinson's racial views, though he was probably more uncertain about segregation than northern justices such as Burton and Minton. Thus, though these Kentuckians were equally committed cold warriors, their support for (or lesser aversion to) segregation may explain why they were less influenced by the cold war imperative. They were also less committed generally to individual rights protection than Black or Douglas. School segregation was not a vexing constitutional problem for them, as their general inclination was to defer to legislatures, traditional legal sources supported segregation, and the policy was congenial, or at least not adverse, to their personal preferences. With law and politics aligned, Vinson and Reed could readily reaffirm *Plessy*.[13]

In December 1952 only four justices were clearly prepared to invalidate school segregation. Two were inclined to sustain it, and three appeared undecided. The justices' informal headcounts confirm deep divisions. In a memorandum to the files dictated the day *Brown* was decided, Douglas observed: "[i]n the original conference, there were only four who voted that segregation in the public schools was unconstitutional. Those four were Black, Burton, Minton and myself. Vinson was of the opinion that the *Plessy* case was right and that segregation was constitutional. Reed followed the view of Vinson, and Clark was inclined that way." Frankfurter and Jackson, according to Douglas, "viewed the problem with great alarm and thought that the Court should not decide the question if it was possible to avoid it," though both believed that "segregation in the public schools was probably constitutional." Frankfurter distinguished between school segregation in the District of Columbia, which he thought violated the due process clause, and in the states, where he thought "history was against the claim of unconstitutionality." In Douglas's estimation, in 1952 "the vote would [have been] five to four in favor of the constitutionality of segregation in the public schools in the States with Frankfurter indicating he would join the four of us when it came to the District of Columbia case." Douglas's dislike of Frankfurter may have colored his perception of Frankfurter's likely vote, but his interpretation is consistent with the conference notes.[14]

Other justices counting heads reached roughly similar conclusions. Frankfurter had "no doubt," he noted in a letter to Reed just days after *Brown*, that a vote in December 1952 would have invalidated segregation 5–4. The dissenters would have been Vinson, Reed, Jackson, and Clark, but not Frankfurter himself, and the majority would have written "several opinions." On another occasion, Frankfurter bragged that he had filibustered the decision "for fear that the case would be decided the other way under Vinson." Reed reported to his law clerk after the initial conference that Vinson probably would join him in dissent, as would at least one other justice (Jackson or Clark). Burton and Jackson calculated between two and four dissenters had the decision been made in 1952–53. These similar headcounts confirm deep divisions. Possibly a bare majority existed to reaffirm *Plessy*.[15]

Worried about the "catastrophic" impact of a divided decision, Frankfurter suggested having the cases reargued on the pretense that the justices required further briefing on issues such as the original understanding of the Fourteenth Amendment and the remedial options available should they invalidate segregation. The justices were less interested in answers than in securing additional time to resolve their differences. Five—Black, Frankfurter, Jackson, Burton, and Minton—voted for reargument, and on 8 June 1953 the cases were rescheduled for the next term.[16]

The principal difficulty with this interpretation—emphasizing deep divisions and the possibility that no majority yet existed for overruling *Plessy*—is that the Court unanimously invalidated school segregation the next term. If the justices were so conflicted in December 1952, how could they have achieved unanimity in May 1954? Perhaps my account treats the conference notes too literally. One commentator suggests, by contrast, that the justices were simply "talking through their concerns about what they knew they were going to do." Frankfurter and Jackson, in this view, were desperately seeking an acceptable path "to the decision that they wanted to reach." The justices' own headcounts are dismissed as "seriously overstated." This interpretation, to its credit, more easily explains the Court's unanimity. Its principal problems are its strained reading of the conference notes and its dismissal of the justices' own headcounts.[17]

That *Brown* was unanimous does not disprove that deep divisions initially existed among the justices. Once a majority existed to invalidate segregation, potential dissenters faced strong pressures to conform. Yet in December 1952 that majority had not yet materialized; only four justices had firmly indicated their willingness to overturn *Plessy*. Then Vinson suddenly died in September 1953. Frankfurter recorded his death as "the first indication I have ever had that there is a God." Eisenhower replaced Vinson with Earl Warren, the governor of California, to whom he felt politically indebted from the Republican convention of 1952. Eisenhower did not appoint Warren to influence the outcome of *Brown*. Apparently he briefly considered appointing John W. Davis, who was defending segregation in his capacity as South Carolina's lawyer.[18]

*Brown* was reargued in December 1953. Warren opened the conference by proposing another informal discussion without voting. On the merits, he declared that the "separate but equal doctrine rests on [the] basic premise that the Negro race is inferior. That is [the] only way to sustain *Plessy*." Yet the "argument of Negro counsel proves they are not inferior." He continued: "we can't set one group apart from the rest of us and say they are not entitled to [the] same treatment as all others. 13th, 14th and 15th Amendments were intended to make equal those who once were slaves." Acknowledging that this view "causes trouble perhaps," Warren could not "see how segregation can be justified in this day and age." Recognizing that the "time element is important in the deep south," Warren concluded that "we must act but we should do it in a tolerant way." Anyone counting heads—and all the justices were doing so—would have recognized immediately that the outcome was no longer in doubt. Warren, together with the four who had already indicated support for overruling *Plessy*, made a majority. Many scholars appreciate Warren's role in securing unanimity in *Brown*, but few recognize that he may also have been instrumental to the outcome.[19]

With the result settled, two factors pushed toward unanimity. First, the justices appreciated that white southerners would receive *Brown* belligerently and perhaps violently. Resisters would exploit any hint of internal Court dissension. Justices disagreeing with the outcome felt pressure to suppress their convictions for the good of the institution. Warren and others persuaded Reed not to dissent, even though he was convinced that *Brown* was wrong. Three days after the decision, Frankfurter wrote to Reed, praising him for resolving the "hard struggle . . . involved in the conscience" of his mind in a manner conducive to the nation's "great good." Jackson left his hospital bed, where he was recovering from a heart attack, to be on the bench when *Brown* was announced, confirming the importance that the justices attached to manifesting unanimity.[20]

A second factor also may have fostered unanimity. Recall that ambivalent justices such as Frankfurter and Jackson experienced *Brown* as a conflict between law and politics. They loathed segregation, but doubted whether it was unconstitutional. After December 1953 they were irrelevant to the outcome, whereas a year earlier they had controlled it. Perhaps they could have endured a disjunction between their personal and constitutional predilections if it affected the outcome, but not for the sake of a dissent. If a majority was committed to invalidating segregation, they would acquiesce, suppressing legal doubts.

Though speculative, this interpretation draws support from the internal history of *Terry v. Adams* (1953), decided during the same term when *Brown* was first argued. The issue was whether the exclusion of blacks by the Jaybird Democratic Association of Fort Bend, Texas—a political club consisting of all whites in the county—qualified as "state action" under the Fourteenth or Fifteenth Amendment. The justices initially voted 5–4 to reject the constitutional challenge, expressing doubt as to "where the state comes in." Even after Frankfurter immediately switched sides, a closely divided decision seemed imminent. Vinson, Reed, Minton, and Jackson planned to dissent, and Jackson drafted an opinion criticizing the majority for sacrificing "sound principle[s] of interpretation." Yet when *Terry* came down, only Minton dissented. Apparently the other three justices, once deprived of control over the outcome, were unwilling to subordinate their political preferences to their legal principles. Similar considerations may explain the Court's unanimity in *Brown*.[21]

*Brown* was hard for justices who approached legal decision making as Frankfurter and Jackson did, because for them it posed a conflict between law and politics.[22] The sources of constitutional interpretation that they usually invoked—text, original understanding, precedent, custom—indicated that school segregation was permissible. The dearth of support in conventional legal sources partially explains the NAACP's reliance on controversial social science evidence, which led Jackson to observe contemptuously that "Marshall's brief starts and ends with sociology." In contrast, these justices' personal values condemned segregation as "Hitler's creed." Their quandary was how to reconcile their legal and moral views.[23]

Frankfurter's self-identity as a judge required separating his personal views from the law. He preached that judges must decide cases on "the compulsions of governing legal principles," not "the idiosyncrasies of a merely personal judgment." In a memorandum regarding the first flag-salute case, Frankfurter noted that "[n]o duty of judges is more important nor more difficult to discharge than that of guarding against reading their personal and debatable opinions into the case." In another case he declined to invalidate a death sentence, notwithstanding his personal opposition to capital punishment, because of "the disciplined thinking of a lifetime regarding the duty of this Court." Frankfurter scorned a former colleague, Frank Murphy—"Dear God," he called him—for his commitment to doing right regardless of law. Frankfurter was so strongly averse to judges reading their personal values into the Constitution that he once favored treating the due process clause "as raising 'political questions' . . . unfitted for the adjudicatory process," because it was so "vague" and "open to subjective interpretation."[24]

Frankfurter undoubtedly abhorred racial segregation. More than any other justice, his personal behavior evinced egalitarian commitments. He served on the NAACP's advisory board in the 1930s, and in 1948 he hired the Court's first black law clerk, William Coleman. Yet Frankfurter insisted, in a memorandum written while *Brown* was pending, that his personal views were of limited relevance to the constitutional question: "However passionately any of us may hold egalitarian views, however fiercely any of us may believe that such a policy of segregation as undoubtedly expresses the tenacious conviction of Southern States is both unjust and shortsighted, he travels outside his judicial authority if for this private reason alone he declares unconstitutional the policy of segregation." The Court could invalidate segregation, Frankfurter believed, only if segregation was legally as well as morally objectionable.[25]

Yet Frankfurter had difficulty finding a convincing legal argument to invalidate segregation. His law clerk, Alexander Bickel, spent a summer reading the Fourteenth Amendment's legislative history, and he reported to Frankfurter: "it is impossible to conclude that the 39th Congress intended that segregation be abolished; impossible also to conclude that they foresaw it might be, under the language they were adopting." Frankfurter was no doctrinaire originalist: he believed that constitutional concepts change meaning over time. But judges were not free simply to write their moral views into the Constitution. In the early 1950s, twenty-one states and the District of Columbia still had mandatory or optional school segregation. Thus Frankfurter could hardly maintain that "evolving standards of social decency" condemned segregation. Precedent strongly supported it. Of forty-four state appellate and federal court challenges to school segregation between 1865 and 1935, not a single one had succeeded. Ordinarily, Frankfurter celebrated stare decisis (the legal doctrine favoring adherence to precedent), calling it "the most influential factor in giving a society coherence and continuity." He recently had reiterated that although stare decisis had less force in constitutional law than elsewhere, he still "pause[d] long before overruling a prior line of constitutional adjudication." Frankfurter conceded at conference that based on legislative history and precedent, "*Plessy* is right."[26]

*Brown* presented a similar problem for Jackson. He too found segregation anathema. In a letter to a law professor friend in 1950, Jackson, who had left the Court for a year to prosecute Nazis at Nuremberg, wrote: "You and I have seen the terrible consequences of racial hatred in Germany. We can have no sympathy with racial conceits which underlie segregation policies." Yet like Frankfurter, Jackson thought that judges must separate their personal views from the law, and he disfavored the frequent overruling of precedent.[27]

Jackson revealed his struggles in a draft concurring opinion, which began: "Decision of these cases would be simple if our personal opinion that school segregation is morally, economically or politically indefensible made it legally so."[28] But as Jackson believed that judges must subordinate their personal preferences to the law, this consideration was irrelevant. When he turned to whether "existing law condemn[s] segregation," he had difficulty answering yes: "Layman as well as lawyer must query how it is that the Constitution this morning forbids what for three-quarters of a century it has tolerated or approved. He must further speculate as to how [to justify] this reversal of its meaning by the branch of the Government supposed not to make new law but only to declare existing law and which has exactly the same constitutional materials that so far as the states are concerned have existed since 1868 and in the case of the District of Columbia since 1791. Can we honestly say that the states which have maintained segregated schools have not, until today, been justified in understanding their practice to be constitutional?"[29]

Jackson's analysis began with the text. As the due process clause of the Fifth Amendment had been interpreted to permit (indeed to protect) slavery, how could the identical Fourteenth Amendment provision bar segregation? Jackson concluded that "there is no explicit prohibition of segregated schools and it can only be supplied by interpretation." Regarding legislative history, Jackson observed that among the Fourteenth Amendment's supporters "may be found a few who hoped that it would bring about complete social equality and early assimilation of the liberated Negro into an amalgamated population. But I am unable to find any indication that their support was decisive, and certainly their view had no support from the great Emancipator himself." He summed up the legislative history: "It is hard to find an indication that any influential body of the movement that carried the Civil War Amendments had reached the point of thinking about either segregation or education of the Negro as a current problem, and harder still to find that the amendments were designed to be a solution."[30]

Turning from words to deeds, Jackson could "find nothing to show that the Congress which submitted these Amendments understood or intended to prohibit the practice here in question." The same Congress that passed the Fourteenth Amendment and every one since had supported school segregation in the District of Columbia. In the late 1860s Republicans in Congress required southern states to ratify the Fourteenth Amendment if they were to regain congressional representation, but they never intimated that school segregation violated the conditions of readmission. Jackson found the behavior of states ratifying the amendment "equally impossible to reconcile with any understanding that the Amendment would prohibit segregation in schools." Eleven northern and border states ratifying the amendment had segregated schools, as did all the reconstructed southern states. As to precedent, northern state courts, as well as a Supreme Court dominated by northerners, had concluded that the Fourteenth Amendment did not prohibit segregation: "Almost a century of decisional law rendered by judges, many of whom risked their lives for the cause that produced these Amendments, is almost unanimous in the view that the Amendment tolerated segregation by state action." Having canvassed the legal sources he considered most relevant—text, original intent, and precedent—Jackson concluded: "Convenient as it would be to reach an opposite conclusion, I simply cannot find in the conventional material of constitutional interpretation any justification for saying that in maintaining segregated schools any state or the District of Columbia can be judicially decreed, up to the date of this decision, to have violated the Fourteenth Amendment."[31]

Jackson's opinion candidly admitted his difficulty in legally justifying a judicial ban on school segregation—a bit too candidly, in the estimation of his law clerk E. Barrett Prettyman, who in response to Jackson's draft noted the need for the nation to believe that Brown was "honestly arrived at, confidently espoused, and basically sound." If the country could "be made to feel . . . that it is a decision based upon law," then segregation "should die in relatively short order, no matter how many legal skirmishes ensue. On the other hand, if the country feels that a bunch of liberals in Washington has finally foisted off their social views on the public, it will not only tolerate but aid circumvention of the decision." Prettyman thought that Jackson's opinion should begin not with doubts and fears, but with a clear statement of his legal position. Yet Jackson's rationale for invalidating segregation occupied just two pages near the end of a twenty-three-page opinion and read like "almost an afterthought." Prettyman advised that Jackson not write as if he "were ashamed to reach [this result]." He nicely captured Jackson's dilemma: the justice was, in a sense, "ashamed" of the result he reached. Jackson admitted to colleagues his difficulty in "mak[ing] a judicial basis for a congenial political conclusion." Unable to "justify the abolition of segregation as a judicial act," he agreed to "go along with it" as "a political decision." Frankfurter did too, but he was less candid about it.[32]

Jackson hesitated to invalidate segregation for another reason as well. He had become skeptical of judicial supremacy, not only because it was inconsistent with democracy, but also because courts were bad at it. Jackson worried that unenforceable judicial decrees bred public cynicism about courts. In a posthumously published book, he wrote: "When the Court has gone too far, it has provoked reactions which have set back the cause it was designed to advance, and has sometimes called down upon itself severe rebuke." In 1954 Jackson wondered if the Court was up to the task of reordering southern race relations. His draft opinion asked why separate but equal had "remained a dead letter as to its equality aspect"; his answer was that it had been "declared and supported heartily only by the judicial department which has no power to enforce its own decrees." Blacks had to sue to enforce equality. But "[t]his was costly, it was time consuming and it was impossible for a disadvantaged people to accomplish on any broad scale." A judicial ban on segregation would be even harder to implement. Litigants would quickly discover "that devices of delay are numerous and often successful," especially as compliance required coercing "not merely individuals but the public itself." Because a ruling against one school district would not bind another, every instance of recalcitrance would necessitate separate litigation. Individuals would bear the burden, as the Justice Department was unlikely to sue, and even if it wished to do so, Congress would probably not appropriate funds. Jackson preferred legislative to judicial action, not from "a mere desire to pass responsibility to others," but because it went "to the effectiveness of the remedy and to the use to be made of the judicial process over the next generation."[33]

Other justices shared Jackson's concern about invalidating a practice apparently sanctioned by traditional sources of constitutional interpretation. Clark conceded that "he always [had] thought that the 14th amendment covered the matter and outlawed segregation. But the history shows different." Vinson, like Jackson, observed that the same congressmen passing the Fourteenth Amendment approved segregation in District of Columbia schools. Several justices worried about overruling an unbroken line of precedent dating back to the 1860s. Clark thought that the Court had "led the states on to think segregation is o.k.," and even Black confessed that perhaps "the long line of decisions bars [the anti-segregation] construction of the amendment."[34]

That the nine justices sitting in 1952—even those less committed than Frankfurter and Jackson to separating law from politics—would be uneasy about invalidating segregation is unsurprising. All were appointed by Presidents Roosevelt and Truman, on the assumption that they supported, as Jackson put it, "the doctrine on which the Roosevelt fight against the old court was based—in part, that it had expanded the Fourteenth Amendment to take an unjustified judicial control over social and economic affairs." Or, as Black stated, Roosevelt had appointed him because he "was against using due process to force the views of judges on the country." For most of their professional lives, these men had criticized untethered judicial activism as undemocratic—the invalidation of the popular will by unelected officeholders imposing their social and economic biases. This is how all nine understood the *Lochner* era, when the Court invalidated minimum wage, maximum hour, and protective union legislation on a thin constitutional basis. The question in *Brown*, as Jackson's law clerk William H. Rehnquist noted, was whether invalidating segregation would eliminate any distinction between this Court and the one from the *Lochner* era, except for "the kinds of litigants it favors and the kinds of special claims it protects."[35]

Thus, the justices wondered if the Court was the right institution to forbid segregation. Several expressed views similar to Vinson's—if segregation was to be condemned, "it would be better if [Congress] would act." Even Black confessed, "[a]t first blush I would have said that it was up to Congress." Jackson had observed in 1950 that he "would support the constitutionality of almost any Congressional Act that prohibited segregation in education." Now he cautioned that "[h]owever desirable it may be to abolish educational segregation, we cannot, with a proper sense of responsibility, ignore the question whether the use of judicial office to initiate law reforms that cannot get enough national public support to put them through Congress, is our own constitutional function. Certainly, policy decisions by the least democratic and the least representative of our branches of government are hard to justify." "[If] we have to decide the question," Jackson lamented, "then representative government has failed."[36]

In the end, even the most conflicted justices voted to invalidate segregation. How were they able to overcome their ambivalence? All judicial decision making involves elements of law and politics. Legal factors—text, original understanding, precedent, custom—range along an axis from determinacy to indeterminacy. Political considerations—judges' personal values, social mores, external political pressure—array along a continuum from indifference to intense preference. When the law is clear, judges will generally follow it, unless they have very strong preferences to the contrary. When the law is relatively indeterminate, judges have no choice but to consult their values and broader social mores. In *Brown* the law—as understood by Frankfurter and Jackson—was reasonably clear: Segregation was constitutional. For justices to reject a result so clearly indicated by legal sources suggests very strong contrary preferences. Had the justices been less certain about the immorality of segregation, they might have followed the legal sources.

Why were these justices so repulsed by segregation when national opinion was divided? One possibility is fortuity: integrationists just happened to dominate the Court in 1954. Had there been five Stanley Reeds, *Plessy* would have been reaffirmed. A more satisfying explanation emphasizes systematic differences between the justices and ordinary Americans. Two prominent ones are level of education and economic status. Justices are very well educated, having attended college and law school—Jackson was a rare exception—and often the most élite ones. They are also relatively wealthy. On many policy issues that become constitutional disputes, opinion correlates heavily with socioeconomic status, with élites holding more liberal views (though on issues of economic redistribution the opposite is true). Early in the twenty-first century, these issues include gay rights, abortion, and school prayer. In 1954 racial segregation was such an issue: 73 percent of college graduates approved of *Brown*, but only 45 percent of high school dropouts did. Racial attitudes and practices were changing dramatically in postwar America. As members of the cultural élite, the justices were among the first to be influenced.[37]

The justices deliberating on *Brown* expressed astonishment at recent changes in racial attitudes and practices. Jackson treated them as a constitutional rationale for eliminating segregation. In his draft opinion, he wrote that segregation "has outlived whatever justification it may have had." Jackson noted that "[c]ertainly in the 1860's and probably throughout the Nineteenth Century the Negro population as a whole was a different people than today. Lately freed from bondage, they had little opportunity as yet to show their capacity for education or even self-support and management." However, he continued, "Negro progress under segregation has been spectacular and, tested by the pace of history, his rise is one of the swiftest and most dramatic advances in the annals of man." This advance "has enabled him to outgrow the system and to overcome the presumptions on which it was based." Black progress was sufficient for Jackson to conclude that race "no longer affords a reasonable basis for a classification for educational purposes."[38]

Other justices made similar observations. Frankfurter noted "the great changes in the relations between white and colored people since the first World War" and remarked that "the pace of progress has surprised even those most eager in its promotion." Burton recorded the encouraging trend toward desegregation in restaurants and the armed forces, and Minton detected "a different world today." Southern justices were no less cognizant of change, though they were more inclined to treat it as justifying judicial forbearance rather than intervention. Clark noted "much progress" in voting and education. Even Reed recorded the "constant progress in [public schooling] and in the advancement of the interests of the negros," and he observed that "segregation is gradually disappearing."[39]

Law clerks' attitudes may be the strongest evidence of the culturally élite bias favoring desegregation. With polls revealing a nation split down the middle, the justices' law clerks almost unanimously favored invalidating segregation, notwithstanding any legal difficulties. Of the fifteen to twenty young men clerking during the 1952 term, only William H. Rehnquist seems to have favored reaffirming *Plessy*. Even those clerking for southern justices, many of whom had grown up with segregation, favored overturning it. Reed reported that he stopped discussing the issue with his clerks because they were so adamant that *Plessy* be overruled. Apparently by the 1950s most highly educated, relatively affluent men in their twenties—even from the South—had difficulty sympathizing with segregation.[40]

The justices did not possess their clerks' anti-segregation youth bias, but they did share the socioeconomic bias. Could Reed, who thought segregation constitutionally permissible and morally defensible, have been persuaded to join *Brown* had his culturally élite status not diminished the intensity of his segregationist sentiment? Reed conceded that "of course" there was no "inferior race," though perhaps blacks had been "handicapped by lack of opportunity." It speaks volumes that an upper-crust Kentuckian who had spent much of his adult life in the nation's capital would have said such a thing. Most white southerners—less well educated, less affluent, and less exposed to the cultural élite—would have demurred.[41]

The justices' culturally élite biases increased the likelihood of their invalidating segregation before national opinion had turned against it. Yet the potential attitude gap between justices and the public is limited; they are part of the larger culture and inhabit the same historical moment. As little as ten years before *Brown*, racial attitudes had probably not changed enough for even a culturally élite institution such as the Court to condemn segregation. The NAACP was wise not to push school desegregation challenges before 1950, as the justices probably would have rejected them. Frankfurter later noted that he would have voted to sustain school segregation in the 1940s, because "public opinion had not then crystallized against it."[42] By the early 1950s dramatic political, economic, social, and ideological forces affecting race relations had made judicial invalidation of segregation conceivable. Slightly more than half the nation supported *Brown* from the day it was decided. Thus *Brown* is not an example of the Court's resisting majoritarian sentiment, but rather of its converting an emerging national consensus into a constitutional command. By 1954 the long-term trend against Jim Crow was clear. Justices observed that segregation was "gradually disappearing" and was "marked for early extinction." They understood they were working with, not against, the current of history.[43]

Given long-term trends in race relations and the Court's traditional constitutional role, perhaps the justices' eventual invalidation of school segregation was inevitable. Jackson predicted, "[w]hatever we might say today, within a generation [segregation] will be outlawed by decision of this Court because of the forces of mortality and replacement, which operate upon it." If Reed was right that segregation would disappear in border states within fifteen or twenty years without judicial intervention, the propensity of constitutional law to suppress isolated practices may have ensured an eventual ruling against segregation. A subsequent generation of justices, finding segregation even more abhorrent, would have been sorely tempted to apply to a shrinking number of holdout states an ascendant national norm against segregation.[44]

But *Brown* was not inevitable in 1954, when seventeen states and the District of Columbia segregated schools, and four more states permitted local communities to adopt segregation at their discretion. *Brown* did not simply bring into line a few renegade states. Reed, who conceded that the Constitution's meaning was "not fixed," thought that the justices could invalidate an established practice only when the "body of people" had deemed it unconstitutional, which one could not plausibly say about school segregation in 1954. Lower courts were not blazing new trails on the issue, as they often do before the high court's momentous constitutional rulings. Before *Brown*, only a single California federal judge had repudiated the voluminous precedent sanctioning separate but equal. As we have seen, significant legal hurdles confronted those justices personally inclined to invalidate segregation. The Court might easily have written an opinion echoing John W. Davis's oral argument: "somewhere, sometime to every principle comes a moment of repose when it has been so often announced, so confidently relied upon, so long continued, that it passes the limits of judicial discretion and disturbance."[45]

Moreover, the probable consequences of invalidating segregation weighed heavily on the justices. The Court had never done anything like this before. Frankfurter observed that although individuals brought the desegregation cases, the justices were effectively being asked "to transform state-wide school systems in nearly a score of States." He cautioned that a "declaration of unconstitutionality is not a wand by which these transformations can be accomplished." Jackson similarly noted that individual lawsuits were "a weak reed to rely on in initiating a change in the social system of a large part of the United States." The justices worried that unenforceable orders might "bring the court into contempt and the judicial process into discredit." Moreover, invalidating segregation would probably produce violence and school closures. Vinson thought that "[w]e can't close our eyes to [the] problem in various parts of [the] country . . . When you force the complete abolition of public schools in some areas then it is most serious."[46]

Several southern states were undertaking crash equalization programs promising rapid redress of educational inequalities. Some justices were tempted to see if southern statesmen, such as their friend and former colleague Jimmy Byrnes, recently elected governor of South Carolina, could deliver on their promises. Vinson observed that in Clarendon County, South Carolina, "you have equal facilities. [It] took some time to make them equal." Reed pleaded with his colleagues to stay their hand, as "10 years would make [black schools] really equal." Many southern white moderates likewise urged the Court to give equalization a chance, while warning that invalidating school segregation would jeopardize southern racial progress.[47]

The justices were not unmindful of these arguments against invalidating segregation. In December 1952 no secure majority existed for overruling *Plessy*. The *Brown* decision was not inevitable. The NAACP's Roy Wilkins was wise to prepare two different press releases as he awaited the ruling. The association could not be certain it would win its case.[48]

## Notes

I am grateful to Muriel Klarman, Seth Klarman, Daryl Levinson, Liz Magill, James Patterson, Jim Ryan, Andrew Schroeder, Mike Seidman, Bill Stuntz, and Stephen Whitfield for helpful comments on a slightly different version of this chapter, which was adapted from my book *From Jim Crow to Civil Rights: The Supreme Court and the Struggle for Racial Equality* (Oxford University Press 2004).

1 See generally Michael J. Klarman, "*Brown*, Racial Change, and the Civil Rights Movement," 80 *Virginia Law Review* 7 (1994).

2 Unidentified and undated press clipping in August Meier, ed., *Papers of the National Association for the Advancement of Colored People* (microfilm, 28 parts, University Publications of America, 1982), part 20, reel 11, frame 27; Mark V. Tushnet, *Making Civil Rights Law: Thurgood Marshall and the Supreme Court, 1936–1961* (New York: Oxford University Press, 1994), 150–51, 165; Richard Kluger, *Simple Justice* (New York: Vintage, 1977), 290–94, 475–76, 523–24, 531, 535–36; Benjamin Muse, *Ten Years of Prelude: The Story of Integration since the Supreme Court's 1954 Decision* (New York: Viking, 1964), 9; Philip Elman, "The Solicitor General's Office, Justice Frankfurter, and Civil Rights Litigation, 1946–1960: An Oral History," 100 *Harvard Law Review* 837 (1987).

3 *Brown v. Board of Education*, 347 U.S. 483, 495 (1954); *Bolling v. Sharpe*, 347 U.S. 497 (1954).

4 James T. Patterson, *Brown v. Board of Education: A Civil Rights Milestone and Its Troubled Legacy* (New York: Oxford University Press, 2001), 116; Tushnet, *Making Civil Rights Law*, 194.

5 I have consulted and am quoting from the conference notes of Burton, Clark, Douglas, and Jackson. The notes are broadly similar, though I am interspersing quotes from each. The conference notes are not transcriptions. I am

quoting from the notes, but one should not assume that they perfectly captured what was said. On the whole, however, they appear quite accurate. See Burton conference notes, School Segregation Cases, 13 December 1952, box 244, Burton Papers, Library of Congress; Clark conference notes, School Segregation Cases, box A27, Clark Papers, Tarlton Law Library, University of Texas; Douglas conference notes, *Brown v. Board of Education* and *Bolling v. Sharpe*, 13 December 1952, case file: Segregation Cases, box 1150, Douglas Papers, Library of Congress; Jackson conference notes, School Segregation Cases, 12 December 1952, box 184, Jackson Papers, Library of Congress. See also Del Dickson, ed., *The Supreme Court in Conference (1940–1985): The Private Discussions behind Nearly 300 Supreme Court Decisions* (New York: Oxford University Press, 2001), 646–54; Kluger, *Simple Justice*, 582–616; Mark Tushnet with Katya Lezin, "What Really Happened in *Brown v. Board of Education?*," 91 *Columbia Law Review* 1867 (1991); Dennis J. Hutchinson, "Unanimity and Desegregation: Decision Making in the Supreme Court, 1948–1958," 68 *Georgetown Law Journal* 1 (1979). I am grateful to Roy M. Mersky at the University of Texas Law Library for permission to quote from the Tom C. Clark collection, and to William E. Jackson and Mary Jackson Craighill for permission to quote from the Robert Jackson Papers.

6  In addition to the conference notes, see Jackson memorandum opinion, 6 January 1954, box 184, Jackson Papers. See also Gregory S. Chernack, "The Clash of Two Worlds: Justice Robert H. Jackson, Institutional Pragmatism, and *Brown*," 72 *Temple Law Review* 51, 85 & n. 162 (1999).

7  *Sipuel v. Board of Regents* (1948) required that Oklahoma either create a separate black law school or else admit a black applicant to the all-white University of Oklahoma School of Law. *Sweatt v. Painter* (1950) ordered the University of Texas School of Law to admit a black man because the separate black law school recently established by the state could not possibly be equal with regard to intangible aspects of legal education, such as the prestige of the institution and the stature of its alumni. *Sweatt* was widely interpreted as interring racial segregation in graduate and professional education.

8  *McLaurin v. Oklahoma*, decided the same day as *Sweatt*, ordered the University of Oklahoma graduate education school to cease segregating—in classrooms, library, and cafeteria—the black man it had admitted pursuant to a federal court order.

9  Roger K. Newman, *Hugo Black: A Biography* (New York: Pantheon, 1994), 91–100, 249–61, 267; Chambers v. Florida, 309 U.S. 227, 241 (1940); Michael J. Klarman, "Is the Supreme Court Sometimes Irrelevant? Race and the Southern Criminal Justice System in the 1940s," *Journal of American History* 89 (June 2002): 138.

10  Kluger, *Simple Justice*, 602; G. Edward White, "The Anti-Judge: William O. Douglas and the Ambiguities of Individuality," 74 *Virginia Law Review* 17 (1988).

11  Mary Frances Berry, *Stability, Security, and Continuity: Mr. Justice Burton and Decision-Making in the Supreme Court, 1945–1958* (Westport: Greenwood, 1978), 59–69, 94–120, 145–46; Linda C. Gugin and James E. St. Clair, *Sherman Min-*

ton: *New Deal Senator, Cold War Justice* (Indianapolis: Indiana Historical Society, 1997), 215, 220–44, 265, 293–94, 310–11; Kluger, *Simple Justice*, 612.

12 Tushnet, *Making Civil Rights Law*, 172–73; *Chicago Defender*, 22 May 1954, 5; John D. Fassett, *New Deal Justice: The Life of Stanley Reed of Kentucky* (New York: Vantage, 1994), 571. See generally Mary L. Dudziak, *Cold War Civil Rights: Race and the Image of American Democracy* (Princeton: Princeton University Press, 2000).

13 Fassett, *New Deal Justice*, 555–56, 559–61; Kluger, *Simple Justice*, 595.

14 Douglas memorandum for the file, Segregation Cases, 17 May 1954, box 1149, Douglas Papers.

15 Frankfurter to Reed, 20 May 1954, Reed Papers; Douglas conference notes, *Brown II*, 16 April 1955, box 1150, Douglas Papers; Fassett, *New Deal Justice*, 567; Kluger, *Simple Justice*, 614; Elman, "The Solicitor General's Office," 829.

16 Frankfurter to Reed, 20 May 1954, Reed Papers, Margaret I. King Library, University of Kentucky; Docket Sheet, *Brown v. Board of Education*, box 1150, Douglas Papers; Frankfurter memorandum for the conference re segregation cases, 27 May 1953, box A27, Clark Papers; Kluger, *Simple Justice*, 614–16; Tushnet, *Making Civil Rights Law*, 194–95.

17 Tushnet, *Making Civil Rights Law*, 194, 215.

18 Kluger, *Simple Justice*, 656; Elman, "The Solicitor General's Office," 840; Stephen E. Ambrose, *Eisenhower*, vol. 2, *The President* (New York: Econo-Clad, 1984), 128; Jeffrey R. Young, "Eisenhower's Federal Judges and Civil Rights Policy: A Republican 'Southern Strategy' for the 1950s," *Georgia Historical Quarterly* 78 (1994): 557 n. 77.

19 Douglas conference notes, *Briggs v. Elliott*, 12 December 1953, case file: Segregation Cases, box 1149, Douglas Papers; Douglas memorandum for the file, Segregation Cases, 17 May 1954, box 1149, Douglas Papers; Kluger, *Simple Justice*, 679, 683, 698–99; Howard Ball and Phillip J. Cooper, *Of Power and Right: Hugo Black, William O. Douglas, and America's Constitutional Revolution* (New York: Oxford University Press, 1992), 177–79; Bernard Schwartz, *Super Chief: Earl Warren and His Supreme Court: A Judicial Biography* (New York: New York University Press, 1983), 82, 106; Patterson, *Brown v. Board of Education*, 60, 64–65; G. Edward White, *Earl Warren: A Public Life* (New York: Oxford University Press, 1982), 163–69.

20 Frankfurter to Reed, 20 May 1954, Reed Papers; Douglas memorandum for the file, Segregation Cases, 17 May 1954, box 1149, Douglas Papers; Kluger, *Simple Justice*, 685, 698; Fassett, *New Deal Justice*, 569–73; Schwartz, *Super Chief*, 89–90, 94, 102; White, *Earl Warren*, 167–68.

21 Dickson, *The Supreme Court in Conference*, 839–41; Jackson, draft dissent, *Terry v. Adams*, 3 April 1953, 1, 9, box 179, Jackson Papers; Terry v. Adams, 345 U.S. 461 (1953); Berry, *Stability, Security, and Continuity*, 126.

22 Melvin I. Urofsky, *Division and Discord: The Supreme Court under Stone and Vinson, 1941–1953* (Columbia: University of South Carolina Press, 1997), 34, 109 n. 112, 130, 217, 223; Adamson v. California, 332 U.S. 46, 68 (1947) (Frankfurter,

J., concurring); Haley v. Ohio, 332 U.S. 596, 602–3 (1947); Frankfurter to Hand, 13 February 1958, Frankfurter Papers, microfilm collection (University Publications of America, 1986), part 3, reel 27, frames 565–68; Felix Frankfurter, "The Red Terror of Judicial Reform," *Felix Frankfurter on the Supreme Court: Extrajudicial Essays on the Court and the Constitution,* ed. Philip B. Kurland (Cambridge: Belknap Press of Harvard University Press, 1970), 158–68.

23  Clark conference notes, School Segregation Cases, box A27, Clark Papers; Dickson, *The Supreme Court in Conference,* 639; Tushnet, *Making Civil Rights Law,* 188–191.

24  My claim is not, I emphasize, that *Brown* cannot be defended in legal terms, only that it cannot be so defended given Frankfurter's and Jackson's particular understanding of permissible legal sources. I am trying to show that *Brown* was a product of judicial values and sociopolitical context. I am not arguing that this makes *Brown* an illegitimate judicial decision. The question of whether *Brown* was rightly decided is one of normative constitutional theory and is beyond the scope of this chapter.

25  Schwartz, *Super Chief,* 77; Kluger, *Simple Justice,* 598; Melvin I. Urofsky, *Felix Frankfurter: Judicial Restraint and Individual Liberties* (Boston: Twayne, 1991), 128–29; Urofsky, *Division and Discord,* 260.

26  Alexander M. Bickel to Justice Frankfurter, 22 August 1953, Frankfurter Papers, microfilm collection, part II, reel 4, frames 212–14; Berry, *Stability, Security, and Continuity,* 142; Douglas conference notes, *Briggs v. Elliott,* 12 December 1953, case file: Segregation Cases, box 1149, Douglas Papers; Note, "Constitutionality of Educational Segregation," 17 *George Washington Law Review* 208, 214 n. 30 (1949); Urofsky, *Division and Discord,* 217, 222; Kluger, *Simple Justice,* 598–99.

27  Justice Jackson to Charles Fairman, 13 March 1950, Fairman file, box 12, Jackson Papers; Chernack, "The Clash of Two Worlds," 52.

28  Whether he intended to publish the opinion is unclear; a heart attack in March 1954 probably prevented him from doing so, even had he been so inclined.

29  Jackson memorandum opinion, School Segregation Cases, 15 March 1954, 1–2, case file: Segregation Cases, box 184, Jackson Papers.

30  *Id.* at 5–7.

31  *Id.* at 7–10.

32  EBP (E. Barrett Prettyman) to Jackson, undated, pp. 1, 3, box 184, Jackson Papers; Burton conference notes, School Segregation Cases, 12 December 1953, box 244, Burton Papers; Kluger, *Simple Justice,* 603–4; Tushnet, *Making Civil Rights Law,* 211–14.

33  Robert H. Jackson, *The Supreme Court in the American System of Government* (Cambridge: Harvard University Press, 1955), 80; Jackson memorandum opinion, School Segregation Cases, 7 December 1953, 8–10, case file: Segregation Cases, box 184, Jackson Papers; Chernack, "The Clash of Two Worlds," 53–54, 59–63, 73–75, 88–89.

34  Douglas conference notes, *Briggs v. Elliott,* 12 December 1953, case file: Segregation Cases, box 1149, Douglas Papers.

35  Jackson to Fairman, 13 March 1950, Fairman file, box 12, Jackson Papers;

Newman, *Hugo Black*, 277; WHR (William H. Rehnquist), "A Random Thought on the Segregation Cases," box 184, Jackson Papers; Robert H. Jackson, *The Struggle for Judicial Supremacy: A Study of a Crisis in American Power Politics* (New York: Vintage, 1941), 321–23; Michael E. Parrish, *Felix Frankfurter and His Times: The Reform Years* (New York: Free Press, 1982), 20–21, 58–59, 165–68.

36 Burton conference notes, School Segregation Cases, 13 December 1952, box 244, Burton Papers; Clark conference notes, School Segregation Cases, box A27, Clark Papers; Jackson to Fairman, 13 March 1950, Fairman file, box 12, Jackson Papers; Jackson memorandum opinion, 7 December 1953, 7–8, case file: Segregation Cases, box 184, Jackson Papers; Douglas conference notes, *Briggs v. Elliott*, 12 December 1953, case file: Segregation Cases, box 1149, Douglas Papers. The justices seem to have ignored the extent to which southern legislatures were unrepresentative, given black disfranchisement and legislative malapportionment. See Michael J. Klarman, "The Puzzling Resistance to Political Process Theory," 77 *Virginia Law Review* 747, 788 (1991).

37 Michael J. Klarman, "What's So Great about Constitutionalism?," 93 *Northwestern University Law Review* 145, 189–91 (1998); Tushnet, *Making Civil Rights Law*, 187–88; George H. Gallup, *The Gallup Poll: Public Opinion, 1935–1971*, vol. 2, *1949–1958* (New York: Random House, 1972), 1250; Melvin M. Tumin, "Readiness and Resistance to Desegregation: A Social Portrait of the Hard Core," *Social Forces* 36 (March 1958): 260–62; Melvin Tumin, Paul Barton, and Bernie Burrus, "Education, Prejudice and Discrimination: A Study in Readiness for Desegregation," *American Sociological Review* 23 (February 1958): 46; Andrew M. Greeley and Paul B. Sheatsley, "Attitudes toward Racial Integration," *Scientific American*, December 1971, 15–16; Lewis M. Killian and John L. Haer, "Variables Related to Attitudes Regarding School Desegregation Among White Southerners," *Sociometry* 21 (June 1958): 161; J. W. Peltason, *Fifty-Eight Lonely Men: Southern Federal Judges and School Desegregation* (New York: Harcourt, Brace and World, 1961), 34–35.

38 Jackson memorandum opinion, 15 March 1954, 1, 19–21, case file: Segregation Cases, box 184, Jackson Papers.

39 Kluger, *Simple Justice*, 684; Douglas conference notes, *Briggs v. Elliott*, 12 December 1953, case file: Segregation Cases, box 1149, Douglas Papers; Burton conference notes, School Segregation Cases, 12 December 1953, box 244, Burton Papers; Douglas conference notes, *Brown v. Board of Education*, 13 December 1952, case file: Segregation Cases, box 1150, Douglas Papers.

40 Kluger, *Simple Justice*, 614; John D. Fassett, "Mr. Justice Reed and *Brown v. Board of Education*," 1986 *Supreme Court Historical Society Yearbook* 53; LCG to Reed, certiorari memo, *Brown v. Board of Education*, Reed Papers; RLR to Reed, certiorari memo, *Davis v. School Board of Prince Edward County*, Reed Papers; *Southern School News*, April 1956, 3; *Southern School News*, June 1956, 13; *Southern School News*, October 1956, 10.

41 Burton conference notes, School Segregation Cases, 12 December 1953, School Segregation Cases, 13 December 1952, box 244, Burton Papers.

42 Douglas memorandum, 25 January 1960, in Melvin I. Urofsky, ed., *The*

*Douglas Letters: Selections from the Private Papers of Justice William O. Douglas* (Bethesda, Md.: Adler and Adler, 1987), 169; see also Tushnet, *Making Civil Rights Law*, 126–27; Jack Greenberg, *Crusaders in the Courts: How a Dedicated Band of Lawyers Fought for the Civil Rights Revolution* (New York: Basic Books, 1994), 110.

43 Douglas conference notes, *Brown v. Board of Education*, case file: Segregation Cases, box 1150, Douglas Papers; Jackson memorandum opinion, School Segregation Cases, 15 March 1954, 1, case file: Segregation Cases, box 184, Jackson Papers; Gallup, *The Gallup Poll*, 1250; Patterson, *Brown v. Board of Education*, 72.

44 Jackson memorandum opinion, 15 March 1954, 1, case file: Segregation Cases, box 184, Jackson Papers; Peltason, *Fifty-Eight Lonely Men*, 249.

45 Jackson conference notes, School Segregation Cases, 15 March 1954, 1, case file: Segregation Cases, box 184, Jackson Papers; Derrick Bell, "*Brown v. Board of Education*: Forty-Five Years after the Fact," 26 *Ohio Northern University Law Review* 171, 172 (2000); Mendez v. Westminster, 64 F. Supp. 544 (S.D. Cal. 1946), *affirmed on other grounds*, 161 F.2d 774 (9th Cir. 1947).

46 Frankfurter memo to the justices, 15 January 1954, 1, Reed Papers; Jackson memorandum opinion, School Segregation Cases, 15 March 1954, 13, case file: Segregation Cases, box 184, Jackson Papers; Clark conference notes, School Segregation Cases, box A27, Clark Papers.

47 Clark conference notes, School Segregation Cases, box A27, Clark Papers; Jackson conference notes, School Segregation Cases, case file: Segregation Cases, box 184, Jackson Papers; Kluger, *Simple Justice*, 336, 345, 481, 499–500, 531–33, 591, 600–601.

48 Tushnet, *Making Civil Rights Law*, 216.

# PART III

Historical Impact: Views from the Grassroots

TOMIKO BROWN-NAGIN

# The Impact of Lawyer-Client Disengagement on the NAACP's Campaign to Implement *Brown v. Board of Education* in Atlanta

The local community study, the predominant model of scholarship in civil rights historiography in recent decades, has produced a greater understanding of the range of actors who contributed to the celebrated achievements of the civil rights movement. Before the ascendancy of this history from the "bottom up," the unique forms of activism and contributions of the common folk had been obfuscated by studies that emphasized the political and legal history of the civil rights movement. Such top-down political and legal histories had focused on the actions of "great men," decision makers who made law in the halls of Congress, garnering pivotal legislative victories such as the Civil Rights Act of 1964, or held forth in court, challenging the legality of segregation in cases such as *Brown v. Board of Education*. Community studies have swept away the view that history is only made in traditional seats of power; these local histories have shown that average, workaday African Americans—women and men who agitated for civil rights in their own neighborhoods, often at great personal risk—also were agents of change. The common folk laid the groundwork for the celebrated achievements of the civil rights movement that ended official sanction for racial segregation.

Although community studies have had an immense influence on civil rights scholarship, we have yet to see the potential of local history fully realized within the subdisciplines of legal history, in particular legal history that assesses the development of the law of equal protection. For instance, few studies combine a detailed analysis of legal developments in a lawsuit with a narrative about the social dynamics in the locale where the case was litigated. In other words, genuine sociolegal history is rare; studies tend either to focus on the thrust and parry of legal argument or on the social history of communities in which struggles for political and civil rights were fought—not both.

In the fiftieth-anniversary year of *Brown*, a point in time when a generation of students includes some who have experienced racially integrated schooling and others who have not, it is fitting to contemplate the full array of factors that contributed to the success or failure of efforts to desegregate public education. Sociolegal scholarship can aid immeasurably in this assessment by illuminating how the unique characteristics of a given community advanced or hindered local school desegregation efforts. In this chapter, I focus on the social context in which the Atlanta school desegregation case, *Calhoun v. Latimer*, was litigated, as a way of shedding light on local factors that influenced the implementation of *Brown* in Atlanta, and by analogy in other large cities.

Although I write in the tradition of the community studies scholarship, there are important differences between Atlanta and the locales that are typically the focal points of local histories. Rural, economically depressed regions of the South where racial violence was the norm and the vast majority of the African American population was abjectly poor dominate community studies; Mississippi Delta counties are prominent subjects of study, for example. Atlanta, by contrast, is a city that experienced consistent economic growth in the decades following the Second World War. Although racial violence occurred in Atlanta and the lines of segregation were drawn tight, the city's fathers, seeking to attract northern investors and encourage economic development, cultivated an image of racial progressiveness. And most importantly, Atlanta has been home to a sizable African American middle class since the late nineteenth century. This distinction was in part an outgrowth of the city's position as the capital of African American higher education: Atlanta boasts the highest concentration of historically black institutions of higher education of any city in the country, including Atlanta University and Morehouse and Spelman colleges. Its middle class, politically active and secure in its educational privilege and relative prosperity, flourished, whereas in other southern locales a black middle class was much smaller and politically less strong. In this way, black Atlanta's demography is similar to that of Chicago or Philadelphia, making the themes here applicable to large, urban centers in the North.[1]

The factors that set Atlanta apart from many smaller southern cities—the presence of a significant black middle class and the white power structure's self-conscious endeavor to cultivate and protect Atlanta's New South image—give rise to the most significant difference between Atlanta and archetypal locales in the community studies scholarship. Local histories typically focus on the interplay of local activists, leaders of national civil rights organizations, and a white majority opposed to civil rights gains. These narratives explain how locally and nationally based civil rights groups together combated white segregationists in the public arena; if tension existed between these groups of activists, it arose from tactical differences, not because either group was marginalized in the struggle to combat racial injustice.

Atlanta was different. In Atlanta, a small group of white and African American élites (a biracial élite) dominated decision making. This élite eschewed the public contestation of issues relating to race, preferring instead to settle challenges to social conventions through settlements negotiated privately by handpicked representatives of each race. Everyday African Americans, as well as most national civil rights organizations, were left on the sidelines, their activism constrained by the élite's desire to exercise control over the terms and pace of civil rights advances.[2] As a result, the social history that I write does not turn exclusively on the interracial axis that is a dominant power relation in community studies scholarship. *Intra-racial* social dynamics in Atlanta exerted an enormous influence on the effort by the NAACP Legal Defense Fund (LDF) to desegregate the city's schools. These social relations are the focus of this chapter.

The particular intraracial social dynamic that is considered here is élite control of the Atlanta NAACP branch, or more specifically the consequences of an inert local branch for LDF's effort to implement *Brown*. The Atlanta example suggests that the history of NAACP branches, although seldom a focus of recent scholarship, is indispensable to understanding why civil rights lawyers were unable to implement the rule of law established in *Brown* in some localities. In exclusively emphasizing the role that white resistance, including intransigent or indifferent federal courts, played in undermining the implementation of *Brown*, historians have undervalued the impact of dynamics within local NAACP branches on the school desegregation effort. This chapter corrects that analytical oversight by demonstrating the significance of local history and local branches. Specifically, it demonstrates how an ineffective NAACP branch, one that had a troubled relationship with the national NAACP and a distant association with the LDF, undermined the LDF's legal strategy. Stated affirmatively, the Atlanta example suggests how important effective branch leadership was to the ability of civil rights lawyers to rally communities around the concept of school desegregation and convince the courts that the right of students to attend desegregated schools must be enforced.

The emphasis placed here on the salience of local branch history suggests another emphasis. By highlighting the role of branch history in the LDF's effectiveness, this chapter makes the larger point that the separation of the national NAACP from the LDF in 1956 undermined the efficacy of civil rights lawyers in ways that have not yet been fully explored. But for the split between the national NAACP and the LDF, these civil rights lawyers might have maintained meaningful connections to their client base through associations with local branch members. Traditionally, however, the split between the two organizations is understood as a mere bureaucratic change prompted chiefly by an investigation by the Internal Revenue Service, as well as by Thurgood Marshall's desire to consolidate his decision-making authority at the LDF by ridding himself of meddlesome interference from Roy Wilkins, executive director of the national NAACP, and competition from Marshall's assistant at the LDF, Robert Carter. And yet, as Mark Tushnet has noted, the separation also had the effect of "eliminat[ing] the formal connection between the LDF and its primary constituency," the membership of the NAACP. This analysis of the Atlanta experience bears out this point and goes further, explaining in detail the ramifications for the work of civil rights lawyers of the organizational change.

The split between the national NAACP and the LDF encouraged a drift by the LDF away from meaningful connections with Atlanta branch members and leaders, and in turn with its clients. As a result, the LDF lacked a unified client group to support its legal efforts at the most crucial stage of the school desegregation campaign; the absence of a close lawyer-client relationship enabled Atlanta's biracial élite, rather than civil rights lawyers and their clients, to control the terms and eventually the outcome of the fight against segregated schools. In this way, the split between the NAACP and the LDF was a turning point in the civil rights movement.[3]

## Branch Decline

The Atlanta school desegregation case, *Calhoun v. Latimer*, was a miserable failure for LDF lawyers. At the case's end in 1973 the city's schools remained almost totally segregated. Moreover, the LDF had suffered the embarrassment of being fired from the case by the president of the local NAACP chapter, Lonnie King, and replaced by a local attorney. King claimed that the dismissal was warranted because the organization's lawyers were out of touch with the values and preferences of their Atlanta clients. After discharging the LDF, King brought *Calhoun* to a conclusion upending two decades of LDF advocacy in Atlanta and rejecting the Supreme Court's holding in *Swann v. Charlotte-Mecklenburg Board of Education* that busing was a legitimate means of achieving substantial school integration. Claiming that the majority of black Atlantans, including local NAACP branch members, had disavowed the LDF's commitment to integrated schools, King negotiated a settlement that minimized desegregation in exchange for administrative control by African Americans of the school system. LDF attorneys, together with civil rights lawyers associated with the ACLU and the Congress of Racial Equality (CORE), objected to the settlement, calling it constitutionally inadequate—a "selling out" of the rights of black students for a "few jobs" for a "few big Negroes." Nevertheless, the federal district and appellate courts, sympathetic to the view that local sentiment should prevail notwithstanding precedent demanding meaningful integration, ignored arguments that Lonnie King was a legitimate representative neither of most black Atlantans nor of the NAACP. Ultimately, the courts rejected challenges to the legality of the settlement and approved the Atlanta school plan.

Lonnie King's claim to be the authentic representative of black Atlanta was questionable in a number of respects. Yet he was able to insinuate himself into the Atlanta school desegregation case. His success was due in part to the LDF's weakness: King was correct in claiming that LDF attorneys were far removed from their clients. A number of factors contributed to LDF's disengagement from its client base, not least the local branch politics that are the focus here.

During the 1960s, when the LDF stepped up its effort to obtain a court order finding "freedom-of-choice" desegregation plans unconstitutional and mandating a meaningful school desegregation remedy, the Atlanta branch of the NAACP was mostly inactive on the subject of school desegregation. Lacking a stable and productive leadership, the branch failed to attract community support. The absence of support was not surprising in light of the hierarchical and undemocratic style employed by the branch's conservative, middle-class leaders. For decades the branch had been controlled by a few old stalwarts, professional men like the lawyer Austin Thomas (A. T.) Walden and the dentist John H. Calhoun, who determined the priorities of the branch in consultation with local businessmen and civic leaders, white and black. Keeping in step with the notion of the "Talented Tenth" espoused by W. E. B. Du Bois, these branch leaders never considered the possibility that workaday African Americans, as opposed to the black élite, would participate in the decision-making process.[4]

During the late 1950s national NAACP officials had begun discussing the branch's difficulties and their embarrassment that a city as prominent as Atlanta could be home to such an ineffectual local branch. A series of internal NAACP memoranda revealed that national leaders perceived the Atlanta branch leaders as weak and the branch itself as unproductive. The branch reached a low point in December 1958, when Calhoun, the long-time branch president, retired under a cloud. Calhoun's resignation came after revelations that he was in personal financial difficulties stemming from his recent divorce, difficulties that "posed embarrassment to the branch." Moreover his remark, published in local newspapers, that the "atmosphere in Atlanta is not right for integration" had embarrassed the NAACP and sparked rumors that Calhoun had "made some sort of deal with public officials" to undermine compliance with *Brown*.[5]

Finding a new leader for the branch proved exceedingly difficult. Few candidates expressed interest in taking the helm, in part because Calhoun and his loyalists limited the pool by insisting on personally approving a successor. Noting the urgent need to have in place a leader of "stature, independence, and considerable leadership ability" in communities like Atlanta where school desegregation battles were at a critical stage, Roy Wilkins was distressed when the branch asked to postpone the election for Calhoun's successor until February 1959. The branch sought delay because of a lack of candidates—a state of affairs that Wilkins found exasperating. In correspondence Wilkins expressed profound disappointment that no one was willing to "carry on the heavy work of one of our most important branches in the South." When the election finally took place on 23 February, Edward K. Weaver, a professor of education at Atlanta University, was elected branch president. But in an astounding move, Weaver resigned from the presidency the very next day, just as local newspapers announced his ascension to the branch's leadership. The reason for his sudden resignation was never revealed.[6]

It was not until December 1959, almost a year after Calhoun's resignation, that a successor was chosen. The new branch president, Samuel W. Williams, would hold the post until 1967 (with the exception of a brief hiatus in 1964–65). The length of Williams's tenure was sufficient to allow him to make a strong impact on the organization's direction, yet he did not do so. Although Williams was dedicated to the cause of civil rights and promised to "overcome" the "internal difficulties which ha[d] afflicted" the Atlanta branch over the years, the energy that he could devote to the branch was limited. In addition to serving as branch president, he was a full-time professor at Morehouse, the pastor of the Friendship Baptist Church, a vice-president of the Southern Christian Leadership Conference, and an adviser to both the Student Non-violent Coordinating Committee and student demonstrators at the Atlanta University Center.[7]

The job of reviving the branch was enormous, and Williams, who was essentially serving part time, was not up to the task of reinvigorating a branch dominated by élites accustomed to acting in step with the white power structure. One of Williams's first acts was to conduct a fund-raising campaign to make the branch self-supporting. Although local businessmen and civic leaders pledged their support for the branch's efforts against discrimination on the golf courses and buses and in employment and education, the branch consistently failed to reach its fund-raising and membership goals throughout the 1960s.[8] Thus despite Williams's promise that the branch would experience a renaissance, national NAACP officials continued to view the branch as deficient. The NAACP field secretary for Georgia, Amos Holmes, was blunt in his assessment: he accused Williams and the branch of inactivity. Even more pointedly, Ruby Hurley, secretary of the NAACP's southeast regional office, accused Williams of having "multiple interests" and "divided loyalties" that undermined the branch's effectiveness. In addition, Hurley decried the continued influence on the branch of the city's black "power structure," which she believed "d[id] not want a vibrant branch." National NAACP leaders seemed loath to respond to Hurley's allegations after Williams reacted to criticisms of his stewardship by maintaining that the "socio-economic background" of Atlanta made true branch leadership impossible. The implication of Williams's statement was that black élites in Atlanta continued to exercise a monopoly over important political and policy matters, including civil rights. The national NAACP accepted Williams's contention that the "old guard" constrained his leadership and proposed to assist him in addressing the problem. Ultimately, however, the national office refused to do anything that might upset social dynamics in Atlanta, reasoning that it should avoid upheaval at the branch during a time when the school desegregation case had reached a critical stage.[9]

Relations between the branch and the national NAACP remained strained when neither group took bold steps toward reform. C. Miles Smith, who briefly served as president of the branch in 1964–65, expressed deep resentment over the perception that the branch was inept. In a letter to the NAACP in September 1964 about the branch's financial difficulties, Smith noted the "few occasions that Atlanta has been mentioned in a favorable light" by national officials. He declared, "we here do not appreciate the total disregard that we receive from the organization as a unit."[10]

The branch's problems continued after Williams resumed the presidency in 1965, and eventually grew so extensive that the branch's very existence was threatened. By 1966 problems had worsened to the point that Gloster Current, the director of branches, was considering disbanding the Atlanta branch outright and replacing it with several smaller branches. Noting that Atlanta's membership had declined to 1,973 in 1965 from 3,547 in 1964, and that a city of Atlanta's size should yield between 10,000 and 15,000 members, Current declared that the branch simply was "not progressing" and bemoaned the unreliability of the "upper middle-class and well-off personalities that had traditionally carried the branch." Current suggested that the proposed system of smaller branches attempt to connect to "ordinary citizens." Claiming that the existing branch held few meetings and that those called were poorly attended, Joe Louis Tucker, field director of the

Georgia NAACP, declared the branch "nothing more than a name." Williams's continued practice of "wear[ing] too many hats" had driven away the branch's most productive members, who recognized that efforts to reach out to Atlanta's working people were stymied by the perception that the NAACP was a "middle-class organization, unconcerned with the problems of the masses." The suggestion that the branch be reorganized seems to have been dropped by 1967, however, when Dr. Albert Davis became the new branch president. Still, the pattern of underachievement continued under Davis's successor, the Reverend R. L. Johnson.[11]

The election of Lonnie King as branch president and successor to Johnson in January 1969 represented a turning point of sorts. King, a former student activist at Morehouse, had been a crucial figure during the early 1960s in demonstrations against merchants who practiced segregation. King had returned to Atlanta as an official with the U.S. Department of Health, Education and Welfare after spending several years in Washington. His reentry into local politics was not smooth, however. King had succeeded to the branch presidency under a cloud. The election that brought him to power was characterized by a lack of interest among the membership and procedural improprieties that violated election protocols set forth in the NAACP's constitution and bylaws. For instance, many members of the committee who had nominated King at a branch meeting on 12 November 1968—and many of the nominees themselves—were not qualified because they were not members in good standing of the branch. As a result of these irregularities, a new nominating session was held, at which qualified nominators again placed King's name in consideration for the presidency. King, as the sole candidate for branch president, was certified the winner of the election in January 1969.[12]

Despite the lack of support for the branch during this period and the peculiar circumstances surrounding his election, King's presidency would prove monumental. He single-handedly ended the LDF's control of the school desegregation case and engineered a settlement that from the perspective of stalwart civil rights lawyers and the national NAACP eviscerated the meaning of *Brown*.

The Split and Lawyer-Client Disengagement

During the late 1950s and into the 1960s, while the Atlanta branch of the NAACP sought to justify its very existence, the LDF's attorneys Constance Baker Motley and Howard Moore, and later Peter and Elizabeth Rindskopf, became the central actors in the Atlanta school desegregation case. LDF attorneys approached the case ambitiously, though their ambition was often stymied by the courts' willingness to indulge the board of education's incremental approach to school desegregation. Atlanta's black élites had for years tolerated the incrementalism of the board, civic leaders, and white businessmen. The willingness of the LDF consistently to challenge local prerogatives on the issue of race and schools therefore represented a radical departure from past practices.

In another sense, however, there were important similarities between local black élites and the LDF lawyers in their approaches to community relations. LDF attorneys, like the local élite, did not seem to value the participation of client communities in the decision-making process, either as a matter of democratic principle or as a matter of litigation strategy. To be sure, different motivations accounted for the attorneys' failure to seek advice from the community or cultivate its support for the cause of school desegregation. Atlanta's black élite tended not to show an interest in the views of the workaday African American, because of both self-interested paternalism and free-market individualism. By contrast, LDF attorneys tended to overlook the input of the average African American because of their unfamiliarity with the dynamics in Atlanta's black communities and their abiding faith in the legal process. Indeed, LDF attorneys became all consumed with questions of legal strategy, altogether neglecting local politics. Ultimately, the LDF's failure to know the community in which it was litigating undermined the efficacy of the aggressive legal tactics that otherwise set the LDF attorneys apart from local élites.[13]

That LDF attorneys were inattentive to the need for strong relationships with client communities may seem odd at first blush. Shortly after *Brown v. Board of Education* was decided, the national NAACP acknowledged that community support was pivotal to successful implementation of the Supreme Court's school desegregation decree. At the NAACP's national convention in July 1954, the general membership adopted a resolution underscoring the importance of nonlegal approaches to the pursuit of equality. The resolution stated that "the enjoyment of many rights and opportunities of first class citizenship is not dependent on legal action, but rather on the molding of public sentiment and the exertion of public pressure to make democracy work. . . . If these rights and opportunities, already sanctioned in law, are to become a reality, the Association and all of its branches must initiate and carry through greatly expanded programs of community action designed to involve the entire membership of the NAACP and influence large circles of citizens beyond our ranks. Such activities, directly influencing the daily lives of our members, will provide the surest means of increasing the membership and influence of the Association."[14]

The national NAACP's early recognition that the formal legal victory garnered in *Brown* would be an empty victory without the support of average African Americans animated its long-standing concerns about the Atlanta branch's ineffectual leadership and failure to thrive. During the crisis of leadership that plagued the branch after John Calhoun's retirement as branch president Roy Wilkins, executive director of the NAACP, made explicit in several letters to Atlanta officials the link between community support and the organization's ability to wage successful campaigns to implement *Brown*.[15]

The national NAACP's concern about the Atlanta branch's ability to pursue school desegregation also reflected the values of the LDF leadership, in particular Charles Hamilton Houston, dean of the Howard University Law School and special counsel to the NAACP, and his protégé Thurgood Marshall. Although Marshall's folksiness and respect for the "little Joes" is legend, both men appreciated the need for civil rights lawyers to hear the counsel and appreciate the sacrifices of African Americans on the local level who participated in NAACP test cases as clients or otherwise supported the organization's initiatives. While researching a case, identifying potential plaintiffs, and preparing for trial, Houston and Marshall often met with local NAACP members, conducted workshops for them, and maintained close communication with local leaders, making it possible to elicit facts and opinions crucial to the success of their case. Houston aptly described the relationship of a civil rights lawyer to his constituency by noting that he was "not only lawyer but evangelist and stump speaker." For his part, Marshall encouraged LDF staff attorneys to maintain close contact with local NAACP membership. "We are here to serve the branches—that is our responsibility," he once remarked. Going further, Marshall made clear that he "believed it was 'dangerous' for the legal work to outpace the development of 'whole-hearted' support in the branches."[16]

By the mid-1960s, however, crucial organizational restructuring had occurred within the NAACP, one that undermined the productive relationship between lawyers and branch members that Houston and Marshall had earlier cultivated. In 1956 the NAACP and the Legal Defense Fund formally separated, a consequence, in the first instance, of an investigation by the Internal Revenue Service that questioned the close working relationship between the LDF, which was tax-exempt, and the NAACP, which because of its political activities was not. The effect of the split was profound. It reduced communication between LDF lawyers and their constituents in the branches. Even Marshall, whose close ties to client communities were widely known, was affected. According to Tushnet, Marshall "spent less time in direct contact with African American communities in the South" during the late 1950s. Constance Baker Motley, an assistant to Marshall in the 1950s who was an attorney of record in *Calhoun*, has also described the grave impact of the split on organizational efficacy. According to Motley, the "separation of the two organizations was the most wrenching episode for us in the entire civil rights struggle" because the organizations' "manpower and resources for implementing *Brown* became divided." The split of the NAACP into two organizations helps to explain why the spirit of cooperation between civil rights lawyers and civil rights clients during Marshall's early leadership of the LDF dissipated when LDF attorneys, led by Motley, took charge of the Atlanta school desegregation case in the late 1950s.[17]

In the end, the LDF's failure to establish close ties to Atlanta's grassroots, coupled with the decline of the local NAACP branch, created significant barriers for the school desegregation campaign. Lacking contact with its client community, LDF's pursuit of equal educational opportunities in Atlanta was confined almost exclusively to the courtroom. Lacking the influence of either workaday citizens, who might have held sustained protests in support of the organization's litigation goals, or the élites of the Atlanta branch of the NAACP, who might have placed pressure on local officials to be more cooperative, the LDF's weapons in the fight against the foot dragging of the Atlanta Board of Education were limited to legal motions and oral arguments before mostly unsympathetic judges.

There was nothing inherently improper about the LDF's exclusive reliance on the court process. But that sort of reliance was wise only if LDF's legal arguments were persuasive to presiding judges and the issues litigated were capable of effective resolution by the conservative white élites who dominated the bench (as well as state and local politics). Neither of these conditions was present in the school desegregation cases, not in Atlanta or in any other southern city. For this reason, it was unwise to pursue school desegregation exclusively by appeal to a court system under the control of white southerners, the vast majority of whom appeared to personally oppose school desegregation.[18] For example, in reflecting on the role of Judge Frank Hooper, who presided over *Calhoun* during this period, Constance Baker Motley stated: "I have never been convinced that he believed blacks had rights that whites were bound to respect. I sized him up not as one of the worst federal judges we had to confront (he was always dignified and courteous) but as one who believed that you make promises to black people and do not keep them—a typical segregationist view."[19]

Indeed, Hooper and the U.S. Court of Appeals rejected the LDF's arguments at almost every turn during the 1960s. Only the Supreme Court's groundbreaking decision in *Swann v. Charlotte-Mecklenburg County* (1971) made it even conceivable for the district and appeals courts to consider ordering a desegregation plan that would bring about a significant degree of school desegregation in Atlanta. In *Swann* the Supreme Court considered how districts should fulfill their obligation to begin operating unitary schools immediately in large urban systems where freedom-of-choice plans were inadequate to achieve desegregation and residential segregation was endemic. Justice Warren Burger's opinion for a unanimous Court established a presumption that single-race schools were unconstitutional and articulated the view that federal judges possessed broad equitable powers to issue remedial orders to achieve desegregated schools. In particular, the Court endorsed the use of numerical racial formulas in formulating desegregation plans and, recognizing the relationship between residential and school segregation, held that officials could gerrymander school attendance zones and extensively use busing to achieve school desegregation.[20]

*Swann* posed significant difficulties for Atlanta's city fathers, who had assumed that residential segregation would enable the city to avoid fundamentally altering school attendance patterns. As far as they were concerned, Atlanta's schools had been desegregated since 1961, when nine black students officially broke the color barrier by attending schools that had been all white for decades. *Swann* threatened this assumption. In light of *Swann*, LDF lawyers proposed to the district court a desegregation plan that would remedy the gross racial imbalance in the city's school system. In 1971 figures showed that 42.4 percent of Atlanta's elementary school students and 50.7 percent of high school students attended schools in which 99 percent of the students were of the same race. These statistics reflected that whites lived at the northern and southern ends of the city, whereas African Americans lived in a broad middle section. The LDF's plan eliminated all one-race schools in the district, using all the techniques approved in *Swann*, including the gerrymandering of attendance zones and the busing of students to schools outside their neighborhoods.[21] This response to *Swann* set in motion a series of maneuvers by a small group of the city's decision makers. They sought to end once and for all Atlanta's "annual agony" of how to deal with school desegregation.

### LDF's Ouster: The Legacy of Branch Decline and Lawyer-Client Disengagement

A settlement of the school desegregation case, negotiated by a few of Atlanta's leading men, made the racial disorder threatened by *Swann* disappear. By agreeing with local whites that the outsiders should be displaced, it was Lonnie King, president of the Atlanta branch of the NAACP, who ultimately sent packing the interloping LDF lawyers from New York. In a blow to the LDF and its supporters, King negotiated a deal with local whites, including school board members who were defendants in the case, that repudiated the integration-oriented remedies for which LDF attorneys had been fighting for decades. King's deal accepted token pupil desegregation in exchange for African American administrative control of the school system. The settlement minimized pupil desegregation to such an extent that 83 of the city's 153 schools, containing 59,064 students, a majority of the system's pupils, were left 90 percent or more black. Among the 83 that were to remain segregated were 45 schools, containing 32,817 students, left with a 100 percent black enrollment. Just 814 white students and 1,951 African American students were to be bused under the plan. Moreover, to the extent that any busing occurred at all, the ACLU and CORE argued, it would be the children of working-class and poor black families (and a few whites) who would bear the brunt of transportation burdens. While it eschewed increased racial balance for pupils, the plan included provisions stating that the school system would increase its support for a voluntary majority-to-minority student transfer program, although the Supreme Court had rejected such a freedom-of-choice program as an ineffective remedy for de jure segregation years earlier.[22] In defending the deal, King argued that he and other Atlantans—not LDF lawyers—were the authentic voice of black Atlanta, and he knew best what these citizens wanted.[23]

As if the substance of the deal were not enough, the LDF had been blindsided in that negotiations to settle the case were taking place at all. The deal had initially been negotiated in secret. When news of the settlement negotiations broke in the local papers, the LDF attorney James Nabrit III denounced the LDF's exclusion from the talks and declared that it would not broker a deal with the school board under any circumstances. At this point King, who had not previously been a party to the litigation, maneuvered his way into *Calhoun* and froze out the LDF. He did so by obtaining powers of attorney from eight of the twenty-eight original plaintiffs in *Calhoun*. Then, acting as the representative of these plaintiffs, King fired Nabrit and hired a local attorney, who was a novice in comparison to Nabrit and other LDF attorneys, to replace the LDF as the representative of the entire plaintiff class. King claimed that LDF attorneys were fired after he had consulted with the plaintiffs, who had enthusiastically supported the LDF's removal. With that, the LDF was ousted from its own case—by a man whose putative constituency was at best unrepresentative of the plaintiff class as a whole and at worst non-existent.[24]

King's ability to exercise such influence in the case can be traced to the decades-long demise of the Atlanta branch of the NAACP. Having secured the branch presidency without any formal opposition and without follow-ing election protocols, King was able to rely on the NAACP's name and historical cachet to assert publicly and in the media that he represented a broad constituency. But there was little to indicate that King represented anything approaching a sizable constituency. Recall that as late as 1970, the Atlanta branch of the NAACP had only fifty active members. Thus in reality King represented himself and the few other members of the black élite who wanted a swift settlement of the school desegregation suits. King was in-deed the legitimate spokesperson for such members of the élite—for exam-ple Lyndon Wade, Benjamin Mays, and Jessie Hill Jr.—but not for others and certainly not for the *Calhoun* plaintiff class as a whole. Yet as president of the Atlanta NAACP, King could claim to represent the branch's member-ship, as an unassuming public did not realize that the branch was virtually defunct. In this way, King was able to insinuate himself into the litigation as *the* voice of black Atlanta. The LDF was thrown out of its own case and the Atlanta branch, long neglected, was the vehicle for the lawyers' ouster.[25]

Four civil rights organizations, including the LDF, the national NAACP, CORE, and the ACLU, objected to King's domination of the case, as well as to the constitutionality of the settlement, but to no avail. The district court was unmoved. Over the organizations' objections, the court brought an end to *Calhoun* on 4 April 1973, when it concluded that the settlement negotiated by King and Van Landingham was "fair, adequate and reasonable."[26]

The potential ramifications of the Atlanta settlement were not lost on LDF attorneys or leaders of the national NAACP. If black Atlanta's repu-diation of school integration was viewed as representative of a trend in African American opinion, civil rights leaders feared, the Supreme Court, already skeptical of imposing racial balance on resistant whites, would end the experiment with school desegregation altogether.[27] In an effort to slow the momentum that may have been created by the Atlanta settlement, the national NAACP responded swiftly to the branch president's breach of NAACP policy. King got his comeuppance: he was ousted as branch president. His dismissal was only a symbolic gesture, however; with the court's approval of the settlement, King had prevailed in both the battle and the war.[28]

The national NAACP and the LDF had contributed in significant ways to what they viewed as the disastrous conclusion of the Atlanta school deseg-regation case. Leaders of the national office had been disengaged from the local branch membership since the mid-1950s, failing to do anything in the face of their awareness that the branch was foundering and unconnected to the "little Joes" who were the putative beneficiaries of the school desegrega-tion campaign. Similarly, LDF attorneys, by developing a single-minded focus on law and the courts after their split with the national NAACP, lost their connection to their client community. As a result, the LDF created a leadership void that was filled by Lonnie King during the most crucial stage of the school desegregation campaign. In this way civil rights lawyers sowed the seeds of their own destruction.

The split between the LDF and the NAACP marked a decline in LDF attorneys' concern for close contact with clients and collaboration with community-based civil rights groups, most obviously the NAACP branches. This development is just one among many intraracial ones at the local level that influenced whether the goals of civil rights legal advocacy were realized. Scholars must give greater attention to how such local factors influenced legal efforts to achieve equality if we are to develop a nuanced legal history of the implementation of *Brown*. More particularly, a deeper and broader analysis of issues internal to the African American community is necessary for a fuller understanding of the advantages and limitations of the civil rights class action as a model for achieving social change.

## Notes

1 Donald L. Grant, *The Way It Was in the South: The Black Experience in Georgia* (New York: Carol, 1993), 205, 239–63; August Meier and David L. Lewis, "History of the Negro Upper Class in Atlanta, Georgia, 1890–1958," 28 *Journal of Negro Education* 2 (spring 1959): 128–39; John Dittmer, *Black Georgia in the Progressive Era* (Urbana: University of Illinois Press, 1980), 151.

2 See chapter 2 in Tomiko Brown-Nagin, "Class Actions: The Impact of Black and Middle-Class Conservatism on Civil Rights Lawyering in Atlanta, 1946–1979" (diss., Duke University, 2002).

3 For the argument that the split resulted primarily from Marshall's egotism, see Juan Williams, *Thurgood Marshall: American Revolutionary* (New York: Random House, 1998), 259–62; see also Mark V. Tushnet, *Making Civil Rights Law: Thurgood Marshall and the Supreme Court, 1956–1961* (New York: Oxford University Press, 1994), 310–11.

4 See Brown-Nagin, "Class Actions," 41–68, 248–56.

5 Confidential Memo on the Atlanta Branch Situation to Roy Wilkins, Gloster Current, and Ruby Hurley, typewritten document, 6 March 1959, box C27, 1959–60 file, NAACP Papers, Library of Congress (LOC); Samuel Williams to Roy Wilkins, typewritten letter signed, 3 December 1959, box C27, 1959–60 file, NAACP Papers, LOC; Warren R. Cochrane to Roy Wilkins, typewritten letter signed, 13 November 1959, box C27, 1959–60 file, NAACP Papers, LOC; V. W. Hodges to Roy Wilkins, typewritten letter signed, 13 November 1959, box C27,

1959–60 file, NAACP Papers, LOC; Program for Banquet Honoring Retiring Atlanta NAACP President John H. Calhoun, typewritten document, 2 December 1958, box C27, 1950–58 file, NAACP Papers, LOC.

6 Roy Wilkins to Dr. C. Clayton Powell, typewritten letter signed, 26 November 1958, box C27, 1950–58 file, NAACP Papers, LOC; Edward K. Weaver to the Rev. Adolphus S. Dickerson, typewritten letter signed, 23 February 1959, box C27, 1959–60 file, NAACP Papers, LOC.

7 Roy Wilkins to Samuel W. Williams, typewritten letter signed, 18 December 1959, box C27, 1959–60 file, NAACP Papers, LOC; Samuel Williams to Roy Wilkinson, typewritten letter signed, 3 December 1959, box C27, 1959–60 file, NAACP Papers, LOC; Ruby Hurley to Gloster Current, typewritten letter signed, 1 November 1960, box C27, 1959–60 file, NAACP Papers, LOC.

8 James O. Gibson to Gloster Current, typewritten letter signed, 15 February 1962, box C27, 1961–63 file, NAACP Papers, LOC; Atlanta Branch NAACP Fall Renewal Campaign Summary Report, typewritten document, 30 December 1966, box C6, 1966–69 file, NAACP Papers, LOC; Gloster Current to Ruby Hurley, typewritten letter, 13 October 1966, box C6, 1966–69 file, NAACP Papers, LOC; A. M. Davis to Lucille Black, typewritten letter signed, 27 October 1967, box C6, 1967 file, NAACP Papers, LOC; Ruby Hurley to Friends of the Atlanta NAACP Branch, typewritten letter signed, 18 July 1969, box C6, 1968–69 file, NAACP Papers, LOC.

9 Amos O. Holmes to Samuel W. Williams, typewritten letter, 11 May 1960, box C27, 1959–60 file, NAACP Papers, LOC; Gloster B. Current to Samuel Williams, typewritten letter, 23 January 1961, box C27, 1961–63 file, NAACP Papers, LOC; Gloster Current to Roy Wilkins, typewritten document, 23 January 1961, box C27, 1961–63 file, NAACP Papers, LOC; Gloster B. Current to Roy Wilkins, John Morsell, Robert Carter, and Ruby Hurley, typewritten document, 21 December 1960, box C27, 1959–60 file, NAACP Papers, LOC; Atlanta Branch Report to Gloster Current, typewritten document, 19 September 1961, box C27, 1961–63 file, NAACP Papers, LOC.

10 C. Miles Smith to Stephen Spottswood, typewritten letter, 23 September 1964, box C27, 1964–65 file, NAACP Papers, LOC.

11 Joe Louis Tucker to Gloster Current, typewritten letter signed, 16 July 1965, box C27, 1964–65 file, NAACP Papers, LOC; Atlanta Branch NAACP Fall Renewal Campaign Progress Report, typewritten document, 11 November 1966, box C6, 1966–69 file, NAACP Papers, LOC; Gloster Current to Joe Louis Tucker, typewritten letter, 2 May 1966, box C6, 1966–69 file, NAACP Papers, LOC; Teressa Stinson to Lucille Black, typewritten letter signed, 9 March 1967, box C6, 1967 file, NAACP Papers, LOC.

12 Chairmen of Standing Committees, typewritten document, 2 January 1969, box C6, 1968–69 file, NAACP Papers, LOC; Donald Hollowell to Gloster Current, typewritten letter signed, 2 January 1969, box C6, 1968–69 file, NAACP Papers, LOC.

13 See chapter 2, sections II–III, in Brown-Nagin, "Class Actions."

14 "Resolutions Adopted by the Forty-Fifth Annual Convention of the NAACP at Dallas, Texas, July 3, 1954," typewritten document, part V, box 682, NAACP Papers, LOC.

15 Roy Wilkins to Dr. C. Clayton Powell, typewritten letter signed, 26 November 1958, box C27, 1950–58 file, NAACP Papers, LOC.

16 On Houston see Genna Rae McNeil, *Groundwork: Charles Hamilton Houston and the Struggle for Civil Rights* (Philadelphia: University of Pennsylvania Press, 1983), 63–106, 131. On Marshall's egalitarianism and the working relationship of Marshall and Houston see Tushnet, *Making Civil Rights Law*, 16–18, 38–39, 311; Williams, *Thurgood Marshall*, xv, 93, 101–9, 143–44, 179–94; Richard Kluger, *Simple Justice* (New York: Vintage, 1977), 182–85, 199, 200, 214–16, 224–26.

17 Tushnet, *Making Civil Rights Law*, 310; see also Constance Baker Motley, *Equal Justice under the Law* (New York: Farrar, Straus and Giroux, 1998), 126.

18 For discussions of southern judges' typical stance on civil rights cases, see for example Tushnet, *Making Civil Rights Law*, 238–40, 251–52. There were notable exceptions to the general tendency among judges to assist local politicos in obstructing compliance with *Brown*, as famously explained by Jack Bass in *Unlikely Heroes* (Tuscaloosa: University of Alabama Press, 1981), the study of four Fifth Circuit judges who supported *Brown*.

19 Motley, *Equal Justice under Law*, 197.

20 402 U.S. at 16–19, 25–32. For a discussion of the negotiations among justices during the process of formulating the Court's final opinion in *Swann*, see Davison M. Douglas, *Reading, Writing, and Race: The Desegregation of the Charlotte Schools* (Chapel Hill: University of North Carolina Press, 1995), 207–14.

21 Plaintiffs' Motion for Adoption of Plaintiffs' Proposed Desegregation Plan and for Other Relief, pp. 1–10, Calhoun v. Cook (N.D. Ga. 30 December 1971), Case File, box 55, folder 3, National Archives and Records Administration (NARA), Atlanta.

22 Plan of Proposed Settlement as Devised and Agreed Upon between Plaintiffs and Defendants in the Above-Captioned Cause, pp. 9–25, Calhoun v. Cook (N.D. Ga. 23 February 1973), Case File, box 55A, folder 5, NARA; affidavit of Michael J. Stolee, pp. 1–15, Calhoun v. Cook (N.D. Ga. 23 March 1973), Case File, box 55A, folder 3, NARA.

23 Plaintiffs' Motion for Adoption of Plaintiffs' Proposed Desegregation Plan and for Other Relief, Staff Desegregation Addendum, pp. 1–4, Calhoun v. Cook (N.D. Ga. 30 December 1971), Case File, box 55, folder 3, NARA; see also Plaintiffs' Proposed Finds of Fact and Conclusions of Law, pp. 9–11, Calhoun v. Cook (N.D. Ga. 30 May 1972), Case File, box 55, folder 3, NARA.

24 Cook v. Calhoun, 409 U.S. 974, 974 (1972); Calhoun v. Cook, 469 F.2d 1067, 1067–68 (5th Cir. 1972); Junie Brown, "School Negotiation Could Be Periled," *Atlanta Journal*, § A, p. 1;. Memorandum to Ruby Hurley from Executive Board of Atlanta Branch NAACP, typewritten document, n.d., box 684, NAACP Papers, LOC.

25 Nathaniel Jones to Roy Wilkins and John A. Morsell, typewritten docu-

ment, 15 November 1972, part V, box 682, NAACP Papers, LOC; Mercedes Wright to Nathaniel Jones, typewritten document, 16 November 1972, part V, box 682, NAACP Papers, LOC.

26  Calhoun v. Cook, 362 F. Supp. 1249, 1249–52 (N.D. Ga. 1973).

27  See Paul Delaney, "Spread of Atlanta School Plan Reported by NAACP Aide," *New York Times*, 22 July 1973, § A, p. 1; "NAACP Suspends Atlanta Officers," *Washington Post*, 9 March 1973, § A, p. 6. The term "counter-majoritarian difficulty" refers to the reality that when courts invalidate legislative acts on equality grounds, they void rules or norms passed by majorities. See John Hart Ely, *Democracy and Distrust: A Theory of Judicial Review* (Cambridge: Harvard University Press, 1980), 73–104.

28  NAACP News Release, "Atlanta NAACP Suspended for Violation of Policy," 10 March 1973, box 683, NAACP Papers, LOC; Minutes of Meeting with Atlanta Branch Officers in New York, 6 March 1973, p. 9, box 685, NAACP Papers, LOC; Transcript of Hearing on the Suspension of Officers and Board Members, Atlanta Chapter, NAACP, 7 April 1973, pp. 9–11, box 685, NAACP Papers, LOC.

CHRISTINA GREENE

# "The New Negro Ain't Scared No More!"

## Black Women's Activism in North Carolina

## and the Meaning of *Brown*

℘ A number of years ago, Michael Klarman unleashed a vigorous debate when he accused civil rights scholars of exaggerating the significance of the Supreme Court's *Brown v. Board of Education* decision in fueling black protest. Klarman argued that the landmark case did more to
provoke a massive wave of white resistance than black insurgency. This
"backlash theory" generated charges of racism against Klarman and coun-
teraccusations that he had disavowed black agency. As the vitriol intensified, however, no one bothered to wonder how attention to black women's
grassroots activism might alter the debate.[1] Indeed, both views—the one
heralding *Brown* as a major turning point and the other diminishing its
impact on black resolve—generally omit African American women, often
define black insurgency too narrowly, and miss critical links between legal
action, community organizing, and direct-action protest. An examination
of local women's activities in Durham, North Carolina, however, illuminates these connections more clearly and helps us to understand how ordinary blacks strove to give meaning to the historic decision in their everyday lives.

The notion that black women and grassroots organizing should figure in
scholarly sparring over the meaning of *Brown* may seem irrelevant. After
all, black determination to desegregate schools initially found expression
largely in the courts rather than in the streets, especially after *Brown II*; and
most attorneys and judges were male. Yet before the first court papers could
be filed, attorneys needed both plaintiffs and community backing, and
African American women and youth, particularly NAACP youth chapters,
were critical to these efforts. By privileging more visible forms of protest,
such as public demonstrations and marches, as indicators of mass black
discontent, we overlook an important arena of grassroots activism, much of
it performed by women. As North Carolina blacks battled to make school
districts comply with *Brown*—whether in challenges to local school boards

or through lengthy NAACP lawsuits—black women's dense associational networks in families, neighborhoods, and leisure settings, as well as in more formal organizations, became important resources in garnering broad community support. African Americans may not have been marching in the streets in overwhelming numbers immediately after *Brown*, but black women were quietly reaching out to their friends and neighbors, building a grassroots foundation for the protracted legal struggles as well as the more visible direct-action protests that lay ahead.

Attracting local backing for school desegregation in the wake of *Brown* depended on newly revived NAACP youth chapters as well as local women. Between 1956 and 1960 NAACP youth in Durham canvassed neighborhoods while black women drew on a long tradition of community work to persuade wary residents to join school desegregation lawsuits.[2] As a result, blacks filed and won more individual challenges to discriminatory school board policies in Durham than in any other city in the state. Many of the same people who participated in the school desegregation campaigns of the 1950s also joined the direct-action protests of the following decade. Moreover, protesters in the 1960s drew on the grassroots base that women and youth had established during the 1950s. Thus, far from arresting black insurgency, *Brown* sparked community organizing drives, conducted largely by women and NAACP youth, to support school desegregation suits, which in turn formed a critical foundation for the sit-ins, boycotts, and demonstrations of the 1960s.

Local women's activities, however, were frequently "invisible," particularly to whites, and they have remained so to many scholars.[3] Newspapers, for example, were unlikely to report that black working-class women at the Walltown Community Center in Durham helped to convince scores of African American families that they should challenge racially discriminatory policies in Durham schools in the years immediately following *Brown*. Nor was it widely known that black tobacco workers stood watch from nearby factory windows as the first African American children made their way through hostile white crowds to attend formerly white public schools. Yet these examples hint at wider community participation in civil rights activity than the absence of overt black protest might otherwise suggest. Dramatic national events such as the prayer vigil in Washington commemorating *Brown* in 1957 may not have drawn the massive crowds that organizers had hoped for; but low black turnout did not necessarily signal black indifference to the court ruling, especially on the local level.[4]

One indication of *Brown*'s impact was the rapid expansion of the NAACP in North Carolina. Much of this growth was attributable to the efforts of black women, who frequently headed membership committees and served as adult advisors to NAACP youth groups across the state. Despite white violence and official attempts to destroy the NAACP in the years after *Brown*, support for the civil rights organization grew markedly in North Carolina, which boasted the largest NAACP membership in the Southeast region. In Durham, high school and college students, among them a substantial number of girls, flocked to the NAACP throughout the 1950s. Adults responded too. By 1954 membership in the Durham NAACP almost doubled from the previous year, making it the second-largest NAACP branch in the state, after that of Winston-Salem. Durham branch membership continued to climb, peaking at just under thirteen hundred and claiming a female majority by 1960.[5]

Although *Brown* spurred an increase in NAACP membership, the organization may have begun to expand even before the court ruling, but in ways that have often been overlooked. Thus even as individual NAACP membership declined by the early 1950s, the number of organizational memberships appears to have risen, perhaps as a way to shield individual blacks from retaliation for associating with the civil rights organization, but also in response to a new NAACP strategy. In 1949, the national NAACP specifically advocated working with local groups, and throughout North Carolina coalitions were formed to press for racial equality. Frank Brower, an attorney in Durham and branch secretary of the NAACP, appealed to local blacks to push their churches, trade unions, fraternal organizations, and other groups "to go on record in behalf of civil rights and to work for passage of legislation." He also noted the importance of women and youth: "If you want anything done, tell the women and the children," he exhorted black residents in 1950. Two days before the *Brown* decision, Louis Austin, editor of the *Carolina Times*, a black weekly published in Durham, specifically connected black associational life with civil rights work by urging that "every lodge, club, fraternity and sorority should make NAACP membership mandatory before allowing anyone to join them."[6] Black women's organizations seem to have taken the lead. In the years before *Brown*, when other black groups in North Carolina avoided public demands to abolish Jim Crow, African American women's organizations called for racial integration and joined the NAACP. In Durham black women's groups such as the Year Round Garden Club, the Little Slam Bridge Club, the Volkamenia Literary Society (which claimed a female majority), the Daughters of Dorcas, the Association of Public School Teachers, local sororities, and several cosmetologists' groups took out organizational memberships in the NAACP. A similar pattern emerged statewide. Between 1954 and 1957 the North Carolina Women's Baptist Home and Foreign Missionary Convention, the Alpha Kappa Alphas, Delta Sigma Thetas, and the North Carolina Federation of Colored Women's Clubs proudly announced their fully paid NAACP life memberships.[7] Black women also used their organizations to solicit individual NAACP memberships; in 1957, for example, a Durham beauticians' group won the NAACP annual branch membership drive. On the national level too, black women's organizations increasingly supported NAACP efforts. In June 1954, just one month after the Supreme Court decision, the national leadership of Jack and Jill of America, Inc., a black mothers' group, asked each chapter to increase its contribution in order to secure a lifetime membership in the NAACP. As northern women wavered, southern black women "in answering for the mothers of the south" insisted "that no mother, northern or southern, would [refuse] life membership" in the NAACP, and the measure carried by a majority vote.[8]

Attention to African American women therefore collapses rigid distinctions between civil rights activity and seemingly apolitical endeavors, including leisure pursuits, and offers us a richer and more expansive understanding of the black freedom movement. A number of scholars have underlined the importance of these "free spaces"—both formal and informal organizations and activities—where those with little power engage in "infra-politics" or pre-figurative politics, laying the groundwork for more public forms of collective protest. Indeed, black women were not simply doing hair, playing cards, or planting flowers. Rather, styling and organizing could and did occur simultaneously. As one beautician in Durham proclaimed, "We supported every effort to free our people."[9]

Affiliation with the NAACP in North Carolina was not as dangerous as in other southern states, but it was not altogether risk free. Tim Tyson has shown that a revived KKK launched a campaign of violence and terror throughout North Carolina in the early 1950s, largely in response to black assertiveness. Anti-communist zealots also took aim at black activists, including women. The House Un-American Activities Committee (HUAC) accused Shirley Temple James, a student at North Carolina College, a historically black institution in Durham, and president of the statewide Intercollegiate NAACP Youth Division, of being a communist sympathizer. Intimidation and even violence, however, often had the opposite effect, cementing rather than deterring black determination. Charles McLean, NAACP field secretary for North Carolina, noted a new sense of "pride" and "confidence" among previously fearful Negroes after *Brown*. "Those who once wanted to keep membership a secret are growing more confident and not only boast of their membership, but wear buttons and display emblems on their cars and front doors," he reported in 1955. Another NAACP official, Ruby Hurley, captured the new spirit of defiance when she declared to a Durham crowd that same year, "In spite of bombs, threats, killings and economic reprisals . . . [white leaders in N.C.] don't seem to know that the New Negro 'ain't scared no more.' "[10] Thus, paradoxically the NAACP solidified its base during the height of the cold war, even as red-baiting and racist violence forced the organization to expel communists and modify its civil rights agenda.

Not only did *Brown* help to revive NAACP branches throughout North Carolina, but it also fueled black resolve to desegregate schools. Just days after the ruling, over a thousand blacks crammed into St. Joseph's AME church in Durham for a pre-election meeting of the Durham Committee on Negro Affairs (DCNA), the largest crowd ever assembled for such an occasion. Clearly school desegregation had assumed renewed importance after *Brown*.[11] Black PTAS rallied the community and sponsored public discussions to "prepare Negro children for public school integration."[12] Shortly after *Brown II*, eight hundred parents together with representatives from the leading black organizations representing a cross-section of Negro Durham signed a petition calling for immediate integration of the Durham public schools. The petition drive was part of a broader statewide campaign by African Americans to urge official compliance with the high court's decision. In one well-publicized effort, three hundred black leaders from across the state converged upon both Governor Hodges and the North Carolina General Assembly to decry "attempts now being made to circumvent the United States Supreme Court's ruling on segregation in public schools." These actions were not simply a response to white intransigence; North Carolina blacks clearly were motivated by *Brown*, and their demands signaled a departure from earlier efforts to equalize school facilities. More importantly, the campaign departed from the Negro élite's typical pattern, especially in Durham, of negotiating behind the scenes with influential whites. Durham blacks knew that it would take more than petitions to dismantle Jim Crow, as they reminded white officials: "most of the gains [we have made] were achieved against the backdrop of coercive action of the courts."[13]

Black fears of white obstinacy were well founded, for local officials found myriad ways to circumvent *Brown*. In 1956 a group of black attorneys inquired whether the Durham school board had developed a desegregation plan or was "contemplating development" of a plan. In response, the superintendent of schools explained that the "segregation committee" was "carefully considering and is continuing the study of the U.S. Supreme Court decision," but was having "difficulty in formulating a recommendation which will meet with sufficient public support to insure the continued operation of our local public schools" and needed more time for "further study." In another example, the school board responded to serious overcrowding in black schools by instituting split sessions and reopening an abandoned white school building for African American students, while leaving vacant classrooms unoccupied in white schools. When parents objected, the board provided buses to transport black students to a segregated school in Walltown, a small, working-class, black neighborhood across town. The Negro PTAS, the DCNA, and the local NAACP rejected these "remedies" and pressed for "prompt and reasonable and good faith efforts" to desegregate the Durham schools. The board simply thanked the parents and activists and assured them that their concerns "would be given consideration."[14]

The state legislature buttressed such local diversionary maneuvers with the Pupil Assignment Act of 1955 and the Pearsall Plan; both measures effectively forestalled school desegregation throughout North Carolina for over a decade by decentralizing decision making and placing the burden of school desegregation on individual blacks. Local school boards in turn received wide latitude and a host of justifications to deny black reassignment requests—without ever mentioning race. Only after exhausting all administrative appeals could blacks seek legal redress. For example, when the Durham school board informed African American parents that it had run out of reassignment forms, blacks made copies of the forms, only to be told that their requests for reassignment were invalid because parents had failed to use the original forms![15] As clever Tar Heel politicians realized, "voluntary segregation" and token desegregation in a few districts proved far more effective than the flamboyant defiance of their Deep South neighbors. North Carolina thus managed to escape federal intervention while maintaining both segregation and its progressive image. These obstructionist tactics worked better than anyone could have predicted. By 1961 North Carolina reported a desegregation rate of .026 percent, lower than in Virginia, Tennessee, Arkansas, or Texas. The state became the envy of segregationists throughout the region, who marveled at Tar Heel ingenuity: "Why if we could be half as successful as you have been, we could keep this thing to a minimum for the next fifty years," remarked one official from Arkansas.[16]

But white intransigence also fueled black resoluteness, and the efforts of youth and women were as important as the attorneys' legal skills. To avert the token desegregation of schools that had occurred in Greensboro, Charlotte, and Winston-Salem, black residents of Durham would need scores of families willing to take on white authorities, first on the school board and then, if these efforts failed, in court.[17] Between 1956 and 1959 the DCNA and the local NAACP, particularly its youth chapters, worked with the black PTAS, the Ministerial Alliance, and neighborhood women to persuade black families to petition the Durham school board for reassignment as required by the Pupil Assignment Act. Providing what the sociologist Belinda Robnett calls "bridge leadership," local women linked ordinary citizens with formal organizations and NAACP attorneys. It was difficult work persuading black working-class parents to take the risks that challenges to segregation might entail. Although the NAACP in North Carolina survived state legislators' efforts to dismantle the organization—bringing more school desegregation lawsuits than in any other state—such attacks by white officials left local blacks fearful and cautious. Many wanted nothing to do with "that mess." In one Durham neighborhood, a rumor circulated that a black woman had lost her housekeeping job at Duke University after her son questioned segregationist policies at the nearby University of North Carolina in Chapel Hill.[18]

Despite these difficulties, in 1957 fourteen African American parents requested reassignment of their children to all-white schools in Durham. Nearly all lived in Walltown or Hickstown, smaller working-class, African American neighborhoods where black students were forced to pass by white schools to attend Negro schools across town. Attorneys reasoned that such gross and blatant segregation would make it easier to prove racial discrimination and demonstrate that the state's Pearsall Plan and Pupil Assignment Act were therefore unconstitutional. After the Durham school board denied the parents' requests and twice rejected appeals from nine of the families, the black community mobilized its resources for the legal battle that lay ahead. In May 1958, a year after the school board denied their requests for reassignment, Mrs. Evelyn McKissick, wife of the attorney and militant NAACP leader Floyd McKissick, and Mrs. Rachel Richardson, a resident of Walltown, filed the first direct legal challenge to Durham's segregated public schools on behalf of their daughters, Joycelyn McKissick and Elaine Richardson, and "others similarly situated." According to Floyd McKissick, Rachel Richardson "was a fighter who understood what would happen in the courts."[19] As the case made its way through the system, local activists maintained pressure on the school board to reassign black students to formerly all-white schools. The combined efforts of NAACP youth and women soon inspired over two hundred black families to join the list of reassignment requests.[20]

Although several local ministers successfully recruited plaintiffs, men often had difficulty convincing residents that they should add their names to the NAACP lawsuits, and the male-dominated DCNA turned to neighborhood women for assistance.[21] The Walltown Community Council (which had boasted an entirely female leadership two years after its founding in the late 1930s) and a local woman whose daughter had agreed to become one of the plaintiffs persuaded scores of families to join the fight. Key neighborhood women—or what the anthropologist Karen Brodkin Sacks calls "center women"—drew on their dense associational and personal networks to overcome black apprehension. For example, Callie Daye, a beautician in Walltown and and head of the Housewives League, added her daughter's name to the list of plaintiffs, undoubtedly reassuring residents.[22] The DCNA, well aware of the cost of ongoing litigation, also relied upon women's fundraising skills. In one successful endeavor called "Tag Days," women utilized their neighborhood connections by asking residents to don tags announcing, "I Gave My Dollar, Did You?"[23]

In August 1959, realizing that a decision on the Durham desegregation suit was imminent, the school board relented and reassigned nine black students, including five girls, to formerly white schools. But the board offered no explanation for denying reassignment appeals brought by the 165 other black students. Moreover, board members continued to use racially identifiable school attendance maps until a federal court order in 1962 forbade the practice. Although blacks filed more reassignment applications in Durham than anywhere else in North Carolina, by 1961 only a handful of students attended formerly white schools. The pattern was similar across the state, where school boards granted only eighty-nine out of a thousand black requests for reassignment.[24]

African American girls were frequently the majority of students who desegregated Durham schools in the early years.[25] Lost athletic opportunities for boys may be one explanation for the slightly larger number of girls, since white schools frequently penalized black male athletes. Parental fears of retaliation against sons for real or imagined contact with white girls may also have been a factor. Although black girls were victims of physical abuse and harassment as well, anecdotal evidence points to black parents' beliefs that boys would be more vulnerable to white violence.[26] After 1954 dire warnings about "miscegenation"—by which whites meant relations between black males and white females—became a rallying cry for white opposition to school desegregation across the South. Few issues had more power to send the defenders of the "Lost Cause" into a frenzy than the volatile mixture of race and sex. The widely publicized "Kissing Case" in nearby Monroe, North Carolina—in which two boys aged eight and ten were arrested for allegedly kissing three white girls and sentenced to a juvenile correctional institute—occurred in 1958 less than two weeks after Robert Williams, head of the Monroe NAACP, and his wife, Mabel, petitioned the Monroe school board to transfer their sons to an all-white elementary school.[27] Despite white hysteria and retaliation, however, African Americans refused to relinquish their struggle to secure a better education for their children.

Black participation in school desegregation included not only those who directly challenged discriminatory policies. At the Walltown Community Center, local college students and teachers ran tutoring sessions for black students in newly desegregated schools, while the *Carolina Times* and the NAACP Youth Council organized a "Freedom Scholarship" college fund for two low-income girls who desegregated Durham High. Local groups such as the Alpha Kappa Alpha sorority gladly contributed.[28] Other residents found ingenious ways to assist these courageous young students. As noted above, black tobacco workers kept watch from factory windows as students came to and from two newly desegregated schools. According to Evelyn McKissick, whose three children were the first to attend formerly all-white schools, "No one could see them but we knew in the street that they were all round . . . the first day especially."[29] In another show of community support, residents rented a limousine from a local undertaker to transport Lucy Mae Jones, the first and only black student to desegregate Brogden Junior High in September 1959. The gesture underlined the solemnity of the event, but it also offered protection from possible white retaliation. Two years earlier, Charlotte, North Carolina, had drawn national attention when a white mob terrorized Dorothy Counts, the lone black student who tried to enter an all-white high school. Lucy Mae distinctly recollected the hostile signs, the insults, and the ominous silence that greeted her as she stepped out of the car that first day.[30] The black community's response to these youthful trailblazers reflected a historic tradition in which African American women helped mobilize their communities to pool resources so that at least some members could secure an education. After *Brown*, however, that tradition was expanded in the hope that all African American children might enjoy the same opportunity.[31]

While black women were instrumental in solidifying broad community backing for school desegregation, they participated in other, less visible ways as well. African American school personnel provided comfort and support to students facing intimidation and physical abuse from white students. Joycelyn McKissick fondly recalled the two black women cafeteria workers at Durham High School who helped her survive those initial days of desegregation.[32] To alleviate some of the isolation that black students endured in the early years of token integration, black women's groups such as Jack and Jill and the Junior Mother's Club organized dances and other social activities for the students. As Evelyn McKissick explained, "I had to keep them from moping and getting lonely."[33]

Despite the community's support, the first students who desegregated Durham's schools undertook a daunting task, educationally, psychologically and socially. The most common complaint was that teachers and administrators failed to discipline white students who abused or harassed black students. Nor were girls immune from physical retaliation. In one incident, twelve white boys surrounded Andree McKissick, Jocelyn's sister, and spat at her on her way to English class; the teacher claimed to have been powerless to intervene, since the episode occurred outside her classroom. Sometimes school officials encouraged such intimidation, chuckling over white pupils' racial epithets. For Jocelyn McKissick, the abuse at Durham High School was particularly severe; one student emptied a fountain pen all over her new yellow dress, while other students tripped her in the hall, shoved her into lockers, and pushed her head into a toilet. Black students were also subjected to humiliating displays of public racism. In a talent show at Durham High School in 1962, a white boy walked onto the stage in blackface with a chain around his neck. When several black students protested to the principal, they were told they "had a chip on their shoulder and shouldn't be mad."

Frequently, whites met black protest with increased harassment, targeting African American girls as well as boys. After black students demonstrated at Durham High School over a speech by Governor Terry Sanford on improving education, a white girl hit Claudia Dixon, other students flung food at her during lunch, and someone scrawled, "KKK will kill all niggers" on her desk. In May 1963, in the wake of the largest black mass demonstrations in the history of Durham, Frances Marrow was shoved into a water fountain from behind and pushed down the stairs at Carr Junior High School. When she asked for permission to leave school, the dean responded that she would only "be running away from the problem." Floyd McKissick's recollections of these early years of desegregation were especially vivid: "The kids would come home from school every day crying. Many of them didn't want to go back . . . [They'd] come home with an inch of hair pulled out of their heads, ink, glue, molasses on them . . . [Teachers] wouldn't let them go to the bathroom sometimes . . . To clean those kids up every day and pray with them at night and send them back to school every day was one hell of a fight."[34]

Early desegregation efforts put intense strains on families too, and black women often bore the brunt. Evelyn McKissick held down a job, worried about her three children at formerly all-white schools, and supported her husband Floyd's activism; but the stress created tension in her marriage and took a toll on her physical health. One girl from another family reported that she and her siblings often went without meals so that their sister could buy her lunch at Durham High. "We didn't have clothes, you know, we wore hand me downs and shoes with holes in them and things like that so that she would look . . . good going to Durham High. . . . It was really traumatic on our family," she recalled.[35]

Black predictions that legal action would be necessary to force compliance with *Brown* proved accurate. Throughout the 1960s obstructionist tactics by white officials forced the NAACP to bring numerous lawsuits against North Carolina school boards. Not until 1970 did Durham finally desegregate its public schools, and then only under federal court order. Across the state, the pattern was similar. In the beginning, few perhaps realized the extent of white resistance or the enormous sacrifices that blacks would bear. In 1950 the *Carolina Times* had poignantly captured the motivation of the maids and janitors, tobacco workers, and teachers throughout the South who would be called upon to endure so much for so long: "it will not be because Negroes are prepared financially to pay the tremendous amount of money that it takes to keep a case in the federal courts," the editors wrote, "but because . . . [they] have been forced to do so to safeguard and make secure the hopes, aims, aspirations and destiny of their children in a world that more and more is becoming intolerable for ignorant and poorly trained people."[36] Like parents nearly everywhere, all they wanted was a better future for their children.

School desegregation was just one of the issues on the black community's agenda in the years after *Brown*. A thwarted sit-in at a segregated ice cream parlor in 1957, a survey of white employers designed to overturn employment discrimination, and a threatened boycott of white merchants were just some of the tactics that black women and men used to break Durham's racial caste system in the late 1950s. Such measures yielded little change, however. Youth in particular were growing impatient. In the fall of 1959 participants at a statewide NAACP youth conference implored adults to adopt more militant strategies and discussed a range of direct-action tactics including "sit-down strikes in eating places such as bus and train stations and *dime stores*" (emphasis added).[37] At the annual meeting of the state NAACP conference in January 1960, the elders insisted that "the first responsibility of our branches this year is to organize [voter] registration drives in every section of the state."[38] Two days later, students in Greensboro ignited a movement across the South that would force adult leaders to reorder their priorities. One week after the sit-in at the lunch counter in Greensboro, about twenty male and female youths conducted a sit-in at Woolworth, S. H. Kress, and Walgreens lunch counters in downtown Durham. By the end of the week, blacks in Raleigh, Fayetteville, Winston-Salem, and Charlotte were staging sit-ins, as the movement spread to other states as well.[39]

Between 1960 and 1963 blacks in Durham launched a wide range of direct-action assaults against segregation in public facilities and discriminatory employment policies in local businesses, with women protestors often outnumbering men. Their efforts culminated in three consecutive days of marches and rallies in May 1963—the largest mass actions the city had ever witnessed. The protests attracted four to five thousand participants, the majority women and girls. According to one observer, "Durham was right on the brink of racial violence."[40] Finally, after several days of mass demonstrations and fourteen hundred arrests (a record number), sporadic violence (mostly by white youth), massive property damage, and weeks of negotiations, the city agreed to desegregate public accommodations.[41]

The community organizing drives that women and NAACP youth waged during the school desegregation campaigns following *Brown* proved indispensable to the sit-ins, marches, demonstrations, and boycotts of the 1960s. Many of the youth activists involved in these protests were drawn from the working-class neighborhoods—particularly Walltown, Hickstown, and the East End—where Floyd McKissick had revived NAACP youth chapters in the 1950s, attracting a large number of girls.[42] For example, Alma Turner and Vivian McCoy, both from working-class families, joined NAACP youth groups in the 1950s, later becoming prominent in the sit-in movement. These were also the same neighborhoods from which black families had stepped forward to challenge the school board's pupil assignments. Marva Bullock, a high school student from the East End, and her younger sister, Linda Mae, were plaintiffs in the NAACP lawsuit against the Durham school board. When the sit-ins began, Marva joined one of the protests at Walgreens, where she was kicked in the stomach by a white man. Joycelyn McKissick and Maxine Bledsoe were among the handful of students who desegregated Durham schools in 1959 and 1960, and both became deeply involved in the direct-action movement in the early 1960s.[43] Charsie Herndon Hedgepath, another plaintiff in the school desegregation lawsuits, became the only woman officer in the Black Solidarity Committee, which waged a seven-month boycott against white Durham merchants in 1968–69.[44]

While most black women remained out of the limelight, they were critical players in Durham's mass protest movement. Not only did they often make up the majority of the protesters, but among youth in particular women also held influential positions in the movement. Some even assumed formal leadership roles. Nancy Grady was president of an active NAACP chapter at DeShazor's Beauty School and was a recognized leader in the student protest movement of the early 1960s. Guytana Horton, a student at North Carolina College, headed the statewide intercollegiate division of the NAACP. Both Jocelyn McKissick and Vivian McCoy were part of an unofficial strategy committee of six students who, under Floyd McKissick's guidance, planned and organized demonstrations throughout the early 1960s. "We didn't have leaders in terms of elected [people]," explained one of the students, "we had people who became leaders . . . because of their activities and . . . because they took the bull by the horn and were there everyday and made the sacrifices. That's who were the leaders."[45]

Student activists often performed similar tasks, regardless of gender. Throughout the 1950s and 1960s both male and female youth canvassed residents in voter registration drives, babysat while adults went to the polls, leafleted, and took charge of the picket lines. Churches offered opportunities for young women activists to address large groups. During the sit-ins of 1960, females made up at least half of the students who visited local churches to solicit community backing for the movement.[46] Thus, much as the Student Non-Violent Coordinating Committee (SNCC) enabled women to assume duties and roles usually reserved for men, so too within NAACP youth groups Durham women seized opportunities for activism and leadership.[47]

As in the school desegregation struggles, the full extent of black women's participation in direct action was not always visible to those outside the community. Age and class as well as gender often shaped the nature of their involvement. Although the movement in the 1960s was dominated by youth, some adult, middle-class women found unobtrusive ways to participate. Mrs. Bessie McLaurin, a teacher at the East End School, attended demonstrations as an "observer" and performed crucial behind-the-scenes tasks, taking charge of the church keys so that movement participants could hold their evening meetings at St. Joseph's AME Church. Mrs. Sadie Hughley, treasurer of the local CORE chapter, frequently led these "debriefing" sessions at the church. Like many of the "mamas" of the movement, Bessie McLaurin, Sadie Hughley, and Evelyn McKissick housed volunteer civil rights workers. Louise Latham, dean of women at North Carolina College, was another adult ally. One of the first black women to desegregate Durham's Central YWCA and the local chapter of the American Association of University Women in the 1950s, Latham was an informal liaison between student protesters and Alfonso Elder, president at North Carolina College, whose position at the state-supported black institution circumscribed more overt support for student demonstrators. Latham also quietly ignored curfew restrictions for female student activists.[48] Although few élite black women visibly supported the movement in the early years, Mrs. Selena Wheeler, wife of the business leader and DCNA head John Wheeler, provided office space which became a convenient resting place for students picketing downtown movie theaters.[49] Middle-class women also organized fundraisers to help defray legal fees incurred by student arrests; and black women's social clubs, sororities, and garden clubs invited students to tell their stories, frequently giving the youth "unsolicited contribution[s]."[50]

Low-income black women also lent their support. A number willingly endured financial hardship to sustain the movement. Norma Royal, wife of a local tobacco worker—and one of the "Tag Day" fundraisers for school desegregation efforts in the 1950s—penned a moving note to the youths at the Durham NAACP explaining, "As a token of appreciation, I send this small [donation], hoping it will help in your (our) fight for freedom. . . . It will be hard to budget. But I feel that I should share part of it with you."[51] Sometimes working-class women even assumed formal leadership positions. Mrs. Margaret Turner, a tobacco worker in Durham, supported her teenage children by walking the picket lines with them, and in 1962 she succeeded Floyd McKissick as statewide youth coordinator of the NAACP.

Working-class women also spearheaded neighborhood protests in the 1960s, adding direct-action tactics to the ongoing legal battle over school desegregation. A fire at the Negro East End School in 1963 catapulted black working-class women into a controversy that drew directly on women's neighborhood networks and leadership. Residents were furious at the school board's decision to implement split sessions in the partially damaged Negro school, rather than allow students to attend only partially filled white schools nearby. School officials remained unmoved by complaints that the split sessions forced black students to lose from 10 to 25 percent of class time each day. The school board even ignored an offer by African American parents to allow segregated classes within the white schools. Neighborhood women such as Christine Strudwick, wife of a tobacco worker and an active member in the East End Betterment Society (one of the community groups that joined the school desegregation struggles of the 1950s), were instrumental in mobilizing the black community. Four hundred predominantly working-class parents, local residents, and members of the East End Betterment Society—three-quarters of them women—signed a protest petition and presented it to the city school board. The next day, five hundred local residents and parents attended a meeting of the East End Betterment Society and voted to boycott the East End School. They set up pickets outside the school—often drawing more girls than boys—and soon local NAACP and CORE youth joined to show their support. Within a week, attendance at the school dropped by 50 percent and "absences" continued to climb. White officials refused to yield, promising only to rebuild the all-black East End School by the fall. But black parents remained steadfast and after three weeks, only 170 out of 750 students were in attendance. Adding legal pressure to street protests, black attorneys included the East End School controversy in a broader legal motion filed with the U.S. district court in 1963, rejecting the court-ordered school desegregation plan formulated by the school board.[52]

Black churchwomen of all classes also backed the freedom movement. Behind the few activist ministers were scores of churchwomen whose moral, spiritual, and financial assistance to the movement and to youth activists in particular was unbounded.[53] As Joycelyn McKissick recalled: "[There was] always a bunch of . . . church women . . . who would . . . be there for us, hugging us and feeding us and making sure everything was just so. Sometimes you knew 'em and sometimes you didn't, but you knew somebody was going to take you in their arms when you walked off that picket line . . . There's no way you can match that kind of contribution."[54]

Emphasis on more visible forms of protest and on traditional areas of leadership, where men were dominant, therefore misses an important dimension of the story and of protest activity in general. As Kathy Nasstrom has observed, by defining leadership so narrowly, we are left with a "composite portrait of civil rights leadership that has a male face." If we look beyond conventional definitions of leadership and public protest, however, black women's participation becomes more visible.[55] The activities of neighborhood women, female students, club women, and churchwomen make clear that black women were critical to the movement. When Mrs. Humely and Mother McLaurin, two cafeteria workers at North Carolina College, made sandwiches for jailed student protesters, they were not simply doing "women's work" but were literally nurturing the freedom movement.[56] William Chafe's comment that "women comprised, in many people's views, the backbone of the demonstrations, always ready to march and picket and get arrested" was true of women not only in Greensboro and Durham but throughout the South.[57]

Most contemporary observers, however, saw only the efforts of a few, heroic black women who had received national media attention, rather than a distinctive, African American female organizational base. In an editorial in the *Carolina Times* in 1957 entitled "The Leadership of Negro Women," Louis Austin praised the "courage and fortitude" of women such as Rosa Parks, Wilhemina Jake, and Autherine Lucy, who had inspired "their men to greater sacrifices and efforts in the struggle for a fuller measure of democracy." Without these women, Austin suggested, the freedom movement would probably never have materialized, leading to "a continuance of Negro lethargy in the deep South and other sections of the nation."[58] But in Austin's portrayal, a few exceptional women inspired the *men*, while the masses of ordinary black women who joined the movement remain invisible. As the movement continued to expand, however, some male leaders conceded their reliance on women's grassroots activism. The North Carolina State Conference of NAACP Branches acknowledged that black women had played a "very important part" in the organization's success. "Women are among the principal supporters of the NAACP and we must do more of utilizing the talent and abilities of our women," a report urged in 1962.[59] Not surprisingly, black women seemed more likely to fully appreciate other women's abilities. Dr. Rose Butler Browne, professor at at North Carolina College, wife of a local minister, and a community leader in her own right, proclaimed, "you get the sisters behind the brothers and between them, anything can be carried forward to success."[60] Similarly, Ella Baker had urged Martin Luther King Jr. and the Southern Christian Leadership Conference to utilize black women's organizations during the Crusade for Citizenship voter registration drive in the late 1950s, a suggestion that King and the other male ministers dismissed. Yet despite these contemporary references to black women's abilities, our "master" narrative too often has relegated women to the margins of the movement.

The community organizing campaigns for school desegregation that African American women and NAACP youth undertook in the 1950s became a key ingredient in the black community's willingness to rally behind the sit-ins and other direct-action protests of the early 1960s. Without their efforts, broader community support for the direct-action movement might well have been far more difficult to attract and sustain. It was not only white intransigence and black frustration that fueled direct-action protest; equally important in forming a grassroots base for later actions were the years that black women and NAACP youth spent canvassing neighborhoods and mobilizing black residents to desegregate local schools in the wake of *Brown*.

Far from arresting black resolve or organizational activity, *Brown* spurred NAACP school desegregation lawsuits in Durham and throughout North Carolina. Lawsuits, however, were not the exclusive domain of male attorneys and judges; rather, they relied upon grassroots, community-organizing drives carried out primarily by women and NAACP youth. *Brown* may well have unleashed a torrent of white opposition to school desegregation in particular, and black freedom in general. But the decision also solidified black determination to secure racial justice in ways that become clearer when we scrutinize women's activities more carefully.

The emergence of mass-based direct action across the South signaled a new direction in the black freedom movement; however, there were important continuities between the 1960s and earlier struggles. By examining women's and NAACP youth activities in the 1950s, both before and after *Brown*, we can observe those connections more easily. Women used their dense associational networks—in neighborhoods, workplaces, and churches, as well as voluntary, professional, and even leisure groups—to organize, mobilize, and lead the black community, first to desegregate public schools and then to abolish racial discrimination in public accommodations. Frequently the links were generational; younger women inherited a historic tradition of community work and racial uplift from mothers, teachers, neighborhood women, and churchwomen that they transformed into collective revolt. In the process, they created a movement that changed not only their lives, but the life of a nation.

## Notes

1 Michael J. Klarman, "*Brown*, Racial Change, and the Civil Rights Movement," 80 *Virginia Law Review* 7 (1994); see the scholarly exchange in the same issue. Charles W. Eagles, "Toward New Histories of the Civil Rights Era," *Journal of Southern History* 66, no. 4 (November 2000): 845–47, provides a summary of the debate. Klarman, "How *Brown* Changed Race Relations: The Backlash Thesis," *Journal of American History* 81, no. 1 (June 1994): 81–118. More recently, Klarman has acknowledged the importance of litigation in mobilizing local black communities. Klarman, "Is the Supreme Court Sometimes Irrelevant? Race and the Southern Criminal Justice System in the 1940s," *Journal of American History* 89, no. 1 (June 2002): 153.

2 There is a rich scholarship on this tradition. See for example Stephanie J. Shaw, *What a Woman Ought to Be and to Do: Black Professional Women during the Jim Crow Era* (Chicago: University of Chicago Press, 1996), and Deborah Gray White, *Too Heavy a Load: Black Women in Defense of Themselves, 1894–1994* (New York: W. W. Norton, 1999). For a fuller discussion of black women's activism in North Carolina during this period see Christina Greene, *"Our Separate Ways": Women and the Black Freedom Movement in Durham, North Carolina, 1940s–1970s* (Chapel Hill: University of North Carolina Press, forthcoming 2005).

3 Recent scholarship has attempted to address this imbalance. For just several examples see Charles M. Payne, "Men Led, but Women Organized: Movement Participation of Women in the Mississippi Delta," *Women in the Civil Rights Movement: Trailblazers and Torchbearers, 1941–1965*, ed. Vicki Crawford, Jacqueline Rouse, and Barbara Woods (Brooklyn, N.Y.: Carlson, 1990), 1–11; Bernice McNair Barnett, "Invisible Southern Black Women Leaders in the Civil Rights Movement: The Triple Constraints of Gender, Race, and Class," *Gender and Society* 7, no. 2 (June 1993): 162–81; Belinda Robnett, *How Long! How Long! African American Women in the Struggle for Civil Rights* (New York: Oxford University Press, 1997); Lynne Olson, *Freedom's Daughters: The Unsung Heroines of the Civil Rights Movement from 1830–1970* (New York: Scribner, 2001); Bettye Collier-Thomas and V. P. Franklin, eds., *Sisters in the Struggle: African American Women in the Civil Rights–Black Power Movement* (New York: NYU Press, 2001); Chana Kai Lee, *For Freedom's Sake: The Life of Fannie Lou Hamer* (Urbana: University of Illinois Press, 1999); Barbara Ransby, *Ella Baker and the Black Freedom Movement: A Radical, Democratic Vision* (Chapel Hill: University of North Carolina Press, 2003).

4 Aldon D. Morris, *The Origins of the Civil Rights Movement: Black Communities Organizing for Change* (New York, Free Press, 1984), 114; Klarman, "How *Brown* Changed Race Relations," 89–90.

5 Although Floyd McKissick was probably the individual most responsible for reviving NAACP youth chapters in Durham, adult women generally served as advisors to NAACP youth chapters in North Carolina. For example, in 1957 there were twelve female and three male advisors among NAACP youth councils and college chapters. Youth Council and College Chapter Officers in North Carolina, box E13, NAACP Papers, III, Library of Congress (LOC). For NAACP membership totals see boxes C381, C142, C141, NAACP Papers, II, LOC; boxes 18, 19, 22, 23, Kelly Alexander Papers, Atkins Library, University of North Carolina, Charlotte; NAACP, "1955 Membership and FFF Goals North Carolina Branches" and "North Carolina Conference of NAACP Branches, State Officers and Branch Officials Meeting," Charlotte, North Carolina, 29 January 1955, Floyd McKissick Papers. When I used the McKissick Papers they were unprocessed at the Hayti Heritage Center in Durham; currently they are at the Southern Historical Collection (SHC), Wilson Library, University of North Carolina, Chapel Hill.

6 *Carolina Times*, 14 November 1950; 4 March 1950, 7, 2; 15 May 1954, 2. Two years later Floyd McKissick contacted every black organization and institution in the city requesting their "100% cooperation" in the NAACP membership campaign. Floyd McKissick to "Dear Fellow Citizen," 11 February 1956, box 7, NAACP folder, William J. Kennedy Papers, SHC, Wilson Library, University of North Carolina, Chapel Hill. Raymond Gavins, "The NAACP in North Carolina in the Age of Segregation," *New Directions in Civil Rights Studies*, ed. Armstead L. Robinson and Patricia Sullivan (Charlottesville: University Press of Virginia, 1991), 114–15. On the importance of NAACP branches in North Carolina before the sit-in movement see also William Jones, "The NAACP, the Cold War and the Making of the Civil Rights Movement in North Carolina, 1943–1954" (M.A. thesis, University of North Carolina, Chapel Hill, 1996).

7 A variety of Negro organizations, including mixed-sex and men's groups, also joined the NAACP, but there appears to have been a preponderance of women's organizations taking out membership. *Carolina Times*, 23 July 1955, 1, 1 August 1953, 6; Charles McLean, North Carolina State Conference of NAACP Branches, 1955 Annual Report, box C142, NAACP Papers, II, LOC; Life Membership Campaign of the NAACP, 10 March 1958, and Mildred Bond to Floyd McKissick, 10 March 1958, Floyd McKissick Papers, SHC, Wilson Library, University of North Carolina, Chapel Hill; Life Membership Roster, 15 September 1960, *The NAACP Honor Guard* (New York: NAACP, ca. 1959), box 23, folder 4, Kelly Alexander Papers, Atkins Library, University of North Carolina, Charlotte; Gavins, "The NAACP in North Carolina," 116.

8 Ninth Annual Convention of Jack and Jill of America, Minutes, 18–19 June 1954, North Carolina College, Durham, North Carolina, box 69, Semans Family Papers, Special Collections, Perkins Library, Duke University.

9 "Black Solidarity Committee Meeting: Emancipation Proclamation Day

Program," 1 January 1969, tape 1, side 1, Nat White Collection, Hayti Heritage Center, Durham, North Carolina; Sara Evans and Harry Boyte, *Free Spaces: The Sources of Democratic Change in America* (New York: Harper and Row, 1986); Robin D. G. Kelley, " 'We Are Not What We Seem': Rethinking Black Working-Class Opposition in the Jim Crow South," *Journal of American History* 80 (June 1993): 75–112.

10  Kelly Alexander to NAACP State Officers, Branch Officials, and Members, 2 February 1957, box 23, folder 1, 1955 and 1956 Annual Reports, North Carolina Conference of State Branches, Charles McLean, 1954 and 1955 Annual Reports, box 22, folders 21, 22, all in Kelly Alexander Papers, Atkins Library, University of North Carolina, Charlotte; Raymond Gavins, "The NAACP in North Carolina," 117; Timothy B. Tyson, *Radio Free Dixie: Robert F. Williams and the Roots of Black Power* (Chapel Hill: University of North Carolina Press, 1999), 61; William H. Chafe, *Civilities and Civil Rights: Greensboro, North Carolina, and the Black Struggle for Freedom* (New York: Oxford University Press, 1980), 70–71, 73; Numan Bartley, *The Rise of Massive Resistance: Race and Politics in the South during the 1950s* (Baton Rouge: Louisiana State University Press, 1969), 96–97; Kelly Alexander to Lucille Black, 26 September 1949, NAACP Papers, II, C141, LOC; *Carolina Times*, 11 May 1957.

11  *Carolina Times*, 29 May 1954, 1. The DCNA was established in 1935; its motto, "A voteless people is a hopeless people," helped make it the most successful black political machine in the South. Dominated by the black male business élite that grew up around the North Carolina Mutual Life Insurance Company (which earned Durham its reputation as "the capital of the black middle class"), the DCNA also included women and working-class blacks, especially from the tobacco unions. However, a survey in the 1950s revealed that working-class blacks saw the NAACP as the most effective black organization. African Americans made up about one-third of the city's total population of 95,000 by the 1960s, and despite the success of the Mutual, the presence of the North Carolina College for Negroes, and a black industrial working class centered around the tobacco industry, most blacks in Durham remained abysmally poor. Walter B. Weare, *Black Business in the New South: A Social History of the North Carolina Mutual Life Insurance Company* (Urbana: University of Illinois Press, 1973); Elaine M. Burgess, *Negro Leadership in a Southern Community* (Chapel Hill: University of North Carolina Press, 1960).

12  *Carolina Times*, 2 April 1954, 4.

13  Petition to the Board of Education of the Public School District of Durham, Durham, North Carolina, 11 July 1955, box 7, William J. Kennedy Papers, SHC, Wilson Library, University of North Carolina, Chapel Hill; *Carolina Times*, 16 July 1955, 1; Marjorie Ann Elvin Foy, "Durham in Black and White: School Desegregation in Durham, North Carolina, 1954–1963" (thesis, University of North Carolina, Greensboro, 1991), 51.

14  Durham *Morning Herald*, 30 July 1957, Wilson Library, University of North Carolina, Chapel Hill; Foy, "Durham in Black and White," 42, 52; Memorandum

to the North Carolina Advisory Committee to the U.S. Commission on Civil Rights from DCNA Education Committee, n.d., box 7, William A. Clement Papers, SHC, Wilson Library, University of North Carolina, Chapel Hill; *Carolina Times*, 16 July 1955, 30 July 1955, 1, 1; W. A. Clement and D. Eric Moore, Statement to Board of Education, 13 April 1959; Minutes, Durham Board of Education, 13 April 1959, Rencher N. Harris Papers, Special Collections, Perkins Library, Duke University.

15 Chafe, *Civilities and Civil Rights*, 50–60, 64–65; Davison M. Douglas, *Reading, Writing, and Race: The Desegregation of the Charlotte Schools* (Chapel Hill: University of North Carolina Press, 1995), 25–49; Ralph Karpinos, "'With All Deliberate Speed:' The Brown v. Board of Education Decisions, North Carolina and the Durham City Schools, 1954–1963" (unpublished paper, Duke University, 1972), 13, 14, Chris Howard Papers, Special Collections, Perkins Library, Duke University.

16 School desegregation statistics and Arkansas official's quote in Chafe, *Civilities and Civil Rights*, 76.

17 As part of the Pearsall Plan, white officials in these three cities were urged to make only a minimal sacrifice (token desegregation) so that segregated schools throughout the state would remain unhampered by federal intervention. Durham initially was included, but the idea was never pursued there. Chafe, *Civilities and Civil Rights*, 58; Durham *Morning Herald*, 30 July 1957.

18 Minutes, DCNA Education Committee, 15 May 1957; "Report of the DCNA Education Committee: 1957," 12 January 1958, and memorandum to the Reverend C. E. McLester and W. A. Clement, DCNA Subcommittee on Education, n.d., box 7, William A. Clement Papers, SHC, Wilson Library, University of North Carolina, Chapel Hill; Douglas, *Reading, Writing, and Race*, 48, 46; Robnett, *How Long! How Long!*; William Fuller to Warren Carr, 1 February 1958, box 3, Asa T. Spaulding Papers, Civil Rights Section, Special Collections, Perkins Library, Duke University; interview with Floyd McKissick by Chris Howard, 30 November 1982, Chris Howard Papers, Special Collections, Perkins Library, Duke University.

19 Foy, "Durham in Black and White," 55–56, 63–69; Karpino, "'With All Deliberate Speed,'" 17–18; Special Meeting: Board of Education, 28 August 1959, and "Elementary Requests Denied, Tuesday, August 25, 1959," box 9, Rencher N. Harris Papers, Special Collections, Perkins Library, Duke University; Rencher Harris to F. L. Fuller, 15 July 1959, and Fuller to Harris, 18 July 1959, box 9, Rencher N. Harris Papers, Special Collections, Perkins Library, Duke University; interview with Floyd McKissick by Chris Howard, 30 November 1982, Chris Howard Papers, Special Collections, Perkins Library, Duke University. Robert Cannon, "The Organization and Growth of Black Political Participation in Durham, North Carolina, 1933–1958" (diss., University of North Carolina, Chapel Hill, 1975), 87–93, 97.

20 Foy, "Durham in Black and White," 65–66, 69; Karpinos, "'With All Deliberate Speed,'" 21.

21 For example, the DCNA thought that Mr. Hennessee "would be of invalu-

able service" in recruiting plaintiffs, but two weeks later, when he had been unable to secure a single name, the DCNA turned to neighborhood women who everyone agreed had "been quite successful in securing plaintiffs from the Walltown area." DCNA Education Committee Minutes, 15 May 1957, 22 May 1957, 29 May 1957, box 7, William A. Clement Papers, SHC, Wilson Library, University of North Carolina, Chapel Hill.

22 Karen Sacks, "Women and Grassroots Organizing," *Women and the Politics of Empowerment*, ed. Ann Bookman and Sandra Morgen (Philadelphia: Temple University Press, 1986), 77–94; Raleigh *News and Observer*, 21 August 1958.

23 Minutes, DCNA Education Subcommittee, 17 April 1956, 15 May 1957, 22 May 1957, 29 May 1957, Minutes of the DCNA Finance Committee, 4 November 1958, box 7, William A. Clement Papers, SHC, Wilson Library, University of North Carolina, Chapel Hill; "Elementary Requests Denied, Tuesday, August 25, 1959," box 9, Rencher N. Harris Papers, Special Collections, Perkins Library, Duke University; "1960 Awards, Plaques, Certificates and Citations," box 23, Kelly Alexander Papers, Atkins Library, University of North Carolina, Charlotte.

24 Karpinos, "'With All Deliberate Speed,'" 18, 21, 22, 30; Chafe, *Civilities and Civil Rights*, 76.

25 Although more boys than girls appealed the board's refusal in August 1959 to grant reassignment—except on the high school level where there were nineteen girls and thirteen boys—in future years girls often accounted for most reassignment requests. Furthermore, more black girls than black boys desegregated Durham schools in the early years. Karpinos, "'With All Deliberate Speed,'" 23–28; Foy, "Durham in Black and White," 73. For lists of students requesting reassignment see Durham Board of Education Meeting Minutes, 3 September 1957, 25 August 1959, 28 August 1959, 21 September 1959, 24 August 1960, 27 July 1961, 31 July 1961, 2 August 1961, 25 June 1962, 26 June 1962, 28 June 1962, 11 July 1962, 1 July 1962, 20 August 1962, 21 January 1963, 16 April 1963, Durham Public Schools Administrative Offices, Durham, North Carolina. By 1964 board members ceased including in school board minutes the names of students requesting reassignment.

26 It is equally likely that the tiny number of black boys accepted to Durham High School (one each in 1959 and 1960) reflects white fears even more than those of black parents. Demographic explanations are not pertinent since the black sex ratio in Durham below the age of eighteen was fairly even in 1960. Kerri Lindland, "Beyond the Law: The Personal Impact of Desegregation in Durham, North Carolina, 1959–1965" (unpublished paper, 1993, typescript in author's possession); 2–3; interviews with Vivian McCoy and Joycelyn McKissick by Chris Howard, Chris Howard Papers, Special Collections, Perkins Library, Duke University; comments by Joycelyn McKissick, Black History Month Celebration, North Carolina Central University, Durham, North Carolina, 10 February 1993 (author's notes); interview with Cora Cole-McFadden by author, 30 March 1993; Audrey Mitchell and Harrison Johnson, comments at Durham Civil Rights Reunion, 8 April 1994, North Carolina Central University (videotape).

27 Tyson, *Radio Free Dixie*, 93, 98–99, and chapters 4–5. *Carolina Times*, 20 December 1958, 2.

28 Lindland, "Beyond the Law," 7; John Edwards to Herbert Wright, 14 September 1961, box E12, NAACP Papers, III, LOC; Gloster Current to Floyd McKissick, 6 October 1961, box C112, NAACP Papers, III, LOC; *Carolina Times* undated news clipping, box C112, NAACP Papers, III, LOC.

29 Lindland, "Beyond the Law."

30 Charles W. Davis to W. A. Clement, 11 March 1959; "Confidential" Minutes of AFSC School Desegregation Program Committee, 14 June 1960, High Point, North Carolina, box 7, William A. Clement Papers, SHC, Wilson Library, University of North Carolina, Chapel Hill; Douglas, *Reading, Writing, and Race*, 72.

31 For the important role of black women in this tradition see Shaw, *What a Woman Ought to Be and to Do*.

32 Comments by Joycelyn McKissick, Durham Civil Rights Reunion, 8–9 April 1994, North Carolina Central University (videotape).

33 *Carolina Times*, 18 October 1952, 5; quote from Lindland, "Beyond the Law," 7.

34 More severe forms of violent reprisal were directed against men, several of whom received death threats. Lindland, "Beyond the Law," 8; statements of Andree McKissick, Durham High School, Frances Marrow, Carr Junior High School, Claudia Dixon, Durham High School, 30 May 1963, box 4, Asa T. Spaulding Papers, Civil Rights Series, Special Collections, Perkins Library, Duke University; interview with Floyd McKissick by Chris Howard, 30 November 1982, Chris Howard Papers, Special Collections, Perkins Library, Duke University; comments by Joycelyn McKissick, Black History Month Celebration, North Carolina Central University, Durham, North Carolina, 10 February 1993 (author's notes); comments by Maxine Bledsoe Thorpe and Harrison Johnson, Durham Civil Rights Reunion, 8–9 April 1994, North Carolina Central University (videotape); interview with Vivian McCoy by Chris Howard, Special Collections, Perkins Library, Duke University.

35 Quoted in Lindland, "Beyond the Law," 11.

36 *Carolina Times*, 14 January 1950, 2. For a discussion of the legal struggle for school desegregation in North Carolina see Douglas, *Reading, Writing, and Race*.

37 *Campus Echo*, 27 February 1959, 2, quoted in Elyse Gallo, "The Emergence of Direct Action: The Early Civil Rights Movement in Durham, North Carolina," (unpublished paper, December 1978), 19, Chris Howard Papers, Special Collections, Perkins Library, Duke University.

38 McKissick quoted in Gallo, "The Emergence of Direct Action," 18. The meeting in Asheville that Gallo dates to 1958 is probably a reference to the meeting held in 1959. Annual Report of the 16th Annual Conference of the North Carolina State Conference of NAACP Branches, Asheville, North Carolina, 8–11 October 1959; meeting agenda, North Carolina State Conference of NAACP Branches, 30 January 1960, box 23, Kelly Alexander Papers, Atkins Library, University of North Carolina, Charlotte.

39  Durham *Morning Herald*, 8, 9 February 1960; *Carolina Times*, 13 February 1960; Chafe, *Civilities and Civil Rights*, 84.

40  My thanks to Leslie Brown for pointing me toward documentary evidence, particularly photographs, which provides an invaluable confirmation of both the written and the anecdotal evidence regarding female participation. See for example photos in the *Carolina Times*, 25 May 1963, 1, the Durham *Morning Herald*, 19 May 1963, and *North Carolina and the Negro*, ed. Capus W. Waynick et al. (Raleigh: North Carolina Mayors Coordinating Committee, 1964), 62. Interview with Quinton Baker by Chris Howard, Chris Howard Papers, Special Collections, Perkins Library, Duke University; Howard, " 'Keep Your Eyes on the Prize': The Black Struggle for Civic Equality in Durham, North Carolina, 1954–1963" (honors thesis, Duke University, 1983), 49, 113, Duke University Archives; Allan P. Sindler, "Youth and the American Negro Protest Movement: A Local Case Study of Durham, North Carolina," 36–55, Paper Presented at the Sixth World Congress International Political Science Association, Geneva, Switzerland, 21–25 September 1964 (unpublished typescript, Durham Public Library), 41.

41  Sindler, "Youth and the American Negro Protest Movement," 46–47; *Carolina Times*, 25 May 1963, 1; Howard, "Eyes on the Prize," 116, 109–20, 130; interviews with Jake Phelps and Wense Grabarek by Chris Howard, Chris Howard Papers, Special Collections, Perkins Library, Duke University; interview with Phelps by Warren Carr, 31 January 1978, Duke Oral History Collection, Special Collections, Perkins Library, Duke University.

42  A similar pattern was evident among boys.

43  Handwritten notes by Buris Toomer and Liticia Thompson concerning man who kicked Marva Bullock, Floyd McKissick Papers, shc, Wilson Library, University of North Carolina, Chapel Hill; McKissick to Basil Paterson, 1 May 1962, Floyd McKissick Papers; McKissick to Edwards, 1 December 1962, Floyd McKissick Papers; interview with McKissick by Chris Howard, 30 November 1982, Chris Howard Papers, Special Collections, Perkins Library, Duke University; Durham *Morning Herald*, 17 March 1962, box 3, Asa T. Spaulding Papers, Civil Rights Section, Special Collections, Perkins Library, Duke University.

44  Women protesters did not always outnumber men and appear to have escaped arrest more often, although not by huge numbers and not in every case. Arrest records can be misleading, however, for police seemed more likely to arrest males, who usually received harsher sentences. With the exception of arrest lists, I discovered only two lists of student protesters with more male than female names. Interview with Mrs. Joyce (Thorpe) Nichols by author, 9 December 1993, Durham, North Carolina (in author's possession); interview with Cole-McFadden by author, 30 March 1993 (in author's possession); "List of Picketers, March 23, 1961," Floyd McKissick Papers, shc, Wilson Library, University of North Carolina, Chapel Hill; Petition for Writ of Certiorari to the Supreme Court of North Carolina, n.d. [ca. January 1961], box 26, Kelly Alexander Papers, Atkins Library, University of North Carolina, Charlotte. For lists of student protesters see Floyd McKissick Papers, shc, Wilson Library, University of North Carolina, Chapel Hill.

45 Gallo, "The Emergence of Direct Action," 32; Rhonda Mawhood, "Tales to Curl Your Hair: African-American Beauty Parlors in Jim Crow Durham," (unpublished seminar paper, Duke University, 1993, in author's possession); "De-Shazor's NAACP Youth Council, 25 April, 1960," Floyd McKissick Papers, SHC, Wilson Library, University of North Carolina, Chapel Hill; interview with John Edwards by Chris Howard, 26 October 1982, Chris Howard Papers, Special Collections, Perkins Library, Duke University.

46 Interview with Vivian McCoy by author (in author's possession); comments by Betty Bledsoe Allen and Alma Turner, Durham Civil Rights Reunion, 8–9 April 1994, North Carolina Central University (videotape); "Members Attending Churches to Make Announcements," ca. 1960, Floyd McKissick Papers, SHC, Wilson Library, University of North Carolina, Chapel Hill.

47 It is not surprising that NAACP youth chapters should have exhibited some of the nonhierarchical traits usually associated with SNCC. The Reverend Douglas Moore and Durham NAACP youth members attended the founding meeting of SNCC in Raleigh; and Ella Baker, adult advisor to SNCC and a staunch proponent of this kind of leadership, made several visits to North Carolina College during the 1960s. Yet NAACP youth chapters were not totally free from the restrictive gender conventions prevalent in the larger society.

48 Chafe, Civilities and Civil Rights, 127; interview with Bessie McLaurin, 20 April 1973, Duke Oral History Collection; comments by participants at Durham Civil Rights Reunion, 8–9 April 1994, North Carolina Central University (videotape); Carolina Times, 13 February 1960, 5; Carolina Times, 23 May 1963, 1.

49 Interview with Lacey Streeter by Chris Howard; interview with Vivian McCoy by Chris Howard, Chris Howard Papers, Special Collections, Perkins Library, Duke University; comments by John Edwards, Durham Civil Rights Reunion, 9 April 1994, North Carolina Central University (videotape).

50 Memorandum to Gloster Current re Callis Brown, n.d. [ca. May 1960], McKissick to Gloster Current, 21 May 1960, box C112, NAACP Papers, III, LOC; "What Makes Durham Tick," n.d. [ca. 1962], Floyd McKissick Papers, SHC, Wilson Library, University of North Carolina, Chapel Hill.

51 Norma Royal to Youth Branch of the NAACP, 10 June 1963, McKissick Papers, SHC, Wilson Library, University of North Carolina, Chapel Hill.

52 The archives of the Durham Morning Herald contain photographs, some of them unpublished, of young girls picketing outside East End School. Petition of Parents and Citizens of the East End Community to the Durham Board of Education, n.d., Floyd McKissick Papers, SHC, Wilson Library, University of North Carolina, Chapel Hill; "To the Durham Board of Education from the East End Betterment League and 378 Parents and Citizens in the East End School Zone," 6 May 1963; untitled news clipping, 8 May 1963, Floyd McKissick Papers, SHC, Wilson Library, University of North Carolina, Chapel Hill; Durham Morning Herald, 13 May 1963, Floyd McKissick Papers, SHC, Wilson Library, University of North Carolina, Chapel Hill; interview with Callina Smith by author, 14 January 1993 (in author's possession); Howard, "Eyes on the Prize," 86–88; Caro-

lina Times, 18 May 1963, 1; Report of the Mayor's Committee on Human Relations to Mayor Evans on the East End School Controversy: Plaintiffs' Opposition to the Defendants' "Plan for Further Desegregation of the Durham City Schools," in *Warren Wheeler, Etc. et al. v. Durham City Board of Education, Etc.* and *C.C. Spaulding, III, Etc. et al. v. Durham City Board of Education, Etc.*, box 4, Asa T. Spaulding Papers, Civil Rights Section, Special Collections, Perkins Library, Duke University.

53 Most scholars focus on the leadership role of male ministers while ignoring the women who accounted for the majority of black church membership, attendance, or both. Morris, *The Origins of the Civil Rights Movement*, 4, 51–63. For a recent effort to address this neglect see Rosetta E. Ross, *Witnessing and Testifying: Black Women, Religion and Civil Rights* (Minneapolis: Fortress, 2003).

54 Vivian McCoy echoed McKissick's views regarding church women. Interviews with Joycelyn McKissick and Vivian McCoy by Chris Howard, Chris Howard Papers, Special Collections, Perkins Library, Duke University.

55 Kathryn L. Nasstrom, "Down to Now: Memory, Narrative, and Women's Leadership in the Civil Rights Movement in Atlanta, Georgia," *Gender and History* 11, no. 1 (April 1999): 115.

56 Comments by Dr. Beverly Jones, Black History Month Celebration, North Carolina Central University, Durham, North Carolina, 10 February 1993 (author's notes).

57 Chafe, *Civilities and Civil Rights*, 125.

58 Jake inspired a bus boycott in Tallahassee, Florida, and Lucy faced down an angry mob at the University of Alabama. *Carolina Times*, 12 January 1957, 2.

59 *Carolina Times*, 14 November 1950; *Carolina Times*, 4 March 1950, 7, 2; report on North Carolina Conference of NAACP Branches, 1962 Annual Convention, box 23, Kelly Alexander Papers, Atkins Library, University of North Carolina, Charlotte; program for Freedom Sunday Worship Service, 27 May 1962, Floyd McKissick Papers, SHC, Wilson Library, University of North Carolina, Chapel Hill.

60 *Carolina Times*, 14 November 1950; *Carolina Times*, 4 March 1950, 2; *Carolina Times*, 27 September 1952, 2.

LAURIE B. GREEN

# The Rural-Urban Matrix in the 1950s South

## Rethinking Racial Justice Struggles in Memphis

Two weeks after the Supreme Court ruled in *Brown v. Board of Education*, local NAACP attorneys in Tennessee helped several African Americans, some of them Korean War veterans, submit applications to Memphis State College, seeking to use the momentum surrounding *Brown* to press for an end to exclusionary racial policies in public institutions of higher education. This strategy is not tremendously surprising; numerous local communities across the South strove to make school desegregation a reality after the decision. There were also efforts to reap the benefits of the Court's striking down of "separate but equal" in public schools by extending its logic to other segregated spheres of public life. Moreover, just as in Memphis NAACP attorneys united with local individuals and families to pursue test cases, recent scholarship has shown convincingly that securing and expanding *Brown* was never simply a legal project pursued by attorneys.

What distinguishes the Memphis case, however, is that the key planning session for the local NAACP's response to *Brown* took place in Mound Bayou, Mississippi, a historically black town due south of Memphis, during a mass outdoor meeting on the eve of the decision sponsored by the Regional Council of Negro Leadership (RCNL), at which the keynote speech was delivered by Thurgood Marshall.[1] The trip to this meeting that Memphis civil rights attorneys took down Highway 61 into the Delta signaled the emergence in the early 1950s of a new relation between rural and urban activism, one that in multiple ways influenced responses to and perceptions of *Brown*. Journeys between the rural Delta and Memphis, the urban hub of a region that extended from the Missouri "bootheel" through Arkansas and west Tennessee to Mississippi, became central to activists' efforts to carve out a new civil rights politics. When the RCNL was viciously targeted by the white Citizens' Council launched in the Delta in reaction to *Brown*, its members became key supporters of the hard-pressed activists. This rural-urban matrix made it difficult to extract desegregation from a far more complex agenda challenging white domination, whether in the plantation region or in the city, leading activists in Memphis to respond to

*Brown* in ways that situated the case within the context of broader issues of racial identity, power, and democracy.

In this chapter, the rural-urban matrix provides a window into the complexity of social protest in the period surrounding *Brown*, allowing us to focus on understandings of racial democracy and equality articulated by various groups of African Americans in the urban South as they responded to *Brown* and pursued other struggles. Recent civil rights studies have taken issue with earlier accounts of the civil rights movement by painstakingly showing that *Brown* itself did not launch the movement; that in fact local struggles had been ongoing since the Second World War, if not before; and that local people, sometimes in conjunction with national civil rights figures, were the engines for the movement.[2] Building on these insights, this chapter argues that when urban black southerners strove to extend the ramifications of *Brown*, they did so within a broader postwar political context that encompassed other heated conflicts as well, from labor and voter registration campaigns to protests against police brutality, in addition to education.

In making this argument, the chapter reaches in a new direction by analyzing the terms in which local people thought about racial justice in the postwar period. Most, to be sure, embraced the Supreme Court's ruling in *Brown* that "separate educational facilities are inherently unequal." Nevertheless, given the multidimensional nature of the struggle in the years surrounding *Brown*—despite the impact of the cold war—urban black southerners also attached other meanings to equality. Demands for desegregation, therefore, encompassed but did not exhaust understandings of racial democracy or justice for urban black southerners in this period. Moreover, local understandings and articulations of democracy were shaped in profound ways by the interchange between plantation and city. African Americans in the city perceived what the Memphis black press in 1955 dubbed a "racial equation" of "master and slave" as a description of not only rural but urban life, leading many to strike out with particular force against urban practices that seemed symbolic of the plantation, whether in contemporary life or in historical memories of slavery. In April 1955, for instance, civil rights attorneys and ministers interrupted their desegregation efforts to launch a new citizens' justice committee when a city judge fined a group of women restaurant workers for disorderly conduct. The workers, most of them women, had quit their jobs to protest their employers' use of an elderly black woman dressed like "Mammy," who rang a bell to attract customers. By challenging racist images of black womanhood and manhood, activists in the 1950s asserted alternative racial identities based on independence, assertiveness, and equality.

Memphis, because of its historical relation to the rural Mississippi Delta region, provides a particularly useful context in which to explore how the rapidly changing, tangled rural-urban relations of the postwar era shaped the activism and political thought of the period surrounding *Brown*, both practically and metaphorically. In a number of ways, the postwar crumbling of the sharecropping system, urban migration, industrialization, and mass culture introduced new sites of struggle and created possibilities for social change in Memphis. After the Second World War not only cotton, migrants, and music but the politics of race traversed the distance between the rural and urban South, whether by radio, newspaper, or personal journeys. Furthermore, as this chapter emphasizes, the rural-urban struggle had profound repercussions for national civil rights agendas and for broader racial politics in the cold war era.

This chapter shifts between the urban and rural South. It first examines racial politics in Memphis on the eve of *Brown*, including the politics of the young civil rights activists who transformed the Memphis NAACP from a nearly moribund organization to the South's largest branch. A second section analyzes the relations of Memphis activists to the Regional Council of Negro Leadership in the Mississippi Delta. The following section returns to Memphis, examining how desegregation campaigns intersected with civic and labor organizing, including the parts played by recent migrants from the same rural counties that had become engulfed in conflict. A brief concluding section outlines the powerful rural-urban crisscrossing that influenced the Memphis sit-in movement of 1960, which coincided with a sharecroppers' movement for voting rights in west Tennessee and the sanitation workers' first organizing drive.

Placing responses to *Brown* within this richly textured fabric illuminates the complexity, contradictions, and potential of the period. To do so, this chapter incorporates cultural studies insights about racial formation and identity making; analysis of political thought among not only élites but working-class activists; and perceptions about urban geographies in the postwar South, emphasizing the permeable borders between rural and urban, local and national. Understandings of place and memory, race and gender, that emerged from the two-way road between the rural and urban South shaped responses to *Brown*. These responses were forged from dynamic local and regional, national and international interchanges. Claims to racial democracy in the *Brown* period, this chapter shows, posited constitutional rights as part of a broader challenge to the "master and servant" relation in the modern urban context.

Two years before *Brown*, in March 1952, Ruby Hurley, southeast regional secretary of the NAACP, wrote to the organization's headquarters in New

York about her frustration over the Memphis branch's "conservative influence" and "little action," asserting that the branch was "dying slowly." Hurley described a tense meeting in which branch leaders had defended their support for a "separate but equal" hospital facility planned by the city, despite the national organization's policy opposing segregation. In contrast, she praised the branch in Indianola, Mississippi, where young veterans had begun to register voters, hold public meetings, and reach out to sharecroppers. "The difference between Indianola and Memphis was an inspiration," she underscored. A year later, after discovering that the Memphis NAACP had barely responded when a black family's newly purchased home was bombed by whites in the neighborhood, Hurley complained that she "could actually cry about Memphis, because the community is ripe for dynamic NAACP leadership."[3] Hurley's words were prescient; by the end of the decade, the NAACP's executive secretary, Roy Wilkins, was touting the Memphis NAACP as "the biggest Branch in the South," and praising its new leaders.[4]

Hurley's critique of Memphis and praise for Indianola contradicted the traditional assessment of the rural South as an unchanging backwater: instead it was Memphis that appeared stagnant. Events surrounding the *Brown* decision would reveal a more dynamic relation between Memphis and the Delta, as resistance and reaction swelled in both places. Even in 1952, however, Hurley's claim about the community's "ripeness" suggests that the branch leaders' "conservative influence" may have been out of step with postwar movements.

As one of the nation's most important cotton markets and a vortex of the hardwood industry, as well as a transportation and distribution center, Memphis had remained bound to the rural economy. City boosters concerned with diversifying and industrializing the local economy in the first half of the twentieth century had successfully attracted northern-based corporations such as Ford, Fisher Body, Firestone, International Harvester, and General Electric by touting the city's low-wage labor force, mostly nonunion until the 1940s. The city's manufacturers in industries based on cotton byproducts and hardwood had kept wages low by relying on successive waves of migrants from the rural Delta, and by exploiting longstanding racial distinctions and hierarchies.[5]

The political culture of Memphis blended elements of urban machine politics with the sort of white domination and social control associated with the plantation South. From the early twentieth century until his death in 1954, the Democratic political machine boss Edward Hull Crump had dominated Memphis politics, largely from behind the scenes rather than as an elected official. Crump promoted a brand of white supremacy based not on disfranchising black voters but on controlling them by bankrolling poll taxes and awarding patronage positions to leaders who delivered votes. He also engaged in coercive tactics, carried out in part by the city police force. Crump never fully crushed independent black political opposition, but he convinced many black religious and business leaders to cooperate rather than resist the machine. His death in October 1954 coincided with the new political opening signaled by the Supreme Court decision.

Hurley's critique of the "conservative influence" in Memphis thus addressed deeply entrenched attitudes developed over the course of several decades of coexistence with the Crump machine. In the 1950s ideological tensions about the thrust of black leadership came to a head over desegregation. At the meeting in 1952 that she described, established leaders ranging from Utillus Phillips, a railroad worker and president of the NAACP branch, to Dr. Hollis Price, president of LeMoyne College, insisted that hospital beds for African Americans were too badly needed for them to reject the city plan. They argued further that opposing the proposal "would mean the death of [the] NAACP in Memphis," Hurley reported. On the eve of *Brown*, these leaders still expected to maintain credibility in their communities despite acquiescing in the Crump machine's sanctioning of "separate but equal."[6]

Hurley clearly disagreed that their wariness of a bolder approach would win support for the NAACP. Indeed, structural upheaval during and after the war had stimulated new forms of resistance by simultaneously altering social and economic life and perpetuating old forms of domination. Put differently, things changed yet remained the same. Memphis had won several lucrative defense and federal housing contracts; however, during the war, corporations such as Ford joined hands with city officials to bypass federal regulations mandating nondiscrimination practices in the defense industry. New housing built with federal support buttressed, rather than weakened, existing segregation patterns. Meanwhile, urban migration intensified. Moving to Memphis offered possibilities for nonagricultural jobs, better schooling, and voting rights, along with modern culture. Artherene Chalmers, for example, stated in an interview that she was thrilled to leave Mississippi in 1941 because she "hated farming." The first thing she noticed was the lamp lights, but she also recalled dancing at Club Handy on Beale Street her first night in town. "They didn't have anywhere in Mississippi to go. Nothing," she declared. Nevertheless, Chalmers could find no job other than in private households as a maid, and she now had to ride segregated city buses. Some migrants secured defense industry jobs, yet faced racist work policies.[7]

Recent migrants discovered new openings for resistance, both informal and formal. Chalmers recalls catching the no. 7 bus home from Sears with her daughter, and then standing by her side as the girl sat next to a white man and refused his demands that she move to the back. Other women and men helped to organize labor unions shortly after moving to the city, not only in industrial workplaces like Firestone but in small manufacturing shops with predominantly black workforces. And in 1945, at the end of the war, the mothers of two young women raped by police officers, along with others in the Binghampton neighborhood—a working-class area with many migrants—sparked a protest movement against police brutality that pressured the Crump machine into prosecuting the police officers.[8]

This turmoil generated an explicit, public critique of local black leaders, especially ministers, deemed overly loyal to the Crump machine. NAACP leaders were not among Crump's allies, but they were not exempt from criticism. When the local NAACP championed protest against police brutality, membership skyrocketed. However, from an apex of 3,540 in 1948, membership then plunged to 731 in 1952, as the branch failed to offer an agenda addressing its working-class constituency. By the time Utillus Phillips retired as the NAACP branch president in 1953 after fourteen years of service, this postwar working-class ferment, combined with criticism from national civil rights figures, indicated a shared desire for a fresh civil rights leadership.[9]

Those who assumed leadership of the Memphis NAACP after Phillips's retirement had harbored concerns about the direction of black leadership well before 1955. Several had graduated from LeMoyne College, a historically black institution, where they had joined the college NAACP, founded in the fall of 1940 by students eager to pursue more open opposition to the Crump machine than that expressed by the adult branch. From its very beginnings, therefore, the youth council not only challenged Crump but communicated with national civil rights officials about shortcomings that its members perceived among established leaders.[10]

The political perspectives of these young civil rights activists had been forged within the crucible of the Second World War, at a time of heightened debate about America's democratic ideals. During the war nearly every black male student at LeMoyne had been drafted, as had many members of the male faculty including Collins George, faculty advisor to the NAACP chapter. Many of the draftees wrote home to the *Private Chatterer*, a campus newsletter edited "for the duration" by female students, that circulated their stories and commentaries about discriminatory practices in the military. A poem titled "I Fought a Battle," for example, listed democratic rights in whose name the war was waged but concluded, "I FOUGHT FOR ALL THESE AND YET / I NEVER KNEW THEM FOR—I AM A / NEGRO." After the war, students drew parallels between problems faced by African Americans and by Africans and Asians in colonized nations. In "Is Justice Possible," for example, a writer for the college NAACP newsletter discussed the exploitation of colonized peoples, asserting that "in Africa . . . the natives are little less than slaves who are ruled by other people who have established themselves as citizens." The writer compared this situation to the American South, where "Negroes do not receive full justice." "Sometimes," he continued, "they do not even receive the benefit of the law, as in the case of a lynching." Other articles reported on speeches about such places as Palestine, South Africa, and India, or argued that America's record on race made it a poor example of democracy to the world.[11]

Some postwar campus writers and activists openly criticized the Crump regime, thereby presenting themselves as an alternative black political voice. One LeMoyne student and veteran, Charles E. Lincoln (later better known as C. Eric Lincoln, a prominent religious studies scholar), described his return to Memphis by Jim Crow train as a journey "back to the world cotton market, back to Beale Street, back to the terrors of the Memphis police brutality, the far-reaching all seeing Cerberus of the Crump machine and the unpleasant daily contact with the little Crumplets." Others lambasted existing black leaders more directly and personally. One writer attacked a column in the local black newspaper by the popular teacher, journalist, and emcee Nat D. Williams on the question "Is the Negro Ready for Democracy?" "To-date many of us have not recovered from a certain sickness at the pit of the stomach, incurred while reading this particular column," he declared.[12]

These emerging black leaders thus posited themselves as representatives of a generation whose political perspective differed from that of their elders. Jesse Turner, an accountant educated at LeMoyne who would later head the Memphis NAACP, first joined the organization in college. After suffering humiliating racism in the army and returning to Memphis after graduate school, he once again sought out the NAACP. Several young attorneys such as Benjamin Hooks, Russell Sugarmon, and A. W. Willis also plunged into civil rights work in the 1950s, as did Maxine Smith and Miriam DeCosta Willis (then Sugarmon).

H. T. Lockard became executive secretary of the local NAACP in January 1955, in the wake of *Brown*. Having joined the LeMoyne College branch in 1941, he spent four years in the military, attended law school in St. Louis, and returned to Memphis in 1951. Lockard concluded that racial conditions there were worse than anywhere he had been. The NAACP branch, in his estimation, was run by "a bunch of courageous old men" who were doing "absolutely nothing." In a letter to the NAACP office in New York just after his election, Lockard described the Memphis branch as "one of the most lethargic in the whole U.S." Lockard asked for advice on "stimulating some interest on the part of our 'silk stocking group,'" but reported optimistically that he had been "swamped with telephone calls as well as many words of encouragement."[13] Lockard and other young civil rights activists thus brought with them a keen sense of urgency about racial democracy in the United States and abroad that they also applied to Memphis. In doing so, they reached out to national civil rights leaders and to the burgeoning rural struggle just outside Memphis.

Two events on the eve of *Brown* illuminate the dramatic influence that the proximity of Memphis to the Delta would have on urban activists' responses to the Supreme Court decision and their efforts to reorganize the local NAACP. First, eager to attract a large audience to the kickoff for the Memphis NAACP's membership campaign in April 1954, branch leaders hopeful of reorganizing the local group after Phillips's retirement in 1953 invited Dr. T. R. M. Howard, president of the Regional Council of Negro Leadership (RCNL) in the Mississippi Delta, to address the meeting. Second, a month later, just ten days before the *Brown* decision, a group traveled down Highway 61 to Mound Bayou, Mississippi, to join more than six thousand African Americans from across the Delta for the RCNL's third annual meeting, where the keynote speaker was Thurgood Marshall. Before Marshall spoke he met with NAACP attorneys, mostly from Memphis, to discuss what initiatives the NAACP should take after the Supreme Court decision, which he expected any day. Two years after Hurley's letter, important bonds had begun to form between rural and urban activists that would influence their perspectives after *Brown*.[14]

According to reports in the Memphis black press, Marshall's mass audience erupted in "thunderous applause" when he traced the current struggle back to the days of the infamous Black Codes after the Civil War, and denounced Mississippi's "peanut head politicians" who sought to perpetuate segregation. The audience similarly applauded when he declared, "We are on a great crusade for freedom and we won't be satisfied in Mississippi or anywhere else in this nation until the shame of segregation and discrimination have been wiped from the records." Overwhelmed, Marshall exclaimed, "This is an unbelievable crowd!" "You couldn't get such a crowd in New York to meet and talk on integration," he declared. "Only in the South is this possible, because here is where the fight is. The weak ones have moved on to Detroit and Chicago while the real ones have remained to fight." Marshall's stunning comment, like Hurley's observation, rejected stereotypes of rural black southerners as passive, even fearful, presenting them instead as the vanguard of the struggle. His strategy meeting with such attorneys as Benjamin Hooks, A. A. Latting, J. F. Estes, A. W. Willis, H. T. Lockard, and the well-known Nashville civil rights lawyer Z. Alexander Looby took place in this context, with Marshall and the attorneys energized by his resounding reception in the heart of the rural Delta.[15]

As was clear from the invitation by the Memphis NAACP to Howard a month earlier, the RCNL had already become an inspiration for city activists seeking new models of independent black politics. In late 1951 the *Tri-State Defender* had hailed the formation of a new "Negro Delta Council." The newspaper, an affiliate of the *Chicago Defender* founded earlier that year, claimed to represent a more outspoken voice than the older *Memphis World*, and accordingly it described the RCNL's founding meeting on 28 December 1951 as a "historic milestone" that would lead to "first-class citizenship."[16]

The chief surgeon at the Friendship Clinic in Mound Bayou, Dr Howard also held positions in Memphis as vice-president of the Tri-State Bank and board member of the Universal Life Insurance Company, linking him to a group of urban business leaders across the South who sought a greater political voice in the early 1950s. Howard first presented the Negro Delta Council as a counterpart to the all-white Delta Council that would address regional economic and political problems. By May 1952, however, he had changed the name to Regional Council of Negro Leadership and challenged the Delta Council's desire to maintain white economic power. Assisted by such young men as Medgar Evers, Amzie Moore, and Aaron Henry, all veterans and NAACP activists, the RCNL mounted spectacular annual meetings with nationally recognized speakers.[17]

Howard explicitly situated the RCNL's mission in relation to driving postwar issues, from migration to the cold war. In his prospectus for the first annual meeting in May 1952, he noted that the state had "lost more people during the last ten years than any other state in the Union," with African Americans constituting 350,000 of the 455,000 that had left. He attributed this to poor schooling for black children, inadequate living conditions, and "the lack of democracy and the insecurity of life for Negroes." Declaring that he had no interest in communism and had "not lost faith in our American democracy," he nevertheless warned that "the cause of Jesus and the cause of Democracy is shuddering throughout the world today because of the inequality of Democracy in regards to Negro rights here in Mississippi."[18]

Howard's prospectus rejected solutions based upon political dependency, in which "white men can go behind closed doors and work out all the Negro's problems and bring them to him on a platter." The RCNL would not " 'Uncle Tom' and come in the back to the [Delta] Council table." The only vehicle to first-class citizenship would be an independent, mass organization uniting representatives from diverse Delta institutions. Howard rhe-torically constructed the RCNL as the region's first militant organization, arguing that "since the days of American slavery," African Americans had been complacent about *"separate but in no case equal facilities,"* leaving the solution up to "the drawn lash of the Supreme Court." Black Mississippians themselves had to secure change. He condemned the lack of public rest-rooms for African Americans, the disproportionate number of blacks at Parchman Penitentiary, and the absence of blacks on juries. He also ad-dressed the "shame, reproach and disgrace" visited upon black women, who were harassed and raped by white men, and lacked protection by black men. "First-class citizenship," therefore, involved a collective agency in which African Americans claimed rather than received citizenship rights. Challenging "separate but in no case equal" also meant squashing rac-ist practices that demeaned black manhood and womanhood. Howard's speech thus couched desegregation within a multifaceted discussion of American democracy.[19]

Howard also connected the empowerment of disfranchised rural Mis-sissippians to a broader national agenda. The RCNL conducted press con-ferences, invited journalists to meetings, and attracted major figures to annual mass meetings. The first mass meeting in May 1952, for instance, drew seven thousand to a speech by Representative William L. Dawson, the first black congressman to appear in Mississippi in six decades, and to a performance by Mahalia Jackson. The *Tri-State Defender* referred to Howard as "a modern 'Moses,'" marveling at the RCNL's militant endorsement of voting rights, "right on Highway 61."[20]

After *Brown*, Memphis activists' relationship to the Delta encouraged them to see themselves as part of an outright war over the future of white domination. With the formation of the white Citizens' Council in Indianola, Delta activists faced a virulent backlash. The RCNL announced its determi-nation to fight the "economic war" planned by the Citizens' Council to pro-tect segregation. When two thousand RCNL delegates met in Mound Bayou in October 1954, they looked to Memphis for support, especially the ability to apply for loans at the Tri-State Bank if denied credit by white-owned banks in Mississippi. In January 1955 a war chest of $1 million was established at Tri-State by bank officials, among them its president, Dr. J. E. Walker, the NAACP's executive secretary Roy Wilkins, and RCNL leaders. The fund, to be built by donors from around the country, would support those affected by the Citizens' Council "credit freeze" against farmers and others involved with voter registration. The *Tri-State Defender* reported weekly on people targeted by the Citizens' Council and on contributions to the war chest, presenting Memphis as central to the struggle over the future of American democracy. "Those citizens and organizations who are depositing funds in the Tri-State Bank of Memphis for the use of the embattled and economically squeezed Negroes of Mississippi," it stated in an editorial, "are fighting a frontline battle for the protection of American principles of fair-play and democracy."[21]

This sense of embattlement escalated in the spring of 1955, when the most massive outpouring to date for an RCNL meeting was followed closely by the first killing of a person singled out by the Citizen's Council. In late April, Memphians joined thirteen thousand others at the fourth annual meeting, where Congressman Charles Diggs Jr. spoke. In a show of defiance against the Citizens' Council, attendance at the mass meeting nearly doubled in size from the meeting in 1954 at which Marshall spoke. Two weeks later, Memphis activists attended the funeral of the Reverend George T. Lee, a leader in the RCNL and the NAACP who had promoted voter registration.[22]

The Delta movement now captured national headlines that made it emblematic of a new race militancy. *Ebony* magazine, published in Chicago, proclaimed that "a new militant Negro" was emerging in the South, describing this militant in gendered terms as "a fearless, fighting man who openly campaigns for his civil rights, who refuses to migrate to the North in search of justice and dignity, and is determined to stay in his own backyard and fight." After Emmett Till's lynching in August 1955, Howard addressed protest rallies in Los Angeles, at Madison Square Garden in New York, and elsewhere. At these appearances he and other speakers connected the lynching to the other deadly violence that followed *Brown*, and made the Delta central to the national struggle for justice.[23]

In Memphis, meanwhile, some twenty thousand black delegates from around the country attended the National Baptist Convention in September 1955, dramatically displaying their intolerance for compromising attitudes. Delegates gathered at Ellis Auditorium shouted down the Reverend H. H. Humes of Mississippi for over thirty minutes, calling him a "traitor" and an "Uncle Tom," in response to the voluntary segregation plan that Humes had recently proposed as a response to *Brown*. Earlier in the convention, the Memphis black press reported, the Atlanta minister Dr. William H. Borders had declared that Humes's comments "were detrimental to all the convention stands for, and that, in a way, Humes had contributed to deaths of three Negroes in his state." These two opposing images of the "new fighting man" and the "Uncle Tom" signaled a changing political context that began before *Brown* but surfaced more dramatically in its aftermath.[24]

In this highly charged atmosphere, the *Tri-State Defender* lambasted the "racial equation" in the Delta, categorizing it as "one of master and servant and rigidly enforced," while others argued that this "racial equation" extended to the city. At a mass meeting in Memphis just after the killing of Lee in May 1955, for instance, Howard reportedly "served notice on the people of Memphis that they themselves are sitting idly by wearing a smug look as regards the situation in Mississippi when in downtown Memphis there exists many of the same conditions which the Negroes in Mississippi have risen up to buck." "Smugness," or complacency, in such views represented an internal barrier to the struggle to "buck" the "master and servant" relation. This relationship between Memphis activists, the rural Delta, and national civil rights politics shaped Memphians' perceptions about their place in the larger struggle after *Brown*, adding urgency to convictions that "first-class citizenship" could not come solely on a platter from the Supreme Court.[25]

In late May 1954 local NAACP attorneys, fresh from their meeting with Marshall, assisted several young African Americans, two of them recently returned from Korea, to apply for admission at Memphis State College. Because *Brown* had not addressed higher education, the NAACP now hoped to extend earlier Supreme Court rulings on graduate programs and law schools that had stopped short of overturning "separate but equal." Most significantly for college students in Tennessee, in 1951 a federal district judge had ruled in *Gray v. University of Tennessee* that African American students refused admission to the university's graduate school and College of Law solely on the basis of race had been denied their constitutional rights under the Fourteenth Amendment's equal protection clause. In *Gray* the judge had not struck down the state's segregated education requirement, but found that the state had failed to provide equal facilities for the black students in accordance with the U.S. Supreme Court's decisions in *State of Missouri ex rel. Gaines v. Canada* (1938) and *Sipuel v. Oklahoma State Board of Regents* (1948), both cases involving law school admissions. The judge also cited the Court's decisions in *Sweatt v. Painter* and *McLaurin v. Oklahoma*. In these cases, both in 1950, the Court ruled that separate facilities provided for black students by the University of Texas Law School and the University of Oklahoma School of Education were inadequate, in part because of intangibles such as black students' inability to benefit from the "rich traditions and prestige" that enhanced their white peers' education. When *Gray v. University of Tennessee* reached the U.S. Supreme Court in early 1952, the Court ruled the appeal moot, since the University of Tennessee had decided to admit the students in the year since the lower court's ruling. Neither *Gray* nor any of these earlier decisions had directly struck down in the realm of higher education the principle of "separate but equal" upheld in *Plessy v. Ferguson*.[26]

By assisting the black applicants to Memphis State, therefore, the NAACP hoped to procure a ruling that explicitly extended the logic of *Brown* to publicly funded colleges. Directly after *Brown II* in 1955, James F. Estes, the attorney in charge of legal redress for the local branch, along with H. T. Lockard, Benjamin Hooks, and A. W. Willis, responded to the refusal by Memphis State to admit the students by filing suit against the Tennessee Board of Education in federal district court. The state board, meanwhile, issued a plan for "gradual desegregation" that stretched out graduate school and college desegregation over several years, did not address secondary schools, and kept the entire plan inoperative unless the courts struck down the segregation mandate contained in the Tennessee state constitution. In October, a federal district judge, Marion Boyd, did find school segregation in Tennessee unconstitutional; however, he agreed to accept the state's plan. Local NAACP leaders ruled this decision a victory, contrasting it to developments in Mississippi, where the legislature was considering a plan to close the schools outright to avoid desegregation; yet they warned that the victory was only partial. Not until 1959, after intervention by the U.S. Court of Appeals for the Sixth Circuit, did the first black students enter Memphis State.[27]

Meanwhile, the new local NAACP leaders involved with this effort to desegregate Memphis State secured enthusiastic, widespread support from all sectors of the black community. They invigorated their campaign with mass meetings featuring prominent veterans of the hard-pressed rural campaigns. A week after Howard's speech in May 1955 inveighing against "smugness," the local NAACP established a fund to support the Memphis State suit. The branch asked local ministers to adopt 3 July as "NAACP Day" and appeal for contributions. In addition, branch members voted to collect money from black workers at businesses and factories, and to establish a committee of one hundred women to canvass homes, headed by Mrs. B. F. McCleave, Miss Rosa Brown Bracy, and Mrs. Gold S. Young. Amazingly, the women's division quickly increased the number of their canvassers to five hundred. The black press added to the momentum by publishing donors' names and amounts (mostly one to five dollars), showing that every contribution was important. To climax this drive, the NAACP asked Harold Flowers, a civil rights attorney from Pine Bluffs, Arkansas—where "White America, Inc.," a home-grown version of the Citizens' Council, had been formed—to speak at a mass meeting.[28]

Civil rights advocates in Memphis also confronted state legislators from the plantation counties of west Tennessee who opposed the Court decision. In December 1954 Senator-elect Charles A. Stainback of Fayette County proposed "pupil assignment" legislation aimed at empowering local school boards to control the placement of students. Similar to legislation passed in North Carolina, the resulting bill was intended to give localities the tools to thwart desegregation, thus enabling the state to avoid directly violating *Brown* itself. In the House the bill's sponsors were from Fayette, Haywood, and Tipton counties, also in west Tennessee. Both houses of the legislature passed the bill in March 1955. However, Governor Frank Clement, whose reelection in 1954 had been secured in part by black voters after his opponent, ex-Governor Browning, had denounced *Brown* and vowed to uphold white supremacy, vetoed the legislation. No liberal, Clement nevertheless declared the legislation unnecessary, since the Tennessee state constitution mandated segregated schools. By 1957 his position had changed from restraint to open obstruction, as he signed a pupil assignment law and other segregation bills, and supported a Manifesto of Protest against *Brown*. By 1957, therefore, representatives of the plantation counties near Memphis set the agenda for the state.[29]

Civil rights and black educational organizations in Memphis sent resolutions of protest to Nashville against Stainback's bill, challenging the extension of planter domination to the entire state and staking their own claims to American democracy and manhood. By sending messages to be read at public hearings, they pitted themselves against what the black press cast as "notorious Dixiecrat strong holds . . . where the Negro residents, although a majority, have long been denied citizenship rights, including the right to vote." James T. Walker, president of the Bluff City and Shelby County Council of Civic Clubs, argued that the bill hit "below the belt" and was "a slap in the face" of Private Edward O. Cleaborn, a black Memphian posthumously recognized as a Korean War hero. The *Tri-State Defender* made its own effort to mold public opinion by invoking the historical memory of the lynching in 1940 of Elbert Williams, who had organized an NAACP branch and registered to vote in Haywood County, and whose killers were never arrested although the NAACP had submitted names of suspects to the FBI. The press reported that at the hearings, Stainback and his colleagues had "denounced Negroes as ignorant, diseased, unclean, dangerous and both unfit and unable to compete with whites." The "leading citizens" of Haywood and Fayette counties, the editors continued, "depend on the availability of Negroes as a cheap, unprotected and terrorized labor supply." Segregation, in this view, stemmed from a plantation system dependent upon subjugated black labor, the denial of citizenship, violence, and racist ideology.[30]

The federal sanctioning of racial equality presaged by *Brown* presented an opportunity for civic groups in Memphis to reshape local black politics by publicly asserting their independence from the Crump machine, in contradistinction to those allied with city officials. The Bluff City and Shelby County Council of Civic Clubs, a coalition of thirty black neighborhood groups, many founded since the late 1940s, declared that both "Negro leaders and the masses" supported integration, although white city leaders had "stated on various occasions that the masses of Negroes and their leaders do not want integration." "What leaders they refer to is not clear," the resolution continued. "This organization desires to let it be known to all and sundry, that its leaders and constituents are pledged to oppose all forms of discrimination based upon race or color." This public rejection of paternalistic claims about the purported satisfaction of black Memphians would be echoed by others.[31]

Such a rejection took on added significance in the complicated political terrain of Memphis in the mid-1950s, which differed from that of the outlying cotton belt. Most city officials avoided open antagonism to *Brown* in the period directly after the decision. The president of the board of education, Milton Bowers, declared that the city would remain within the law, suggesting that it might comply with the Supreme Court. For the coming year, however, there would be no changes in city schools, according to its superintendent Ernest Ball, since the Tennessee constitution required segregation and the Court had not yet ruled on implementing *Brown*. Over the next year the board proceeded in a style typical of the Crump machine, soliciting black support by trumpeting various building projects to enhance and expand "Negro schools." The Shelby County board, which administered schools outside the city limits, announced that as usual, black schools would close for six weeks during cotton-picking season.[32]

White spokesmen cast themselves as critical of racial "extremism" on both sides, being sure to distance themselves from black civic activism while also acknowledging its electoral significance. With the state legislature's elimination of the poll tax in 1951, two black business leaders, Dr. J. E. Walker, a Democrat, and Lt. George W. Lee, a Republican, had organized a Non-Partisan Voters League, which together with the Bluff City and Shelby County Council of Civic Clubs tripled black voter registration, from 7,000 to 22,000. Civic club members, especially women, lobbied neighbors to register and attended mass voter rallies such as one held at Metropolitan Baptist Church in January 1954, where the featured speaker was the president of the National Baptist Convention, Dr. J. H. Jackson. In response to this growing activism, an aspiring white politician, Edmund Orgill, established his own moderate voice by publicly castigating Representative Pat Sutton, Senator Estes Kefauver's opponent in the Democratic primary in 1954, for his proposal to introduce a constitutional amendment obstructing *Brown*. Orgill, who would run for mayor of Memphis in 1955, declared his support for the city's plan to "work out its problem within the law." The *Commercial Appeal*, one of the city's two daily newspapers, greeted the *Brown* decision by counseling "calmness, reason, and . . . cooperation," while the *Press-Scimitar*, a long-time opponent of Crump, characterized America's support for democratic principles of "equal opportunity" as key to winning the cold war.[33]

For black voters, the *Brown* decision's intersection with the elimination of the poll tax and death of Boss Crump appeared to offer an unprecedented political opening in 1955, since the Crump machine had long been the public face of white domination in Memphis. The death of Crump in October 1954 and that of Mayor Frank Tobey in the following September had presented reformers with a chance to win the municipal elections in 1955. "For the first time in many years," the black press declared, "the voters of Memphis will go to the polls without the shadow of implied or real 'boss' machinations." Civic clubs opened all stops to increase black voter registration to sixty thousand. More than two hundred ministers formed the Ministers and Citizens League, hiring women to supervise a door-knocking campaign in every majority-black ward in the city. The Veterans Voters Movement, composed of veterans of the Second World War and the Korean War and headed by J. F. Estes of the NAACP, launched a drive to register ten thousand voters, in which two thousand veterans would drive five registrants each to the courthouse.[34]

Despite this unified voter registration campaign, groups disagreed about how to choose between mayoral candidates unlikely to support their interests. Black voters expressed reservations about both candidates. Orgill, they argued, had no record of supporting black rights beyond his backing of the new "Negro hospital," Collins Chapel Memorial. Critics of the former mayor Watkins Overton questioned his autonomy from Crump. Ultimately, the majority supported Orgill, swinging the election in his favor, and underscoring black voters' rejection of the white machine. However, Overton won support in wards that included a significant middle-class presence, such as Orange Mound, and from Republican leaders ranging from Lt. Lee to Benjamin Hooks.[35]

Disagreement over the mayoral race contrasted with black voters' strong unity on two other points. First, since neither mayoral candidate, however reasonable he sounded, could be counted on to promote *Brown*, black voters solidly supported a black school board candidate, the Reverend Roy Love. Black Memphians cared deeply about education. Indeed, many women who migrated to the city in the postwar period did so to secure a better education for themselves or their children. Black residents took great pride in their schools and educators; however, most felt indignant about conditions resulting from the city's segregation plan, including overcrowded facilities and inferior resources, such as out-of-date books previously used by white students. Love lacked white support, however, and lost.

Second, black Memphians expressed overwhelming concern with police brutality. "Here in Memphis, as in many Southern cities," the *Tri-State Defender* asserted, "Negroes have long endured a callous, disrespectful, and sometimes brutal expression of an administration's racial policies through the police." They perceived the city commission system as conducive to police abuse, since commissioners had little accountability to the electorate. At a banquet of the Non-Partisan Voters League, for example, a minister related a story about a father who had been arrested and fined while taking his son to the hospital. Only the officers' confidence that they would be backed up by "the top brass" could explain this "disregard for the Negro," the minister declared. At meetings, black citizens queried candidates about their plans for stopping police brutality. During the mayoral elections of 1959, police brutality sparked mass political rallies, a clear sign that Orgill's election had not resolved the problem.[36] Thus, as black voters sorted out their perspectives at this critical juncture, they placed equal emphasis on police brutality and school segregation, viewing them as features of urban life that they compared to the white dominance of the plantation.

In this period following *Brown*, black workers, many of them women, further interrupted local political discourse by provocatively making urban problems of labor into issues of racial justice. Significantly, even as most black leaders were endorsing the candidacy of Henry Loeb in 1955 for commissioner of public works—over a decade before Loeb as mayor became infamous for his determination to crush the sanitation workers' strike of 1968—a group of women at a political rally cautioned against support for Loeb because of the "business policies of the Loeb Laundry-Cleaners establishment," as the press obliquely reported it. Indeed, at the end of the Second World War workers at Loeb's laundry had struck against poor working conditions, especially a piecework system that made them work at a dangerous speed. The women's prescient critiques failed to deter endorsements of Loeb, allowing him to sail into office with considerable black support (he would lose that support in 1959, when he campaigned for mayor on an openly segregationist platform).[37]

Another protest by women workers in 1955 captured far more immediate attention, placing a gendered symbol of the plantation, the "Mammy" image, at the center of public discourse and sparking a struggle against racist courtroom procedures that paralleled the campaigns for desegregation and political change. Distraught over their employers' decision to seat Mrs. Savannah Keys outside a downtown restaurant with a bandana wrapped around her head, ringing a bell to attract customers, several employees of Joel's Patio decided to approach their employers. The owners of the restaurant were white women who had already placed a black "Mammy" rag doll in the window to promote their southern fare. For the employees, the use of a living elderly woman raised disrespect to an intolerable level. According to Mrs. Marie Taylor, who approached the employers on behalf of the group, she was told: "Look, if you all don't like it, get your clothes and get out." When she and five others, all but one female, decided to leave, the employers locked the door and called the police, who arrested the employees. Mrs. Taylor reported that one arresting officer became verbally abusive: "[He threatened to] 'knock my brains out' if he ever caught me on the street." Jailed and charged with disorderly conduct and disturbing the peace, the employees were sentenced by Judge Beverly Boushe, who fined them $11 to $26 on each count.[38]

Although the incident leading to the arrests was prompted by indignation over the use of an elderly woman as a subservient black female stereotype, the "Patio 6" case rapidly inspired a protest movement against racial injustice in the courtroom. Press coverage of the arrests drew a number of observers to the trial. A. A. Latting, the NAACP attorney who defended two of the employees, strategically requested the highest fine for his clients so that it would meet the minimum required for an appeal. Later that week, AME and Baptist ministers convened a meeting to hear reports from Mrs. Taylor and from the Reverend W. L. Powell, presiding elder of the South Memphis District of the AME Church. Powell argued that the judge had made the proceedings "purely a racial matter" and that his fellow ministers had the responsibility to speak out on behalf of these "heroes in a common place." Those in attendance organized the Memphis Citizens Committee for the Promotion of Justice, led by the funeral home director T. C. D. Hayes and the prominent Baptist minister Dr. S. A. Owen, and hired Latting and Hooks to pursue the appeals. The "Patio 6" case and the Citizens Committee for the Promotion of Justice became vehicles, in part, for challenging white images of black womanhood, including icons of slavery such as the "Mammy" persona, popularized by American mass culture. The black press also portrayed the Citizens Committee's fight against racial bias in the courtroom as being "in line with the best traditions of American democracy," as well as a "Christian action." Such conflicts over identity and justice became central to rejecting the "master and servant" relation.[39]

Working-class black Memphians, many of whom were recent migrants from the outlying cotton region, also seized on *Brown* in more direct ways, drawing on their multiple roles as NAACP members, civic club leaders, and labor activists to challenge segregation in various spheres of urban life.

At Firestone, for example, Clarence Coe, originally from Fayette County, joined other black union activists in initiating a desegregation suit against Firestone, charging the company with maintaining segregated seniority lists, pay scales, and facilities. Matthew Davis, also a Firestone worker originally from rural west Tennessee, recalls that black workers held meetings to talk about racist job restrictions and segregated water fountains and restrooms. These working-class migrants posed a formidable challenge to the racial structures in Memphis, suggesting that urbanization did not end but rather politicized their desires for changed conditions of life and labor.[40]

One civic club with a strongly working-class and migrant membership, the Binghampton Civic League, issued pointed challenges to segregation, underscoring the urban culture of political assertiveness that Coe and Davis reflected. In 1956 O. Z. Evers, a postal employee and the league's president, filed a bus desegregation suit against the city after he refused to move to the back of a bus and was ejected from it. Two years later, the Binghampton Civic League petitioned the City Commission for complete desegregation of the zoo, fairgrounds, public parks, and recreational facilities. "For four years now, the Negro has adopted a 'wait-and-see' attitude towards integration in public recreational facilities here in Memphis," the letter began. And in 1959 the club demanded to know why African Americans were excluded from employment in city government, calling for an immediate end to this situation.[41]

The decision in 1959 by a group of city sanitation workers, many of them migrants from rural west Tennessee now living in Binghampton, to approach O. Z. Evers for help in organizing a union powerfully illustrates the way labor and racial justice issues intersected with political activism in the period after *Brown*. Throughout the 1950s workers in both industrial workplaces like Firestone and small manufacturing shops with predominantly black workforces continued to organize, even after the most vicious red-baiting of the McCarthy era, including the interrogation of labor activists during hearings of the Senate Internal Security Subcommittee conducted by Senator James Eastland in Memphis in 1951. Sanitation workers, who were precluded from unionizing by the exclusion of public employees from the Wagner Act (1935), first began organizing during the late 1950s, even earlier than has been generally recognized by historians.

Because the city reserved garbage collection jobs for black men while assigning supervisory jobs to whites, workers interpreted derogatory treatment as both exploitative and racist. For example, Evers declared that the workers had to deal with "biased foremen who will lay men off for several days for little or no cause." Workers from rural areas likened their long hours to those of field labor. "It was the same thing that you would put on farmhands—can-to-can," recalled Clinton Burrows. "That means get up as early as you can and leave when they tell you you can . . . sunup to sundown." A series of spirited meetings and rallies held in neighborhood churches in Binghampton involved hundreds of workers and their wives in early 1960, the period when the Memphis sit-in movement began. When the Public Works commissioner, William Farris—elected to replace Loeb, who had become mayor—refused to negotiate, eight hundred of twelve hundred workers voted to strike, backed by Teamsters Local 984. The Teamsters then precipitously dropped their support. The plans fell apart in the face of Farris's threat to fire workers who joined a union, and his claim that the workers had no complaints of their own but were being riled up by "outsiders." Despite this initial failure, the workers and their wives, assisted by Evers, had begun to develop a community spirit that in 1968 would prevail over the intimidation and paternalism that Farris articulated.[42]

Black working-class civil rights and labor activism during this period became part of the rural-urban matrix that led activists and others to respond to *Brown* as one facet of a larger, more complex struggle for racial justice. By 1960, the year when student sit-ins swept the South, the complex urban-rural dynamic that had shaped responses to *Brown* and other dimensions of racial politics in the 1950s had produced a striking new confluence of events. Even as the sanitation workers in Memphis rallied, students at the city's historically black colleges LeMoyne and Owen seized the moment to launch their own sit-ins, targeting first the public library and other taxpayer-funded institutions and then lunch counters. This sit-in movement, which some considered one of the most intensive in the South,[43] included sons and daughters of migrants, who had inherited stories of rural racial violence but by now had their own memories of police harassment and indignities on city buses. All of them had become fed up with what they perceived as stalling by city officials since *Brown* and too impatient to wait for legal decisions. In isolation the sit-ins might appear as the capstone of desegregation efforts galvanized by *Brown*. When seen in conjunction with other movements occurring at the same time, however, it becomes evident that even these hallmark protests of the Freedom Movement addressed desegregation as the crux of a far more multidimensional racial justice movement.

The sit-ins overlapped not only with the sanitation workers' organizing and the election rallies of 1960 but also with the sharecroppers' movement for voting rights in Fayette and Haywood counties. This remarkable confluence of protest was firmly rooted in the rural-urban matrix of the 1950s. In Fayette County, the third-poorest county in the nation, with a two-thirds black majority among the nearly 25,000 residents, only seventeen African

Americans voted between 1952 and 1959. Many recalled the lynching in 1940 of Elbert Williams, which the *Defender* had invoked in its attacks in 1955 on west Tennessee state legislators' attempts to block school desegregation. This memory had also been kept alive by the Tennessee NAACP, which singled out black disfranchisement and the "reign of terror" in west Tennessee as key problems to address throughout the 1950s.[44]

When local residents renewed voter registration efforts, their proximity to Memphis became crucial. Activists in Fayette County recall listening to coverage of voter registration drives on Memphis black radio. News about J. F. Estes's campaign to register veterans prompted Mt. Zion Church in Fayette County to invite him as a guest speaker in 1958. He then helped fourteen men, most of them veterans, to register, and also helped a group in Haywood County to form a voters' league. When threats of economic reprisals kept all but one registrant in Fayette from voting in November, Estes filed complaints with the state election commission. He was again in the news in early 1959, when in response to death threats prompted by a radio broadcast on his project to register veterans, he vowed that he had "no intention of leaving": "the fight for first-class citizenship must continue."[45]

As a result of these exchanges, the family of the Reverend Burton Dodson retained Estes's services in April 1959. Dodson, a fugitive since 1940 when he fled a Klan mob, was accused of killing a deputy sheriff during a crossfire. As his attorney, Estes became the first African American to appear in the Fayette County courthouse as counsel rather than as the accused. "Farmers in the area postponed Spring plowing to witness the drama," the *Tri-State Defender* reported. For some, like Square Mormon, this display of citizenship and masculinity was riveting. The trial was "the first thing that really give me and lots more people an ideal," he recalled. "[T]he main thing [was] that people need to stand on their foot and as a man, that truth could be found and justice could be found somewhere." Mormon and others launched an all-out voter registration campaign after the trial. Hundreds lined up at the courthouse on the one day of the month when registration was scheduled, with over five hundred registering in April and May alone. When officials obstructed further registration, Estes filed complaints with the federal civil rights commission. After registrants were barred from voting in the August primary, with Estes's help residents chartered the Fayette County Civic and Welfare League.[46]

In Memphis, meanwhile, a swirl of events was transforming the Freedom Movement. In August 1959, at a spirited "Freedom Rally" sponsored by the "Volunteer Ticket" campaign, speakers supported black candidates while denouncing the mayoral candidate Henry Loeb and the "Uncle Toms" whom the speakers accused of continued support for segregation. The guest speaker, Dr. Martin Luther King Jr., declared that he was "delighted beyond power of word to see such magnificent unity." In the following January, Hooks, Sugarmon, and others organized huge rallies to protest the exclusion of blacks from a national auto show held downtown. However, at a meeting of the NAACP Southeast Regional Conference in Memphis in February after the lunch counter sit-ins in Greensboro, Ruby Hurley declared, "The Negro youth have just about lost patience with their adults." Within a month, students at LeMoyne and Owen had initiated the sit-in movement.[47]

As headlines about arrests, mass meetings, and NAACP legal defenses grabbed headlines in the black press, spiraling developments forged close ties between Memphis activists and the Fayette and Haywood county share-croppers' movement. John McFerrin, president of the Fayette County Civic and Welfare League, reported that local merchants had blacklisted residents who registered to vote, refusing to sell them "furnishings" for planting or fuel for machinery. When McFerrin hastily established a store and service station, gasoline distributors throughout the region refused to sell to him and he received death threats from the Citizens' Council. By the fall fourteen hundred voters had registered for the national elections, but hundreds had been evicted from their homes and were living in a "tent city."[48]

The Memphis NAACP, intensely busy with a sit-in movement, now revisited the role it had played with the RCNL. In July 1960 members delivered food and clothing to families who had been denied credit. The branch established a relief fund, served as a clearinghouse for material and financial support sent from around the country, and helped residents of Fayette County to charter a local NAACP. In December, with over three hundred sharecropper and tenant farm families facing homelessness and destitution, Estes, Lt. George Lee, and other black leaders sponsored a civil rights "yuletide" program featuring Mahalia Jackson, aimed at raising money and lifting the spirits of the evicted families.[49]

This latest rural-urban relation unfolded in a national context, at a time when civil rights activists were responding to a rapidly changing political landscape. In New York in July 1960, Roy Wilkins called on NAACP branches to boycott national oil companies whose dealers refused delivery, and he requested that branches send financial and material aid to Memphis for Fayette and Haywood counties. In Chicago the young CORE activists Sterling Stuckey and James Foreman established a national Emergency Relief Committee to coordinate relief, and they traveled to west Tennessee themselves, in a forerunner of the journeys to the rural Deep South that would be made by activists in later years.[50] In Memphis the rural voting rights movement had taken on national and international implications, becoming a "litmus test for American democracy," as the black press put it.

The *Tri-State Defender* referred to Fayette County as "Little Africa," a reference to its system of white domination and the movement for black liberation. Editorials blasted both European and American arguments that Africans were not prepared for self-government, and insisted upon citizenship rights for black people in west Tennessee.[51]

As can be seen from this confluence of movements in 1960, the rural-urban matrix of the postwar era had powerful implications for the struggles surrounding *Brown v. Board of Education*. It ensured that protesters approached school desegregation as part of a broader and complex set of problems revolving around rights, power, and identity, problems that the black press had summed up as a "racial equation" based on "master and servant." In practical terms, urban activists' engagement with rural struggles made it impossible to separate their own responses to *Brown* from the dramatic conflicts over white domination that surfaced in the rural Delta areas of Mississippi, east Arkansas, and west Tennessee. Likewise, the increasing presence of working-class migrants from these same areas made problems of police brutality and labor especially potent and symbolic, even in advance of the sanitation strike in 1968 that made "I AM A MAN" a popular rallying cry. Those who protested against police brutality or became union activists also joined civic clubs and the NAACP. Therefore, demands for school desegregation—and even desegregation of other public institutions—were not compartmentalized from these other struggles.

Political rhetoric about American democracy took on competing and highly charged meanings in the cold war era. One of the most powerful articulations of democracy during these years came from the Supreme Court, when it reinterpreted the Fourteenth Amendment to the Constitution as barring the notion of "separate but equal" put forth in *Plessy v. Ferguson* and established desegregation as the basis for racial equality in modern life. The far-reaching implications of the Court's opinion have dominated much legal, political, and historical scholarship over the half-century, and for good reason. But the Supreme Court's postwar redefinition of equality and its challenge to American democracy never set the limits for popular understandings of racial justice among African Americans in the postwar South. Even as individuals and organizations hailed *Brown* as the greatest development since the Emancipation Proclamation (the words used by the Bluff City Council in Memphis), and seized upon it to press for desegregation in public schools and other institutions, they continued to face and attempted to push forward on deeply rooted problems and issues that the Court did not—and perhaps could not—address.[52]

As this chapter has shown, within the crucible of the urban South of the mid-1950s, African American activists in different domains celebrated

*Brown* as a crucial federal sanctioning of racial justice, and strove to make its promises into realities in schools and elsewhere. However, neither its mandate for desegregation nor its definition of equality exhausted activists' own complex and contested understandings of democracy that rejected white racist conceptions of black manhood and womanhood, as well as a politics of complacency or caution among themselves. The rural-urban matrix of the postwar South offers a fresh vantage point for analysis, one that allows us to see that amid the multidimensional struggles of the period, an ideological struggle was also being waged at the grassroots, one in which individuals and groups attempted to redirect black politics at this propitious moment. As they did so, notions of place and memory, race and gender provided a language for articulating the struggle.

## Notes

1 " 'We'll Fight Bias to Finish Line'—Marshall," *Tri-State Defender*, 15 May 1954; "Round Table Discussion at Mound Bayou," *Tri-State Defender*, 22 May 1954; Alex Wilson, "Leaders Map Campaign to Aid Victims of Race Credit 'Freeze' in Mississippi," *Tri-State Defender*, 8 January 1955; "We Weep for Mississippi," *Tri-State Defender*, 8 October 1955.

2 See for example John Dittmer, *Local People: The Struggle for Civil Rights in Mississippi* (Urbana: University of Illinois Press, 1994); and Charles M. Payne, *I've Got the Light of Freedom: The Organizing Tradition and the Mississippi Freedom Struggle* (Berkeley: University of California Press, 1995).

3 Ruby Hurley, Southeast Regional Office, Report from Field Trip, 27 March 1952, group II, box C186, Memphis, Tennessee, 1951–55 folder, Papers of the NAACP, Library of Congress; Hurley to Gloster Current, 5 August 1953, group II, box C222, 1953 folder, Papers of the NAACP, Library of Congress; Hurley to Current, 21 August 1953, group II, box C224, Reports: 1953–54 folder, Papers of the NAACP, Library of Congress.

4 Membership in 1952 was 731; in 1960 the branch reported that it had enrolled 5,200. H. T. Lockard to Gloster Current, 10 February 1955, group II, box C185, Memphis, Tennessee, 1951–55 folder, Papers of the NAACP, Library of Congress; Report from Workshop of Tennessee NAACP Branches, 13 May 1951, group II, box C221, Southeast Regional Office, Correspondence 1951, January–June, Papers of the NAACP, Library of Congress; Lucille Black to Maxine Smith, 19 May 1960, group III, box C146, Memphis, Tennessee, 1960, Papers of the NAACP, Library of Congress. See also Minutes of Memphis NAACP, 24 July 1960, Maxine Smith NAACP Collection, Memphis and Shelby County Archives, Memphis.

5 On Mississippi boosters' efforts to attract industry by touting low wages see James C. Cobb, *The Selling of the South: The Southern Crusade for Industrial Development, 1935–1990*, 2d ed. (Urbana: University of Illinois, 1993).

6  Hurley, Report from Field Trip, 27 March 1952.

7  Interview with Artherene Chalmers by author, Memphis, 15 August 1995, Behind the Veil: Documenting African American Life in the Jim Crow South Collection, Center for Documentary Studies, Special Collections, Duke University (tape recording); interview with Eddie May Garner by author, Memphis, 22 July 1997 (tape recording in author's possession); Aubrey Clapp to Mayor Walter Chandler, 18 June 1943, Papers of Walter Chandler, box 17, Welfare Department 1943 folder, Memphis and Shelby County Archives, Cossitt Library, Memphis.

8  Interviews with Chalmers and Garner. On the police brutality protest movement see Laurie B. Green, "Battling the Plantation Mentality: Consciousness, Culture, and the Politics of Race, Class and Gender in Memphis, 1940–1968" (diss., University of Chicago, 1999; book forthcoming 2005), chapter 3.

9  Utillus Phillips to Leah Brock, 7 February 1950, group II, box C187, Tennessee State Conference, 1948–50 folder, Papers of the NAACP, Library of Congress. For membership statistics see H. T. Lockard to Gloster Current, 10 February 1955, group II, box C185, Memphis, Tennessee, 1951–55 folder, Papers of the NAACP, Library of Congress; Report from Workshop of Tennessee NAACP Branches, 13 May 1951, group II, box C221, Southeast Regional Office, Correspondence 1951, January–June, Papers of the NAACP, Library of Congress.

10  "College Chapter to Celebrate 8th Anniversary," Beacon, 30 November 1948, newspaper 34 box, LeMoyne–Owen Archives, Memphis; Daniel Dean Carter to Thurgood Marshall, 8 January 1941, Papers of the NAACP, part 18, group II (Bethesda, Md.: University Publications of America, 1994), 28:976–77 (NAACP microfilm).

11  Cpl. W. E. Jackson, "I Fought a Battle," 31 August 1945, Private Chatterer, newspaper 34 box, LeMoyne–Owen Archives; "Is Justice Impossible?" 26 September 1949, Beacon, newspaper 34 box, LeMoyne–Owen Archives.

12  Charles E. Lincoln, "Night Train to Memphis," 14 February 1946, LeMoyne Democrat, newspaper 34 box, LeMoyne–Owen Archives; C.T. 50, "Charlie's Chats," Democrat, 23 April 1948, newspaper 34 box, LeMoyne–Owen Archives.

13  Turner, Hooks, and Lockard all attended LeMoyne. Interview with Allegra Turner by author, Memphis, 21 August 1995, Behind the Veil: Documenting African American Life in the Jim Crow South Collection, Center for Documentary Studies, Special Collections, Duke University (tape recording); "Draft Boards Continue after LeMoynites," LeMoyne Democrat, 20 February 1942, newspaper 34 box, LeMoyne–Owen Archives; H. T. Lockard to Gloster Current, 23 March 1955, group II, box C185, Memphis, Tennessee, 1951–55 folder, Papers of the NAACP, Library of Congress; Lockard to Walter White, 17 January 1955, group II, box C185, Memphis, Tennessee, 1951–55 folder, Papers of the NAACP, Library of Congress; interview with H. T. Lockard by author, Memphis, 23 July 1997 (tape recording in author's possession).

14  "NAACP Kicks Off Drive April 4th," Tri-State Defender, 3 April 1954; " 'We'll Fight Bias to Finish Line'—Marshall," Tri-State Defender, 15 May 1954; "Round Table Discussion at Mound Bayou," Tri-State Defender, 22 May 1954.

15 Raymond F. Tisby, "To Be Free by '63, Marshall Urges," *Birmingham World*, 11 May 1954.

16 "Mississippi Civic Leader Urges Better Deal," *Tri-State Defender*, 1 December 1951; "Dr. Howard Proposes a Delta Negro Council," *Tri-State Defender*, 15 December 1951; Daryl F. Grisham, "Launch Negro Delta Council: Leaders Meet at Cleveland, Miss. Dec. 28," *Tri-State Defender*, 22 December 1951.

17 George F. David, "Deep in the Delta," *Journal of Human Relations* 2 (spring 1954): 72–75; "The New Fighting South: Militant Negroes Refuse to Leave Dixie or Be Silenced," *Ebony*, August 1955, 69–74. For more on Henry, Moore, and Evers and their involvement in the RCNL see Payne, *I've Got the Light of Freedom*, 31–33, 37–38, 49, 58–59; Dittmer, *Local People*, 32–33.

18 Dr. T. R. M. Howard, Prospectus of the First Annual Meeting of the Mississippi Regional Council of Negro Leadership, 2 May 1952,Vivian G. Harsh Research Collection of Afro-American History and Literature, Chicago Public Library.

19 *Id.*

20 "Expect 10,000 at Delta Regional Leadership Council Meet May 2nd," *Tri-State Defender*, 3 May 1952; " 'Vote for Lawmakers Who Defend Rights,' " *Tri-State Defender*, 10 May 1952; "Highlights Of Delta Council Voters Campaign," *Tri-State Defender*, 10 May 1952; " 'Don't Get Mad . . . Get Smart,' " *Tri-State Defender*, 17 May 1952.

21 "Mississippi Faces Economic War," *Tri-State Defender*, 9 October 1954; L. Alex Wilson, "Leaders Map Campaign to Aid Victims of Race Credit 'Freeze' in Mississippi," *Tri-State Defender*, 8 January 1955; "Meeting the Neo-Kluxism Challenge," *Tri-State Defender*, 5 March 1955.

22 Hurley to Current, 27 May 1955, group II, box C225, Southeast Regional Office: Reports, 1955, Papers of the NAACP, Library of Congress; "The New Fighting South," 69–70.

23 "The New Fighting South," 69–74; "Donate $10,000 at Till Rally In Los Angeles," *Tri-State Defender*, 22 October 1955.

24 "Confab Rebukes, Humiliates Rev. Humes for 'Selling Out in Mississippi," *Tri-State Defender*, 17 September 1955. For more on the Mississippi conflicts over school desegregation see Dittmer, *Local People*, 41–59.

25 "We Weep for Mississippi," *Tri-State Defender*, 8 October 1955; "Won't Be Deterred from Goal, Says Dr. Howard," *Tri-State Defender*, 28 May 1955.

26 *Gray v. Board of Trustees of the University of Tennessee*, 97 F. Supp. 463 (1951), *vacated as moot*, 342 U.S. 517 (1952). See also *State of Missouri ex rel. Gaines v. Canada*, 305 U.S. 337 (1938); *Sipuel v. Board of Regents of the University of Oklahoma*, 332 U.S. 631 (1948); *Sweatt v. Painter*, 339 U.S. 629 (1950); *McLaurin v. Oklahoma State Regents*, 339 U.S. 637 (1950). The quotation is taken from the Court's decision in *Sweatt*.

27 "Try to Enter Memphis State: Refusal of President Is Ignored," *Tri-State Defender*, 5 June 1954; "Gird to Push Memphis State Case: Will Go to High Court If Forced," *Tri-State Defender*, 12 June 1954; "Let's Don't Confuse The Mem-

phis State Issue," *Tri-State Defender*, 19 June 1954; "Sectional Bias Now, Claims NAACP," *Tri-State Defender*, 11 September 1954; "Approve Fund to End MSC Barrier," *Tri-State Defender*, 4 June 1955; "Official to Answer on Admitting Five to MSC," *Tri-State Defender*, 18 June 1955; "Lower Barriers for Grad Students to Memphis State," *Tri-State Defender*, 22 October 1955; "Court of Appeals Puts 'Heat' on Judge Boyd in School Case," *Tri-State Defender*, 7 February 1959; "Negro Students Expect to Enter MSU in Fall," *Tri-State Defender*, 11 July 1959; "Negro Students Won't Bow to Bias at MSU," *Tri-State Defender*, 19 September 1959.

28 "Won't Be Deterred from Goal, Says Dr. Howard," *Tri-State Defender*, 28 May 1955; "Approve Fund to End MSC Barrier," *Tri-State Defender*, 4 June 1955; "NAACP . . . ," *Tri-State Defender*, 25 June 1955 [title and first page of article missing from microfilm]; "See Success in NAACP's Fund Drive," *Tri-State Defender*, 9 July 1955; "Atty. Flowers to Speak for NAACP Meet," *Tri-State Defender*, 23 July 1955; "Universal Workers Give $115 to NAACP Drive," *Tri-State Defender*, 30 July 1955; "Profit Group in Arkansas for Race Bias," *Tri-State Defender*, 19 February 1955; "New 'KKK' Unit Rears Its Head," *Tri-State Defender*, 2 April 1955; and "Negro Club Council Upholds Court Edict," *Commercial Appeal*, 4 July 1954.

29 "12,000 Help to Swing Sen. Kefauver Victory," *Tri-State Defender*, 14 August 1954; "First Move to By Pass Rule of High Court," *Tri-State Defender*, 18 December 1954; " 'Mum' about Biased Bill," *Tri-State Defender*, 12 February 1955; "New Bill Hits Mixing Students," *Tri-State Defender*, 26 February 1955; "Hot Potato for Gov. Clement," *Tri-State Defender*, 5 March 1955; "Governor Vetoes 2 Bills," *Tri-State Defender*, 26 March 1955; Roger Biles, "A Bittersweet Victory: Public School Desegregation in Memphis," *Journal of Negro Education* 55 (1986): 473. On the North Carolina legislation see William H. Chafe, *Civilities and Civil Rights: Greensboro, North Carolina, and the Black Struggle for Freedom* (New York: Oxford University Press, 1980), 50.

30 "3 Leaders Rap Stainback Bill," *Tri-State Defender*, 26 February 1955; "Bill Seeks to Thwart Integration in Tenn.," *Tri-State Defender*, 5 March 1955.

31 "Negro Club Council Upholds Court Edict," *Commercial Appeal*, 4 July 1954; "Refute 'Hint' Negroes Don't Seek End of School Barriers," *Tri-State Defender*, 24 December 1955.

32 "Orgill Lashes Rep. Sutton in TV Speech," *Tri-State Defender*, 24 July 1954; "City Education Board Stands Pat on Bias," *Tri-State Defender*, 21 August 1954; "5 Schools to Expand under New Program," *Tri-State Defender*, 5 March 1955.

33 Green, "Battling the Plantation Mentality," 217–24; interview with Matthew Davis by author, Memphis, 17 July 1997 (tape recording in author's possession); interview with Lillie G. Kirklon by author, Memphis, 18 August 1995, Behind the Veil: Documenting African American Life in the Jim Crow South, Center for Documentary Studies, Special Collections, Duke University (tape recording); "National Baptist President to Address Voters Rally," *Tri-State Defender*, 16 January 1954; "Orgill Lashes Rep. Sutton in TV Speech," *Tri-State Defender*, 24 July 1954; "12,000 Help to Swing Sen. Kefauver Victory," *Tri-State Defender*, 14 August 1954; Biles, "A Bittersweet Victory," 472.

34 "Thousands Mourn Loss of Mayor Frank Tobey," *Tri-State Defender*, 17 September 1955; "Now Is the Time," *Tri-State Defender*, 20 August 1955; "Voting Strength Is Now 40,774," *Tri-State Defender*, 30 July 1955; "Mass Meeting Friday Spurs Campaign for More Voters," *Tri-State Defender*, 8 October 1955; "Veterans Voters Movement Starts Drive to Get 10,000 Registered," *Tri-State Defender*, 15 October 1955.

35 "The Memphis Political Scene," "Hear Glowing Reports of Drive for Orgill," and "Leader Lauds Overton Record and Platform," *Tri-State Defender*, 11 November 1955; "Voters Are Together" and "Pick Candidates for Campaign," *Tri-State Defender*, 22 October 1955; "Weight of Record Vote Cast Helps Orgill; Rev. Love Bid Impressive," *Tri-State Defender*, 19 November 1955. Black Republicans had an important political presence in Memphis even in the 1950s, when many black leaders worked to thwart efforts by an ascendant all-white faction to gain party control. See for instance Nat D. Williams, "Six Making Political History," *Tri-State Defender*, 17 July 1954, on campaigns by six black Republicans in the "old Guard" faction.

36 "Dr. Love Opens Campaign: Commission Plan Hit," *Tri-State Defender*, 10 September 1955; "The Memphis Political Scene," *Tri-State Defender*, 5 November 1955; "Voters Are Together," *Tri-State Defender*, 22 October 1955; "20,000 Negroes behind Council's Effort to Meet with Armour and Stop Police Brutality," *Tri-State Defender*, 17 October 1959. Orgill was declaring his loyalty to southern segregation by 1957, amid the backlash to *Brown*. His political waffling would result in such a drastic loss of political support that he would withdraw from the mayoral race in 1959, leaving the path clear for Henry Loeb, an avowed white supremacist. See Green, "Battling the Plantation Mentality," 314–17.

37 "The Memphis Political Scene," *Tri-State Defender*, 5 November 1955; "Loeb's Laundry Workers Strike," *Memphis World*, 21 August 1945.

38 "6 Employes Revolt over Bell Ringer," *Tri-State Defender*, 23 April 1955; "All-Out Fight Looms in 'Patio 6' Case," *Tri-State Defender*, 30 April 1955.

39 "6 Employes Revolt over Bell Ringer," *Tri-State Defender*, 23 April 1955; All-Out Fight Looms in 'Patio 6' Case," *Tri-State Defender*, 30 April 1955; "Seek Justice in 'Patio Six' Case," *Tri-State Defender*, 5 May 1955.

40 Interview with Betty Coe Donahue by author, Memphis, 19 July 1997 (tape recording in author's possession); interview with Matthew Davis by author, Memphis, 17 July 1997 (tape recording in author's possession); on Clarence Coe see Michael K. Honey, *Black Workers Remember: An Oral History of Segregation, Unionism, and the Freedom Struggle* (Berkeley: University of California Press, 1999).

41 "Sues to End Park Bias," *Tri-State Defender*, 10 January 1959; "Showdown Begins on Bus Bias February 27," *Tri-State Defender*, 28 February 1959; "Evers Criticizes City's Position on Parks, Zoo," *Tri-State Defender*, 14 March 1959; O. Z. Evers et al. to City Commissioners, *Tri-State Defender*, 13 August 1958; "Civic Club and NAACP in Hot Exchange," *Tri-State Defender*, 12 March 1960; O. Z. Evers et al. to Honorable Edmund Orgill, 9 November 1959, and Orgill to unnamed recipient, 16 December 1959, both in Papers of Edmund Orgill, box 16,

Negroes (1) folder, Mississippi Valley Collection, Special Collections, University of Memphis.

42 Burrows quoted in Cornell Christion, "Blood and Strife Bought Dignity for City Workers," *Memphis Commercial Appeal*, 28 February 1993; "Evers, Farris Lock Horns on Union," *Tri-State Defender*, 6 February 1960; "200 Sanitation Men Cheer Union Plans," *Tri-State Defender*, 19 March 1960; "Sanitation Men Ready Petition," *Tri-State Defender*, 9 April 1960; "Sanitation Men Ready to Strike," *Tri-State Defender*, 7 May 1960; "Sanitation Strike Gets 2 Week Delay," *Tri-State Defender*, 15 May 1960; "Sanitation Workers Set to Strike," *Tri-State Defender*, 25 June 1960; interview with Robert L. Beasley by the Memphis Sanitation Strike Project, Memphis, 10 July 1991, Sanitation Strike Collection, Special Collections, University of Memphis (transcript); interview with Taylor Rogers by author, Memphis, November 2000 (tape recording in author's possession); interview with Robert Worsham by author, Memphis, 24 April 2001 (tape recording in author's possession); Thomas W. Collins, "Unionization in a Secondary Market," *Human Organization* 6 (summer 1977): 138.

43 Benjamin Muse, Southern Regional Council, quoted in Christopher Silver and John V. Moeser, *The Separate City: Black Communities in the Urban South, 1940–1968* (Lexington: University Press of Kentucky, 1995), 97; testimony by Russell Sugarmon in U.S. Commission on Civil Rights, *Hearings before the United States Commission on Civil Rights: Hearings Held in Memphis, Tennessee, June 25–26, 1962* (Washington: Government Printing Office, 1963), 107–8.

44 Robert Hamburger, *Our Portion of Hell: Fayette County, Tennessee: An Oral History of the Struggle for Civil Rights* (New York: Links Books, 1973), 3–5; on C. P. Boyd see Richard A. Couto, *Ain't Gonna Let Nobody Turn Me Round: The Pursuit of Racial Justice in the Rural South* (Philadelphia: Temple University Press, 1991), 32–34; Gloster Current, "Which Way Out?," *Crisis* 68 (March 1961): 133–35; "Resolutions Adopted by the 6th Annual Conference of Branches of the State of Tennessee NAACP," October 1952, and press release from Tennessee State Conference of NAACP Branches, 27 November 1953, both in Papers of the NAACP, group II, box C187, Tennessee State Conference 1951–55 folder, Library of Congress.

45 On Tom Rice see Couto, *Ain't Gonna Let Nobody Turn Me Round*, 32; On Minnie Jameson, George Bates, and June Dowdy see Hamburger, *Our Portion of Hell*, 33, 66–73; Burleigh Hines, "Tells Background on Fayette Vote Fight," *Tri-State Defender*, 5 December 1959; "Leaders Back Atty. Estes in Vote Registration Campaign," *Tri-State Defender*, 14 March 1959; Current, "Which Way Out?"

46 "Man Who Escaped Mob Faces Murder," *Tri-State Defender*, 4 April 1959; M. L. Reid, "Rev. Dodson Gets 20 Years; Seeks New Trial," *Tri-State Defender*, 11 April 1959; "Fugitive Life Fine Compared to Penitentiary, Says CME Minister," *Tri-State Defender*, 11 April 1959; "Deny New Trial to Rev. Dodson," *Tri-State Defender*, 23 May 1959; "Negroes in Fayette DID Try to Register," *Tri-State Defender*, 13 February 1960; interview with Square Mormon in Hamburger, *Our Portion of Hell*, 47; Hines, "Tells Background on Fayette Vote Fight"; "Voteless Negroes to Testify," *Pittsburgh Courier*, 23 January 1960.

47 "Bury Uncle Toms at Rally," *Tri-State Defender*, 8 August 1959; "Negroes Up in Arms over Auto Show Snub," *Tri-State Defender*, 23 January 1960; "Protest Group Becomes Permanent!," *Tri-State Defender*, 30 January 1960; "NAACP Youth Resolve to Extend Sit-Ins All over Southeast Area," *Tri-State Defender*, 27 January 1960; "Jail Fails to Stop 'Sit-Ins'" and "Negroes at Fever Pitch, Vow All-Out Support of Students," *Tri-State Defender*, 26 March 1960.

48 "Negroes in Fayette DID Try to Register," *Tri-State Defender*, 13 February 1960; "Squeeze Tightens in Fayette," *Tri-State Defender*, 7 May 1960; Hamburger, *Our Portion of Hell*, 3–82.

49 Minutes of Memphis NAACP executive board and branch meetings, June 1960–February 1961, Maxine Smith NAACP Papers; "Fayette Gets Help, More Coming," *Tri-State Defender*, 16 July 1960; "Urge 'Don't Buy' from Oil Companies," *Tri-State Defender*, 16 July 1960; "Seek Charter for NAACP in Fayette," *Tri-State Defender*, 30 July 1960; "M. Jackson to Sing at Ellis," *Tri-State Defender*, 24 December 1960.

50 "Urge 'Don't Buy' from Oil Companies," *Tri-State Defender*, 16 July 1960; "Help from Chicago for Fayette Co.," *Tri-State Defender*, 24 September 1960; "300 Face Eviction for Registering," *Tri-State Defender*, 17–23 December 1960; correspondence regarding Fayette and Haywood counties, group III, box C146, Papers of the NAACP, Library of Congress.

51 "The Boycott in Fayette County," *Tri-State Defender*, 2 July 1960; "The Boycott in Fayette County" and "Republic of Congo on Trial," *Tri-State Defender*, 16 July 1960.

52 On the cold war implications of *Brown* see Mary L. Dudziak, *Cold War, Civil Rights: Race and the Image of American Democracy* (Princeton: Princeton University Press, 2000).

MADELEINE E. LÓPEZ

# New York, Puerto Ricans, and

# the Dilemmas of Integration

La segregacíon escolar no es constitucional, dice la Corte.

—*La Prensa*, 18 May 1954

The Supreme Court Rules School Segregation Unconstitutional.

—*New York Times*, 18 May 1954

℘ The impact of *Brown v. Board of Education* was greater than the justices of the U.S. Supreme Court or the American public could have possibly imagined. Almost immediately, the scope of the ruling expanded beyond the American South and the dismantling of legalized segregation in tax-supported institutions. New York offers a fascinating example. On 24 December 1954 the New York City Board of Education issued a response to the Supreme Court decision, noting: "the board is determined to accept the challenge implicit in the language and spirit of the decision. We will seek a solution to these problems and take action with dispatch."[1] Jim Crow and public school segregation were not simply a southern problem, and educational officials invoked the city's tradition of liberalism to take action.[2]

The doctrine of "separate but equal" did not solely affect African Americans. People of color across the racial spectrum endured segregation in both de facto and de jure forms throughout the country. To date, scholars have devoted little attention to the issue of segregation and the meaning of *Brown* beyond the black-white and southern parameters of traditional civil rights historiography.[3] This bias has marginalized the experiences of other racial and ethnic communities in relationship to *Brown* and left unexplored the decision's broader ramifications in battles over the desegregation of public schools.

The experience of Puerto Ricans in New York City reflects the multifaceted nature of *Brown* and its broad reach in American life and politics. Puerto Ricans brought new meaning to the struggle for desegregation and the historical implications of the landmark ruling. In this chapter I discuss how Puerto Ricans, at the public policy and grassroots levels, reshaped

*Brown* to emphasize the centrality of language, an essential part of their cultural and political identity, in the struggle for educational equality. Puerto Rican educators and community activists interpreted *Brown* on their own terms. Defined by their historical and cultural experiences, Puerto Ricans made the marker of language, not race, their site of action. This effectively challenged the black-white conception of segregation in New York and forced city education officials to include Puerto Ricans in municipal desegregation efforts. Simultaneously, the reinterpretation of *Brown* revealed the determination of the Puerto Rican community to demand equal educational opportunity for their children. Examining *Brown* from the perspective of New York City and its Puerto Rican community demonstrates how a complete assessment of the decision's full impact has only begun.

## Neighborhood Schools

The Second World War and its aftermath brought forth two of the largest demographic changes in the history of the northern United States: the African American Great Migration from the South and the Puerto Rican Great Migration from the island.[4] Because of wartime employment opportunities, between 1940 and 1950 the population of African Americans in New York rose from 328,000 to 750,000.[5] Similarly, 58,500 Puerto Ricans had migrated to the city by 1954, bringing the size of the community to 254,880. A decade earlier, Puerto Ricans numbered in the city only 61,463, and any movement from the island was negligible in official census records.[6] As many European immigrants once had, African Americans and Puerto Ricans arrived in New York City sharing dreams of economic opportunity.[7] Like earlier immigrants, both groups settled into racial and ethnic enclaves, sometimes by choice but most often because institutionalized housing discrimination provided no alternative.[8] As a result, racial and ethnic residential segregation became further entrenched in New York's demographic fabric.

Neighborhood segregation inevitably translated into segregated public schools. To address this situation, city educators and urban planners organized neighborhood schools with four goals in mind: cheap, safe transportation of children; a small school population; learning in a familiar environment; and a close relationship between school and community,[9] a notion strongly supported by the New York State Education Department.[10] State administrators believed that neighborhood schools promoted important educational values, which in turn led to more effective participation by parents and other supportive citizens.[11] Commenting on the importance of neighborhood schools to the life of the city, the state's commissioner of education, James Allen, wrote: "The present difficulty is in the changing character of many neighborhoods, not in the concept itself. . . . It will take time to correct this situation, to restore racial balance in these areas. In the meantime, the school is the agency that can do something about the problem, which can be modified to overcome the injustices caused by segregation and achieve the educational and social values inherent in integration."[12] Likewise, parents saw neighborhood-based schools as an integral part of community networks and thus fiercely protected their continued existence.

Despite their usefulness, neighborhood schools obviated any implementation of proposed integration efforts in New York City. New York State offered little help in this area, placing all the responsibility on individual school districts.[13] In response, the city took steps to promote educational initiatives rather than address segregation as a systemic issue. For a decade after the *Brown* decision, special service programs such as the "Demonstration Guidance Program" and "Higher Horizons" preoccupied school administrators. While these programs attempted to equalize city schools through additional funding, remedial instruction, counseling, and other special services, little was done to actually desegregate schools.[14] At the heart of the matter were different understandings among administrators and parents of the place that neighborhood schools occupied in the integration process.

While administrators understood neighborhood schools as traditional, safe, and convenient, African American and Puerto Rican parents also expected educational quality. They were keenly aware that such schools tended to be available only outside their own neighborhoods. While parents laid great stress on improving their local schools, they nevertheless reserved the option of placing their children elsewhere until this improvement took place. Such action, however, remained a last resort. African American and Puerto Rican parents would have preferred improvements in their neighborhood schools to transfers and busing. This is why integration plans like Open Enrollment and free transfer plans, or one-way busing, did not work. Instead they exacerbated tensions and were seen by parents as an attempt to circumvent real change.

Parents eventually turned to school boycotts.[15] Pockets of chaos erupted as parents and administrators clashed over which changes needed to take place and how. In 1958 African American parents in Harlem withdrew their children from public schools and created their own freedom school. They rejected busing, the Board of Education's only proposed remedy for inferior, overcrowded facilities. As the movement for integration grew in the early 1960s, boycotts became a powerful negotiating tool.[16] The largest occurred in February 1964, when nearly 500,000 students stayed away from school.[17]

As African American and Puerto Rican parents fought on their children's behalf, school administrators began to criticize the increasing rate of de facto segregation in the ten years following *Brown*. In early 1965 Irving Anker, principal of Benjamin Franklin High School and later the city's schools chancellor, wrote: "The implications for northern public school de facto segregation are most serious because there appears to be a population pattern forcing changes in the schools quite independent of the policies of any one board of education."[18] Recognizing the declining number of white students, administrators increasingly saw the futility of the Board of Education's integration efforts. As Anker stated, "It becomes more and more apparent that each new plan is but a new act of desperation. Failure to recognize this as the central issue—keeping a reasonable proportion of whites in the public schools—will result in continuing school segregation."[19]

In the midst of these disputes, Commissioner Allen ordered the city's superintendent of schools, Calvin Gross, to assume all accountability in matters of school desegregation. In 1963 Allen wrote to Gross, "At this stage the initiative for planning the means for eliminating imbalance is in your hands." He also noted, "Few problems facing the schools in our State and elsewhere have ever given local school officials the opportunity to use their imagination, initiative, leadership and resources in the way this one does."[20] Allen presented desegregation to Gross as an opportunity rather than a problem for local school officials. He ordered the school board to reflect on its progress toward integration. However, Allen continued to define an integrated school as one that that was more than 50 percent white, an impossibility in a racially heterogeneous New York City. Calvin Gross and the Board of Education struggled with this task. This period of confusion marked the beginning of a new regional discussion on racial classification within a black-white dichotomy. Puerto Ricans, like Mexican Americans in Texas who also confronted a narrow racial classification system in the wake of *Brown*, listened to this discussion: despite attempts to marginalize them they took it upon themselves to develop a system for defining racial groups and how they fit into the city's desegregation efforts.[21]

Race and Puerto Ricans

In 1963 the New York City Board of Education published a report entitled "Progress Towards Integration and Plans for the Immediate Future." This report divided school integration goals into two categories: equality of educational and vocational opportunities and the promotion of ethnic inte-gration.[22] Significantly, the report discussed Puerto Ricans and African Americans as one group without distinction. For Gross, the report proved inconclusive because it did not provide clear data; one could not tell which group—Puerto Rican or African American—benefited from the proposed solutions.

Seeking clarification, Gross inquired about the data, which in the past had been collected and reported only for African Americans. Allen replied: "Although my request contemplated information on schools with 50% or more Negroes only, in order to have the total picture for New York City, data on Puerto Rican pupils is also necessary. For each of the schools, report the number and percent of each category, namely Negro, Puerto Rican, Other."[23] His response illustrates several key points: the confusion caused by the city's racial classification system; the difficulty of factoring Puerto Ricans into the state's integration plans; and the slow pace at which the city's demographic reality was officially recognized. That noted, the situa-tion in New York City had compelled Allen to alter his previous request by including Puerto Ricans. This marked the beginning of an effort at the administrative level to effectively address the city's diverse population and was a sign that the black-white parameters of the desegregation debate were beginning to expand.

Simultaneously, Puerto Rican officials in the Migration Division Office of Puerto Rico in New York internally inquired about the steps toward integra-tion. Ralph S. Rosas, who worked in the office, questioned the data given for Puerto Ricans in the "Progress Towards Integration" report. Though he be-lieved in the importance of the report, particularly on the instructional front, he still found the data insufficient, as Puerto Ricans and African Americans remained grouped together. In December 1963 Rosas asked the director of the Migration Division Office, Joseph Monserrat, to inquire about the data and find out which programs specifically targeted and assisted Puerto Rican children. There was apparently no response to this memo.[24]

In the following years, internal debates continued regarding Puerto Ri-cans and their place in many of the city's proposed projects. Throughout the highest levels of the New York State Education Department, the diffi-culty of distinguishing between Puerto Ricans and African Americans re-mained a troubling one. As late as 1968 Lorne H. Woollatt questioned the categorization of Puerto Ricans. Seeking to comply with a data request from the Office of Civil Rights, Woollatt asked which of the five categories described Puerto Ricans: Negro, American Indian, Oriental, Spanish Sur-named American, and Other.[25] In a handwritten note, James Allen himself questioned whether the state should classify Puerto Ricans as "other." After further investigation, Allen wrote to Woollatt on 31 May 1968, explaining that according to the U.S. Department of Health, Education and Welfare the category "Spanish Surnamed American" included "persons considered in school or community to be of Mexican, Central American, South American, Cuban, Puerto Rican, Latin American or other Spanish speaking origin."[26] The Spanish-surnamed category, which ultimately encompassed Puerto Ricans, was not an automatic choice for a group that had previously been classified within rigid black-white racial categories. This process of self-reflection slowly pushed education officials in New York to realize that the problem of desegregation existed within a more complicated matrix that included blacks, whites, and Puerto Ricans.

Articulating a Space for Puerto Ricans

City education officials prepared the Allen report after the first major school boycott in February 1964. Its publication promoted ethnic integration, rather than racial integration, as the focal point of desegregation discussions. "We prefer, however, to speak of desegregation rather than integration or ethnic balance," its author noted, "since the segregated school is the evidence of the difficulty and must therefore be the target of the corrective effort."[27] The report defined a public school as ethnically segregated in New York City if in 1963 less than 10 percent of its enrollment was African American, Puerto Rican, or belonging to some other group. The debate of the preceding year over categorizing Puerto Ricans framed the awareness of the administrators. Researchers reached an understanding that racial classification could not encompass whites, African Americans, and Puerto Ricans, and past efforts to classify Puerto Ricans within a black-white binary had proved ineffective. The researchers even cast doubt on their own past data collection—data on which they based their recommendations. In a report entitled *Desegregating the Public Schools* (1964), the New York State Board of Education observed: "The terms, Puerto Rican and White are most doubtful, since most Puerto Ricans were classified as Whites in the 1960 Census. Nevertheless, we employ the three terms, Negro, Puerto Rican, and White on the ground that they are fairly accurate and commonly understood."[28] Nevertheless, uncertainty continued over how to factor Puerto Ricans into the city's integration plans. An outmoded system of racial classification continued to hold sway, even as dramatic demographic changes rendered it increasingly inadequate to the tasks at hand.

The Allen report was marked by a very pessimistic tone regarding the city's desegregation progress. It concluded that Open Enrollment, a plan that offered African American and Puerto Rican students the opportunity to transfer to designated receiving schools which were predominately white, had no significant effect on integration and that at the elementary level it actually increased segregation. The report concluded that this program failed because it depended entirely upon the voluntary choice of African American and Puerto Rican parents.[29] Parents had good reason to hesitate in sending their children into potentially hostile environments. The Free Choice Transfer Policy, a program initiated in 1963 which allowed children in schools with a "high" percentage of African Americans and Puerto Ricans to transfer to any school where space was available, was also considered incapable of reducing the city's level of segregation.[30] The report ended by expressing little hope for future success: "We must conclude that nothing undertaken by the New York City Board of Education since 1954, and nothing proposed since 1963, has contributed or will contribute in any meaningful degree to desegregating the public schools of the city. Each past effort, each current plan, and each projected proposal is either not aimed at reducing segregation or is developed in too limited a fashion to stimulate even slight progress toward desegregation."[31] Nearly a decade after *Brown*, efforts to desegregate New York remained stagnant.

For Puerto Ricans, the turmoil surrounding the efforts of city bureaucrats to create and successfully implement integration plans had an unintended consequence. It created a space for Puerto Ricans to formulate an agenda of their own in support of the needs of their children. Previous studies of ethnic groups in New York have erroneously assumed that Puerto Ricans had no interest in mobilizing around desegregation issues and no influence over the process.[32] Because integration was largely framed in black-white terms, the parameters of the debate did mute the voice of Puerto Ricans. It did not, however, stop their participation. Puerto Ricans remained highly involved in the education of their children and took advantage of every opening, no matter how small, to demand a say in how and under what conditions they would be taught.

A pivotal moment in the efforts of Puerto Rican parents and activists to insert themselves into debates over school integration occurred during the Conference on Integration in the New York City Public Schools, held in 1963 at Columbia University.[33] This event provided Puerto Ricans with a rare public opportunity to voice their own perspective on integration struggles. The goal of the conference was to offer tangible solutions for school integration to the city of New York. Together, the participants advanced the following propositions: the government at all levels must commit itself financially to education so that schools can have flexible policies; foundations need to bear the cost of research; and total community involvement is necessary.[34] Puerto Rican involvement at the Columbia conference was limited in scope. The Office of the Commonwealth of Puerto Rico Migration Division stood as the lone Puerto Rican representative out of twenty participating organizations. Two staff members from the Office of the Commonwealth of Puerto Rico, Max Wolff and Rosa Estades, sat on the thirty-one-person conference planning committee. Until the 1960s New York City viewed this office as the official spokesperson for the Puerto Rican migrant community. However limited, its presence at least ensured that the perspective of Puerto Ricans would be represented at the conference.

Born in Puerto Rico, Joseph Monserrat was one of the conference's eight principal speakers. Like thousands of other Puerto Ricans, Monserrat migrated to New York City after the Second World War. He graduated from Benjamin Franklin High School and later studied social work at the New School for Social Research and Columbia University. An active member of the Puerto Rican political leadership, he led the Migration Division Office and sat on the New York City Board of Education. Monserrat promoted active participation in the city's pluralistic ethnic culture.[35] In his conference presentation, he confronted the ambiguous place of Puerto Ricans in the city's racial classification system. "I welcome this opportunity to discuss with you what has been called a 'Puerto Rican View of School Integration,'" he began. "This title would seem to imply that Puerto Ricans view the question of school integration somewhat differently from others. As a matter of fact—we do."[36] This introduction initiated a discussion that distinguished between two minority communities in New York City: Puerto Rican and African American. Monserrat inserted a Puerto Rican view of race into the desegregation debate that until then discussions had sorely lacked.

As his first goal, Monserrat demonstrated the varied historical experiences of African Americans and Puerto Ricans. "In a multi-cultured democratic society such as ours," he noted, "integration must not and cannot mean submerging or forgetting the specific content and values of one's own past, whether as an individual or as a member of a group."[37] Puerto Ricans did not and could not conform to America's existing conceptions of race: "In discussing the issues of integration in New York City schools, Negroes and Puerto Ricans are referred to constantly almost as if they were one and the same. They are not. Unlike the Negro, we Puerto Ricans are not a race. We are, at most, an ethnic group. As such, some of us are 'white,' some of us are 'Negro' and some of us are so-called 'mixed.'"[38] The grouping of Puerto Ricans with African Americans marginalized the Puerto Rican voice in discussions of school integration.

As Monserrat explained, categorizing Puerto Ricans as a race was the product of the postwar migration to New York City and the resulting efforts to "fit" Puerto Ricans into state bureaucrats' integration plans for the city's schools. He explained: "It was not until after 1946 that we became a 'race,' that an identifiable descriptive stereotype had been created for us. In 1954 we discovered that our children, along with Negro children, were being described as 'X' children who attended 'X' schools. There also were some other children who were called 'Y' children and they attended 'Y' schools. We also learned at that time, that when the 'X' schools were compared with the 'Y' schools it was discovered that the 'X' school buildings were older and somewhat less well-equipped than the 'Y' school buildings; also, that there were fewer regular teachers in the 'X' schools."[39]

The racial identity ascribed to Puerto Ricans by state officials, according to Monserrat, proved not only inadequate to addressing the particular needs of Puerto Ricans in school debates. Like Mexican American activists in Texas, Monserrat found that the classification also led to a fundamentally flawed strategy for confronting segregation. "From a 'racial' point of view," he noted, "the all-Negro school is in fact completely segregated. On the other hand, because of the racial background of the Puerto Rican child, an all–Puerto Rican school may well be, from a 'racial' point of view, the most integrated of schools."[40] Acknowledging the distinctiveness of Puerto Rican racial ideology was necessary for *Brown* and school integration to be truly effective.

Monserrat's discussion foreshadowed those of recent scholars of Puerto Ricans in articulating and historicizing Puerto Rican conceptions of race. Once in New York City, Puerto Ricans encountered a system of racial classification that differed in substantive ways from the system they lived with in Puerto Rico. As Clara Rodriguez explains in her seminal essay "The Rainbow People," "in Puerto Rico, racial identification was subordinate to cultural identification, while in the U.S., racial identification, to a large extent, determines cultural identification. Thus Puerto Ricans were first Puerto Ricans, then *blanco/a* (white), *moreno/a* (dark), and so on, while Americans were first white or black, then Italian, West Indian or whatever. This is not to say that Puerto Ricans did not have a racial identification but rather that cultural identification superseded it."[41] For Monserrat, the privileging of race in debates over public school education submerged the broader concerns of Puerto Ricans that flowed not from their understanding of themselves as a race, but from their understanding of themselves as a distinctive people, with a distinctive culture tied closely to their language.

As Juan Flores has argued, the Great Migration was a defining historical event in the shaping of Puerto Ricans' consciousness of themselves as a people and a nation. Homage to Taino (indigenous) and African roots and a reverence for the island of Puerto Rico as a homeland played important roles in the shaping of this consciousness. Flores maintains, however, that the Spanish language was the foremost cultural symbol and theme in organizing the community in New York City.[42] Although African Americans and Puerto Ricans had much in common—the experience of migration, ties to a real and imagined African past, as well as rampant discrimination in access to adequate housing and schooling in New York City—Puerto Ricans' particular identification with and desire to preserve the Spanish language in their new geographic setting marked a significant point of departure. In New York City, loyalty to the Spanish language became an important marker of Puerto Rican identity. Through the issue of language, more so than race, Puerto Ricans began to assert themselves in city politics, particularly in relationship to debates about equality in public school education.

Puerto Ricans' emphasis on language marked a key difference in how they understood and defined the struggle in the city's public schools in relationship to African Americans. At the practical, day-to-day or grassroots level, however, Puerto Ricans and African Americans found much in common. The renowned Puerto Rican author Piri Thomas recalls in his memoir how white New Yorkers: "couldn't decide whether I was a nigger or a spic so they called me both."[43] Thomas, who like many Puerto Ricans shared physical characteristics with African Americans, still identified himself as Puerto Rican, even when others failed to do so. Despite clear cultural differences, the shared social positions of Puerto Ricans and African Americans led to cooperative efforts that informed Puerto Rican activism in significant ways. In 1964, for example, when the chairman of the education committee of the Brooklyn NAACP, Milton Galamison, and other black leaders led a boycott against the city's public schools, a handful of Puerto Rican leaders, including the community activist Evelina Antonetty, joined them. The experience of participating in the African American civil rights struggle, as Juan Gonzalez has recently argued, played an important role in the development of Puerto Rican leadership.[44]

Such participation also sharpened the perception among Puerto Ricans that they needed to create their own sociopolitical vehicles to address concerns specific to their community. In the mid-1960s, as debates over school integration and equality continued, Puerto Rican parents and community leaders confronted the herculean task of forming their own educational and political agenda for progress. They began to build neighborhood institutions with the aid of federal anti-poverty funds, joining other grassroots organizers in challenging racial and class injustice.[45] When Monserrat spoke at Columbia, he challenged Puerto Ricans to join a crusade for improving their children's educational opportunities. Puerto Rican parents responded and in doing so came into their own as a political force, articulat-

ing their own political agenda out of the turmoil surrounding debates over
school integration.


## A Community in Action

Examining the efforts of the United Bronx Parents, Inc. (UBP), demonstrates how a migrant community emerged as a viable political force. Established in 1965 by Puerto Rican parents in the South Bronx, the UBP was a
grassroots, self-help organization that focused specifically on correcting the
unresponsiveness of the city's public schools to the needs of Puerto Rican
children, who had been neglected by the various and ineffective integration
plans launched by the city. Since 1957 the number of African Americans in
public schools had risen by 53 percent and of Puerto Ricans by 38 percent,
while whites' share of the total student population had decreased from
68 percent to 53 percent in 1964.[46] Despite an increase in enrollment
numbers, city schools failed to meet the needs of Puerto Rican children.

The UBP responded to this neglect by formalizing its service agenda and
increasing membership through a grant from the Department of Health,
Education and Welfare. By 1967 increased funding allowed for expanding
UBP services into the areas of health care, housing, welfare, and juvenile
justice, although schools remained the primary focus. These additional
funds enabled the UBP to establish satellite offices throughout New York.
Through its Parent Leadership Training Program, each branch remained focused on the needs of children and parental empowerment.[47] As its founder
Antonetty explained it, the UBP was created to address the concerns of
parents and provide the community with "expertise, insight, new information, resources, criticism and contacts."[48] Keenly aware of the fragility of the
impoverished, migrant community being served, Antonetty stressed the
flexibility of the group. The continued arrival of migrants from Puerto Rico
necessitated an accommodating approach to community issues and a respectful adherence to their cultural norms and language. Like many grassroots organizations during the War on Poverty, the UBP focused on alle-
viating immediate needs while working toward long-term improvement.

The UBP's plan for improving the education of Puerto Rican children was
to create an effective monitoring system involving knowledgeable parents.
As a result, the UBP concentrated on training parents to advocate, even
agitate, for their children in schools. While it served the varied needs of
Puerto Ricans, its principal work involved class and case advocacy.[49] Antonetty emphasized to parents and community activists the significance of
education to unlocking upward social mobility.[50] The UBP placed the re-

sponsibility of raising educational standards on the parents themselves. One organizational flyer, "Homework: How Can It Help Your Child Learn," advised parents to participate in their children's homework and to be aware of the assignments their children received. Antonetty encouraged parents to demand that their children have the best educational experience and that the schools set the highest standards for their children.[51] Among other activities, Puerto Ricans openly criticized sociological studies that had labeled their children as "disabled learners" and "culturally deprived."[52] Through her writing, Antonetty challenged presumed notions of Puerto Rican inferiority and inability to learn. The UBP encouraged parents to expect equal opportunity and a good education as the standard for their children. In this sense the UBP resembled educational advocacy groups for African Americans, which used educational reform as a mechanism for larger political objectives. By the late 1960s the UBP was getting results.

A principal component of the UBP's effort was empowering parents within the public school buildings themselves. Too often, school buildings were a bastion of intimidation. The UBP encouraged parents to view themselves as the equal of their children's teachers and to assume ownership of their community schools. Bilingual organizational flyers instructed parents on "How to Prepare for a Good Parent-Teacher Conference" and pushed them to view schools as a community institution. "A Good School Involves Its Students in the Life of Their Community," read one flyer, and "[t]he community gives life to the school." Antonetty worked to formalize the process of getting Puerto Rican parents involved in schools and helped to inform schools of community expectations for them. As the UBP understood it, "Parents and the general community should have major decision-making, not merely advisory, power on all levels—from local school policy decisions to national legislation and regulation."[53]

The UBP pressed for change in New York City public schools on a number of fronts. A critical concern was that teachers treat students with respect and sensitivity and that schools meet their particular needs, especially with respect to language. In addition to urging parents to become more deeply involved in the life of the schools, to question teachers' methods, and to intervene on their children's behalf, the UBP charged parents with protecting their children from ill-fitting desegregation policies. More specifically, the UBP supported efforts to ensure bilingual education and attention to Puerto Rican culture in the public school curriculum. The UBP directed parents to confront the learning barriers faced by their children. This effort centered on the preservation of Spanish as an essential component of Puerto Rican cultural identity. The UBP called on parents to demand bilingual and bicultural programs in the city's schools. It also called attention to the lack of Puerto Ricans in school administrative and teaching posts. Taking a page from the African American civil rights movement, the UBP encouraged parents to pressure the federal government for funds and the local government for representation in decisions concerning their children's schooling.[54]

The UBP saw the law as a means to educate and mobilize the community. It actively monitored developments in the courts and legislatures that affected the educational future of Puerto Rican children. It set out to train its staff and the community on their rights in the new legal environment after the U.S. Supreme Court held in *Lau v. Nichols* (1974) that the absence of remedial language assistance denied a meaningful education to Chinese-speaking students in San Francisco and after ASPIRA, a prominent Puerto Rican political and educational organization in New York City, in 1974 won a consent decree from the New York City Board of Education which established standards for bilingual education.[55] Antonetty took the lead in training parents in their legal rights and those of their children. By emphasizing the significance of these cases, the UBP instilled in Puerto Rican parents a sense of legal rights consciousness that translated into demands for an educational system reflective of their social and cultural needs.

Like the Student Nonviolent Coordinating Committee in the South, the UBP trained parents to help each other rather than depend on the agency to advocate on their behalf. As a result, parent organizers did the majority of the advocacy work as volunteers rather than as paid professionals. The UBP provided the environment of trust and the knowledge necessary to empower parents on behalf of their children, while community members learned to work together to protect their children in the city's educational system. By the late 1970s not only did the UBP advocate bilingual and bicultural education for its community, but it also campaigned for community control of schools, easier access by parents to their children's school records, a reduction in suspension cases so that more children would remain in school, and an increase in educational options, including a more liberal transfer policy and free bus passes.[56]

Three decades after the mass arrival of Puerto Ricans to New York, the UBP helped Puerto Rican parents to develop a stance in educational politics. The demand of Puerto Rican parents—the right to determine and secure the best educational experience for their children—did not differ from those of other parents. As Puerto Ricans entered the schools, bilingual education became the vehicle through which to express ethnic identity and particular concerns. It was the cornerstone in their fight for educational equality because they believed it guaranteed the best schooling experience possible for their children, who had limited English proficiency.

Bilingual education also guaranteed that the Spanish language and Puerto Rican culture would not be viewed as a hindrance to success in the broader life of the community. In part, it was a matter of recognition and cultural validation. Parents saw Spanish as "their language." The teaching of that language was viewed as a connection between their homes and the public schools. To be fully recognized in the system of public education, the Spanish language had to become part of the dialogue between teachers, administrators, schools, and parents. More importantly, for a child to succeed, to be educated in a supportive and productive learning environment, Puerto Rican parents felt that the home language had to be introduced as an educational tool. For many Puerto Ricans, empowerment in schools and the broader political life of New York City required that the Spanish language be a central part of their children's educational experience. It was a matter of educational quality and cultural inclusiveness.[57]

As Puerto Ricans migrated in growing numbers to New York City after the Second World War, they arrived in a city that like the nation as a whole was grappling with a long history of racial exclusion and discrimination. In 1954 *Brown v. Board of Education* elevated the question of Jim Crow segregation and equality in public schools to a new level of debate and conflict. The debate was too often couched in uniquely southern terms and the problem viewed too frequently through the lens of white and black. Puerto Ricans soon found themselves deeply immersed in questions of integration and equality in the public school system in New York City. Because of the confining terms of the debate, Puerto Ricans battled to make themselves heard and to develop a political agenda that addressed their specific concerns as a community. Through the UBP Puerto Ricans worked to personalize the debate and reform efforts that flowed from *Brown*. They worked to liberate themselves from the black-white binary which regulated debates about school reform in the early 1960s. More importantly, they worked to liberate their own children from discriminatory practices. Members of the UBP addressed the need for school integration on their own terms, eschewing the racially polarized strategies of the city's education officials. Instead, they worked to persuade parents to advocate on their children's behalf by focusing on the specific cultural needs of the Puerto Rican community, especially the need for bilingual and bicultural education. Puerto Rican participation in the early integration battles of New York was a learning experience. In a short time, community groups, such as the UBP, became full-fledged participants in the educational politics of the country. Through the UBP, parents demanded cultural recognition and demanded that their children receive the best education possible.

The UBP is an example not only of Puerto Rican creativity and activism in

New York City but of the multifaceted impact of *Brown*. The significance of the decision transgressed both regional and racial boundaries. While *Brown* dismantled Jim Crow segregation in public schools, a highly visible manifestation of structural inequality, it simultaneously provoked a more wide-reaching debate about education and equality in America at large. It brought to the surface a whole range of issues of concern to racial and ethnic communities in addition to southern African Americans. Though this chapter focuses on New York City, the battles that took place there demonstrate the importance of rethinking *Brown* and its legacy in light of the demographic diversity of every American city. The issues of segregation and desegregation, education, access, and equality have touched the lives of many. Contrary to previous popular and academic assumptions, Puerto Ricans were active in struggles around school integration in the wake of *Brown*. If the terms of the debate muted their voices or marginalized their concerns, they battled in myriad ways to change these terms and influence outcomes. They formed their own political and cultural organizations, raised their voices, and participated in educational politics less than thirty years after their mass arrival in the continental United States. While unique, the Puerto Rican experience reminds us of the need to broaden our geographic and race-based conceptualizations of the meaning and consequences of *Brown*. Only in doing so will we come to a full appreciation of the historic decision.

## Notes

I would like to thank Jeremy Adelman, Carlos Decena, Sarah Igo, Kevin Kruse, Peter Lau, Felix Matos Rodríguez, Elizabeth Todd, and Chad Williams for their assistance and encouragement throughout the writing of this chapter.

1  *New York Times*, 24 December 1954.

2  Diane Ravitch, *The Great School War: A History of the New York City Public Schools* (Baltimore: Johns Hopkins University Press, 2000), 252.

3  The startling exception has been the work on Mexican American children in public schools. See: Guadalupe San Miguel, *"Let All of Them Take Heed": Mexican Americans and the Campaign for Educational Equality in Texas, 1910–1981* (Austin: University of Texas Press, 1987); Benjamin Marquez, *LULAC: The Evolution of a Mexican American Political Organization* (Austin: University of Texas Press, 1993); George Sánchez, *Becoming Mexican American* (New York: Oxford University Press, 1993); David Gutiérrez, *Walls and Mirrors: Mexican Americans, Mexican Immigrants, and the Politics of Ethnicity* (Berkeley: University of California Press, 1995).

4  Oscar Handlin, *The Newcomers: Negroes and Puerto Ricans in a Changing Metropolis* (Cambridge: Harvard University Press, 1959); Virginia Sánchez-Korrol,

*From Colonia to Community: The History of Puerto Ricans in New York City* (Berkeley: University of California Press, 1994).

5  Ravitch, *The Great School War*, 242.

6  Sánchez-Korrol, *From Colonia to Community*, 224. The period between 1946 and 1964 is known as the Great Migration. During these years the largest number of Puerto Ricans migrated from the island. Their communities grew in East Harlem, the South Bronx, and the Lower East Side. For more on this see Clara Rodriguez, *Puerto Ricans: Born in the USA* (Winchester, Mass.: Unwin Hyman, 1989).

7  While other European immigrants have been able to go through a whitening process and integrate themselves according to their whiteness, this has not happened en masse for Puerto Ricans. For a concise summary on all that is white see Peter Kolchin, "Whiteness Studies: The New History of Race in America," *Journal of American History* 89 (June 2002): 154–73; Noel Ignatiev, *How the Irish Became White* (New York: Routledge, 1995); David R. Roediger, *The Wages of Whiteness: Race and the Making of the American Working Class* (New York: Verso, 1991); Matthew Frye Jacobson, *Whiteness of a Different Color: European Immigrants and the Alchemy of Race* (Cambridge: Harvard University Press, 1998).

8  For early accounts on housing discrimination see Leonard Covello, "A Community-Centered School and the Problem of Housing," *Educational Forum* 7 (January 1943): 133–43; Oscar Handlin, *The Newcomers: Negroes and Puerto Ricans in a Changing Metropolis* (Cambridge: Harvard University Press, 1959); Robert W. Peebles, "Interview with Leonard Covello," *Urban Review* 3 (January 1969): 13–18.

9  For more on neighborhood schools see Allan Blackman, "Planning and the Neighborhood School," *Learning Together: A Book on Integrated Education*, ed. Meyer Weinberg (Chicago: Integrated Education Associates, 1964), 49–56.

10  After making a commitment to integration in 1955 the New York City Board of Education created a Commission on Integration to investigate zoning and teacher assignments. As the commission began hearings, the Public Education Association launched a census on the student population. Board of Education of the City of New York, *Toward Greater Opportunity: A Progress Report from the Superintendent of Schools to the Board of Education* (New York, June 1960), 1.

11  State Education Commissioner's Advisory Committee on Human Relations, "Guiding Principles for Dealing with Defacto Segregation in Public Schools" (Albany, N.Y., 17 June 1963), 3.

12  James E. Allen Jr. to Calvin E. Gross, 2 August 1963, transcript in Allen's files at the State Archives, Albany, N.Y.

13  In 1963 the Board of Education wrote: "Participation by the local communities themselves in developing and working out the pattern to accomplish these objectives will give strength to our program. If the proposals for progress come from the communities themselves, they will then have ample reason to see that these proposals work and will find satisfaction in their accomplishments. Therefore, every opportunity will be given to the communities to work out their own

destinies without premature action from central headquarters." Board of Education of the City of New York, *Progress toward Integration* (New York, December 1963), 3.

14 In 1956 Dr. Kenneth Clark's subcommittee of the Commission of Integration initiated the Demonstration Guidance Program. This program sought to equalize schools by providing additional services that would improve academic achievement. The Higher Horizon program began in 1959. Seen as a tool to equalize educational opportunities, this program offered remedial instruction, cultural activities, and extra counseling to all children beginning in the third grade. However, because of insufficient funds few students benefited. For more on this see Ravitch, *The Great School War*, 260–61.

15 Nathan Glazer and Daniel Patrick Moynihan, *Beyond the Melting Pot: The Negroes, Puerto Ricans, Jews, Italians, and Irish of New York City* (Cambridge: M I T Press, 1963), 46–47.

16 Meyer Weinberg, *A Chance to Learn: A History of Education in the United States* (Cambridge: Cambridge University Press, 1977), 114.

17 Leonard Buder, "Schools in City Will Open Today Despite Boycott," *New York Times*, 14 September 1964, 1.

18 Irving Anker, "Our Northern Cities: Toward Integration or Segregation?," *Strengthening Democracy* (New York: Board of Education of the City of New York, February 1965).

19 *Id.*

20 James E. Allen Jr. to Calvin E. Gross, 2 August 1963, New York State Education Department, Albany, 4.

21 The Mexican American struggle in Texas was multifaceted and changed over time. From early efforts by the League of United Latin American Citizens (L U L AC) to classify their children as "white" to a radical grassroots switch in the early 1970s seeking a "nonwhite" racial status, their struggle is not so much about identity as it is a continual battle against discrimination. A discussion on the shift in consciousness as well as historical insight can be found in Guadalupe San Miguel's *Brown, Not White: School Integration and the Chicano Movement in Houston* (College Station: Texas A&M University Press, 2001).

22 Board of Education of the City of New York, *Progress toward Integration*, 1.

23 James E. Allen Jr. to Calvin E. Gross, 2 August 1963, New York State Education Department, Albany, 1.

24 Subsequent reports do not distinguish between the groups. Memo from Ralph S. Rosas to Joseph Monserrat, Commonwealth of Puerto Rico Migration Division Office, New York, 19 December 1963.

25 Memo from Lorne H. Woollatt to James E. Allen Jr., New York State Education Department, Albany, 10 May 1968, James E. Allen Papers, New York State Archives, Albany.

26 Memo from James E. Allen Jr. to Lorne H. Woollatt, New York State Education Department, Albany, 31 May 1968, Allen Papers, New York State Archives, Albany.

27 New York State Board of Education, *Desegregating the Public Schools* (Albany, N.Y., 1964), 1.

28 *Id.* at 2.

29 For example, in September 1964 about 110,000 elementary pupils were offered the opportunity to transfer yet only 2,000 applied and only 1,800 ultimately transferred, or less than 2 percent of those eligible. The authors of the report found that the number of segregated, predominantly African American and Puerto Rican schools in New York City increased over five years, from 12 percent to 22 percent at the elementary level, from 10 percent to 19 percent at the junior high level, and from 0 to 2 percent at the senior high school level. About three-quarters of the city's schools showed no change in their percentage of Negro and Puerto Rican students. *Id.* at 4–5.

30 *Id.* at 7.

31 *Id.* at 8.

32 Glazer and Moynihan, *Beyond the Melting Pot*, 47.

33 Gordon J. Klopf and Israel A. Laster, *Integrating the Urban School: Proceedings* (New York: Teachers College, 1963).

34 *Id.* at 10–11. This was very unlike the many other academic conferences held in New York City throughout the 1960s. See Proceedings of the Invitational Conference on Northern School Desegregation (New York: Yeshiva University, 1962); Hubert H. Humphrey, *School Desegregation: Documents and Commentaries* (New York: Thomas Y. Crowell, 1964).

35 For more on Joseph Monserrat see Michael Lapp, "Managing Migration: the Migration Division of Puerto Rico" (diss., Johns Hopkins University, 1990).

36 Joseph Monserrat, "School Integration: A Puerto Rican View," *Integrating the Urban School: Proceedings*, 60.

37 *Id.* at 64.

38 *Id.* at 66–67.

39 *Id.* at 65.

40 *Id.* at 13.

41 Rodriguez, *Puerto Ricans*, 52

42 Juan Flores, " 'Qué assimilated, brother, yo soy asimilao': The Structuring of Puerto Rican Identity," *Divided Borders: Essays on Puerto Rican Identity* (Houston: Arte Publico, 1993); Juan Flores, "Broken English Memories: Languages in the Trans-Colony," *From Bomba to Hip-Hop: Puerto Rican Culture and Latino Identity* (New York: Columbia University Press, 2000), especially 57.

43 Interview with Piri Thomas, cited in Clara E. Rodriguez, "The Rainbow People," *Puerto Ricans Born in the USA* (Boulder: Westview, 1989), 272.

44 David Rodgers, *New York City and the Politics of School Desegregation* (New York: Center for Urban Education, 1968), 139–40; Juan Gonzalez, *Harvest of Empire* (New York: Penguin, 2000).

45 Another example of mobilization by Puerto Rican parents is documented in Tom Roderick's *A School of Our Own: Parents. Power, and Community at the East Harlem Block Schools* (New York: Teachers College Press, 2001).

46 Anker, "Our Northern Cities," 1.

47 Evelina Antonetty, "History of United Bronx Parents, Inc.," 5–6, United Bronx Parents Records, Center for Puerto Rican Studies in New York City, box 2, folder 14 (hereafter cited as "UBP Records").

48 Antonetty, "History of United Bronx Parents, Inc," 7.

49 See Sánchez-Korrol, *From Colonia to Community*.

50 *Id.* at 10.

51 United Bronx Parents, Inc., "Homework: How Can It Help Your Child Learn," UBP Records, box 2, folder 11.

52 National Conference of Puerto Ricans, Mexican-Americans, and Educators on the Special Educational Needs of Urban Puerto Rican Youth, *"Hemos trabajado bien": A Report* (New York, 1968).

53 United Bronx Parents, Inc., "How to Prepare for a Good Parent-Teacher Conference" and "A Good School Involves Its Students in the Life of Their Community," UBP Records, box 2, folder 11; Emile Schepers, *Law and Community Advocacy: A Case Description of the Use of the Law by United Bronx Parents* (Chicago: Center for New Schools, 1978), UBP Records, box 2, folder 14.

54 Schepers, *Law and Community Advocacy*. For more on the efforts of Puerto Ricans in reforming public schools see Melissa Rivera and Pedro Pedraza, "The Spirit of Transformation: an Education Reform Movement in a New York City Latino/a Community," *Puerto Rican Students in U.S. Schools*, ed. Sonia Nieto (Mahwah, N.J.: Lawrence Erlbaum, 2000), 223–45.

55 Schepers, *Law and Community Advocacy*, 9.

56 *Id.* at 22–25.

57 Catherine E. Walsh, *Pedagogy and the Struggle for Voice: Issues of Language, Power, and Schooling for Puerto Ricans* (New York: Bergin and Garvey, 1991); Ana Celia Zentella, *Growing Up Bilingual* (Oxford: Basil Blackwell, 1997). For more on the language and public schooling for Latinos see Antonio Darder, Rodolfo D. Torres, and Henry Gutiérrez, eds., *Latinos and Education: A Critical Reader* (New York: Routledge, 1997).

# PART IV

# Life, Law, and Culture in Post-*Brown* America

WALDO E. MARTIN JR.

# "Stretching Out"

## Living and Remembering *Brown*,

## 1945–1970

Get an education. It's the one thing the white man

can't take away from you.

On 17 May 1954 Melba Pattillo was a seventh-grade student at the all-black Dunbar Junior High School in Little Rock, Arkansas. That same Monday, the Supreme Court announced its epochal ruling in *Brown v. Board of Education*, declaring segregated schools for black and white children unlawful, overturning its own decision in *Plessy v. Ferguson* (1896) and enshrining school integration as a national ideal. For young Melba, however, the moment was fraught with tension, not jubilation. She later recalled: "The adults around me behaved so strangely that their images became a freeze-frame, forever preserved in my mind. I learned lessons on that day that I will remember for the rest of my life." As her teacher told the class about the just-announced decision, "she appeared frightened and nervous" and "spoke breathlessly." To her friend Carl's query—"Does this mean we have to go to school with white people?"—the teacher replied: "Yes, maybe. But you needn't concern yourself with that." Melba remembered that her teacher, as she dismissed the class for the day, had a facial expression that betrayed anguish rather than the celebratory mood that she claimed the decision should evoke.[1]

On her way home, Melba took her usual "shortcut across a vacant block, through a grassy field filled with persimmon trees . . . [where] ripened fruit littered the ground to make walking a hazardous, slippery adventure." As she started to trek across the persimmon field, she encountered "a big white man, even taller than my father, broad and huge, like a wrestler," who tried to lure her into his car with candy. When she refused and took off running, he ran after her, "talking about niggers wanting to go to school with his children and how he wasn't going to stand for it." When she stumbled over an untied shoelace and fell, he attempted to rape her. As she bravely fought off the vicious attack, her enraged attacker shouted: "I'll show you niggers the Supreme Court can't run my life."

Marissa, an older, mentally challenged girl who had tormented Melba and her friends in the past, now came to her rescue, beating the rapist on the head with her leather book-bag, enabling both of them to escape to the safety of Melba's home. There, soothed by her Grandma India and her parents, Melba came to understand that she had just been the victim of an attempted rape, a crime about which she previously knew nothing. She took a cleansing bath; her Grandma burned the clothes she had been wearing; and after much discussion, the grown-ups decided not to report the attempted rape to the police. Seeing her father cry for the first time, Melba took in his tear-soaked words: "We ain't gonna call the law. Those white police are liable to do something worse to her than what already happened."[2]

Many prayers later Melba was able to handle better the trauma that the attempted rape had caused. She confided in her diary: "It's important for me to read the newspaper, every single day God sends, even if I have to spend my own nickel to buy it. I have to keep up with what the men on the Supreme Court are doing. That way I can stay home on the day the justices vote decisions that make white men want to rape me."[3] Nevertheless, when her teacher later asked for volunteers who would be willing to integrate Central High, which was all white, Melba signed on. In short order, she became one of the Little Rock Nine, all of whom endured extreme white hostility and violence for their valiant efforts. As the title of her autobiography proclaimed: "Warriors Don't Cry."

In the conventional historical narrative of the modern civil rights struggle, both the *Brown* decision (1954, 1955) and the Montgomery bus boycott (1955) are awesome, inspiring triumphs. Between these two freedom struggle highs of the mid-1950s sits an equally salient low: the gruesome lynching of Emmett Till, a black male teenager, in Money, Mississippi. Whereas *Brown* showed the nation's highest court responding affirmatively to escalating black demands for an end to statutory Jim Crow and the bus boycott showed blacks effectively organizing to overcome Jim Crow on public buses, Till's lynching stands in dreadful counterpoint, a terrifying example of extreme racist white opposition to any black gesture seen as violating Jim Crow mores. A searing interruption of the triumphal narrative of liberation, Till's lynching is a tragic reminder that any honest narrative of African American liberation and progress must fully treat the perils, costs, and setbacks as well as the prospects, benefits, and triumphs—the downside as well as the upside.

African American memories and stories of Till's lynching and its fallout, set temporally against memories and stories of the earlier *Brown* decision and the later Montgomery bus boycott, can tell us a lot about the cultural, social, and even intellectual history of *Brown*. This kind of broad contextual understanding of the meanings and consequences of *Brown* requires careful analysis of the decision as a social, cultural, and ideological force, not only as a legal, constitutional, and political one. How do we assess the impact of *Brown* on the developing black freedom struggle? What do the events of the mid-1950s tell us about America's developing integrationist ethos and worldview? And to what extent has *Brown*, understood broadly as a social and a cultural phenomenon, influenced the lives of all Americans, but especially blacks and whites, since the mid-1950s? To ask these questions is to assume that *Brown* is central to both the history of the black liberation movement and the history of integrationism, or desegregation, in schools and other institutions.

To gauge the influence of *Brown*, we must look carefully at many episodes in the years 1954–55 and their short- and long-term ramifications. Equally important, we must closely inspect and analyze the lived experiences of ordinary folks. We can obtain a richer and more satisfying historical understanding of *Brown* by considering how blacks have witnessed, understood, and written about *Brown* in their own lives.

One key measure of the complex way in which blacks responded to and fashioned *Brown* and its possibilities is the stories they have told and continue to tell about the place of *Brown* in black life and the movement. Unraveling how blacks have seen *Brown* operating within the textures and rhythms of black life and the movement is the focus of this chapter. This project illustrates that for blacks themselves, the decision, whose prospects and perils in many ways persist, has constituted a means rather than an end of the continuing African American freedom struggle. It has been an important flank in a struggle that necessarily has many flanks and great complexity.

The argument here is twofold, and the two strands are interwoven. First, *Brown*, when seen in terms of its immediate as well as its long-term historical context, shows a more multifaceted and complex set of meanings and consequences than heretofore acknowledged. *Brown*, Till's lynching, and the Montgomery bus boycott are episodes that belong to the same historical moment. And seen together, though refracted through the lens of *Brown*, these events and what they signify—inspiring black insurgency and horrific white counterinsurgency, triumph and tragedy, hope and despair—pointedly illuminate the emerging civil rights struggle of the mid-1950s, and in particular the centrality of education to that struggle.

The second and interrelated argument is that by viewing *Brown* in this more broadly contextual manner, we gain a better understanding of the role of *Brown* in African American history and memory, notably as expressed in the autobiographical and biographical imagination. By taking seriously the various ways in which *Brown* in this sense figures in African American efforts to "narrate the self" and to "narrate the world,"[4] we glimpse private and affective as well as public and rational meanings and consequences attached to *Brown*. *Brown* emerges as a telling window on African American consciousness and African American narrative and historical sensibilities. It likewise emerges as a telling window on a large and transformative historical moment and that moment's very own defining site: the growing civil rights insurgency.

In a letter from Folsom prison in California in mid-1965, Eldridge Cleaver, an ex-rapist who became the era's most famous ex-prisoner turned black revolutionary, used the *Brown* decision of ten years earlier to mark a critical shift in his personal consciousness as well as collective black consciousness. In the opening essay in *Soul on Ice*, the series of polemical pieces that made him a sensation, *Brown* is a watershed. Recalling what he had thought of *Brown* as an eighteen-year-old prisoner who had been deeply immersed in "street life" rather than his people's liberation struggle in the early 1950s, Cleaver wrote that he lacked "the vaguest idea of its . . . historical importance. But later, the acrimonious controversy ignited by the end of the separate-but-equal doctrine was to have a profound effect on me. This controversy awakened me to my position in America and I began to form a concept of what it meant to be black in white America." Cleaver explained: "I'd always known that I was black, . . . [but] I'd never really stopped to take stock of what I was involved in."[5] Over time, the huge social fallout from *Brown* forced Cleaver to undertake a searching personal re-evaluation of his life and its meaning. Indeed that very fallout, notably the tortured trajectory of integrationism in theory and practice, has profoundly influenced national and international life ever since.

For Cleaver, *Brown* came to signify that pivotal moment when the "atmosphere of Novocain," or drug-like somnambulance necessitated by accommodationism, gave way to an increasingly aggressive nonviolent direct action movement. Heralded by the Montgomery bus boycott, this emerging militant black consciousness framed and propelled the emerging modern black freedom struggle. "Nurtured by the fires of the controversy over segregation," Cleaver continued, "I was soon aflame with indignation over my newly discovered social status, and inwardly I turned away from America with horror, disgust, and outrage."[6] Over a decade later, as a key figure in the revolutionary Black Power phase of the modern black freedom struggle,

Cleaver would be among those questioning the efficacy of the nonviolent civil disobedience exemplified by the southern movement led by Dr. Martin Luther King Jr. Cleaver would also be among those deeply questioning the logic and results of the integrationism epitomized by *Brown*.

Speaking before an NAACP rally in Atlanta where seven thousand people celebrated the ninety-fourth anniversary on 1 January 1957 of the Emancipation Proclamation, King himself noted a shift in his people's consciousness similar to that noted by Cleaver. King detected the evolution of that shift throughout the first half of the twentieth century, as blacks became increasingly urban, industrial, better educated, and better off economically. He observed "all of these forces conjoined to cause the Negro to take a new look at himself. Negro masses all over began to reevaluate themselves. The Negro came to feel that he was somebody." In fact, "with this new sense of dignity and this new self-respect, a new Negro came into being." This "new Negro," King suggested, made the integrationist logic of the *Brown* decision necessary, even inevitable. Seen in that light, the Montgomery bus boycott which he had helped to lead resulted in significant measure from the struggle of this "new Negro" to get rid of Jim Crow once and for all.[7]

Like Cleaver and King, John Lewis, a leader of the Student Non-violent Coordinating Committee (SNCC) and later a congressman from Atlanta, found much to celebrate in *Brown* and the bus boycott as a young teenager. As for Till's lynching, Lewis wrote: "I was shaken to the core by the killing of Emmett Till. I was fifteen, black, at the edge of my own manhood just like him. He could have been me. That could have been me, beaten, tortured, dead at the bottom of a river. It had been only a year since I was so elated at the *Brown* decision. Now I felt like a fool."[8] A fellow SNCC leader, Cleveland Sellers, concurred with Lewis's judgment that Till's lynching was " an incident . . . that no one could ignore": "[It was] the atrocity that affected me most." Like Lewis, and untold numbers of black male adolescents in particular, at the time Sellers identified strongly with Till. Throughout the black community of Denmark, South Carolina, moreover, Sellers recalled the lynching as having a most unsettling impact. He would later write, "There was something about the cold-blooded callousness of Emmett Till's lynching that touched everyone in the community. We had all heard atrocity accounts before, but there was something special about this one."[9]

In September 1961, as a SNCC organizer, Sellers reiterated that anti-black violence and intimidation were directed toward blacks generally, not just those associated with the movement. When four black fishermen discovered, near the location of Till's lynching, an unidentified black male body "in a cloth sack and weighted down with one hundred pounds of rocks," terrible memories of Emmett Till's "bloated corpse" flooded back. Similarly, in 1964 during the Freedom Summer campaign, the sight by Sellers of his SNCC colleague Wayne Yancey's dead body again led to eerie flashbacks of a grossly disfigured Till. By now, for many, the grisly photographs of Till's lynched body had become emblematic of racist violence against blacks, notably black men. In this case, Yancey, the victim, had died from an apparent head-on collision. His "face was badly mangled. And his body was bruised and torn by several deep cuts. Blood was everywhere." Sellers remembered being "immediately reminded of the magazine pictures of Emmett's corpse."[10]

Till's lynching was alleged to have been committed in a barn near the home of Mae Bertha and Matthew Carter. As a result, Naomi Carter, thirteen years old at the time, remembered that when her parents were away from home after dark, "the younger children always hid inside the house." In her classic movement autobiography *Coming of Age In Mississippi*, Anne Moody remembered Till's lynching as cataclysmic. The episode gave her "a completely new insight into the life of Negroes in Mississippi." She argued that the lynching affected her—and by extension countless other black female adolescents—in much the same way as it affected their male cohorts like Lewis and Sellers. Even as a black girl, she, like the black boys she knew in her community, felt intensely vulnerable to racist murder in the aftermath of the lynching. For her, the lynching immediately came to symbolize a frightening vulnerability of blacks generally to murderous white violence against them. The alleged cause, or reason, for such evil was clear in her young mind: the simple fact of being black in a white supremacist world. "Before Emmett Till's murder," she wrote, "I had known the fear of hunger, hell, and the Devil. But now there was a new fear known to me—the fear of being killed just because I was black. This was the worst of my fears. I knew once I got food, the fear of starving to death would leave. I also was told that if I were a good girl, I wouldn't have to fear the Devil or hell. But I didn't know what one had to do or not do as a Negro not to be killed. Probably just being a Negro period was enough, I thought."[11]

Till's lynching affected Moody in several other revealing ways. For one, she now came to understand that the shocking local incidence of unsolved murders of blacks, especially black men, was not the result of "an evil spirit," as her mother had explained in seeking to shield her as a child from an unconscionable reality. Rather, it was the work of evil white men. In a manner similarly revelatory, in her search to uncover information about Till's lynching Moody uncovered the courageous and inspirational work of the NAACP with the help of Mrs. Rice, a sympathetic homeroom teacher. This most important black civil rights organization, Moody learned, had sought valiantly yet unsuccessfully to convict the guilty parties in Till's lynching. Precisely because of its unwavering anti-racist work, of course, the group was increasingly anathema to the white South. Some states like Mississippi went so far as to outlaw the NAACP. Mrs. Rice also provided Moody with a chilling history of the unchecked, bloody, and often murderous trail of white violence against blacks in the South.[12]

These political education and consciousness-raising sessions strongly influenced Moody. She began to bond with her knowledgeable and engaged mentor. "Mrs. Rice got to be something like a mother to me," she recalled. "She told me anything I wanted to know. And made me promise that I would keep all this information she was passing on to me to myself. She said she couldn't, rather didn't, want to talk about these things to the other teachers, that they would tell Mr. Willis [the principal] and she would be fired. At the end of that year she was fired."[13]

Most compelling, even chilling, was Moody's subsequent admission that in part because of all she uncovered in her quest to comprehend Till's lynching, she learned to hate. "I was fifteen years old when I began to hate people," she explained. "I hated the white men who murdered Emmett Till and I hated all the other whites who were responsible for the countless murders Mrs. Rice had told me about and those I vaguely remembered from childhood. But I also hated Negroes. I hated them for not standing up and doing something about the murders. In fact, I think I had a stronger resentment toward Negroes for letting whites kill them than toward the whites. . . . It was at this stage of my life that I began to look upon Negro men as cowards."[14]

On the unforgettable day when Melba Pattillo prepared to join her fellow black students who were to integrate Central High in Little Rock, the ghost of Till reemerged. It would appear that the haunting and conjoined memory of the attempted rape at the hands of her white male assailant on the very day the *Brown* decision was announced also reemerged. Conrad, Melba's brother, half-jokingly reminded her not to look the whites directly in the eyes. He explained: " 'Remember what happened to Emmett Till?' " Pattillo recalled that her brother's "expression changed as his eyes lit up with monstrous delight. I thought about Mr. Till, who had been hanged and tossed in the Mississippi River because he looked white folks in the eye." Till's lynched body here as elsewhere in countless contexts graphically signified the potentially fatal cost of black transgression of the racial status quo. As a symbol, a memory, and a reality, Till's lynched body reinforced the black dread and fear of transgressing the Jim Crow barriers so central to white supremacy and its maintenance.[15]

Black responses to the high court rulings in *Brown* and *Brown II* ranged from enthusiastic embrace to vigorous opposition, with a cautious hope and optimism characterizing the dominant response.[16] The young teenager John Lewis, for one, was euphoric: "I remember the feeling of jubilation I had reading the newspaper story—all the newspaper stories—that day. Everything was going to change now." While happy about the news and supportive of the decision, Lewis's parents, reflecting a commonplace and seasoned black wisdom, were not quite ready to try forcing compliance onto a recalcitrant white South. Like so many blacks of their generation, Lewis maintained, they were wary of "trying to push things" too far too quickly. "Right or wrong didn't matter to them as much as reality."[17]

Andrew Young, an associate of King who later became mayor of Atlanta and ambassador to the United Nations, recalled the same moment as one that caused "a change in our belief in what was possible." Ralph Abernathy, another of King's close lieutenants, reconstructed a mealtime conversation with King and Vernon Johns, King's predecessor at Dexter Avenue Baptist Church in Montgomery, where a sense of hope dominated: "We talked about the oppression of our people and about the growing belief that a sea change was taking place. We all agreed that *Brown versus the Board of Education* had altered forever the conditions on which the continuing struggle would be predicated. No longer was the law unambiguously on the side of Jim Crow. It now appeared as if the law was on our side, that the federal government might even be pressed into service in our fight for freedom."[18]

While blacks hoped that the decision spelled the death knell of Jim Crow and the white supremacist worldview and power structure which sustained it, they knew all too well that in many ways the struggle to end Jim Crow and white supremacy had merely entered a new phase. Nevertheless, it must be borne in mind that *Brown* evoked a largely positive response among blacks. Those like W. E. B. Du Bois who saw the decision unfolding against the extraordinarily repressive backdrop of cold war anti-communist hysteria thought the decision a step in the right direction: part of "the price of liberty." Du Bois correctly foresaw, however, that ultimately realizing the mandate of *Brown* would be extremely difficult. A few observers, like Zora Neale Hurston, actually opposed the *Brown* decision because they thought it reiterated stereotypical notions of black cultural insufficiency. Such black critics also regarded as a serious mistake the notion that integration, especially as represented in school desegregation, was a panacea for America's race relations woes. If they were not separatists of the Black Muslim (Nation of Islam) variety and opposed to integration per se, they often preferred the strategy of equalization within separate, if not Jim Crow, spheres.[19]

In fact, a critical distinction must be drawn between two at times competing visions of integration. The first vision has represented integration primarily as a means to equalize access to a quality education, especially the resources associated with that education. The second has represented integration as a social as well as educational phenomenon. As a result, it has given added emphasis to the spatial arrangement of blacks and whites in the same classrooms. Needless to say, blacks have historically been far more concerned about the former than the latter.

Integration's inherent ambiguities ignited all kinds of revealing debates, small and large. Anne Moody observed that any time her employer, Mrs. Burke, wanted to engage her in a serious conversation, it generally happened while Anne was ironing, so as to reiterate her dependency and confirm her own complicity in her subordination. Anne had other kinds of understandings, however, and let that be known. On the occasion of mounting local white opposition to *Brown*, Mrs. Burke asked Moody, in the course of her ironing ritual, what she thought about the prospect of school integration. Rather than feign ignorance or give Mrs. Burke the answer she wanted—that Anne was dead set against it—she sketched out a hopeful yet unrealistic scenario including her employer's son Wayne and his friends, a scenario that she knew would enrage her employer. "I don't know, Mrs. Burke, I think we could learn a lot from each other. I like Wayne and his friends. I don't see the difference in me helping Wayne and his friends at home and setting in a classroom with them. I've learned a lot from Judy and them. Just like all Negroes ain't like me, all white children I know ain't like Wayne and Judy and them. I was going to the post office the other day and a group of white girls tried to force me off the sidewalk. And I have seen Judy with one of them. But I know Judy ain't like that. She wouldn't push me or any other Negro off the street."[20]

Similarly, in Deborah E. McDowell's *Leaving Pipe Shop: Memories of Kin* we glimpse ordinary black folks fashioning lives within the constraints of *Brown*. All the while, like blacks everywhere, in their daily lives they wittingly and unwittingly contest as well as accommodate those very constraints. Here, however, *Brown* operates more as backdrop, a subtext, to a rich, deep, and evocative examination of the process of coming of age in the time of *Brown*. From the vantage point of the all-black working-class community of Bessemer, Alabama, on the outskirts of Birmingham, we learn: "Pipe Shop Elementary was still fully segregated when I first walked through its double doors in 1956, two full years after the *Brown* decision declared segregation unconstitutional. . . . Pipe Shop Elementary was still segregated when I left to start junior high at Brighton. When what passed for desegregation made its sluggish way to Bessemer, long after *Brown* was the law of the land, the school did not survive the change, but in 1956 it was alive with learning about Alabama, the 'Cotton State' deep in the 'Heart of Dixie.' And about the Pilgrim fathers."[21] The emphasis here is on surmounting and transcending the limitations of time and place, as well as living life as joyfully and meaningfully as possible within those limitations.

In Birmingham at about the same time, Angela Davis was in junior high school. For her, *Brown* similarly functioned effectively as an autobiographical and historical backdrop and subtext. But also for her, the rhetorical purpose was ostensibly more militantly political: to demonstrate in crushing detail the fundamental inequity, wrong, and tragedy of segregation. In addition to devastating critiques of the racist curricula, Davis provided compelling descriptions of the physical disparity between the white and black schools in her world. Tuggle, her elementary school, "was all the shabbier when we compared it to the white school nearby. From the top of the hill we could see an elementary school for white children. Solidly built of red brick, the building was surrounded by a deep-green lawn. In our school, we depended on potbellied coal stoves in winter, and when it rained outside, it rained inside." Davis described her junior high school, Parker Annex, as "a cluster of beaten-up wooden huts not much different from what we had just left." Students referred to the two primary buildings as "Shack I, Shack II."[22]

As the recollections of McDowell and Davis attest, popular black articulation and understanding of notions like desegregation and integration in schools and beyond were rather inchoate throughout much of the 1950s. Integration as both a guiding philosophy and a central goal of the black freedom struggle only took shape slowly, and it did so principally through the agency of the NAACP's successful litigation campaign against Jim Crow, notably in the late 1940s and early 1950s.[23] Popular embrace of the notion proceeded in fits and starts as a mass movement gathered steam and key leaders, especially Dr. Martin Luther King Jr., increasingly conceptualized and concretized the idea.

Like King and the increasingly influential black writer James Baldwin, an array of mid-century religious and secular leaders, scholars, intellectuals, activists, and policymakers thought and wrote about the visions brought forth by *Brown* and its integrationist thrust and how those visions might be realized. At Roosevelt University in Chicago and elsewhere, James Forman and his colleagues "argued over the merits of integration, which we took to mean total absorption into the mainstream of American life." Foreshadowing James Baldwin's classic jeremiad *The Fire Next Time*, many in Forman's crowd concluded forcefully: "Who wants to integrate into a burning house?"[24]

Most ordinary black folks struggled on dutifully, trying to square the demands of a positive and inspiring series of court victories with an all-too-often dreadful race relations reality. A decade after *Brown*, the Mississippi sharecroppers Mae Bertha and Matthew Carter bravely sent seven of their thirteen children to integrate the all-white public schools in Sunflower County. Ms. Carter recalled that she had first heard of the decision from a church friend. At the time she had never heard of desegregation. But as she began to piece together what it meant, her apprehension emerged pointed and clear. White opposition notwithstanding, the prospect of integrated schools gladdened her, she explained, "because when that day come our children won't be starting to school in November, and stopping all the time to pick cotton. I know they will start in September and go nine months like the white children."[25]

For the Carters, as for most blacks, the key issue remained how best to achieve equal educational opportunity for their children, all the while struggling to make a living in a South where Jim Crow and its remnants have persisted long after *Brown*. Rather than fixate on the intense southern white opposition to school integration, they labored in various ways, like Mae Bertha and Matthew Carter, to make the most of *Brown* and its offshoots as a means of undermining Jim Crow and white supremacy. They pragmatically adapted *Brown* to an escalating black freedom insurgency: the civil rights movement (1945–65), the black power movement (1966–76), and beyond. Within that continuing struggle, *Brown* has meant many, at times conflicting, things.

Yet one point remained clear: legal victories were essential to the ongoing black freedom struggle. Nevertheless, few blacks truly believed that integrated schools and an integrated society would come easily and quickly. Nor did the vast majority believe that legal victories alone would usher in either integration or "America, the Beautiful." Yet most had no idea how hard, even intractable, the struggle to realize integrated schools and an integrated society would in fact be. With its hard-earned and important victory in *Brown*, the NAACP validated once and for all the viability of legal action in an evolving multi-front war against Jim Crow and white supremacy. The courts had become a critical arena of struggle. Dismantling American apartheid legally and constitutionally was essentially a court matter. Dismantling it culturally, ideologically, socially, politically, economically, and institutionally in space and time, however, has been another matter altogether. As of 2004, as a society we are still engaged on that flank in a series of battles with shifting aims and on shifting terrain.

Not surprisingly, therefore, the substance and tenor of concurrent black responses to *Brown* often lacked the emotional and psychological investment, and the intensity, associated with Till's lynching and the Montgomery bus boycott. Cases like Melba Pattillo's, in which the impact was not only personal but also horrific, were the exception that proved the rule.

Septima Clark, the legendary South Carolina educator and exponent of the Citizenship Schools—which taught blacks how to master the rudiments of voting in the late 1950s and 1960s, before the Voting Rights Act of 1965— keenly captured this wise detachment. At the time Clark taught in an all-black elementary school in the Charleston public school system. When news of the *Brown* decision came, she was attending the Highlander Folk School, a progressive alternative institution in rural Tennessee dedicated to fomenting social change in the South. Referring to the decision, Septima Clark remembered: "We were really happy over that, and I felt wonderful. But I didn't yet have the feeling that this thing was really a part of me." Having enlisted in the battle to integrate Central High, however, Melba Pattillo and the few others like her could forcefully claim otherwise.[26]

*Brown* plainly signified pivotal government action in support of the free-dom struggle. Fundamentally, that government—in this case, the Supreme Court—represented white male power responding to black challenges and demands: the intensifying black freedom struggle. Till's lynching, however, was a frontal white attack on black humanity. The viciousness and notoriety of that crime ensured that it would resonate more deeply among blacks than *Brown*, whose immediate meanings were hopeful but debatable. On a far more positive note, the Montgomery bus boycott heralded black re-sistance and exemplified the possibilities of concerted mass black social protest.

While there had been innumerable and scattered mass black protest actions at the local level throughout the South before, even black bus boy-cotts, the Montgomery action singularly touched a national nerve as well as a black nerve. It deeply inspired black America and catalyzed the mass social insurgency that came to be identified as "the movement." Angela Davis recalled that as a teenager in Birmingham, she and a few friends staged a series of bus protests in solidarity with the Montgomery action. The other black riders prevailed upon her and her cohorts to desist, how-ever. Melba Pattillo Beals captured well the dominant contemporaneous black view of the boycott: "I felt such a surge of pride when I thought about how my people had banded together to force a change. It gave me hope that maybe things in Little Rock could change." Even more rhapsodically, John Lewis has recently claimed, "With all that I have experienced in the past half century, I can still say without question that the Montgomery bus boycott changed my life more than any other event before or since." In fact, the glorious example of the boycott helped to undercut his boyhood anger and disappointment at the strident opposition to the *Brown* mandate among hometown whites in Pike County, Alabama.[27]

By demonstrating conclusively to blacks themselves, as well as mid-twentieth-century America, that blacks could indeed unite in a successful long-term protest action, the boycott "had a very significant effect on the consciousness of black people throughout the United States," according to James Forman, a stalwart of SNCC. It vividly refuted the charges of fundamental disunity, fatalistic otherworldliness, and racial inferiority that dogged blacks everywhere. "These self-destructive attitudes, these self-fulfilling prophecies of 'we can't get together'" were resolutely overcome and shown to be false by the boycott. Forman deeply admired what he saw as "the cultural effects of the boycott in changing the mass psychology of black people, showing them that we could do things as a group."[28]

Televised images of the intense white opposition to the bus boycott touched in a different way the Cuban exile Assata, future activist in the Black Liberation Army. She would ultimately write: "Only the news concerning Black people made any impact at all on me. And it seemed that each year the news got worse. The first of the really bad news that I remember was Montgomery, Alabama. . . . It was a nasty struggle. Black people were harassed and attacked and, if I remember correctly, Martin Luther King's house was bombed." For Assata, the saga only continued with the battle to integrate Central High in Little Rock. "Then came Little Rock. I can still remember those ugly, terrifying white mobs attacking those little children who were close to my own age. When the news about Little Rock came on, you could hear a pin drop at my house. We would all sit in front of that box, watching my people being attacked by white mobs, beaten and water-hosed by police, arrested and murdered. Then the news seemed too real."[29] The racist violence at Little Rock indeed shocked the nation and the world. For the mature Assata and a growing number of blacks in the mid-1960s and later, the lesson was clear: the benefits of *Brown* and integration were not worth the costs. These blacks in time moved toward a revolutionary, often Black Nationalist, cause.

The boycott nonetheless represented for a vast number of Americans, white and black, transformative social action, not just egalitarian constitutional and legal rhetoric with enormous potential, like *Brown*. For that potential to be realized, thoughtful and committed blacks understood that they would have to take the upper hand and make the most of *Brown*. The decision supported and sustained the movement, which blacks themselves primarily made. As James Forman thoughtfully discusses in *The Making of Black Revolutionaries*, the boycott, for all its weaknesses and limitations, demonstrated conclusively the absolute necessity for black mass-based protest action to uproot Jim Crow and white supremacy. Illustrating an effective set of organizing and mobilizing tools, he argued, the boycott plainly showed the way. Aggressive black social and political action had to complement and push forward legal and constitutional action.[30]

Sympathetic coverage in the mainstream news media, support within key segments of the white community, along with a well-organized and deeply committed black community and the charismatic leadership of King, helped to make the bus boycott a defining moment of the civil rights movement. The mass action electrified and galvanized blacks throughout the country. It verified the evolving and spreading black feeling that a black social movement was in fact emerging. Beals recalled her grandmother's revealing characterization of the black mood in the mid-1950s: "Our people were stretching out to knock down the fences of segregation." Lewis explained that in 1955 "no one was using the term 'movement' quite yet, but they would before the year was out, because the nearly century-old struggle for black Americans' civil rights, spurred by the *Brown v. Board* decision, was now finally coming to a head. Things were truly beginning to 'move,' both for bad and for good. Lines were starting to be drawn, and blood was beginning to spill."[31]

*Brown* was potentially revolutionary rhetoric, stunning and significant, but nonetheless fundamentally a court ruling that had to be accepted by the larger society and enforced by the government to become real, to become effective. This was the rub. Hence, the pervasive black caution, even skepticism, regarding how schools and other institutions would be integrated has been not only understandable and realistic but also quite necessary. As Ralph Abernathy observed of black America in the mid-1950s: "Though we were told the law would be applied equally throughout the land, we were skeptical. We had heard that before." Over time blacks saw the limits and constraints of *Brown* with greater clarity and deeper understanding.

Pauli Murray (1910–85) led an extraordinary and inspiring life, overcoming obstacles to become a lawyer, civil rights activist, teacher, feminist, and Episcopalian priest along the way. An unsung heroine of the modern African American freedom struggle, Murray was a keen observer of twentieth-century race relations. She was particularly insistent and persuasive regarding the necessity of treating the movements for racial and gender equality as both primary and mutually supportive struggles. One of a handful of pioneering black women lawyers at mid-century, in 1951 she wrote *States' Law on Race and Color*, a widely used text on civil rights law. Her personal stake in the *Brown* decision was clear. In 1938 the University of North Carolina had denied her admission to its graduate school because of her color. She fought back, writing a series of editorials critical of the university for its Jim Crow admission policies. Subsequently, as the only woman in her law school class at Howard University in the early 1940s, she endured the sexist hostility of many of her male colleagues.[32]

Over the next decade or so Murray met and surmounted a great deal of opposition in her quest to expand her legal training and to practice law.

*Brown* immediately tapped into her idealism. She wrote at the time: "The Supreme Court has set the example for future conduct by combining moral and constitutional integrity with wisdom of high order. . . . It has indicated an orderly procedure of moving forward with patience and restraint." Even she did not envision, however, the extremes of patience and restraint that would eventually be called for. As Andrew Young noted, there was "no dramatic change in the South immediately in the wake of the Supreme Court decisions." Similarly, John Lewis recalled, "*Brown v. The Board of Education* notwithstanding, nothing in my life had changed."[33] The ambiguous implementation decree in *Brown II*—to integrate the schools with "all deliberate speed"—translated into southern white evasion, avoidance, and outright rejection: in effect, massive resistance.

A necessary and cogent way to think about *Brown* and its aftermath is certainly to see it as most scholars do: that is, as a spur to the movement. It is equally important to see the powerful white backlash to *Brown*—the refusal of the South and the nation as a whole to support the decision in the short term—also as a spur to the movement. As Abernathy observed of the March on Washington in 1963, the shadow of *Brown* loomed heavily over the 250,000 gathered at the Lincoln Memorial. This troubling shadow contributed to the fiery passion animating the official festivities, notably the "militant" speeches. "*Brown*," Abernathy ruefully recalled, "had been handed down earlier, yet most of the schools in the South were still segregated. Though segregated public transportation had been ruled unconstitutional in 1956, there was still segregation on the buses throughout the region. And still black workers were underemployed and underpaid."[34]

King gave classic voice to the mounting and understandable black frustration with the excruciatingly slow pace of change in the racial status quo in his justly famous "Letter from Birmingham City Jail," written at the height of the Birmingham campaign. To the charge of the clerics in Birmingham and many in the nation at large that his people demanded too much too soon, King's response was clear and pointed: "Frankly I have never yet engaged in a direct action movement that was 'well timed,' according to the timetable of those who have not suffered unduly from the disease of segregation. For years now I have heard the word 'Wait!' It rings in the ear of every Negro with a piercing familiarity. This 'wait' has almost always meant 'never.' . . . We must come to see with the distinguished jurist of yesterday that 'justice too long delayed is justice denied.' We have waited for more than 340 years for our constitutional and God-given rights."[35]

King understood that while patience was indeed a virtue, it had its limits. And he knew that for his people the limits were fast approaching. As he explained, "There comes a time when the cup of endurance runs over, and men are no longer willing to be plunged into an abyss of injustice where they experience the bleakness of corroding despair." His people's impatience, he observed, was both "legitimate and unavoidable." In her unforgettable song "Mississippi Goddamn," Nina Simone captured this mood perfectly:

> Don't tell me, I'll tell you,
> Me and my People just about due.
> I've been there, so I know.
> They keep on saying, "Go slow."

Rejecting these incessant and disturbing pleas for blacks to "Go slow" in their freedom quest, Simone retorted: "But that's just the trouble—Too slow."[36] "All deliberate speed" plainly had to be speeded up.

The escalating frustration of blacks with the pace of change in their status and prospects had enormous consequences. As Abernathy noted of the national caution in implementing the Civil Rights Act of 1964 and the Voting Rights Act of 1965, blacks refused the prospect of being "given a beautifully wrapped box with nothing inside."[37] Rising national postwar expectations of progress were heightened by the movement, making it imperative that substantive change be effected in the racial status quo. The illusion of change or concessions, or only minor change, was increasingly unacceptable. This expanding spiral of expectations contributed significantly to the Watts insurgency (1965), the black insurgencies in other cities in the late 1960s, and the Black Power movement of the late 1960s and early 1970s.

Through it all, the cry for a meaningful and relevant education was clear. Equally clear was the demand for equal educational opportunity. It was precisely at this moment that the federal government began to put teeth into its commitment to school integration. One goal motivating the government to act at this time was plainly political and urgent: to undercut the rising and threatening tide of black militancy. Just as the legalism of the campaign led by the NAACP against Jim Crow had given way in the 1950s to the nonviolent direct action of the southern struggle, the latter gave way to an increasingly oppositional and complex struggle after the victories of the classic civil rights movement. As the federal government between 1965 and 1975 endeavored to desegregate public schools, the Black Power phase of the movement gave increasing emphasis to demands for black community empowerment, educational relevance, and black studies curricula. On one level, these demands exacerbated tensions surrounding school desegregation, as innumerable whites felt increasingly put upon by increasingly assertive black students and black advocates. On another level, these demands were absolutely imperative to ensure that school integration, or black education in all-black or segregated institutions, better served the interests of black students who were all too often ill served in either setting.

Deep-seated concern over the state of black education in this period led many activists to commit themselves, in the words of William Van Deburg, "to educational reform at all levels." Some fought to reform existing schools and make them work for young blacks. Van Deburg writes that these activists "focused on making the public schools community-based and -controlled centers of individual and group empowerment." He further explains: "Treating black children as creative, educable . . . (rather than as aberrant or dysfunctional . . . ), these revamped institutions would emphasize racial and cultural difference in a positive way—by nurturing a youngster's sense of self and instilling self-respect for collective responsibility and action."[38]

In the late 1960s and early 1970s others sought to establish alternative institutions to provide black students with a nurturing and supportive black education that would inoculate them against the "socialization in whiteness" endemic in "traditional schooling." In 1966 the Black Panther Party had expressed this widespread concern forcefully in the fifth point of its Ten Point Party Platform and Program: "We want education for our people that exposes the true nature of this decadent American society. We want education that teaches us our true history and our role in the present-day society. We believe in an educational system that will give to our people a knowledge of self. If a man does not have knowledge of himself and his position in society and the world, then he has little chance to relate to anything else."[39]

Similarly, on a growing number of black and white college campuses many black student activists sought to create strongholds of liberation and laboratories for the study of the African American experience. Recognizing that knowledge was power and that higher education had a great deal to do with ordering societal power relationships, campus militants demanded major curriculum reforms. Here, as elsewhere, increased control of the learning environment and the creation of a relevant course of study were key agenda items.[40] The institutionalization of African American, ethnic, and Third World studies, often within distinctive departments, has transformed American higher education. This too is a legacy of the sense of black hope and efficacy epitomized by both the modern battle for black education and the movement, all of which *Brown* shaped significantly.

# Notes

This chapter was revised while the author was a fellow at the Center for Advanced Study in the Behavioral Sciences (2002–3). I am grateful for the financial support provided by The Andrew W. Mellon Foundation.

*Epigraph.* Gabrielle Morris, *Head of the Class: An Oral History of African-American Achievement in Higher Education and Beyond* (New York: Twayne, 1995), xx.

1 Melba Pattillo Beals, *Warriors Don't Cry: A Searing Memoir of the Battle to Integrate Little Rock's Central High* (New York: Pocket Books, 1994), 22.

2 *Id.* at 25–27.

3 *Id.* at 27–28.

4 Achille Mbembe, "African Modes of Self-Writing," *Public Culture* 14:1 (winter 2002): 262; V. P. Franklin, *Living Our Stories, Telling Our Truths: Autobiography and the Making of the African-American Intellectual Tradition* (New York: Oxford University Press, 1995).

5 Eldridge Cleaver, *Soul on Ice* (New York: Dell, 1968), 3.

6 *Id.* at 3–4.

7 Martin Luther King Jr., "Facing the Challenge of a New Age," *The Papers of Martin Luther King, Jr,* vol. 4, *Symbol of the Movement, January 1957–December 1958,* ed. Clayborne Carson et al. (Berkeley: University of California Press, 2000), 76, 77.

8 John Lewis with Michael D'Orso, *Walking with the Wind: A Memoir of the Movement* (New York: Simon and Schuster, 1998), 57.

9 Cleveland Sellers with Robert Terrell, *The River of No Return: The Autobiography of a Black Militant and the Life and Death of* SNCC (New York: William Morrow, 1973), 15.

10 *Id.* at 50, 104.

11 Constance Curry, *Silver Rights* (Chapel Hill, N.C.: Algonquin, 1995), 51; Anne Moody, *Coming of Age in Mississippi* (New York: Bantam Doubleday Dell, 1968), 121–26, quotes on 121, 125–26.

12 Moody, *Coming of Age in Mississippi.*

13 *Id.* at 128.

14 *Id.* at 129.

15 Beals, *Warriors Don't Cry,* 44; Stephen J. Whitfield, *A Death in the Delta: The Story of Emmett Till* (Baltimore: Johns Hopkins University Press, 1988).

16 Waldo E. Martin Jr., ed., *Brown v. Board of Education: A Brief History with Documents* (Boston: Bedford, 1998), especially 199–229.

17 Lewis, *Walking with the Wind,* 54, 55.

18 Andrew Young, *An Easy Burden: The Civil Rights Movement and the Transformation of America* (New York: Harper Collins, 1996), 90; Ralph David Abernathy, *And the Walls Came Tumbling Down: An Autobiography* (New York: Harper and Row, 1989), 126.

19 Manning Marable, *W. E. B. Du Bois: Black Radical Democrat* (Boston:

Twayne, 1986), 200; Zora Neale Hurston, "Court Order Can't Make Races Mix," (Orlando) *Sentinel*, 11 August 1955, reprinted in Martin, ed., *Brown v. Board of Education*, 209–12.

20  Moody, *Coming of Age in Mississippi*, 153.

21  Deborah E. McDowell, *Leaving Pipe Shop: Memories of Kin* (New York: Scribner, 1996), 67.

22  Angela Davis, *Angela Davis: An Autobiography* (New York: Random House, 1974), 90, 100.

23  This is a crucial yet ignored development treated more fully in the forthcoming study by Patricia A. Sullivan, *Going the Distance: A History of the* NAACP (New York: New Press, forthcoming).

24  Forman, *The Making of Black Revolutionaries: A Personal Account* (New York: Macmillan, 1972), 85; James Baldwin, *The Fire Next Time* (New York: Dell, 1963).

25  Curry, *Silver Rights*, 49.

26  Cynthia Stokes Brown, ed., *Ready from Within: Septima Clark and the Civil Rights Movement* (Navarro, Calif.: Wild Trees, 1986), 31.

27  Davis, *Angela Davis*, 101; Beals, *Warriors Don't Cry*, 28; Lewis, *Walking with the Wind*, 58.

28  Forman, *The Making of Black Revolutionaries*, 85.

29  Assata Shakur, *Assata: An Autobiography* (Westport, Conn.: Lawrence Hill, 1987).

30  Forman, *The Making of Black Revolutionaries*, 84–85, 104–5.

31  Melba Pattillo Beals, *Warriors Don't Cry*, 28; Lewis, *Walking with the Wind*, 56–57.

32  Pauli Murray, *Song in a Weary Throat: An American Pilgrimage* (New York: Harper and Row, 1987).

33  *Id.* at 400; Young, *An Easy Burden*, 89; Lewis, *Walking with the Wind*, 56.

34  Abernathy, *And the Walls Came Tumbling Down*.

35  "Letter From Birmingham Jail, April 6, 1963," cited in Clayborne Carson et al., eds., *Eyes on the Prize: America's Civil Rights Years: A Reader and Guide* (New York: Penguin, 1987), 116.

36  Cited in Nina Simone and Stephen Cleary, *I Put a Spell on You: The Autobiography of Nina Simone* (New York: Pantheon, 1992).

37  Abernathy, *And the Walls Came Tumbling Down*, 385.

38  William L. Van Deburg, ed., *Modern Black Nationalism: From Marcus Garvey to Louis Farrakhan* (New York: NYU Press, 1997), 158. For a good introduction to how this phenomenon occurred within colleges and universities see William L. Van Deburg, *New Day in Babylon: The Black Power Movement and American Culture, 1965–1975* (Chicago: University of Chicago Press, 1992), 64–82.

39  "What We Want, What We Believe: Black Panther Party Platform and Program," Van Deburg, *New Day in Babylon*, 249.

40  Van Deburg, *Modern Black Nationalism*, 158.

MARK V. TUSHNET

# The Supreme Court's Two Principles of Equality

## From *Brown* to 2003

### *Brown* and the Choice between Desegregation and Integration

When Thurgood Marshall stood up to argue *Brown v. Board of Education* for the third time in April 1955, he knew that his arguments were legally airtight and politically porous. Eleven months earlier the Court had held school segregation unconstitutional, saying that "[s]eparate educational facilities are inherently unequal," and that segregating children on the basis of race "generates a feeling of inferiority as to their status in the community that may affect their hearts and minds in a way unlikely ever to be undone."[1]

The third argument session was devoted to determining the remedy for the practices already held unconstitutional. As the Court grappled with that question, it anticipated a wide range of issues that would arise over the next fifty years. The questions went well beyond school desegregation, encompassing racial discrimination in employment and, eventually, discrimination on the basis of religion and disability. The fundamental question was this: What does the equal protection clause protect against or, even more broadly, what notion of equality are Americans committed to? Two versions of equality competed in the discourse of equality in American law. In one, equality was satisfied so long as no decision maker adopted policies intending to make racial minorities—or, eventually, other minorities and even, in the context of affirmative action, members of majority groups—worse off. In the other, equality required the elimination of practices that contributed to the subordination of racial or other minorities, whether intended or not. Each discourse was continually present in constitutional deliberations about equality.

The issue arose in the remedy argument in *Brown* in the following way. In an ordinary case, the remedy would be simple. Long-established law held that constitutional rights were, in the law's jargon, personal and present. They were personal in the sense that each person adversely affected by a constitutional violation was entitled to some remedy, and they were present in the sense that the remedy should be provided as soon as possible. The remedy for an unconstitutional statute that separated children in school on the basis of race would be straightforward: eliminate race as a basis for assigning students to schools. As Judge John J. Parker put it in discussing the South Carolina companion case to *Brown*, the Supreme Court's holding meant that the Constitution "forbids discrimination, . . . [that is,] the use of governmental power to enforce segregation."[2] The personal and present right to government decisions that ignored race could be vindicated by simple orders directing schools to ignore race in assigning students to schools.

Calling this remedy a requirement for "immediate" desegregation, Marshall acknowledged that schools might not be able in a month or two to devise student assignment plans that ignored race; school boards would have to identify where African American and white children lived, calculate school capacities, devise assignment plans that matched residence with capacity, and the like. These administrative problems, as Marshall referred to them, might delay desegregation for several months, perhaps to the second semester of the 1955–56 school year or even to the 1956–57 school year in extreme cases. But it was clear to Marshall that immediate desegregation, understood in this way, could be completed quickly, and the rights of African American schoolchildren vindicated.

Marshall's legal argument about the remedy for unconstitutional segregation was unassailable, although a few justices picked around its edges when Marshall presented it to them. At the same time, however, the argument was politically vulnerable on two fronts. The first, and the one most strongly present in the minds of the Supreme Court's members, was enforcement in the Deep South. Everyone involved in the desegregation suits, including Marshall, knew that the Deep South would resist desegregation fiercely and perhaps violently. From the Supreme Court's point of view, the problem was to devise a remedy that might accomplish something without impairing the Court's standing as the nation's primary institutional defender of constitutional rights. Ordering immediate desegregation—the rapid development of student assignment policies that ignored race—might not accomplish anything, and would certainly harm the Court's reputation in the Deep South.

The second source of political vulnerability came from the largest part of the African American community and its liberal supporters. The campaign against segregation was not, for them, merely a campaign to cleanse the statute books of laws referring to race. It was a more substantial effort to transform race relations in the United States. Token integration that left many African American children in largely nonwhite schools was not what these activists sought, and yet it might be the result of immediate desegregation or simple nondiscrimination.

The Court's solution to its political dilemma was to borrow a tradition from the equity courts, rarely invoked in constitutional litigation, allowing the courts to devise complex remedies for complex problems. The famous formulation was that courts should order desegregation to occur "with all deliberate speed."[3] The Court's decision about remedy was shot through with tensions that in the end shaped the law of race discrimination in important and to some extent unexpected ways. These tensions pervaded the law of race discrimination in the early 1950s. The Court was torn between what later came to be called an anti-discrimination rule and an anti-subordination rule.[4] Under the former, the equal protection clause barred government from predicating its decisions on race; under the latter, the clause barred the government from actions that sustained a system of racial subordination. In the context of the segregation cases, Judge Parker articulated the distinction in asserting that "the Constitution does not require integration. It merely forbids discrimination."[5]

That *Brown* could be understood in two ways—as requiring only desegregation or as requiring integration—reflects deeper differences about the nature of equality under the Constitution. Those who see equality as equality of opportunity would treat *Brown* as a case requiring only desegregation, meaning here the opportunity to attend school without regard to race; those who see equality as equality of outcome would treat *Brown* as a case requiring integration. Equality of opportunity naturally inclines toward focusing on the reasons that decision makers have for their actions, developing legal tests requiring intentional discrimination, while equality of outcome naturally inclines toward focusing on the patterns that result from what decision makers do, without regard to what they had in mind. The anti-discrimination and anti-subordination theories attempt to capture these distinctions.

The anti-discrimination and anti-subordination approaches to equality have coexisted as long as the modern Court has confronted issues of race discrimination. During the early stages of the Court's efforts to dismantle the American system of apartheid the Court did not clearly distinguish between the two approaches. The anti-discrimination approach probably dominated in the Court's and the public's articulated understandings of what equality required, yet the anti-subordination approach, whose role in articulated doctrine may have been secondary, influenced and to some extent was the only defensible justification for much of what the Court did. In the 1960s and early 1970s the Court came close to articulating the anti-subordination approach as the predominant one, drawing on its expe-

rience in school segregation cases and on recently enacted civil rights statutes in approaching that conclusion. The practical implications of the anti-
subordination approach and changes in the political climate led the Court
to reaffirm, perhaps even more forcefully than before, the view that the
Constitution required anti-discrimination, not anti-subordination. Still,
some important statutes could be understood only by assuming that Congress had taken the anti-subordination approach, and even in the domain of
constitutional law a large and persistent minority of justices, supported by
important voices in the legal academy and the general public, kept the anti-
subordination approach alive.

This chapter examines the cycles of the law of equality. After describing
how the anti-subordination approach provided the best explanation for
some prominent early Supreme Court decisions, including its decision on
remedy in *Brown*, the chapter turns to the Court's ambivalent rejection of
anti-subordination in favor of anti-discrimination in the 1980s and 1990s.

Early Decisions Obscure the Difference

The analytic tension between anti-discrimination and anti-subordination
had already arisen, almost unnoticed, in the controversial case of *Shelley v.
Kraemer*.[6] The case involved a state court decision enforcing a covenant
restricting the sale of a home to whites only. The Court considered two
questions in *Shelley*. The one that attracted the most attention was whether
the action by a state court in enforcing the covenant was "state action"
subject to the restrictions placed on state action by the equal protection
clause. The Court gave the obvious answer, that the action of a state court
was state action.

The Court then turned briefly to the merits, and found that the enforcement of a racially restrictive covenant violated the Constitution. That
holding implicated the distinction between anti-discrimination and anti-
subordination. The state court's action would clearly have violated the equal
protection clause if, in enforcing the restrictive covenant, the state court
had held that it would enforce *only* restrictive covenants limiting sales on a
racial basis. Such a rule would itself have been cast in racial terms and, with
a qualification that I note below, could be held unconstitutional without
much difficulty. But the state court in *Shelley* was actually enforcing a different rule, one that required it to enforce *all* covenants restricting the sale
of property so long as the covenant did not exclude an unreasonably large
number of potential buyers from the transaction.[7] *That* rule was not cast in
racial terms. The rule that the state court followed, in other words, com-

plied with the requirement of non-discrimination. In holding the enforcement of the racially restrictive covenant unconstitutional, the Court necessarily implied that there was something wrong with a system of apparently neutral rules if it had the effect of maintaining a system of racial superiority and subordination.

Referring to a property owner's rights as "personal," the Court dismissed the argument that courts would enforce racially restrictive covenants against whites as well as against African Americans: "Equal protection of the laws is not achieved through indiscriminate imposition of inequalities."[8] That statement too took the anti-subordination side. The Court had dealt with many cases in which state officials imposed disadvantages on African Americans, for example through statutes that disqualified African Americans from jury service.[9] The baseline against which these statutes were measured was the rights of white persons, and the Court found it easy to explain why rules that placed African Americans below that baseline denied equality to African Americans. But rules like the one applied in *Shelley* lowered the baseline for whites and African Americans alike. To find such a rule unconstitutional, the baseline had to be something other than the rights to which white people were entitled. Rather, the baseline had to be something like the set of rights that people would have in an integrated society. Yet that is precisely what the anti-subordination principle meant, and in dismissing the "equal imposition of inequalities" as plainly impermissible the Court in *Shelley* implicitly though obscurely endorsed that principle.

In an analytic sense, *Brown* was a replay of *Shelley*. The Court's decision proceeded on the assumption that material conditions in the schools for whites and African Americans were equal. There was, in other words, an equal imposition of inequality: African Americans could not go to school with whites, and whites could not go to school with African Americans.[10] In holding segregation unconstitutional, the Court must have been endorsing the anti-subordination principle. But as we will see, that principle has far-reaching implications, and the Court was understandably nervous about accepting those implications, out of concern for its own standing and power and out of concern about the scope of social reordering that the anti-subordination principle, fully enforced, would require.

The Court's decision on the merits in *Brown* provided some support both for the view that the Constitution required only desegregation or nondiscrimination and for the view that it required integration or anti-subordination. The Court quoted a finding made in the Topeka case: "Segregation *with the sanction of law* . . . has a tendency to [retard] the educational and mental development of negro children and to deprive them of some of the benefits they would receive in a racial[ly] integrated school system."[11]

This finding blurred the distinction between non-discrimination and integration: The reason for the adverse effects on learning was legally sanctioned segregation, not the mere separation of the races unaccompanied by legal sanction. Yet the loss was measured not against what children would learn in schools to which they were assigned without regard to race but rather against what they would learn in integrated schools. The Court's own reference to the "feeling of inferiority" generated by racial separation could have been read to refer to a feeling generated by *the law* but more naturally reads as a reference to a feeling generated by the separation itself.

The *Brown* opinion on remedy referred to the "personal interest of the plaintiffs in admission to public schools as soon as practicable on a non-discriminatory basis." This language suggested agreement with Marshall's position. The opinion then noted the existence of possible "obstacles in making the transition to school systems operated in accordance with . . . constitutional principles." A later sentence suggested that these obstacles included such matters as "the physical condition of the school plant, the school transportation system, personnel, revision of school districts and attendance areas," and the associated need to change local laws and regulations. Here too the opinion might have been taken to echo Marshall's position, acknowledging that the requirement of immediate desegregation had to be tempered by relatively modest administrative concerns.

The only hint of what really concerned the Court came in an almost self-contradictory assertion by the Court: "it should go without saying that the vitality of those constitutional principles cannot be allowed to yield simply because of disagreement with them." Everything else in the opinion indicated that the natural remedy would be immediate desegregation. It took no deep insight to see that the Court's decision to allow "deliberate speed" rather than to require immediate desegregation flowed precisely from concern about what should go without saying, that is, from the Court's concern that orders requiring immediate desegregation would be ignored—and constitutional principles in practice would "yield"—because of resistance predicated on disagreement with the Court.

The Court's decision on remedy had to be rationalized legally, and the rationale—the anti-subordination principle—shaped the law of discrimination over the next decades. School systems could immediately accomplish desegregation, understood as the elimination of government reliance on race, in assigning students to schools. The "all deliberate speed" formulation implied that the Constitution required something other than simply eliminating reliance on race. The candidate for what the Constitution did require was obvious. The alternative, as characterized by Judge Parker in rejecting it, was that the Constitution required integration, that is, the actual co-presence of African American and white children in the same schools. Accomplishing *that* would indeed be difficult, and giving systems time to work out plans that produced integration made sense in a way that giving them time to eliminate reliance on race did not.

### The Brief Dominance of the Anti-Subordination Principle

The Supreme Court stayed away from the details of desegregation for a decade after *Brown*, intervening only in the extraordinary circumstances of the Little Rock desegregation crisis, which attracted worldwide attention and the deployment of U.S. military forces. School boards working within the "all deliberate speed" framework developed a number of responses. Most consistent with the integrationist interpretation of *Brown* were so-called grade-a-year plans, in which all children in one grade were assigned to schools without regard to race; when implemented, these plans generally led to integrated schools, particularly in small districts and in the high schools of larger ones. Most consistent with the non-discrimination interpretation were "freedom of choice" plans, which allowed students to choose for themselves which schools they attended, subject only to minor administrative constraints imposed by school capacity. Other plans were nominally consistent with the non-discrimination interpretation. Some school systems, usually urban ones, took advantage of pervasive racial residential segregation to substitute pure neighborhood assignment policies, sometimes drawing the borders carefully to ensure that the neighborhood schools would actually be schools for whites or African Americans. This tactic was unavailable in many locations, particularly in rural districts where residential segregation was less pervasive. Other systems adopted complex student assignment policies that enumerated a number of criteria like student or parental interest for assigning students to particular schools. Nominally neutral on race because race was not one of the listed criteria, and therefore nominally consistent with the non-discrimination view of *Brown*, these policies were usually transparent efforts to categorize by race without saying so, as the student assignment policies were implemented in ways that ensured the assignment of all white students to one set of schools and all African American students to another. Litigators might find it difficult to challenge gerrymandered neighborhood school districts or student assignment plans that were administered in a racially discriminatory manner, but such evasions posed no serious analytic problems: The evasions were plainly inconsistent with the non-discrimination interpretation of the Equal Protection Clause.[12]

Freedom-of-choice plans were another matter. In a sense, they presented the courts with a new visit to the problem of state action. Typically, student choices under freedom-of-choice plans produced schools that were racially identifiable, a term that came into common use much later in the course of desegregation litigation. But the choices were *the students'*, not the state's. State government made no racially discriminatory choices in setting up freedom-of-choice plans, unless the courts were prepared to say that employing racially neutral rules in a social setting where government decision makers could confidently predict obtaining racially identifiable schools as a result was itself an act of racial discrimination. But in saying that, the courts would be adopting the anti-subordination view of the equal protection clause.

The Supreme Court considered the constitutionality of freedom-of-choice plans in 1968. *Green v. County School Board* involved such a plan in a rural district with two schools and little residential segregation.[13] After three years in operation, the results were clear: no white children attended the school that had been operated for African Americans before *Brown*, and only 115 African American children attended the white school. The Court noted the long delay between *Brown* and the school board's first adoption of the freedom-of-choice plan, and concluded that school boards had to "come forward with a plan that promises realistically to work, and promises realistically to work *now*." The opinion also said that plans had to promise to "convert promptly to a system without a 'white' school and a 'Negro' school, but just schools."[14] The Court's emphasis on plans that "worked" marked its commitment to the integrationist interpretation of *Brown*. Under Judge Parker's "desegregation, not integration" approach, a freedom-of-choice plan necessarily worked to eliminate what the anti-discrimination approach identified as the only relevant constitutional vice, the use of race-based criteria in governmental decision making. The idea of needing something more to demonstrate the workability of a plan made sense only if the Court meant that the Constitution did require integration. The Court's commitment to an integrationist interpretation of the Constitution continued in later cases that measured systems' progress toward complying with the Constitution by assessing whether the systems had racially identifiable schools.[15]

The Court's long abstention from school desegregation cases meant that the Court confronted the choice between the anti-discrimination and anti-subordination approaches in a new political environment. The civil rights movement had made demands for large-scale changes in race relations that were far more plausible in the 1960s than they had been in prior decades. Civil rights activists in the 1930s and 1940s believed that anti-discrimination would lead to integration, and so saw no need to develop an alternative interpretation of equality's requirements.[16] Southern resistance to desegregation brought the tension between the anti-discrimination vision of equality and the integrationist vision to the fore. The integrationist vision was prominent in the civil rights movement of the 1960s, but to make sense of it a new interpretation of equality, the anti-subordination one, had to replace the anti-discrimination one as dominant one. Civil rights activists in the 1960s, that is, sought to reverse the relative position of anti-discrimination and anti-subordination.

The Civil Rights Act of 1964, coupled with the enactment of substantial programs of federal aid to education, made Southern resistance to desegregation increasingly costly, because the Act directed that federal money could not flow to districts that continued to discriminate.[17] The Act's ban on discrimination in employment unexpectedly turned out to provide a model for developing a doctrinal structure on which the anti-subordination principle could be elaborated.

Title VII of the Civil Rights Act banned race discrimination in private employment. That ban raised the same questions that a ban on race discrimination in public education did. Clearly, the ban meant that employers could not predicate their employment decisions on race alone; in banning what came to be known as disparate treatment, the statute extended at least the anti-discrimination approach to the private sector. Did it do more? The answer came in so-called disparate impact cases, where employers used criteria for employment and promotion that did not expressly refer to race but nevertheless had differential effects on whites and African Americans. With no dissent, the Supreme Court held in 1971 that Title VII did call into question employment practices with a disparate impact. The case, *Griggs v. Duke Power Co.*, involved an employer who had previously engaged in racially discriminatory disparate treatment.[18] When Title VII took effect, the company said that applicants for vacant positions in traditionally white job categories had to pass a newly instated aptitude test and have a high school diploma. These requirements had a disparate impact on African American applicants, and the Court held that the employer could use them only if the employer showed the requirements to be a "business necessity." Chief Justice Warren Burger's opinion said that Title VII was aimed at eliminating patterns of discrimination, and at overcoming the effects of past discrimination.

*Green* in 1968 and *Griggs* in 1971 were the high points in the Court's commitment to an integrationist or anti-subordination view of equality. Analytical difficulties associated with the anti-subordination approach, and a political backlash against the more expansive claims of the civil rights movement, pushed the Supreme Court, with a new set of members appointed by more conservative presidents, to move fairly rapidly to—or back to—the anti-discrimination principle.

## The Anti-Discrimination Principle Becomes Dominant

Civil rights litigators pressed the courts to adopt the rule that statutes with a disparate impact on African Americans violated the Constitution unless the government could demonstrate extremely strong reasons for adopting the statutes. The Supreme Court rejected that position in *Washington v. Davis*, decided in 1976.[19] The case involved a job test for positions on the police force in Washington, D.C.: Job applicants were required to pass a test measuring vocabulary and reading comprehension. The plaintiffs showed that white applicants passed the test at a higher rate than African American applicants, and, they claimed, the city had not shown that the test measured qualities important to success as a police officer. The Court rejected the argument that the test was unconstitutional (unless there was a strong justification for its use) simply because of its disparate impact. Justice Byron White, writing for the Court, firmly asserted that the equal protection clause was violated only when governments adopted practices with a discriminatory purpose. In rejecting the proposition that disparate impact alone raised constitutional questions, Justice White wrote: "A rule that a statute designed to serve neutral ends is nevertheless invalid, absent compelling justification, if in practice it benefits or burdens one race more than another would be far reaching and would raise serious questions about, and perhaps invalidate, a whole range of tax, welfare, public service, regulatory, and licensing statutes that may be more burdensome to the poor and to the average black than to the more affluent white."[20] Here Justice White relied on the empirical correlation between race and wealth. His point was that many statutes with a disparate racial impact were enacted for reasons associated with wealth rather than race. Much that matters in American society is distributed on the basis of market prices, and a disparate impact theory would require the courts to supervise legislatures' efforts to address problems created by that fact. Legislatures enact statutes that only partially eliminate the effect of the price system on the distribution of goods. But as Justice White understood, a disparate impact theory would tell the courts to direct legislatures to go even further, and to eliminate racial disparities resulting from market distribution. That, as he noted, would work a large change in the entire system of legislation and, importantly, markets in the United States.

The sweeping effects of a disparate impact theory might be limited, though. There were two courses obviously available. As the Court noted in *Washington v. Davis*, the disparate impact rule was not that statutes with a disparate impact were automatically invalid, but that such statutes could be justified by showing that they served a "compelling" need. The possibility of justification was the constitutional parallel to the "business necessity" defense available under Title VII. The difficulty with transferring the idea to the constitutional context is that the justifications for government actions are more complex than the profit-oriented calculations of businesses. Typically, for example, a government could say that it adopted a policy with a disparate racial impact because, though the government knew that the policy would have a disparate impact, eliminating that impact would have been quite costly, and the government believed that spending the money on other programs—education or national defense—was more important. If courts found such justifications adequate, the disparate impact standard would be toothless; if they rejected such justifications, the courts would become deeply involved in determining the contours of government programs generally.

Alternatively, governments might be given the opportunity to show that the racial disparities were a statistical artifact, disappearing once one controlled for variables like wealth. If statistical analysis showed that the only apparent explanation for disparate impact was race, though, the practice would be unconstitutional. The Court considered, and rejected, this possibility, in *McCleskey v. Kemp*, a challenge to the death penalty as administered in Georgia.[21] Warren McCleskey had been convicted and sentenced to death for killing a police officer who interrupted a robbery. McCleskey's lawyers gave the Court a statistical study showing racial disparities in the imposition of the death penalty in cases like McCleskey's. The study examined the possibility that something other than race accounted for the disparities, and demonstrated, in terms generally acceptable to statisticians, that nothing other than race could explain the pattern of outcomes. The Supreme Court assumed that the study was valid, but nonetheless held that McCleskey could not prevail on his constitutional claim unless he showed that some particular decision maker—the prosecutor, the jurors, or the judge—relied on McCleskey's race as a reason for subjecting him to the death penalty.

Justice Lewis F. Powell's opinion for the Court gave several reasons for rejecting McCleskey's claim, of which two are important here. First, he echoed Justice White's concern in *Davis*, writing that accepting McCleskey's claim would raise serious questions about the entire criminal justice system, because, he assumed, similar racial disparities pervaded that system. Second, Justice Powell pointed out that without locating a particular decision maker who intended to discriminate, the courts would face a difficult task in remedying the disparate outcomes.[22] In dissent, Justice William Brennan responded to the concerns of Justice Powell by saying that the concerns "suggest a fear of too much justice."[23] Both justices were right. Pursuing a disparate impact theory would indeed require large-scale changes in law and practices, and such changes might well be required for the United States to achieve racial justice. The moment at which politics seemed to make such changes possible passed, and the courts' commitment to the anti-discrimination principle rather than the anti-subordination principle fit well with what the political system was willing to do regarding race.

School desegregation cases in the 1980s and 1990s demonstrated the political limits of the anti-subordination principle. *Green* seemed to adopt integration as the goal of school desegregation. Achieving integration in urban areas characterized by severe residential segregation required quite substantial changes in accepted practices; in particular, it required severely limiting the scope of student assignment to neighborhood schools and required instead that students be transported to schools outside their neighborhoods. The American public as a whole was willing to accept such changes, sometimes reluctantly, when desegregation was confined to the South, and when desegregation was understood as a reasonably direct remedy for core practices of racial apartheid expressed in statutes requiring that students of different races go to different schools. When desegregation efforts moved north, though, opposition to the integrationist, anti-subordination interpretation of *Brown* grew.[24]

Opponents of "busing" in the North pointed out that proponents of integration could not point to anything like the southern state laws requiring racial segregation before *Brown*. As they conceded, sometimes grudgingly, civil rights litigants could occasionally show that once in a while school authorities made decisions with race in mind: School boards altered the lines for assigning children to schools when racial residential patterns changed, and located new schools to ensure that the schools would be racially identifiable. But, opponents of the integrationist interpretation argued, these decisions were neither as widespread nor as troublesome as the laws requiring segregation in the South had been. In the North, they claimed, racial separation in the schools resulted far more from residential patterns, themselves the product of decisions by individual families rather than decisions by public officials. Imposing the same kind of remedy in the North that had been imposed in the South seemed to them to go too far. And the effort to desegregate northern schools and urban southern schools seemed increasingly futile—or seemed to require long-term and far-reaching judicial supervision of the schools—as white families moved from the cities to the suburbs.

In the 1970s the Supreme Court began to dismantle the basis for thinking that *Brown* adopted the integrationist view. It held that judges could not require the participation of suburban school districts in desegregation plans unless, as was rarely true, the suburban districts had somehow collaborated with the urban ones to sustain patterns of racial identifiability.[25] Then, in a series of cases in the 1990s, the Court permitted and eventually directed the federal courts to withdraw from supervising desegregation efforts even in states that had had laws requiring segregation before *Brown*.[26] By the end of the century, the Supreme Court had essentially abandoned the project of achieving integration in the schools through deliberate constitutional policy. If integration resulted from racial diversity in a school district, of course the courts would not interfere, but the courts would do almost nothing to promote integration. Nor were there substantial efforts, either on the national level or in state governments, to promote racial integration in the schools.

The abandonment of integration as a policy goal was connected to the other area in which the anti-discrimination principle prevailed over the anti-subordination principle: affirmative action. The integrationist interpretation of *Brown* sometimes *required* public authorities to take race into account: To ensure that a school was not racially identifiable, school authorities had to pay attention to the race of the students they were assigning to each school, for example. Affirmative action programs had the same characteristic of making race relevant to public decision making. Like the integrationist program, affirmative action came under increasing attack as its scope spread.

Initially, affirmative action programs were designed to address intentional discrimination that was difficult to identify.[27] Employers who did not want to employ African Americans might use hiring techniques that effectively concealed their intentions. Affirmative action programs directing employers to search out African American applicants, or even directing them to show that they employed African Americans in rough proportion to the number of African Americans qualified for the jobs, were ways of ensuring that employers did not violate the anti-discrimination principle. As affirmative action programs gained political support, their rationale shifted. In part, affirmative action programs came to be justified as a means of rectifying past discrimination. An employer who had deliberately refused to hire African Americans in the past could "remedy" that wrong by adopting an affirmative action program.[28]

The idea of affirmative action as a remedy gradually changed, making affirmative action a technique for implementing the anti-subordination principle. Affirmative action came to be described as a remedy for "societal" discrimination. At this point affirmative action became linked to the disparate impact theory and the anti-subordination principle. The idea behind disparate impact theory was that *something* caused racially disparate patterns of outcome, even if no one could identify a particular actor who intended to impose disadvantage. Disparate impact theory, that is, was predicated on the idea of societal discrimination. And as we have seen, disparate impact theory, with its emphasis on patterns, was one way of translating the anti-subordination principle into constitutional doctrine.

Affirmative action was relatively uncontroversial when it was limited to outreach programs and even when it was designed to smoke out and remedy past acts of discrimination by the actor adopting the program. As their scope expanded, affirmative action programs became intensely controversial. The Supreme Court too was uncomfortable with affirmative action programs. It tried to treat such programs within the anti-discrimination framework, where, because they expressly relied on racial categories, they fit quite awkwardly. The Court struggled to develop a doctrine that simultaneously respected the anti-discrimination approach and yet preserved some room for affirmative action programs. The doctrinal technique was to hold that affirmative action programs were subject to the anti-discrimination principle, and therefore could be justified only by compelling interests. In its first confrontations with affirmative action programs, the Court held that the best justification for expansive programs—that they were efforts to overcome societal discrimination—could not be invoked to defend affirmative action's constitutionality.[29]

### The Persistence of the Anti-subordination Principle

By the turn of the century the anti-discrimination principle had clearly prevailed over anti-subordination. Yet the anti-subordination approach to equality continued to have its supporters in the academy, in the general political system, and even in the courts. Many of the Supreme Court's decisions endorsing anti-discrimination against anti-subordination were decided by 5–4 votes. When the Court definitively held that affirmative action programs in government contracting had to be evaluated in light of the anti-discrimination principle, it went out of its way to emphasize that although such an evaluation required the programs to be examined skeptically and given "strict scrutiny," strict scrutiny need not inevitably be fatal to affirmative action programs.[30] Justifications for affirmative action might be available in other contexts that would not be available with government contracting or employment. In particular, the idea that affirmative action promoted a valuable educational goal—commonly called "diversity"—gave some hope to the large number of proponents of affirmative action in colleges and universities.

The Supreme Court vindicated those hopes in 2003, when it upheld an affirmative action program for admission to the University of Michigan's law school, even as it invalidated a more rigid and numbers-driven program at the school's undergraduate college.[31] Relying heavily on briefs filed by leaders of the nation's military and its major corporations, the Court found that diversity in university classrooms did indeed serve a compelling interest in ensuring that the nation's leadership positions would be occupied in significant numbers by racial minorities. As Justice Antonin Scalia suggested in his dissent, the Court's analysis also suggested that affirmative action in employment could be justified by diversity concerns as well. Justice Sandra Day O'Connor's opinions in the two cases rested squarely on the anti-discrimination theory, but demonstrated how that theory could be used to reach goals easily compatible with anti-subordination ideas.

Justice O'Connor's opinion in the law school case observed that American society was one "in which race unfortunately still matters." A separate opinion by Justice Ruth Bader Ginsburg drew on that observation in support of an approach invoking the anti-subordination tradition. Ginsburg's opinion stressed "the effects of centuries of law-sanctioned inequality" and detailed the "large disparities" between the life conditions of racial minorities and those of whites. Her opinion shows that the anti-subordination theory remained available in constitutional law even in 2003, after decades during which most of the justices clearly preferred the anti-discrimination theory.

As we have seen, the deepest analytic problem with disparate impact theories is their need to accommodate justifications for practices that have a disparate impact. In a 1989 decision *Ward's Cove Packing Co. v. Antonio*, the Supreme Court attempted to loosen the definition of "business necessity," which could justify employment practices with disparate impact.[32] *Griggs* had said that employers had to demonstrate business necessity, and took the term *necessity* to mean something close to "nearly essential for the business's safe and efficient operation." *Ward's Cove* placed the burden of demonstrating the *lack* of business necessity on plaintiffs, and changed the definition of "business necessity" to allow any practices that "serve[d], in a significant way, the [employer's] legitimate employment goals." Congress responded to this decision in the Civil Rights Act of 1991, which returned the burden of proof to the employer and adopted a definition of business necessity that while ambiguous, still seemed to favor employees more than the Court's definition. The importance of the Act lies less in its explicit provisions than in the simple fact that it was enacted, albeit after a complex struggle between Democrats in Congress and President George H. W. Bush. The Act's adoption showed that anti-subordination ideas still had significant purchase in the nation's political arenas, even if their hold in the courts had weakened substantially.

Both in the context of race and elsewhere, the idea that practices with disparate impact were problematic—an idea, as we have seen, that is intimately connected to the anti-subordination approach—continued to have real force. Federal agencies implemented rules that directed them to deny federal funds to state agencies whose practices had a disparate impact. The Supreme Court rejected the argument that private plaintiffs could file lawsuits to enforce the disparate impact regulations, and its opinion was grudging at best in accepting the regulations themselves.[33] The Court's decision had an important practical effect because the federal administrative agencies charged with enforcing the regulation had relatively few resources with which to do so. But again, the staying power of the disparate impact regulations shows that anti-subordination ideas continued to affect the public understanding of discrimination.

Indeed, the major civil rights statutes of the 1980s and 1990s were almost pure anti-subordination statutes. The Voting Rights Act of 1982 responded to a Supreme Court decision holding that the Fifteenth Amendment's guarantee of a right to vote without regard to race prohibited only intentional discrimination—an anti-discrimination decision—by enacting a statutory ban on voting practices that have racially discriminatory outcomes. The Supreme Court in turn applied the statute without suggesting that its anti-subordination approach was somehow inconsistent with constitutional notions of equality.[34]

The two most important examples from the 1990s are the Americans with Disabilities Act, passed in 1990, and the Religious Freedom Restoration Act, passed in 1993. In both statutes Congress built upon a provision adopted in 1972. The Civil Rights Act of 1964 prohibited discrimination based on religion. The agency administering the Act interpreted this to require that employers "make reasonable accommodations" for the religious practices of their employees, if the employer could do so without "undue hardship." The lower courts divided over whether the agency's interpretation was consistent with the Act. After the Supreme Court split 4–4 over that question,[35] Congress amended the Act in 1972 to endorse the agency's position and to require that employers accommodate their employees.

By the 1990s the idea that prohibiting discrimination entailed a requirement of reasonable accommodation had substantial political support. Congress was increasingly attracted to the idea that employers and governments should adjust their practices to accommodate the needs of groups
who had historically been the targets of intentional discrimination. The
idea of accommodation flowed in the first instance from the idea of disparate impact. For example, it might be convenient and cheap to set up voting
booths inside public schools built years ago, but such schools might not be
readily accessible to people in wheelchairs. The voting authorities might
not intend to make it difficult for such people to vote, but their decision
clearly has a more substantial adverse impact on people who must use
wheelchairs than it does on people who need not. The idea of accommodation requires the voting authorities to do something to address the disparate impact of policies that are not cast in terms of treating people with
disabilities differently from people without them. The idea of disparate
impact, in turn, flows more easily from the anti-subordination principle
than from the anti-discrimination principle. We might be uncomfortable in
asserting that the voting authorities discriminated against the disabled in
the ordinary sense of intending to impose costs on them; rather, the problem is that difficulties of access to voting booths perpetuate their lower
social status.[36]

The Americans with Disabilities Act, passed in 1990, is a disparate impact statute, requiring employers and public agencies to accommodate
their practices to the needs of persons with disabilities. The Religious Freedom Restoration Act follows the same model. In 1991 the Supreme Court
held that the First Amendment's protection of the free exercise of religion
did not invalidate state laws that were not themselves cast in terms of
religious exercise but had a disparate impact on some religious practices.[37]
For example, a state could apply its general prohibition of the use of psycho-
active drugs to the use of peyote in a religious ceremony, and it could apply its usual zoning rules to churches, even if that limited the ability of
churches to locate where their congregants lived. Congress responded with
the Religious Freedom Restoration Act, which prohibited governments
from imposing substantial burdens on religious exercise, unless they could
show that such burdens were the least restrictive method of advancing a
truly important government interest. Again, this is a disparate impact statute requiring some substantial accommodation of government programs
to the particular needs of the religiously observant.

The Supreme Court was not comfortable with these statutes. Indeed, it
held the Religious Freedom Restoration Act unconstitutional, although
not on grounds directly relevant to the discussion here.[38] The Court's in-

terpretations of the Americans with Disabilities Act have been quite restrictive, with respect to both who is covered by the statute and which accommodations are required.[39] Still, Congress's actions showed that the anti-subordination perspective on equality retained considerable political support even as the Supreme Court appeared to be committed to the anti-discrimination perspective.

One reason for the persistence of the anti-subordination view is that those who are attracted to it can reframe their concerns in ways that fit comfortably with an anti-discrimination approach. This means they are always in a position to agree that anti-discrimination might be the dominant approach while preserving the possibility of reviving the anti-subordination approach when they are in a position to do so. The argumentative moves fall into two broad categories. First, those who are attracted to the anti-subordination approach can argue that existing distributions of burdens and benefits result from historical practices that were discriminatory in the sense of the anti-discrimination principle. The Court may have found it easy to invalidate Duke Power Company's requirement that job applicants have a high school education because Duke Power had discriminated in the past, and drew its employees from an area where schools had been segregated by race before and after *Brown*. A similarly expanded vision of the relation between present conditions and past intentional discrimination could reduce the real-world impact of choosing the anti-discrimination principle instead of the anti-subordinationprinciple. The more willing one is to treat existing patterns as the residual effects of past discrimination, the easier it is to understand how expansive "remedies" are as justified by the anti-discrimination principle as by the anti-subordination one.

Second, consider policies that do not use racial categories as a basis for imposing burdens on anyone, but that have a disparate adverse impact on African Americans. One could address these policies within an anti-discrimination approach by claiming that the policies resulted from a selective indifference on the part of policymakers to the interests of African Americans: The policies would not have been adopted, the argument would go, had the racial distribution of burdens and benefits been reversed.[40] Further, one could argue, selective indifference might result from psychological phenomena, sometimes labeled unconscious racism,[41] that are analytically indistinguishable from the intentional discrimination condemned by the anti-discrimination approach.

The existence of these argumentative strategies does not, of course, mean that those attracted to the anti-discrimination principle will accept the arguments. They may conclude that unconscious racism does not actually fall within the scope of that principle. They may conclude that the effects of past discrimination, as they understand discrimination, have become so attenuated that it is improper to describe policy responses as remedies for past discrimination. The Supreme Court's decisions in the 1990s authorizing courts to withdraw from supervising the operation of previously segregated schools seem to endorse that conclusion, as does its refusal to allow governments to justify affirmative action programs as responses to "societal discrimination," understood here to refer to the present effects of past intentional discrimination.

Again, however, the point is not that the anti-discrimination principle and the anti-subordination principle are analytically the same. Rather, the point is that the availability of these argumentative strategies means that the anti-subordination principle will never entirely disappear from legal-political discourse. The course of public deliberation on race since the 1950s has been one in which the anti-discrimination principle has usually prevailed over the anti-subordination one, but in which on occasion the anti-subordination principle has emerged to shape policy and public understanding.

*Brown* identified the possibility that the equal protection clause embodied *either* the anti-discrimination principle *or* the anti-subordination principle. It did not, however, choose between them. The tension between the two approaches appears to be a permanent one in the way Americans understand the Constitution's requirement of equality. One question, for scholars, is "Which principle will be predominant and which subordinate under what circumstances?"[42] Another question, for policymakers and the public, is "Which choice should we make?" The authors of the affirmative action decisions of 2003 expressed the hope that affirmative action would be unnecessary by 2028. Expressing that hope was the Supreme Court's way of signaling that *it* did not want to grapple with affirmative action for years to come. The rest of the country—ordinary citizens and policymakers—do not have the luxury of avoiding the question of whether the nation is committed to the anti-discrimination theory or the anti-subordination one. That question remains open as the United States addresses issues of equality in the twenty-first century.

## Notes

1 Brown v. Board of Education, 347 U.S. 483, 494 (1954).
2 Briggs v. Elliott, 132 F. Supp. 776, 777 (E.D.S.C. 1955).
3 Brown v. Board of Education ("Brown II"), 349 U.S. 294, 301 (1955).
4 See Paul Brest, "Foreword: In Defense of the Antidiscrimination Principle," 90 *Harvard Law Review* 1–54 (1976); Ruth Colker, "Anti-Subordination

above All: Sex, Race, and Equal Protection," 61 *New York University Law Review* 1003–66 (1986).

5  Briggs v. Elliott, 132 F. Supp. 776, 777 (E.D.S.C. 1955).

6  334 U.S. 1 (1948).

7  For a discussion, see Mark Tushnet, "*Shelley v. Kraemer* and Theories of Equality," 33 *New York Law School Law Review* 383–408 (1988).

8  334 U.S. at 22.

9  Strauder v. West Virginia, 100 U.S. 303 (1886).

10  The classic exploration of this aspect of *Brown* is Herbert Wechsler's notorious essay "Toward Neutral Principles of Constitutional Law," 73 *Harvard Law Review* 1–35 (1959).

11  347 U.S. at 494.

12  See Yick Wo v. Hopkins, 118 U.S. 356 (1886).

13  391 U.S. 430 (1968).

14  *Id.* at 442.

15  See, e.g., United States v. Montgomery County Bd. of Education, 395 U.S. 225 (1969); Columbus Board of Education v. Penick, 443 U.S. 449 (1979).

16  For a discussion, see Mark Tushnet, *Making Civil Rights Law: Thurgood Marshall and the Supreme Court, 1936–1961* (New York: Oxford University Press, 1994), 176–77.

17  For a discussion of the role of federal funding in inducing desegregation, see Gerald Rosenberg, *The Hollow Hope: Can Courts Bring about Social Change?* (Chicago: University of Chicago Press, 1991), 97–100. Indeed, the school board in *Green* adopted its freedom-of-choice plan only when threatened with a loss of federal funds.

18  401 U.S. 424 (1971).

19  426 U.S. 229 (1976).

20  *Id.* at 248.

21  481 U.S. 279 (1987).

22  As Justice John Paul Stevens pointed out in dissent, the study on which McCleskey relied showed racial disparities only in what the study characterized as an intermediate set of murders. The racially disparate impact could have been eliminated by confining the death penalty to a different set of cases, where juries almost invariably imposed the death penalty. *Id.* at 367 (Stevens, J., dissenting).

23  *Id.* at 339 (Brennan, J., dissenting).

24  For a general discussion see James T. Patterson, *Brown v. Board of Education: A Civil Rights Milestone and Its Troubled Legacy* (New York: Oxford University Press, 2001).

25  Milliken v. Bradley, 418 U.S. 717 (1974).

26  Board of Education of Oklahoma City Schools v. Dowell, 498 U.S. 237 (1991); Freeman v. Pitts, 503 U.S. 467 (1992).

27  For an overview see Hugh Davis Graham, *The Civil Rights Era: Origins and Development of National Policy, 1960–1972* (New York: Oxford University Press, 1990).

28 The term "remedy" is somewhat out of place here. Affirmative action programs do not necessarily provide employment or other benefits to people who themselves have been denied a job by the employer operating the affirmative action program. Instead, they provide the benefit to some members of the class of people who, as a class, have been subject to discrimination.

29 The most explicit rejection occurred in Wygant v. Jackson Board of Education, 476 U.S. 267, 274 (1986).

30 Adarand Constructors, Inc. v. Pena, 515 U.S. 220, 237 (1995).

31 Grutter v. Bollinger, 123 S. Ct. 2325 (2003); Gratz v. Bollinger, 123 S. Ct. 2411 (2003).

32 Ward's Cove Packing Co. v. Antonio, 490 U.S. 642 (1989).

33 Alexander v. Sandoval, 532 U.S. 275 (2001).

34 Thornburg v. Gingles, 478 U.S. 30 (1986).

35 Dewey v. Reynolds Metal Co., 402 U.S. 689 (1971).

36 I note, however, the possibility of distinguishing between discrimination based on disability, which might require accommodation, and discrimination based on race, as to which accommodation of assertedly distinctive racial characteristics might be problematic.

37 Employment Division, Oregon Dept. of Human Resources v. Smith, 494 U.S. 872 (1990).

38 City of Boerne v. Flores, 521 U.S. 507 (1997). Congress responded in turn with a narrower statute that it believed addressed the Court's concerns. Religious Land Use and Institutionalized Persons Act, 42 U.S.C. 2000cc–2000cc-5.

39 See, e.g., Sutton v. United Air Lines, Inc., 527 U.S. 471 (1999); Toyota Motor Mfg., Inc. v. Williams, 534 U.S. 184 (2002).

40 Brest, "Foreword."

41 Charles R. Lawrence III, "The Id, the Ego, and Equal Protection: Reckoning with Unconscious Racism," 39 Stanford Law Review 317–88 (1987).

42 For a discussion of the circumstances under which stronger and weaker principles prevail, see Philip A. Klinkner with Rogers M. Smith, The Unsteady March: The Rise and Decline of Racial Equality in America (Chicago: University of Chicago Press, 1999).

DAVISON M. DOUGLAS

# *Brown v. Board of Education* and Its Impact

# on Black Education in America

℣ Americans have long maintained a near religious faith in the possibilities of education for social and economic uplift.[1] Indeed, since the
emergence of the common school movement during the 1830s and 1840s,
social and economic advancement has remained a central rationale for
education. "Let every child in the land enjoy the advantages of a competent
education at his outset in life," commented Horace Eaton, the first state
superintendent of education in Vermont, during the antebellum era, "and
it will do more to secure a general equality of condition than any guarantee
of equal rights and privileges which constitutions or laws can give."[2] Writing in 1944, the distinguished Swedish sociologist Gunnar Myrdal identified education as central to the American ethos: "Education has always
been the great hope for both individual and society. In the American Creed
it has been the main ground upon which 'equality of opportunity for the
individual' and 'free outlet for ability' could be based."[3] Ten years later, the
Supreme Court of the United States would observe in its landmark decision
in *Brown v. Board of Education*, "it is doubtful that any child may be reasonably expected to succeed in life if he is denied the opportunity of an education."[4] President Lyndon Johnson declared during the 1960s that proper
education could prevent poverty and backed up that claim with a large
increase in federal funds for public schools.[5]

This faith in education has been characteristic of all racial and ethnic
groups, but has been particularly strong in the African American community. For most of our history, African Americans have viewed education
as essential to their quest for social, economic, and political equality. Although many blacks have expressed frustration at the inability of education
to move them into the mainstream, faith in the potential of education has
remained strong. As the historian Kevin Gaines has noted, "African Americans have, with an almost religious fervor, regarded education as the key
to liberation."[6]

During the past half-century, many Americans have also developed a deep
faith in the ability of courts to produce social change in the face of the

unwillingness of the elected branches of government to pursue reform agendas. Indeed, a broad range of interest groups—environmentalists, civil rights groups, welfare rights activists, consumer advocates, women's groups, disability activists, school finance reformers, abortion rights proponents and opponents—have embraced litigation as a centerpiece of their strategy for reform during the past few decades.[7] Many of these groups would agree with the assertion of Aryeh Neier that "[s]ince the early 1950s, the courts have been the most accessible and, often, the most effective instrument of government for bringing about the changes in public policy sought by social protest movements."[8]

This faith in education as an engine of uplift and in courts as effective instruments of social policy converged in the Supreme Court's decision in *Brown*, in which it declared de jure segregation in public education an unconstitutional deprivation of the rights of black children to "equal educational opportunities."[9] In so doing, the Court helped to unleash a revolution in public education in America, although a revolution that cannot be attributed to the *Brown* decision alone. Indeed, the central holding of the *Brown* decision—that state-mandated racial segregation in public schools was unconstitutional and must come to an end—did not take full effect for more than a decade, when Congress entered the fray by enacting the Civil Rights Act of 1964 and the Office of Education of the Department of Health, Education and Welfare issued guidelines designed to enforce Title VI of the new legislation.

As we look back on *Brown* from the perspective of a half-century, what has been its impact? Certainly the decision has had a profound effect on the judiciary and its emergence as an important instrument of institutional reform. Although some scholars question the efficacy of judicially directed social reform,[10] *Brown* unquestionably helped reshape the judiciary's role in American life by inspiring many interest groups to pursue their goals through litigation.

*Brown* has also played an important role in the larger black freedom struggle, granting to the cause of racial equality the imprimatur of the highest court in the land. Particularly during the first decade after *Brown*, the decision offered the developing civil rights movement both an important legal precedent and a "moral resource"[11] in its struggle for racial justice. The Montgomery bus boycott, for example, ultimately prevailed when the courts struck down bus segregation in a lawsuit that relied in significant measure on *Brown*.[12] Moreover, the virulent white reaction to *Brown* helped to fuel the civil rights movement, which in turn led to the significant anti-discrimination laws of the mid-1960s that went far beyond the school context.[13] *Brown* also helped open the door to legal challenges to other educational inequities such as the exclusion of the children of illegal aliens from the public schools, various educational practices that discriminated on the basis of gender, and educational barriers to children with special needs.[14]

But what has been the impact of *Brown* on the education of black children in America? The Supreme Court in *Brown* found that state-mandated school segregation deprived black children "of equal educational opportunities."[15] Has *Brown* in fact produced equal educational opportunity for African American children? The answer is extraordinarily complicated. First of all, it is impossible to assess the impact of *Brown* without considering the larger context of the decision—other court decisions that both preceded and followed it and a variety of congressional and administrative actions designed to enforce its mandate. As scholars such as Michael Klarman and Gerald Rosenberg have noted,[16] the effect of the *Brown* decision itself was more modest than many observers have noted and did not reach fruition until the elected branches of government threw their weight behind the decision's desegregation imperative during the mid-1960s. This chapter's consideration of the impact of *Brown* on the education of black children is thus an assessment not just of the Supreme Court's decision but of desegregation actions by all three branches of government.

An assessment of *Brown* and its effect on the education of African Americans depends in part on how one defines the central thrust of the decision. In the early years, *Brown* was viewed primarily as an "anti-segregation" decision in which the Court had held that de jure school segregation was unconstitutional. By the late 1960s a competing understanding of *Brown* as an "integrationist" decision became dominant. Proponents of this perspective argued that *Brown* required school boards not only to end race-based pupil assignments but to take affirmative steps to overcome racial separation in schools caused by residential segregation. In the face of political and legal resistance to implementation of this integrationist construction of *Brown*, a third view of the decision gained prominence during the late 1970s and 1980s that deemphasized racial mixing in favor of providing greater resources for minority schools as a means of enhancing the educational opportunities of minority children. The "success" of *Brown* thus depends in part on how we define what the decision sought to achieve.

As we approach the fiftieth anniversary of *Brown*, de jure segregation has been eliminated and racial mixing in public schools, at least in the South, is greater than in 1954. But the hope that *Brown* and its associated judicial, legislative, and administrative actions would accomplish the long-sought "uplift" goal of raising African Americans to an even ground with whites has not been fully realized. Blacks still have inferior social and economic outcomes in comparison to whites. To some extent, the failure of *Brown* to redress these larger social and economic inequalities between blacks and whites must be viewed as part of the inherent limitations of education as an engine of social reform. As the distinguished black educator Horace Mann Bond wrote in 1934: "Of one thing, at least, we can be sure: that is the unsoundness of relying upon the school as a cure-all for our ills."[17] In recent years, many scholars have invited us to consider more closely the impact of economic class in addition to race on the long-term prospects of schoolchildren. As the black sociologist William Julius Wilson wrote in his influential book *The Declining Significance of Race*, "[r]ace relations in America have undergone fundamental changes in recent years, so much so that now the life chances of individual blacks have more to do with their economic class position than with their day-to-day encounters with whites."[18] Indeed, in America there remains a significant overlap between class and race, as the poor are disproportionately members of minority groups. Particularly in America's largest cities, disadvantaged black—and Hispanic—students continue to languish in schools that are frequently underfunded in comparison with their suburban counterparts, especially when one considers that urban schools typically have greater financial needs given the array of social and economic problems that beset so many urban schoolchildren.

But some recent research suggests other causes for poor black educational outcomes. In their book *No Excuses: Closing the Racial Gap in Learning* (2003), Abigail Thernstrom and Stephan Thernstrom argue that the poor educational outcomes (and presumably life outcomes) of many black children are due in significant measure to family structures, including the high incidence in the black community of single-parent homes.[19] Similarly, Christopher Jencks and Meredith Phillips argued in 1998 that "[c]hanges in parenting practices might do more to reduce the black-white test score gap than changes in parents' educational attainment or income."[20] America has made significant strides in improving the education of minority children during the past half-century. But the outcomes for so many minority children, particularly poor children in urban school districts, suggest that considerations of how best to provide all children with an "equal educational opportunity" must continue.

## The Integrationist Vision of *Brown*

During the first few years after the *Brown* decision, many observers conceived of it as merely barring the use of race in pupil assignments. For example, Judge John Parker of the U.S. Court of Appeals for the Fourth

Circuit offered a highly influential interpretation of *Brown* in 1955 in an opinion involving the school district in Clarendon County, South Carolina, one of the original defendants in the *Brown* case: "[w]hat [the Supreme Court] has decided, and all that it has decided, is that a state may not deny to any person on account of race the right to attend any school that it maintains." If, Judge Parker continued, a school district opens its schools "to children of all races, no violation of the Constitution is involved even though the children of different races voluntarily attend different schools, as they attend different churches. . . . *The Constitution, in other words, does not require integration. It merely forbids discrimination.* It does not forbid such segregation as occurs as the result of voluntary action. It merely forbids the use of governmental power to enforce segregation."[21] Parker's oft-quoted statement that *Brown* "does not require integration" would be used by many southern judges during the 1950s and 1960s to limit the obligation of local school districts to integrate their schools.

Although much of the white South initially resisted implementing this anti-segregation mandate, by the late 1960s pupil assignments based explicitly on race had largely been eliminated. During the late 1960s, however, many argued that *Brown* not only forbade state-mandated segregation but also required racially mixed public schools. The U.S. Office of Education issued guidelines in 1966 claiming that southern school districts achieving "little or no actual desegregation" were not in compliance with "constitutional and statutory requirements." The Office of Education specified the percentage of minority children that must attend racially integrated schools in order for school districts to retain their eligibility for federal education funding.[22] One year later, in 1967, Judge John Minor Wisdom of the U.S. Court of Appeals for the Fifth Circuit embraced this notion that *Brown* required actual integration in a highly significant decision involving several school districts in Alabama and Louisiana: "The Court holds that boards and officials administering public schools have *the affirmative duty* under the Fourteenth Amendment to bring about an integrated, unitary school system *in which there are no Negro schools and no white schools—just schools.* Expressions in our earlier opinions distinguishing between integration and desegregation must yield to this affirmative duty we now recognize."[23]

The U.S. Supreme Court expressed agreement with Wisdom's construction of *Brown* in *Green v. New Kent County* (1968),[24] the Court's most important school desegregation opinion since *Brown*. The Court in *Green* held that a rural Virginia school board "must be required to . . . fashion steps which promise realistically to convert promptly to a system without a 'white' school and a 'Negro' school, but just schools."[25] Responding to the argument that "freedom of choice" pupil assignment plans were consistent with the "anti-segregation" imperative of *Brown*, the Court responded: " 'Freedom of choice' is not a sacred talisman; it is only a means to a constitutionally required end—the abolition of the system of segregation and its effects. If the means prove effective, it is acceptable, but if it fails to undo segregation, other means must be used to achieve this end. The school officials have the continuing duty to take whatever action may be necessary to create a 'unitary, nonracial system.' "[26]

After *Green*, compliance with *Brown* in the South would be measured by whether black and white children were actually attending school together. In the process, *Brown* came to stand for the actual integration of public schoolchildren. Outside the South, many educational reformers during the post-*Brown* era also framed the debate about equal educational opportunity in America in terms of integration. In 1963, for example, the commissioner of education for the state of New York, though his state was under no obligation to desegregate, deemed any school with more than 50 percent minority students to be racially imbalanced and therefore, by definition, failing to provide an equal educational opportunity.[27] In 1965 the Massachusetts Advisory Committee on Racial Imbalance and Education also urged the elimination of racial imbalance in public schools as a necessary condition to providing equal educational opportunity for minority children.[28] To some extent, this integrationist focus was influenced by the views of many social scientists during the 1960s concerning the deficiencies of black culture and the need for social assimilation through integrated schools.[29]

Under this integrationist construction of *Brown*, the decision enjoyed mixed success. Although virtually no racial integration took place in the eleven states of the Old Confederacy during the first decade after *Brown*, leaving only about 1 percent of southern black children attending a racially mixed school on the decision's tenth anniversary,[30] pupil mixing substantially increased after Congress enacted the Civil Rights Act of 1964 and the Office of Education issued its guidelines providing for the withholding of federal education funds from school districts that failed to meet its desegregation standards. At the same time, after the Supreme Court's decision in *Green* in 1968, lower federal courts finally began to insist that southern school districts engage in pupil mixing to comply with the desegregation mandate of *Brown*. The Supreme Court's decision in *Swann v. Charlotte-Mecklenburg* (1971),[31] which legitimated the use of school busing to desegregate urban school districts beset with significant residential segregation, had a particularly significant impact on patterns of southern school desegregation. The results were impressive. Whereas in 1968 only 18 percent of southern black schoolchildren attended majority-white schools, by 1972 that figure was 46 percent, rendering the South the most integrated region in the nation.[32] The number of southern black schoolchildren attending schools with more than 90 percent black enrollment declined from 77.5 percent in 1968 to 24.6 percent in 1980. Although white flight in many southern cities would affect those integration gains, the South would remain the most thoroughly desegregated area in the United States.[33]

The effect of *Brown* on patterns of racial integration outside the South was far less dramatic. Indeed, racial isolation in northern and western schools actually increased during the 1950s and 1960s because of two important demographic shifts: a significant influx of black and other minority residents into the cities[34] and an equally significant outflow of white residents from cities to suburbs.[35] For example, between 1940 and 1965 the black percentage of the total population increased from 8 to 27 percent in Chicago, from 9 to 29 percent in Detroit, and from 4 to 18 percent in Los Angeles.[36] By 1980 only 28 percent of the white population in the metropolitan areas of the Midwest and Northeast lived in inner cities, compared to 77 percent of the black population.[37]

These demographic shifts exacerbated the problem of residential segregation that had beset northern cities since the early twentieth century, creating a degree of racial separation "unimaginable to the architects of the municipal segregation ordinances of the early part of the century."[38] The correlation between residential segregation and racial separation in the public schools was obvious. As the Harlem Tenants Council noted after *Brown* in 1954: "Segregation in education, now outlawed by the Supreme Court, cannot really be eliminated until segregation in housing, too, is outlawed."[39]

The increase in residential segregation caused by the influx of minority residents to cities and the outflow of white residents to suburbs provoked a similar increase in racial isolation in many northern school districts.[40] In Pittsburgh, for example, the proportion of black students enrolled in predominantly black schools increased from 45 to 67 percent at the elementary school level and from 23 to 58 percent at the secondary school level between 1945 and 1965.[41] In New York City, 41 percent of the city's black and Puerto Rican schoolchildren attended predominantly minority schools in 1957; by 1965 that number had climbed to 58 percent.[42] Moreover, by 1965 the proportion of black elementary school students attending majority-black schools in Chicago, Dallas, Detroit, Houston, Los Angeles, and Philadelphia ranged from 87 to 97 percent.[43] Whereas whites were a majority in all of the nation's largest school districts except Washington in 1950, by 1980 every big-city school district in America had a student population that was at least two-thirds minority and most were at least three-fourths minority.[44]

While much of the nation, particularly the South, experienced a decline between 1968 and 1980 in the percentage of black children attending predominantly black schools, a few heavily urban northern states, including New Jersey and New York, experienced an increase in the percentage of black children attending predominantly black schools during those same years. By 1980 the five states with the highest proportion of black students attending schools with at least a 90 percent minority population were all northern states with large urban populations: Illinois, New York, Michigan, New Jersey, and Pennsylvania.[45] Although some of this increase in racial isolation in northern urban schools during the 1970s was due to white flight in response to court-ordered school desegregation, northern cities with no court-ordered school desegregation also experienced an increase in racial isolation in the schools.[46] By the same token, the proportion of Hispanic students in the United States attending predominantly minority schools increased from 55 to 68 percent between 1968 and 1980.[47] Since 1980 the percentage of Hispanic students attending predominantly minority schools has steadily increased.[48]

At the end of the twentieth century, more than 80 percent of the nation's minority students lived in metropolitan areas, which in most instances were divided into inner-city school districts where most students were minorities and suburban school districts where most students were white.[49] In the nation's largest cities, over 93 percent of black and Hispanic students attended schools that were overwhelmingly nonwhite.[50] Moreover, as a result of residential segregation, racial isolation in public schools today, in contrast to 1954, is typically due to "racial disparities *between* [school] districts rather than segregative patterns *within* districts,"[51] a problem which, as we shall see, has become virtually impossible to solve.

As American urban school districts became increasingly nonwhite, integrationist reformers sought to involve neighboring suburban school districts, which tended to be overwhelmingly white, in multi-district, metropolitan-area desegregation plans. But the Supreme Court's decision in *Milliken v. Bradley* (1974),[52] involving the Detroit schools, sharply limited the authority of federal courts to issue metropolitan-area desegregation orders involving multiple school districts. *Milliken* foreclosed the possibility of school integration in many northern and western cities in which school district lines kept suburban white children separate from inner-city minority children. Although the schools in some major cities were desegregated in the wake of the Supreme Court's school busing decision in *Swann*, including cities like Charlotte and Tampa with large school districts encompassing both center-city and suburban areas, the Court's decision in *Milliken* foreclosed racial integration in many of the nation's largest cities with more fragmented school districts. In some northern cities, such as New

York, Chicago, and Philadelphia, no serious desegregation efforts were ever launched despite extensive racial isolation in the public schools.[53] By the end of the twentieth century, the four states with the most significant racial isolation for black children—New York, Illinois, Michigan, and New Jersey—were each fraught with highly fragmented school districts that made desegregation impossible within the constraints of the *Milliken* decision.[54]

As federal courts—South and North—began to allow school districts to terminate their busing plans during the late 1980s and early 1990s, racial isolation in the public schools further increased. By 1991 the percentage of black students in schools with a student population more than half minority returned to levels predating the Supreme Court's decision in 1971 in *Swann*, which had had such a dramatic effect on urban segregation patterns.[55] Moreover, during the 1990s racial homogeneity in America's public schools further increased, as courts nationwide continued to allow school districts to jettison busing plans in favor of a return to racially homogeneous neighborhood schools.[56] Even Charlotte, whose schools were at issue in *Swann*, the Supreme Court's landmark decision that permitted extensive school busing to desegregate urban schools, and which subsequently fashioned a desegregation image for itself as the "City that Made it Work,"[57] was recently directed by a federal court to end its thirty-year history of school busing.[58] If the impact of *Brown* is measured merely in terms of the extent of racial mixing in the public schools, then *Brown* did achieve some success, particularly in the rigidly segregated South, but those integrationist gains have begun to erode and will continue to do so.


Envisioning Educational Equality in Non-Integrationist Terms

On the fiftieth anniversary of *Brown*, the integrationist construction of the decision is in serious retreat. Both the popular and academic press regularly proclaim an end to the school integration era.[59] Public and scholarly conversations about equal educational opportunity have increasingly shifted away from the issue of racial mixing and more to issues of school funding or educational alternatives such as private school vouchers for poor children.

Many factors account for this shift. As racial mixing became increasingly difficult if not impossible in large urban school districts with few nonminority students, and because the Supreme Court in *Milliken* declined to order multi-district desegregation remedies, an increasing number of proponents of minority education began to urge non-integrationist alternatives to equal educational opportunity, such as improved funding for minority schools. In 1977 the Supreme Court, in another decision involving the Detroit schools (*Milliken II*), held that governmental defendants could be required to fund remedial and compensatory education programs in inner-city, predominantly minority schools as an alternative to racial mixing.[60] *Milliken II* opened the door to litigation strategies designed to capture greater resources for urban, heavily minority schools as opposed to greater racial mixing.

By 1979, the twenty-fifth anniversary of *Brown*, even a few NAACP attorneys questioned the integrationist construction of the decision, suggesting that the equal opportunity mandate of *Brown* could be met through greater financial support for minority schools. Robert Carter, one of the NAACP litigators in *Brown*, articulated this broader vision of the decision: "While we fashioned *Brown* on the theory that equal education and integrated education were one and the same, the goal was not integration but equal educational opportunity. . . . If [equal educational opportunity] can be achieved without integration, *Brown* has been satisfied."[61] Derrick Bell, a former NAACP attorney involved in many of the school desegregation suits of the 1960s, also questioned his organization's emphasis on racial mixing, which Bell characterized in an influential article in 1980 as "in some cases inferior to plans focusing on 'educational components,' including the creation and development of 'model' all-black schools."[62] "The educational benefits that have resulted from the mandatory assignment of black and white children to the same schools are . . . debatable," Bell claimed. "If benefits did exist, they have begun to dissipate as whites flee in alarming numbers from school districts ordered to implement mandatory reassignment plans."[63] Looking back on years of frustration, Bell wrote in 1986: "rather than beat our heads against the wall seeking pupil-desegregation orders the courts were unwilling to enter or enforce, we could have organized parents and communities to ensure effective implementation for the equal-funding and equal-representation mandates."[64]

By the 1990s many African Americans had rejected the integrationist paradigm that dominated earlier discussions of how best to insure equal educational opportunity for all children, favoring instead a return to neighborhood schools.[65] For example, in 1993 Alex Johnson, a black law professor at the University of Virginia, wrote an article subtitled "Why Integrationism Fails African-Americans Again," in which he suggested that "*Brown v. Board of Education* and its explicit adoption of integrationism" was "a mistake."[66] Giving voice to the frustrations of many African Americans about the failure of racial mixing to improve their status in American society, Johnson conceded that his perspective constituted a break with the past. "Twenty or thirty years ago this Article would not have been written," Johnson noted. "The views presented . . . would have been so far outside the mainstream that, frankly, they would have been unthinkable by an African-American scholar."[67] To be sure, many proponents of minority education continued to insist on the importance of racial mixing to achieve equal educational opportunity,[68] but the decline in support for school integration in the minority community was striking.

Skepticism about integration as the best way to achieve equal educational opportunity has deep roots in African American history. Throughout the nineteenth century and the early twentieth, many African American leaders favored racially separate schools because of fears that their children would be mistreated in racially mixed schools, the refusal of school boards to let black teachers teach in integrated classrooms, and the loss of community cohesiveness.[69] For many blacks, racially separate schools with black teachers provided a far better learning environment for their children than did integrated schools with uncaring white teachers and classmates. The celebrated conflict between W. E. B. Du Bois and the NAACP during the mid-1930s over the importance of integrated schools is but one example of this long-standing divergence of opinion within the black community.[70]

During the 1960s, and increasingly thereafter, many in the black community criticized the integrationist construction of *Brown* championed by the NAACP in its long struggle for racially integrated schools.[71] To some extent this opposition to integration was a reaction to some of the assumptions embedded in the integrationist perspective about the inferiority of black culture and the need for contact with whites to improve black performance. The Congress of Racial Equality, for example, expressed this view in its amicus brief in the *Swann v. Charlotte-Mecklenburg* school busing case:

> When normal standards of educational excellence are applied to Black schools under segregation, it becomes clear that they are inferior to White schools. This is a fact with which no one can argue. Unfortunately, it has caused those who did not in the past and do not now understand the true nature of segregation to arrive at the faulty conclusion that all-Black schools are inherently inferior under any set of circumstances. . . . The "inherently inferior" theory is not only spurious on its face but insidiously racist in its implication that Black children . . . must mix in order to be equal. Blacks who subscribe to this theory are suffering from self-hatred, the legacy of generations of brainwashing. They have been told and they believe that it is exposure to Whites *in and by itself* that makes Blacks equal citizens.[72]

Many blacks also lamented the loss of black teachers and principals as a result of desegregation, and the closure of many black schools. As it had for more than a century, the integration of black and white children typically meant the replacement of black teachers with white ones. Between

1968 and 1970 alone, school districts in the Deep South reduced the total number of black teachers by 1,072 while increasing the number of white teachers by 5,575. At the same time, 20 percent of the black principals in Deep South states lost their jobs, while the number of white principals increased.[73] In recent years, a number of scholars have celebrated the "good black school" that was lost in the wake of the integrationist focus of *Brown*.[74]

Because achieving or retaining integrated schools in much of America is impossible in light of residential segregation and the end of court-ordered busing plans, in recent years the pursuit of equal funding for minority schools has displaced integration as the central educational strategy for improving minority education, and on the litigation front school finance has replaced school desegregation as the predominant focus of suits to secure equal educational opportunity. Although in 1973 the Supreme Court in *San Antonio v. Rodriquez* refused to prohibit unequal school funding under the equal protection clause of the U.S. Constitution,[75] state courts on state law grounds have granted relief in many recent lawsuits challenging unequal funding.[76] In fact, between 1973 and 1997 sixteen state supreme courts found state systems of funding education not in compliance with state constitutional provisions; these decisions helped to reduce funding disparities.[77] At the same time, a number of state legislatures engaged in their own equalization efforts, often in response to a state court decision.[78]

Despite these successes, heavily minority urban schools frequently get less funding than largely white suburban schools.[79] A study by the General Accounting Office in 1997 found that suburban school districts outspend urban school districts in almost every major city in the United States, a sharp reversal from 1950. The average spending gap between urban and suburban is 24 percent, but in some cities the disparity is as much as 100 percent. A few examples will suffice. Per pupil spending in the mostly black Baltimore city school system in 1998 was $4,101; statewide, the average was $5,887. In the mostly black Philadelphia school system, per pupil expenditures in 1998 were $4,455 compared to a statewide average of $5,212. Nationwide, urban school districts spent on average $4,500 per student in 1994, while the national average was $5,066.[80] Moreover, urban school districts, educating large numbers of poor and minority children, often require greater resources than suburban school districts do to cope with the array of concerns that disproportionately affect their students: health problems, developmental disabilities, hunger, violence, single-parent families, and lower parental education and participation.[81] At the same time, urban school districts often face greater competition than suburban school districts for tax dollars because of the greater demand for government-provided social services in urban settings.

For some critics, such as Gary Orfield of Harvard, these funding inequities between rich and poor school districts will be difficult to overcome if schools remain racially and ethnically separate. Indeed, for years many proponents of school integration, such as the NAACP, have argued that the best way for minority children to capture a fair share of educational funds is to attend school with white children. During the first few decades after *Brown*, many black parents favored integrated schools for precisely that reason. In light of the dismal record of funding black education during the pre-*Brown* era, particularly in the South, certainly one of the beneficial effects of *Brown* was to improve the amount per pupil available to black children who attended racially mixed schools. Moreover, although school busing plans tended to move black children to white schools rather than vice versa, black schools, when called upon to educate white children, frequently received extra resources that had not been forthcoming in the past. Thus, many proponents of minority education fear that the abandonment of racial integration as an educational goal will inevitably undermine minority efforts to secure a fair share of limited educational resources. Orfield, for example, has argued that the poor educational outcomes of many urban minority schools will unfairly breed cynicism about the capabilities of minority schoolchildren and further erode financial support for their education: "[When] the policies of resegregation are accepted by courts and community leaders as educationally sound, the blame for the pervasive inequalities that remain tends to be shifted to minority families and communities, the teachers, and the educational leaders. When discrimination is declared cured, the system can no longer be blamed. . . . The predictable failure of inner-city segregated schools then feeds cynicism and generates attacks on the entire system of public education. The failure often reinforces white stereotypes about what critics describe as the inferior culture of minority families, reinforcing growing suburban resistance to providing state resources to heavily minority urban school systems."[82]

Whether Orfield is unduly pessimistic remains to be seen. The history of black education for the past sixty years does suggest that school authorities have often been most willing to provide additional funds to minority schools when such action served white interests. Hence, during the 1940s and early 1950s many southern school districts made great strides toward equalizing black teacher salaries and supporting black schools to avoid the possibility of court-mandated desegregation.[83] After *Brown*, traditionally black schools that began to educate white children often received an influx of resources. As public schools in America become increasingly resegregated, one of the most important issues confronting those interested in minority education is how to procure sufficient resources to adequately educate the many poor minority children who live in urban communities with an array of problems that impede their learning process. Because of general resistance to providing additional financial resources to schools populated by poor children with limited political influence, increasing attention will be directed toward alternative strategies for urban education, such as private school vouchers.

By the same token, some scholars increasingly urge that the effect of non-economic factors on educational outcomes be considered. For example, in their landmark book *The Black-White Test Score Gap*, Christopher Jencks and Meredith Phillips argue that successful theories for understanding the gap between black and white academic performance "will probably pay more attention" to family patterns and to "psychological and cultural differences."[84] The debate over the causes of poor educational outcomes among many black children will continue.

### *Brown* and Its Impact on Black Education

Given the limitations of the integrationist agenda of *Brown* and the ongoing difficulty of securing financial support for the educational needs of many poor minority children in racially isolated urban schools, what have been the tangible gains for African American education during the last half-century?

Particularly in the South, *Brown* (and the threat of a decision like it during the 1940s and early 1950s) helped produce significantly greater educational resources for black children and reduce the gross disparities in educational funding between white and black schools. Much of this improvement has taken place in racially mixed schools, but many predominantly black schools are also significantly better supported than before *Brown*. As the NAACP lawyer Jack Greenberg has noted, "[b]efore *Brown* there may not have been a single black school in the South equal to its white counterpart. Afterward, many schools attended mostly by blacks equaled or at least approximated white schools in physical quality."[85]

The effect of this improvement in educational resources has been noticeable. Before *Brown* educational opportunities for blacks, particularly in the South where the majority of then lived, were extremely limited. In 1940 only 7.7 percent of blacks over the age of twenty-five in the United States had completed four years of high school, compared to 26.1 percent of whites. That same year, 41.8 percent of blacks over the age of twenty-five had less than five years of education, compared to only 10.9 percent of whites.[86] Since *Brown*, black high school graduation rates and college attendance rates have sharply increased. Among blacks aged twenty-five to twenty-nine, the proportion who had completed high school rose from 55 percent in 1970 to 75 percent in 1980 to 83 percent in 1986.[87] By the mid-1990s blacks finished high school in the same percentage as whites and about half of black high school graduates went on to college (compared to two-thirds of whites), which constituted a dramatic increase since 1954.[88]

Moreover, the performance of minority students on achievement tests has substantially improved since *Brown*, and the gap between the performance of white and nonwhite students has narrowed though it has not been eliminated. For example, between 1970 and 1994 black students made stronger gains in science, mathematics, and reading achievement tests than whites did, although they continued to lag behind their white counterparts.[89] In some communities, the achievement gains were more dramatic. In Charlotte, for example, achievement test scores for both black and white students were significantly higher in 1980 than they had been in 1968 before implementation of the city's busing plan.[90] There is some evidence, however, that the achievement gap between white and black children in Charlotte has been widening since the late 1980s.[91]

To what extent are these improvements in black educational outcomes due to the elimination of segregated schools as opposed to factors unrelated to racial mixing? Before *Brown* there was scattered evidence that black children actually fared better in single-race schools than in racially mixed schools because of the nurture and support of black teachers. Studies conducted during the 1920s found that black students attending segregated schools in border-state cities tended to have higher school attendance and graduation rates than black students attending racially mixed schools in northern cities.[92] Yet since *Brown* some data have indicated the contrary— those black children who attended racially mixed schools enjoyed superior educational outcomes compared to those who remained in single-race schools.[93]

Are these gains attributable to the benefits of racial mixing? Some scholars argue that the achievement gains of black children in racially mixed schools have more to do with the children who wind up in integrated schools than with the fact that they are racially mixed. For example, black children from middle-class backgrounds are more likely to have attended racially mixed schools than black children from poor backgrounds. Studies consistently show a correlation between the economic status of children and their educational performance (although the strength of that correlation is debated).[94] Hence, the rising achievement levels of children in racially mixed schools may well have had more to do with socioeconomic status, as James Coleman famously argued, than with racial mixing.[95] For example, student achievement test data consistently correlate with the level of parental education.[96]

Despite the educational gains of many black children during the past thirty years, *Brown* has not eliminated the poor social and economic outcomes of many racial minorities in America, particularly blacks and Hispanics. The underclass in America's cities, consisting in significant measure of racial minorities, remains largely unaffected by the educational reforms provoked by the Court's decision in *Brown*. Jack Greenberg, though enthusiastic about the larger effects of *Brown*, concedes that the decision has not reached many poor blacks in urban ghettos: "Along with the gains, there has come into being a large group of unemployed, uneducated, poorly supervised children. The income gaps between upper, middle, and lower classes are growing, faster within the black than in the white community, with the largest concentration among blacks at the lower end. . . . [The benefits of *Brown*] were never universally enjoyed by black Americans."[97]

This raises the question whether education can in fact be the instrument of liberation that African Americans and other racial minorities have long hoped for. The evidence of the past fifty years suggests that the educational reform efforts unleashed by *Brown* did have certain positive effects, but failed to overcome the gap between the haves and the have-nots. As we move further into the twenty-first century, therein lies one of America's greatest challenges.

## Notes

1 David Tyack and Larry Cuban, *Tinkering toward Utopia: A Century of Public School Reform* (Cambridge: Harvard University Press, 1995), 1.

2 Quoted in Henry J. Perkinson, *The Imperfect Panacea: American Faith in Education* (New York: McGraw-Hill, 1991), 12.

3 Gunnar Myrdal with Richard Sterner and Arnold Rose, *An American Dilemma: The Negro Problem and Modern Democracy* (New York: Harper and Row, 1962), 882.

4 Brown v. Board of Education, 347 U.S. 483 (1954).

5 Tyack and Cuban, *Tinkering toward Utopia*, 27.

6 Kevin K. Gaines, *Uplifting the Race: Black Leadership, Politics, Culture in the Twentieth Century* (Chapel Hill: University of North Carolina Press, 1996), 1.

7 Lee Epstein, "Interest Group Litigation during the Rehnquist Court Era," *Journal of Law and Politics* 9 (1993): 639–706; Gregory A. Caldeira and John R. Wright, "Amici Curiae before the Supreme Court: Who Participates, When, and How Much?," *Journal of Politics* 52 (1990): 782–806.

8 Aryeh Neier, *Only Judgment: The Limits of Litigation in Social Change* (Middletown: Wesleyan University Press, 1982), 9.

9  Brown v. Board of Education, 347 U.S. 483 (1954).

10  During the 1970s a few prominent commentators identified various institutional and political constraints on the ability of courts to have a meaningful impact on social policy. Stuart A. Scheingold, *The Politics of Rights: Lawyers, Public Policy, and Political Change* (New Haven: Yale University Press, 1974); Donald L. Horowitz, *The Courts and Social Policy* (Washington: Brookings Institution, 1977); Joel F. Handler, *Social Movements and the Legal System: A Theory of Law Reform and Social Change* (New York: Academic, 1978). In more recent years, scholars examining the impact of litigation on specific policy areas have also questioned the influence of the judiciary on social policy. For example, the use of litigation to improve the welfare system and to enhance the status of poor people has received considerable attention, as has the effect of environmental litigation on environmental policy. Martha F. Davis, *Brutal Need: Lawyers and the Welfare Rights Movement, 1960–1973* (New Haven: Yale University Press, 1993); R. Shep Melnick, *Regulation and the Courts: The Case of the Clean Air Act* (Washington: Brookings Institution, 1983).

Particularly in the area of racial reform, critical theorists argue that courts are unwilling and unable to effect significant racial change because of their inherent conservatism and adherence to legal rules that do not confront the realities of racial oppression. Examples include Derrick A. Bell Jr., *And We Are Not Saved: The Elusive Quest for Racial Justice* (New York: Basic Books, 1989); Girardeau A. Spann, *Race against the Court: The Supreme Court and Minorities in Contemporary America* (New York: NYU Press, 1993). For these critics, litigation at best creates an illusion of progress that masks a failure of substantial empowerment for African Americans. Gerald Rosenberg, relying on extensive empirical research, reached similar conclusions in his book *The Hollow Hope: Can Courts Bring about Social Change?* (Chicago: University of Chicago Press, 1991), in which he argued that courts have had much more limited success in securing gains for African Americans than is popularly believed.

11  Mark Tushnet, "The Significance of *Brown v. Board of Education*," 80 *Virginia Law Review* 173, 182 (1994).

12  Browder v. Gayle, 142 F. Supp. 707 (M.D. Ala. 1956), aff'd, 77 S. Ct. 145 (1956).

13  Michael Klarman, "*Brown*, Racial Change, and the Civil Rights Movement," 80 *Virginia Law Review* 7–150 (1994).

14  Tyack and Cuban, *Tinkering toward Utopia*, 26.

15  Brown v. Board of Education, 347 U.S. 483 (1954).

16  Klarman, "*Brown*, Racial Change, and the Civil Rights Movement," 7–150; Rosenberg, *The Hollow Hope*.

17  Horace Mann Bond, *The Education of the Negro in the American Social Order* (New York: Octagon, 1934), 12.

18  William Julius Wilson, *The Declining Significance of Race: Blacks and Changing American Institutions* (Chicago: University of Chicago Press, 1978), 1.

19  Abigail Thernstrom and Stephan Thernstrom, *No Excuses: Closing the Racial Gap in Learning* (New York: Simon and Schuster, 2003), 133–37.

20  Christopher Jencks and Meredith Phillips, eds., *The Black-White Test Score Gap* (Washington: Brookings Institution Press, 1998), 25.

21  Briggs v. Elliott, 132 F. Supp. 776, 777 (E.D.S.C. 1955) (emphasis supplied).

22  Davison M. Douglas, *Reading, Writing, and Race: The Desegregation of the Charlotte Schools* (Chapel Hill: University of North Carolina Press, 1995), 124–25.

23  United States v. Jefferson County Board of Education, 380 F. 2d 385, 387 (5th Cir. 1967) (emphasis supplied).

24  391 U.S. 430 (1968).

25  *Id*. at 442.

26  *Id*. at 440.

27  Diane Ravitch, "Desegregation: Varieties of Meaning," *Shades of Brown: New Perspectives on School Desegregation*, ed. Derrick Bell (New York: Teachers College Press, 1980), 42.

28  Ravitch, "Desegregation," 43.

29  Ravitch, "Desegregation," 42.

30  Southern Education Reporting Service, cited in Rosenberg, *The Hollow Hope*, 50.

31  Swann v. Charlotte-Mecklenburg Board of Education, 402 U.S. 1 (1971).

32  Donald Nieman, *Promises to Keep: African-Americans and the Constitutional Order, 1776 to the Present* (New York: Oxford University Press, 1991), 179.

33  Stephan and Abigail Thernstrom, *America in Black and White: One Nation, Indivisible* (New York: Simon and Schuster, 1997), 341.

34  During the 1950s and 1960s the black population of many northern cities dramatically increased. In Boston, for example, there were 40,000 blacks in 1950 (5 percent of the total population) and over 100,000 in 1970 (about 17 percent of the population). Henry L. Allen, "Segregation and Desegregation in Boston's Schools, 1961–1974," *From Common School to Magnet School: Selected Essays in the History of Boston's Schools*, ed. James W. Fraser, Henry L. Allen, and Sam Barnes (Boston: Trustees of the Public Library of the City of Boston, 1979), 110.

35  Gary Orfield, *Must We Bus? Segregated Schools and National Policy* (Washington: Brookings Institution, 1978), 50–51.

36  Adam Fairclough, *Better Day Coming: Blacks and Equality 1890–2000* (New York: Viking, 2001), 298.

37  Harvey Kantor and Barbara Brenzel, "Urban Education and the 'Truly Disadvantaged': The Historical Roots of Contemporary Crisis," *The "Underclass" Debate: Views From History*, ed. Michael B. Katz (Princeton: Princeton University Press, 1993), 371.

38  David Delaney, *Race, Place, and the Law, 1836–1948* (Austin: University of Texas Press, 1998), 182.

39  Martha Biondi, "The Struggle for Black Equality in New York City, 1945–1955" (diss., Columbia University, 1997), 383.

40  For example, from 1957 to 1965 the number of black children enrolled in the New York City public schools increased by 64 percent, but there was a decline

of 13 percent for "other students," a category composed largely of white children. Lisa Yvette Waller, "Holding Back the Dawn: Milton A. Galamison and the Fight for School Integration in New York City: A Northern Civil Rights Struggle, 1948–1968" (diss., Duke University, 1998), 239.

41 Laurence Glasco, "Double Burden: The Black Experience in Pittsburgh," *City at the Point: Essays on the Social History of Pittsburgh*, ed. Samuel P. Hays (Pittsburgh: University of Pittsburgh Press, 1989), 90.

42 Waller, "Holding Back the Dawn," 237.

43 Kantor and Brenzel, "Urban Education and the 'Truly Disadvantaged,'" 374.

44 *Id.*

45 Gary Orfield, *Public School Desegregation in the United States, 1968–1980* (Washington: Joint Center for Political Studies, 1983), 8–10.

46 Kantor and Brenzel, "Urban Education and the 'Truly Disadvantaged,'" 376.

47 Orfield, *Public School Desegregation*, 12–14.

48 Orfield, *Dismantling Desegregation: The Quiet Reversal of Brown v. Board of Education* (New York: W. W. Norton, 1996), 59–60.

49 *Id.* at 292.

50 *Id.* at 61. Moreover, by 1986 the twenty-five largest urban school systems contained 30 percent of the nation's Hispanic school population, 27 percent of the black population, and 3 percent of the non-Hispanic white population.

51 Charles Clotfelter, "Public School Segregation in Metropolitan Areas," *Land Economics* 75 (1999): 487, 502.

52 418 U.S. 717 (1974).

53 James S. Liebman, "Desegregating Politics: 'All Out' School Desegregation Explained," 90 *Columbia Law Review* 1463, 1470 (1990).

54 Orfield, *Dismantling Desegregation*, 60.

55 *Id.* at 54.

56 In recent years, courts have terminated school desegregation plans in a variety of cities, including Charlotte, Buffalo (Arthur v. Nyquist, 904 F. Supp. 112 (W.D.N.Y. 1995)), Denver (Keyes v. Congress of Hispanic Educators, 902 F. Supp. 1274 (D. Colo. 1995)), Savannah (Stell v. Board of Public Education, 860 F. Supp. 1563 (S.D. Ga. 1994)), Oklahoma City (Dowell v. Board of Education, 778 F. Supp. 1144 (W.D. Okla. 1991), *aff'd*, 8 F.3d 1501 (10th Cir. 1993)), and Wilmington, Delaware (Coalition to Save Our Children v. State Board of Education, 901 F. Supp. 784 (D. Del. 1995), *aff'd*, 90 F.3d 752 (3d Cir. 1996)). School districts that have been declared unitary have typically experienced an increase in racial isolation. See, e.g., Catherine Freeman, Benjamin Scafidi, and David L. Sjoquist, .*Racial Segregation in Georgia Public Schools, 1994–2001: Trends, Causes, and Impact on Teacher Quality* 26 (Atlanta: Andrew Young School of Policy Studies, Georgia State University, 2002), 26.

To be sure, some courts continue to insist on racial mixing. For example, a federal judge in 1996 ordered racial balance in the schools in Rockford, Illinois, as a means of improving black achievement. Thernstrom and Thernstrom, *America in Black and White*, 346.

57 Douglas, *Reading, Writing, and Race*.

58 Capacchione v. Charlotte-Mecklenburg Schools, 57 F. Supp. 2d 228 (W.D.N.C. 1999).

59 See for example Wendy Parker, "The Future of School Desegregation," 94 *Northwestern University Law Review* 1157, 1157 (2000) (noting that "either desegregation cases are dead or, at the very least, the death knell has sounded"); James E. Ryan, "Schools, Race, and Money," 109 *Yale Law Journal* 249, 254 (1999) (noting that school desegregation is in its "twilight phase"); Bradley W. Joondeph, "Skepticism and School Desegregation," 76 *Washington University Law Quarterly* 161, 161 (1998) (noting that the "curtain falls on court-ordered desegregation nationwide").

60 Milliken v. Bradley, 433 U.S. 267 (1977).

61 Robert Carter, "A Reassessment of Brown v. Board," *Shades of Brown*, ed. Bell, 27.

62 Derrick A. Bell Jr., "*Brown v. Board of Education* and the Interest-Convergence Dilemma," 93 *Harvard Law Review* 518, 528 (1980).

63 *Id.* at 531.

64 Bell, *And We Are Not Saved*, 112–13. See also Kevin Brown, "Has the Supreme Court Allowed the Cure for De Jure Segregation to Replicate the Disease?," *Cornell Law Review* 78 (1992): 1; Alex M. Johnson Jr., "Bid Whist, Tonk, and United States v. Fordice: Why Integrationism Fails African Americans Again," 81 *California Law Review* 1401 (1993).

65 For example, black mayors in several major cities, including Cleveland, Denver, and Minneapolis, have endorsed the termination of school desegregation plans. Davison M. Douglas, "The End of Busing?," 95 *Michigan Law Review* 1715, 1731 n. 67 (1997). Many black parents prefer a return to neighborhood schools even if that means the end of racially mixed schools. Drew S. Days III, "*Brown* Blues: Rethinking the Integrative Ideal," 34 *William and Mary Law Review* 53, 54 (1992); Orfield, *Dismantling Desegregation*, 343.

66 Johnson, "Bid Whist, Tonk, and *United States v. Fordice*," 1401, 1402, 1409.

67 Johnson, "Bid Whist, Tonk, and *United States v. Fordice*," 1401, 1409.

68 See, for example, Orfield, *Dismantling Desegregation*; John A. Powell, "An 'Integrated' Theory of Integrated Education," forthcoming, *North Carolina Law Review*.

69 Davison M. Douglas, "The Limits of Law in Accomplishing Racial Change: School Segregation in the Pre-Brown North," 44 *UCLA Law Review* 677, 697–701, 712–19 (1997).

70 See for example W. E. B. Du Bois, "Does the Negro Need Separate Schools?," *Journal of Negro Education* 4 (1935): 328.

71 Bell, *Shades of Brown*, vii.

72 Congress of Racial Equality, "A True Alternative to Segregation: A Proposal for Community School Districts," Amicus Curiae Brief, *Swann v. Charlotte-Mecklenburg*, February 1970, 36.

73 Jack Greenberg, *Crusaders in the Courts: How a Dedicated Band of Lawyers Fought for the Civil Rights Revolution* (New York: Basic Books, 1994), 391.

74 See for example Vanessa Siddle Walker, *Their Highest Potential: An African American School Community in the Segregated South* (Chapel Hill: University of North Carolina Press, 1966).

75 San Antonio School District v. Rodriquez, 411 U.S. 1 (1973).

76 For example, thirteen days after the Supreme Court's decision in *San Antonio v. Rodriquez*, the New Jersey Supreme Court found that the state's method of funding education violated the state constitution's guarantee of a "thorough and efficient" education for all children. Robinson v. Cahill, 62 N.J. 473, 303 A.2d 273 (1973).

77 Douglas S. Reed, *On Equal Terms: The Constitutional Politics of Educational Opportunity* (Princeton: Princeton University Press, 2001), 15–35.

78 U.S. General Accounting Office, *School Finance: State Efforts to Equalize Funding between Wealthy and Poor Districts*, GAO/HEHS-98-92, June 1998.

79 For a contrary view see Thernstrom and Thernstrom, *America in Black and White*, 351 (noting that urban school districts in 1988–90 were better funded than suburban school districts).

80 "The Persisting Myth That Black and White Schools Are Equally Funded," *Journal of Blacks in Higher Education* 22 (winter 1998–99): 17.

81 Orfield, *Dismantling Desegregation*, 83.

82 *Id.* at 332–33.

83 Douglas, *Reading, Writing, and Race*, 22.

84 Jencks and Phillips, *The Black-White Test Score Gap*, 43.

85 Greenberg, *Crusaders in the Courts*, 510.

86 Diane Ravitch, *Left Back: A Century of Failed School Reforms* (New York: Simon and Schuster, 2000), 374.

87 Greenberg, *Crusaders in the Courts*, 398.

88 James Patterson, *Brown v. Board of Education: A Civil Rights Milestone and Its Troubled Legacy* (New York: Oxford University Press, 2001), 188.

89 U.S. Department of Education, National Center for Education Statistics, *Report in Brief: NAEP 1994 Trends in Academic Progress* (Washington: Government Printing Office, 1994), 7; Digest of Education Statistics (1997), at http://nces.ed.gov/pubs/digest97/d97t118.html.

90 Douglas, *Reading, Writing, and Race*, 249–50.

91 Thernstrom and Thernstrom, *America in Black and White*, 357–59.

92 For example, black students attending segregated high schools in Washington, Baltimore, and St. Louis were found to have higher attendance and graduation rates than black students in integrated high schools in New York, Boston, and Philadelphia. Guy Michael Fultz, " 'Agitate Then, Brother': Education in the Black Monthly Periodical Press, 1900–1930" (diss., Harvard University, 1987), 94, 207. Kelly Miller wrote in the *Chicago Defender* in 1922 that blacks had higher enrollments in segregated schools "[i]n Washington, Baltimore, St. Louis and Kansas City, where separate Colored schools are maintained, there is a much larger enrollment of Colored pupils in the higher levels of instruction than in

Philadelphia, New York and Boston, where the schools are mixed." Quoted in Chandler Owen, "Mistakes of Kelly Miller: Reply to Kelly Miller on Segregation in Education," *Messenger* 4 (1922): 422. Similarly, a study of New Jersey schools in 1925 comparing racially mixed schools in the state's northern counties with segregated schools in the southern counties found that "Negro students enter high schools in larger proportions from segregated schools, and graduate in greater numbers than those who attend mixed schools." Lester Granger, "Race Relations and the School System," *Opportunity* 3, no. 25 (1925): 329; Granger, "Race Relations and the School System," 357; Fultz, " 'Agitate Then, Brother,' " 207. A study in 1929 of fifty northern and border state cities with populations of at least 100,000 found that black children had a higher attendance and graduation rate from high school in cities with only single-race schools than in cities with both integrated and segregated schools. L. A. Pechstein, "The Problem of Negro Education in Northern and Border Cities," *Elementary School Journal* 30 (1929): 192, 194.

93  Patterson, *Brown v. Board of Education*, 188. Other data do not support the view that black children in racially mixed schools have made greater educational progress. Thernstrom and Thernstrom, *America in Black and White*, 358.

94  Freeman, *Racial Segregation in Georgia Public Schools*, 18. Abigail Thernstrom and Stephan Thernstrom, however, argue that the correlation between economic status and educational outcome is weaker than often assumed. Thernstrom and Thernstrom, *No Excuses*, 124–30.

95  Patterson, *Brown v. Board of Education*, 188.

96  U.S. Department of Education, National Center for Education Statistics, *Report in Brief*, 7; Digest of Education Statistics (1997), at http://nces.ed.gov/pubs/digest97/d97t118.html.

97  Greenberg, *Crusaders in the Courts*, 515–16.

PETER F. LAU

# Conclusion

## *Brown* and Historical Memory

In June 2003 the U.S. Supreme Court upheld the constitutionality of the University of Michigan's affirmative action policy for law school admissions by a slim 5–4 majority. Writing for the majority, Justice Sandra Day O'Connor reluctantly acknowledged the continued significance of race in American life. "Just as growing up in a particular region or having particular professional experiences is likely to affect an individual's views," she explained, "so too is one's own, unique experience of being a racial minority in a society, like our own, in which race unfortunately still matters." By acknowledging that race "still matters" nearly fifty years after *Brown v. Board of Education*, O'Connor challenged an increasingly prevalent notion that the civil rights revolution of the 1950s and 1960s settled the problem of race in the United States once and for all by establishing the principle of equality under the law for all citizens. At the same time, however, O'Connor sought to establish a time frame for ending race-based decision making in admissions to public institutions of higher education. "We expect that 25 years from now," she wrote, "the use of racial preferences will no longer be necessary . . . to further a compelling interest in obtaining benefits that flow from a diverse student body." If the passing of fifty years was not enough to signal the demise of race in the nation's most prestigious educational institutions, the Court was saying, in effect, an additional twenty-five ought to be sufficient to complete the task. The problem with the Court's formulation is that the history of race and racial discrimination in the United States has seldom progressed in such a straight line. Indeed, the court's ruling lacks the historical lens that the essays in this book offer.[1]

One hundred years before the Supreme Court issued its most recent ruling on racial justice in the United States, W. E. B. Du Bois, the African American intellectual who was a forceful advocate of black equality, prophetically declared that "The problem of the twentieth century is the problem of the color-line,—the relation between the darker and lighter races of men in Asia and Africa, in America and the islands of the sea." Writing less than fifty years after the close of the American Civil War and the formal end of institutionalized racial enslavement, Du Bois sought to come to terms with the rising tide of Jim Crow segregation, disfranchisement, and lynch mob terror in American life, and he linked the future of African-descended people in the United States to that of people of color around the world. Confronted with the particularly brutal reality of race in the opening years of the twentieth century, Du Bois remained optimistic about the future and set forth an agenda for racial advancement and democratic reform that placed education and forceful protest at its center. In contrast to today's Supreme Court, Du Bois did not posit a day when race would cease to matter, either in the United States or in the larger world. Race, as he understood it, was so central to American history and life (and to world history) that to imagine an America in the absence of race was more than mere folly; it was, quite simply, impossible. Rather than hope for an America without race, Du Bois sought to create an America in which it would be "possible for a man to be both a Negro and an American, without being cursed and spit upon by his fellows, without having the doors of Opportunity closed roughly in his face." The social reality of race, Du Bois might just as well have written, could not be wished away. The struggle for racial equality necessitated a transformed consideration of race in American life, *not* an end to the consideration of race itself. Indeed, America's particular history required that race be made a resource for creating a more democratic society and cease to serve as a source of exclusion from it.[2]

This volume of essays represents a challenge both to the notion that race has ceased to exist as a significant factor in American life and to the notion that progress over race, segregation, and discrimination is either inevitable *or* impossible. Race, to be sure, is not something fixed in time and bears only the faintest relation to biological fact—the scientific and social science communities have provided ample proof of that. To acknowledge that race is neither a fixed essence nor a biological fact, however, is not the same as arguing that race has not or does not continue to shape real human lives. To the contrary, race has been central to America's understanding of itself from the earliest decades of its colonial past. It has given shape to American visions of freedom, to economic systems, to the development of an industrial working class, to demographic patterns, to the alignment of major political parties, to artistic innovation, social movements, history, and the law.[3] For all the violence, exclusion, and discrimination based on race, there are related stories of human struggle, creativity, and triumph that have invested the history of race in America with quite different meanings. *Brown* embodies both the abject horror and ignoble beauty of race in America. It suggests that race is so intertwined with all that America abhors *and* values that to imagine a time when the nation ceases to take race into account is to imagine a time beyond the existence of America itself. That time may come, but a twenty-five-year time frame for its demise seems premature at best.

As the fiftieth anniversary of *Brown* is celebrated and then recedes into the historical past, the importance of the legal decision will no doubt be reaffirmed. The decision will be celebrated justly for sweeping away the legal doctrine of "separate but equal" and for challenging the United States to live up to its loftiest ideals of freedom and equality. Although there will be ample criticism of the decision's legal premises and social ineffectiveness, the decision will retain its status as a landmark Supreme Court ruling and a pivotal event in American history. Too often, however, the grand events of American history are remembered shorn of their social—their human— contexts. They become, in effect, relics of the historical past, praised or criticized, but detached from the present because they are larger than life. My hope is that this collection helps to keep the human spirit of *Brown* alive. As it makes plain, the history of *Brown* has been filled with far too much disagreement and conflict, hope and despair, struggle and violence, to be stripped of its human dimension and flattened to serve any single political purpose.

The United States is currently undergoing a demographic revolution in which understandings of race, ethnicity, and citizenship are being rede- fined in ways we can barely conceive, let alone fully comprehend. Fifty years ago, race and segregation were defined principally in terms of white and black, even as Asian Americans, Native Americans, Mexican Americans, Puerto Ricans, and numerous other individuals and groups experienced pervasive discrimination and fought to have their voices heard in local communities and the larger nation. Today, the demographics are trans- formed and the array of people demanding the opportunity to shape their own lives and the society around them is more diverse and louder than ever. As never before, there is a need to recognize just how central race and segregation have been to American life and to openly confront the his- tory and legacy of both. Race and patterns of discrimination will certainly change during the next twenty-five years—they always have. But they will not disappear. What is needed, and this collection helps point the way, is an understanding of how race can serve as a resource for making a more equal and democratic society. The current option is not to ignore race or wish it away. It is, rather, to recognize its significance and work to harness its capacity for human advancement.

*Brown* was a momentous legal event, but it was a far more important social and cultural one, precisely because it forced an open confrontation with the nation's history of race and segregation. As the product of decades of social struggle, the decision in turn helped to make possible a larger human struggle against inequality in all its forms. That struggle, to be sure, continues. So long as it does, *Brown* will remain a source of inspiration and controversy. Today, it is up to all of us to understand how *Brown* has shaped the course of human history and to begin charting a path to the future that is informed by the possibilities and limitations that flow from that history.

## Notes

1  Grutter v. Bollinger, 123 S. Ct. 2325, 2341, 2347 (2003).

2  W. E. B. Du Bois, *The Souls of Black Folk* (1903; reprint, Boston: Bedford, 1997), 45, 39.

3  For just a few examples see Eric Foner, *The Story of American Freedom* (New York: W. W. Norton, 1998); Nathan Irvin Huggins, "The Deforming Mirror of Truth," *Revelations: American History, American Myths*, ed. Brenda Smith Huggins (New York: Oxford University Press, 1995); Robin D. G. Kelley, *Freedom Dreams: The Black Radical Imagination* (Boston: Beacon, 2002); David Levering Lewis, *When Harlem Was in Vogue* (New York: Alfred A. Knopf, 1981); Edmund S. Morgan, *American Slavery, American Freedom: The Ordeal of Colonial Virginia* (New York: W. W. Norton, 1975); David R. Roediger, *The Wages of Whiteness: Race and the Making of the American Working Class* (New York: Verso, 1991).

# Bibliography

Abernathy, Ralph David. *And the Walls Came Tumbling Down: An Autobiography*. New York: Harper and Row, 1989.

Adams, David Wallace. *Education for Extinction: American Indians and the Boarding School Experience, 1875–1928*. Lawrence: University Press of Kansas, 1995.

Anderson, James D. *The Education of Blacks in the South, 1860–1935*. Chapel Hill: University of North Carolina Press, 1988.

Balkin, Jack M., ed. *What "Brown v. Board of Education" Should Have Said: The Nation's Top Legal Experts Rewrite America's Landmark Civil Rights Decision*. New York: New York University Press, 2001.

Beals, Melba Pattillo. *Warriors Don't Cry: A Searing Memoir of the Battle to Integrate Little Rock's Central High*. New York: Pocket Books, 1994.

Bell, Derrick A., Jr. *And We Are Not Saved: The Elusive Quest for Racial Justice*. New York: Basic Books, 1989.

Bell, Derrick A., Jr., ed. *Shades of Brown: New Perspectives on School Desegregation*. New York: Teachers College Press, 1980.

Brown, Cynthia Stokes, ed. *Ready from Within: Septima Poinsette Clark and the Civil Rights Movement*. Navarro, Calif.: Wild Tree, 1986.

Chafe, William. *Civilities and Civil Rights: Greensboro, North Carolina, and the Black Freedom Struggle*. New York: Oxford University Press, 1980.

Chafe, William, Raymond Gavins, and Robert Korstad, eds. *Remembering Jim Crow: African Americans Tell about Life in the Segregated South*. New York: New Press, 2001.

Child, Brenda J. *Boarding School Seasons: American Indian Families, 1900–1940*. Lincoln: University of Nebraska Press, 1998.

Cleaver, Eldridge. *Soul on Ice*. New York: Dell, 1968.

Crawford, Vicki, Jacqueline Anne Rouse, and Barbara Woods, eds. *Women in the Civil Rights Movement: Trailblazers and Torchbearers, 1941–1965*. Bloomington: University of Indiana Press, 1993.

Curry, Constance. *Silver Rights*. Chapel Hill: Algonquin, 1995.

Davis, Angela. *Angela Davis: An Autobiography*. New York: International, 1974.

Dittmer, John. *Local People: The Struggle for Civil Rights in Mississippi*. Urbana: University of Illinois Press, 1994.

Douglas, Davison M. *Reading, Writing, and Race: The Desegregation of the Charlotte Schools*. Chapel Hill: University of North Carolina Press, 1995.

Dudziak, Mary L. *Cold War Civil Rights: Race and the Image of American Democracy*. Princeton: Princeton University Press, 2000.

Eagles, Charles, ed. *The Civil Rights Movement in America*. Jackson: University Press of Mississippi, 1986.

Fairclough, Adam. *Race and Democracy: The Civil Rights Struggle in Louisiana, 1915–1972.* Athens: University of Georgia Press, 1995.

———. *Teaching Equality: Black Schools in the Age of Jim Crow.* Athens: University of Georgia Press, 2001.

Foreman, James. *The Making of Black Revolutionaries.* Seattle: University of Washington Press, 1997.

García, Mario T. *Mexican Americans: Leadership, Ideology, and Identity, 1930–1960.* New Haven: Yale University Press, 1989.

Gavins, Raymond. "Fear, Hope, and Struggle: Recasting Black North Carolina in the Age of Jim Crow," *Democracy Betrayed: The Wilmington Race Riot and Its Legacy,* ed. David S. Cecelski and Timothy Tyson. Chapel Hill: University of North Carolina Press, 1998.

Greenberg, Jack. *Crusaders in the Courts: How a Dedicated Band of Lawyers Fought for the Civil Rights Revolution.* New York: Basic Books, 1994.

Gutiérrez, David. *Walls and Mirrors: Mexican Americans, Mexican Immigrants, and the Politics of Ethnicity in the Southwest, 1910–1986.* Berkeley: University of California Press, 1996.

Honey, Michael. *Southern Labor and Black Civil Rights: Organizing Memphis Workers.* Urbana: University of Illinois Press, 1993.

Irons, Peter. *Jim Crow's Children: The Broken Promises of the Brown Decision.* New York: Viking, 2002.

Klarman, Michael J. *From Jim Crow to Civil Rights: The Supreme Court and the Struggle for Racial Equality.* New York: Oxford University Press, 2004.

———. "Is the Supreme Court Sometimes Irrelevant? Race and the Southern Criminal Justice System in the 1940s." *Journal of American History* 89 (June 2002): 119–53.

———."How *Brown* Changed Race Relations: The Backlash Thesis." *Journal of American History* 81 (June 1994): 81–118.

Klinkner, Philip A., with Rogers M. Smith. *Unsteady March: The Rise and Decline of Racial Equality in America.* Chicago: University of Chicago Press, 1999.

Kluger, Richard. *Simple Justice.* New York: Alfred A. Knopf, 1976.

Lawson, Steven F. *Running for Freedom: Civil Rights and Black Politics in America since 1941.* Philadelphia: Temple University Press, 1991.

———. "Freedom Then, Freedom Now: The Historiography of the Civil Rights Movement." *American Historical Review* 96 (April 1991): 456–71.

Lewis, John with Michael D'Orso. *Walking with the Wind: A Memoir of the Movement.* New York: Simon and Schuster, 1998.

Lofgren, Charles A. *The Plessy Case: A Legal-Historical Interpretation.* New York: Oxford University Press, 1987.

Low, Victor. *The Unimpressible Race: A Century of Educational Struggle by Chinese in San Francisco.* San Francisco: East/West, 1982.

Márquez, Benjamin. *LULAC: The Evolution of a Mexican American Political Organization.* Austin: University of Texas Press, 1993.

Martin, Waldo E., Jr., ed. *Brown v. Board of Education: A Brief History with Documents*. Boston: Bedford, 1998.

McDowell, Deborah E. *Leaving Pipe Shop: Memories of Kin*. New York: Scribner, 1996.

McNeil, Genna Rae. *Groundwork: Charles Hamilton Houston and the Struggle for Civil Rights*. Philadelphia: University of Pennsylvania Press, 1983.

Moody, Anne. *Coming of Age in Mississippi*. New York: Bantam Doubleday Dell, 1968.

Morris, Aldon. *Origins of the Civil Rights Movement: Black Communities Organizing for Change*. New York: Free Press, 1984.

Murray, Pauli. *Song in a Weary Throat: An American Pilgrimage*. New York: Harper and Row, 1987.

Orfield, Gary, and Susan Eaton. *Dismantling Desegregation: The Quiet Reversal of Brown v. Board of Education*. New York: New Press, 1996.

Patterson, James T. *Brown v. Board of Education: A Civil Rights Milestone and Its Troubled Legacy*. New York: Oxford University Press, 2001.

Payne, Charles M. *I've Got the Light of Freedom: The Organizing Tradition in the Mississippi Freedom Struggle*. Berkeley: University of California Press, 1995.

Ravitch, Diane. *Left Back: A Century of Failed School Reforms*. New York: Simon and Schuster, 2000.

Robison, Armstead, and Patricia Sullivan, eds. *New Directions in Civil Rights Studies*. Charlottesville: University Press of Virginia, 1991.

Rosenberg, Gerald. *The Hollow Hope: Can Courts Bring About Social Change?* Chicago: University of Chicago Press, 1991.

Ruiz, Vicki L. *From Out of the Shadows: Mexican Women in Twentieth Century America*. New York: Oxford University Press, 1998.

Sánchez, George J. *Becoming Mexican American: Ethnicity, Culture, and Identity in Chicano Los Angeles, 1900–1945*. New York: Oxford University Press, 1993.

Sánchez-Karrol, Virginia. *From Colonia to Community: The History of Puerto Ricans in New York City*. Berkeley: University of California Press, 1994.

San Miguel, Guadalupe. *Brown, Not White: School Integration and the Chicano Movement in Houston*. Houston: University of Houston Press, 2001.

——. *"Let Them All Take Heed": Mexican Americans and the Campaign for Educational Equality in Texas, 1910–1981*. Austin: University of Texas Press, 1987.

Sarat, Austin, ed. *Race, Law, and Culture: Reflections on Brown v. Board of Education*. New York: Oxford University Press, 1997.

Sellers, Cleveland, with Robert Terrell. *The River of No Return: The Autobiography of a Black Militant and the Life and Death of SNCC*. New York: William Morrow, 1973.

Shakur, Assata. *Assata: An Autobiography*. Westport, Conn.: Lawrence Hill, 1987.

Sullivan, Patricia. *Days of Hope: Race and Democracy in the New Deal Era*. Chapel Hill: University of North Carolina Press, 1996.

Takaki, Ronald. *Strangers from a Different Shore: A History of Asian Americans*. Boston: Back Bay, 1998.

Tamura, Eileen H. *Americanization, Acculturation, and Ethnic Identity: The Nisei Generation in Hawaii*. Urbana: University of Illinois Press, 1994.

Thernstrom, Stephan, and Abigail Thernstrom. *America in Black and White: One Nation, Indivisible*. New York: Simon and Schuster, 1997.

Thomas, Brook, ed. *Plessy v. Ferguson: A Brief History with Documents*. Boston: Bedford, 1997.

Tushnet, Mark V. *Making Civil Rights Law: Thurgood Marshall and the Supreme Court, 1936–1961*. New York: Oxford University Press, 1994.

——. *The NAACP's Legal Strategy against Segregated Education, 1925–1950*. Chapel Hill: University of North Carolina Press, 1987.

Tushnet, Mark V., with Katya Lezin. "What Really Happened in *Brown v. Board of Education?*" 91 *Columbia Law Review* 1867–1930 (1991).

Tyack, David, and Larry Cuban. *Tinkering toward Utopia: A Century of Public School Reform*. Cambridge: Harvard University Press, 1995.

White, Deborah Gray. *Too Heavy a Load: Black Women in Defense of Themselves*. New York: W. W. Norton, 1999.

Whitfield, Stephen J. *Death in the Delta: The Story of Emmett Till*. Baltimore: Johns Hopkins University Press, 1988.

Williams, Juan. *Thurgood Marshall: American Revolutionary*. New York: Random House, 1998.

Wollenberg, Charles. *All Deliberate Speed: Segregation and Exclusion in California Schools, 1855–1875*. Berkeley: University of California Press, 1976.

Wolters, Raymond. *The Burden of Brown: Thirty Years of School Desegregation*. Knoxville: University of Tennessee Press, 1992.

Young, Andrew. *An Easy Burden: The Civil Rights Movement and the Transformation of America*. New York: Harper Collins, 1996.

Yung, Judy. *Unbound Feet: A Social History of Chinese Women in San Francisco*. Berkeley: University of California Press, 1995.

Zangrando, Robert L. *The NAACP Crusade against Lynching, 1909–1950*. Philadelphia: Temple University Press, 1980.

# Notes on the Contributors

TOMIKO BROWN-NAGIN is an associate professor of law and history at Washington University (St. Louis). She is a graduate of Yale Law School, where she was an editor of the *Yale Law Journal*, and was a law clerk for Robert L. Carter of the U.S. District Court for the Southern District of New York, one of the principal attorneys in the *Brown* litigation. She earned a doctorate in history at Duke University and is currently working on a manuscript concerned with the NAACP's educational equity campaign in Atlanta from 1958 to 1979.

DAVISON M. DOUGLAS is a professor of law and the director of the Institute of Bill of Rights Law at the William and Mary School of Law. He is the author of *Reading, Writing, and Race: The Desegregation of the Charlotte Schools* (University of North Carolina Press, 1995) and many articles on race and public education, of which one received the History of Education Society Award for the best article published during the 1994–95 biennium and another received honorable mention for the same prize in 1996–97. He has also edited several books, including most recently *Redefining Equality* (Oxford University Press, 1998).

RAYMOND GAVINS is a professor of history at Duke University. He is the author of *The Perils and Prospects of Southern Black Leadership: Gordon Blaine Hancock, 1884–1970* (1977) and a co-editor of *Remembering Jim Crow: African Americans Talk about the Segregated South* (New Press, 2001), and he has published many essays on race in America. He is the co-director of "Behind the Veil: Documenting African American Life in the Jim Crow South," a collaborative research project based at Duke University.

LAURIE BETH GREEN is an assistant professor of history at the University of Texas at Austin. She has been a Rockefeller Postdoctoral Fellow, the recipient of a Woodrow Wilson Dissertation Grant, and visiting assistant professor of history at the University of Chicago, where she received her doctorate. She is completing a book on the politics and culture of race, class, and gender in Memphis from 1940 to 1968.

CHRISTINA GREENE is an assistant professor in the Department of African and African American Studies at the University of Wisconsin, Madison, after five years at the University of South Florida. She is the author of *Our Separate Ways: Women and the Black Freedom Movement in Durham, North Carolina, 1940 to 1970*, forthcoming from the University of North Carolina Press. She earned her doctorate in history from Duke University.

BLAIR L. M. KELLEY is an assistant professor of history at North Carolina State University. Her dissertation, a history of black protest around the segregation of streetcars in three southern cities at the beginning of the twentieth century, uses a lens of race, class, and gender to explore the emergence of Jim Crow and multiple forms of black protest thought and activity. She earned her doctorate in history from Duke University.

MICHAEL J. KLARMAN is the James Monroe Professor of Law and a professor of history at the University of Virginia. He is the author of *From Jim Crow to Civil Rights: The Supreme Court and the Struggle for Racial Equality* (Oxford University Press, 2004). He has also published many important essays related to *Brown v. Board of Education*, including "*Brown,* Racial Change, and the Civil Rights Movement," 80 *Virginia Law Review* 7–150 (1994).

PETER F. LAU earned his doctorate in United States and African American History at Rutgers University in January 2002. He has been a research fellow of the Institute for Southern Studies at the University of South Carolina, the John Hope Franklin Center for Documentary Studies at Duke University, and the Avery Research Center for African and African American History and Culture at the College of Charleston. He is currently completing a book entitled *Freedom Road Territory: The Politics of Civil Rights Struggle in South Carolina during the Jim Crow Era* and teaching at Lincoln School in Providence, Rhode Island.

MADELEINE LÓPEZ is an assistant professor in the Department of Latin American and Puerto Rican Studies at Lehman College, City University of New York. She is currently completing her doctorate at Princeton University, where she is writing a dissertation on bilingual education in New York City and Puerto Rico between 1940 and 1960.

WALDO E. MARTIN JR. is a professor of history at the University of California, Berkeley. He is the author of "*A Change Is Gonna Come": Black Movement, Culture, and the Transformation of America* (forthcoming) and *The Mind of Frederick Douglass* (University of North Carolina Press, 1984). He edited *Brown v. Board of Education: A Brief History with Documents* (Bedford/St. Martin's, 1998) and co-edited *The Encyclopedia of Civil Rights in the United States* (Macmillan, 2000).

VICKI L. RUIZ is a professor of history and Chicano/Latino studies at the University of California, Irvine. Her recent book *From Out of the Shadows: Mexican Women in Twentieth-Century America* (Oxford University Press, 1998) was named a Choice Outstanding Academic Book. She is also the author of *Cannery Women, Cannery Lives: Mexican Women, Unionization, and the California Food Processing Industry, 1930–1950* (University of New Mexico Press, 1987) and the editor or co-editor of three anthologies, including *Unequal Sisters: A Multicultural Reader in U.S. Women's History* (Routledge, 1990, 1994, 1999). She has served as president of the Berkshire Conference on the History of Women and is currently president-elect of the Organization of American Historians.

CHRISTOPHER W. SCHMIDT is completing a dissertation entitled "Postwar Liberalism and the Origins of *Brown v. Board of Education*" in the History of American Civilization Program at Harvard University. He has taught at Phillips Academy and Dartmouth College, and is a fellow at the Miller Center for Public Affairs at the University of Virginia for 2003–4.

LARISSA M. SMITH is an assistant professor of history at Longwood State University in Prince Edward County, Virginia. She is completing a book entitled *Where the South Begins: Black Politics and Civil Rights Activism in Virginia, 1930–1951*. She earned her doctorate in the Department of History at Emory University under the direction of Dan Carter.

PATRICIA SULLIVAN is the associate director of African and African American Studies at the University of South Carolina. Since 1996 she has been a research associate at the W. E. B. Du Bois Institute for Afro-American Research at Harvard University. Along with Waldo E. Martin Jr., she has been co-director since 1995 of a series of summer institutes sponsored by the National Endowment for the Humanities at Harvard University on the civil rights movement. She is the author of *Days of Hope: Race and Democracy in the New Deal Era* (University of North Carolina Press, 1996), editor of *Freedom Writer: Virginia Foster Durr, Letters from the Civil Rights Years* (Routledge, 2003), and co-editor of *New Directions in Civil Rights Studies* (University Press of Virginia, 1991) and *The Encyclopedia of Civil Rights in the United States* (Macmillan, 2000). She is currently working on a book entitled *Struggle toward Freedom: A History of the National Association for the Advancement of Colored People*.

KARA MILES TURNER is the assistant dean for administration at the College of Liberal Arts, Morgan State University. She is completing a book on the black educational struggle from 1865 to 1995 in Prince Edward County, Virginia, one of the school districts that provided the setting for the *Brown v. Board of Education* litigation. She earned her doctorate in history at Duke University.

MARK V. TUSHNET is the Carmack Waterhouse Professor of Constitutional Law at Georgetown University Law Center. A former law clerk for Supreme Court Justice Thurgood Marshall, he has written several works on race and American law, including *Making Constitutional Law: Thurgood Marshall and the Supreme Court, 1961–1991* (Oxford University Press, 1997), *Making Civil Rights Law: Thurgood Marshall and the Supreme Court, 1936–1961* (Oxford University Press, 1994), *The NAACP's Legal Strategy against Segregated Education, 1925–1950* (University of North Carolina Press, 1987), and *The American Law of Slavery, 1810–1860: Considerations of Humanity and Interest* (Princeton University Press, 1981). Most recently he is the author of *The New Constitutional Order* (Princeton University Press, 2003). He has also edited or co-edited sixteen other books and written over two hundred articles and book chapters. He has received many awards, including a John Simon Guggenheim Memorial Fellowship, a Rockefeller Foundations Humanities Fellowship, and the Littleton-Griswold Prize of the American Historical Association.

# Index

Index   397

*Library of Congress Cataloging-in-Publication Data*

From the grassroots to the Supreme Court : Brown v. Board of Education
and American democracy / edited by Peter F. Lau.
p. cm. — (Constitutional conflicts)
Includes bibliographical references and index.
ISBN 0-8223-3475-5 (cloth : alk. paper) ISBN 0-8223-3449-6 (pbk. : alk. paper)
1. Segregation in education—Law and legislation—United States.
2. Race discrimination—Law and legislation—United States. 3. United States—
Race relations. 4. Brown, Oliver, 1918–Trials, litigation, etc.—History. 5. Topeka
(Kan.). Board of Education—Trials, litigation, etc.—History.
I. Lau, Peter, F., 1971– II. Series.
KF4155.F76 2004
344.73'0798—dc22
2004013135